The Question of Being

The Question of Being

A Reversal of Heidegger

Stanley Rosen

Yale University Press

New Haven and London

Grateful acknowledgment is given to
the following for permission to reprint: *Philosophiques,*
Revue de la Société
de Philosophie du Québec and *Review*
of Metaphysics.

Designed by Sonia L. Scanlon.
Set in Sabon type by Rainsford Type, Danbury, CT.
Printed in the United States of America by
Book Crafters, Inc., Chelsea, Michigan.

Library of Congress Cataloging-in-Publication Data
Rosen, Stanley, 1929-
The question of being : a reversal of Heidegger / Stanley Rosen.
p. cm.
Includes bibliographical references and index.
ISBN 0-300-05356-8 (acid-free paper)
1. Metaphysics. 2. Heidegger, Martin, 1889-1976—Contributions in
metaphysics. 3. Plato—Contributions in metaphysics.
4. Platonists. 5. Nietzsche, Friedrich Wilhelm, 1844-1900—
Contributions in metaphypsics. I. Title
BD111.R65 1993
110 – dc20   92-34934
CIP

A catalog record for this book is available
from the British Library.
The paper in this book meets the guidelines
for permanence and durability of the Committee on
Production Guidelines for Book Longevity
of the Council on Library Resources.

10 9 8 7 6 5 4 3 2 1

In Memoriam
David R. Lachterman
(1944–1991)

The law of chaos is the law of ideas,
Of improvisations and seasons of belief.
Ideas are men. The mass of meaning and
The mass of men are one. Chaos is not
The mass of meaning. It is three or four
Ideas or, say, five men or, possibly, six.

In the end, these philosophic assassins pull
Revolvers and shoot each other. One remains.
The mass of meaning becomes composed again.
He that remains plays on an instrument
A good agreement between himself and night,
A chord between the mass of men and himself,
Far, far beyond the putative canzones
Of love and summer. The assassin sings
In chaos and his song is a consolation.
It is the music of the mass of meaning.
And yet it is a singular romance,
This warmth in the blood-world for the pure idea,
This inability to find a sound,
That clings to the mind like that right sound, that song
Of the assassin that remains and sings
In the high imagination, triumphantly.

—from Wallace Stevens,
Extracts from Addresses to the Academy of Fine Ideas

Contents

Contents

Introduction

In this book, I propose to investigate the thesis of Martin Heidegger that European philosophy from Plato to Nietzsche is the history of metaphysics, or of what Heidegger also calls Platonism. I shall be primarily concerned with the beginning and the end of this history: with the ostensible origin of metaphysics in Plato and with its culmination in Nietzsche. This will require a considerable amount of textual analysis, but my intentions are philosophical rather than philological. The question before us, What is Being? is raised in the first instance by Heidegger, although the answer, to the extent that there is an answer, has a different inspiration. My "reversal" of Heidegger is at the same time a reconstruction of the spirit of Platonism, a spirit that must renew itself in each generation, like a firebird that is reborn from the ashes of refutation.

The texts I have chosen to analyze were selected because they enable us to understand what is fundamental in Heidegger's thesis and by extension in his interpretation of Plato and Nietzsche; no attempt has been made to provide an exhaustive account of Heidegger's views or of the history of their development.[1] I take my bearings by Heidegger because of his decisive influence in our time, an influence that repeats the fate of Nietzsche, as rhetoric and journalism provide an ever-gaudier and increasingly meretricious substitute for what Hegel called the infinite labor of Spirit. It is not, however, simply because of his reputation or influence that Heidegger is the main figure in this study. I do not wish to substitute one form of meretriciousness for another. Heidegger's interpretation of Platonism, and so of metaphysics, is in my opinion the greatest obstacle to the contemporary understanding of the nature of metaphysics, and so too of philosophy. This is due to the power of his intelligence and the extent of his learning, however perverse may be the use to which he puts these very considerable attributes.

In particular, his authority and his thought stand behind the widespread conviction, even among the self-styled "analytical" philosophers, that the history of philosophy is at an end and that we have arrived at a postphilosophical age. More precisely, it is Nietzsche who stands behind this conviction; and Heidegger's interpretation of Nietzsche has become canonical for our time. The entire debate among our leading schools of philosophy has been seriously distorted by Heidegger's influence, which has also contributed to a concealment of the true nature of the problem by encouraging a spurious distinction between analytical and continental philosophers.

This distinction produces the absurd impression that precision, conceptual clarity, and systematic rigor are the property of analytical philosophy, whereas the continentals indulge in speculative metaphysics and cultural hermeneutics or, alternatively, depending upon one's sympathies, in wool gathering and bathos. No intelligent person is taken in by the gestures toward "pluralism" that have presumably rectified the situation. Nevertheless, at a deeper level than that of the conference of academicians or the awarding of research grants, the influence of the wool-gatherers and the hermeneuticists has been steadily filling the void that surrounds the *technè* of analytical philosophy. I predicted almost twenty-five years ago that this would inevitably occur, since there is no analytical justification for analysis.[2] The attempt to acquire such a justification from fashionable political and cultural views of the moment has left the analysts naked before the assaults of continental doctrines, one of which, namely, that logic and mathematics are poetry or perspectival constructions of the will to power, stems from Nietzsche, and the other, namely, that logic and logical or analytical philosophy are the incarnation of technicity, and so are a posthumous excrescence of Platonist metaphysics, stems from Heidegger.

The sociology of professional philosophy is of interest only in the sense that no progress can be made until the rubble is removed from the public highway. This book is concerned with the machines by which the rubble may be removed, not with the rubble itself. Let me repeat that I write in a spirit of reconstruction, not refutation. My fundamental intention, to employ a Nietzschean distinction, is active rather than reactive: I have a proposal to make about the next step in philosophy. Technical precision and speculative metaphysics must be unified in a step *downward,* out of the thin atmosphere of the floating island of Laputa or of the balloons in which so many of our advanced thinkers are currently suspended, back into the rich air of everyday life. As will soon become evident, I understand this step to be equivalent to a sound application of genuine Platonism. We cannot orient ourselves outside the cave because our initial attempt to do so led not to illumination, but to blindness and sunstroke. I do not recommend that we remain in the cave, but rather that we try to distinguish between it and the heavens by regaining our sight of the surface of the earth as well as of the horizon.

Genuine Platonism is timeless, not reactionary; one may agree with Heidegger that it has more to do with the Enlightenment than with the obscurantism of Teutonic invocations of Wotan and the forest paths of the Schwarzwald. Heidegger criticizes Plato's famous comparison of the Idea of the Good to the sun on the grounds that this image expresses the utility of beings rather than their uncoveredness in the Being-process.

In reply, I borrow Hegel's warning that philosophy must strive not to be edifying; mere edification is stultifying. Very far from attempting to deny Heidegger's point of interpretation, I shall argue that utility is an essential component of goodness. But what I mean by goodness has very little to do with a metaphysical doctrine of Platonic Ideas in the traditional sense of that expression. As part of the aforementioned step downward, I shall try to show how the doctrine of the Ideas, as explained by Socrates himself, emerges from a commonsensical reflection on the nature of ordinary experience.

There is a sense in which I regard myself as an ordinary-language metaphysician, provided that this appellation not be transformed into a technical doctrine in its own right. Whether one speaks of *phronēsis*, common sense, or (as does Heidegger) of *Vorsicht* and *Umsicht,* one is very close not merely to Aristotle's practical treatises, but to the practice of Socrates in the Platonic dialogues.[3] This practice has consequences that go beyond common sense, but there are different beyonds, not all of them identical to Laputa. However this may be, it is important to make clear at the outset that I am not advocating a return to metaphysics in the Aristotelian sense of the science of being qua being.

Metaphysics has an ambiguous reputation in the late-modern epoch, for reasons which are intrinsic to the enterprise and which go back to the origins in classical antiquity. The term does not appear in Aristotle, who is nevertheless burdened with the responsibility for having initiated the science that it names. This is not the place to rehearse the long story of the origin of the name and the various conceptions of the content of the science that have arisen during the past 2,500 years. Whether the term "metaphysics" means "the things coming after the physical things" or "the things beyond the physical things" is of little importance for the investigation I am about to undertake.[4]

What is decisive for our purposes is Heidegger's contention that metaphysics in the sense of the science of being qua being, and so as the attempt to think the being of beings rather than Being, originates in Plato's turn (presumably under the influence of Being rather than through some personal idiosyncrasy) from truth as uncoveredness to the truth about that which is uncovered.

Heidegger, of course, does not claim simply that metaphysics is Platonism. He also claims to be engaged, as the passive yet resonant medium of destiny, in the preparation of "another beginning," or a return to the original manifestation of Being to the archaic Greek thinkers and poets, a return that will not, however, repeat the almost immediate errors of the first beginning, errors that should be regarded as the errance of Being itself, which concealed its very concealment within the mask of beings. Presumably the end of metaphysics, that is to say, its oddly Hegelian working out of all its fundamental forms, of which the last is the mature teaching of Nietzsche, is the sign of future salvation, a sign that is incarnated in Heidegger as the second coming. We should not begrudge Heidegger the assumption of the robes of prophecy. This is after all a costume that has been irresistible to all the great thinkers of our race. We must nevertheless beware of false prophets. Our task, to borrow an expression from Nietzsche, is to philosophize with a hammer; and to give this image a Heideggerian inflection, we must strike the doctrine of the prophecy like a bell, to see if it rings true or if it shatters under pressure.

Among the various things that one can learn from Heidegger is, oddly enough, how to strip philosophy of its academic or scholastic shell and bring it to life. Unfortunately, one can also learn how to suffocate life by the very terminology that is intended to preserve it. Let me illustrate this point by introducing in more detail Heidegger's general thesis about the history of metaphysics. In the *Introduction to Metaphysics*, Heidegger asserts that "philosophy is extra-ordinary questioning about the extra-ordinary."[5] The hyphens (which appear in the German original) are intended to emphasize that one must go outside or beyond the ordinary ways of thinking and speaking when engaging in philosophical thought. As one could therefore expect, Heidegger's texts are filled with neologisms and obscure paraphrases, usually rooted in etymological analyses of philosophically important terms that take us back to classical Greek and occasionally to Sanskrit and Old German. The purpose of these analyses, however, is not to shift us from one set of technical terms to another. It is instead to discover (literally, to uncover) the original experience that is contained within language prior to its encrustation by derivative modes of expression.

As one examines Heidegger's etymologies, it soon becomes evident that, in his view, a revelation or manifestation of the truth occurred in archaic Greece that was superior in its purity to subsequent manifestations.[6] This revelation is elicited by analyses of certain crucial terms, in particular "nature" (*phusis*), "truth" (*alētheia*), and "light" (*phōs, phaos*) or "shining" (*phainō*).[7] In his analysis of these terms, Heidegger cites the thinkers of the time, poets as well as philosophers. One might therefore assume that he is attempting to substitute archaic for modern technical terminology or one set of extraordinary thoughts for another. There is no doubt that Heidegger's paraphrases of the original content of the aforementioned expressions strike the contemporary reader as peculiar. But they are not technical in the modern sense of the term; that is to say, they are intended to make explicit how language responds to the manifestation of truth in everyday experience.

Let us take as an example Heidegger's account of the original sense of *phusis*. The root *phu* means "growing" or "emerging" and thus is connected conceptually to the root *pha* of words like *phaos* and *phainō*, all designating light, visibility, or presence as a showing-forth. *Phusis* is accordingly explained as "that which emerges from itself" or "self-opening unfolding." One thinks here of a plant that grows up from the earth and spreads its leaves or flowers in the sunlight, thereby becoming visible to human beings. Thus far, the account is straightforward and does not depend in any way on extraordinary philosophical doctrines. It is intended to express how the early Greeks experienced natural, and in particular living, phenomena. But at this point, the analysis takes an unexpected turn. In the text from which I have just cited, Heidegger goes on to say that "*phusis* is Being itself, thanks to which the thing first becomes and remains observable."[8]

In making this statement, Heidegger intends to convey the following point. From the time of Plato onward (and perhaps earlier), philosophers conceive of "Being" as a general term that expresses what is common to all things. By "thing" is meant any definite or identifiable entity whatsoever. Incidentally, in developing this point, Heidegger blurs the distinction between *phusis* and the Greek expressions for art and custom, a distinction which he of course knows and often discusses. He even includes human history within the domain of *phusis*.[9] This extended use of *phusis* covers over the original sense of "growth" or "emergence" as a characteristic of life. One could say that the same ambiguity is contained in the philosophical use of *ta phusika* to include inanimate bodies, terrestrial as well as heavenly. The underlying notion is that *ta phusika,* or what we call in English "natural beings," are those things that emerge from a process of manifestation that is complete in itself and does not depend upon human invention or production.

Phusis is then for Heidegger the process of emergence, not the things, beings, or *ta phusika* that emerge. The emergence process, however, is different not only from the things that emerge, but from the properties, if there are such, that are common to everything whatsoever. By directing our attention to the visible thing, and so to visibility or presence as the property that is common to and thus defines anything whatsoever, Plato is said to conceal from our view the process of emergence or of rendering visible. He misdirects our attention from Being to beings, and by way of his attention to the visible "look" of beings, or the so-called doctrine of Ideas, to the "being of beings." The relatively direct accessibility of beings or things leads us to attempt to define the process of emergence not in its own terms, but in the terms of the properties common to beings or things.

Heidegger does not deny that Being "presents" itself as concealed by beings or things. On the contrary, he insists on it. But he claims that this concealment was understood in principle by the thinkers prior to Plato and in particular by Heracleitus, as is shown from an analysis of the fragment "nature loves to hide" (*phusis kruptesthai philei*): "*Phusis* is the play of emergence in self-concealment, [a play] that hides in the act of emancipating that which emerges into the open, that which is free."[10] Plato initiates the shift in attention from awareness of Being as the play of presence and absence to a conception of Being as pure or genuine (*ontōs on*) presence, namely, as the presence of the look, that by which we identify what a thing is: the *idea*.[11] From this point on, philosophy is defined by the Platonic standard. I will come back to a more detailed account of what this entails. But first I want to make a general observation about Heidegger's procedure.

The turn from *phusis* to Being is without doubt a turn from ordinary to extraordinary ways of thinking and speaking. This is evident from the fact that there is no single word in Greek that corresponds to Being (*Sein*) as Heidegger employs it. Heidegger shows very clearly the different senses of the participle *on,* the articular infinitive *to einai,* the abstract noun *ousia,* and so on.[12] More precisely, it is not the Greek equivalent to "being" or "to be" that approximates to his use of *Sein* but rather *phusis.* One could therefore say that Being conceals itself in its initial presentation as *phusis.* This is not a mere playing with words; according to Heidegger, "Language is the house of Being. In this housing lives Man."[13] And again: "In the word, in language, things first come to be and are."[14] How we speak is determined by how Being manifests itself to us: "The thinker has only corresponded in speech to what is awarded to him by speech."[15] "Speech" should be understood here as *logos* in the original sense of *legein,* "to collect": "The original gathering gatheredness that continuously holds sway within itself."[16] In this sense, *logos* and *phusis* "are the same."[17] To be human thus means to gather together within thinking the being of beings.[18]

The sense of Being is of course not for Heidegger a mere linguistic expression. Etymological exercises are arbitrary unless we see the sphere of the affairs (*Sachbereich*) to which the old words correspond.[19] As Heidegger says toward the end of the second volume of his *Nietzsche* studies, "Recollection that is oriented by the history of Being returns to the claim of the silent voice of Being and to the manner of its voice. ... The thinker can never say what is his ownmost. That must remain unspoken, because the speakable word receives its determination from the unsayable."[20] Being, in the original sense of *phusis,* is language, in the original sense of *logos,* not as a spoken discourse but as a process of gathering-together that is a concealed self-presentation; human beings are the "place" within which this process is revealed, and the Heideggerian definition of human being is that of the animal who is possessed by *logos,* not the animal who possesses *logos.*[21]

In sum, how we speak is determined by what is given or revealed to us. The fundamental question of philosophy is thus precisely: *What* is given to us? This is my formulation, not Heidegger's. For him, a *what* is a being or definite thing, not Being or the emergence-process. On the other hand, Heidegger would agree that Being does not give itself to us in a straightforward manner, unmasked as itself. It cannot do so because the expression "as" refers to some particular thing: this is given *as* that, and so we speak in predicative discourse of one thing "as" another (i.e., as one of its properties).[22] There is then a fundamental ambiguity running through Heidegger's thinking in all of its various stages, an ambiguity that corresponds to the fundamental question. We cannot say "what" is given to us because the given is not a "what." Thus Heidegger says of the "other beginning" or alternative to metaphysical philosophy for which he hopes to prepare us, "It is no longer a question of discussing 'about' something and of exhibiting something objective, but of being conveyed to the E-vent."[23]

The term "E-vent" (*Er-eignis*) is, according to Heidegger, "since 1936 the leading word of my thinking."[24] It is impossible to translate straightforwardly into English, and Heidegger gives a wide range of senses or paraphrases, of which perhaps the simplest and most illuminating is that it is "the way of Being itself."[25] A more complete exposition would require extensive discussion of the word translated here as "way": *Wesung*, "waying" or "manner of proceeding," not "essence" or "nature" in the traditional senses. Suffice it to suggest that *Wesung* is prior to nature or essence in that these latter are determined by how Being (which Heidegger in this context spells *Seyn*) presents itself. Strictly speaking, the E-vent is not a happening, if by this last expression we refer to something definite, some identifiable event or thing. With respect to the E-vent, *nothing happens;* the E-vent eventuates.[26]

If I am not mistaken, there is a relatively straightforward way in which to restate this crucial thesis, despite its apparent obscurity. In fact, I have already conveyed the substance of the thesis in drawing the distinction (following Heidegger) between *phusis* and the Platonic *idea*. The *idea* presents us with the nature or essence of "what" shows itself and thus serves as a ground or foundation, a standard by which to define the being that exhibits a look of such and such a kind. *Phusis*, however, is not a standard or a foundation to which one can appeal in order to define the nature or essence, the "genuine" being of a thing. *Phusis* is a *way* rather than the *nature* of the way; it is free or unpredictable happening, not a standard to which we may appeal but the mysterious presentation of standards, and hence it is the process of the changing of standards, of the "giving" now of one standard, now of another.

In slightly different terms, let us define "nature" to mean "what a thing is by virtue of its constitution." In this sense, nature serves not merely as a standard but as a necessary or grounding standard. Despite the colloquial reference to "unnatural behavior," we cannot act contrary to nature in the sense just defined. I note in passing an important consequence. Those who speak of "unnatural behavior" or "action contrary to nature" are committed, whether they recognize it or not, to an understanding of nature as divided against itself. This division is covered over by the distinction between natural laws and natural ends. But there are no natural laws that prevent us from behaving contrary to natural ends.

In the sense just defined, "natural occurrences" are occurrences which are determined to transpire in accord with a procedure that is always or for the most part (as Aristotle puts it) the same. Fire always burns in the same way, given the same conditions. Human beings generate other human beings, not rabbits or monkeys, by sexual intercourse. The term "natural" can then be extended to refer to human praxis; for example, as just noted, certain conduct is said to be "in accord with nature" if the action conduces to the fulfillment of human perfection. On the other hand, if the notion of nature is unknown or repudiated, we speak of the "ways" of human beings in order to indicate that their actions follow no standard, are not grounded in a foundation that is expressed in the constitution of their being, but simply happen to be what they are. In this case there are no perfect human beings, but only different ways in which human beings happen to be.

This rough and ready distinction between "nature" and "way" permits us to understand the main sense attributed by Heidegger to "E-vent." We put to one side the original or genuine sense of *phusis*. "Way" is now prior to "nature." There is no sense or foundation behind or beneath what happens. The happening of "what happens" just is or happens. On the other hand, "what" happens is this or that epoch of *Seinsgeschichte*, that is, not of history in the ordinary sense but in the sense of a particular way of experiencing, and so thinking and speaking about, Being. The standard thus becomes "what happens" in the decisive sense of this term. But there are many standards, no one of them authoritative for any epoch other than its own. And if we come to understand the "eventing" of the E-vent, as I may perhaps refer to it, then we are freed, in any but a nominal or conventional sense, from obedience to *any* standard. To state this more carefully, either we are required to accept whatever standard we are given, simply because it is given; or else we may do as we please. Heidegger does not state the alternatives in this way. The problem is that he states no alternatives in an explicit manner but leaves everything sufficiently vague as to justify either of two distinct inferences.[27] The happening of the E-vent is thus understood as the freedom of human being; there are no principles, no foundations, and so no standards other than those we freely accept. But why we should accept them, other than because they are given, is unclear.

At this point, I believe, one finds the deepest and most genuine ambiguities in Heidegger's thinking. On the one hand, he regularly invokes us to "overcome" the limitations of metaphysical or thing-oriented thinking in behalf of a new way of thinking, namely, the thinking of the E-vent (or more simply, of Being as emergence-process). On the other hand, there seems to be nothing here to think "about." No wonder Heidegger always insists that he is "on the way toward speech" or preparing the way for "another beginning" rather than actually speaking in the sense of answering questions or formulating a doctrine. And there is a closely associated second ambiguity. Heidegger does not advocate the "destruction" of metaphysics in the sense of wiping it from the face of the earth or obliterating it from human memory. On the contrary, he wishes and believes that we are required to preserve metaphysics, albeit now as freed from its limitations. By the same token, Heidegger does not advocate the destruction of tradition or, for example, of bourgeois civilization, despite his predilection for peasants and forests and his concerns about the age of technology.[28]

We cannot avoid describing Heidegger as an extreme conservative, namely, as someone who denies the applicability of his doctrine of the E-vent to political, social, or moral activity.[29] In very simple and direct terms, Heidegger accepted Nietzsche's critique of modern democracy and liberalism, of the vulgarization of European culture, of the arrival of the "masses," and in short, of the culmination of nihilism in the forces of progress and Enlightenment. His political actions during the Nazi regime have often been explained, by himself and his admirers, as owing to his desire to liberate Europe not from "standards" or "traditions," but from the barbarism represented by dominance of the metaphysically equivalent United States and Russia.[30] Heidegger wished to return Germany and, through its dominance, Europe to the very tradition that made the Germans the metaphysical people.

This is one of the main themes of the Hölderlin lectures of 1934/35. Heidegger is continuously calling upon the German "folk" to reaffirm the greatness of its tradition and its destiny. But he expresses the way in which this is to be done with so much vagueness as to leave historical action indistinguishable from an openness to Being: "*The 'Fatherland' is Being itself* which from the ground up carries and ordains the history of a folk as one that exists."[31] And again: "The truth of a folk is that openness of Being, from out of which the folk knows what it wants historically, insofar as it wills itself, wills to be itself."[32] In sum, Hölderlin must become "the power of the history of our folk." Heidegger then adds, "To join this cause is 'politics' in the highest and genuine sense, so much so that who here effects something is not required to speak about the 'political.' "[33] What is to be effected here? Surely not radical freedom in the sense of a complete acceptance of all forms of behavior, but rather an authentic mode of acting in the resolute acceptance of destiny as defined by history, that is, by tradition. Yet it is entirely unclear why this should be so.

Not long after his resignation as chancellor of the University of Freiburg, Heidegger underwent a well-publicized and frequently mystified "turn" (*Kehre*) which may here be described very briefly as acceptance of *Gelassenheit*, "releasement toward Being," or in Heidegger's language toward the "activity of regioning" (*Gegnet*) that opens up regions within which Being occurs.[34] This is the theme that underlies the attitude toward the e-venting of the E-vent. We have to wait for the next gift of Being or for the return of the gods who, as Hölderlin put it, have flown away from this parlous time. But while we are waiting, what should we do? Heidegger's postmodern admirers are fairly clear on this point: they orient themselves by the rejection of foundations in order to advocate a deconstruction of bourgeois civilization or, in the extreme case, anarchy.[35]

Very simply stated, openness to Being, or to that which regions, is compatible with doing nothing or with doing anything at all. Anarchism is as compatible with Heidegger's ambiguous doctrine as is extreme conservatism and even despotism. There is no reason, foundation, ground, or principle intrinsic to the E-vent to give us any guidance or to restrict us in any way whatsoever on this delicate point. It therefore remains permanently unclear why Heidegger's resolution of the problem of nihilism is not itself nihilism on the grand scale.[36] Let me emphasize that I am not restricting myself here to political or moral nihilism. Either the E-vent is thinkable or it is not. If it is thinkable, then there must be some content to our thoughts, in which case the E-vent is thought "as" such and such, which is directly contrary to Heidegger's intentions. On the other hand, if we are to avoid "thinking" the E-vent in any sense that connotes content peculiar to the E-vent itself, since there is nothing in Being "about" which to think, we are left with the sole alternative of thinking about *what* eventuates, that is, about beings.[37]

The most that can be said for Heidegger's "other beginning" is that it somehow purifies or exhilarates us for the task of thinking beings. But since it makes no positive contribution to the substance or content of that thinking—on the contrary leads us to believe that the beings which we think, and so what we think about them, are all temporary, "free" in the sense of groundless or unprincipled happenings—the edification incidental to releasement to the E-vent or that which regions must soon decay into the lassitude of thinking about the merely contingent, the random, and the arbitrary. Heidegger of course claims that original thinking places beings in a new light by situating them within the process of emergence, or the E-vent. But what we gain by freeing beings from subjectivity and consequent distortion by the will to will, we lose because of the ungrounded pointlessness of the gift of disclosure. Abolition of a metaphysics of values leaves everything valueless; abolition of a metaphysics of substances leaves everything without substance. This is as good a description of nihilism as I can propose.

I now return to the question What is given to us? My point is not at all that Heidegger is completely mistaken, but rather that he is partially correct. Heidegger's etymologies rightly indicate how philosophical thinking emerges not from the emergence-process, but from everyday thinking. But Heidegger is mistaken to think that we need to return to the archaic Greeks in order to recover the original or genuine manifestation of *phusis*. He is no doubt right in maintaining that the subsequent history of philosophy has covered over many original insights with the dross of countless technical productions and doctrines. But if the original Greek experience was indeed original or genuine, how is this genuineness known to us moderns, who exist in the late stages of European nihilism? How in particular did it become accessible to Heidegger? If Heidegger is an instrument of destiny or a prophet, how can we understand his prophecy except by comparing his revelation of the genuine senses of the crucial Greek terms with our understanding of our own experience?

Heracleitus himself (to mention no others) did not invent the original senses of *phusis, alētheia,* and *logos* in a moment of divine frenzy while sitting in his stove, separate from the multitude. His "dark" sayings are rooted in the revelation of *phusis* to the Greek people and domiciled in their language, which is not, like Heracleitus's sayings, an extraordinary transformation of the everyday, but the everyday itself. I of course do not mean to suggest that all Greeks were philosophers, but rather that Greek philosophy, as interpreted by Heidegger, originates in the way that Greeks speak about ordinary events, such as the growth of a flower or the gathering in of the harvest or the daily tasks of the artisan or the discussions about right and wrong that transpire in the agora.

No doubt Heracleitus radicalizes this everyday language or brings it to a peak of concentration that surpasses ordinary speech in its revelatory power. But the language that he is radicalizing is everyday Greek. Just in this way, Heidegger radicalizes everyday German as he develops his own "technical" terms. Neither in the first case nor in the second is the procedure one of leaping outside of ordinary language in order to create a radically new tongue that can thus be understood by no one but the inventor. No doubt *Er-eignis* is a peculiar term with a range of senses that are hard to define in ordinary German. But it comes from the ordinary German word *Ereignis* and is explained by means of ordinary words like *eignen* ("belongs to") and *äugen* ("watch out for"), just as *Gegnet* is explained with reference to *Gegend* ("region") as well as to *Offenheit* and *versammeln* ("openness" and "gathering"). So too Heidegger, in his most powerful evocations of the ambiguity of the "question of Being," begins from simple reflections about beings: a piece of chalk, the school building next to his seminar hall, the heavens and the earth, the gods and the mortals.

But these are the things that we are given: a piece of chalk, a flower, a building, a tree, a man or a woman, a star, and so on in endless diversity, which is the same as endless specificity or "whatness." Of course, we are given these things in various combinations and relations, as emerging from and disappearing into a totally familiar and yet ineffable "region" or "openness"; but the region or openness would not itself be given except as the region *of* the things, as the openness from which and into which the things emerge and disappear. Heidegger is right to say that Being presents itself in a concealed form. He is wrong to try to persuade us to think Being apart from its modes of concealment. Nor can we think the "dialectic" of disclosure and concealment apart from what shows itself and disappears without relapsing into the logic of Hegel.[38]

Heidegger's guiding concern is to arrive at a thinking of Being (other names are employed) that both questions and commemorates rather than defines, specifies, or calculates, or in other words to avoid thinking Being in terms of beings, rather than the reverse. Thinking that orients itself by beings is metaphysics or Platonism. Platonism has completed its historical destiny in the later teaching of Nietzsche. I cite from a paper written in 1964 and published two years later in French; the German publication dates from 1969. The title of the paper is "The End of Philosophy and the Task of Thinking." In the course of answering the question To what extent has philosophy arrived at its end in the present age? Heidegger says, "Throughout the entire history of philosophy, Plato's thought in derived forms remains continuously the standard. Metaphysics is Platonism. Nietzsche characterizes his philosophy as reversed Platonism. With the reversal of metaphysics, which was already carried through by Karl Marx, the most extreme possibility of philosophy is achieved. Thus it has reached its end. To the extent that philosophical thinking is still pursued, it arrives only at epigonal renaissances and their varieties."[39]

We are now in a transitional period, in Heidegger's view, one which requires us to reappropriate metaphysics in such a way as to "release" ourselves from its grip and thus to prepare ourselves for the other beginning that enables us to think Being, that is, to be conveyed into the E-vent. It is unclear whether the transitional period is itself a gift of Being, presented to humankind through the person of Heidegger, and so an "e-vent" that is bound to occur, or whether we must ourselves act in such a way as to insure our entry into the promised land. Like all prophetic doctrines of history, of which Marxism is an alternative example, Heidegger's teaching cannot coherently resolve the relation between destiny and freedom.

In either case, namely, as a consequence of the necessary acceptance of the gift or as a free act, we must according to Heidegger detach ourselves from the grip of Platonism. My own claim is rather different. I shall first attempt to show that what Heidegger calls Platonism is more properly entitled Aristotelianism. This will clear the way for an account of the true difference between the questioning of Plato and that of Heidegger. The difference is not that of the road taken by both on their philosophical travels, but rather of how each proposes to see the sights on the way. The reconstruction of Platonism will lead us back not to Pindar and Heracleitus, but to what is just under our noses, and so is both present and absent in the everyday senses of those terms.

In the second half of this book, I shall turn to the fundamental points in Heidegger's interpretation of Nietzsche, paying special attention to the two volumes of university courses and essays published in 1961. Again, my intention here is not to provide an exhaustive scholarly account of that interpretation, but to understand and to assess the adequacy of Heidegger's joint contentions that (1) Nietzsche is a reversed Platonist; (2) his Platonism is the culmination of metaphysics; and (3) the inner sense of metaphysics is nihilism. In this way I hope to free metaphysics from the charges that have been leveled against it by Heidegger and his followers, by presenting a different and more accurate portrait of Platonism, a portrait in which there is room for the best features of Nietzsche and Heidegger as well. If the history of Western philosophy is the history of metaphysics, my goal is to defend metaphysics against the new way of thinking recommended by Heidegger.

Finally, my book is not intended as a scholarly report on Heidegger's philosophical career. I have immersed myself in the Heideggerian texts, as in those of Plato and Nietzsche, not out of historical curiosity but in order to clarify the present manifestation of the perennial philosophical question: What is to be done? Those who, like Heidegger and Lukács, followed Plato's example in going to Syracuse failed to grasp the significance of his publication of the failure of that act. One may agree instead with Heidegger that theory is the highest form of activity. The reason for this, however, is that theory is noble and good but not edifying.

I

Platonism

Platonism Is Aristotelianism

1

Platonic Ideas

By Platonism Heidegger means primarily, indeed, almost exclusively, the doctrine of Ideas. Heidegger discusses this doctrine in a wide variety of texts ranging over a period of fifty-odd years. If one studies closely this presentation of Plato in Heidegger's writings, a certain shift is evident from the initial to the later account. Alain Boutot, for example, notes that Heidegger began by seeing in Plato and Kant his precursors but ended by distancing himself from the entire history of philosophy.[1] He also observes that in the period defined by the preparation of *Being and Time,* the a priori character of the Ideas is understood as intrinsically temporal but not yet as nihilistic.[2] This latter development seems to be associated with Heidegger's intensive study of Nietzsche during the 1930s and 1940s; it is the interpretation resulting from this study that is of central, but not exclusive, interest to us. In this chapter, I want to present a summary account of what I take to be the four main points in Heidegger's evolving understanding of Plato's doctrine of Ideas. The first two may be stated briefly; the third requires a considerably lengthier exposition. The fourth point will make clear the Aristotelian perspective of Heidegger's interpretation of Platonism.

1.   Plato shifts his attention from the original Greek understanding of Being as *phusis,* or the process by which things of a certain look emerge into view, to "the *shining forth* of the *look* itself, [to] what the *view* offers *for* observation," namely, "the enduring presence, *idea,* the face in its nature as a look."[3] In other words, Plato concentrates upon the look as the foreground of *phusis;* the process by which the look comes into the light is now relegated to the background, as in the image of the cave in the *Republic:* "Uncoveredness is named in its various stages, but it is now thought from the standpoint of how it makes what shows itself accessible in its look [*eidos*] and how it makes this self-manifesting [*idea*] visible."[4] The original distinction between coveredness and uncoveredness is present in the distinction between the cave

and the surface of the earth, but this is subordinated to the role of fire and sunlight as that which allows what appears to shine forth in visibility.[5] *Alētheia* in its original sense as uncoveredness is now subordinated to the dominance of the Idea, and so too the notion of truth changes from uncoveredness to that of the correct measurement or calculation of the look as accessible to human cognition: to the correspondence or likeness of the description to the original.[6]

2.   The light by which the Ideas are rendered visible is itself transformed into an Idea, namely, the Idea of the Good, which is represented in the *Republic* by the image of the sun. Being as the process of emergence is replaced by the expression of the accessibility of the emergent entity to human understanding and hence of the serviceability or utility of things to the discursive, calculative intelligence. The Good is "that which makes the thing [*das Seiende*] useful or capable [*tauglich*] to *be* a thing. Being shows itself in the character of making possible and conditioning. Here the decisive step for all of metaphysics is taken."[7] Heidegger means by this last remark that the Idea is the prototype for the modern notion of *Sollen,* the Ideal or the perfect original to which the being aspires, and so the precursor to the Nietzschean doctrine of Being as value.[8] To say this in another way, the "utility" of the looks of beings makes them valuable to mankind as instruments for the satisfaction of the will. To be is to be visible or present to the calculative intellect, and so eventually to be manipulable or producible in accord with the human will.

3.   As the first two points imply, there are according to Heidegger two levels in the Platonic discussion of the Ideas. The underlying level of the original revelation of Being is covered over by the new doctrine of the accessibility and utility of what shows itself in a determinate way. But there is an additional ambiguity in the new doctrine itself. Plato understands the Ideas to be enduring preordinations of their copies or instances in the world of genesis and, as such, independent of the process by which they are apprehended. At the same time, he conceives of the Ideas by analogy with the model of the craftsman or handiworker. The Ideas are like blueprints which the divine artificer consults in the construction of beings of corresponding looks. Intrinsic to the model of the divine craftsman is the notion of the blueprint as itself constructed,

more precisely, as a product of the imagination. The divine craftsman is thus, contrary to Plato's intention, the prototype for the modern conception of Being as produced by the process of cognition. It also incorporates into Platonic ontology what may be called the utilitarian component of technical production.

This ambiguity in the Platonic doctrine as understood by Heidegger leads to an ambiguity in his critical analysis of Platonism. Heidegger so to speak alternates between "deconstructing" the intended doctrine by the application of original etymologies and "projecting" subsequent developments in the history of philosophy back into Plato's explicit account. Plato himself thus appears as an indistinct amalgam of original Greek views and disastrous innovations, innovations which are rooted in the elusiveness of Being's mode of presentation. As a result, it is not always clear whether Heidegger is criticizing the orthodox understanding of the doctrine of Ideas or reading his own "original" doctrines into the subterranean structure of the Platonic texts.

I will consider two different discussions by Heidegger of the productionist thesis, one dating from 1927 and the other from 1936/37. The first text is contained in a seminar given at Marburg University under the title *Fundamental Problems of Phenomenology*.[9] The context is that of a clarification of the phenomenological foundation of the distinction between essence and existence. More broadly stated, Heidegger describes the development from the Greek conception of Being as production to the modern doctrine that we know only what we make. In the section that concerns us,[10] Heidegger begins by listing the Greek concepts that underlie the medieval term *essentia*. These include *morphē, eidos, to ti ēn einai, genos, phusis, horos, horismos,* and *ousia*. We see here Heidegger's implicit assimilation of Platonic to Aristotelian terminology. The Idea as that which faces or stands before us is the prototype of the essence as that which stands beneath (*hupokeimenon*) the properties of the perceived entity.

Heidegger goes on to clarify the relation between *morphē,* "shape" or "form," which he translates as *Gepräge,* "mark," "characteristic," or "imprint" (the stamping of a coin), and *eidos,* literally, "look," (*Aussehen*). The word *morphē* refers originally to the shape of the perceived entity. "It means not only the spatial configuration but the total stamp of a thing, from which we read off what it is."[11] In ordinary Greek usage as explained by Heidegger, the model for the understanding of perceived entities is the productive activity of the craftsman: the activity of stamping lends to the produced entity its characteristic look, the *eidos* by which we see what has been produced. More generally, in the case of sense-perception, "the *eidos* or look of a thing is founded or grounded in its *morphē* or stamp."[12] The paradigm of the craftsman, and so of Being as production, is then according to Heidegger already to be found in the Greek understanding of sense-perception; if this is so, however, Plato's productionist metaphysics must be authentically Greek. Or are we to assume that Homer, Pindar, and Heracleitus had a different understanding of the *morphē* and *eidos* of the perceived being?

Heidegger does not answer this question; instead, he claims that in Greek ontology, by which he means primarily Platonism, the fundamental relation between *eidos* and *morphē* in the model of sense-perception is reversed. In perception, we apprehend the *eidos*, or look, via the *morphē*, or shape; I identify a dog or a cow as a being of such and such a kind by virtue of its phenomenological configuration, which is primarily (but not exclusively) physical. In Platonist ontology, however, the particular phenomenological configuration or "stamp" of the particular dog or cow is explained by, and so grounded in, the *eidos*, understood as prior to and independent of the particular dog or cow, in the way that a blueprint is prior to and independent of the artifact to be constructed in its light. As Heidegger expresses this, we move via a constructive conception (*Auffassen*) from the eidetic look (the blueprint) to the production (*Herstellen*)[13] of the perceived being. The focus of the paradigm of the craftsman thus shifts from perception to thinking.

Heidegger illustrates his point with the example of the potter. That which is "stamped" is a creation of the imagination (*Gebilde*). The potter shapes (*bildet*) a pitcher out of clay. "All shaping of a creation [*Alles bilden von Gebilden*] is carried out via the guiding thread and the standard of an image [*Bild*] in the sense of a model [*Vorbild*]."[14] In other words, the ontological meaning of *eidos* and *idea* is derived from the paradigm of production or craftsmanship; "the creation that is shaped in accord with the model" (the image or "idea" in the craftsman's mind) "is as such the likeness [*Ebenbild*] of the prior image" (as I here translate *Vorbild*). The prototype of the Platonic Idea is thus the pattern existing in the craftsman's mind by which he anticipates what he intends to produce. "The anticipated look, the pre-image [*Vor-bild*] points out the thing as it is before the production and how it ought to look when produced."[15] The continuous occurrence of the word *Bild* in this passage has the effect of underlining the pictorial or visual characteristics of the Idea or look; thinking is for Plato in the first instance a seeing with the eye of the soul, and sight (as Aristotle notes at the beginning of the *Metaphysics*)[16] is the sense that discerns the greatest number of differences, that is, determinations or properties. This is of importance for understanding Heidegger's interpretation of the Idea as the prototype of the category.

Of more immediate importance, however, is the assimilation of the blueprint (my term) or model to the status of a *Gebilde*. The model or pre-image in the case of the craftsman is an image of the imagination (*fantasia*). "The *eidos* as the anticipatory look in the imagination of what is to be stamped [i.e., imprinted onto the appropriate matter] presents the thing in accordance with that which it already was and is, prior to all actualization."[17] The principal function of the paradigm of the craftsman is to insinuate the activity of the imagination into Platonic ontology, contrary to Plato's intention. We see here an early example of what is today called deconstruction. The Aristotelian doctrine of *fantasia* as the middle term in perception between sensation and cognition is transferred by Heidegger to Platonist ontology in such a way as to anticipate the modern process by which the understanding is first united with and eventually subordinated to the will and the imagination.

The Platonic Idea is accordingly understood as the prototype of the Leibnizian perception or viewpoint and thus of the Nietzschean perspective. What Plato takes as the look of the being is in fact how the being looks to human cognition. Furthermore, in a way that is not fully compatible with the function assigned to the imagination, the Idea is now conceived as a *possibility* rather than as an actuality. The Idea is called an "anticipatory look," which Heidegger tacitly assimilates to the Aristotelian essence, or *to ti ēn einai* ("the thing in accordance with that which it already was and is"); and this in turn is taken in the modern, not the Greek or Aristotelian sense as "prior to all actuality." We see here an excellent example of Heidegger's tendency to insert his own doctrines into texts which he is ostensibly interpreting as deviations from the original manifestation of truth.

Finally, and closely connected with the reversal in status of actuality and possibility, the sentence we are studying imputes the origin of the a priori to the doctrine of the form as Ideal, and thus as "possibility" in the sense of that which allows the production of the thing. The *eidos* or the *to ti ēn einai,* that which the thing is in advance of production and which is the power through which it is produced, "provides the family of the thing, its descent, its *genos.*"[18] I note that for Heidegger the Platonic Idea and the Aristotelian *eidos* are intrinsically the same conception; Aristotle simply makes explicit in his doctrine of *ousia* what is implicit in the Platonic understanding.

Heidegger gives a similar analysis of *phusis,* "growing," "generating," "generating itself," that is, a production of the thing in accord with the look as model of what the thing ought to be. In other words, Plato wishes to maintain that nature, unlike the craftsman, works from perfect models; its paradigmatic looks are prior to the imagined models of the craftsmen and permanent rather than themselves created expressions of what the thing ought to be. But the model of the craftsman dominates over the intended doctrine. Plato holds that the natural look or Idea is the truth of the thing, the true or genuine thing itself (or what Plato will call the *on ontōs on*). It is the perfection of the thing, *to teleion,* and, as prior, permanent, and complete, it is that which we capture in the definition (*horismos,* another Aristotelian term).[19] But the use of the craftsman-model undercuts Plato's intentions in the manner described a moment ago.

A difficulty in Heidegger's interpretation is now apparent. The craftsman produces an artifact from materials that do not in themselves contain the form or nature of the item produced; one can therefore correctly say that the craftsman manufactures or constructs the artifact, which has no life or principle of growth of its own. A bed, for example, does not give birth to another bed; if it is true that the carpenter "uncovers" or brings to emergence the being of the bed, what he brings to emergence is not the same as what grows or emerges by nature. *Phusis* is the principle of that which grows or emerges from entities of its own kind; exactly the same, incidentally, is the inner sense of *natura,* from which we derive our ostensibly non-Greek conception of "nature." *Nascor* means "to be born," not "to be assembled or manufactured."[20] We say that artists "give birth" to their artworks in a metaphorical or derived sense. At the same time, by replacing nature as the principle of origination, the artist reveals something in addition to the artifact, namely, the human soul or creative activity, which is different from the activity of *phusis* and which "uncovers" different looks. Heidegger glosses over the sense of growth in the root *phu-* in favor of emergence, which is then as it were rendered homogeneous in the three cases of *phusis, technē,* and *poiēsis*. But growth is not the same as manufacture.

The pertinence of this difficulty will emerge more directly when I discuss Heidegger's analysis of the discussion of the Idea of the bed in book 10 of the *Republic*. Meanwhile, let me restate in summary form Heidegger's central contention: the concept of the existing thing (*realitas*), which is fixed initially in Greek ontology and which serves as the standard throughout the history of philosophy, consists of relations expressing the human activity of production, more specifically, of what pertains to the producibility of that which has been produced.[21] That which has been produced lies before one (i.e., is a *hupokeimenon*) as ready for use; this includes man-made tools as well as the things produced by nature. Things are understood as *ousia;* in ordinary language, "property," what lies ready to hand, is available or disposable. The philosophical sense of *ousia* follows directly from this and defines the mode of being of a thing as "availability" (*Verfügbarkeit*) or, as we also say, its presence to hand (*Vorhandenheit*), which belongs to it on the basis of its having been produced.[22]

So too the senses of *essentia* have emerged with respect to the conception of the activity and result of production. "The fundamental concept of *ousia* emphasizes on the other hand more the producedness of the produced in the sense of what is ready at hand as disposable."[23] In other words, it shifts from the activity of production to the status of the result as a production: as that which is present. This is as far as we need to follow Heidegger's analysis; I note only that in a later paragraph (14), he attributes the same understanding of Being to Kant: "A genuine understanding of an existing thing [*Seienden*] in its Being is present only to the creator-being [*Urhebersein*] of this thing. In the *production* of something lies the primary and direct reference to the Being of a thing. And this means: *Being of a being* signifies nothing other than *producedness*."[24]

By way of transition to the second text, the following remark is in order. The first stage of the doctrine of productionist metaphysics defines beings as productions, and the Being of beings in two ways. The first way, producibility, corresponds to existence; the second way, producedness, corresponds to essence. In Greek, one may designate these two ways as corresponding to the *on* and the *ousia,* respectively. It is illuminating to connect the present analysis to the subsequent investigation of the verb *einai* in the *Introduction to Metaphysics,* in which Heidegger shows that there is no one sense of "Being" that is common to or unites the various senses designated by the participle, the copula, and the infinitive.[25] As we shall see below, "common" (*koinon*) is understood in the sense of "universal," that is, the Idea or *eidos* as common to all of its existing instances.[26] That is, Heidegger assimilates the community of the Idea with its instances into the analogical unity underlying substance and the other categories, in order to obtain a universal or general concept of Being that is initiated by Plato and remains the defining mark of Platonism throughout its history. This is not compatible with Heidegger's own (in my view correct) thesis that there is no common doctrine of Being in Plato and for that matter in Greek thought altogether. I shall come back to this difficulty.

I can now turn to the second presentation of Plato's productionist metaphysics, which occurs in volume I of the *Nietzsche* lectures and essays.[27] Heidegger is discussing the relation of art to truth in Plato and in particular in the *Republic.* As he did not do in "Plato's Doctrine of Truth," however, Heidegger takes his bearings not by the allegory of the cave, but by the discussion in book 10 of the carpenter and the Idea of the bed. As will become evident when I examine the details, this discussion is clearly related to the analysis of 1927, which I have just summarized, by the theme of the paradigm of craftsmanly production. It should be said at once that Heidegger does not discuss the relation between the dramatic structure of the *Republic* and its philosophical significance. He therefore says nothing about an underlying reference to the original Greek doctrine of Being as uncoveredness. In particular, he does not raise the question of the relation between the conversation about the Ideas in the middle books of the *Republic,* of which the allegory of the cave is a part and which emphasizes the importance of mathematics, and the conversation about the Idea of the bed in book 10, which is part of the more general treatment of the quarrel between philosophy and poetry.

Still more precisely, Heidegger does not raise the question about the dubious status of the ostensible Idea of the bed, and so of the dangers that ensue from taking this text as definitive for an understanding of the Platonic doctrine. At the very least, it would seem that if Socrates takes seriously his example of the Idea of the bed, then there is a difficulty intrinsic to the doctrine of Ideas that is made explicit by the difference between *phusis* and *technē*. This difficulty is suppressed or concealed by Heidegger's interpretation of the Ideas as possibilities rather than as actualities. If there is an Idea of the bed, then there must also be Ideas of every possible artifact, including those which will never be invented by human beings. A sound understanding of the doctrine of the *Republic,* and by extension of Platonism, thus requires one to determine why Socrates introduces the example of the bed in book 10. This presumably has something to do with the shift from the link between mathematics and dialectic in the middle books to the reconsideration of the political significance of poetry in the last book.

Heidegger's shift from actuality to possibility dissolves the regular link in the dialogues between genuine being (*ontōs on*) and being by nature (*phusei*). This is closely connected to the shift from growth to emergence; artifacts are now taken to emerge in the same way as natural beings. So too the distinction between discovering and making dissolves. Heidegger is thereby able to treat the doctrine of the Ideas as the prototype of modern subjectivity; the model of the craftsman is thus the prototype for the productive *ego cogitans.* Underlying these shifts as accomplished by Heidegger's interpretation is the thesis that truth and Being are to be understood primordially or originally as uncoveredness.[28] Modernity presumably arises from the mistaken interpretation of *technē* as manufacture, and so of natural production as technical in this sense. Otherwise expressed, it arises from the shift, initiated by Plato, from uncoveredness as a property of beings to uncovering as an activity of the thinker-maker.

Heidegger's tendency to assimilate *technē* or *poiēsis* into *phusis* and to understand both as producing, not in the sense of manufacturing but of bringing forth from out of uncoveredness,[29] is therefore the basis or crucial element in his entire interpretation of Greek philosophy and by extension of the history of Western metaphysics as Platonism. The deconstruction of Plato proceeds by the ostensible demonstration of the concealment of uncoveredness by uncovering. In fact, the deconstruction is a construction assembled from bits and pieces of the Platonic corpus, which stands to Platonism as the Idea of the bed stands to the doctrine of Ideas. Heidegger does however note that this stage of the Platonic thinking about Ideas is not the highest,[30] presumably for the reason that it is connected to the development of conversations about the city. Why this consideration would not also be true of the allegory of the cave is not evident. Nor does Heidegger suggest, in the course of his analysis, that we are to give a subordinate status to the results he claims to establish.

To turn now to the most important details, after a very brief reference to mimesis, Heidegger cites the statement by Socrates (whom he identifies in a parenthesis with Plato) to this effect: "We are accustomed to pose [*tithesthai*] a single sort of form, one each corresponding to each [case of] the many, to which latter we apply the same name" (596a5–8: I have translated the Greek directly, not Heidegger's German translation). The verb *tithesthai* will be of considerable importance later, when I turn to a careful analysis of Socrates' speech in the *Phaedo* in which he explains how he arrived at the "hypothesis" of the Ideas. When used in the middle voice to express mental action, it is normally translated as "assume" or "lay down." A *hupothesis* is something that one lays down as a foundation upon which to support something else.

Heidegger notes correctly that the *eidos* is not a concept but a look (*Aussehen*), just as he did in the text of 1927. The look is the presence of the many, the same in each instance, their Being as present, and as so determined with reference to the look.[31] Each one of the given many is identified by reference to the monad of its uniform look.[32] The monad (as I have translated "das Eine") endures despite all changes suffered by the individual instances exhibiting that same look; this oneness of the look points out what the thing that we encounter "is." "Steadfastness" or "continuance" (*Beständigkeit*) thus belongs to Being as understood by Plato.[33] In developing this point, Socrates has introduced the general example of *skeuē*, vessels, implements, baggage, gear, and so forth; the term is here applied specifically to household objects such as the bed and the table.

Why does Socrates refer to beds and tables instead, say, of introducing natural beings such as plants or animals? Without penetrating deeply into the text, one may say that it is obvious that Socrates wishes to reduce the stature of the poet, who is the natural rival to the philosopher in the struggle to educate their fellow-citizens. Socrates therefore characterizes the poet as a producer of fantasms or inaccurate copies of the household artifacts produced by the craftsmen. He thus ignores the difference between poetry and painting, but more generally he disregards the fact, regularly illustrated by his own citations of poets throughout the *Republic,* that the mimetic artist, in the principal examples of the poet and musician, imitates the states of the human soul, not artifacts. By making the god a craftsman, Socrates detaches the *poiētēs* from his traditional association with the divine; by shifting from poetry to painting, Socrates is able to ignore the fact that artistic mimesis is an expression of the human soul, not a copying of entities, whether natural or produced.

Heidegger ignores the political context of the discussion of the bed in order to impose his ontological interpretation onto an apparently suitable passage. I shall show that the central point of Socrates' metaphor is to distinguish the god from craftsmanship or fabrication and not, as Heidegger claims, to establish him as a fabricator. Furthermore, assuming that the discussion in book 10 of the *Republic* is a fair basis for the understanding of Platonism, Socrates' interpretation of the divine craftsman is compatible in an essential respect with Heidegger's own account of the genuine or original Greek doctrine of Being. The craftsmanship of the god is that of the gardener (*phutourgos:* 597d5), not that of the carpenter. In growing the Idea of a bed, the god thus exhibits Heidegger's understanding of the original Greek sense of Being as *phusis,* or emergence. But the emergence of the Idea by nature is not the same as the emergence of the bed by manufacture. Even if we allow that there is a natural Idea of the bed, what it uncovers cannot be the same as the look uncovered by the carpenter's bed. This is rendered invisible by the assimilation of growth into emergence on the one hand and by the claim that emergence in Platonism is manufacture on the other.

In the text we are now studying, what interests Heidegger primarily is the function of the paradigm of the craftsman. This leads him (as in the previous example) to attribute to Plato the conception of Being as "the production of something created."[34] It must be the case that, by concentrating upon the look as accessible to the calculative intelligence, and so as useful for rendering things of that look disposable to human intentions, Plato not only degrades *technē* from disclosure or uncovering to producing or creating; he also comes to understand beings as "implements" like beds and tables that are designed by a divine craftsman for the sake of human utility. As usual, Heidegger presents Plato as the initiator of a doctrine that overlays elements of authentic Greek thinking with a patina of misunderstanding; he sees Plato as the initiator of what will evolve into a doctrine of "utilitarian" productionism in which the divine craftsman is no longer a god but mankind, whether *in propria persona,* as the transcendental ego or Absolute I, or finally as the will to power, understood as the will to will.

The *dēmiourgos,* or craftsman, is one who makes implements like beds and tables for the *dēmos,* or people, that is, for everyday life. But even he must make his implements "by looking to the Idea."[35] And neither he nor any other craftsman can make the Idea itself, which is "preordinated" and to which he is "subordinated." In other words, Heidegger acknowledges or rather insists upon the fact that it is not Plato's intention to initiate an ontology of subjective production. On Heidegger's reading, Plato is necessarily unaware of the implications of his own use of the paradigm of the craftsman, just as he is (mysteriously) unaware of the peculiar consequences of referring to an Idea of a manufactured thing like a bed. There is in this sense no merely practical activity; even the craftsman is a theoretician in the sense of one who looks to the Idea. To which I add the converse: on Heidegger's account, there is no purely theoretical activity. Being, and hence knowing, are both making. Once again, Heidegger is silent on the important question of political activity, or what Aristotle calls *praksis.* This would seem to be neither theory nor production. Heidegger's silence is justified in the sense that there is no notion comparable to Aristotelian *praksis* in Plato. But the absence of a distinction between *praksis* and *poièsis* in Plato is crucial to the question of the Platonism of Nietzsche, and so for Heidegger's interpretation of metaphysics. It is therefore not to his advantage that Heidegger overlooks this point.

Heidegger engages next in an extended discussion of *poiēsis* and *mimesis,* which may be summarized as follows. Socrates introduces the example of someone who "makes" the whole by rotating a mirror through an angle of 360 degrees. The mimesis of the whole that is contained in the entire series of reflections is not a *Her-stellen* in the sense of producing a second cosmos that is a replica of the first, but rather in the sense of a *Bei-stellen,* or "placing before" or "to one side of" the original, the look of that original in something else, namely, the mirror.[36] The mimesis containing the same look is an image, or a *phainomenon,* as opposed to things that truly are (*onta ge pou tēi alētheia*). The image is "made" but nothing is fabricated. Heidegger concludes from this that *poiēsis* is not to be understood as "manufacture," that is, the bringing into existence of a previously nonexistent construction that duplicates the look of an already existing original. In other words, on this point Plato apparently retains the original or genuine Greek understanding.

The difference between phenomena and things that truly exist is then explained by Heidegger not as an opposition of "appearance" in the sense of illusion on the one hand and Being on the other, but rather as the contrast between two different types of presence: the existent as on the one hand "self-manifestation" (*sich Zeigende*) and on the other as the unobstructed (*das Unverstellte*).[37] In other words, both the image in the mirror and the beings reflected in the mirror are on an ontological par in the sense that both are "uncoverings" or "presentations" of the same look, namely, the Idea, although in different ways. Heidegger develops this point by making use of an example of a house. The look of the house, which here replaces the Idea of the bed, is now said to "manifest itself" in both cases, namely, in the mirror image and in the structure of stone and wood.[38] So the look is "the same" in both cases. What is *not* the same is the *tropos,* or manner, in which the Idea manifests itself as "the purest" being.

The two tropes of manifestation correspond to the reflection and the carpenter's house, respectively. There must then be two forms of production, that of the carpenter or demiurge and that of the image-maker or painter (and here the *zōgraphos* replaces the mirror). Heidegger is commenting on 596e4–7 in the *Republic;* note that neither in the Greek text nor in Heidegger's interpretation is there at this point any reference to the look itself (Heidegger's "house") as a product of demiurgy. However, Heidegger infers from the example of the mirror that the same Idea of the house is present, albeit in two different ways, in the constructed house and in its image. But in Socrates' example, there is no reference to an Idea; the mirror produces an image of the world of genesis. The distinction between *phainomena* and *tēi alētheia* furthermore implies that the look is not the same in the two cases. A mirror image of the heavens is not the same as a direct perception of it. To come back to the house, we can dwell within it, but not within the painting of a house. Yet it is part of the essence or nature of a house that it is a human dwelling-place. It is therefore quite misleading to infer from the pictorial resemblance of an image to a three-dimensional being that both exhibit the same look, where by "look" is meant the genuine being of each.

Nevertheless, Heidegger extends the sameness of the look (despite different degrees of clarity) to the third level of images. Heidegger's terminology is also confusing in another respect. He takes the constructed house of stone and wood to correspond to the unobstructed or truly existing house, in contrast to the image in the mirror. In fact, however, if we put to one side the discussion of the mirror and turn (as Heidegger himself does) to the question of the Idea of the house, the constructed house is a secondary or phenomenal, and the image is a tertiary or fantastic, representation of the genuine self-manifestation of the Idea of the house. Furthermore, if the look is the same in all three cases, then either the looks of all three houses are instances of production or none is. This will militate against Heidegger's interpretation as well as against common sense if it can be shown that Socrates does not intend to attribute demiurgic manufacture to the god whose labor assists nature in growing the Idea of the bed.

Thus when Socrates says that the painter "does not make truly what he makes" (*ouk alēthē poiei ha poiei*),[39] he means that the carpenter gives us a less obstructed view of the Idea of the bed than does the painter. But "less obstructed" cannot mean that the Idea is present within the bed. It must mean rather that the bed of the carpenter is a more accurate image of the natural bed than is the painting, because the carpenter is said to have constructed his bed in accord with a look at the Idea. But the view obtained by the carpenter cannot itself be incorporated into the bed. If it were, there would be no essential difference between genuine being and the being of a phenomenon. This distinction is impossible to convey in the Heideggerian conflation of nature, *technē,* and art as *Her-vor-bringen.*

Let me emphasize this crucial point. If there is an Idea of the house or the bed, then the carpenter's house or bed is as much a "painting" of the Idea as the image-maker's bed is a "painting" of the carpenter's product. It is one thing for the carpenter to look at the Idea of the bed in order to make his own and something else again for the Idea of the bed to be exhibited *by nature* in the emergent bed. To anticipate a later point: the Idea of the cow is emergent within as intrinsic to all cows, whose genuine nature it expresses. If god is a gardener who grows the

Idea of the cow in the garden of nature, one can say that the converse is also true: cows themselves grow by exhibiting the Idea of the cow. There is no manufacture here, but two types of growth. But if god is also a carpenter who constructs the Idea of the bed, the converse is not true. Beds do not grow or for that matter assemble themselves by exhibiting the Idea of the bed. The Idea of the bed is *external* to the bed; a mediation is required by the activity of the carpenter. This mediation, the productive labor of the carpenter, thus expresses primarily not the Idea or look of the bed, but the appropriation of the look to human needs.

Again, to remain within the terms of the Socratic metaphor, the god does not stand to the Idea of the bed and the constructed bed as he stands to the Idea of the cow and the existing cow. By making the Idea of the cow, the god also makes cows. But by making the Idea of the bed, the god does not also make beds. The expression "god" thus stands for nature itself, not for a divine carpenter or even a gardener. There is as it were an *ontological* difference between the two kinds of work, natural and technical or demiurgic: the resultant "looks" are therefore different, not the same.

The bed of the carpenter is not a perfect being, but only "like" such a being (597a5–7). Yet according to Heidegger, the perfect look of the bed is manifested in both the image and the constructed bed. Heidegger does not explain the difference between the self-manifestation of the look and the likeness of that look. If the likeness is also a self-manifestation, then there is no difference between original and image. But this is entirely contrary to Plato's presentation. In saying this, I do not mean to suggest that Plato himself explains the relation between the original and the image. On the contrary, he does not.[40] But he asserts it; and it tends to disappear in Heidegger's analysis.

Suffice it to say that when one actually focuses on the details, Plato's text is more precise than the clarification of it that is offered by Heidegger. Sometimes, of course, Heidegger can be extremely illuminating. But often he misleads or conceals instead of uncovering or bringing into the open. To come back to the text, it is correct to say that the carpenter, according to Socrates in book 10, has consulted the Idea of the bed in anticipation of carrying out his production. On the other hand, so far as Socrates' statement goes, there is no reason to believe that the painter or image-maker looks at the Idea; instead, he looks at the constructed bed. He is looking at something that itself "looks like" the Idea of the bed.

When Socrates says at 597a10–11 that the carpenter's bed will be "dim" or "obscure" (*amudron*) with respect to the truth, he should be understood to mean that the bed will be less true than the Idea of the bed, not that there is a dim manifestation of the Idea within the fabricated bed. A dim manifestation is, precisely on Heidegger's interpretation, a contradiction in terms.[41] Manifestations of Ideas are maximally bright. The fabricated bed will be less true than the Idea, but more true than the painting, again, not because the Idea is manifested in the former but not in the latter, but because the carpenter has looked at the Idea whereas the painter has not. At the same time, to look at the Idea of the bed is not the same as to allow the Idea to emerge from or within the bed. Dimness with respect to the truth is a sign of a difference in being and hence in looks; it cannot be explained merely as owing to a difference in the *tropos,* or manner of presentation, of the same truth.

In sum, Socrates is about to maintain that the three processes of natural growth, demiurgic production, and image-making issue in radically different entities. On the basis of Heidegger's "original" definitions, the processes, regardless of their sources, must "disclose" the same look. But Socrates says of the Idea of the bed that "it exists in nature" (*en tēi phusei onta*). In the Heideggerian interpretation, the natural bed must also be disclosed by the carpenter's bed and its copy in a painting or a mirror. There is so to speak no "ontological" distinction between *theōria* and productive practice. Socrates does claim in this passage that the "natural" bed has been "produced" (*ergasasthai*) by god (507b5–8). By presenting god as a craftsman, or *phutourgos* (597d5: literally, a gardener), Socrates speaks in the voice of the "original" understanding of *phusis* but as the emergence of growth, not simply as emergence or uncovering. If the Idea of the bed is to be taken as standing for the Ideas altogether, then these become analogous to plants that are grown by God in the garden of genesis.

In this case the Idea of the bed is not a bed in the sense of a manufactured artifact but rather the look that is copied by manufactured beds. The look of a plant is not the same as that of a product of carpentry. There cannot be a homogeneity of looks in the three cases of Idea, bed, and painting. The disclosure of the look in the garden of nature is nothing like the disclosure processes of the arts and crafts. The look grows like a flower or a tree; it is not assembled by the god from other materials like stone and wood; but neither is it a copy of some existing bed, like the reflection in a mirror or a painting of a bed. The work of the divine gardener consists in acts like the planting and tending of seeds, not in copying something else in an artifact. Socrates distinguishes carefully between divine "gardening" and human making. When words like *apergazesthai* (bringing to perfection, making: 597c2) or *epistatēs* (supervisor or foreman: 597b13) are applied to god, they must be interpreted on the basis of the root sense of *phu-,* which is, as Heidegger always insists, "growth" or "emergence from itself." God neither makes or fabricates like a craftsman, nor does he supervise the manufacture of Ideas by subordinate workers. When Socrates says that god wished to be the "maker" (*poiētēs*) of a single genuine bed, he clarifies this making as a "growing" or "engendering" (*mian phusei autēn ephusen:* 597d3; cf. c4–5).

In other words, Socrates introduces the notion of divine gardening as a kind of making in order to carry out a comparison with *technē,* which for him includes arts like painting. The point of the comparison is to show that god is not a *technitēs* or a *poiētēs* in the same sense as the carpenter or painter. We can therefore agree with Heidegger's observation, noted above with respect to the mirror image, that *poiēsis* is not necessarily or primarily "manufacture." It is a serious question whether this comparison is intended to explain the nature of the Ideas in the most fully developed sense. Heidegger himself says that it is not;[42] yet he goes on to take the passage as decisive for our understanding of the origin of metaphysics in Plato.[43] In order to do this, he must ignore (or overlook) the fundamental sense in which the central metaphor is not that of manufacture but of gardening. Furthermore, Heidegger claims that Plato introduces the entire discussion in order to make clear how the same look can manifest itself in three different ways.[44] But the same look is not manifested in three different ways. The manifestation of the look takes place in the garden of nature; the carpenter copies this look, and the mimetic artist copies the copy (598b1–5); the copy is a *phainomenon,* and the copy of the copy is a *fantasma.*

To refer to the production of phenomena or manufactured beds and fantasms or reflections as instances of self-manifestation is to erase the very point that Socrates is attempting to establish. Strictly speaking, if the same look is revealed in three different procedures, then the crafts and arts should be sufficient bases for the study of Being. When Socrates says that the manufactured bed and painting are dim in comparison to truth, he means that they show us a copy of a self-manifestation, not the manifestation itself. As I have already stated, Socrates never explains how the image is able to "look like" the original without being that original. But Heidegger never explains how the same look is manifested in all three processes; he never explains what it means to say that *phusis* is emergence or that Being is presencing. He starts from "the that," to employ one of his favored Aristotelian expressions: this is what happens.

Heidegger thus arrives at the following decisive explanation of the unity or singularity of the Idea of the bed, and so, by extension, of each singular look with respect to each aggregate of generated things (*ta polla*). The ground for the singularity of the Idea does not lie in the fact that if there were two Ideas, both would be subordinated to their common look (in other words, the paradox of the third man would be generated), although Socrates says exactly this at 597c7–9. Instead, says Heidegger, it is because God wished to be "the maker of the genuine bed" (*ontōs klinēs poiētēs ontōs ousēs:* 597d1–2), and not of this or that bed, that he grew one bed by nature. In his translation, Heidegger says that God wished to be "der wesende Hervorbringer des wesenden Dinges," that is, the genuine bringer-forth of the genuine bed (*wesenden* here must be understood in conjunction with *walten* and *Unverborgenheit*). He then summarizes the entire analysis in the following words:

> Because God wanted to be such a God, therefore he allowed e.g. the manufacture of the bed [*Bettgestelle*] to go forth "in the unity and singularity of its nature [*Wesens*]." In what is then for Plato the essence of the Idea and therewith of Being finally grounded? In the fastening together of producing [*In der Ansetzung eines Schaffenden*], the essentiality of which appears to be preserved only then, when its production is unique, a one, by which one can account for that superelevation from the representation of a multiplicity to the representation of its unity.[45]

In the balance of the section, Heidegger reinstitutes the Platonic distinction between carpentry, or *technē,* and the arts, or *mimēsis,* by noting that the former copies the Idea, whereas the latter is "third from the king" in Plato's expression; that is, he copies a copy.[46] I note that he continues to believe that the Idea is dimly visible in the painting: "In this medium . . . the look is unable to manifest itself purely as such"; that is, it manifests itself dimly or impurely. It is not hair-splitting to insist that in the image there is no *sich Zeigen* at all in Heidegger's precise sense of that expression. He himself cites Plato's (i.e., Socrates') conclusion about the relation between *Kunst* (mimetic art) and truth as follows: "Art [*mimētikē*] stands far from the truth." Heidegger explains the meaning of this assertion: "What [the artist] produces is not the *eidos* as *idea* (*phusis*), but *touto eidōlon*," that is, an image.[47] Continuing: "This is only the appearance of the pure look; *eidōlon* means a small *eidos,* not only in the sense of measurement, but as insignificant [*ein geringes*] in the manner of manifesting and shining forth [*des Zeigens und Erscheinens*]."

This final assertion almost but not quite cancels the earlier contention that there are three different ways in which the same look manifests itself. But the more important point is that Heidegger attributes a "productionist" account of Being to Plato on the basis of the discussion of the Idea of the bed and the inferiority of mimesis to both *technē* and philosophy. The passage selected as paradigmatic for the Platonic doctrine of Being is thus especially ambiguous with respect to Heidegger's own intentions. It seems that Socrates accepts Heidegger's account of the meaning of *phusis;* but Heidegger as it were suppresses this implication of the Platonic metaphor and interprets it from the standpoint of the productive crafts, thereby reversing Plato's own evident intentions. But it is also true that Socrates distinguishes sharply between *phusis* on the one hand and both *technē* and *mimēsis* on the other, a distinction that Heidegger tends to blur even as he is insisting upon it. And the same can be said for the distinction between *technē* and *mimēsis.*

4. Side by side with the interpretation of the Idea as a product analogous to that of the craftsman (and so not in the genuine sense of what grows by nature) is Heidegger's claim that the Platonic doctrine of Being, like that of all "metaphysicians" after him, is a "general" or "average" conception of what is common to beings of different types. I quote from the seminar on phenomenology of 1927:

Platonism Is Aristotelianism

21

A look at the history of philosophy shows that very soon, various regions of beings [*Seienden*] were uncovered: nature, space, soul, [but also] that they nevertheless could not be grasped in their specific Being. Already in antiquity there arose an average concept [*Durchschnittsbegriff*] of Being, that was applied to the interpretation of all beings of different regions of Being and their modes of Being. But the specific Being itself in its structure could not be explicitly formulated and delimited as a problem. Thus Plato saw very well that the soul and its Logos is another being [*Seiendes*] than the sensuous existent. He was not however in a position to delimit the specific mode of Being of this being in distinction from the mode of Being of any other being or non-being; but for him as well as for Aristotle and the period extending to Hegel and especially for his successors, all ontological investigations busy themselves with an average concept of Being in general.[48]

In this passage, Heidegger means by an "average concept of Being" one that empties Being of its content in order to apply it to all regions or types of beings. This concept of Being is referred to in the opening pages of *Being and Time* with an initial citation from Aristotle: " 'Being' is the 'most universal' concept: *to on esti katholou malista pantōn.*"[49] Heidegger points out that the universality of Being is not that of a genus. It is rather to be explained as the unity of analogy.[50] Being stands to the various regions of beings, classified in the categories, as health stands, among other things, to the physician, medicine, and the physician's patient. Heidegger says in *Being and Time* that Aristotle, despite all dependence on Plato, places the problem of Being "on a fundamentally new basis. But neither was he able to illuminate the darkness of this categorial association."[51]

I should note that the universality of the concept of Being relative to the categories is not the same as the "community" of the Idea with respect to its instances. This point is obscured because Heidegger talks about beds rather than, say, cows. The "look" of the cow has in common with all natural cows not the being but the *way* of being, that is, the particular order assumed within each instance such that all instances show the same look. On the other hand, the universal "Being" has in common with all categories not a look, but the property of being itself. This property is universal in the sense that it is not a definite or identifiable look at all; otherwise put, it is the emptiest of all properties precisely because everything whatsoever possesses it. It need not be stressed that only beds possess the look of the genuine bed. If there were actually an Idea of the bed, one could perhaps suggest that there is a unity of analogy between the look of that Idea and the looks of the constructed bed on the one hand and the painted bed on the other. Even here, however, the terminology would be forced, since the "look" is synonymous with the nature or genuine being of its instances, and the look of a carpenter's bed is different by nature from that of its ostensible Idea on the one hand and its image in a painting on the other.

In what sense is there an "average concept of Being" in Plato? In fact, and contrary to Heidegger's early claim, the answer is: in no sense. Heidegger would be justified to hold that there is no doctrine of Being, no ontology of any kind, in Plato, but rather a variety of presentations, some starting from analytical considerations of experience, others formulated in myths about the destiny of the soul, of what are variously called Ideas, forms, and greatest genera, as well as natures and powers. No doubt Plato was unable to delineate either Being in its specific structure or the specific mode of Being of the distinct types of beings; but the reason may have been that there is no such specific structure, whether of Being in general or in each of its modes.

However this may be, Plato's Ideas are certainly not Aristotelian categories. Whether one regards the development from Plato to Aristotle as a progress or a decline, the Platonic Idea becomes in Aristotle an *eidos* in the sense of an *ousia,* namely, the specific form that is exhibited by natural particulars. The Idea of the cow stands to particular cows as the species-form "cow" stands to particular cows. But the species-form is not the "most universal" concept of Being. It is rather a single category within the table of categories, and not even the being that possesses instances of the various categories. It is the individual cow, not the species-form, that possesses properties, that is, items from the respective categories, one of which is a species-form.

When Aristotle uses the expression "being qua being," he is referring to the fact that whatever is, is a structure of species-form plus at least one item from each of the remaining categories. "Being qua being" is neither a particular being nor a "common" being in the sense that the Idea is common to all instances showing the same look. One might call being qua being a relation or a concept, whether or not one regards it as an analogy. The relation or concept may be said to be present in every being not as an identifiable and hence determinate look, that is, as the look of this particular type of being, but rather as the structure that is exhibited by all beings. The structure is not determinate or particular; it is universal. The Idea, on the other hand, is not universal; it is merely common to a specific set of beings. The closest Plato comes to discussing the question of the structure common to Ideas is in such dialogues as the *Sophist,* the *Philebus,* and the *Parmenides,* in which he gives various accounts of such properties as being, sameness, otherness, oneness, manyness, the limited, the unlimited, and so on. These discussions are not only inconclusive in themselves and as a totality; they are also quite different from presentations of the Ideas as looks. The difference between these two kinds of discussions underlines my earlier assertion that there is no "average concept of Being" in Plato.

Nevertheless, Heidegger tends to slide from *koinon* to generality when discussing the Ideas, in such a way as to prepare for the thesis that the underlying sense of Being in Plato and Aristotle is the same.[52] In other words, the *eidos* and the Idea as look are assimilated via *phusis* to the *on hēi on,* Aristotle's "being qua being."[53] This can be illustrated clearly by way of the *Introduction to Metaphysics.* In summarizing a discussion of *phusis* and *logos,* Heidegger says of the transitions in Greek philosophy, "*Phusis* becomes *idea* (*paradeigma*); truth becomes correctness. The Logos becomes a proposition, it becomes the place of truth as correctness, the origin of the categories, the fundamental proposition about the possibilities of Being. 'Idea' and 'category' are in the future the two titles under which Western thinking, doing, and estimating, existence in its entirety, stands."[54]   This passage must be integrated into Heidegger's general thesis that Western philosophy is metaphysics from the time of Plato onward. And metaphysics, to cite a representative text, "states what is being as being [*das Seiende als das Seiende*]. It contains a *logos* (proposition) about the *on* (being [*das Seiende*]).... Metaphysics busies itself in the region of *on hēi on*" and so on.[55] In short, metaphysics is "knowledge about the categories as the determinations of the Being of beings."[56] If however metaphysics is Platonism, then, despite the difference between Plato and Aristotle, Platonism is Aristotelianism. In other words, the differences between Plato and Aristotle are those between the originator of metaphysics and his greatest pupil. Aristotle develops Platonism; he does not change it.[57]

Heidegger apparently understands the evolution from the Idea to the table of categories to be mediated by the accessibility of the definiteness of the look to discursive intelligence. Although one can give vague descriptions of *phusis* as a process of emergence, it is clearly impossible to assign that process any definite properties without reifying it or transforming it into a particular being. I want also to observe that to speak of emerging, coming into view, shining forth, and so on is not to talk about anything in particular but of anything whatsoever; Heidegger's preferred understanding of *phusis,* and so of Being, is at least as "general" or "universal" and so as "empty" as the Aristotelian table of categories and its associated concept of being qua being.

But this criticism or comment to one side, one can state the properties of the look of a bed, a cow, or some other determinate being. Again a distinction must be drawn here; to state the properties or some of the properties of a bed or a cow is not the same as to state the properties of the Idea of the bed or of the cow. The look of a bed or a cow is entirely specific qua look (although of course it is not something that can be precisely or exhaustively described); if there is such a thing as a Platonist ontology or metaphysics of Being, in a sense that is prototypical for Aristotle's being qua being, then it must consist of statements about Ideas as ontological entities of a certain type, not as distinct looks. The properties of the look of a cow are specific to that look; the properties common to all Ideas are not specific to the look of the cow. Not all Ideas look like cows.

For whatever reason, Heidegger does not draw this distinction. He focuses instead on two other points: (1) the reification of Being as a determinate look; and (2) the community of the Idea as look with respect to the things exhibiting that look. From the first point, he derives the ancestry of Aristotle's categories from the Idea as look; from the second point, he derives the generality or universality, and so the "emptiness" in the sense of "averageness" of the metaphysical conception of Being. But these two points are incompatible with one another. Aristotle's enumeration of the categories is rather casual, but the categories themselves are quite precise and in no sense vague or general. The generality or universality of the concept of Being is not that of the table of categories; it seems rather to characterize the copula, which as Heidegger notes from time to time is used even with respect to Being (as when we say, "Being is a concept"). Heidegger infers from this that we must understand "Being" in advance of our use of its various names,[58] but the closest he comes to clarifying this understanding is by way of the previously described generalities about emergence, presencing, concealing and revealing, and the like.

My own view, which I propose to develop in the next chapter, is in partial agreement with Heidegger. I agree that we must understand "Being" prior to engaging in analyses of its various uses. However, I disagree with him in believing that the preawareness or preunderstanding is given within and can be explicated in terms of everyday experience and language, thanks to the accessibility or disposability to human intelligence of things or beings. As I noted earlier, Heidegger himself in his most lucid moments begins with an analysis of everyday modes of speaking about our encounters with beings. He runs into trouble when he attempts to turn away from these encounters to a meditation on the process through which what we encounter is presented to us. But apart from what we encounter, *there is no encounter.* As Heidegger wisely says, "Nothing happens."

Aristotelianism

Heidegger's distinction between Being and beings may be understood as a post-Hegelian revision of an Aristotelian insight. Although there is no direct or explicit analogy in Aristotle to what Heidegger calls Being, one can see in the latter a residue of the Aristotelian formulation of the relation between being and thinking. For Aristotle, the *eidos,* or species-form, or "being" in the fullest and primary sense of the term, is given to human cognition on the occasion of perception of the particular of such and such a kind,[59] via enactment in the passive or potential intellect. This corresponds very roughly to the Heideggerian doctrine of the "gift" of Being to human thought. Being is accordingly not produced by humankind, but the attempt to master Being through technical or productive thinking plays a crucial role in the determination of beings.[60] Heidegger thus separates the receptive thinking of Being from the productive thinking of beings, while retaining the Hegelian understanding of both as temporal processes.[61]

Let this general remark introduce the following conclusion from my previous discussion of Heidegger's account of the Platonic Ideas. Although Heidegger and his successors refer to metaphysics as Platonism, what they actually understand by this term would be better (although of course not perfectly) described as Aristotelianism. Despite what has been called his aporetic or even dialectical presentation, Aristotle, unlike Plato, directs us toward a first philosophy, traditionally called metaphysics on however ambiguous a basis, that is explicitly referred to as the science (*epistēmē*) of being qua being. Despite a certain amount of what could be called advertisement of the merits of a science of dialectic, that is, of a science of the Ideas, Plato never presents us with any instances of how such a science would function. In subsequent chapters I shall argue that it would be much better to refer to Platonism as an attempt to think the whole, rather than to define the ontological constituents of the whole. Heidegger is of course well aware of this way of characterizing metaphysics;[62] unfortunately he understands it to refer to the attempt to think being in its totality or in other words being qua being (but not Being).

One can, and indeed must, distinguish between two senses of *epistēmē*, or "knowledge," in Aristotle. As I shall indicate, we know the first principles and causes in a way different from the manner in which scientific or demonstrative knowledge is obtained about the distinct species of beings. But my point is not that Aristotle advocates demonstrative knowledge in metaphysics; it is rather that Aristotelianism, or the historical development of metaphysics, alias Platonism, turns upon the suppression of the difference between the aforementioned two senses. Whether in approbation or condemnation, metaphysics comes to be identified with demonstrative knowledge, via predicative discourse, of pure forms.

This situation does not arise without assistance from Aristotle. Being qua being is defined by means of a categorial structure which itself rests upon the conception of *ousia* as the independent owner of properties. It thus looks very much as though the science of being qua being is predicative discourse, or the assertion of the properties of *ousia* (translated as both substance and essence). Since *ousia,* understood as essence, is the species-form, Aristotelian metaphysics is at bottom the thinking of pure, eternal forms that are discovered or received rather than produced, whether by the origination-process of Being or by human cognition.

As we shall see, there is no demonstrative knowledge of essence for Aristotle; hence the categories are, strictly speaking, irrelevant to the explanation of how we apprehend or know, and hence possess an *epistēmē*, of being in its primary sense of *eidos*. But the categories are directly relevant to the question of the structure of being qua being. In order to keep straight the situation within the *Metaphysics*, we have to distinguish between knowledge of the *eidos*, or essence, which arises by noetic intuition, and knowledge of being qua being. This latter is knowledge not of the *eidos*, but of the *on* as consisting of form and matter.

The first category contains the answers to the question What is it? which we address to each being: it is an *ousia* in the sense of essence or species-form. The other categories (and Aristotle's lists vary) classify all remaining properties of the being. These properties are not of the *eidos* but of the *on*, or being. Whereas each such property is accidental in the sense that it could have been otherwise, Aristotle intends the categories as a schema of properties which are necessary in the general sense that every *on*, understood as a composite of form and matter, must possess one or another property from every category in the schema.

With a crucial exception that I will mention in a moment, being qua being thus refers to the structure underlying beings, namely, to be an instance of a species-form with properties that are classifiable according to the categories. The exception is discarnate form, God or the pure thinking of thinking. This leads to the vexed question of whether metaphysics in the sense of "first philosophy" can be the same as "theology," or knowledge of God, the highest being.

We do not need to take a stand on this question because it is not central to our present concern: the development of metaphysics understood today (wrongly) as Platonism. As to the doctrine of actuality and potentiality, developed in book *Theta* of the *Metaphysics*, it constitutes in one sense a separate analysis of the problem of being, and in another sense it is subordinate to the understanding of *eidos*. Since it is with *eidos* that I am primarily concerned, I shall put to one side the distinction between actuality and potentiality, on which I have written elsewhere.[63]

To summarize by way of transition: there is no single science of being in the Aristotelian corpus, but there is a science of being qua being that has determined the historical destiny of metaphysics. In the Platonic dialogues, by contrast, there is also no single science of being qua being, but at most a variety of discussions of Ideas or pure forms that cannot be reduced to a common, well-defined doctrine. Furthermore, there is an elaborate presentation of the human soul in terms of the erotic desire for the Ideas, of which one finds only a pallid vestige in book *Lambda* of the *Metaphysics*. Eros is not itself an Idea but what one might almost call, in Hegelian terms, negative excitation. There is in Plato no speculative dialectic to correspond to this psychic excitation, nor is there a *logos,* in the sense of a complete discursive account, of the origin of the cosmos or Whole (*to holon*), the Platonic analogue to Hegel's (and Heidegger's) "das Ganze." Neither God, man, nor world, the three principal topics of metaphysics, is in Plato accessible to the predicative or analytical discourse concerning determinate formal structure.

I have argued elsewhere that there are striking parallels between the Platonic and the Heideggerian ways of philosophizing and do not wish to repeat that discussion.[64] For my present purposes, it is pertinent to say instead that both the speculative dialectic of Hegel and the "originative" thinking of Heidegger reflect in their opposition to traditional metaphysics a dependence upon Aristotle that is also visible in their admiration for him. The simplest way in which to explain the centrality of Aristotle for both German thinkers is to say that each is concerned, Hegel in a positive sense and Heidegger as its sharp critic, with the notion of a science of the ultimate structure of the whole. Otherwise put, Hegel replaces metaphysics by the "first philosophy" of the *Science of Logic,* whereas Heidegger clearly regards philosophy as nothing other than "first philosophy," albeit not as a science but as an inquiry into Being.

My general suggestion, then, is that the postmodern identification of metaphysics as Platonism, even allowing for the distinction between the enigmatic dialogues of Plato and his historical influence, is not merely a crude oversimplification; it is largely on the wrong track. The ontological interpretation of Platonism is wrong in itself because it omits one of the two crucial components of the Platonic tradition: the doctrine of Eros or, more comprehensively, the dependence of *logos* upon *muthos*. As to the theory of Ideas, it is an invention of nineteenth-century historical scholarship, based not upon the Platonic dialogues but upon Aristotle.

In sum, the most evident implication of the Platonic dialogues as fictional dramas or poems is that there is no science of being qua being and certainly none of Being or the whole. Aristotle, on the other hand, clearly refers to the science of being qua being in conjunction with the categories and predicative assertions. Whether or not the name "metaphysics" derives from the classification of Aristotle's manuscripts by Andronicus of Rhodes, metaphysics as we know it (but not necessarily as it ought to be known) is a product of Aristotle and the Aristotelian tradition, not of Platonism.

What can be said, however, is that the turn away from the primacy of form to the primacy of the formation-process, although it seems to have more in common with Christian speculation than with Greek philosophy, is certainly related to the Platonic doctrine of Eros. But since the pejorative sense of metaphysics refers to the notion of pure forms, this observation serves only to emphasize the inaptness of the designation of metaphysics as Platonism. As one might put it, the Aristotle of the Aristotelian tradition created metaphysics by ignoring the Platonic reservations with respect to discursive as opposed to mythical thinking and by replacing the mythical or hypothetical[65] doctrine of Ideas with the scientific doctrine of species-forms.

In order to avoid confusion, I must immediately qualify the assertion that metaphysics is Aristotelianism by noting that it is intended to bring out the inner sense of the Heideggerian thesis that metaphysics is Platonism. Once we discard fashionable contemporary ideologies and study the history of philosophy in detail, it becomes apparent that there are many different types of metaphysics. Any attempt to answer the question What is metaphysics? that takes its bearings by the actual uses of the term will soon dissolve into an endless series of particular historical and doctrinal analyses. The multiplicity of the conceptions of metaphysics is itself no doubt due to the fact that what we mean by this term is a consequence of what we mean by philosophy. It is tempting to conclude that nothing serious can be said about metaphysics unless we ourselves engage in it.

In what follows, it is not my concern to give a balanced, comprehensive picture of Aristotle's development of his contention that "being is said in many ways."[66] Neither shall I analyze in detail the ambiguities of his contention that "being" is a *pros hen legomenon*, that is, a term applied with respect to the sense of *ousia*, but not in such a way (*kath'hen*) as to define a single science. The key point is that the investigation of what is said *kath'hen legomenon* belongs to one science of a single species of beings; this science assumes the species as given and attempts to acquire demonstrative knowledge of beings of this species.

The *pros hen* distinction, as we saw previously, is intended to convey the fact that the items in the remaining categories are called "being" with respect to the first category. I believe that this is a crucial source of confusion for the subsequent development of metaphysics. The fact is that, by Aristotle's own doctrines, the items in the remaining categories are properties of the composite being (*on*) or substance. To say that they are called "being" with respect to *ousia*, or essence, confuses two distinct points: (1) The properties classified in the other categories are called "being" with respect to the substance whose properties they are, not with respect to the essence, or *eidos*, of that substance; (2) The substance is called "being" primarily with respect to its essence.

To these two points, I may add a third: as the primary sense of being, *eidos* is also the foundation of the structure of being qua being. But it is not itself being qua being. Putting to one side the problem of God or the highest being, mentioned above, as an added complication that does nothing to simplify matters, one can see that there is a dualism intrinsic to Aristotle's treatment of being. He draws no distinction akin to Heidegger's between Being and beings, but he does distinguish between form and being qua being, although they are closely related, as I have just noted. The turn to a Heideggerian "Being" arises, I suspect, from the fact that *eidos* is a configuration of essential properties, the necessary unity of which cannot be established by discursive reason.

This point needs development. There seem to be only two possible ways in which we can know the *eidos*. Either we arrive at this knowledge by apprehending its properties, which we are then able to state in a series of predicative assertions as belonging to, and indeed as constituting, the essence; or else we intuit or perceive intellectually the *eidos* in its unity and identity. The first alternative is of course excluded for Aristotle, since to know an *eidos* is to possess its definition, and there is no predication in a definition.[67] But there is a deeper difficulty in this alternative. If it is asserted, we must distinguish between essential and accidental properties of the substance; obviously no essence can have accidental properties. But in order to specify the essential properties, we must know the essence.

In other words, we cannot know one before the other; hence we must know them simultaneously. What Aristotle says of the specific difference must hold for all essential properties: there is no predication here. There is no "before and after" with respect to the essential properties;[68] they are a fully given, internally articulated unity. We cannot predicate them of anything because there is nothing in the essence *other than* the essential properties of which to predicate them. They belong, so to speak, to themselves. Accordingly, the essence must be known by intellectual perception, or *noēsis,* exactly as Aristotle says in the *Posterior Analytics.*[69]

The *eidos* or essence is intuited all at once; no demonstration is involved in grasping it. But there is also no demonstration in the science of being qua being, which consists primarily in the presentation of the schema of the categories and the justification of the *pros hen* status of descriptions of being qua being. The categories, as the German philosophers from Kant onward objected, are not "deduced" by Aristotle. And within the categories, the distinction between *ousia* in the sense of composite separate substance and the properties of this substance depends upon a combination of intellectual intuition and sense-perception. If there is any demonstrated knowledge in metaphysics, it must be subsequent to and dependent upon predemonstrative knowledge.

Let me recapitulate. In order to know being qua being, we must verify the distinction between essences and accidents or, what comes to the same thing, between substances and essences. This verification rests upon intellectual intuition; that is, it is prediscursive or metascientific. As has often been noted, the Aristotelian science of being qua being rests upon the givenness within pretheoretical experience of separate and composite particulars like man, dog, horse, but also tree, stone, star, and so on. To this we can add the following important point. Intellectual intuition is not an occult or theoretical power reserved for metaphysicians; it is the power of human thinking par excellence, by which we apprehend a given pattern of properties as constituting a separate particular of such and such a kind.

In the *Nicomachean Ethics*[70] Aristotle says that *epistēmē* is *hupolēpsis,* that is, "taking up" into the intellect and thereby forming a conception "of the universals and of necessary beings, which are the principles of demonstration and of every science (for science is via *logos*); but there is neither science nor *technē* nor *phronēsis* of the principles of that which is known." As I have already noted, meta-physics, or first philosophy, is *sophia* or *epistēmē*[71] in the sense of the theoretical study of "the first principles and causes." But this formu-lation has to be rendered more precise by distinguishing between the apprehension of the principles and highest causes of the first science, which can occur only through *nous* or intellectual perception, and the *apodeikseis,* or demonstrations, that follow from these perceptions.

In this context, one should note briefly an aporia concerning the universal. The *Posterior Analytics* states that the *kath' hauto,* that is, the *ousia* or *eidos,* is universal.[72] This doctrine seems to be denied in a number of passages in the *Metaphysics.*[73] I find the texts to be mutually inconsistent and those in the *Metaphysics* to be obscure beyond the possibility of secure interpretation. But regardless of whether *ousia* is universal or not, it cannot be known by demonstration. Hence meta-physics, understood as first philosophy, is not demonstrative knowledge.

On the other hand, many have refused to believe that metaphysics is nothing more than a dialectical presentation of the conflicting opinions about being. Their position would gain in strength if they could show what demonstrations, based upon the noetic perception of essences, make up the *epistēmē* of first philosophy. Whether or not they can produce such demonstrations from Aristotle's texts, their argument itself supports my main contention: Aristotle, willingly or otherwise, is the source of the confusion that leads to the notion of metaphysics as rational knowledge of eternal form.

Metaphysics (as distinct from first philosophy) arises from the attempt to furnish a body of demonstrated truths about essences. This attempt is associated historically with the categorial structure that Aristotle introduces in conjunction with his very cryptic account of the science of being qua being in book *Gamma* of the *Metaphysics.* One could say that the categories, understood as the properties of being (separate substances), are replaced with categories of the essential properties, not of this or that essence (since these would differ from case to case) but of essence as such. This step is encouraged by the so-called *pros hen* relation, which gives the impression that the properties in the remaining categories are called "being" with respect to the first category of *ousia.* In other words, being qua being is now understood, tacitly or explicitly, as essence, the primary sense of being. As is entirely clear in Kant, what is essential to a being is furnished it by the transcendental ego via the categories. The distinction drawn by Aristotle between essence and being qua being accordingly collapses.

For Aristotle, the most important (but not the only) part of what it means to be is to have an essence. Essences are particular identities; they share a universal in the genus, but each is distinguished from the other by its differences, the most important of which is the ultimate difference. What we have understood by the essence is expressed in a definition. The definition (*horismos*) states the genus and the ultimate difference; but these are derived from observation and so from perception, both sensuous and intellectual. To repeat an earlier observation, there is no predication in a definition, no before and after with respect to the essential properties, because these are given simultaneously to intuition, that is, they actualize all at once, not in an order. Hence none belong to some other property; there is no owner of essential properties in the essence. At this point, a new interpretation becomes possible. The givenness or visibility or presence of the essential properties may be conceived as concealing an underlying and invisible owner, what one could call the substratum of the essence itself, or Being, namely, that which has no properties because it is not a particular, but rather a universal, or being qua being in a new sense: that which is common to all beings.

But the *eidos* is an *atomon eidos;* it is presented at once and as a unity. It cannot be either assembled from below by a combination of predicative statements or arrived at by analysis from above, that is, by the division of the genus, even assuming that we knew all the differences of each genus. But we are left in the dark concerning the identity of virtually all differences other than such reliable examples as "rational" and "featherless."

I believe we arrive at the following conclusion: there cannot be a demonstration of the *eidos,* and hence there is no scientific knowledge of it, whether or not we call it universal. It is impossible to verify the content of an intellectual intuition, since this is the foundation or precondition for all scientific verification. There is accordingly no science, that is, no discursive knowledge consisting of predicative statements, statements that say something about something, of the primary sense of being, namely, *eidos.* Metaphysics, in order to be understood as the discursive analysis of being qua being, then becomes dependent upon

Platonism

a metadiscursive assertion of essence, and this in turn leads in two directions, both fatal for our science.

Either (1) metaphysics devolves gradually into a descriptive phenomenology in which we exchange assertions about how essences look to us or else (2) it is replaced by a linguistic conventionalism, with rules or definitions that *stipulate* what shall count as an essence in each case. As one could also put this, metaphysics devolves either into the arbitrariness of looking or the endless discussion of the rules of discussion: into voyeurism or chatter.

This is in fact precisely what has transpired in the course of the history of philosophy. From the present standpoint, we may regard this history as the steady repudiation of the given, that is, of everyday experience as a more reliable source of the units to be analyzed than any theoretical construction purporting to give those units or their structure not as they appear, that is, show themselves, but as they are, that is, in accord with a paradigm or model that abstracts from the phenomena in order to reconcile their ostensible inconsistencies. The repudiation of Aristotle by Aristotelianism thus leads inevitably to history, understood as the endless record of the production and rejection of models of ontological structure.

There can be no doubt that Aristotle intended metaphysics to be the science of being qua being in a sense having nothing to do with historical process, whether in the transcendental or human senses of that expression. At the same time, it is impossible to doubt that the weaknesses intrinsic to his textual presentation of metaphysics, and so to Aristotelianism (in the sense above defined, as analogous to the Heideggerian use of "Platonism"), gave rise to the gradual triumph of phenomenological and linguistic historicism.

Unity and Identity

My argument to this point has been intended to suggest that Aristotelianism, or the metaphysics of being qua being as form, leads directly, because of aporiai internal to its original presentation by Aristotle, to a metaphysics of activity, not of course in the Aristotelian sense of *energeia,* but in a sense much closer to the Platonic notion of Eros as self-differentiating psychic formation, in a way not dissimilar to what Hegel calls negative excitation. Eros, however, is transformed from pure

Platonism Is Aristotelianism

negative desire for separate forms into a "transcendental" process of formation. Eros does not merely differentiate the psyche into a variety of human types, each defined by what it loves. Erotic desire is now conceived as a double process: that of desire and of the satisfaction of desire by the production of the forms it seeks.

If we take classical metaphysics to be defined as Aristotelianism, together with its extension into the modern period in the guise of Cartesianism, but also of Neo-Kantian positivism and phenomenology, and on the other hand if we define "process" metaphysics to be exemplified by German Idealism and Hegel, but also by post-Idealist thinkers like Nietzsche and Heidegger, to say nothing of the postmoderns, then the following historical observation is valid. The turn from the classical to the process metaphysics is in an essential sense a return from Aristotelianism to Platonism. Ironically, this partial return to Plato has been identified, especially from the time of Nietzsche forward, as anti-Platonism.

It is of course not my intention to maintain that Plato's various discussions of the Ideas, however sketchy or poetic, amount to a genuine anticipation of Idealism or of Nietzschean and Heideggerian doctrines of formation-process. I have, however, suggested that Plato's reticence in discussing the Ideas as well as his various indications, especially perhaps at *Phaedrus* 248a1ff, of the perspectival vision of the Ideas by even the most philosophical of human beings, together with his separation of the forms from the intellect, which is set into motion by erotic desire rather than instantaneously actualized by noetic enactment of the form, all incline in a restricted but significant degree toward the eventual development of the metaphysics of *Trieb* and *Selbstbewusstsein,* and so too to a speculative dialectical logic in which the eidetic elements are "woven" together into formal structure by the very attempt to think these elements separately.

It could of course be argued that the shift from the "separation" thesis of Platonism to the Aristotelian doctrine of the enactment of the forms within the potential intellect is the first critical step in rendering them accessible to the shaping or constructive powers of the discursive and (eventually) the imaginative intelligence. I myself agree that this shift was influential in the ultimate development of modern philosophy. But in itself, it could not account for the developments I have sketched above because no role is given to psychological processes of reflection,

Platonism

imagination, and construction. Strictly speaking, Aristotle's doctrine of thinking casts no light on how individual human beings ("substances" in the earlier terminology) are able to cognize the forms that (in some sense or another) are universally enacted, not by their particular intellectual faculties, but by the propertyless or formless *nous*.

I want now to suggest that, very far from having been overcome in its identity as Platonism, metaphysics is today more prominent than ever, and if not precisely as Platonism, certainly in a sense closer to Plato than to Aristotle. Metaphysics is possible precisely because *it is not actual*. I mean by this that the repudiation of the science of being qua being, in the sense of a discursive or deductive knowledge of pure form, has reopened the way for a more diverse understanding of what it is to know and hence too of what it is to be a form, that is, the structure of what appears.

In the balance of this section, I want to put historical speculations largely to one side and try to make my point in purely analytic or theoretical terms. Stated with introductory brevity, this point is that metaphysics is rooted in a silence that corresponds directly to the discontinuity between our noetic reach and our dianoetic or discursive grasp. I limit myself in this section to illustrating this discontinuity by some remarks about unity and identity.

We saw from our consideration of Aristotle that there are very strong reasons to distinguish between the intuitive or prediscursive foundations and the discursive development of metaphysics, understood as an *episteme* of being qua being. Despite Aristotle's contention that the sense of being qua being is given by the schema of the categories, it is rather the case that the primary sense of being qua being is *ousia* in the sense of *to ti ēn einai* or *eidos*. Putting Aristotle to one side at this point, I wish to consider the nature of the difficulty presented by a metaphysics of pure form.

Each form is both a unity and an identity. It is an identity in the sense that we can distinguish it from all other forms, and this requires that it possess an internally articulated structure of subeidetic elements. But it is also a unity in the sense that all subeidetic elements cohere in the given identity as "this identity here, and none other." The point may seem obscure, but it can be made indirectly as follows. The identity of each form is different from all the others; but the unity of every form, qua unity, is the same. The unity underlies the identity; it is visible in the coherence of features as this one identity. Otherwise put, each identity is both one and many; it is many as a plurality of subeidetic elements, but one as a single identity.

If we ask the question of something, What is it? the correct answer is to give its identity. But that which allows the identity to present itself as this identity rather than as a transient multiplicity of formal traits is its unity. This is the unity that Kant attempts to impose onto psychological associations via the synthetic activity of the transcendental ego. But his description of the transcendental ego as well as of its functions is the stipulation of identities.

The transcendental ego is constituted as the transcendental unity of apperception, which has a determinate identity that is given by the specification of the powers of reason and the understanding, hence as the regulative Ideas, the table of categories, and so on. This identity might be otherwise, given some other account of the conditions for the possibility of discursive thinking in beings like ourselves. But the properties or faculties constituting the alternative identity would be unified within some equivalent to the transcendental unity of apperception.

One cannot arrive at an ultimate unity by a series of syntheses, but only at an identity. And this identity could have been otherwise. The unity that is projected by the transcendental ego, however that set of conditions is identified, is not a sum of functions, not in other words a multiplicity, but the condition for the unity of each and every identity. The identity of the transcendental ego is already marked by unity, which can hardly be explained as spontaneous self-unification. Whereas every analysis presupposes a synthesis, only unities can synthesize. A synthesis is a synthesis of units of identity. And the condition of synthesis is transcendental unity.

We can of course make various remarks about the properties of unity as such; but these all beg the question by assuming that we possess an intuitive grasp of unity, since the properties we designate are all either negative or relational. Unity is of course not many, just as it is visible as a relation of a multiplicity of units (each of which is subject to the same distinction). But each unity is not many in precisely the same way; and its visibility as a relation of units is not itself a relation that can be analyzed but can only be asserted. There is no law of unity, comparable to the law of identity, $x = x$ (which may also be written out more fully in the language of the predicate calculus).

The distinction between the unity and identity of form is pivotal for understanding the absurdity of the attempt to derive an alternative to metaphysics by distinguishing between Being and beings. A distinction between Being and beings can be drawn in only two ways. Either we refer to that which is common to every being (= *on, rēs, Seiendes*), or we refer to some origination-process of beings. In the latter case, however, we arrive at what is unspeakable in any language that attributes thing-properties to things, since such a language could succeed only in reifying Being or transforming it, whether in metaphors or through an ostensibly literal description, into a being. This takes place, for example, in Heidegger's later philosophy, in which thing-words like "frame" and "round dance" are employed as metaphorical circumlocutions to evoke the sense of Being.

In the first of the two aforementioned alternatives, namely, the attempt to list the properties common to every being qua being, we might, like Aristotle, develop a schema of categories which organize into distinct types all the properties of any being whatsoever. But Aristotle's properties belong not to being qua being in his own definition as *ousia*, that is, species-form; they belong, like species-form itself, to substances, that is, to separate and compound beings, each with its own unity and identity. The many senses of being make it finally impossible to answer the question What is *the* sense of being? Despite the primacy of *eidos*, there is no one sense of being underlying the diversity of senses in Aristotle's analyses. Each sense is a distinct identity. The ground of these identities is in each case their unity, which is always the same and always inaccessible to discursive analysis.

It is impossible to maintain that being qua being is the schema of categories itself, since that would reduce being to discourse or a *façon de parler*.[74] If one states conversely that being qua being is the exemplification of the structure represented schematically by the categories, then being qua being is transformed into a relation, namely, the relation of possessing a given structure. But, as is already obvious in the lack of a rigorous formulation of the schema, the givenness of the relation is indeterminate.

More precisely, each categorial schema is a multiplicity and hence a particular identity, not a unity. Those who demand a transcendental deduction of the categories (as did Fichte of Kant) have understood that the demonstration of the completeness of a proposed table of categories is dependent upon a demonstration of the necessity of the unity of that table. But there is no demonstration *of* unity; it is rather *from* unity, for example, the transcendental unity of apperception, that all demonstrations derive their own unity.

So too in the case of forms. It must be shown that all the features of a certain look are in place; but the attempt to show this depends upon an antecedent grasp of the completeness of the look. And what does completeness mean here? That all the features are in place; that is, that the look is a unity. But this is given; this we see. We see it, but we cannot describe it. What we describe is the identity of the look that is given as a unity. This is what Aristotle means by saying that thinking is coming to rest, not change, and that the species-form is enacted at once, not as a progressive or sequential synthesis of before and after. This is why there is no demonstration or predication of essential properties but rather intellectual perception.

In logical terms, the relation of essence and attribute is that of "belonging." But belonging is not itself a phenomenological property; we may perceive one attribute as associated with another, but we cannot analyze the appearance except by imposing logical definitions, that is, linguistic stipulations, onto how things look to us. To say "p belongs to S" is to state a logical form that we stipulate as regulating associations of a certain kind. But these stipulations do not as it were superimpose the property of unity onto our perceptual associations. Again, the unity of the associations must be present as the condition of the visibility of the identity in any particular instance. And this is so whether we are Kantians or Aristotelians. Unity does not arise from predication; predication assumes, that is, is with respect to, a unity to be identified.

The perception of any identity rests upon the unity of that identity as well as of cognition or apprehension. But perception is also the occasion for the mutual presence of unity in the two senses. The unity of what one could call being qua being is given in, but not by, perception, and so it is presented within everyday, pretheoretical experience. We therefore tend to confuse unity with identity, that is, with the multiplicity of the given as identifiable. The combination of these two facts leads to the blurring of identity and the dissolution of unity. And this in turn transforms the relation from a metaphysical into a stipulative or conventional rule of language use, as I argued above.

To be is to have an essence and so to possess both essential and accidental properties; but nothing can be said to verify the essentiality of the former, which accordingly become indistinguishable from the latter properties. We can attempt to avoid this difficulty by shifting from a schema of substantial properties (including essence as the property of the ultimate substrate) to a Platonic schema like the alphabet of noetic elements introduced in the *Sophist* by the Eleatic Stranger. The justification for such a shift would be that we require formal properties of every being, not an indeterminate relation or an indeterminate list of the properties of beings, that is, of *rēs* or *Seienden*.

The problem with a noetic alphabet of a Platonic kind is that its elements, such as being, one, same, other, and so on, cannot be understood or analyzed in themselves, since none of them has an internal structure. Even if we postulate their independent being, we can do so only by implying that each of the others is combined with the element "being." As to "being," what can we say of it, without making use of the other elements? The attempt to constitute a metaphysics of noetic or eidetic elements leads inevitably to a dialectical logic of the Hegelian variety. And this is to say that the process of attempting to think the elements becomes involved in the statement of the relational nature of the elements. Language, as it were, both assimilates the forms and bifurcates into the set of forms and the process by which they are cognized.

By referring to a categorial schema, we imply that being qua being is a structure rather than an element or entity, such as an *on, rēs,* or thing. This has two opposite dangers. First, the structure becomes hard if not impossible to distinguish from a particular conceptual analysis of beings, and in this way, being, understood as the being of beings, turns into discursive thinking. Second, the structure is in each of its exemplifications a unity and an identity in two distinguishable senses: (1) as this being here, for example, a man, but also (2) as this particular structure, common to all beings, rather than some other structure, for example, the Kantian categories. Even if we grant that the identity is in both cases discernible, nothing can be said about the unity of these identities. Hence no reason can be given as to why these identities should not change, that is, *lose their identity,* and so become historicized.

Again, Aristotle makes no attempt to answer this last question; he begins from the "that" (*to hoti*) and offers no explanation of why there are beings or how a man is a man, other than to say, "Through his *ousia* or *eidos*." But this is to grant the facticity of metaphysics, and so its contingency: we are on the road to doctrines of transcendental temporality and historicity as well as to linguistic conventionalism. In fact, the Aristotelian solution to all these problems is precisely the one that has been rejected by his contemporary "analytical" interpreters, who are all Neo-Kantians or Wittgensteinians and believe that stipulative rules as well as a doctrine of predication will define all questions as well as their possible answers.

In my view, however, what we require is neither rules nor predications, hence certainly not a schema of categories, but a straightforward assertion of noetic perception. We cannot explain the unity of a given identity, and this means finally that we perceive it. But to perceive unity is also to perceive Being, and precisely in the sense of being qua being, that is, the being of beings. Being underlies being qua being and is accessible to us in its gift of unity. Unity, so to speak, is the ultimate substratum of identity. Being is not a structure because structure is always particular or possesses an identity, and so is this structure as opposed to that structure.

If the preceding analysis is on the right track, then the consequence is plain: metaphysics is rooted in the silence of noetic perception, not of this form as this form, but of this or that form as unity, that is, as a unified identity. Once we have the perception, then discourse, or analysis of the identity, and so metaphysics proper, becomes possible. Noetic perception designates the units of being and hence of thinking. But it does not provide us with an account of the "essential structure" of unity because there is none. For this reason, identities may change without in any way violating the omnipresence of unity.

These changes are no longer to be explained as changes in the conceptual map by which we carve up reality, that is, by linguistic conventions or stipulations. Instead, changes in conceptual maps are to be explained as shifts in our perception of identities. The extralinguistic status of the identities is given by their unity because unity can never be given by linguistic rules. We cannot decide to consider a certain cluster of formal elements as a unity if it is visibly dissolving. Nor can we be mistaken about the unity of identities; all mistakes are about identities. And we establish the identity about which we make mistakes because of the unity through which that identity is given. I would therefore say that Aristotle is right to orient metaphysics by everyday experience and noetic perception. It is Aristotelianism that errs in seeking for a discursive science of metaphysics.

I am under no illusion that the preceding paragraphs will suffice to persuade my readers of the claim, to which I subscribe, that unity is a sign of Being. My hope is that they will serve to indicate how metaphysics is possible even though not actual. It may be easier to accept the refutation of the claim that metaphysics is a science of being qua being in the sense of the derivation of a schema of categories. And I see no alternative to the thesis that metaphysics is possible if and only if we can distinguish between formal identity and Being. But at the same time I hold strongly to the view that nothing or next to nothing can be said about Being. And this is why I contend that metaphysics is rooted in silence. Unity reveals itself as concealed by a particular identity. This is the ancestor of the Being that reveals itself as concealed by a particular being.

I come now to my conclusion. Being qua being, *pace* Aristotle, is neither a categorial schema nor the exemplification of a structure. And *pace* Heidegger, it is indeed that which is common to all beings, but in a sense very close to his own understanding of a Being that must be distinguished from every *rēs* or *Seiendes*. Whereas I deplore Heidegger's own attempt to develop a "new" or "poetic" thinking about Being, I judge it to be a defective version of Platonism, namely, the attempt to elicit the senses of Being in myths, poetic dramas, and even in simple accounts of how philosophy emerges from everyday life. My objection to Heidegger is not that he engages in poetry, but that he is a bad poet.

From this standpoint, metaphysics does not depend upon silence; but neither does it depend upon the elaboration of a spurious new language. Metaphysics depends upon the ordinary language of everyday life, as deepened and articulated by poetic imagination. But this in turn is rooted firmly in the silence of the given. We cannot talk sensibly unless we see what we are talking about. All attempts to derive seeing from talking (or from writing) lead finally to the chaos of infinite chatter, which is refuted not by some alternative metaphysical hypothesis, but by life itself.

I have presented the essential points of Heidegger's interpretation of the Platonic doctrine of Ideas, which is for him the core of Platonism and so of Western philosophy, alias metaphysics. I have provided some clarifying critical remarks, but the bulk of my criticism of Heidegger will be contained in a more detailed analysis of Plato's own presentation of the doctrine of Ideas. For Heidegger, the doctrine of Ideas fulfills four main functions: (1) it leads to the forgetting of the concealment of Being by beings; (2) it introduces a kind of ontological utilitarianism or instrumentalism that itself gives rise to Idealism and to Nietzsche's metaphysics of value; (3) it replaces the original Greek understanding of Being as *phusis,* that is, a process of emergence, with a productive conception of Being as patterned on the fabrication of the craftsman; (4) it is the prototype for, and in fact is intrinsically the same as, Aristotle's doctrine of the categories and being qua being. Stated with extreme and introductory concision, my replies to these four points are as follows: (1) Being is indeed concealed by beings; this is why we must always orient ourselves by beings and not attempt to orient ourselves by Being; (2) the accessibility of beings to humankind is a good thing (no pun intended); (3) there is no productionist doctrine of Being in Plato; there is, however, a doctrine of life as practico-productive, in a sense that I shall explain later; (4) Plato's Ideas are prototypes of Aristotle's species-forms but not of his categories or of being qua being.

In addition, I have argued in this chapter that what Heidegger and his students call Platonism is better named Aristotelianism. I have also explained why I regard a science of being qua being as both impossible and a diversion from the understanding of the genuine nature of Platonism. My task in the next two chapters will be to present a more accurate account of Platonism than is available from Heidegger. Only then will we be in a position to consider the details of Heidegger's interpretation of Nietzsche, and so too of Nietzsche's interpretation of Plato.

One last point: the doctrine of Ideas is not the totality of Platonist metaphysics but is instead an element—an extremely important one, but nevertheless an element only—of a broader doctrine, which Socrates calls in the *Phaedo* a *logos.* The primary sense of *logos,* as will become apparent in a subsequent chapter, is not "language" but, as Heidegger is fond of putting it, a "gathering" or "collecting." By way of anticipation, let me say here that *logos* is a gathering in the sense of a community between being and thinking; the Ideas are the middle term in this community. In order to understand more precisely what this

Platonism

means, I want first to rethink the thoughts by which Plato tells us that Socrates arrived at the "second sailing" of the Ideas. In so doing, I shall make use of some elements of Heidegger's account of the original sense of crucial Greek terms; but the results will be different in fundamental ways from those arrived at by Heidegger.

Socrates' Hypothesis

2

Preliminary Remarks

Having prepared the way for a direct approach to the Platonic Ideas, I turn to the dialogue *Phaedo*. My reason for choosing the *Phaedo* rather than some more apparently technical passage from the *Republic*, the *Sophist*, or the *Philebus* is that in the *Phaedo*, Socrates explains the connection between the "hypothesis" (100a2) of the Ideas and the fundamental conception of philosophy as a way of life. As we shall see, it is not ontology that motivates the turn to the Ideas but the need to render *theōria* harmonious with the intention to act for the best. In order to certify the rationality of the scientific investigation of beings, we require a sense of rationality that applies to life as a totality, and so to the contrast between one way of life and another. But physics and ontology do not supply us with this sense of rationality. The intention to act for the best is a fundamental characteristic of everyday or pre-theoretical life. If we begin with ontological analyses of the structure of intelligibility, we shall never arrive at human existence as it is actually lived. According to Socrates, however, if we begin with the everyday expression of human intentionality, which is not phenomenological, so to speak, but directed toward the better rather than the worse, and so toward happiness or blessedness, we will arrive at the hypothesis of the Ideas and in this way preserve the wholeness of human life.

Socrates imitates this wholeness in a story about the course of his life as a philosopher. The story is recounted at the edge of the everyday, namely, within a prison cell during the last hours of Socrates' life. The prison cell is a political location that is at the same time detached from the city; prisoners are banished from political life, yet executed in accord with the *nomos*. The city that has made possible the generation of Socrates and, I may add, of the Socratic understanding of philosophy is about to enforce his destruction. In this way, Plato connects the theme of presence and absence in the cosmos with that of human existence. Socrates is both present in and absent from the city; at the moment of approaching death, he is able to see his life as a whole, namely, as a harmony of presence and absence. What is conveyed by the context of the story, but not within the story itself, is the danger of the philosophical life or in other words the paradoxical incompatibility of the best human life with the political association that alone makes such a life possible.

As a resident of his cell, Socrates is in the process of transcending *doksa* from within. In fact, we witness the gradual departure of life from his limbs as the poison takes effect. We witness the death for which Socrates' entire philosophical life has been a preparation. The story that he tells reflects the same preparation as it took place over the course of that lifetime. That preparation is not technical in the sense of possessing a formal structure consisting of eidetic looks. On the contrary, it is technical in what Heidegger calls the authentic Greek sense of "being at home" within the whole. As we shall see, Socrates asserts explicitly that what he has to say here about the Ideas is no different from what he has said elsewhere. This statement refers to the "positing" (100b5) of beauty considered in itself (*auto kath' hauto*) and other such cases. Although these Ideas are "frequently mentioned" (*poluthrulēta*) in the dialogues, there is no uniform account of their nature. What is common to the various discussions of the Ideas is not ontological analysis but recognition of their function in the economy of a rational existence.

The variety of expositions of the nature of the Ideas, and the fact that these expositions are more poetic and mythical than analytical or ontological, supports the inference that Socrates (and indeed Plato) has no fully elaborated conception of the Ideas as separate entities. This does not alter his conviction that the Ideas are the "strongest" (100a4) or "most steadfast" (100d8) hypothesis in the following sense. They account for the presence within the flux of genesis of identifiable unities or beings of a definite look. It does not however follow that, in making beings intelligible, the Ideas are themselves fully intelligible. In order to identify a being, I must perceive its "look." If this identification is to be steadfast or reliable, the look must endure in the sense that it is not dissolved or modified by the transformations of genesis. But recognition that a being has such and such a look is not the same as understanding what it is to be a look. To mention only the most important and controversial point, namely, in what sense the Ideas may be said to exist *auto kath' hauto,* the evidence of the dialogues is inconclusive. The Greek expression is certainly employed to attribute to the Ideas the steadfastness of identity and unity. However, Socrates' story in the *Phaedo* makes no mention of the separate existence attributed to the Ideas in the myth of the soul presented in the *Phaedrus.*

So much for the preliminary sketch of the motivation underlying the story told by Socrates in the *Phaedo.* I turn now to the details. Socrates has been attempting to persuade his interlocutors, who are spending his final hours with him in the prison cell in Athens, that the soul is immortal. This proof is required if they are to be liberated from the fear of death. Socrates says that in order to do this, one must give an account "concerning the cause of genesis and destruction" (95e8ff.). The word translated as "cause," *aitia,* means literally responsibility or blame, and so an accusation of blame. Allow me to digress for a moment on the interesting connection between this word and *katēgorein,* from which the word "category" is derived. The verb *katēgorein* means to level an accusation against someone; it consists of a preposition *kata* and the verb *agoreuein: kata* here means "against"; *agoreuein* means "to speak," more precisely, to speak in the agora, that is to say, in the public square or marketplace, where the nobles used to assemble in order to conduct legal business; by extension, the verb means "to address the assembly." A *katēgoria* is an accusation of responsibility or blame made in public, so that the blame can be fully visible to all. Heidegger occasionally cites this etymology;[1] it brings out the inner connection between "presence" and the role of categories in the definition of being or, as Aristotle says, of being qua being, hence of what Heidegger calls the "Sein des Seienden."

Heidegger associates *katēgoria* with the Platonic Idea and thereby with the Aristotelian *hupokeimenon* which underlies the predications classified in the table of categories. But there are no categories in Plato. It is Aristotle who introduces the technical sense of "category." Thus, to level an accusation in this sense is to say something of something, *ti kata tinos,* and thereby to formulate a predicative assertion, in which we identify something "as" or by means of something else, namely, a defining property. The categories are the table of defining properties, the things we attribute to other things; the "other things" own the properties and are identified by them.

This raises a problem I touched upon in chapter 1: strictly speaking, the identification of the owner by his property is not an identification of the owner himself. If you ask me, "Who is that man?" and I reply, "He is the man with the blue guitar," then I have not identified the man himself but merely picked him out as one who owns a blue guitar. You will then say, "No, no, I am not interested in what he owns; I want to know who he is." To come closer to the Aristotelian situation, you will ask me not "Who is that man?" but "What is that?" or perhaps "What is a man?" The "what" points not to the personal identity of the man in question, but to that which necessarily and indispensably marks him as a man. Is this something that he owns or is it the man himself, understood as the owner? Is to be a man to be marked by something or to be something that is so marked?

The distinction between owner and property is connected with the table of categories in the following manner: The owner must possess one item from every category in the list, but knowledge of the series of items thus possessed is not the same as knowledge of the owner himself. This is clear from the fact that the first category is *ousia,* or "essence." But the essence, which states most fundamentally what the owner is, cannot itself consist of items from the other categories. We can therefore ignore the other categories and concentrate on the statement of the essence. The essence of man is "rational animal" (and we can also ignore here the complications arising from the occurrence of other essential definitions of man, such as "political animal" and "featherless biped"). In order to understand the meaning of the expression "rational animal," one must sooner or later rely upon an intuition, that is, a precategorial but also a preousiological or prediscursive apprehension of what it is to be a rational animal. It thus turns out that the accusation of responsibility that is expressed by the table of categories points the blame in the wrong direction. Reflection on the table of categories tells us that the owner *cannot* be identified by his possessions. In fact, we cannot identify the owner's possessions until we have identified the owner.

By saying "what it is to be a rational animal," I perhaps unavoidably obscure what is at issue here. The word "what" suggests that I am about or ought to answer the question What is a rational animal? with another definition, of the form "A rational animal is an *xy*," where *xy* stands for the concatenation of two essential properties, still more essential than "rational" and "animal" because they somehow explain the peculiar unity of these last two and thereby bring us directly to the answer to the question What is a man? But this is not so. "Rational" and "animal" may each be subject to further analysis, but this analysis will not bring us closer to what it is to be a man; it will take us farther away. "Rational" and "animal" are intended by Aristotle to exhibit in their concatenation the "what" in question; a finer analysis will show us not what it is to be a man, but (perhaps) what it means to be rational, for example, to obey the laws of logic; or what it means to be an animal, for example, to possess a soul. But man may not be the only rational being; apart from the gods, some people claim that computers are rational beings. And man is certainly not the only animal.

Let us assume that man is indeed the only rational animal. What we want to know is just this: What is a rational animal? Now of course we cannot know this unless we can state what it is to be rational and what it is to be an animal. But this still leaves unanswered the question what it is to be both, that is, the living unity of the two. Do we simply glue together two parts, rational and animal, in order to make the whole being "man"? Is the rational part external to the animal part? Since no other animal is rational, how does man acquire rationality? And if man acquires rationality, then what is it that does the acquiring here? Is it an animal? No, because animals other than man are not rational. A man exists if and only if "animal" and "rational" coexist. But we do not understand what the "co-" means in "coexist." It is easy to see how all of this bears upon the question of the soul. We cannot tell whether it is immortal if we do not know what it is. But it is far from apparent that the soul is a certain configuration of properties. If it is an owner of properties, then we do not know the soul by knowing its properties.

In sum, predicative statements, tables of categories, and the distinction between *hupokeimenon,* or "that which stands beneath," that is, supports or owns, and *sumbebēkota,* or properties, literally, what meets, joins, or comes to an agreement, will not answer the question What is a man? This is not to suggest that they are useless. They are very helpful for analyzing our discursive accounts of what we already understand by some prediscursive faculty. We must already understand not simply what "rational" and "animal" mean, but what it means to say that these two "stand together." Do they stand together as properties owned by something else? Or is their standing together the being of the owner? In the latter case, it may be true that to be a man is to be a rational animal, but "being" is something quite different, namely, standing together. I repeat: Aristotle provides an articulated analysis of the sense of "standing together," an analysis based upon our antecedent awareness of what has that sense, not via a discursive understanding of "whatness," but by recognizing its occurrence in this or that intuited thing. We see what this means when we perceive any identifiable thing whatsoever as not merely identifiable but also as a unity or a unit, that is, as a one in many. But this is one way in which to explain what Plato means by *eidos* or *idea*.

For Plato, the *eidos* of man is not the *ousia*, taken as "rational animal," that is, as a way in which two properties stand together. The *eidos* here is the look of man that must be apprehended in order for any predicative statements or essential definitions to be uttered. One could of course say, and say rightly, that Aristotle also requires that the *eidos* be intuited intellectually. But he emphasizes the discursive analysis of the content of the intuition as providing us with a *logos* of the being of man; the *logos* is the discursive exhibition of the inner ratio of essential parts constituting the being "man." To put this in another but related way, for Aristotle, the apprehension of the *eidos* "man" occurs as the actualization of the unity of that *eidos* and the active intellect. Stated as simply as possible, the *eidos* "man" actualizes, that is, *is* or possesses its being not simply in the individual man who is standing before me, but coevally in my own thinking.

Not only does the man own his properties, but I own the man qua owner. Hence discursive thinking has the being of the man *in its grasp;* and so the analysis of the structure of the content of intellectual intuition purports to provide us with a definitive answer to the question What is man? One could therefore say that in a sense, Heidegger's exposition of the Greek conception of being as *parousia*, or presence, holds good for Aristotle, although strictly speaking, *parousia* in Aristotle means the presence of an attribute to an *ousia*, or essence. It does not mean the presence of the essence itself because the essence is not graspable in itself but only via its essential properties. This aside, however, the Aristotelian *eidos*, or species-form, "man" is indeed present within my thought as well as within the individual, perceived human being.

The Platonic *eidos*, on the other hand, is "absent" from my thinking or separated from it; hence I cannot fully grasp it and so there is no adequate discursive analysis of what I have seen in viewing an Idea.

Furthermore, the *eidos* is not a structure of owner and properties, concerning which I must still explain how the standing together of the two distinct components constitutes the being in question. The viewing of the Idea of man is not the apprehension of man *as* something else, for example, rational animal; it is rather the viewing precisely of man. One may say, "That thing over there looks like a man," but one cannot say, "John looks like a man" because John *is* a man, and this means in turn that John exhibits the look of a man. This look is the Idea. I repeat: the expression "looks like" is inappropriate when applied to a man with respect to himself, that is, with respect to the Idea "man." John does not look like the Idea of man, nor does the Idea of man look like John. There is no verbal equivalent to the look of a man; to the contrary, all verbal accounts of what it is to be a man depend upon the prior recollection of the look or Idea "man."

In looking for the *aitia*, then, Socrates is not leveling an accusation, or *katēgoria*, in the sense of identifying this as that or saying something of something. To say something "of" something is not to render present but to separate oneself from or to render absent, in the statement itself, that of which the predicate names a property. In a sense, of course, the absent owner is present as represented by the name or subject-term that stands for the *ousia*. But the name is an identification mark, not itself a predicate; it marks what has been discerned or apprehended by the eye of the soul, not what is present within discursive intelligence. On the other hand, the presence of the Socratic "look" or Idea is verified by the intelligibility of what exhibits that look, not of the look itself as a separate entity. One could perhaps say that the presence of the Idea is concealed by the presence of its instance. The Idea as it were disappears in the fulfillment of its function as the *aitia* of disclosure. It is in this way that Plato and Aristotle both anticipate the Heideggerian doctrine of the interplay of presence and absence.

Now let me come back to the more immediate setting of the *Phaedo*. Socrates recounts to Cebes, his interlocutor at this point in the drama, what has befallen him (*ta ge ema pathē*) in his effort to discover the *aitia* of generation and destruction. Let us note carefully the context. Simmias and Cebes are young intellectuals who aspire to philosophy, not philosophers. Second, they are afraid of death, and Socrates wishes to release them from this fear. Third, Socrates is himself about to die; he is as it were providing his young interlocutors with an anecdotal or biographical statement rather than with a theoretical analysis; this biographical statement is a kind of summing-up that is adapted to the capacities of the audience and to the circumstance that has brought them together. There is something tragic about the episode, in the sense that the hero of the Platonic drama is about to die.

On the other hand, there is also something comic about the dialogue, in which Socrates is said to laugh quietly on two separate occasions,[2] and which shows him as continuing to discourse on philosophical topics even as the fatal effect of the hemlock moves slowly upward from his limbs to his torso. Socrates, one could say, exhibits in his demeanor the look of philosophical courage, which, like all genuine virtue, is ostensibly equivalent to knowledge. The implication is that since he does not fear death, he must possess knowledge of the immortality of the soul; for without that knowledge, as Cebes claims, and as Socrates restates his point, "anyone, unless he is mindless," must fear death (95d6ff.). Socrates is portrayed as the philosophical hero who, unlike the tragic hero, does not bemoan his approaching demise. But there is a hint of exaggeration here which might make us smile if not laugh out loud. Are there any human beings like Socrates or is he an Idea?

Socrates indicates that in order to be free of the fear of death, we must know the *aitia* of generation and destruction. Socrates is free of the fear of death. The implication is that Socrates knows this *aitia*. If he does, incidentally, then it is surely false that he knows only that he knows nothing. If he does not know the *aitia*, then either he is not free of the fear of death or that freedom is not dependent upon such knowledge. And there is an even more important ambiguity in the dramatic function of Socrates' story. Socrates explains how he was led to the hypothesis of the Ideas, but not how this hypothesis guarantees the immortality of the soul. In the section of the dialogue immediately following the story, Socrates asserts that the presence of an Idea guarantees the exclusion of its opposite; for example, the Idea of evenness excludes the Idea of oddness (103e9ff.). From this he shifts to the assertion that life is the opposite of death and that, since the soul is the principle of life, it is, as opposite to death, immortal (105c6ff.). But this argument is worthless, as is almost immediately obvious.

The presence of the soul guarantees the life of the body, but it does not follow from this that the soul continues to exist in separation from the body. One could perhaps argue that there is an Idea of the soul which persists even when the individual person dies. But not only does Socrates fail to assert, let alone to establish, that there is an Idea of the soul. Even if we grant this, the Idea of the soul is not the same as the individual human soul. There is no reason to assume that the "look" of the soul is itself alive; but if we attribute life to it, this cannot be the same as my or your individual life, for if it were, either the Idea would die when we cease to exist or else its immortality would amount to the destruction of our separate personalities. This is, incidentally, the same distinction as that made in the *Phaedrus* (245c5ff.) between the soul as the "principle of change" (*archē kinēseōs*) and the individual or personal soul as represented by the figure of the winged charioteer and his team of horses. The story in the *Phaedo* thus contributes to a rhetorical persuasion, but not to a philosophical demonstration, of the immortality of the soul. This is not irrelevant to our understanding of Socrates' conception of what Heidegger would call ontology.

But I want to focus attention now on a different aspect of the problem. It is important for us to know whether Socrates is truly courageous. I suggested a moment ago that Socrates is portrayed as a kind of Idea of courage. Socrates is attempting to instill courage in his companions: to be the *aitia* of their courage. How does he do this? It cannot be merely through his speeches, since the same arguments expressed by someone else, for example, someone who was weeping, pale, and shaking, would not be very convincing. How do we recognize courage in Socrates? If I say, "Socrates is courageous," you will ask, "How do you know that?" What am I to reply? Am I required to describe the traits in Socrates' demeanor that are indicative of courage? How can I do this if I do not know what courage is; and if I know this, can I define courage?

What counts as the defining properties of the look of courage? Is that look identical with the *morphē,* or spatio-temporal disposition, of Socrates' perceivable attributes? Certain things can be said without hesitation. Socrates is calm rather than agitated; he speaks in his normal voice and does not break down from time to time; he does not weep but laughs quietly on two occasions. Let these aspects of his behavior serve as representative of a fuller list. The fact is that someone might exemplify those traits without being philosophically courageous. In other words, if the danger of death is not imminent, and one's thoughts are engaged on other topics, it is quite easy even for a coward or for one who fears death excessively to be of good humor. We attribute

Platonism

courage to Socrates because he is about to die; in fact, he is in the process of dying during the last minutes of the conversation. And he knows that he is about to die. This shows us that "knowledge" of the Idea of courage is not the same as knowledge that Socrates is courageous.

But there is more to be said on this issue. For Socrates might be dissembling his fear of death in order to preserve a posthumous reputation for courage. Whether he laughs or weeps, he will die in either case; hence he might as well seem to be courageous. And seeming to be courageous is "looking like" a courageous man but not actually exhibiting the look of courage, which is by definition absent here. It is much more far-fetched, but it is not impossible to suggest that Socrates might also be courageous in fact but wish to appear to be cowardly for some reason. He might wish to present himself as afraid in order to bolster the morale of his companions by legitimating their fears, since they will not, despite any arguments that he may put forward, be rendered impervious to the terrors of death. Socrates could then wish to show that fear of death and philosophy are not incompatible. I am not suggesting that this is a likely eventuality, and of course, Socrates in fact shows no fear of dying at any time in the dialogues. But my point is that there is no logical connection between courage and the perceivable look of courage. We cannot say with apodictic certitude that he who is courageous will die with equanimity; perhaps the philosopher has not yet finished his investigations or is in the midst of his most important work and becomes outraged at the impending permanent interruption. Even if this outrage does not deteriorate into despair, it manifests itself in quite a different set of behavioral traits than those which mark Socrates in the *Phaedo*. And outrage is at least related to fear; we are outraged because we fear that something we despise is about to occur.

If these considerations are sound, they point to an important distinction. There is a relation, but also a discontinuity, between the *morphē*, or perceivable shape of courage, and the Idea. Courage is a state of the soul; under normal circumstances, it will produce certain typical responses which we perceive and recognize; conversely, fear produces under normal circumstances the opposite responses. But under abnormal circumstances, the responses may be feigned or they may be atypical and so ambiguous. By "normal" we mean that which usually occurs; our experience tells us that under normal circumstances, the look of courage in the face of death is exhibited by traits which are the same as those that define Socrates' behavior in the prison cell during the last hours of his life. By "abnormal" we mean what does not usually happen under circumstances of such and such a kind. In other words, we cannot identify the abnormal except by way of contrast with the normal. The normal is the measure or standard; let us call it here the *eidos* or *idea* of courage. This is the same result at which we arrived earlier when considering the relation between the *morphē* and the Idea in the case of the look of the perceived entity.

Here the body is of interest to the extent that it exhibits the nature of the soul. We are looking for the measure of a psychic virtue, not for the family to which an animal belongs. The measure is not identical with any precisely defined set of observable characteristics. If however a sufficient number of the characteristics are exhibited, then we detect the look of courage. What we mean by "sufficient" cannot be quantified; it will vary from circumstance to circumstance. As my examples were intended to suggest, there are certain occasions on which we may be misled. But in what are we being misled? Not with respect to courage itself, but rather with respect to whether the person whom we are observing is genuinely courageous.

We can then misapply the measure or standard, but this entails that we apprehend that measure or standard. In the particular case of courage, one might wish to say that if we could directly apprehend Socrates' soul, then we would know unmistakably whether he was genuinely courageous. This may or may not be true, but in fact, we cannot directly apprehend Socrates' soul. What we apprehend is our own soul; we infer from Socrates' perceptible behavior to the state of his soul, and what licenses this inference is not a logical deduction or set of axioms and rules for valid inference but knowledge of ourselves. And in apprehending our own soul, we do not see a picture; the "look" of the soul, in other words, if it were equivalent to a visual configuration, would still require interpretation in the same way that the visual configuration of Socrates' behavior traits in the *Phaedo* requires interpretation. How does one carry out this interpretation? Not directly by the application of hermeneutical principles, for example, Whoever looks like this is courageous. For we still have to determine what the look is that stamps someone as courageous.

My point is not that we cannot identify the look of courage. I believe that we can and that we normally discern it in perceptible behavior, for example, the look on someone's face, the sound of his voice, the steadiness of his hands and limbs, and so on. But the look of courage is not the same as those perceptible traits. We can err in taking what "looks like" courage for the look of courage itself. But this is possible only because (1) we apprehend the look of courage, and (2) we can apprehend it even in a fantasm or false image, such as that of the coward who feigns courage. The coward who looks like a courageous man, in looking like that man exhibits the look of courage. The fantasm that constitutes his being "looks like" but is not courage. But the look of courage does not "look like" the fantasm of the dissembling coward. The fantasm reminds us of the look of courage; it stimulates us, as Plato would say, to *recollect* the Idea of courage. And as soon as we understand this, we also understand that it is not the fantasm that we discern as the look or Idea, even though the fantasm was the occasion for that discernment. In sum, we are not wrong about the Idea of courage; but we can be wrong about its *appearance* or manifestation in this or that particular person.

A technical point: if the fantasm looks like the original of courage, why does not the original look like the fantasm? If *A* resembles *B*, must not *B* resemble *A*? This takes us directly to the heart of the problem of the Platonic Idea. According to the Eleatic Stranger in the *Sophist* (235c8ff.), a fantasm is an inaccurate image that is accommodated to human perspective so as to look like the original. This being so, an accurate image, or *eikon*, does not accommodate to human perspective and so does not look like the original, although it is an accurate copy of it. So we have to distinguish between "looks like *A* to us" and "genuinely exhibits the look of *A*." It follows from this that we are unable to perceive the Ideas as they actually are because these are not accommodated to human perspective. *The vision of the Ideas is perspectival.* Note that Heidegger claims this or something very close to this. But I am not making a Heideggerian interpretation of this point. My contention is that the original look shows itself to human beings not through its identity with the false image, but as distinct from that image. The image does not show us the original; it reminds us of it. This is what Plato means by recollection. In Socrates' mythical language, we saw the original in another stage of existence, when we were souls detached from bodies and led up to heaven by the gods. And this is absolutely necessary if we are to be able to distinguish between false and accurate images. If our view of the original is not independent of the image, then we cannot measure or judge the image to be inaccurate. Differently stated, the image becomes the original, since we have no access to the Idea except by way of images.

This does not solve the problem of originals and images by any means. For example: if accurate images look to us as though they were inaccurate, how can we identify them as accurate? Are we to say that an accurate image is one that looks inaccurate? We could say this only if we could see the original independently of the image. But even so, is there no difference between an accurate image that looks inaccurate and an inaccurate image that also looks inaccurate? If I draw a caricature of a friend, don't I know that my friend does not in fact look like the caricature? However these problems are to be resolved, the first step must be to insist that the look of the original is not conveyed directly through the look of the image. We can decide whether Socrates is or is not truly courageous, that is, whether he is an accurate or an inaccurate image of courage, only if we can see the Idea of courage apart from the image. Second: suppose that we can see the Idea independently of the images. In this case, must we not say that an inaccurate image, that is, one accommodated to human perspective, is accurate *for us,* whereas an accurate image is accurate in itself? Not quite. What we need to say is this: strictly speaking, there are no accurate images of Ideas in the human domain because an accurate image is just the look of the Idea itself. All images are inaccurate.

In other words, it is not possible to apply the discussion of images in the *Sophist* to the analysis of the Platonic Ideas without various modifications. This is because there is no ontology or discursive account of the nature of being, whether of Being or of the being of beings. Discourse is imagery; words are copies, and inexact copies, of things, which in turn may be called inexact copies of Ideas. Discourse is regulated by the prediscursive "recollection" of the Idea. The literal meaning of Idea is "look," but the term is used here metaphorically, in order to play upon the difference between hearing and seeing, hence between speech and vision. *Logos* in the sense of speech does not simply reveal or uncover (*apophainesthai*); hence discursive thinking cannot simply arrive at truth or uncoveredness (*alētheia*). *Logos* itself conceals what it reveals or reveals in a concealed manner.

This is why the shift from *logos* to logic is so appealing. In logic we study only the pure forms of syntax or what one could call the relations of the imagic content of *logos*. The imagic content is concealed revelation; the images are inaccurate. We know them to be inaccurate in one of two ways: either because we have access to the Ideas or because, lacking such access, we can never arrive at stability or agreement in our analysis of that content. When access to the Ideas is blocked, we are left with the indeterminateness of images, which is multiplied, not clarified, by the work of discursive analysis, since discourse is itself the production of images. The turn to logic is a turn away from images, and so from discourse, or toward an imitation of the vision of the Ideas, namely, to a vision of logical form, which vision occurs in silence (cf. Wittgenstein's *Tractatus*).

As soon as we start to analyze logical form, however, the blurring or multiplying of discourse covers over our intuition of form, and the result is the production of "philosophies" of logic, that is, alternative interpretations of the primordial vision, which is thus dissolved or transformed into rules, that is, into discursive statements, which, since there are no longer any originals or because access to the originals is blocked, refer to nothing but to other discursive statements. The result is an infinite discourse, or interminable chatter, all disguised by the cosmetic of technical intricacy.

It follows from this that Plato's Ideas are not intended as topics of metaphysical or ontological analysis leading to a systematic theory or account of the structure of the whole. They are a hypothesis—in Plato's view no doubt a necessary hypothesis—that is required in order to account for order and intelligibility in our everyday life. This hypothesis obviously is the result of, and itself issues in, speculations of varying degrees of precision. But arguments leading to the necessity of the hypothesis are quite different from discursive accounts, whether in natural or formal languages, of the nature of the Ideas themselves. This is exactly what Socrates conveys by means of the story that he tells to Simmias and Cebes in the last hours of his life. In sum, the Idea is not a detached original in the sense of a model that is copied by the image. A dog is not an image of the Idea of the dog in the sense that a photograph of a dog is an image of the living dog. If this were so, the original would itself have the look of a dog, and we would again have to distinguish between the "original" and its look. If the Idea provides the dog with its look, it must do so in some way other than by cognitive copying. The Idea *is* the look, not in the sense of a *morphē,* but in a sense connected with that of *logos.* This will become evident as we pursue our study of Socrates' account in the *Phaedo.* Let me turn now to the stages in Socrates' pursuit of the *aitia* of generation and destruction.

Stages Along Life's Way

When Socrates was young, he experienced a marvelous desire for the wisdom "which they call investigation concerning nature" (96a6–8). Note first that Socrates says "which they call." The "they" is reminiscent of Heidegger's "das Man." Socrates himself would not now call it the investigation concerning nature; that is, he would now distinguish "physics" from the investigation of the Ideas. The Greek word for investigation is *historia.* A *historia* is an inquiry into something by looking for oneself or by talking to someone who saw or participated in the events one is investigating. "It seemed to me to be *huperēphanos* to know the *aitias* of each thing, through what each thing comes to be and through what it perishes and through what it exists" (96a8ff.). The word *huperēphanos* means primarily "arrogant" or "hybristic" and is used rarely in a good sense to mean "splendid." The *huperēphanos* person looks down on others; here Socrates indicates that the physicist looks down on human affairs because he regards them as trivial in comparison with his own investigations. Socrates goes on to say that he investigated "the properties [*ta pathē*] of heaven and earth" (96b9f.); this is the period of his life that is satirized in Aristophanes' *Clouds.*

After engaging in this investigation, Socrates decided that he was ungifted for it because it led him to forget what he had previously known. He gives two examples of this. First, he used to know that persons grow through eating and drinking. In other words, the analysis of growth and decay in terms of elements, ratios of elements, atoms, natural forces, and so on leads us away from our everyday understanding of human motivation as well as from the commonsense explanation of everyday events. Second, he used to think that one horse or person was taller than another horse or person by so many cubits, and that numbers increased by the addition of units and decreased by the subtraction of units. But the study of mathematics led him to ignorance concerning such problems as this: when one is added to one, does the first one or the second become two or do they each become two by addition? How, he asks, can the division of one cause it to become two, when division is the opposite of addition, which also caused one to become two? In sum, this method of studying natural causes led to the loss of knowledge of the everyday context of physics as well as of commonsense clarity about the behavior of numbers (96c2–97b7). Socrates includes what would today be called philosophy of mathematics in the study of physics or natural causes. In other words, the first procedure he followed was mathematical physics.

In his second stage, he turned to the doctrine of Anaxagoras, according to which "it is *nous* that orders and is the *aitia* of all things" (97b8ff.). Socrates interpreted this to mean that intellect arranges everything in the way that is best for it. At this stage, he turns from mathematical to what he assumes will be teleological physics. But once again he is disappointed. Anaxagoras is just like the mathematical physicists in that he talks of the elements; that is, as we would say, he gives a materialist explanation of natural phenomena. This leads again to the loss of commonsense knowledge. Instead of explaining that Socrates is sitting in his prison cell because he has been condemned to death, the Anaxagorean explanation is by way of the physical constitution of his body.

Note that Socrates says in this passage that, since the Athenians condemned him to death, it is best for him to sit here and undergo his penalty (98e1ff.). He also says that this is why he is having the present conversation with his companions. In other words, had the Athenians not condemned him to death, the conversation would not have occurred. This makes clear the political context of the discussion. Differently stated, this is an everyday discussion, not a technical discourse on ontology. In order to understand discussions on ontology, or on mathematical physics, it is necessary to understand the everyday context within which they occur. And this is not merely because of general considerations about the emergence of ontological analyses from the activities of the *Lebenswelt*; more precisely, we say different things under different circumstances. We cannot understand Socrates' speeches unless we take into account the circumstances under which they are uttered.

Socrates then draws the following distinction. An *aition* is one thing; something else is the instrument by which the *aition* exercises its function as *aition* (99b2ff.). The *aition,* that which is responsible for human acts, is the conviction that to do so-and-so is best. If one acts for the best, then one is, as the *aition* of one's own behavior, blameless. There can be no *katēgoria*. Let me put this into modern terminology. Mathematical physics leads to what is called determinism or the reduction of the human to the physical, and the physical to a set of natural laws. Note parenthetically that this terminology continues to fit the modern situation at least through the first half of the nineteenth century, if not beyond that point. We no longer speak of natural laws in the same sense as Newton, but the essential meaning is the same.

Of even greater importance for our purposes is the fact that the *aition* is not the Ideas but human intention. It is I who act for the best, not the Ideas, and not even the Idea of the good. There is, in other words, a systematic ambiguity in Socrates' story that we already noticed with respect to the discontinuity between the hypothesis of the Ideas and the purported immortality of the soul. The Ideas are the "causes" of the being of the things that undergo generation and decay. The stability or steadfastness of the identities of these things enables us to employ them wisely or foolishly and thus to act for the better or for the worse. But the hypothesis of the Ideas is in itself insufficient to explain rational choice. We also require the hypothesis of the soul. Unfortunately, the soul is no more directly accessible to analytical investigation than are the Ideas. In telling how he turned away from beings to the Ideas, Socrates is telling us how his soul guided his conduct, but he is not explaining the nature of the soul or demonstrating its immortality.

The larger theoretical issue is as follows. In the everyday world, there is no question that each person does what he or she thinks is best. There are of course enormous disagreements concerning what is best. But no one claims to do what is worst for oneself or harmful or even useless. Science and technical philosophy lead us to lose the belief that we act on the basis of conscious motives, and so that intelligence governs our actions, even if it is a defective or mistaken intelligence. Instead, we come to believe, or to fear, that the experience of consciousness, and

Platonism

so of responsible action, is illusory because the "laws" of physics are determinist. Even if these laws are replaced by statistical generalizations, we do not regain the freedom of conscious or intentional action. Instead, our behavior is explained statistically or by generalizations over which we personally have no control; consider sociology or psychology.

So the question arises: Why should we disregard our everyday knowledge of purposive behavior? Is this disregard not based upon the conviction that there is no difference between the soul and the body or that the soul is just how the body behaves or that there is no soul? And if there is no soul, how can there be a mind or intellect? Absent an intellect and a soul, there is of course no sense to the distinction between "better" and "worse." Under some conditions, this happens; under other conditions, something else occurs. I do not propose to investigate this problem in any detail. There is no demonstration of free will, but only its exercise, as for example in the attempt to produce demonstrations of the freedom of the will. The inference toward which Socrates is arguing is this: the hypothesis of the Ideas allows us to preserve our everyday knowledge, and so too the context of scientific or technical thinking, including the technical thinking of philosophy.

This can be so only if the hypothesis of the Ideas is not itself a *scientific* hypothesis, one which is based upon the presupposition of the comprehensive validity of mathematical physics, that is, of its correctness as an account of the whole, which includes human life. Please note: the hypothesis of the Ideas is not based upon the assumption of the invalidity of mathematical physics. But it allows us to preserve everyday knowledge together with mathematical physics. A second inference follows at once: the hypothesis of the Ideas cannot itself suffice to explain the whole; in particular, it cannot explain thinking or the various properties or powers of the soul, including the desire for or love of the Ideas. The soul might conclude that what is best for it is to attempt to view the Ideas; but this conclusion is not "caused" by the Ideas. The most that could be said is that we are compelled to this conclusion by the force of Eros. But Eros is a god or daimon, not an Idea. Platonism cannot be equated with the so-called theory of the Ideas.

So much for Anaxagoras. Socrates then asks Cebes, "[Would you like to hear of my] second sailing with respect to the investigation of the *aitia*?" (99c9ff.). We are about to hear of the hypothesis of the Ideas. The presumption is that the Ideas are responsible for generation and destruction. More accurately, they are responsible for the identity and unity of beings that undergo generation and destruction. The stage in Socrates' life that is marked by the turn to the Ideas is not a third sailing because there is no intrinsic difference between the doctrine of Anaxagoras and that of the mathematical physicists. The difference between the first and the second stage is a shift in position, not a new journey. Socrates introduces the radical shift from the first to the second sailing in a puzzling manner: "It seemed to me, then, after these events, when I had ceased to investigate *ta onta*..." (99d4). In the first stage, Socrates studied *phusis,* or the beings that exist by nature. Is this not also the task of the philosopher?

Interestingly, the same question arises in Aristotle's *Metaphysics, E* 1, 1026a25ff. Aristotle says there that if there is no other *ousia* besides those composed by nature (*para tas phusei sunestēkuias*), physics (*hē phusikē*) will be the first science. In other words, let us divide the whole into two components, the natural and the artificial. The natural is that which occurs through its own *archē* or *aitia,* whereas the artificial arises through the *aitia* of human activity. But man is a natural being; therefore the underlying *aitia* of the artificial is the natural. It seems to follow that the fundamental science or inquiry is the inquiry into nature.

This problem, incidentally, is transmitted to the modern epoch, during which the quarrel persists as to whether human activity can be understood on the basis of physics, that is, the study of natural beings, including man considered as a body, or *rēs extensa.* The sense of the term "nature" undergoes considerable change, but the underlying problem is more or less the same. Does man have one nature or two? In other words, is the nature of the soul different from that of the body? Or is what we call the soul merely an epiphenomenon of the body? Eventually this debate gives rise to the assertion that man has no nature, that he is what Nietzsche calls "the not yet constructed [or completed: *festgestellt*] animal."

This problematic can be restated as follows: either physics is the first science or else we must choose between the study of God and the study of human being. If we reject the study of God on the grounds that there is no natural theology, given God's supernatural status, then the first philosophy must be the study of human being, that is, not of the natural being called *Homo sapiens* but of the nonnatural being who produces his own sense in a way reminiscent of nature's production of its own alterations. Strikingly enough, the choice of the study of man as the first philosophy is inseparable from the Aristotelian definition of man as the *zōon logon echon*. *Logos* is here understood as discourse, whether spoken or written. The Christian notion of God as *logos* is thus transformed into the post-Christian notion of man as *logos*.

In sum, the detachment of man from *phusis* leads to the primacy of speech or discursive intelligence. *Phusis* itself is silent, which is no doubt why mathematics is the appropriate instrument for apprehending its structure. When speech is no longer regulated by nature, the faculties of the imagination and the will are soon emancipated. This emancipation takes modern, in particular, late modern, philosophy on a different path from that chosen by Socrates. This difference is relevant to our investigation because it shows how dubious is the identification of Western metaphysics with Platonism. Socrates also seems to be turning away from *phusis* toward *logos* in the text we are studying. But the turn, as we are about to discover, is not toward human speech as its own *aitia;* it is instead a turn to the Ideas.

Nietzsche is then mistaken to regard himself as a reversed Platonist on the grounds that he rejects the Ideas. This rejection leads either back to the pre-Socratic physicists, with the will to power and the eternal return being simply poetic expressions of Nietzsche's restitution of *phusis* as fate; or forward into the chaos of unprincipled discourse, whether spoken or written. Discourse emancipated from *phusis* as well as from the gods or from their philosophical substitutes, the Ideas, has no *aitia*, not even itself. Antifoundationalism, as it is today called, means just this: nothing is responsible. The rejection of the Ideas leads to pre- or post-Platonism. But it is merely perverse or sophistical to call either of these the ultimate stage of Platonism.

These are the historical consequences of Socrates' second sailing. He turns away from *ta onta* in the following precise sense: the study of the alterations, changes, and motions of natural beings does not explain human life. Attribution of the *aitia* of generation and destruction to *phusis* in this sense forces us to jettison our understanding of ourselves as beings who act in accord with what they think best. Natural motions, considered in themselves, are neither good nor bad, better nor worse; they merely are. Of course, they may be beautiful to human perception;

but this is because we see beauty in the order and in the splendor of the heavenly bodies and so on. Our vision of beauty is not itself a natural motion.

There are no measurements by which to define the presence or the perception of beauty. Socrates does not say that he turned away from physics because it is false, but because it had bad consequences for him. We can understand this to mean that physics must be supplemented by another inquiry which allows us to preserve both physics and our everyday understanding. Human nature is not reducible to or derivable from nonhuman nature. If then there is an ontological root to the two senses of nature, it is unclear, to say the least, what light this root casts upon human existence. Perhaps the Socratic myth, which deals with the cosmos as a whole, and so with the city and the soul as reflections of the cosmos, is a human artifact designed to give a human sense to the whole. This has a bearing on the outcome of the famous quarrel between philosophy and poetry.

I want to make a second point here. Human beings act in accord with what they think best. So far as we know, they are the only beings who do this. At least up to this point in Socrates' story, there is no reason to attribute to him a teleological physics. Socrates has said nothing as yet to license the inference that he regards pre-Socratic physics as inadequate because it does not explain natural motions, and so forth in terms of what is best for natural beings. Since man alone acts in accord with a *telos,* there is, as I have in effect just noted, apparently a bifurcation in nature. The bifurcation can be bridged, if not entirely removed, by showing that there is a "supernatural" criterion which is ultimately responsible (the *aitia*) for the choices that we make, and that this supernatural criterion is also responsible for the changes of the natural beings.

Up to a point, the Ideas constitute such a criterion. In order to employ this criterion, while at the same time preserving physics as an independent science, Socrates makes the Ideas responsible not for the changes of the heavenly bodies, but for their being: for their *ousia* (101c3). The Idea provides the heavenly body with a stable look that is *independent* of the changes of the body qua body. But there would be no body of this sort, undergoing changes of this precise kind, unless there were a unity and identity underlying the body as changing, which unity and identity tell us both *that* a body is changing and *what* body or what kind of body is changing. In addition, the Ideas are the *aitia* of justice, beauty, and goodness, to mention only these virtues or excellences of the human soul. In sum, the Ideas provide a unification of the sources of theory and practice; otherwise stated, they offer a bridge across the bifurcation between nonhuman and human nature. But it is the soul that must traverse the bridge.

The Second Sailing

Now, to continue with Socrates' account. First, to repeat, Socrates gives up, in a restricted sense previously defined, the investigation of *ta onta*, that is, *ta phusika*. He therefore decides that he must be careful to avoid the misfortune that befalls those who "contemplate and observe carefully" (*theōrountes kai skopoumenoi*) the sun during its eclipse. "For some of them ruin their eyes unless they look at its icon in water or something like that" (99d4ff.). In other words, even if he does not study the natural changes, he must still avoid the danger of attempting to look directly at the being that undergoes these changes. Remember the famous icon of the sun in the *Republic*. Does Socrates mean to imply here that one cannot see the Idea of the Good directly? If so, dialectic is impossible. All philosophical discourse, since it proceeds with words, is by way of icons. But it will be apparent in a moment that this is not quite Socrates' view.

In our passage, Socrates says that one must not contemplate beings directly with the eyes and the other senses; but he does not advise us to look at them directly with the intellect or the eye of the soul. The soul will be blinded by the direct regard of *ta pragmata*, a rather general expression that includes deeds as well as things. In order to avoid the blinding of the soul, it occurred to Socrates "to take flight to *tous logous* and to look for [*skopein*] the truth of the beings in them" (99e1ff.). This statement is close to the key premise of those modern philosophers for whom language or discourse is primary. Nevertheless, a fundamental difference will emerge shortly. First, Socrates now denies the accuracy of his earlier icon (*eikazo:* "I express myself in an icon") concerning the sun: "I do not at all agree that he who investigates beings in *logois* is looking in icons any more than is he who investigates beings in *ergois*" (99e6–100a2).

The reference to the sun is an icon; the reference to *logoi* is not; that is, it is not a recommendation to employ icons in the investigation of the beings. Accordingly, *logoi* cannot here refer to "words" or artifacts of the discursive faculty which are produced as surrogates for beings, hence as signs or icons. The *logoi* to which Socrates refers are not "propositions" or statements "about" the Ideas, any more than they are concepts. The attempt to connect these *logoi* to Aristotle's categories is mistaken. This is emphasized by the comparison with the study of *erga,* or deeds. A deed is not an image of something else but an original. Of course, a courageous deed exhibits the Idea of courage; but the deed itself is not an image of the Idea because courage is not a deed but a state of the soul.

Furthermore, Socrates did not in fact give up studying the beings, as he asserted at the beginning of the passage I am analyzing. His intention is still to discover the truth of the beings; this truth is not accessible in the science of (mathematical) physics. But neither is it accessible in speech qua imagery; that is, it is not accessible in speech taken as detached from but representing the beings. *Logos* means here something that is common to being and to speech. To retain the visual metaphor, what we see in the *logos* must be the same as what we would see if we were able to look directly at the beings without blinding the soul. This same look, that is, the look that is the same in both cases, is the Idea.

At this point in the analysis, we have to face a difficulty. Socrates advises us to look into the *logoi* in order to find more conveniently the truth of the beings. If that truth is the Ideas, are these the same as or different from but accessible within the *logoi*? Let me suggest the following formulation, which is based in part upon the technical discussion of modes of being and knowing in the *Republic* and the *Philebus.* The *on,* or being, has a *phusis,* or nature, that consists of an order or ratio (*logos*) of elements of intelligibility. The *logos* can be transferred into speech by a two-stage process: first the *logos* is apprehended by *nous* or *noēsis;* then this apprehension is "copied" by the *dianoia* in the icons of language. This copy or "judgment" is inscribed into the soul by what Socrates calls in the *Philebus* (38a6ff.) the psychic demiurge who writes. What he has written (the *doksa*) is then the mediate original for the copy made by the other demiurge in the soul, the painter (who produces the perceived image, or *morphē*). This two-stage process enables us to grasp or to "see" the *logos* and thereby to see the truth or "openness" of the *on.* As present within or apprehended by the intellect, the *logos* is clearly different from the *on,* since otherwise the being and the intellect would be identical. On the other hand, as exhibiting the ratio of intelligibility of the being in question, the *logos* is the same as that being in the sense that both have the same look or Idea.

Let me underline this last point. The look cannot be different in the two cases of the being and its correlative *logos,* since then there would be no such correlation or coincidence, in which case we could not see the same truth in the *logos* that obtains in the being. The *logos* would in other words be at most an image of the look of the being, which Socrates denies, and at worst, some other look entirely. On the other hand, the *logos* cannot be the same as the being, since in that case there would be no need to look into the *logos* as a more accessible way into seeing what is contained in the being. Above all, we must not make the mistake committed by linguistic philosophers, who take the *logoi* to be statements about the beings. This amounts to the replacement of the Ideas by discursive rules or concepts.

Perhaps I can convey my general conclusion as follows: the *logos* is ontologically distinct from the being (*on*), but formally it is the same. The eidetic look is the same in both cases. This is why the truth of the being can be discerned by looking into the *logos.* Thus the Idea that is the truth of the being is visible in the *logos.* And the *logos* is the middle term, according to Socrates' own words, that makes genuine being accessible to thinking. Stated in a preliminary manner, the *logos* is the community of being and thinking. We arrive at the *logoi* by thinking about beings. It is not thinking in the sense of the product or activity of subjective consciousness, and it is not the being which is independent of consciousness and has a certain look. The genuine being, the Idea, is the eidetic intelligibility of the being about which we inquire. But it does not follow from this that the being is fully intelligible to us. What we apprehend or perceive is the Idea. Finally, there cannot be a complete discursive analysis of the Idea because discourse works with images, on the basis of what Socrates calls elsewhere a recollection of the original. There is always a gap between "vision" and speech. So much for general conclusions; now for the details.

The visual metaphor is essential in giving us a primary orientation with respect to Socrates' second sailing. But it cannot be finally satisfactory because it is an icon. The sense of sight is as it were an icon of the cognition of Ideas. This is also apparent in Socrates' reference to those who investigate the beings *en tois ergois,* in deeds. We see that a certain person is performing a deed, for example, a potter makes a pot or a general leads his troops into battle. But we do not see the deed in the same sense that we see the motions of the person. What is it that transforms our perception of the moving body or bodies into a perception of a deed? We understand that the person is a general; we know what it is to engage in a war, and so on. None of this is perception of a motion or measurement of changes by the methods of mathematical physics. We understand the intentions of the human beings whose motions we are perceiving; we understand these because we understand the souls of the actors. And this understanding does not come from perception but from our inner understanding of ourselves: precisely from that which scientific psychology excludes under the title of introspection, reliance upon anecdote, recourse to occult entities, and so on.

It is not unreasonable to suggest that the understanding of deeds is prior, both chronologically and as it were ontologically, to the understanding of beings. We understand what to do in order to satisfy our desires before we understand the natures of the beings that satisfy our desires. We know how to run away from danger, how to defend ourselves against attack, what it is to express our love, and a thousand other things, none of which requires us to know the natures of the beings with respect to which our deeds are performed. In this sense *praxis* is more fundamental than *theōria* as well as more urgent. And we understand deeds because we understand intentions; we know the *aitia,* or what is responsible for the series of motions in the bodies we are perceiving.

We know this because we "know" ourselves, not in any theoretical sense but by virtue of our own nature; we know ourselves as *aitia.* This knowledge is not arrived at by way of sense-perception and certainly not by vision. We cognize, intuit, feel, apprehend, are aware of . . . ; there is no precise term to designate this kind of direct knowledge. The knowledge emerges spontaneously from within us, not as solipsists or detached cogitating egos and certainly not from a physics-oriented scientific investigation, but from ourselves as immersed within the everyday, and so, among other things, as beings who turn to scientific investigation because we understand before making that turn why it is best to do so. We know ourselves as the beings who look to the *logoi.*

Platonism

This is not the same as knowledge of Ideas; it is self-knowledge or obedience to the command of the Delphic oracle.

The look in the *logos* is the same as the look of the being. The former is not an icon of the latter. I said previously that the *logos* is the ratio of the intelligible elements of the being; it is the being as it looks or is intelligible to the human intellect. As to the being itself, that is something else; we can know only how the being looks. We may talk endlessly, in the Heideggerian style, of letting beings be and of truth as uncoveredness, that is, as something that is independent of the act of seeing or understanding. The fact remains that what is uncovered is what we see to be uncovered. In one sense, this is perspectivism; but it is not relativism because the accessibility of the beings, which is made possible by the Ideas and which Heidegger criticizes as utilitarianism, allows us to confirm or disconfirm what we personally see. The validity or genuineness of the *logos* is established by the comprehensive consideration of its effects: of what it is responsible for as *aitia*. Coherence, in other words, is not a property of propositions or even at bottom of the relation between propositions and beings. It is a property of the cosmos or whole. As to talk about uncoveredness apart from what is uncovered or about the clearing within which uncoveredness occurs, that is empty talk, talk about nothing.

As a ratio, the *logos* is both the identity of the being, that by virtue of which we know it to be the being that it is, hence, what it is; and it is also the unity of that identity, that by virtue of which the identity coheres and is available as what it is to our intelligence. I observe parenthetically that according to Aristotle there are as many senses of "one" as there are of "being." To be anything at all is always to be one; to be one is always to be something or another. To be anything at all is to be something or another, and this differs from case to case. But the unity of the differing cases is always the same, as is the being. "Being" and "one" are virtual if not actual synonyms. If this is so, then there is nothing to be said about "being" understood as that which is common to every individual or unitary being. But there is something to be said about the particular identity of each being: namely, by answering the question, What is it? Unity is always the same; identity is always different. Being is unity and identity. This is, incidentally, not the same as the Hegelian expression "identity of identity and nonidentity," that is, "identity of identity and difference." Identity is not the same as unity. There is no unity in Hegel; the place of unity is filled by the circularity of the concept, that is, by the perpetual differentiation of identities.

So this is how Socrates "launched himself" (*hōrmēsa*) on his second sailing. He then states his general procedure, namely, the procedure which he arrived at after having abandoned physics and avoided the dangers of what would today be called ontology or the effort to view the beings directly. The Greek reads as follows: *kai hupothemenos hekastote logon hon an krinō errōmenestaton einai, ha men an moi dokei toutōi sumphonein, tithēmi hōs alēthē onta, kai peri aitias kai peri tōn allōn hapantōn tōn ontōn, ha d'an mē, hōs ouk alēthē* (100a2–7). A tentative translation: "And positing in each case a *logos* which I judge to be the strongest, I establish [take my stand on the *logos*] as true whatever seems to me to agree with it, whether with respect to the cause or to any other things whatsoever; what does not [agree with the *logos*], I establish to be untrue."

At this point a possible equivocation occurs in Socrates' account. Initially, he says that he turned to *tous logous* in order to avoid the danger of blinding his soul by looking directly at the beings by means of his senses. This can mean either that he turned away from cognition rooted in sense-perception to various ways of grasping beings by discursive thinking alone or else that he turned to the *logos* or ratio of intelligibility that corresponds to each of the perceivable beings. The plural *tous logous*, in other words, can refer here either to rational accounts in general or to the Ideas in particular. There is of course no doubt that Socrates is about to introduce the hypothesis of the Ideas. But it is of considerable importance to know whether the hypothesis of the Ideas is merely one *logos* or hypothesis among many, and so a "model" or construction of the discursive reason.

In the immediate sequel, Socrates denies that the study of beings by the inspection of *logoi* (*ton en tois logois skopoumenon ta onta*) constitutes a study of beings via images, as in the case of studying the sun through its reflected images. This assertion, together with the co-ordination of *logoi* and *erga* (99e6ff.), shows that Socrates is referring to "originals" rather than to discursive copies or interpretations. The turn away from the sensed beings is a turn to their genuine being, or *ousia*, not to a hypothetical construction. The participle *hupothemenos* must therefore mean to enjoin, demonstrate, or propose what one has determined to be true and not to suggest or to suppose for the sake of argument. We can unpack the sense of Socrates' condensed manner of expression as follows. The *logos* is a ratio of intelligibility which shows the intellectually rather than the sensuously apprehended "look" or Idea of each being.

When Socrates says that he posits in each case a *logos,* he is presumably referring to the Idea that corresponds to each type of being. On the other hand, by referring to each *logos* so posited as "the strongest," he raises the suspicion that he is speaking here of one among a variety of possible accounts. If the second alternative is correct, *logos* refers here not to a particular Idea, but to the doctrine or hypothesis of the Ideas in general. I do not believe that the passage allows us to decide which of these senses is intended. There may well be a blurring together of the two distinct senses of "explanation" or "account" and "ratio" or element of the account. But the senses are related by the fact that in neither case is Socrates referring to a "hypothesis" in the modern sense of a linguistic construction. At the same time, it is important to notice that the doctrine of Ideas is indeed a "hypothesis" in the sense of something laid down to be true, not as a deductive inference from previously established premises or principles, but as a general conclusion from everyday experience. What counts as true is that which agrees with the posited *logos*. The *logos* itself, that is, the doctrine of Ideas, cannot be "true" in the same sense as propositions which are accepted on the basis of the doctrine. This is why Socrates must have recourse to stories, myths, and metaphors in expounding the doctrine of Ideas.

In sum, Socrates has turned away from beings to *logoi*. By the latter, he does not mean icons, and so certainly not signs. The truth of the being is accessible in or is the same as the truth of the *logos*. But a distinction is required at this point. Socrates chooses the "strongest" *logos*. In other words, he chooses from a multiplicity of candidates. The hypothesis (*logos*) that he chooses is that of the intelligible ratios (*logous*). But the ratios are not themselves hypotheses in the sense of linguistic constructions. And the hypothesis itself is validated by the presence in everyday experience of stable and identifiable unities, by means of which we are enabled to act for the better. The "strength" of the hypothesis is not formal but existential. It is rooted in the *erga* rather than in abstract interpretations of the *erga*. If this were not so, then there would be no basis, external to an arbitrary or subjective choice, for choosing between one *logos* and another. The decision as to the strength of the *logos* must be rooted in some characteristic intrinsic to how things are and not simply in how I wish them to be or in how I make them to be by a primordial decision concerning how to talk about them. It is fair to say that Platonism stands or falls on the rationality of taking one's bearings by our ability to distinguish between better and worse decisions in everyday life. In this sense Heidegger is correct to refer to the "utilitarian" nature of the doctrine of Ideas. But the utility of the Ideas is grounded in the utility of beings. The actual meaning of "use" is here nothing more nor less than "practice" or "activity." The beings allow us to exist, and the Ideas are responsible for the beings.

It follows that some *logoi* (= hypotheses) must "uncover" more than others. I think that the Heideggerian term is quite helpful at this point. Socrates does not say that all the *logoi* he considers, other than the one he chooses, are false. Strength is not the same as truth, and weakness is not the same as falsehood. The strongest *logos* reveals the most; it uncovers the whole. The weaker *logoi* are partial or perspectival, like the *logos* of mathematical physics. The Socratic hypothesis is a *logos* that is perspectival only in the sense that it shows us the broadest perspective. It is not quite, but almost, synoptic; not quite, because it does not explain the soul, but almost, because the soul cannot be understood on any other basis. So *logos* has an "ontic" sense here; it renders the *on* visible to or, as Heidegger would say, as unconcealed before, the intellect.

Logos does not "discover" or render unconcealed by means of discourse what is in itself covered over. The rendering in question is not of something by something else—of a thing by a statement or speech. The *logos* itself contains the openness or unconcealment of the being. Henceforward I shall refer to the openness of the *logos* as an abbreviation for the openness of the *logos* as the openness of being. The *logos* is what Heidegger calls the uncoveredness of the being as it is accessible to human intelligence. Conversely, the intellect is also openness, but it is not yet clear whether this openness is the same as or different from the openness of the *logos*. In one sense, of course, they must be different because "openness" in the intellect means (1) open to receive something else, and (2) open to oneself, that is, not just to receive but to think what it has received. Openness in the *logos* means instead open to be received by something else, specifically, the intellect. If the *logos* were also open to itself, it would be the same as the intellect, and we would move from Platonism to Hegelianism. Truth would then be not of *onta,* but of *noēsis,* or what Hegel calls *Geist.*

But in another sense, the openness of the *logos* must be the same as the openness of the intellect. As open to itself, the intellect thinks not itself, but that which it receives, that which has been furnished to it; and what has been furnished to it is the openness of the *logos.* One could object that the intellect may also think itself; but if this is possible, the intellect somehow doubles: the openness of the intellect is as it were filled by itself. And this is possible only if the intellect possesses a determinate form. If it did, however, it would not be open but closed. Otherwise put, if the intellect is to think itself, it must have a *logos,* or form. But if it has a form, then it cannot think, since thinking is openness to all other forms or the absence of a form of its own. We may be aware of ourselves as thinking something in particular, but this is not the same as thinking: it is not the same as the activity attributed by Aristotle to God: thinking thinking itself. The self, in other words, is the same as the intellect in God alone, but certainly not in human beings.

To continue, the openness of the intellect must be the same as the openness or visibility of what it thinks. For if not, there would be two different truths; the act of knowing something would in fact be the knowing of something else (such as oneself); but this is impossible. To know a cow is not to know one's own intellect. We resolve the puzzle as follows. That which is open to be received (the *logos*) is other than that which receives; but as what has been received by the apprehension of the intellect, it is the same. The intellect (as distinguished from the soul) cannot think itself because it has no particular look or *logos;* it is pure receptivity. Nor can it think anything other than the *logos,* as has just been explained; for then knowing something would in fact be knowing something else instead. In sum, the openness of the *logos* and the openness of the intellect coincide in the act of thinking. I have been using the word "openness" as a synonym for "truth." Now replace "openness" by "look" in the double sense of the act and the result, and we have the Idea.

Some readers will undoubtedly have been thinking of Aristotle as I offered the preceding analysis. How does this analysis of the passage from Plato's *Phaedo* differ from the Aristotelian doctrine of the actualization of the species-form, or *eidos,* in the passive (that is, receptive) intellect? The first thing to be said is that the similarity between the two thinkers should come as no surprise, whether on the basis of Heidegger's or of a more orthodox interpretation of the history of philosophy. Whether we call Aristotle a Platonist or simply note that his entire philosophy is a revisionary commentary on the doctrines of his teacher, there is nothing surprising about discovering a point of very close similarity at the heart of the two accounts of thinking. But close similarity is not the same as identity. Aristotle clearly believed himself to be in disagreement with Plato. Was he mistaken?

In order to bring out the difference between Plato and Aristotle, which, although crucial, is in my opinion much narrower than is normally assumed, we have to remind ourselves of a previous distinction. "Openness" in the case of the intellect has two senses; these are, to repeat, (1) open to receive and (2) open to oneself. But "openness" in the case of the being means just open to be received. The being is not open to itself; it is not the same as thinking and certainly not the same as the intellect. This means that even if there were no intellect, there would be beings. The beings would stand open to be received even if there were nothing to receive them. This is not true in Aristotle's analysis. The openness of the being is precisely its truth or actuality as now being thought. The *eidos,* or species-form, can be distinguished from the activity of noetic thinking as the content of a thought is distinguished from the thought. But this distinction is not ontological or, to use a quasi-Aristotelian word, it is not substantial. Of course there can be no thought without a content; to think is to think something. But the something that is thought is not thereby ontologically separate from the process of thinking.

From this crucial standpoint, we can say that Aristotle is an Idealist; it is not by chance that Hegel preferred him to Plato. Aristotle places the being itself within the act of thinking itself; Plato separates these. It is the *logos* that is the same in both being and thinking. Stated with maximum simplicity: the ratio of the intelligible elements is the same in the being as it is in the noetic apprehension of that being. The ratio of intelligible elements is that by which a being both is what it is and is open to being thought. But the being of what is being thought is not the same as the being of that which is doing the thinking. Aristotle in effect collapses the distinction between the being of what is available for thinking and the being of thinking. His so-called realism or empiricism, that is, the fact that he starts with particular beings or residents within the everyday world of genesis, is entirely illusory. These particular beings owe their being to their *eidos,* or species-form, which itself actualizes in thinking, not in the particular being itself, apart from being thought (via perception). Stated crudely: if there were no thinking about rabbits, if no one were thinking a rabbit, there would be no rabbits. And if no one were thinking anything, there would be no *eidē,* or species-forms.

On the other hand, there is no difference whatsoever between Plato and Aristotle on this crucial point: the look or ratio of the being, that is, the Idea, if it is to be apprehended by the intellect, must be apprehended in itself, not in or as an image. This is because images cannot be identified except via the look of the original. *If* there is such a thing as a vision or recollection of the Idea, it cannot be the vision or recollection of some look other than the look one is actually viewing or recollecting. In other words, the doctrine of separate Ideas makes no sense whatsoever. Either we perceive the Idea or we do not. As the look of a being, the Idea cannot be some other look when we view it. The view is the same, whether we start from the side of the being or from the side of the viewing intelligence. Beings and intellects are separate; but they are bridged by *logoi,* and so, by looks or Ideas. For this reason, the intellectual faculty by which we apprehend the *logoi* of *onta* cannot be the *dianoia,* or discursive intellect, because this faculty proceeds by way of words and hence through the manufacture of icons. I have followed Plato by calling the faculty with which we know *logoi* by the name of *noēsis. Noēsis* cannot manufacture anything; it rather furnishes the original look to the *dianoia,* which then manufactures an icon of that look for transmission in discourse. *Noēsis* is not production but acquisition or reception.

The distinction between the *logos* and the being is explicitly made by Socrates himself; I have not interpolated it into the text by an act of hermeneutical violence. What I have done is to offer an explanation for the meaning of this distinction. The *logos* is the ratio of intelligible elements; it is intelligibility. As such, it exhibits the genuine being or the Idea. But the intelligibility of a being can hardly be different from my apprehension of that intelligibility; if it were, in apprehending the intelligibility of something, I would be apprehending the intelligibility of something else. But this is the principle of deconstruction, or of the thesis that reading is in fact writing; it is not the thesis of Platonism. The thesis of Platonism, at least as it emerges from the *Phaedo,* is rather that the truth in the *logos* is the same as the truth in the being. This truth is the openness or what we call the Idea of the being, that is, the Idea of the cow.

In my formulation, following Socrates, the Idea is the genuine being, the *ontōs on,* because it is the intelligibility or truth of the being. The Idea is also *ontōs on* in contrast with the spatio-temporal or generated particular. As the look or ratio that allows the particular to stand open to the cognitive faculties, namely, as this thing here, of such and such a kind (the terminology is Aristotelian but in no way un-Platonic), the Idea genuinely is the look of the genuine being of the generated, illusory icon of the original. There is, however, a slight qualification of the orthodox version. If I may be permitted to preserve Plato's own visual metaphor, the Idea is the *face* of the genuine being of the particular.

But surely Plato did not require Aristotle to explain to him that if the genuine being of the particular is separate from it, in some other place, if further it is some other look or some other being, then the entire analysis falls to the ground. And whether Plato did or did not need Aristotle to explain this, he clearly understood it, as is more or less obvious from the *Parmenides,* to say nothing of the difference between the mythical accounts of ostensibly separated, Hyperuranian Ideas and prosaic analyses of eidetic form in dialogues like the *Sophist* and *Philebus.* But the most serious reply, of course, is that the literal formulations of the ostensible doctrine of Ideas differ from one dialogue to the next; it is the task of the philosopher to think through the problem in such a way as to make it intelligible, and only secondarily in such a way as to reconcile the various texts with one another. In fact, it is only if we have thought through the doctrine in as coherent a form as possible that there is any hope of reconciling the diverse Platonic texts with one another, texts which demand to be interpreted as dramatic, poetical, or metaphorical accommodations of an intrinsically intractable problem to the differing standpoints of human beings of diverse capacities and interests.

I must bring this line of reflection to a conclusion. Suffice it to say this: if the Idea is separate from thought, then it is unintelligible. If we remember or recollect it in the form of an image, that image either has the same look as the Idea or a different look. If the look is the same, then the Idea is the same as separate and as thought, in which case it is not separate. If the look differs, then it is a different look, and we are not thinking the Idea at all, but something else. So the Idea cannot be separate from thought. But if the Idea is inseparable from thought, and the genuine being of instances, that is, images, that look like it, then the result is Idealism, not separation of Ideas from genesis. The only way out of these difficulties is to make the Idea common to being and thinking while at the same time distinguishing being from thinking. *The Idea is what is thinkable in Being,* which I now spell with a capital *B* to bring out my criticism of Heidegger. The Idea is not the reification of Being, the perspectival projection that conceals Being; it is instead the accessibility of Being.

To return now to the meaning of *hupothemenos,* Socrates begins by putting forward as a basis, that is, as something that will sustain his thinking, the *logos* that he judges (*krinō*) to be the healthiest or most powerful (*errōmenestaton*); the one that will keep him upright, prevent him from slipping or falling down, that is, from failing to conclude his investigation. What Socrates puts forth is not an invention, a "hypothesis" in the modern sense of a theoretical construction, and so a conceptual artifact or pattern which is to be imposed onto the phenomena in order to make them orderly and coherent. Socrates arrives at a *logos* by judging or distinguishing (*krinein*) among *logoi* themselves; he separates accounts of looks or ratios and selects the healthiest one as the basis for continuing to live a rational life. What he stands on is not an *on* but a *logos;* this is the turn or second sailing. We cannot look directly at the *onta;* to do so would be to blind the soul. So we have to look at the *logoi.*

The *logoi* (the content of the hypothesis) are not icons; they have the same look, the truth or openness or unconcealedness of the *onta.* And to the extent that what is genuinely is genuinely intelligible to the gods (as in the myth of the Hyperuranian beings), we may say by analogy that what is fully or most fully intelligible to us is genuinely for us. *For us:* this is the inescapable element of perspectivism, but it has nothing to do with relativism, since the perspective is the same in principle for every human being. But no human being can see the back of the moon by the unassisted act of vision; we cannot see the other side of the stars or Hyperuranian beings but only their faces, the faces that are turned toward us.

Whatever harmonizes or sounds in unison with the *logos* (either in the general sense of the hypothesis of the Ideas or in the particular case), whether with respect to *aitia* or anything else, "I put forward as true." *Tithēmi* is used here, not *hupotithēmi*. Socrates puts forward truth on top of that which he has placed beneath; the *logos* sustains and establishes truth. This does not mean that truth is a covering, like bricks or stones, built on top of a now-invisible foundation. The true *sumphonei*, it sounds in unison; it is the same look as that of the basis or hypothesis. And this raises our final query, which I shall address in detail in the next section. The look, truth, or Idea is the same in the *logos* or ratio of intelligibility and in the being, only more accessible to us in the former than in the latter. What then is the difference between the Idea and the *logos*? If the *logos* is neither a concept nor a proposition but nevertheless communicates the truth or Idea of the being to the intellect, what is the medium of communication, if not the Idea itself?

The Middle Term

In order to investigate the truth about beings, Socrates grounds his investigation in *logoi* that exhibit the same truth one would find if one were able to look directly at the beings. The truth in question is that of the nature of the being, what it genuinely is, and so, it is the exhibition of what Socrates calls elsewhere *ontōs on*, "genuine" or "true" being. This true being is often compared to the look of the thing; the truth is *of* the thing, not of being qua being, and certainly not of what Heidegger calls Being (*Sein*). The truth, or the true being, of a cow is not the truth about being per se, but about the cow. The *logos*, as the intermediary between the being and the human intellect, must have something in common with both. Furthermore, there are degrees of strength or comprehensiveness by which *logoi* (= hypotheses) are distinguished, just as some things look better than others. The best-looking hypothesis is that which enables us to harmonize as much as possible of our experience. Such a harmony is rooted in the greatest possible community between being and thinking. That which is common to both is obviously the visible or intelligible truth of the being; for the intellect, in apprehending the Idea, sees the truth in question. The great difficulty in understanding Socrates' speech lies in the following delicate point. The *logos,* or intelligible ratio, must be distinct from and yet, as a look, the same as the being that we are investigating. If it were not distinct from and more accessible than the being, we would not need to and indeed could not consult it as the route to the discovery of the truth of the being itself. But if the look were not the same, there would be no point in examining the *logos,* for in so doing we would be seeing something other than what we were looking for.

Ideas are the looks of beings, and so how beings look to us; but they are not projections effected by the act of human looking or thinking or distortions of how beings present themselves in their genuine uncoveredness apart from thinking. Socrates evidently means to suggest that the Ideas or looks are accessible within, but are themselves different from, the *logoi* in which they are presented. This is evident from the etymology of the two words. *Idea* comes from *horao* and *eidomai,* to see, whereas *logos* is derived from *lego,* to gather, pick up, and so to collect or bind together. If we pick up and arrange elements, such as lines of various curvature, colors of various hue, and so on, the results of this collection might be a picture or sketch. The picking up and arranging that leads to the picture is not the same as the picture itself. On the other hand, the picture, as the end-stage of the picking up and assembling, is indeed the *logos* in its fullness or genuineness of being. The picture is the *ontōs on* of the *logos* and, derivatively, of the being (e.g., the cow).

In formulating this distinction, I have removed the Socratic equivocation between the sense of *logos* as "hypothesis" and *logoi* as ratios of intelligibility in order to try to explain how the Idea is in one sense the same as, and in another different from, the *logos* in the second sense, namely, as the community of being and thinking. The gathering-together or collecting of thinking must be the same as the gathering-together or collecting that culminates in the looks of beings. The formulation, if taken literally, is unsatisfactory because it seems to adopt the paradigm of the carpenter or to imply a divine fabricator of Ideas. It becomes more acceptable if we think of the Ideas as possessing an internal structure of their own, one which is composed not of looks, but of elements like same, other, one, many, being, nothing, and so on.

In order to avoid problems of this sort, we have to distinguish between *logos* as the ratio of being and thinking and *logos* as human discursive intelligence. Socrates certainly implies this distinction, but it is blurred by the unremarked use of *logos* in two different senses, as I have now explained at length. *Logos* in the first sense refers to human discursive intelligence, namely, as exercised in the production of a hypothesis. We consider our everyday experience, which is predicated upon the stability of beings, despite the changes they undergo; this consideration is of course discursive or calculative in nature, even though it culminates in a general conclusion that cannot be demonstrated logically to follow from the antecedent consideration. In the second sense, however, a *logos* is not a discourse but that about which we speak. If human beings put together lines and colors at random, the resultant look is an invention of our imagination or else of mere random arrangement. In order for the look to be *ontōs on,* it must guide the arrangement of *legein* or be accessible in advance of the ostensible composition of the picture. But this problem does not arise at the ontological level. Suppose that, as is appropriate to the realm of eternity, there is no disjunction between the "picking up" and the resultant picture; instead, there is a ratio of elements that provides the intellect with a look or cognitive picture, and that it is the apprehending of this cognitive picture that allows us to proceed to the attempt to ascertain the natures of the elements within the ratio or to state, not as a picture but as a *formula,* the ratio of elements.

To sum up, *logoi* in the sense of hypotheses are ways of viewing the whole; some are better than others, which is to say that they may be rank-ordered on the basis of comprehensiveness or, more colloquially, on the goodness of their looks. The *logos* of the Ideas is not itself an Idea; it is the presentation of the whole as a community of being and thinking, a presentation in which the community is itself explained by the accessibility of the looks of things to thinking or, in the Socratic idiom, to the eye of the soul. It is this *logos,* in which the Ideas (exhibited in *logoi* or ratios of intelligibility) are the middle term between being and thinking, so to speak, that Socrates selects as the strongest and that he establishes as the basis for subsequent reasoning. We may use the term "hypothesis" to mean the founding *logos;* but this is not a conjecture or purely perspectival construction. When Socrates says that the beings are visible in the *logos,* which is no more an image than are the *erga,* or deeds of everyday life, he means that the order of the whole exhibits the Ideas; he is not here referring to a hypothesis that is produced by our speech about that order. The *logos* as hypothesis is not the *logos* of human discursive thinking but its ground.

Let us go back again to the turn away from the direct inspection of the beings. This is the same as a turn toward an indirect investigation into the beings, namely, by way of ratios of intelligibility. Socrates must mean that he turned from one stance to another with respect to the beings. As we saw earlier, two standpoints or perspectives were abandoned: (1) that of natural science or mathematical physics; and (2) that of looking directly at the beings, something which mathematical physics does not do. Despite Socrates' metaphor of the sun, it is not immediately evident what is meant by a direct inspection of the beings. In an earlier section, I referred to this as the "ontological" stance, but the term is one of convenience rather than clarification.

Let me try to be more precise. Apparently the truth of the beings is not directly accessible to us. If I look directly at a cow, there must be a sense in which I am "blinded" or cannot see. Socrates wishes to convey something like the following distinction. The cow qua being is an item of genesis, hence is itself a series of changes and is variously accessible to a variety of viewpoints. Not only does the cow undergo change, but so do we as we observe it. Not only do we change our position but we are also undergoing changes in our sense organs. How do the anti-Platonists or enemies of the Ideas explain our ability to recognize a cow by way of sense-perception? According to them, the identity of the cow is arrived at by a series of constructions from the initial sense-data; more accurately, it is a ratio of two sets of changes, those in the cow and those in us. However the details may go, the result is a ratio, whether in the sense of a Kantian rule or in the post-Kantian sense of a concept, to which is associated an image or picture. The rule allows us to identify the sense-object as a cow.

On this analysis, we do not identify the cow by looking directly at it. There is, so to speak, no cow standing available to direct inspection, but a series of changes awaiting interpretation through the mediation of another series of changes. The result of the interpretation will vary as the changes vary, but variations are with respect to the identity of the cow, so let us stay with this identity. The identity of the cow is not the directly observed cow, but a concept together with a picture. The picture is the sense-image, but this does not provide us with the cognized identity of the cow. It is instead identified by the concept of the cow. Now the most striking fact about the concept or rule is that it is relative to a ratio of changes. Let us call this ratio the *logos*. The *logos* provides the intellect with the concept. The picture, as a product of sensation, is a derivative entity that may be ignored here. This leaves us with the concept or rule as the anti-Platonist's substitute for the Platonic Idea. The middle term between being and thinking is the rule.

The fact that pictures are banished to a subordinate role is not enough to affect the analogy between anti-Platonism and Platonism. For as I have already argued, the Idea is not really to be understood as a visual phenomenon or a picture. The Idea allows us to understand that we are perceiving a cow. Now of course, the Idea does not explain to us in discursive language what it is to be a cow; in order to learn this, we must turn to zoology. But what of the rule or concept of the anti-Platonist? What does it explain? In the case of Kant, little or nothing. The concept or rule for perceiving empirical objects is very general; for example, the rule for perceiving a dog is that a dog is a four-footed animal.[3] Kant cannot specify this rule any further without turning the shape of the dog from an empirical and contingent appearance into a product of the understanding, that is, into a transcendentally constituted object. Exactly like contemporary students of perception who take their bearings by neurophysiology and artificial intelligence, Kant wants the perceived shape of the dog to be contingent, not a priori. It is up to the progress of science to tell us what dogs or any other empirical object may be. In short, the rules must be transient.

The Kantian rule, then, is not accessible to the analytic intelligence, not available to a precise restatement in discursive terms of the ratio of the object of sense-perception. As in the case of the more empirically minded anti-Platonist, the concept of the cow is entirely contingent and certainly imprecise; it is nothing more than a general statement of those observed features of the cow which are currently taken to serve as identifying properties. The concept of the cow is as much in flux as the cow. The image of the cow is a contingent artifact of the structure of the sense organs which we happen to possess; it is not the look of the being of the cow. Instead, it is the look of the nonbeing of the cow; that is, it is the simulacrum of the cow because cows and all other objects of sense-perception seem to everyday or prescientific experience to be beings which we identify accurately by means of their looks, but are in fact invisible ratios of changes or ratios that are visible, if at all, via or as the productions of the mathematical intelligence. And these productions not only do not look like cows; they do not tell us anything definite about the being of the cow.

I venture to assert that no equations have been published which purport to define the nature of the cow. The mathematical analysis of neurophysiological reactions takes us entirely away from the domain of cows and trees to another domain, general in nature, in which what look like cows and trees are in fact mathematically measured waves or ratios of waves. This domain is not even the domain of the neurophysiology of the anatomical laboratory, let alone of the bodies of living residents of the everyday world. It is also interesting that thus far the neurophysiological approach has not been able to explain how we perceive anything at all, that is, any object whatsoever, whether a cow or a tree, and certainly not how we integrate all sensations into the visual field. The transition from waves to cows is still a mystery to science; that transition is not by way of mathematical equations.

One would therefore be justified in saying that the scientific account of perception, and so the rejection of the Platonic Ideas in favor of rules and concepts of discursive reason, has cast no light whatsoever on the problem Plato tried to solve: namely, how do we perceive cows? It has instead answered the question What is the being of the cow? by saying that there are no cows or that cows are nonbeings. For reasons of this sort, Socrates abandoned the pre-Socratic equivalent of mathematical physics. But our analysis has suggested that mathematical physics did not fail because it looked directly at the cow, that is, at the beings. It failed because it looked away from the beings to the ratios of their changes. In so doing, it looked to the *logoi*. If we are to distinguish Socrates' approach from that of the physicists or the contemporary neurophysiologists who take their bearings by mathematical physics, then we must turn to a different *logos*. We must, in other words, turn to a hypothesis about intelligible ratios that, although it alters our perspective onto the beings, does not direct us to something other than the beings we set out to understand. And once more: this is not to abandon science or even neurophysiology but to try to preserve the beings of the everyday world which are the direct occasions, the basis, for science.

My hypothesis is this: no one can look directly at the beings; every look at the beings is at the *look* of a being, not at a being. The look mediates, and so is the middle term between, being and thinking. By "look at" I mean "focus on," "pick out," hence "attempt to identify" and so "attempt to understand and explain." These are distinguishable stages of a continuous process by which we attempt to isolate elements or strands in the continuous weave of the web of everyday life. The web is continuous; hence there is no element in the continuum that emerges or stands apart from the continuum except on the basis of a criterion that is not itself ingredient in that continuum.

In other terms, the domain of genesis is indeed in flux. This being so, there are no identifiable objects in the domain of genesis. That is why Kant recognized the inadequacy of empiricism, as represented in particular by Locke and Hume. Regardless of the inadequacy of Kant's own account, he saw the correct problem and was on the right track. The correct philosophical alternative on this point is Plato or Kant. How can we make sense of genesis? The attempt to force an explanation out of genesis itself simply will not work because the attempt does not belong to genesis. The desire to identify the beings of the objects of perception is not directed to the changes within genesis, since they have no being as such objects. The desire is directed toward the ratios of changes, which ratios are intelligible to the extent that they do not themselves change. And the agent of desire is of course the individual human being, who seeks to understand how it is possible to live a rational life.

The turn away that is a turn toward the correct perspective with respect to the beings is then a turning to a hypothesis that is not itself a product of genesis but instead *articulates* genesis, that is, renders it intelligible. The turn to the *logos* is nothing more and nothing less than the turn toward thinking about the beings, rather than the attempt to think them directly. Contrary to Heidegger's censures, we have to think the beings *as* something. In our initial attempt to make sense out of everyday experience, we turn directly toward the beings as products of genesis, and so as in the process of generation and decay. This leads us first to the elements (water, fire, air, earth) and forces (love, hate) and then to the shapes (lines, circles, triangles) and numbers out of which generation and decay build up and dissolve the beings of genesis. But this in turn amounts to the reduction of the content of everyday understanding into the elements, forces, and formulae of mathematical physics. The turn directly to the beings is thus shown to be itself a turn away from the beings, but a turn that is equivalent to reductivism: the beings are reduced to elements of genesis. In order to turn away from reductivism, we must turn back to the everyday intelligibility of the beings because there is nowhere else to turn. The ratios of change are now seen as identical in their looks with the looks of the everyday beings, and by "look" is here meant not the *morphē* of sense-perception, but the intelligible *eidos,* the look that shows itself, and so is present to, *noēsis.*

Mathematical physics teaches us that every explanation of genesis is in fact an explanation of something other than the objects of sense-perception, which are finally seen to be *fantasmata,* or inaccurate images, of an original intelligible structure. Philosophy teaches us that the originals of mathematical physics are incommensurable with our everyday understanding of life, without which understanding mathematical physics would itself be impossible. This is what Socrates has been telling us by means of his story to Cebes. The story is a myth about *logos.* The myth is man-made, but the *logos* is not.

We need to take one more step in our consideration of the *logos* within which the Ideas function as the middle term. According to Socrates, what he has just said is the same as what he has always been saying (100b1). In other words, although the account of the study of the beings is accommodated to the nature and needs of Cebes (and the other interlocutors), it is not in principle different from what Socrates discussed with Glaucon in the *Republic* or with Phaedrus in the *Phaedrus,* to mention two examples. Socrates says that he will now undertake "to exhibit the form of the cause" (*epideiksasthai tēs aitias to eidos*) "with which I have been busy."

He goes back for his starting point to the much-discussed Ideas: "I lay it down [*hupothemenos*] that there is a certain beauty itself [*auto kath' hauto*] and good and greatness and all the rest" (100b1–7). The expression *auto kath' hauto* means that something is to be taken as what it is apart from everything else. This does not entail that the *kath' hauto* item exists or stands altogether apart from its instances. For example, we may consider that each beautiful thing is beautiful by virtue of the fact that it exhibits beauty, and that beauty is the same in each beautiful thing, just as goodness is the same in each good thing, and so on. We can then consider beauty with respect to itself, but our consideration is of beauty as present in the same way in each beautiful thing, not as separate from these things.

It is worth pausing for a moment to ask whether this contention about the *kath' hauto* property of, say, beauty is reasonable. Could it not be objected that a vase is beautiful in a way that differs from the beauty of a poem, and that the beauty of a string quartet is different from each of the first two types of beauty? To shift examples, it is true that one human being differs in appearance, personality, aptitude, and so on, from another. But if there is an Idea of the human being, it must express the genuine being of any human being whatsoever, a genuine being that is independent of the variations just noted. The same does not seem to be true in the case of beauty. All human beings will possess a body and a soul, but not all souls will be the same in intelligence, courage, moderation, and justice. What is there in the case of beauty that is analogous to the body and the soul in the case of the human being? The common response to diverse artworks, namely, that all are beautiful, is not an expression of something in the work of art but in us. Socrates assumes otherwise, but what is the basis for this assumption? In the case of human beings, it is plausible to contend that regardless of how we respond to them, they all possess certain intrinsic or essential properties, such as a soul or an intellect. In the case of beauty, Socrates appears to be tacitly applying standards of taste, for which there is no plausible evidence to assume a corresponding Idea or *logos* of intelligibility.

I do not believe that the dialogues provide us with any plausible reasons for accepting an Idea of beauty, in distinction to Ideas of mathematical forms, logical relations, and perceivable entities. Socrates assumes that a well-ordered soul will perceive beauty as the expression of well-ordering, and that this "well-ordering" is not a matter of taste but a manifestation of genuine or true beauty. But I do not propose to argue the point further, as it is not central to my main concern. Let me continue instead with the crucial issue of the meaning of *auto kath' hauto*. I want to show now that the usual alternative to Platonism, namely, an appeal to abstraction and concept-formation, does not succeed in eliminating, but is merely another version of the fundamental *aporia* concerning the "separateness" of the Ideas.

We normally apply the term "abstraction" to the process by which we consider a property by itself. Under normal circumstances, we do not claim that the property exists by itself, but that, as a property, it must belong to some owner. This is more or less Aristotle's procedure, but whether we consider its occurrence in Aristotle or in common-sensical reasoning, the key point is to explain how the property, which has no subsistence apart from its various owners, can nevertheless subsist in our thoughts. For example, the color green is a property of the surfaces of various kinds of bodies. Suppose that we are examining a sample selection of green bodies and I ask you, "What is the color of these bodies?" You will reply, "Green." In so doing, you have perceived each body to be green and "abstracted" from your series of individual perceptions the color that is common to them all. You have considered green itself, taken apart from the bodies of which it is a color; but you will certainly not contend that green itself exists by itself, apart from the bodies of which it is the color. What then does it mean to "abstract" in this case? What have you dragged out of or removed from the bodies? You did not squeeze out their color, thus leaving them colorless, with a pool of green to one side. Neither is your answer based upon a simultaneous viewing of, say, ten individual images of green bodies, as though they were ten paintings in a room in the museum. For you must still explain how you discern the same color in all the images or paintings. Whether there is a shift from sense-perception to thinking or whether thinking takes place within or together with sense-perception, the situation is the same: to identify abstraction as the process of thought by which we arrive at a general idea of a property that is common to many bodies or things is not at all to explain what thinking is or how it goes about arriving at the general idea. If for example we possessed a complete account of the neurophysiological processes that accompany the activity of abstraction, this would not explain the shift from the perception of individual instances to the thinking of the general idea. At a certain point in the sequence of discharges of electrical energy, there would be a mental transition from individual perceptions to the general thought. We might then say, "Discharge no. 25 occurs when the agent reports the occurrence of a general idea, whereas at discharge no. 24, the agent was still considering particular cases."

But this would not explain the *mental* or cognitive shift, which, as mental, is not itself the same as or reducible to an electrical discharge or chemical reaction or something of that sort. In order to explain the mental shift, as opposed to the neurophysiological process, we would have to shift from neurophysiology to the analysis of thinking. But what would we analyze? Abstraction is not a multiplication; it is a unification. The multiplicity is given by the individual acts of sense-perception; if we analyze or take these apart, we will arrive at the components of sense-perception, not at the mental act of abstraction.

In fact, there is no possible discursive or analytical explanation of the power of abstraction because there is no structure to take apart. A phenomenological description of the steps by which the process of abstraction supposedly occurs in our thinking is no more an explanation of that process than is the detailed description of the neurophysiological processes that accompany abstract thinking. Furthermore, if we were to analyze the abstract idea of green, we would not arrive at the unity of the thought but would dissolve it into different thoughts. And so too with the process of thinking; unity is always presupposed by each act of analysis.

Kant refers to this unity as the synthetic unity of apperception. Kant maintains, to state it with maximum simplicity, that thinking itself unifies. Thinking is a unity of a particular kind, namely, a synthetic unity of a manifold of all possible objects of thought, that is, a manifold in which objects cannot appear except by being thought. To come back now to Socrates, his approach is as it were the reverse of Kant's. Kant attributes to the power of thinking the activity of constituting general ideas or, in our previous terminology, abstractions. He attributes this, of course, not to the powers of the individual or living thinker, but to the transcendental ego, that is, to the power of thought understood as the conditions for the possibility of thinking anything whatsoever in a rational manner. Kant's hypothesis rests upon the assumption that it is evident what it means to think rationally. To pursue this point, however, would take us entirely away from our main line of inquiry. Socrates differs from Kant by attributing unity or generality to the object of thought rather than to thinking.

The disadvantage of Kant's hypothesis is that by designating thinking as the unifying agent, he makes the intelligible world into an artifact of intelligence. The disadvantage of Socrates' hypothesis is that by designating the object, that is, the Ideas, as the truth of the natural beings, he deprives the thinker, that is, human being, of unity in any sense other than that of subordination to the Ideas. In Kant, all human beings are agents of unity; in Plato, unity is accessible only to the philosopher, and at the price of his humanity. The peculiar feature of the difference between Plato and Kant is that the two doctrines, although opposed to one another, have the same practical consequences.

Since the table of categories and the rules by which thinking spontaneously unifies the world are both derived not from an a priori understanding of thought, but from the world as we know it, the former must change as our knowledge of the world changes. The doctrine that the world is constituted by thought leads to the gradual devolution of unity into multiplicity. Thought devolves from the transcendental to the historical. The doctrine that thought is constituted by the world (or cosmos) has precisely the same result; as our knowledge of the world or cosmos evolves, so must our knowledge of the Ideas. But this is equivalent to the dissolution of the unity of the Ideas: in our standard example, the Idea of the cow dissolves into ideas, that is, concepts or points of view concerning the cow.

The Platonist claims that the Idea of the cow is always the same, regardless of the steady growth or refinement in our knowledge of cows. At the same time, he must claim that the apprehension of the Idea of the cow is by way of cows. Nor, as Aristotle convincingly argued, can the Platonist rescue the unity of the Idea of the cow by separating it entirely from the multiplicity of our perspectives on cows. This separation is contradicted by the thesis that the Idea is the look of the cow; a look cannot be in one place and that of which it is the look in another.

We can of course attempt to modify or abandon Platonism for some version of Aristotelianism by saying that the intellect "abstracts" the look of the cow from a multiplicity of perceptions of cows; but no one can explain what is meant by "abstracting." And the analysis of the faculty of abstraction terminates in the precise claim of Platonism; namely, that the look of the cow is both in the cows and separate from them as present in our thinking. This has one of two results: either the look or (in Aristotle's sense) the essence of the cow is said to be furnished to cows by the activity of thinking or else the look of the cow is an invention of thinking and cows have no standard look at all, as in Kant. In either case, abstraction is in fact not drawing the look out of the cows but imposing it onto them.

However one considers the matter, the shift from the traditional Platonic Idea to the doctrine of abstraction accomplishes nothing of fundamental importance. It makes no more sense to say that cows are instances of the abstract concept "cow" than it does to say that individual cows "participate" in the Idea of the cow, namely, in cowiness taken apart by itself (100c5f.). In order to be an instance of a concept, something must exhibit the essential properties exhibited by the concept; that is, the look of the individual cow must be precisely the look of the concept "cow." The ostensible difference between the look of the cow as thought and the look of the cow as ingredient to and constitutive of the cows in the field is no more and no less intelligible than the ostensible difference between the look of the *logos* and the look of the natural being in Socrates' story. As a matter of fact, the look must be the same in the two pairs. Furthermore, to take cowiness or the look of the cow by itself, apart from individual cows, is so far as I can see indistinguishable from entertaining an abstract concept of the cow.

There is one difference between the two doctrines that is normally insisted upon, and I myself have discussed it at length. The Idea is supposed to subsist independently of our thinking or apprehending it, just as it is said to be separate from that which intermittently participates in it. The abstraction or concept, on the other hand, is supposed to exist nowhere but in our thoughts. I have already pointed out that this duplicates the problem of the ostensible separateness of the Ideas from their participants, with the added disadvantage that being is now identified with thinking.

In order to overcome this disadvantage, the concept must be distinguished from the act of conceptualization. In this case the concept of the cow is neither the particular look of some historical cow nor an intellectual artifact, but an independent, cognizable being that reveals the truth about cows. In other words, it is the Platonic Idea. Such a concept can be neither generated nor destroyed, like historical cows; nor does it come into being and pass away as we think or cease to think it. It is forever itself, apart from its appearances, both in cows and in our thoughts. This is the type of Platonism that one finds attributed to Frege, Cantor, and Gödel or, more generally, the Platonism of modern mathematics. In mathematics, however, one talks of sets, geometrical forms, numbers, and so on rather than of cows, beauty, or goodness. What I shall call conceptual Platonism is frequently confused with Kantianism, but these are two distinct accounts of the status of abstract entities, as we have now seen at sufficient length.

Platonism

So much for our consideration of the doctrine of abstraction: for Socrates, being and thinking are separate but in such a way that being is accessible to thinking. For Kant, the accessibility of being to thinking is explicable only on the hypothesis that the two are an identity within difference. This is the starting point for Hegel. Whereas the question of the difference between Kant's transcendental philosophy and German speculative Idealism is of interest in its own right, it falls outside the perimeter of my present inquiry. I leave it at the following parenthetical observation: For Hegel, it makes no sense to deprive the transcendental ego of spirituality or self-consciousness, which cannot be derived from the pure logical properties of the transcendental ego and which, if restricted to human beings, whether considered phenomenally or noumenally, is then separate from the rules or concepts constituted by the actualization of the conditions for the possibility of being and thinking. For Hegel, Kantian dualism is at bottom indistinguishable from Platonism in its traditional interpretation. Kant unifies being and thinking only at the level of abstractions, rules, or concepts. The identity within difference of being and thinking is nothing more than the conceptual or objective side of the Absolute; in Kant, this side is still detached from the subjective side.

To summarize the main features of my analysis of the Idea: we must distinguish between the *morphē* or shape, of the perceptible element in a cognition and the *idea* or *eidos,* namely, the intelligible look that presents itself within the *logos* as the truth of the natural being. The *morphē* of perception is a fantasm; remember that it can vary with the circumstances of perception. The *logos* is accessible to the reflective consideration of our everyday experience of a thing, event, psychic modification, or relation. The term *on* or *onta,* "being" or "beings," stands for any and all of these items of experience. Every attempt to view the beings directly leads to a consideration of something else: the properties of the being, its formal structure, an abstract concept, and so on. This "something else" is the *logos.* There are also alternative interpretations of the *logoi,* or ratios of intelligibility. These alternative interpretations are unfortunately also designated by the word *logos* in Socrates' story, but the word must here refer to the general account of *logoi* or ratios, not to the ratios themselves. In order to judge among alternative *logoi,* Socrates adopts the criterion of reconciling his understanding of beings in the light of everyday experience with a philosophical or theoretical or epistemic understanding.

Everyday experience is the given; it is the starting point and the context for all theoretical accounts of beings, and hence of being. This is not at all to say that the ultimate structure of being is cognitively accessible from the looks, faces, or surfaces of things. Even our own deeds are not self-explanatory and require analysis. But it is the *logoi* and *erga* of everyday experience that we analyze in each case. In a slightly different formulation, no theoretical analysis of the natures of beings is adequate if it excludes or renders unintelligible my own intentions and motivation to act for the best. Remember that even the fantastic element of sense-perception (the *fantasma*) is adopted to the everyday human perspective. Cows may be other than they appear, but it is the appearance, or *phainomenon,* that renders the cow accessible to us.

Finally, the look or Idea is both present and absent. It is present as the original of the image embodied in the *morphè,* and so as that which provides us the criterion or reference point for the various perspectives that we open up in our investigations of the nature of the cow. But it is absent to discursive or analytic intelligence, which articulates the aforementioned perspectives in the light of the Idea, light which cannot itself be made the content of an analysis, and so which remains a hypothesis, but a hypothesis that is justified by the fact of its illumination, by what it allows us to see and to explain.

Socrates refers in our passage to the presence of the Idea with three different terms: *metheksis* (from the verb *metechein:* 100c6), *parousia,* and *koinōnia.* Thus he says that he bids farewell to the *aitiai* that are put forward by others; "I hold for my part to this, simply, artlessly [*atechnos*] and perhaps foolishly, that nothing else makes a thing beautiful but the presence [*parousia*] or communion [*koinōnia*] of beauty itself, in whatever way or manner it may have occurred. I am not yet able to affirm this [i.e., the manner of the occurrence] with confidence, but only that all beautiful things come to be beautiful by the beautiful [itself]." This is, incidentally, one of just two occurrences of *parousia* in Plato,[4] a term that Heidegger equates with the Platonic doctrine of Being. But that which is present can also be absent; in the particular case, the Idea of beauty is no longer present in what ceases to be beautiful.

In the assertion of *parousia,* Socrates also makes clear the absence of the Idea from discursive intelligence. The recourse to the *logos* of the Idea is the safest reply that Socrates can make to the question of the *aitia* (100d9ff.). In his consideration of the other examples, such as those of size and number, Socrates states explicitly that one must reply to attacks on the hypothesis of the Ideas by examining its consequences in order to determine whether they agree or disagree with each other; and so too with the consequences of rival hypotheses (101d3ff.). This is entirely different from a direct and detailed justification of the hypothesis in itself. But no such justification is possible, since the hypothesis provides us with the basis of all justifications or explanations. Every attempt to deduce the hypothesis from its consequences presupposes the validity of the hypothesis, that is, the hypothesis itself provides us with the pertinent consequences. This is as true in mathematical physics or modern science as it is in philosophy. Every explanation of the whole is circular because the whole is itself a circle.

Presence and Absence

3

The Whole

Heidegger regularly defines metaphysics as the attempt to think "das Seiende im Ganzen,"[1] an expression that may be translated as "the existent altogether" or "the being of beings altogether." Metaphysics thinks Being as the being of beings, "from the part of, and with respect to, beings."[2] In other words, it thinks the totality of beings, not as a sum of individual things, but from the standpoint of being qua being.[3] This thinking is intrinsically *Vorstellen*,[4] literally, "placing before," a representational thinking in which the thinker places the being that is to be thought before his intellect as that which lies beneath (*hupokeimenon*) or is accessible to his gaze: the Idea. The fundamental conceptions here are those of accessibility, definiteness, permanence, and presence as visibility. In Heidegger's later writings, genuine thinking, which, in contrast to metaphysics or philosophy since Plato, is in harmony with *logos*, or the voice of Being,[5] is primarily hearing, not seeing.[6] "In the word, in its continuing presence [*Wesen*], hides that which gives," that which gives Being.[7]

Genuine thinking is no longer to be understood as the knowledge of formal structure, but as an attentiveness to and questioning of the voice whose saying is at once the clearing and covering or veiling giving of the world.[8] It is important to emphasize that the voice is not that of the giver of Being, but rather that in which there "hides that which gives." One cannot help thinking here of Jaweh, who hides from Moses even as he communicates with him in speech. This interplay of silence and speech, as emblematic of the absence that lurks within every presence, is implied in the Hölderlin lectures of the thirties, in which poetic activity (*Dichten*) is regularly defined as a pointing out and opening up, as for example of the world, of inwardness, of the realm within which the gods once dwelt and from which they have now flown away.[9] All of these "openings" are dimensions waiting to be occupied with something that is now absent, whether this be the destiny of the Folk or the ministrations of a God. The same point is present in a completely explicit manner in a previously cited text dating from 1941 and included in the *Nietzsche* volumes: "The thinker can never say what is his ownmost. That must remain unspoken, because the speakable word receives its determination from the unsayable."[10] Whether we consult the texts of the early or the late Heidegger, we find an insistence upon the interplay of presence and absence. Metaphysics is defective because it defines Being as presence, and this is essentially because presence is understood as visibility. The visible is the look or form. Genuine thinking, on the other hand, orients itself by language and, more particularly, by speech, not simply in itself but as a sign of the unsaid. One may suppose that speech is superior to vision as a paradigm for thinking because it is more fluid, more a giving and taking of thoughts than a presentation of determinate structures. We can listen without seeing what is being said or who is speaking. Thus we can attend to the process of speech, whereas the vision of looks prevents us from attending to the process of seeing. Otherwise put, the vividness of the presence of the look distracts us from considering what cannot be seen in any event: absence.

The same notion seems to underlie Heidegger's preference for the pre-Socratic thinkers who, unlike Plato and Aristotle, think being, *to on*, verbally, that is, as a participle rather than as a substantive.[11] For Heidegger, *logos* is a gathering of Being, not a specification of a look or a ratio.[12] The whole is thus not a formal structure but that into the midst of which we are "thrown" or "projected" by our thinking itself.[13] It is everything thinkable, everything that we might encounter; and so, it includes nothingness, *das Nichts*, since we would not encounter nothingness without having thought *das Seiende im Ganzen*. As omni-inclusive, the whole is that which we question, not that which we define or fully understand but that which most needs to be understood: "The name 'the existent altogether' [*das Seiende im Ganzen*] thus names the most questionable and is therefore the most questionable word."[14]

The whole, *das Ganze*, is for Heidegger that which concerns the philosopher, whether we understand that person to be a thinker or only a metaphysician. The whole is the interplay of presence and absence that defines the totality of beings but is not itself a being. This is more or less the same sense that is attributed to the expression *to holon* (the whole) and sometimes to *to pan* (the all) in the Platonic dialogues. The whole is the totality of beings, arranged as a cosmos, which includes the human and the divine but which is an ordering rather than itself a being or element in that ordering.[15] It is to the whole that the philosophical soul reaches out in yearning (*eporeksesthai*) for everything divine and human.[16] Philosophy is the love of the whole of truth,[17] and hence it is the love of the whole, not as a sum of entities but as an ordering that bestows truth and excellence upon all things in accordance with their rank or place in the order.

Even if it should be objected that philosophy is for Plato the love of the Ideas, which are fully present, one must not forget that knowledge of the Ideas is necessarily by way of their instances, that is, by way of what shows itself: *ta phainomena*. The Ideas are fully visible or entirely illuminated in themselves, but not to us. Since we must recollect them or attempt to see them within the images that reflect them, we can say with perfect accuracy that the Ideas are also *absent*. Human beings are not capable of grasping full presence. It is all very well to say that *ta onta,* in the sense of the generated things, whether natural or artificial, are not or do not possess genuine being. They are nevertheless part of the whole, and so they must be known, even if only as other than or as covering over the very Ideas which they reveal.

One may therefore say that the whole, as understood by Plato and portrayed in his dialogues, is both presence and absence, and absence in two senses. First, the Ideas are themselves concealed or veiled by the beings that present them or remind us of them. Second, if there is an Idea of the individual human soul, it is not one that can be understood by *logos* in the sense of discursive or calculative thinking. Divine speech would be required; mortals must make do with likenesses or myths.[18] The soul, as erotic, is continuously changing its shape, dying and being reborn; it is not an Idea but a process of emergence and disappearance, a perpetual philosopher who is also a sorcerer, poisoner, and sophist.[19] Philosophy is not and cannot possibly be solely the attempt to think the Ideas, that is, to answer the question What is Being? It is also, and in the first instance, the attempt to answer the question Who and what am I?[20]

In sum, philosophy understood as Platonism is the love of the whole truth, and thus it is a desire to know the whole; first and foremost, it is the divine compulsion to know oneself and in particular to know whether one knows anything. As I would restate this, I must know myself because it is I who am open to the whole. I cannot know the whole or know whether the whole is knowable unless I know myself. That this pursuit of self-knowledge is not vulgar egoism is conveyed by Socrates' contention in the *Phaedo* (64a7ff.) that philosophy is a preparation for dying. This is not the place to attempt to reconcile the diverse paradigms presented by Plato of the philosophical life. The point I wish to make is that philosophy is in fact a way of life, whether human or divine; it is not simply pure noetic gazing upon Ideas. Life is not an Idea; neither is the whole.

Adventures in the Lifeworld

I want now to begin the procedure of enriching the rather abstract sketch that has just been given of the whole, and I shall do this initially by providing a sample analysis of how we arrive at an understanding of the related phenomena of presence and absence on the basis of everyday life and the reflection that it engenders. My analysis begins from everyday life itself, not from a passage in a Platonic dialogue. It is intended to provide the general framework for the interpretation of the doctrine of Ideas presented in the previous chapter. Heidegger's analysis of the "average everydayness" (*durchschnittliche Alltäglichkeit*) of *Dasein* is his version of what Husserl presents as the analysis of the lifeworld (*Lebenswelt*). Both of these approaches may be initially described as Kantian revisions of the Greek *doksa*. Everydayness and the lifeworld are structures constituted in the first case by the existential activity of *Dasein* and in the second by transcendental subjectivity, which is, so to speak, concealed from itself within the natural attitude (as Husserl calls it) of everyday life. The task of the Heideggerian and the Husserlian phenomenologists is at bottom the same: to describe the structures of everyday life. Were I to follow the same approach, my next step would be to offer a description of the structure of the copresence of the individual person to the world, as lived or experienced within the natural attitude.

In this case, however, my description would itself be provided by the phenomenological type of thinking that is not itself resident within the lifeworld. I note again that Heidegger's intention is to describe the "clearing" process by which or within which Being shows itself to mankind, in the paradigm-case through the mediation of the epochal thinker. My intention is different. Both the thinking of Being (or what approximates to such thinking) and the analytical description of the structures and rank-orderings of what presents itself are derivatives from everyday thinking. In order to preserve the unity of the whole, I must show how subsequent types emerge from everyday thinking. But this cannot be done if I begin with their separation and then attempt to subject the everyday to an analysis "from above."

I start with a simple question. How do we know what does not show itself? Let me first give my answer to this question: we know what does not show itself on the basis of what does show itself. I cannot tell you why there is something rather than nothing, but I can say that if there were nothing at all, there would be no one to think the unthought and so no one to think absence. Nothing would be absent because to be absent is to be absent to someone who is present. This is no doubt why Aristotle says that nonbeing is dependent upon being. Something may be present as absent in the metaphorical sense that we infer its absence or know what is absent on the basis of what we know to be present. Here is an example. I enter John's apartment during a party, look around, do not see him, and say, "John is absent." I know that it is John who is absent because I am in his apartment; I know John when I see him, and he is not here.

John's absence from his apartment is total in the sense that he is not partly there and partly not there. John's clothes, his furniture, his stereophonic equipment, photographs of him, and even what one might call his aura or scent are present; but John is not there. One could thus have a real sense of John's presence, but a sense of John is not John himself. There are also other kinds of absence, however. For example, an acorn exhibits the absence of an oak tree in a sense different from the absence of John from his apartment. The acorn is not yet, but will turn into, the oak tree. How do we know this? Originally, because we have seen acorns sprouting and growing into oak trees. This experience, incidentally, underlies the science of trees, or biology. The laws governing the development of acorns are derived from countless experiences that things of this sort behave in such and such a way. The point is not fundamentally different from the inference that if you combine two parts of hydrogen with one part of oxygen, the result will be water. This result is not due to the fact that the elements obey laws passed by some divine monarch. We may interpret the result in this way, but there is no evidence, the monarch is not present; the connection between the

Platonism

hydrogen and the oxygen is not present as an instrument of compulsion in advance of their combination.

But this is somewhat beside the point; I make this remark merely to indicate that we would not speed up our progress by turning from everyday experience to its scientific study, whether in the phenomenological or some other sense of that expression. The problem that concerns us has nothing directly to do with science. If there is such a thing as the scientific study of everyday life, it is possible only for those who know how to live; and this knowledge is not itself scientific. One should perhaps also observe that there is no such thing as a scientific study of Being. The scientist begins with beings or processes that are accessible to measure and manipulation. And he or she studies them from a definite viewpoint, namely, to determine their natures, how they work, how they came into existence, how we can use them for our own intentions, and so on. Most important, perhaps, is that what the scientist means by "nature," and so the nature of a being or process, is determined by the need to measure and manipulate. He does not ask, What is being qua being or What is Being? And the scientist does not attempt to account for everyday experience in its own terms; to the contrary, he assumes that genuine structure is concealed by ordinary experience.

On this score, Heidegger's thesis about the concealment of Being is in accord with the underlying assumptions of modern science, although Heidegger of course does not accept the need to measure and to manipulate or to master nature for the satisfaction of human needs. For Heidegger, the attempt to master is a form of concealment. More generally, and thus in an expression that would apply to Plato as well, science emerges from everyday life and has its roots there. Everyday life is not itself scientific and has to be understood in its own terms. Heidegger is again closer to modern science than is Plato on this point; Heidegger employs a much more developed technical terminology and a more explicit or prosaic mode of description and analysis than does Plato. Despite Heidegger's admiration for poetry and his attempt to develop a poetic mode of thinking, he remains a scholastic and in that sense a product of the advent of rationalist science, whereas Plato, for all his rationalism and praise of mathematics, remains a poet.

To come back to the acorn, the oak tree is absent because it has not yet begun to be present as an oak tree. On the other hand, the oak tree is potentially present because, under certain circumstances, acorns grow into oak trees. Furthermore, as the oak tree is growing, it is both present and absent for as long as it fails to reach its full stature; and even then, it will begin to decay, and so to be both present and absent in another sense. Yet in all these cases, just as in the different case of John and his apartment, we use the term "absent" with respect to what is present. Let us look at this set of cases more closely. John was said to be absent not simply or generally, but from his apartment. What does this mean? Is John's existence linked to his apartment? No, of course not; he might be found at the university or on the sidewalk of the street next to his apartment building or on an airplane or anywhere at all. It is true that normally he is in the United States, in Pennsylvania, in State College, and perhaps even for the greatest part of the day, in his apartment. John is an apartment dweller, but it is not part of the conditions of his being that he stay in his apartment.

Instead, there is a set of places where John might be found; this set can be more or less defined by another set of facts or relations that hold true of John, for example, that he is an American citizen who teaches or studies at the Pennsylvania State University. If we know the members or most of the members of the second set, then we can fill in, with some order of increasing probability, the members of the first set. All this being so, we will be able to regard it as abnormal if John is not in his apartment at, say, 2 A.M. on a weekday night. But this abnormality does not entail that John no longer exists, that he has ceased to be. He might have died, of course; perhaps he is lying dead in a smashed automobile in some ditch. But then he will be a corpse, not a nullity. Let this suffice: the point is that John is absent from a context, which must itself be present, although not of course in the same sense that John is present when I find him standing in his living room. John is absent because he is normally here or because it was reasonable for me to have expected him to be here, given the present circumstances. And that means that he was previously here under similar circumstances; or, if the circumstances obtain for the first time, as for example at a housewarming party, then we say that John is absent because we expect a resident to be present at his housewarming party.

I interject a remark at this point about Heidegger. In *Being and Time*, Heidegger attributes our recognition of the web of relations constituting the world of average everydayness to the experience of reaching for a tool and finding that it is absent.[21] But everyday life cannot be conceived by analogy with the workshop of the craftsman or farmer. I do not reach for John in the way that I reach for my hammer. The most that could be said is that in looking for John, I intend to engage in the *praksis* of social conversation. But *praksis* is not *poiēsis*. The tools of the craftsman are employed in the production of artifacts or in the modification of nature. As we saw in a previous chapter, Heidegger attributes the Greek, and in particular the Platonist, conception of Being to the adoption of the paradigm of the *technitēs;* in fact, it is precisely this model that applies to his own analysis of *Dasein*. What Heidegger does not seem to notice is that in Plato, life is indeed practico-productive; but this is not the same as to say that beings are tools or the products we make with tools. I will return to this later. Let us continue with our reflection on the absence of John from his apartment.

We do not need to be a metaphysician, but only a moderately thoughtful person, to begin to wonder about why John is absent. And this may lead us to ask, "Who is John, anyhow? What do I really know about him? What sort of person would be absent from his own housewarming?" If someone were to ask, "What is it to be John?" the question would no doubt initially puzzle us, but it becomes less puzzling when it emerges from the context of our interest in his absence. This interest could also be evoked by some bizarre act performed by John in our presence. How would we take our bearings in the attempt to answer this question? Surely in the same way that we explain what we mean when we say that John is absent. First we must have seen or somehow directly encountered John or been informed about him by someone who has directly encountered him or heard about him indirectly from someone who has heard enough of him to speak to us about him, and so on. What do all of these ways have in common? All of them begin with the presence of John, either directly or within a set of relations that is itself present by virtue of what we know about him. No one expects John to manifest himself suddenly ex nihilo, any more than we expect him to disappear or conceal himself instantaneously. John comes and goes in a variety of ways; these comings and goings are of John himself, John "in person" and not as a simulacrum; it is this personal or direct coming and going that is accessible to someone, and so that can be reported to someone else, and so to us, that enables us to speak of John's presence or absence.

Now let me draw out another aspect of this situation: it is the coming and going of John that interests us here, not the coming and going of his clothing, his umbrella, his cane, his briefcase, his cigarettes, the money he carries in his pockets, and so on. John is something definite: a man, not a pair of trousers or an umbrella. How do we know this? Metaphysics is of no help to us here; we are not looking for a definition or doctrine of being qua being and certainly not of John qua John. We of course perceive John and thereby identify him as a man. But what if we had made a perceptual error, and he was actually a mannikin or an android like Commander Data on *Star Trek* or some other thing that we took to be John? What if it was in fact Herbert or Arthur whom we saw? We can verify our initial identification by adding to the number of perceptual soundings that we take, but when have we taken enough? When can we be sure that we are not deceived?

Most of us will realize that these questions have no genuine substance outside the confines of a seminar in epistemology or ontology. When I deliver a lecture, no one in the auditorium is in any doubt concerning my identity as a human being, although they may not know my name or the details of my biography. I *might* perhaps be a leprechaun or a satyr, and the members of my audience *might* be under hypnosis because of rays that Martians are training on the auditorium from some point in outer space. It is also possible that the moon is made of luminous green cheese, but that we take it for a stellar body because of the hypnotic rays of the aforesaid Martians. All of this might be so in a fantastic sense of "might be" that carries no weight when contrasted with our communal experience, our knowledge of science, and the laws of probability themselves.

But put all this to one side. If we are being hypnotized by Martians, then it is also possible for us to discover this, to develop antihypnosis screens, and thereby to perceive things as they are. The hypothesis of the Martians carries no more weight than does the example of the stick that looks bent when it is placed in water. And the point is once more the same: you might be mistaken about my identity, but this error could be corrected, in which case you would find out who I am. You would find this out because I am who I am: this is not a property that is restricted to God (although God may have said, "I am that I am"). If on the other hand you could never in principle find out that I am a Martian or someone other than the person you take me for, this is because I am not a Martian but just the person you see.

Platonism

———————————————

By analogous reasoning, we cannot be disturbed by arguments, today quite fashionable, according to which the identity of objects is relative to the nature of the perceptual organs of the perceivers. Imagine that we are together in an auditorium and that you perceive me by means of heat emissions rather than by refracted light. You would no doubt see something other than what you see when looking at me in what is for us the normal manner. But similar effects could be produced by artificial instruments or by physically maiming your sense organs. The variation in your sense organs is one thing; the variation in my identity is something else again. For example, if I were to be perceived by heat-sensitive creatures, I would not thereby turn into a fire. What is heat for one perceiver and light for another must have a nature that permits it to register in one way on heat-sensitive organs and in another on light-sensitive organs. There cannot be a science of perception at all if we simply make up our perceptions out of an intrinsically propertyless prime matter.

It is therefore true that what we call form or appearance, and so the discussion of what Plato calls in his dialogues Ideas, when these terms refer to physical entities, are influenced by the particular perceptual apparatus that we in fact have. But the Idea is not primarily a painting or photograph of something; it is the intelligibility of the thing. What I shall call for the moment the phenomenological Idea, for example, of a cow, is the look that cows have in a world like ours, inhabited by beings who perceive as we do. This look is visible to beings like us as the physical shape, or *morphē*, of the cow; but the visibility or intelligibility of the cow is not the same as its physical shape. If we lived in some other world which also contained cows but in which all of our perceptual organs were different, then no doubt the phenomenological look of the cow would also be different.

But this does not affect the doctrine of Ideas, and it is of no interest whatsoever to those of us who live in this world rather than in our science fiction fantasies. I use the word "normal" to refer to the look of a being in this world. The normal phenomenological Idea of the cow is precisely the look of cows in this world, not of cows in any world whatsoever, that is, in any kind of perceptual situation, however bizarre. It is not a telling criticism of Plato's doctrine of Ideas to say that cows might look quite different from the way in which they normally look. If they did look different, then the phenomenological look exhibited by them would be different in a quite trivial sense from what I have called the normal look.

This little exercise does however teach us something of value. The phenomenological Idea of the cow, the particular cowy look that enables us to say, "There goes a cow!" cannot be the essence of the nonphenomenological nature of the cow. The cow as phenomenon is a *morphē* that is rendered intelligible by the cow as *noumenon*, a Kantian expression that I somewhat riskily adapt to Platonic purposes. *Noumenon* means "that which is thought." What we think is the Idea. Let me rephrase this. How the cow looks, that is, its *morphē* in this world, is essential to the apprehension or "recollection" of the Idea of the cow. Abnormal cows will have abnormal looks, that is, looks having a quite different *morphē* from that of the cow in our world. So this abnormal cow will exhibit a different Idea, namely, the Idea of a being that *looks like this,* whatever "this" may be in a given world. To the extent that what it is to be a cow is independent of the *morphē,* to that extent the Idea of the cow will be the same in all worlds, that is, under all perceptual circumstances. The cow remains what it is, regardless of how we perceive it.

So one could say this: visible or perceptual shapes of cows are *fantasmata,* that is, images adjusted to the visual perspective of residents existing under such and such perceptual conditions, in order to exhibit for them the Idea or the original of the cow in its true cowyness. Those of us who live in the normal world will begin their investigation of abnormal cow-looks by looking at normal cows. The normal cow, or cow-look, is *present;* with respect to it, the abnormal looks are absent. We can go on to specify the circumstances under which the normal look will be replaced by an abnormal look, but only because of the presence of the circumstances under which the normal look obtains. We must point directly or indirectly to the present circumstances and say, "These will be changed." To say "these," however, is to say that the present circumstances are not only present but that they are more or less definite.

A brief comment about Darwinism: the same considerations I have sketched about changes in perceptual organs apply to Darwinism. The Idea of a cow is exhibited by, but independent of, the fantasm or *morphē* of the cow. The *morphē* changes; when the cow is no longer a cow, the shape is no longer that which we associated with cows. We are now looking at a different animal. But the changes in the phenomenal cow have nothing to do with changes in what it is to be a cow. If the Platonic Idea of the cow is separate from historical cows, then the disappearance of cows from history is not going to affect the Idea of the cow. Darwinism poses a problem for Aristotelianism, but not for Platonism.

I return once more to John. However perceptually various John may be, we can find and identify him in the normal world. In fact, we must have done so in order to be able to speak about his variations and of course about his absences. It is John about whom we are speaking, and this means that John is not just a figure of speech. Of course, I have invented John as an example, but I am not thereby contradicting myself because John is an Ideal type in the Husserlian rather than the Weberian sense of the term. John could be, and in fact is, you and me. I can find you and you can find me. Talk about John is just shorthand for talk about you and me.

To continue: John has an identity that allows him to be identified. It is this identity that licenses our perceptual identifications and which one could say is missed by our perceptual misidentifications. John is present in his proper identity, whether or not I successfully identify him. The fundamental level of that identity is the property "human being." I understand originally or fundamentally what it is to be a human being not as a result of a scientific education and not thanks to perceptual experience, but rather because *I* am a human being, and part of being a human being is to possess the ability to identify other human beings. It is this ability that enables me to identify my perceptions of X as exhibiting the presence of a human being, say John.

It is exactly the same ability that allows me to misidentify John. To say that human beings can be fooled about the identification of something as a human being is to say that they know what it is to be a human being. And this in turn means not that they know infallibly in each particular case that X is a human being, but that they know what Plato calls the Idea of the human being. This is why they can correct their errors of identification; it is also why no one can state in advance or with precision how many additional attempts are required in order to make the correct identification. It all depends upon the circumstances: the lighting, the distance of the thing to be identified, the quality of my vision, the mood I am in, and so on.

I think we must conclude that I do not identify John as a human being solely or originally through my perceptions. One could of course distinguish between sensations and perceptions and say that perceptions already contain identification-judgments whereas sensations do not. But this would just move the problem back one stage. My perception (as contrasted with my sensations) enables me to identify John because (on the present hypothesis) it is already the result of existential knowledge of which things are human beings. And this existential knowledge is not knowledge of some paradigmatic human being in another world or separated from all actual human beings. At the same time, it is not knowledge of this or that actual human being. It is, as Aristotle might put it, the knowledge of the actuality of human being.

Note that I have no such existential knowledge of aardvarks, piranhas, or hole-boled grebes. I can identify them as animals because I myself am an animal; in order to identify them as mammals, fish, and birds, respectively, I would require special knowledge. This means that if there is a Platonic Idea of the aardvark, I must indeed recollect it in some way other than the way in which I recollect the Idea of a human being. I want to interpolate a remark about the problem of alien beings, that is, those who have developed on other planets. By "alien" is presumably meant "nonhuman being." But this is a mistake in terminology. The Klingons, for example, in the television show *Star Trek* are humans in accord with Aristotle's definition of "animals that possess *logos*." When I see a Klingon, I identify him or her as a funny-looking human being, not as something alien to me in the way that an aardvark or a termite is alien.

I do not claim to possess a mystical power of intuition that enables me to say, upon first glancing at someone, "There is a bacteriologist from Cincinnati named John Smith." Neither can I, as a result of my initial glance, provide you with an ontological explanation of what it is to be a human being. I claim just this: we recognize beings of our own kind by virtue of the underlying unity of that kind, that look, which is not phenomenological in the simple sense of a picture or photograph, but which has to do with a not fully analyzable synthesis of properties, the most important of which is the recognition of another consciousness, that is, of a sentient being whose responses, even if unexpected, are not unintelligible but could have been our responses.

The point I am trying to make here does not require me to provide a detailed analysis of how we recognize each other as human beings. I wish to claim rather that such recognition emerges from the primacy of one's own consciousness of oneself as someone of such and such a kind. By "such and such" I am not referring to precise knowledge of an essence but rather to a living core of awareness that I am who I am, and so to the fact that it is I who am surprised, who wonder, and who understand. And this in turn is intended to serve as the basis for saying that we identify nonhuman beings, events, processes, and relations as a result of or with respect to our self-recognition. I marvel at the heavenly motions because I see how they are both more orderly than my motions but also beyond my capacity to alter them, simply by performing my normal repertoire of physical motions or intellectual intentions. I am frightened of wild beasts because I know that they are dangerous to me. I am curious about the properties of nonliving bodies on the surface of the earth because they are harmful or useful, beautiful or unusually ugly, and so on.

It has nothing to do with a doctrine of subjectivity or the Cartesian *ego cogitans* to say that I find my way with respect to myself. One instance of finding my way is to know that it is John who is present (or absent), not some inanimate object and not a perceptual illusion. I want to underline the following point: I may not be able to explain with any clarity who or what I am, but practical as well as theoretical thinking presupposes that I am acquainted with, and in that sense know, myself to be something of approximately the following kind: someone who desires, marvels, imagines, hopes, thinks, and so on, and who knows that he is doing these things. This is the foundation from which I proceed to answer the question What is it to be John?

It is also the foundation from which I conclude that what is present is either John or something else, but in every case something. And if it is John, then it cannot be something else. The process of completing the analysis of John's identity may be endless, but it cannot be arbitrary. When I say, "John is absent" or when I ask, "Who is that?" I am either referring to someone in particular or asking someone else to identify the person to whom I am referring. I am referring to John, that is, a human being, or to a human being whose name may be John or something else. But I am not referring to articles of clothing, an umbrella, a cane, the contents of trouser-pockets, and so on.

Since we identify beings with respect to ourselves as the one who inquires, it would make no difference to the story I have been telling if I used the example of an umbrella or a hat in order to illustrate the difference between presence and absence, instead of the example of John. By speaking of another human being, I was able to introduce a variety of related points as well as to exclude certain problems that are artificial but frequently raised obstacles to our inquiry. On the other hand, by so doing I may have raised a question about the relation between thinking and being that needs to be answered.

Thinking Is Not Making

If synoptic thinking originates in my copresence with the world or as the whole (but not as the "all" in the sense of the sum of its parts), does it follow that the I is after all indistinguishable from the Kantian transcendental ego? Is it not the case that the "I think" must accompany every act of cognition, and so that it is finally impossible to distinguish between the world we think and the thinking of the world? The first and perhaps the main thing to be said about these questions is that they arise because of a failure to appreciate the difference between everyday experience and an interpretation of that experience. Differently stated, it is one thing to interpret some particular event within everyday life and something quite different to offer an interpretation of the ontological status of everyday life itself.

There are many events in everyday life in which the "I think" does not accompany consciousness or in other words in which we are conscious but not self-conscious. Examples of such events are solving mathematical problems, being absorbed in a film, drama, or novel, and in general thinking deeply about something other than oneself. This does not mean that the I is not copresent with whatever it is that has engaged my attention. It remains true that if someone is "lost in thought," he can be found again, either by himself or by someone else; and he can find or remember the thoughts themselves as *his* thoughts. Both recoveries are made by virtue of the presence of the whole as in each case the copresence of the world and the I. The person who looks for me or who calls me back to self-attention by shouting, "Wake up!" is present within the same world in and to which I am present. We may well say of someone who has apparently been lost in thought or perhaps daydreaming but who is now attending to us again, "At last; he's back." We might also ask the person, "Where were you?" Both questions are posed against the backdrop of the same kind of normal presence that

Platonism

allowed us to inquire after John's whereabouts when we noticed that he was missing from his party.

Actually to disappear from the world for a temporary interval is something much more drastic than being lost in one's thoughts while still maintaining residence in that same world. If I disappear for a finite time from this world, then either I am temporarily nonexistent or else I have taken up residence in another world. But to be lost in one's thoughts is not the same as to disappear; for example, others may be watching my body as well as the play of expressions on my face, the twitches in my nostrils, and so on; or, if no one is with me at the time, someone could easily enter the room and see me in my chair, oblivious to my surroundings and presumably to myself as well. And there would be other ways in which to determine my absence, such as by my checking the clock, the objects on my desk, and so on. For note carefully: if there is no evidence whatsoever that I have disappeared temporarily or been temporarily nonexistent, then I have not disappeared. The seamlessness of my fit in the world is undisturbed. To worry about the contrary possibility is like worrying about whether one's neighbor is a Martian, even though there is no basis for imagining that he might be. And very similar procedures could be used to verify or refute the claims of those who believe that they have taken up temporary residence in another world.

Contrary to fact examples based upon what we can imagine without violating the principle of noncontradiction are as distant from everyday life as Kant's transcendental philosophy or Fichte's absolute ego. I discussed this question some years ago in *The Limits of Analysis*[22] and will not repeat myself here. Suffice it to say that what is today called the metaphysics of modal logic is based upon the assumption that the principle of noncontradiction is independent of physics and, at a more fundamental level, that logic is independent of experience. This assumption has been dissolved by two different but related tendencies in twentieth-century philosophy: (1) the reduction of logic to experience, and (2) the triumph of imagination over reason. But the net effect of these tendencies is to reconstitute the import of the initial assumption by transforming logic into poetry.

I can indeed imagine a world in which my desk is a block of ice, although it looks to me exactly as though it had been constructed from wood. I can also imagine a world in which elephants ride on the backs of kings. But the fact, if it is a fact, that these examples do not violate the formal principle of noncontradiction is no reason for me to take them seriously when considering the nature of the world in which I actually exist. I can imagine whatever I like, including the inapplicability of the principle of noncontradiction. But if I cannot distinguish between reason and the imagination, then philosophy is impossible. It is impossible not on metaphysical grounds, but because everyday life is then also impossible. How we should respond to the metaphysics of modal logic is not to be determined by mathematical analyses of syntax but on the basis of what procedures are sanctioned by how we actually live. I cannot live from hour to hour or day to day without distinguishing between reason and the imagination. And the compulsion of the world refutes the vapid contention that there is no basis for making this distinction. This is why philosophy must take its bearings by everyday life.

To continue with the main line of argument: Examples of being lost in thought are useful because they show how to distinguish between copresence as a fact about me, or the I, and the world, on the one hand, and my attention to that copresence on the other. It remains true, as initially asserted, that I cannot think any thoughts that are separate from me or that are not my thoughts but someone else's. It also remains true that philosophical thinking requires me to think about myself as copresent with the world. But it does not require me, while engaging in philosophical thought, to be thinking simultaneously and continuously about myself or saying to myself at each instant, "I think that..." But now I want to make a different point. I agree with Kant that my own unity depends upon my ability to identify every thought or other event of consciousness that I have or undergo as *my* thought or event. In order to do this, however, I must first know who I am. Otherwise, I can scarcely say, "This thought is mine."

In other words, the attempt to arrive at the thesis of the unity of self-consciousness by a theoretical principle or argument itself depends upon our knowing who we are, and so that we are already a unity. By the same token, there is no way in which to derive or demonstrate the origin of self-consciousness from a formal analysis of consciousness because the analysis depends, both for its execution by one person and its intelligibility to another, on the existence of self-conscious persons. Kant would no doubt claim that the thesis of the transcendental unity of apperception is a necessary *explanation* of the unity of empirical con-

Platonism

sciousness. My reply, however, is that there is nothing transcendental about the unity of empirical consciousness.

Kant transforms empirical into transcendental unity because he regards this as necessary in order to attribute the unity of the object of thought to the functions or rules of thinking, and so to justify what he calls "synthetic a priori judgments." Those who deny the necessity of such judgments or their possibility or who believe the inconveniences stemming from Kant's assumption to outweigh the advantages will turn to another assumption, as for example the Platonic assumption that the unity of the thing must precede the activity of thinking, even if that activity adds to or regulates the presentation of the thing. The basis for making this choice is everyday life, not metaphysical speculation. We have to decide which *logos* provides the strongest foundation for thinking the whole. Kantianism cannot be justified by the synthetic a priori judgment because judgments of that kind exist only within the world as interpreted by Kant.

In making these remarks, I have been attempting not to refute Kantianism but only to deny that there is any compelling reason to accept it. We are compelled to accept not what we can imagine, but what life forbids us to deny. Stated positively, if our intention is to account for the totality of human experience, the only plausible accounts are those that explain the most with the fewest encumbrances. And under no circumstances are we compelled or even permitted to adopt an explanation that is incompatible with the facts of everyday life. There will always be those who contend that there are no facts of everyday life or that everyday life is a theoretical, indeed, an imaginary, construction. We normally refer to people of this sort as being mad; if they prefer to call themselves philosophers, then they are presumably open to the evidence. The burden is on them to explain the illusory nature of the world in which they speak and we consider what they say.

Nothing compels me to regard the things about which I think, whether directly or indirectly, as themselves *Gedankendinge*, entities having no existence except within my thoughts. The whole, as I have been calling the copresence of the world and the I, is, as I have also emphasized, not the sum of things that happen within it. For example, my encounter with a cow occurs within the whole, but the cow is not a constituent of the whole as copresence. The cow is a resident of the world, with which I am copresent as another resident, and in particular, as that resident who, among his various adventures, encounters beings, such as cows. By "copresence" is meant just this: whatever I encounter in the world, it is *I* who encounter it. By "whole" is meant that I cannot encounter anything anywhere else but in the world. In thinking the whole, I attempt to make sense out of the world within which I find myself, and it is precisely the independence of the beings I encounter, and so the causes of the events in which I am engaged, that forces me to ask at almost every moment, "What shall I do next?" And so I am obliged to think about the possible courses of action, in order to do what is best. This is as true of theory as it is of practice; for as Heidegger says, *theōria* is the highest form of activity. And finally, when I am lost in my thoughts, I do not encounter things in the world; I may, for example, be on the roof of the cosmos, viewing the Hyperuranian beings; for such viewing, after all, is not bodily, and so not worldly at all. But it hardly follows that, assuming the thinking of Ideas to be possible, they are themselves *Gedankendinge* in the sense of productions of the process by which I think them.

After this somewhat fanciful but nevertheless necessary flight, let us return to John, if we can do so despite his absence. Words like "presence" and "absence" refer to some set of coordinates, and these in turn refer to some observer who determines them. John is absent from his apartment; the apartment was selected by him and identified as his, either directly or indirectly, by him to his friends, including me. If this were not so and were it not expected that he be present on the occasion of his housewarming party, then it would make no sense to say that he is absent. In this sense we may legitimately say that his absence depends upon me or some equivalent observer. But unless I or my equivalent arranged for his absence, as for example by having him murdered the night before, by having sent him a false telegram from his mother telling him to return to the parental home immediately, or by some other device, I am not responsible for his absence.

Again, "absence" means "absent from . . ." and "absent to . . ." The "from" and the "to" refer, directly or indirectly, to an observer. But since the mere act of my observation does not remove John from where I expected to find him, just as it would not bring him back if I continued to stare at the spot on the floor where I expected and wished to see him, we must distinguish between presence and absence on the one hand and being and nonbeing on the other. John's absence from the apartment is not a guarantee of his nonexistence. He might be visiting a sick uncle in response to a genuine telegram. But what if John is in fact dead, and so will never again be present within this world? Is he not then fully and definitively absent? Unfortunately, the situation is not a simple one; it will require us to draw a distinction between being and existence, and so between nonbeing and nonexistence.

I will make the distinction in the following way: existence is narrower than being. Whatever exists, is, but not everything that is, exists. Plato and Heidegger existed at one time, but now that they are dead or no longer exist they may be said to "be" in the sense that we may encounter the consequences of their former existence, whether we actually do so or not. But Sherlock Holmes and Commander Data do not exist and never have existed, and, as far as we know, never will exist. But they may be said to "be" in the sense that they are characters in a work of fiction which has effects on our existence, to the extent that we become familiar with those works. I do not encounter evidence of the existence, past, present, or future, of Sherlock Holmes. I cannot, for example, read his monographs any more than I can read the accounts of his adventures written by Dr. Watson. But I can read those accounts as written by Arthur Conan Doyle, who did exist.

In accord with my distinction, square circles and other "impossible" objects possess being within some fictional context, as for example the context of possible-worlds semantics or, more familiarly, in counter-examples invented by imaginative philosophers to make or to invalidate theories. But we have very little concern with objects of this sort in our general reflection on everyday life. Sherlock Holmes is of course another matter, and I have tried to deal with this case in a way that seems quite close to ordinary, as distinguished from philosophical, procedures. Even some philosophers, for example, P. F. Strawson, would proceed in the way I have just indicated so far as fictional characters are concerned. I see no harm in modifying the suggested terminology by saying that Sherlock Holmes "exists" in the stories of Arthur Conan Doyle, provided we understand what this means, namely, that he is a fictional character, and so has his being in the modality of fiction or fantasy, which precludes his existing in the world as an I whom I might encounter during my next visit to 221B Baker Street.

I have, however, introduced the distinction between being and existence in order to deal with human beings and events in the world other than encounters with fictional persons or impossible objects. To summarize, a being may or may not exist, and it may never have existed. A formerly existent being who is now dead continues to participate in being, but not in existence. As nonexistent, John (assuming him to be dead) will never again appear in person. But he cannot be said to be entirely absent so long as some consequence of his former existence remains accessible within our worldly experience. His apartment, for example, may be filled with his possessions; if he was a famous author, his books may be found in the library and his thoughts in the minds of his readers, and so on. There are no impossible beings of which no one has ever thought or ever will think. But it is possible that there are beings which no one will ever encounter. For this reason, being and presence cannot be synonyms. And absence is no guarantee of nonexistence; it is, however, a guarantee of being, since to be absent is to be absent from someone, and hence either once to have been actually present to that observer or potentially present. Holmes and Watson can never be absent because they were never present.

This is as far as I need to go with this analysis. I regard it as useful simply because it establishes a problem for those who wish to identify being with presence on the one hand and nonbeing with absence on the other. More fundamentally, however, it suggests that terms like "being," "existence," and their negatives are systematically ambiguous or that with sufficient ingenuity we could devise puzzles to show the defects of any attempt to develop a complete and consistent ontological terminology. Could we not, for example, speak of the presence of an absence as well as the absence of a presence? All this has obvious implications for the possibility of developing a science of being *qua* being, but also for the possibility of an ostensibly more genuine thinking of Being. If what we mean by "being" depends upon how we decide to employ our terms, this is a good sign that, apart from linguistic stipulations, we do not in this case know what we are talking about.

My point is not that "being" is a syntactical or logical term only, but rather that it cannot be discussed coherently without reference to *what* is or exists. It is not by chance that philosophers like Kant insisted that "being" is not a predicate. When we hear statements like "John is" we are impelled to inquire "Is *what*?" The expression demands analysis in a way that "John is a man" or even "John is present" do not. Suppose that the correct analysis is this: "John is a being." But what does the predicate-term "being" mean here? I suggest that it means either that to be is to be a thing or else that what is, is. The second expression is of course an empty tautology, whereas the first reifies being and in so doing makes it accessible by way of the properties of a thing, or of *what* shows itself; as Heidegger says, to be is thus the present as that which is present, not as the presencing-process. The situation becomes more complicated, not less so, when we factor in problems about the difference between being and existence on the one hand, and presence and absence on the other.

The statement "John exists" does satisfy us in a way that "John is" does not. Why is this? I believe it is because "exists" conveys to us the notion of a definite type of being, namely, a spatio-temporal resident in the world, as distinguished from a resident of our thought or imagination. We can easily say that Sherlock Holmes exists in the imaginary world of Conan Doyle's stories or that centaurs do not exist in this world but they might in some other world. But to do so is to employ "exists" as a term indicating presence in a world, whether this world or some other, and so "presence to" a living observer in such a way as to satisfy the criteria for actual as opposed to imagined or merely conceived being. But what are those criteria? If we are going to allow the metaphysics of possible worlds, how shall we define "exists" in such a way as to distinguish it from "is"? From a logical standpoint, there is no significant difference between the two words; whatever may be counted or named may be said to exist for logical purposes. But concepts or *Gedankendinge* may be counted or named; hence there is no discernible difference between being and existence. We can talk about, count, and therefore calculate with respect to anything we wish. There are, in other words, restrictions implicit in naming and counting, and so in talking or calculating, but none concerning what we name or count.

On the face of it, it seems to be perfectly reasonable to argue in something like the following manner. It makes no difference whether you say "is" or "exists"; this is a matter of linguistic convention. The fact is that there are things: human beings, animals, plants, rocks, stars, and so on. Each of these things is just itself, namely, a human being, an animal, a rock, and so forth; but, as itself, it is also something else, namely, a being. We can argue about terminology here, namely, about whether to speak of existents, beings, entities, essences, and so on. But the dispute itself shows that we recognize what is obvious: to be a thing is to be. This is what everything has in common; as common to all things, it is different from the individual thing-identity in each case, and so it is something distinguishable about which we can speak. So we can ask, "What is a being?" And this requires us to understand being.

Heidegger has himself pointed out the most obvious difficulty in this line of reasoning. To ask What is being? (or What is Being?) is to presuppose that we know the answer, since we are able to understand the use of "is" in the question. Differently stated, the question What is . . . ? is applicable only to something or another; "is" here is already understood to designate a thing, and so the question demands the identification of a *what*, namely, what Aristotle calls a "this something." But being is not and cannot be a thing, since it is common to everything whatsoever. There is no thing standing apart from persons, cows, trees, and stars which has the peculiar nature or "whatness" of constituting the being of persons, cows, trees, stars, and so on. But neither is there anything identifiable that is added onto persons, cows, and so on in order to allow them to be persons, cows, and so on.

When we attempt to construct a table of categories or properties that define what it is to be anything at all, we must assume in advance what we mean by "to be." For example, Aristotle's categories, as normally applied, would exclude Sherlock Holmes or Zeus from the roster of beings. Aristotle did not arrive at his decision concerning what exists by consulting his table of categories. He arrived at his table of categories by rendering more or less precise his general views on what kinds of things exist. And the same is true concerning his doctrine of individual and species-*ousiai* (normally but wrongly translated into English as "substances"). But the greater precision of his categories does not make them superior in all ways to his general views. On the contrary, the fluidity of those general views is much more appropriate to the intrinsic ambiguity of the question of being. As to the question of Being, the situation here is even worse, since we are not permitted to talk about beings, and not even about the being of beings. As Heidegger notes in passages that I have already cited, we are talking about nothing. But this is why Being is not the central category in Hegel's Logic; in other words, it is why Heidegger's meditations do not constitute an advance upon what he calls Hegelian metaphysics. Differently stated, Heidegger

Platonism

is quite wrong to call Hegel a metaphysician in the sense that he himself gives the term.

If we subject Platonism to a Heideggerian critique yet remain faithful to the Greek injunction to provide a rational account (*logon didonai*), the result, for better or worse, is Hegel's Logic. But this in passing. To come back to categories, apart from their arbitrariness, which is due to their excessive specificity, they do not identify a thing or entity called being. They simply list properties possessed by beings of a definite sort, that is, definite both in the sense that we can ask of them, "What is it?" and in the sense that nothing counts as a being that lacks the properties constituting the table of categories. As I noted previously, "being qua being" is not itself a being. Heidegger is perfectly correct to say that talk about being qua being is talk about beings, that is, things or entities, not about Being. But if one puts to one side the limitations of categories, the attempt to talk about being qua being is intelligible in a way that the attempt to talk about Being is not.

My point is not that there is no Being; this is an unintelligible claim. My point is that we cannot talk coherently about Being. Even the injunction against such talk is incoherent. The difficulty with Heidegger's language is not that it is theoretically complex or technically sophisticated; the difficulty lies in the fact that he is not talking about anything at all, as he himself insists. Otherwise put, he is attempting to talk about the beingness of beings without referring to the being of beings, and so without referring to anything that is a this or a that, a something or another. But this is like trying to talk about the fishiness of fish without referring to fish.

I must now bring this line of argument to a close. Its function in the present context is to assist us in distinguishing between being and thinking. The main point of the argument is not that it provides me with technical terminology to make this distinction. On the contrary, I must have made the distinction in order to introduce technical terminology. The distinction is made not in metaphysics or in ontology, but in everyday life. If we do not take our bearings by everyday life, then we can make up any technical terminology we like. Ontology and metaphysics are then miraculously transformed into poetry, whether of the mathematical or the nonmathematical species. Does Sherlock Holmes exist? Of course not; we know that he is a fictional character. But can we demonstrate that he does not exist by rendering precise our use of terms like "is" and "exists"? Not in the slightest. Either the senses of these terms are derived from ordinary usage or they are not. If they are not, then they are arbitrary poems; I am free to construct a poem, buttressed by logical symbolism and precisely worded definitions, in which Sherlock Holmes exists.

But if the senses are indeed derived from ordinary life, then ordinary usage is more precise, not less, than technical analysis, whether mathematical, metaphysical, or semantical. So far as "is" and "exists" are concerned, I am an adamant ordinary-language philosopher. Genuine precision here consists in adhering to the precision, and so to the great flexibility and hence to what is from a formalist or ontological standpoint the imprecision, of ordinary usage. Now what does ordinary usage tell us about the difference between being and thinking? That they are not the same; and this message cannot be challenged by any philosophical doctrine whatsoever. This statement will seem preposterous to many of my readers; here is what I mean by making it. Idealists and realists all conduct their lives, even that portion of their lives devoted to theorizing, on the unchallenged assumption that there is a difference between being and thinking. When an Idealist prepares himself to think, he first attends to his bodily needs and then arranges a comfortable locale, such as a leather chair in a book-filled study or a seat beneath a shade-tree; he does not try to satisfy his bodily needs by thinking to himself that they are satisfied, and he does not think about sitting in a chair made up of thought.

Before the reader condemns me for my naivete or failure to negotiate the ontological difference, let the following principle be considered: If philosophy is the pursuit of truth, and our purpose is to explain the world, or Being, then our explanations must in fact be true. If they are true, then we must believe them, and if we believe them, then they must govern our lives, whether we like it or not. But no one can live a life of applied Idealism. If the Idealist protests that the distinction between being and thinking is an illusion, the normal reply to assertions of illusion is to expose them. In order to expose the illusoriness of the distinction between being and thinking, the Idealist must prove that the chair he is sitting in is a thought. How will he do this? By "deconstructing" the chair into its constituent pieces? Obviously this will not take him very far.

Platonism

The Idealist cannot proceed by performing any physical operations on things, since this would only prove their existence as distinct from thought. He must therefore proceed by mere thinking. But this seems to beg the question. More specifically, if we are told that for subtle theoretical reasons, the distinction between being and thinking is untenable, the correct reply is that the distinction between being and thinking is itself not obscure or at least is radically less obscure than the subtle theoretical distinctions, which must accordingly be wrong. In short, no theory can be correct that falsifies the circumstances to which all theoreticians must conform if they are to be in a position to theorize. Idealism is in fact no different from Materialism; both begin by pointing to a dualistic world and telling us that dualism is an illusion. But the elements of the correct explanation, whether Idealist or Materialist, are just the two components of the initial dualist situation. One theorist claims that matter is in fact thought or Idea; the other claims that Idea is in fact matter. Both thereby grant the initial distinction between matter and Idea or thought.

What problem are we trying to solve when we ask ourselves whether things exist only in our thoughts? This one or one very much like it: Can I arrange, by simply thinking it to be so, for John suddenly to appear in his living room, from which he is currently absent? The answer to this question is no. Can I give a precise explanation of why this is so? Yes, strangely enough I can. I tried to conjure John up by thinking him to be present, and it did not work. The obduracy of things in general to my wishes, thoughts, and desires is quite certain and quite precise, and it forces me to take steps to deal with that obduracy, in some cases by formulating complicated philosophical doctrines. But if I am truthful, what these doctrines will explain is why the obduracy exists, not that it is an illusion or that, at some deeper metaphysical plane, it does not exist.

Not even Kant claims that John is a product of my thinking, and Nietzsche does not suggest that I can conjure John up by willing him to appear on the spot. The complicated doctrines of Kant and Nietzsche address themselves to different problems. But these doctrines both begin from the need to revise our everyday opinions about life because of some inadequacy in those opinions. The doctrines should be judged primarily on the old-fashioned criterion of whether they save the phenomena in the sense of correcting the inadequacy. This criterion is one that emerges from everyday life itself: it is everyday life that requires explaining, not some other dimension of existence or being. Of course we shall have to reject many of our opinions about everyday life. But we cannot reject everyday life as well; for if we do this, then there is nothing to explain. There are no longer inadequate opinions; there are merely different opinions.

To conclude: (1) the fact that I am copresent with the world does not mean that I produce the world by thinking it; it means that I cannot think about the world without thinking about myself. Life is in fact perspectival; we do see the world from various angles. What the perspectivist philosophers usually overlook or deny to be possible is that each of us can assume the perspective of his neighbor. I can change my angle of vision. I can as it were rotate with respect to the world, but I cannot rotate myself out of the world. (2) If "being" is taken apart from "what is," then we cannot arrive at a precise and coherent account of what we mean by "being." But we can say this: terms like "presence" and "absence" are obviously closely connected with "being" and "nonbeing," but they are not synonymous. It is possible to be without being present to anyone; what has not been present cannot be said to be absent. (3) Philosophical doctrines are required in order to clarify the obscurities of ordinary or everyday life. But no doctrine is worth holding if it renders everyday life unintelligible or claims that it is an illusion. At the same time, there is no philosophical doctrine or definition of what constitutes everyday life. There will always be disagreement about what needs to be explained and what does not. This is why one must first be wise before one can be a philosopher.

Making a Life

The transcendental philosopher, as we have seen, assures us that everyday life cannot be explained in its own terms. My reply is that transcendental philosophy cannot be explained in the terms of everyday life. All arguments for making the transcendental turn are circular; they are presented from beyond the turn. Not merely does everyday life not *seem* to be a world of appearances with which the process of cognition veils over things in themselves; it *is not* such a world. The difference between how things appear to me and how they actually are is a distinction that is drawn within everyday life itself, as I have now shown

Platonism

at sufficient length. Illusions of sense-perception, distinctions between everyday perception and the refined analyses of science, differences of religion, moral principles, social perspective, and so on; all of these are familiar to us as evidence not that the world is an illusion or that it is unknowable in itself, but rather that the world is knowable from the outset. We understand these differences because they all emerge from a horizon of intelligibility. The secrets of the world are available.

Nothing, however, that I have said thus far is intended to suggest that life is simply a matter of gazing at the looks of things or that these looks are directly accessible in their full purity. We have to make our way within the world, which we can do thanks to the accessibility not of looks as looks, but of things having looks of such and such a kind. A cow is accessible to me, not the Idea of the cow. When Socrates refers to the doctrine of Ideas as a hypothesis or founding *logos,* he does not mean that he first considers competing theoretical explanations of life, chooses the one that he believes to be strongest, and then begins to live. His inspection of competing *logoi* is based upon his already having lived or rather upon the reflection that life demands *as* we live it. The look of the cow imposes itself upon us by our encounter with the cow, not by epistemological and ontological meditations.

But it is not merely the look of the cow that imposes itself on us; the cow does so as well, and in a more direct manner. I can take a variety of attitudes toward the cow. I can ignore it, admire its tranquillity, study its digestive system, drink its milk, eat its flesh, or defend its right not to be eaten, to mention just a few possibilities. The cow presents me with a network of possibilities, but therefore with a problem. What shall I do? What is the best stance to take with respect to the cow? And of course the same network, together with the same problem, is posed by everything that I encounter. It would be better in some ways to say that life is itself a network of possibilities, together with the problems these raise, rather than to formulate the point as though problems arise from the encounter of two independent entities, my life and a cow or some other entity. But this formulation carries with it the danger of reducing the cow to the status of a network of possibilities within my life, rather than to that of a being that I encounter in the world as I live my life.

I can ignore the cow or let it be; but I do not have this luxury with respect to everything that I encounter. If I do not eat the cow or some other animal, then I must eat plants or die. If I do not study the anatomy of the cow, I must study other animals and engage in dissection as well as medical experimentation or else I and others will die through a want of medical knowledge. I must either tear up the soil and thus destroy its vegetation in order to build roads, sidewalks, and buildings as well as sewage systems and the other paraphernalia of urban life; or else I must decide to live in the fields and walk on the grass, as though I were myself a cow. But even cows eat grass. On the other hand, they do not think, daydream, write poetry, or study other cows or their neighbors the birds and the insects. Cows, so far as we know, do not meditate the emergence-process of Being. Let us therefore say farewell to those who choose, somewhat artificially, to live the life of the cow and consider our own situation.

Everyday life is a unity of looking and doing, and doing is either complete in itself or it issues in a product that is distinct from the deed. These three activities are called by Aristotle theory, practice, and production. Whereas knowledge is involved in all three activities, they differ most simply as follows. Theoretical activity is for the sake of knowing as an end in itself; practical activity employs knowledge for the sake of the act as an end in itself; productive activity employs knowledge to produce an artifact that is separate from the act and the end toward which the act was directed.[23] Political and ethical activity fall under practice; ethics is a part of politics because it deals with the virtues and the pursuit of happiness, and these cannot be pursued in isolation.[24] Aristotle also speaks in certain passages as though theoretical activity were the highest type of practice, namely, activity that is neither for the sake of action involving others nor for the sake of an artifact.[25] Conversely, he says in the *Metaphysics* that knowledge of the first principles and causes, that is, of the theoretical science or first philosophy, "is supreme among the sciences, and more a ruler than a servant" because "it knows that for the sake of which each thing must be done [*prakteon*]."[26]

What is of special interest to me here, however, is the attribution of a political nature to the human being. Since politics falls under practice, and practice is for its own sake, it follows that the polis, that is, the completion of man's political nature, and so the means for the achievement of the natural end of happiness to the extent that this is available to the nonphilosopher, is not a product. Neither the theoretical nor the practical life is productive, and this is true whether practice is for its own sake or for the sake of others. In the Platonic dialogues, on the contrary, it is never said that man is by nature political. Furthermore, as is well known, Plato does not divide human activities or the corresponding sciences into three kinds, as does Aristotle. The typical division of the arts and sciences in the dialogues is into the theoretical on the one hand, namely, those which acquire knowledge without producing anything, and on the other, those which produce something.[27]

Before I explore the significance of Plato's classification of the arts and sciences, let me try to state in a precise manner the root of the Aristotelian thesis concerning man's political nature. In the *Politics,* Aristotle infers from his preliminary inspection of the primitive forms of association that the city is the culminating or complete growth[28] of four earlier types of association: (1) the sexual union of man and woman, which arises from the natural desire "to leave behind another like oneself" (1252a24ff.); (2) the association of natural ruler (one who possesses forethought) and natural slave (one who lacks this intellectual capacity: 1252a30ff.); (3) the household, which arises from the association of the first two types to satisfy in accord with nature the daily needs of sex, nourishment, shelter, and daily labor (1252b9ff.); (4) the village, which arises in order to provide utility (*chrēseōs heneken*) that goes beyond the daily needs just noted; Aristotle does not state in what such utility consists (1252b15ff.). This constitutes a lacuna in his presentation; there is no reference to nature in this stage of the development. One could cite the thesis that political life, in the primitive form of patriarchy, originates in the village (b20ff.); but what needs to be demonstrated is that political life is natural, and this does not follow from the first three stages of the presumed growth.

The fifth and culminating stage is the polis, which arises as an association of many villages. Aristotle cites the autarchy of the polis; it is the last stage of growth required for self-sufficiency in the sense of the capacity to satisfy the natural needs noted in stages 1 through 3 (1252b27ff.). In addition, Aristotle says that the polis comes into existence for the sake of life, but that it endures for the sake of living well. He then says that the polis is "therefore by nature" because it is the *telos,* or fulfillment, of the previous associations, "and nature is a telos": "for whatever each thing is when it has completed its genesis, this we say to be the nature of each thing, such as of man, of the horse, of the household" (b31–34).

Aristotle apparently assumes that the village is natural because it is a necessary stage on the path of growth from the sexual pair to the polis. But the polis is said to be natural (1) because it is the limit of growth and (2) autarchy is the telos and the best, that is, the highest or most comprehensive good. This line of argument is marked by the following difficulties: (1) The city does not grow out of the prior four stages in the way that an adult grows out of a child or a horse grows out of a colt. Human beings initiate the process of growth at several steps, and in particular by shifting from villages to cities. It should also be noted that some persons choose not to reproduce, whereas others are so superior to the normal or the usual, and so the natural, human being as not even to require participation in political associations. (2) Furthermore, the form of the mature horse defines a self-sufficient or independent horse in the sense of a separate *ousia;* there is nothing more that a horse can do to become more of a horse. But human beings can initiate an association of cities into an empire. Aristotle of course regards this as "unnatural," for reasons that he will give later; but these reasons cannot be deduced from the natural growth of the city itself. They are derived from a conception of how human beings *ought* to live or, in other words, from Aristotle's understanding of what it is to be a human being.

To come now to the most important point: (3) Aristotle probably assumes that the polis is natural because it allows those human beings with forethought and sufficient wealth or birth to live well, that is, to acquire *eudaimonia.* It is far from obvious that *eudaimonia* is accessible only within the limits of the polis. But there is a deeper problem. It is also not self-evident that *eudaimonia* is accessible even within the polis. And this, I am quite certain, would be Plato's objection to the Aristotelian thesis that man is *by nature* a political animal, that is, that nature furnishes us with the means to obtain *eudaimonia,* namely, the polis. For Plato, on the contrary, no one is capable of achieving *eudaimonia* but the philosopher. This is closely connected to Socrates' assertion in the *Republic* that the purpose of the city they are building in speech is not to make the guardians happy (*eudaimones*), although it would not

Platonism

be surprising if they were to be the happiest of mortals; the purpose is to make the polis as happy as possible.[29]

I can now return to the Platonic classification of the arts and sciences. The various discussions of this classification in Plato are by no means entirely consistent with one another, but the distinction between discovering or acquiring and making or producing is uniform. It therefore looks as if political action (which of course includes ethical action) must be either theoretical or productive. Heidegger's "authentic" etymologies to one side, Plato, like Aristotle, is quite plain about his intention to separate theory and in particular the Ideas, which are the highest goal of our contemplation, from production. But there does seem to be a solid basis in the dialogues for the claim that Plato holds something like the view that life, understood as everyday practice,[30] is productive. In other words, even if there is a kind of theoretical knowledge about politics, the implementation of that knowledge is a kind of production, not (in Aristotle's sense) a kind of practice.

This point is of considerable interest in itself, and it will be of great importance later, when I discuss the relation between Plato and Nietzsche. In the immediate context, the point is central to our understanding of Platonist metaphysics as "being at home in" and consequently thinking the whole. It is part of my overall argument that human freedom is not restricted but rather facilitated by the determinate looks of things, and that by means of these looks we are able to engage in the process of constructing, and so reconstructing, our lives. Even in the extreme case of the *Republic,* which is too complex to be fully clarified in the present study, Socrates regularly speaks of the just city as a painting or an artifact made by philosophical artists or "demiurges."[31] He also refers to the city as a paradigm "laid up in heaven";[32] one could therefore apply Heidegger's interpretation of the implications of the demiurge-paradigm to political life. The city is made in accord with an "Ideal" or blueprint. That the mimesis is not simply a reading of a blueprint is suggested by 6, 498e2, where Socrates says that their discussion has been *apo tou automatou,* "spontaneous."

I propose to look more carefully at a passage in the *Philebus* which discusses the division of the arts; Socrates is the principal interlocutor and the main topic is the good life. More specifically, the discussion is concerned with the rank-ordering of intelligence and pleasure within the mixture of attributes that make up the good life. This continuous characterization of the good life as "a mixture and blend" sets the tone for the underlying theme of practico-production; the good life is a *sunkrasis* that we make after praying to Dionysus or Hephaestus or whichever god is responsible for supervising mixtures.[33] The passage that is of specific concern to us begins at 55d1. Science is divided into two parts: (1) demiurgic and (2) "that which is concerned with education and nurture" (*to de peri paideian kai trophēn*). Although this opposition reminds us of the distinction between the productive and the nonproductive sciences, it is not the same. It suggests more immediately the distinction between the banausic knowledge of the handworker and the aristocratic formation of the upper-class citizen. Socrates does not exclude production from "education and nurture." In fact, he disregards the latter as soon as he mentions it and devotes the remainder of the diaeresis to the demiurgic part. That education and nurture is not equivalent to the theoretical sciences is plain from the fact that Socrates will shortly classify "philosophical arithmetic" as a subspecies of demiurgy, which is puzzling in itself and which violates the procedure followed in other classifications.[34]

The next step is to distinguish within the branch of *cheirotechnikē* ("handicrafts" is here substituted for "demiurgy") the epistemically purest part from the part that is less pure (55d5). The former will be the "hegemonic" element in each *technē*. "If someone were to separate from all *technai* the component of numbering, measuring, and weighing, the remainder in each *technē* would be so to speak trivial" (55e1–3), namely, what is accomplished by guesswork, experience and practice, and reliance upon random activity, all of which are made strong "by care and effort" (55e5–56a1). As examples of *technai* in which there is reliance upon inexactness, guessing, and chance, Socrates cites music at some length and mentions medicine, farming, navigation, and generalship in addition (56a3-b3).

The arts just mentioned will be interpreted by Socrates to possess a small hegemonic component of arithmetic. In book 4 (400d6ff.) of the *Republic,* Socrates brings out the importance of harmony and measure in music, properties which require the hegemony of number and ratio. So too in the *Sophist* (252b1–261c10), the Eleatic Stranger uses the two paradigms of the alphabet and musical composition to designate the "mixing" or "blending" of formal elements (*stoicheia*) into intelligible structure.[35] In the *Philebus,* despite frequent reference to harmony, measure, mixing, and blending, music is treated not as the art of composition, but as that of performance. From the Greek standpoint, it is banausic to acquire excessive skill as an instrumentalist. Socrates' other examples, with the possible exception of farming, are also peculiar, since they are not normally associated with the handicrafts. Generalship, for example, is a political art, not a productive *techne*. The net effect of this passage is to diminish the separation between doing and making. Of more importance is the degree to which arithmetic exercises hegemony over activity, whether the latter is in Aristotle's sense productive or practical.

Socrates turns next to those arts in which there is greater use of measurement and tools, with correspondingly greater exactness; the paradigm here is building (*tektonike:* 56b4–6), more specifically, carpentry or the working of timber, as in house construction or shipbuilding (56b8–c2). He then certifies the bifurcation of "what are called the *technai*" on the basis of the previous discussion. The criterion is exactness (*akribeia*) in the work done (*en tois ergois* can mean either the activity or the product of work); the less exact part contains those arts which resemble (the performance of) music, and the more exact arts resemble carpentry (56c4–6). Socrates' own division, however, is not "exact" because the previously mentioned arts of counting, measuring, and weighing, which play more or less hegemonic roles in the less exact arts, are themselves classified under the more exact arts.

The more exact arts are themselves divided into two, following a distinction between what Socrates calls philosophical and vulgar (*ten ton pollon*) arithmetic (56d1–6). Vulgar or unphilosophical arithmetic consists of calculation and measurement used in carpentry and commerce (*logistike kai metrike kata tektoniken kai kat'emporiken*). It employs "unequal units" in its counting, by which Socrates means a number associated with a collection of things, for example, "two armies," "two cows," or "two anythings." Philosophical arithmetic, on the other hand (the geometry and calculation used by those who are fully trained in philosophy), employs exclusively homogeneous monads (56d9–57a2). This distinction is of great interest in the study of Greek mathematical theory, but it cannot be pursued here.[36] The important point for us is that Socrates is distinguishing between pure and applied arithmetic or, in other words, between acquiring pure knowledge (= theory) and practico-production.

Vulgar arithmetic exerts its hegemonic function both in the less and in the more exact arts. More precisely, vulgar arithmetic plays a dual role in the more exact branch of demiurgy. In the less exact branch, it was alluded to as the ruling component, yet its role in these arts was said to be negligible in comparison with the role it plays in the more exact arts. "Hegemonic" means something like "superior" rather than like "ruling" in these cases; the superior element is precisely *not* the ruling element in the less exact arts. In the more exact arts of everyday or nonphilosophical life, the arithmetical art plays a greater role, but one which is closer to that of a "guide" than a "ruler" (*hegemon* can be translated in either way). What we may call the genuinely hegemonic role is played by the philosophical arithmetic that employs pure monads exclusively, and so has no dealings with practico-production at all. This form of hegemony is a rule without subjects, as it were.

In the less exact arts, we classified *technai* and made use of the role played in these cases by arithmetic. In the more exact arts, we divided not only *technai* but arithmetic itself. House building is an example of a more exact use of vulgar arithmetic. But the contrast here is not between building artifacts out of wood and building them out of some material that is more amenable to exact measurement. The contrast is between building out of wood and building out of pure monads, that is, between production and theory, which is not building in the same sense as carpentry. And most surprising of all, philosophical arithmetic is classified under demiurgy, not under education and nurture, which is not, as I noted previously, identical with pure nonproductive knowledge.

Socrates makes use of this division of the sciences at 61c9ff. when he turns to the blending (*sunkrasis*) of the life that is best for mortals. The division was supposed to teach us that truth is connected with purity and exactness or, as we may say, with an abstraction from the body, a principle that Socrates applies to pleasures as well (57d3ff.). Pure truth, however, like pure intelligence, cannot be even the first or hegemonic element in the mixed life that is best for mortals; that honor goes to "the measured and the appropriate," which is to be found "somewhere in measure," that is, in the mixture of the various components, among which are included intelligence and pleasure, resulting in the good life (64e9, 65b10, 66a4). Intelligence turns out to be third and pure pleasures of the soul fifth in the list of six levels of "possessions" or components in a life.

The various rankings of the goods with which the *Philebus* culminates are extremely confusing, and no attempt will be made here to provide a thorough interpretation of this most obscure of the Socratic dialogues. What does stand out throughout the conversation, however, is that we have to produce our lives from components which are furnished partly by nature and partly, perhaps largely, by our own constructive efforts. Socrates never suggests that we produce the pure monads of philosophical arithmetic or any of the psychic attributes from which our life is composed. But the good or mixed life is not given to us, and it does not grow up within the garden of nature. I may be born with intelligence, for example, but I am not born with moderation and the ability to act at the appropriate moment. The pure monads of philosophical arithmetic are furnished by nature, but I must employ them in order to produce a philosophical life. The capacity to experience pleasure is natural, but not the capacity to restrict oneself to pure pleasures, to moderate amounts of impure pleasures, and so on.

The initial oddity of the location of philosophical arithmetic under demiurgy is now removed. The various divisions and classifications of the arts and sciences in the Platonic dialogue are all ad hoc; they are determined by the thematic context of the particular conversation, not by a set of general rules or for that matter by a productionist theory of Being. This observation also applies to the discussion of the Idea of the bed in book 10 of the *Republic* (see chapter 1). As the example of the *Philebus* shows, we cannot say even that Plato follows without deviation the rule of separating the productive from the nonproductive arts, if by "separating" is meant classifying under distinct branches of a diaeresis.

What we can say, however, is that Plato never presents human beings as being by nature political. This is undoubtedly why he does not distinguish practice from production. As the *Republic* makes explicit, there is no practical virtue in Aristotle's sense. The only philosophical virtue is wisdom or philosophy itself; all other virtues, including justice, are "demotic" or political,[37] and so they must be produced, as for example in the extreme case by philosophical demiurges. None of this is to deny that Socrates regularly consults nature in the process of constructing his recommendations for human life. But the paradigms he consults are themselves derived from the distinction between what is alone "divine" or given by nature, namely, philosophy, and demotic or nonphilosophical life. Even in the *Statesman,* in which the royal art of politics is classified under the epitactic branch of the gnostic arts, it is identified as being concerned with the generation of living beings, and the art itself is compared to weaving. The art of producing citizens is like that of producing artifacts from the warp and woof of the brave and the gentle natures.[38]

I want to make one more use of the *Republic* in this connection. In book 4 (445c1ff.), Socrates summons Glaucon to join him "as from a lookout tower," where he seems to see "one *eidos* of virtue and an endless number of vices." Socrates thus leads his companion to a "perspective" that is beyond good and evil. This is the genuinely philosophical perspective, namely, the synoptic perspective of the "dialectician" or philosopher.[39] The word *eidos* is not used here in the sense of the Platonic Idea, but even if it were, the point would be the same. The philosopher surveys the whole and in so doing stands beyond or outside of nature, in particular when he is attempting to legislate for human beings or, as Nietzsche puts it, to produce a new breed of mortals. Socrates is of course not Nietzsche; but we are required to see that for him as for his distant successor, man is the not-yet-constructed animal.

We have traveled a long distance in this chapter, and I shall be brief in summarizing it. Heidegger is right to identify metaphysics as immersion in the whole, but wrong to identify Platonist metaphysics as immersion that attends primarily, even exclusively, to the thinking in propositional statements of the properties of being qua being. Platonist metaphysics is primarily the attempt to think the whole in the sense of attempting to be at home in it; hence wisdom is more like *phronēsis* or what comes to mean in Aristotle "practical intelligence" than it is like dialectic or the science of free men[40] or the quasi-mathematical dialectic of the *Republic,* which, unlike diaeresis in the *Sophist,* reasons exclusively with Ideas.[41] On the basis of the evidence of the Platonic dialogues, there is no reason to suppose that dialectic in the second sense is possible; as to dialectic in the first sense, or diaeresis, the only fully developed examples we are given are the obviously comical ones of the sophist and the statesman.

I certainly do not intend to deny either that diaeresis was of importance to Plato or that he dreamed of a science of pure dialectic. I do intend to assert that the importance of these "sciences" in the comprehensive economy of the Platonic dialogues has been exaggerated by generation after generation of excessively serious students, for whom philosophy is fundamentally metaphysics understood as the science of being qua being, a science that has itself in more recent times been assimilated into or identified with mathematics (thereby, incidentally, missing Socrates' explicit distinction in the passage from the *Republic* just cited between mathematics and dialectic).[42]

The whole is where we find ourselves; what we do there is to make use of what it gives us and to adjust to what it takes away, in the unceasing and indivisible harmony of presence and absence, in order to carry out the task of making a life.

Reversed Platonism

II

Nietzsche's Platonism

4

In previous chapters, I directed attention toward Platonism, both as understood by Heidegger and in itself. This has prepared the ground for a study of the relation between Nietzsche and Plato. More precisely, as the title of this chapter makes clear, I want first to establish the sense of Nietzsche's reversed Platonism. This in turn will provide the basis upon which to evaluate the key elements of Heidegger's interpretation of Nietzsche. My penultimate goal is to determine the sense, if any, in which Nietzsche may be said to represent the end of philosophy understood as metaphysics, that is, as Platonism. The completion of the process of historical and conceptual desedimentation is intended to provide a secure basis for the consideration of the merits of my answer to the question of Being.

Heidegger's interpretation of Nietzsche may be understood very broadly as the attempt to explain the inner sense of the following remark from Nietzsche's Notebooks for 1870/71: "My philosophy *reversed Platonism:* the farther removed from true beings, all the purer more beautiful better it is. Life in illusion [*Schein*] as goal."[1] The immediate sense of this remark seems plain. In Plato's dialogues, the Ideas are normally referred to as the purest and most beautiful of beings; the life devoted to their apprehension is regularly described as the best (and even as the only good) human existence. Nietzsche is either denying the existence of the Ideas or asserting that they should be repudiated. Instead of moving toward the Ideas, we are told to move deeper within "false" in the sense of "illusory" beings or, as one could also say, we are directed away from the ostensible truth of the Ideas toward the greater value of art. This orientation is better for life.

At first glance, Nietzsche thus seems to reverse the Platonic subordination of art to truth. As we have already seen, however, the situation in Plato is more complicated. The process of life is practico-productive and not simply the pure pursuit of truth by way of the Ideas. One could of course insist that the production of life is regulated in Plato by the perception of the truth, as grounded in the vision of the Ideas. But the truth must be accommodated to the understanding of the citizens, and there is a fundamental difference between the accessibility of truth to the philosopher-kings or masters of the art of dialectic and to the non-philosophers, who are to be persuaded by the noble lie to adhere to the mythical foundations of the just city.

In the Heideggerian interpretation, Nietzsche's reversal of Platonism is essentially metaphysical. Nietzsche rejects the world of Ideas and thereby liberates the world of genesis from its subordinate or derivative role as illusion. The world of genesis is the true and only world. At the same time, Heidegger's attribution of a fundamental metaphysical doctrine to Nietzsche, and so of a continuation of Platonism, vitiates the significance of Nietzsche's own practico-political conception of the nature and function of the philosopher. In my opinion, Heidegger is right to notice a Platonist dimension in Nietzsche's thinking, but wrong in his description of the proportions of that dimension. This is because Heidegger's interpretation of Plato is defective in much the same way as is his interpretation of Nietzsche. Neither thinker is a metaphysician or ontologist in Heidegger's use of that term; for both, the philosopher takes his bearings in the pursuit of the best way of life. And this does not conflict with, but guarantees, the distinction between truth and art. Art is an instrument that is employed in the production of the truth about human existence.

I therefore also agree with Heidegger's understanding of Nietzsche as a careful thinker and writer and so reject the view of Nietzsche that is prominent in contemporary scholarship, namely, that he is an epigrammatist and inspired disciple of Dionysus with no comprehensive doctrines. Like Heidegger, I am a "rationalist" in the simple sense that I deny the predominance of Dionysus over Apollo in Nietzsche. In more straightforward terms, even if one wishes to associate Dionysus with inspiration, it remains true that the lucidity of philosophical understanding and the articulation of a comprehensive philosophical politics are incompatible with intoxication. This is of course not to deny the key role played by Dionysus in the economy of Nietzsche's thought. But Dionysus, both in Greek myth and in Nietzsche's explicit statement, is associated with destructive ecstasy, certainly not with philosophical inspiration. He who would create must first destroy; but creation is not spontaneous intoxication. It is intentional. The preponderant mass of

Nietzsche's writings entirely contradicts the now-fashionable doctrine of creative spontaneity.

One more preliminary remark is in order. The statement about his reversed Platonism stems from Nietzsche's Notebooks for 1870–71, a period in which he still held to the "artist-metaphysics" of *The Birth of Tragedy*. I will cite below the passage from 1876/77 in which Nietzsche disowns this doctrine. Heidegger, despite his insistence that the thought of the late, post-Zarathustran Nietzsche breaks radically with all prior writings, nevertheless takes his bearings by the early assertion of reversed Platonism. This is justified not by reference to the metaphysical nature of the reversal of truth and art, but by a political difference between Plato and Nietzsche. This difference is not metaphysical because it is rooted in agreement concerning the task of the philosopher as a follower of Apollo or as one who views the totality of human history from a synoptic perspective "beyond good and evil." Nietzsche's metaphor is essentially Platonic and is anticipated by Socrates in a previously cited passage in book 4 of the *Republic* (445c1ff.), at the conclusion of the discussion of the virtues of the soul, when he invites Glaucon to join him in looking out over the forms of virtue and vice "as from a lookout tower."

On Heidegger's reading, Nietzsche's adherence to the eternal return is conclusive evidence that he has not escaped from metaphysical Platonism but only reversed it, or favored becoming over being. On my account, the adherence to the eternal return is articulated not in a metaphysical account of Being, but in the claim to have understood the sum of the total stages of human historical possibility. One could also say that by rejecting the Platonic Ideas, Nietzsche liberates the practico-political function of the philosopher from all metaphysical constraints; but by retaining the Platonic conception of the synoptic vision of the philosopher with respect to human nature, or historical possibility, Nietzsche preserves the key thesis of Platonism. The philosopher is a double being who dwells within a historical perspective, marked by the decadence of the closing of a historical cycle, and so with access to all of the finite number of types of human soul. This access is the gateway not into historical time, but out of it, to what Nietzsche, following Pindar, calls the land of the Hyperboreans.

I shall have to investigate all aspects of this introductory impression of the sense of reversed Platonism. Let me begin by citing two passages from Heidegger that make plain the most important aspect of his own understanding of that sense. In the first, Heidegger explains that Nietzsche intended not simply a "reversal" (*Umdrehung*), but a "switching off" of that is also a "removal from" Platonism (*Herausdrehung*) and by that means an overcoming of nihilism. This would require the destruction of the two-worlds theory, and so of both the real world of the Ideas as well as the illusory world of genesis. The latter, in other words, could now be genuinely affirmed, together with the world of *Geist,* or human spirit, as the one true world, and so as the source and residence of value.[2]

In the second passage, Heidegger reflects upon the sense in which one may speak of the end of metaphysics as its resurrection in a derived form in which it will furnish materials for a new construction of the world of knowledge (*Wissen*): "What however does 'end of metaphysics' mean? Answer: the historical moment in which the *essential possibilities* of metaphysics are exhausted. The last of these possibilities must be that form of metaphysics in which its essence is reversed. This reversal is completed, not only actually, but also *consciously,* if however in different ways, in Hegel's and Nietzsche's metaphysics."[3]

Heidegger goes on to explain this last possibility of metaphysics as the attempt to invert the Platonist primacy of the object over the subject. For my present purposes I need to say only that Heidegger wishes to return to the pre-Socratic understanding of Being as the unveiling of presence and absence or, still more simply, to the notion of truth as the presencing of beings rather than as a property of looks (how beings look to human intelligence) or propositions about looks. Reversed Platonism, on the other hand, is the fulfillment of the implicit meaning of the Platonic doctrine of Ideas: substance is subject (Hegel) and subjectivity is perspectivism (Nietzsche).

As I suggested above, Heidegger is correct in his general thesis that reversed Platonism continues to be a form of Platonism. He is, I think, mistaken in understanding this reversal in essentially metaphysical terms, unless we replace the conception of metaphysics as the attempt to think being qua being by the conception of metaphysics as a thinking of the whole. As a preliminary version of my hypothesis, I would say that Nietzsche reverses the rank of the theoretical and the practico-productive elements in the Platonic conception of philosophy. One must certainly acknowledge that Nietzsche did not believe in the existence of the Ideas. But then, if Plato believed in them, this belief had nothing to do with metaphysics in the Aristotelian sense as adapted by Heidegger. Whatever the status of Plato's beliefs, Nietzsche, as part of his reversed Platonism, retains the general Platonist understanding of the nature of the philosopher and, correlatively, of the conception of philosophical *paideia:* of the political task of the philosopher as the attempt to produce a new human type. "Politics" must here be understood in the Greek sense as the formation of the soul of the citizen.

As I argued in part 1, the doctrine of the Ideas is a hypothesis that is required to account for the stability and intelligibility of beings in everyday life. We are able to live precisely because of the utility of such beings, but the utility of the hypothesis is confirmed by the exigencies of existence, not by an act of will or the imposition of a protosubjective perspective on the part of the philosopher. The question, in other words, is not How shall I conceive of the world in order to exercise my will to power? but How must I conceive of the world, granted its obvious nature? Furthermore, the hypothesis of the Ideas, although it gives rise to much conjecture on the nature of these presuppositions of stability and intelligibility, does not furnish them with discursive intelligibility. The attempt to see the Ideas themselves is always described in the dialogues in a poetic, mythical, or metaphorical manner. It is true that the nature of the soul is also invariably discussed in mythical terms, but the same cannot be said of the desire for happiness or the need to distinguish between better and worse lives. Unlike the Ideas or the nature of the soul, this need is directly accessible to us; to employ once more a Nietzschean metaphor, it is the gateway into the depths of the soul and thus to the Ideas. If we do not enter that gateway, we run the risk of perishing in the abyss of ontology.

In what follows, Nietzsche's Platonism will be represented by a metaphor that he himself adopted from Pindar. In *Pythian* 10, Pindar speaks of the Hyperboreans, a mythical race of blissful people who dwell in the far north and who are free from sickness and death; he writes, "Neither by ship nor by journeying on foot will you discover the marvelous way to the Hyperboreans" (11. 29–30). The Hyperboreans worship Apollo, who is said to spend the winter months with them and who delights "in their perpetual feasts and hymns." The Muse is always present to the Hyperboreans, whose life is free from the dictates of Nemesis.

Stated with maximum concision, my thesis is that the Hyperboreans express the Apollonian essence of Nietzsche's Dionysian music. Dionysus is in the first instance the intoxicated destructiveness that must precede creation. Apollo represents the lucidity of the synoptic or trans-perspectival vision that enables the philosophical lawgiver to create a new table of values. At this point there is an ambiguity in Nietzsche's metaphorical language. The actual creation of a new epoch or race of mortals is described both as Apollonian, or in keeping with Platonic intentionality, and as a Dionysian expression of the will to power. But this expression of the will to power is a consequence of philosophical lucidity and thus serves as the instrument of the demiurgic nature of the philosopher.

There are two references to the Hyperboreans in Nietzsche's published texts. The first dates from 1880 and is contained in *Human, All Too Human*. Here Nietzsche says that the happiness of the child is as mythical as the happiness of the Hyperboreans: "If happiness dwells on earth at all, thought the Greeks, then it is certainly as far away from us as it can be, perhaps yonder at the edge of the earth."[4] What Nietzsche means by calling happiness mythical becomes apparent only nine years later in *The Antichrist* (1889), one of the last writings he approved for publication. Nietzsche refers to himself as a Hyperborean in the first and seventh paragraphs of this work, thereby marking off a segment which, as Colli and Montinari tell us in their commentary, "was the preface to the *Will to Power* under the title *We Hyperboreans*, according to the plan of 26 August, 1888."[5] This identification with the Hyperboreans occurs in more than one manuscript.[6]

In the first paragraph of the segment from *The Antichrist*, Nietzsche says, "We are Hyperboreans—we know well enough how far apart we live. Neither by land nor by water will you find the way to the Hyperboreans: Pindar already knew about us. Beyond the North, the ice, and death—our life, our happiness.... We have discovered happiness, we know the way, we have found the exit from entire millennia of the labyrinth." Nietzsche goes on to contrast the Hyperboreans with modern man: "This tolerance and *largeur* of the heart, that 'pardons' everything because it 'comprehends' everything, is silence for us. Rather to live in the ice than under modern virtues and other south winds!"[7]

In this text, happiness is explained as the discovery of the exit from the labyrinth, an exit that is equivalent to the attainment of the lookout tower described by Socrates in the *Republic,* or in other words to the ascent beyond good and evil, and so outside or beyond the labyrinth of finite historical perspectives. The philosophical life is thus identified with Platonic contemplation not of the Ideas, but of human existence. Happiness is for Nietzsche as much as for Plato detachment from merely human life; but it is not the extinction of conscious life so much as the destruction of one's historical limitations.

Nietzsche makes this point explicitly in the foreword to *The Case of Wagner,* published in 1888: "What does a philosopher require of himself as the first and last thing? To overcome his time within himself, to become 'timeless.' With what must he undergo therefore his hardest struggle? With that precisely whereby he is the child of his time. Well! I am as well as Wagner the child of this time, that is to say a decadent: except that I understood this, I defended myself against it. The philosopher in me defended himself against it."[8]

As the earlier passage makes explicit when read in its entirety and as is confirmed by Nietzsche's regular insistence upon his uniqueness, the exit from the labyrinth is an accomplishment of neither the ancient nor the modern Hyperboreans, but of Nietzsche alone. Nietzsche claims for himself the discovery that the goal of the bravery required to negotiate this exit is the will to power, which he identifies as the good. In a text that is of crucial importance, Nietzsche states in paragraph 3 the problem to which this understanding of the good gives rise: "not what will supersede Mankind in the succession of natures ... but which type of man one ought to *breed,* ought to *will,* as of higher worth, more deserving of life, more certain of a future."[9]

In the last paragraph of this passage, Nietzsche identifies Christian pity as what is most unhealthy in our "unhealthy modernity." "To be a physician here, to be inexorable here, to use the knife here—that belongs to us, that is our form of philanthropy, thereby are we philosophers, we Hyperboreans!"[10] In short, the happiness of the Hyperboreans lies in the philosophical attempt to produce a new type of man. This happiness is mythical in two senses. First, it is not itself within history or the world of political activity but beyond the ice of the farthest north, in a land sacred to Apollo, the god of Socrates. Second, it is expressed in Apollonian music and hence not in philosophy or in poetry, understood as opposed to one another, but in a unity of the two.

The general thesis of the philosopher as Hyperborean was known to Plato; Nietzsche, however, modifies Platonism by giving to poetic construction a higher place in the economy of the philosophical life than does Plato. One can grant to Heidegger that Nietzsche's insistence upon the willful nature of the creation of new laws, values, and human types is due to the rejection of the hypothesis of the Ideas. But the replacement of one hypothesis by another, in this case of the Ideas by the assertion that Chaos is at the heart of becoming, is not the same as the articulation of a metaphysics. As we shall see later, Heidegger attempts to explain Nietzsche's hypothesis of Chaos as a subjectivist version of the hypothesis of the Ideas. In so doing, he identifies the ostensible laws of Chaos with those of productive thinking, thereby unconsciously employing an Aristotelian rather than a Platonist model.

We are not yet prepared to investigate this issue. Let us proceed step by step. The passages cited from *The Antichrist* and *The Case of Wagner* introduce us to the political or comprehensive version of Nietzsche's doctrine of destructive creation. They bring to mind Socrates' instruction to Glaucon in Plato's *Republic*[11] that in order to found the just city of philosopher-kings it will be necessary to "rusticate" everyone over the age of ten. In accepting the challenge "to bring forth a nature that is elevated beyond the entire species 'man,' " Nietzsche was prepared to sacrifice himself and "those who are closest to me," in other words, his epoch and thus his own historical identity.[12] Socrates speaks of persuasion whereas Nietzsche has recourse to the knife. The sharpness of the rhetoric is greater in Nietzsche, but the theoretical point is the same. Man is not, as Aristotle asserts, by nature a political animal. Citizens must be made by *muthos*. But this means that their antecedent mythical existence must first be unmade (as by Socrates' attack on Homer and, more broadly, on the poets).

Just as Plato presents his production of a new human type in the myth of the dialogue, and while wearing the mask of Socrates, so Nietzsche introduces his unfinished task in the persona of a Hyperborean. The myths are in one sense an interpretation of or perspective onto the nature of the philosopher. But the nature is the same in both myths, which are timeless or nonhistorical in their content. This is why

Socrates expels what I shall call historical or innovative poetry from the just city, whereas he and his companions will construct the city in speech "just like those who tell tales in myth."[13] The discursive image is supplemented later[14] by a comparison of the making of the just city to the production of a painted statue. Still later, Socrates says that "we have made a paradigm in speech of the good city."[15] The conversation in the *Republic* is not the same as "the paradigm laid up in heaven" which the philosopher establishes in his soul.[16]

The difference is this. The city as spoken by Socrates to his companions is a portrait of *praksis*, which shares less in the truth than does discourse (*leksis*),[17] or the conversation that might have been conducted by Socrates with genuine philosophers like Plato. The city constructed in the *Republic* is already accommodated to *praksis*. There are thus two forms of speech, as Socrates clearly indicates, which may be designated as philosophical and political. Political speech is perspectival or the entrance into history by philosophy, which is not itself perspectival but Hyperborean. Whereas founders of the city are not poets in the traditional sense,[18] the guardians, and so the philosophers within the city, as we have already seen, are so educated as to become "demiurges of the city's freedom."[19] This education is primarily musical or poetic in the comprehensive sense of the production of images of the good that are the food of the soul.[20] The political good is the harmony in the soul of ruling and being ruled.[21] This is temperance, which is stained like a dye into the souls of the guardians and forced onto the souls of the workers.[22]

Temperance is thus virtually indistinguishable from justice, the condition in which each part of the soul minds its own business with respect to ruling and being ruled.[23] Temperance and justice are both artifacts of intelligence as well as perspectival accommodations by intelligence to the guardians and workers, respectively. Intelligence is the ability to care for the city as a whole.[24] Wisdom is thus distinct from the other *technai* because these have specific goals.[25] The *technē* of wisdom is to produce good citizens or to make guardians through the use of the *nomos* of the city.[26]

The crucial *nomos* is in fact a kind of witchcraft that charms the guardians into believing that what is useful to themselves is identical to what is useful for the city.[27] A noble lie is needed to persuade the rulers if possible, but in any case their subjects, of the natural hierarchy of human souls.[28] The noble lie is a medicinal myth[29] that is useless to gods but useful to mortals in the form of medicine (and is not to be confused with the genuine lie in the soul, hated by gods and mortals alike).[30] Even the guardians must be forced to do or act (*poiein*) in such a way "that they will be good demiurges of their own production."[31] As the Athenian Stranger puts it to his interlocutors in the *Laws*, "We ourselves are poets, who have to the best of our ability created a tragedy that is the most beautiful and the best."[32] This is even truer of Socrates in the *Republic*, in which the art of breeding a new type of citizen is stated with unusual frankness. There is not a word of the description of this art with which Nietzsche would disagree.

We can now define the point around which turns what Nietzsche calls his "reversed Platonism." It is the conception of the comprehensive political intention of the philosopher. I cite from *Beyond Good and Evil*: "The philosopher as we understand him, we free spirits—as the man of the most comprehensive responsibility, who has the conscience for the total development of mankind."[33] Like Plato, Nietzsche employs "multiplicity and the art of disguise"[34] to exercise the genuine art of philosophy: "*The authentic philosophers . . . are commanders and lawgivers; they say 'let it be so!'*"[35]

For Nietzsche, the greatness of man is his "comprehensiveness and multiplicity," and the philosopher is the greatest of all men because he assumes responsibility for the total development of mankind.[36] Just as Plato imitates in the dialogues all fundamental human types, so Nietzsche says of himself, "I want to live through all of history in my own person and make all power and authority my own."[37] This, I believe, is one sense of Nietzsche's famous epigram "Everything deep loves the mask."[38] The philosopher conceals himself in his assimilation of the various personalities exhibited by the human soul. The philosopher understands by becoming what he is, namely, the totality of the human spirit.[39]

Nietzsche refers to Plato's self-concealment as follows: "*prosthe Platōn opithen te Platōn messē te Chimaera*" (Plato in front, Plato in the back, the Chimaera in the middle).[40] The philosopher is the monster who conceals his fire-breathing demiurgy beneath a mask that is itself bold enough to distract the attention of the more conventional reader. The mask is the expression of the superior person's instinct for rank,[41] and it is the decisive mark of the philosophical hybris: "The superior soul has reverence for itself."[42] The mask accordingly reveals to a kindred spirit that which it conceals from others, namely, the Hyperborean nature of the philosopher, to which Nietzsche refers when he says that in Plato the world is seen entirely from the standpoint of the eye of Apollo.[43] Nietzsche's reversed Platonism is also a reversal of the early doctrine of *The Birth of Tragedy*, according to which Dionysus is the inner core of things, or the Idea of which the Greek heroes are images made by Apollo.[44]

I remind the reader of the ambiguity noted earlier in the nature of creativity. Dionysus, of course, continues to represent the frenzy of creativity: "In the negation also of the most beautiful illusion, Dionysian happiness achieves its pinnacle."[45] But negation is not creation. We cannot however simply assume that Apollo is the creator-god, for the reason that has already been given. Creation as such is still Dionysian; the disciple of Apollo does not produce anything (unless we interpret the healing art of the physician as a cryptic reference to the production of a new, healthier version of mankind) but instead contemplates and so decides what is to be done. This is, I think, an inextricable confusion in Nietzsche's doctrine. In the same text, incidentally, Nietzsche reassesses *The Birth of Tragedy* as a youthful work of romantic confession based upon an "artist metaphysics."[46] Eight years before this, Nietzsche made a note warning the readers of his previous works "that I have given up the metaphysical-artistic viewpoints which ruled those works essentially; they are pleasing but cannot be maintained."[47] Dionysus now stands for "the happiness of becoming," that is, of the negation that is the necessary condition for creativity and perhaps of creativity itself. This begins from and culminates in Apollonian contemplation. It produces the illusion of stability for the non-Hyperborean, the happiness of human existence that is life in illusion, far from true Being: the goal of reversed Platonism on behalf of the nonphilosopher. The happiness of the Hyperborean, on the other hand, has nothing to do with human existence in the ordinary or artifactual sense of the term. Just as Plato employs myth to produce a timeless illusion of happiness, so Nietzsche employs the frenzy of Dionysus in the hand of Apollo to produce an image of Apollonian vision.

Human existence in the normal or historical sense is perspectival and depends upon an immersion in illusion as though it were actual and stable. The structure of this illusion or perspective is defined by its table of values. Hyperborean existence, on the other hand, is happiness of quite another kind: "My philosophy—to extricate mankind from illusion at any risk! Also no fear in the face of the destruction of life!"[48] In Platonic language: stable illusion for the citizens of the city of *praksis;* freedom from illusion for the genuine, transpolitical Hyperboreans. As we have already seen, in accepting the challenge "to bring forth a nature that is elevated beyond the entire species 'man,' " Nietzsche was prepared to sacrifice himself and his historical or perspectival identity.[49] This point is expressed very well in the following passage from *The Twilight of the Idols:* "In order to live alone, one must be either a beast or a god—says Aristotle. This omits the third case: one must be both— philosopher."[50] Beast and god—but not a historical person.

For a Platonic antecedent that at the same time brings out a subtle difference between Plato and Nietzsche, one should consult the passage early in the *Phaedrus*[51] in which Socrates says that he has no leisure for the scientific interpretation of religious myths because he is fully occupied with the need to know himself, to determine whether he is a monster like Typhon or something that is more gentle and shares in the divine. Nietzsche collapses the Socratic disjunction into a conjunction.

Art Is the Truth of Life

Let us now inspect more closely the relative excellence of art and truth. Heidegger introduces his discussion of Nietzsche's remark about reversed Platonism immediately following a brief commentary on the relation between truth and beauty in Plato's *Phaedrus.*[52] The juxtaposition is inspired by Nietzsche's contention that he has "experienced through living" (*erlebt*) that art is worth more than the truth.[53] What this means is clarified by a slightly earlier entry in Nietzsche's notebook of the same year: "Art and nothing but art. It is art that is the great enabler of life, the great seducer to life, the great stimulus to life."[54] In this connection I cite *Beyond Good and Evil,* in which Nietzsche says that it is not the truth or falsehood of a judgment that counts, but "how far it is life-promoting, life-sustaining."[55] In short, art is worth more than the truth *for life.* This is not the same as to say that truth is worthless or that there is no truth. It is not the same as to say that art is worth more than the truth for the philosopher or Hyperborean.

The philosopher as Hyperborean encompasses the whole, not by thinking the Ideas but by assuming the masks of each fundamental type or possibility of the human spirit. If we define each mask as a perspective, one which to be sure is capable of resolution into an unending regression of subperspectives but which dominates these latter as a fundamental stage of the finite sequence constituting the eternal return of the same, then we may be in a position to offer a plausible reconciliation of the two apparently divergent aspects of Nietzsche's teaching. When Nietzsche says elsewhere that there is no truth, he does so while developing his doctrine of world-interpretation.[56] But he also claims that the truth of this doctrine is accessible to the Hyperborean, who dwells beyond good and evil.

The reference to the Hyperboreans is intended to express the impersonal truth intrinsic to Nietzsche's loneliness. Loneliness is the psychological or personal manifestation of the existential isolation of the genuine philosopher. Nietzsche speaks of his isolation frequently; a paradigmatic text is his letter to Franz Overbeck of 12 November 1887: "I was in this way already as a child alone; I am still alone today, in the 44th year of my life."[57] The question is not one of Nietzsche's psychological detachment but rather of his philosophical mission and nature. In a letter that testifies to his sense of a new period of creative production, one in which he hopes to go entirely beyond everything he has accomplished to date (1887), Nietzsche says, "Now, when I must make a transition to a new and higher form, I require first of all a new estrangement, a still higher depersonalisation [*Entpersönlichung*]."[58] These texts could be multiplied; they are all anticipated in the previously cited note, in which Nietzsche refers to the solitude of the philosopher as the synthesis of the god and the beast who need not and cannot live in the polis.

In what sense is the philosophical hermit[59] the resident of a world? When Nietzsche speaks of his complete superiority to all of his contemporaries, including Wagner,[60] and indeed, to all Europeans, living or dead,[61] when he says that he writes for himself alone,[62] that he belongs to the breed of posthumous men[63] who will be understood only after they are dead, are we to attribute all these statements and countless others like them to his incipient madness? Or do they not make perfect sense in the context of Nietzsche's conception of the philosopher as prophet, lawgiver, and world-creator, who must breed a new race of readers capable of exemplifying his doctrines? Let me underline that

Nietzsche's Platonism

149

Nietzsche does not create his fellow Hyperboreans, among whom he includes Heracleitus, Empedocles, Spinoza, Goethe,[64] Dostoyevski, and Stendhal,[65] and (at least in *Human, All Too Human*), Epicurus and Montaigne, Plato and Rousseau, and Pascal and Schopenhauer. But if we accept his invocation to exist within the world produced by Nietzsche's laws or table of values, then our estimation of previous Hyperboreans will change.

The life of the philosopher, who combines the natures of the beast and the god, does not take place in the world but is rather a solitary process of world-creation. At the same time, of course, the philosopher is a human being who must also live within a world and in that sense become subject to the laws he has himself promulgated. From this standpoint, it is plain that there are no genuine or pure Hyperboreans; the metaphor is an expression of a spiritual characteristic. It defines the deepest or highest tendency of the philosophical nature. This is the background against which we must assess Nietzsche's assertion that art is worth more than the truth. Art *is* the truth—for life. Let us now look at some representative passages in which Nietzsche speaks of life. In noting the ambiguity of this term, I shall also be illustrating the central ambiguity in Nietzsche's thought. In a fragment from 1885/86, Nietzsche writes, " 'Being' [*Das "Sein"*]—we have no other representation of it than 'life.'—How therefore can anything dead 'be'?"[66] But Nietzsche also says that "there is no 'Being' behind doing, acting, becoming; the 'doer' is simply invented as an addition to doing—doing is everything."[67] This statement is connected to Nietzsche's rejection of the independence of the ego, which he regularly reduces to physiological affects, and these in turn to points of force emerging from the will to power.[68]

In other words, reality is for Nietzsche in fact *Schein,* on which I shall have more to say below; for the time being we can translate it as how things appear from a given perspective. But *Schein,* or the perspectival, is itself intrinsically will to power.[69] The intellect, will, and sensations all depend upon our values; these correspond to our drives (*Triebe*) and their conditions of existence. "Our drives are reducible to the will to power," which is the last fact.[70] "From within each of our fundamental drives there is directed outwards a differentiated perspectival evaluation of all events and lived experiences [*Erlebens*]. . . . *Man as a multiplicity of 'Will to Power': each with a multiplicity of means of expression and forms.*"[71] Despite Nietzsche's assertion that the will to power is the last fact, we must go one level deeper. Strictly speaking, there can be no will since there is no ego or subject and certainly no transcendental or Absolute Ego. The will to power is not a self-conscious or teleological force; at bottom it is Chaos.

" 'Chaos of the all' as exclusion of every purposiveness of activity is not in contradiction to the thought of circular motion"—Nietzsche is here referring to his doctrine of the eternal return of the same—"the latter is precisely an *irrational necessity,* without any formal, ethical, [or] aesthetic intention."[72] According to Nietzsche, "The world is altogether not an organism but Chaos."[73] I cite one more passage from the Notebooks of 1888: "Will to power as knowledge not 'knowing' but schematizing, imposing onto Chaos so much regularity and forms as suffice for our practical requirements."[74] Note that there is no explanation as to how one aspect of Chaos, namely, ourselves as practical agents, organizes or schematizes Chaos as a whole to "appear" as a world that suffices for our practical needs. How are we ourselves, who possess practical needs, "schematized"? The answer can only be that Chaos differentiates itself into changing bundles of perspectives that themselves produce the illusion of subjectivity or the unity of the self. In sum, Being is life; life is will to power; will to power is Chaos.

If we combine Nietzsche's doctrine of the prophet-philosopher as lawgiver, and hence as the one who is fundamentally responsible for the rank-ordering or values by which a world is defined,[75] with the doctrine of perspectivism and interpretation, it follows that art is "worth more" than the truth for life as it is lived within a world. To the extent that the philosopher is also a human being or even a superman, he too must live in a world; but this does not encompass or explain his world-creating activity, which is transworldly or Hyperborean. The deepest problem in Nietzsche is not how to combine the doctrine of philosophical truth, and so the truth of Nietzsche's own teaching, with the doctrine of perspectivism and interpretation. It is instead how to understand the relation between the philosopher or highest representative of the will to power, and so the creator-lawgiver, with the intrinsic nature of the will to power as Chaos.

If the world is a self-creating and self-sustaining organism[76] or, as Nietzsche expresses the point in his late period, "a work of art that gives birth to itself,"[77] then how can it be created by the philosopher and his disciples? When Nietzsche speaks in a more exoteric or political vein, he refers to world-creation by a master race that produces itself in the process of stamping a form onto Chaos, a form, incidentally, that originates in acts of terrifying violence.[78] This in turn can be understood as a kind of perturbation of Chaos itself. The philosopher must then serve as a kind of shaping and accelerating force that inflects the will of the master race to his own will to power, but who in so doing is himself a more concentrated expression of the internal excitations of Chaos. In sum, all talk of self-conscious direction of the will to create a world is exoteric; the deeper or esoteric teaching is that philosophical understanding is encapsulated in the Spinozist *amor fati*.[79]

In a fragment entitled "My new way to 'Yes' " Nietzsche identifies the Dionysian affirmation of the world as the highest stance accessible to a philosopher; "my formula for which is *amor fati*."[80] Dionysus is not only the god of creation; he is also the god of destruction. To repeat, "Dionysian happiness achieves its peak in the negation of the most beautiful illusion"[81] or in other words in a return to Chaos. This is because one must first destroy in order to create, as Zarathustra teaches his future disciples.[82] Creation and destruction are both forms of Chaos; the philosopher is the highest expression of what one can call only the self-affirmation, but hence the self-consciousness, of Chaos. Nietzsche never explains how this is possible; it is the equivalent in his doctrine to what Heidegger, following Aristotle, calls *to hoti,* the way things are, the given. We also see here a stubborn residue of German Idealism.

We shall have to study later in careful detail this "metaphysical" core of Nietzsche's teaching. I introduce it here in order to provide the context within which one may distinguish between the philosophical activity of world-creation and the human or superhuman life within a world. It is in this context that we are able to understand the assertion that art is worth more than the truth. Art is worth more than the truth for the preservation of the illusion that what is visible (*Schein*) exists for us not as a mere product of the will, but in such a way as to sustain human life, to satisfy our practical needs. This greater value of art in no way cancels or invalidates truth. The quarrel with Platonism must be seen as a quarrel concerning what is valuable for life, granted Nietzsche's analysis of the nature of life as Chaos. The quarrel is therefore also about truth; not about whether there is any truth, but rather about what is true. All of Nietzsche's invocations to creativity, overcoming, the continuous transvaluation of values, and so too the invocation to return to the earth or to repudiate the supersensible world of Platonic Ideas as well as doctrines like Christianity, which is Platonism for the people, must therefore be understood as part of Nietzsche's own production of illusion for the sake of life.

To say this in another way, let us assume that Platonism is indeed the doctrine of the Ideas. In this case, according to Heidegger's own procedure, Nietzsche's reversed Platonism would be a replacement of the Ideas by an alternative "metaphysical" doctrine of being qua being. As Heidegger also in effect asserts, Nietzsche's metaphysical teaching is contained in the twin doctrines of the will to power and the eternal return. But these doctrines themselves reduce to the thesis that Being is intrinsically Chaos. What returns eternally is the finite number of comprehensive permutations of Chaos. Nietzsche is then, if a metaphysician at all, a metaphysician of Chaos. Since the Ideas are the Platonic expression of permanent order, it is dubious whether one could refer to a metaphysics of Chaos, or the absence of order, as reversed Platonism.

Of more immediate interest, however, is the following anomaly in Heidegger's account. In the Platonic dialogues, the doctrine of the Ideas is never fully explained, but it is never denied. Whereas the dialogues are esoteric documents in the sense that they advocate one teaching for the few and another for the many, the doctrine of the Ideas is part of both teachings. Nietzsche, however, does not teach consistently and uniformly that creation and order are merely an illusory manifestation of Chaos. Chaos is the first principle of radical creativity, but it is not and cannot be the first principle of the fundamental Nietzschean doctrine of rank-ordering. The distinction between the noble and the base, or between the synoptic vision of the Hyperborean, who is beyond good and evil, and the perspectival vision of the nonphilosopher or historical individual, is never reduced by Nietzsche to Chaos. On the contrary, it expresses the two fundamental, and fundamentally different, responses to the fact of Chaos. This distinction is the root of Nietzsche's Platonism. What one could therefore by an exercise of poetic license refer to as Nietzsche's metaphysics of Chaos does not apply to his doctrine of human nature.

We may thus make the distinction, following Nietzsche, between his "philosophy" and his "task": (1) "My philosophy—to drag mankind out of *Schein* at any risk! and also no fear concerning the going to ground of life!"[83] (2) "My task: man as poet, as thinker, as God, as power, as compassion."[84] The task, or the political enactment of the teaching, is also referred to in a previously cited note as "my demand" or "challenge": "to produce a nature that stands superior to the entire species 'man': and for the sake of this goal to sacrifice myself and 'those nearest' [to me]."[85] Nietzsche is thus guided by the same practical goal as is Plato: to extract humankind, in the persona of the philosopher, from *Schein*. And there is a close analogy to Plato's practical task: to produce a new race of beings by means of a comprehensive doctrine that is political in the sense that it requires philosophers to be kings. As to the philosopher himself, he is outside the doctrine in the same sense that he is outside the Platonic cave.

Inside the cave, so to speak, the artist is superior to all previous philosophers. Nietzsche's reversed Platonism, when seen in this way, amounts to the rule of artists as agents or surrogates of masked philosophers. And this is not so much a reversal as an exaggeration of the role of the artist; it is, in other words, an extension of the creative type understood as the mask worn by the philosopher, but not as the philosopher beneath the mask. Here again is the previously noted ambiguity in Nietzsche with respect to synoptic vision and law giving or world making. Nietzsche does not separate with precision the philosopher as Hyperborean and as world-creator. As outside of history, the philosopher is a Hyperborean. As the productive force of history or the shaper of chaos, the artist is a world-creator. The creation of a world is Apollonian to the extent that it is rooted in the vision of the Hyperborean and carried out in accord with an elaborate theoretical program based upon knowledge of human nature. It is however Dionysian to the extent that creation must be preceded by destruction, by the happiness of the obliteration of antecedent forms that are already in decline.

That the superiority of art to truth is not unqualified is indicated by the following passage from the Notebooks of 1885: "We defend the artist and poet and whoever is a master therein; but as a nature that is of a higher type than these, who are only capable of something as the merely 'productive human beings,' we do not mistake ourselves for them."[86] As Nietzsche says in the *Genealogy of Morals,* artists "were at all times valets of a morality or philosophy or religion."[87] Praise for the artist in the traditional sense applies only within *Schein;* outside *Schein,* the genuine artist is the philosopher who imposes his comprehensive perspective onto mankind, and so onto Chaos. As I have already indicated, Nietzsche makes it entirely explicit in his Notebooks from 1876/77 that the early "metaphysics of art" as represented by *The Birth of Tragedy* has been repudiated.[88] The value of the artist in the conventional or nonphilosophical sense of the term is entirely "exoteric" or political; it is thus subordinated to the rhetoric of the philosopher.

For added clarification, I call attention to the following fragment from 1888: "The will to appearance [*Schein*], to illusion, to deception, to becoming and changing, is deeper, 'more metaphysical' than the will to truth, to actuality, to Being; pleasure [*Lust*] is more original than pain; pain is itself only the consequence of a will to pleasure (—to creating, forming, levelling to the ground, destroying) and, in the highest form, a type of pleasure."[89] Paradoxical though it may sound, we are entitled to say that for Nietzsche, the will to appearance, illusion, and so on is *truer* than the will to truth, actuality, and so on; and by "truer" is meant here "more valuable for human life."

What is Heidegger's formulation of the relation between Plato and Nietzsche with respect to the connection between truth and art? Heidegger takes his bearings by the *Phaedrus*. He explains the function of Eros as that of "being raised beyond oneself and being attracted by Being itself."[90] By "Being" (*Sein*), Heidegger means here the Ideas.[91] Eros thus corresponds to what Nietzsche calls "intoxication" (*Rausch*). The possibility of executing the apprehension of Ideas as Ideas is grounded in Eros by way of the Idea of Beauty, which is "most lovable and at the same time most visible" (*erasmiōtaton* and *ekphanestaton*). The beautiful thus serves to illuminate the domain of the Ideas, to make them visible and so present to the intellect; as Heidegger expresses this, the beautiful "brings Being forward [*zum Vorschein bringt*]."[92]

The corresponding situation in Nietzsche is as follows: "The truth, that is, the true as the enduring, is a species of *Schein*," which latter we can now translate as both illusion and the shining of what appears, only as a human perspective, not as the process by which the Idea points itself out in the illumination of the Idea of Beauty. *Schein* "justifies itself as the necessary condition for the maintenance of life. It soon becomes clear, however, from a deeper reflection, that all appearance [*Anschein*] and all seeming [*Scheinbarkeit*] is possible only when in general something shows itself [*sich zeigt*] and comes forward [*zum Vorschein kommt*]."[93] This last expression is the tandem of "brings forward," used above with respect to the role assigned by Plato to the beautiful in connection with Being. The passage concerning Nietzsche continues, "What makes possible such an appearing [*Erscheinen*] in advance is the perspectival itself. This is the genuine shining [*Scheinen*], *zum sich Zeigen-bringen*," as Heidegger says in a phrase that is difficult to render in English.[94]

In other words, *Schein*, understood as illusion only in contrast to the Platonic Idea, but in itself as the shining of that which presents itself as becoming (compare Hegel), and so as that which brings itself forward as appearing rather than as permanent, is the perspectival. The being of that which appears and shows itself to human beings is determined by the human activity of looking at, by the standpoint or viewpoint from which human beings regard the process of becoming. This is the inner truth of Platonic *noēsis*, or the gazing upon Ideas as ostensibly separate from and independent of the activity by which we view them, although according to Heidegger Plato does not recognize this or leaves it unthought. Being is thus for Nietzsche not merely becoming; in addition, as that which shows itself as coming to be, it is perspectival. Hence one can say that for Nietzsche, Being is interpretation.

Nietzsche himself expresses this most pithily in a fragment from 1885/86, to which I alluded above: "World-interpretation, not world-explanation."[95] The following text gives us a fuller statement of what this means and connects the function of interpretation to the previous discussion of truth, falsehood, and the several senses of *Schein*:

> That the value of the world lies in our interpretation (that perhaps somewhere still other interpretations than the merely human are possible—), that interpretations up to now are perspectival valuations, by virtue of which we sustain ourselves in life, that is to say in the will to power, for the sake of the growth of power, that each elevation of human being brings with it the overcoming of narrower interpretations, that each accomplished strengthening and expansion of power opens new perspectives and signifies belief in new horizons—this runs through my writings. The world that concerns us is false, i.e. is no fact [*Thatbestand*] but an inventing and rounding off of a meagre sum of observations; the world is "in flux" as something that is coming to be, a perpetually self-

shifting falsehood that never comes nearer to the truth: for—there is no "truth."[96]

There is no truth, that is to say, in the sense of a stable world existing independently of our perspectival interpretations. Otherwise, the sense of the passage is self-explanatory. To it, we may add a remark about the function of beauty in Nietzsche. In a fragment from 1883, Nietzsche says, "I count as beautiful (considered historically): what becomes visible to the most admired man of an epoch [*Zeit*] as an expression of that which is most worthy of admiration."[97] Heidegger cites a different fragment in which Nietzsche speaks of the beautiful as an affirmation and goes on to the following generalization: "The beautiful is that which we estimate and admire as the paradigm [*Vor-bild*] of our nature."[98] In Heidegger's account of Plato, the Idea of the beautiful lights up the realm of independent and permanently present Ideas toward which our Eros attracts us. In Nietzsche, the beautiful is the expression of our own will to power, to which we are attracted by Dionysian intoxication. Just as being is defined by the perspective of the viewer, so the visibility of the being radiates out from the activity of looking, which is not *theōria* but self-affirmation.

The same ambiguity concerning the relation between metaphysical Chaos and human nobility is apparent in Nietzsche's statements about art and Heidegger's interpretation of those statements. Stated generally, the Nietzschean analogon to beauty in the world of the Platonic Ideas is the perspective, which is itself defined by the values of the creator. In Plato, however, there is a rank-ordering of perspectives; more precisely, the only adequate perspective is that of the philosopher, who alone adequately loves, and so contemplates, the Ideas. There is then for Plato only one truly noble world, the cosmos as articulated by the philosopher. Nietzsche, however, vacillates between two different formulations of the equivalent element in his thinking. On the one hand, the beautiful is straightforwardly explained as that which the most admired man of the age himself admires: in other words, it is the force underlying the will to power. This formulation escapes from relativism only by equating nobility with quantity of power; in Heidegger's interpretation, the plurality of Platonic Ideas is represented in Nietzsche by the plurality of perspectives: whatever shines forth in any given determination of Chaos. But this leaves unintelligible the basis for the rank-ordering of alternative worlds. Heidegger's metaphysical or ontological reading takes its bearings by the functional or structural understanding of perspectives (in accord with the ostensible analogy between the perspectives and the Platonic Ideas). Heidegger thereby ignores or minimizes the problem of rank-ordering. Some illusions are better or more noble than others. This cannot be explained on ontological grounds. The expression of power is not the same as spiritual excellence, as Nietzsche himself insists in his criticism of Stoicism.[99]

So much for the connection between art and truth as the inner content of the significance of Nietzsche's reversal of Platonism. One could describe Heidegger's presentation of this connection as a long commentary on what he calls Nietzsche's principal assertion on art: that it is the greatest stimulus to life.[100] I want next to consider closely the section in Heidegger's lectures entitled "Nietzsche's Reversal of Platonism."[101] In this section Heidegger first summarizes his discussion of the relation between beauty and truth in Plato and then proceeds to illustrate Nietzsche's reversal by way of an analysis of one of the latter's most famous texts: the section in *Götzen-Dämmerung* entitled "How the 'true world' finally became a fable."[102]

From Truth to Fable: Stage 1

Nietzsche's text is divided into six parts, each of which corresponds to one stage in what Heidegger calls the history of Platonism. Whereas the biblical God takes six days to create the world, Nietzsche dissolves it in six steps. The unspoken implication is that the seventh day will be devoted to a new creation ex nihilo rather than to rest and contemplation. The first part opens as follows: "The true world attainable by the wise, the pious, the virtuous—he lives in it, he is it." There follows a parenthetical sentence that serves as a commentary on the first part: "(Oldest form of the Idea, relatively clever, simple, convincing. Paraphrase of the statement 'I, Plato, am the truth.')" Nietzsche treats the world from the outset as the product of philosophical thought. It is neither an epoch of the evolution of the Absolute, as in Hegel, nor a gift of Being, as in Heidegger, but a human perspective. The perspective is relatively clear and simple: the wise man (whose wisdom is moral in character) not only attains to, but is, the "true" world. The world is the projection of a way of life, which is itself a camouflage of the will of the sage, exemplified by Plato.

In support of Nietzsche's thesis, one might cite the *Philebus*, 28c6ff., in which Socrates says, "The wise all agree, thereby exalting themselves, that intellect (*nous*) is king for us of heaven and earth." This passage comes closer than any other in the Platonic corpus to expressing Nietzsche's interpretation of the origin of the true world. But there is a fundamental difference. Socrates says that the philosophers exalt themselves by making *nous* their king; he does not say that they are or that *nous* is the truth; instead, he means that *nous* apprehends the truth. By "heaven and earth," Socrates means the cosmos, not "the true world." The cosmos is the order that is accessible to *nous*. To the extent that man is a part of the earth who aspires to the heavens, it is true that man and thus in particular human thinking is a part of the cosmos. One could say even that *nous* shares in the ordering of the cosmos because the order is disclosed as such only to *nous*. But this is not to derive the order from the will. *Nous* could be called the perspective onto the cosmos, but it is the synoptic perspective that is the same for all who attain to it. *Nous* is not the will; there is no independent will in Plato. This is why Socrates subordinates the desires to the intellect in the soul of the philosopher. And the erotic desire of the philosophical intellect is not the will, that is, not a projection from the intellect outward or the constitution of a world, but a force from above and outside the soul that comes down into it and raises it to the heavens.

A world, on the other hand, is a projection of an intelligence, whether in the Kantian or the Nietzschean sense. The word *Welt* carries the sense throughout Nietzsche's writings of human perception, which is gradually identified as the will to power. Two representative texts: (1) "The world cannot be better than man; for how could it exist except as human sensation? [*Empfindung*]."[103] (2) "*This world is the will to power—and nothing beyond that!*"[104] In Nietzsche, *Empfindung* replaces *nous;* the world is projected from within outward. But this explains the origin of the world as it were from within the perspective of the *Schein*, that is, the perspective of how the world appears to human beings themselves. Paraphrases of the assertion "I, Plato, am the truth" are necessarily all versions of the attempt to create a world by schematizing or organizing Chaos. In fact, however, Nietzsche, as we saw, conceives of the world as a work of art giving birth to itself. It is not the will of the historical personage, Plato, that creates the world, but Chaos, manifesting itself as the world of classical antiquity on the one hand and Plato's transforming will on the other. Chaos schematizes or organizes itself by its own random excitations, which produce "the world of Plato."

Heidegger's interpretation of Chaos in Nietzsche does not coincide with the Nietzschean texts. In a crucial passage, Heidegger says that Chaos for Nietzsche is not an arbitrary *Durcheinander* or *Gewühl*, that is, a swarm or hurly-burly of *Empfindungen*. Instead, it is "das leibende Leben," which may be translated as "corporealizing life." As such, it is not disorder but "that jostling, streaming flow of excitation, whose order is *hidden,* whose law we do not immediately know."[105] A few pages later, Heidegger associates Chaos with *praksis* and says that the former is schematized in *Lebensvollzug,* that is, in the acts executed in daily life. The horizon of a perspective, which rules via schematization, is thus both the mastery of Chaos and the manifestation of Chaos as Chaos.[106] The world shows itself as the securing of duration or existence thanks to this perspective. Accordingly, "reason [*Vernunft*] together with its concepts and categories does not develop initially from the need for the mastery of Chaos, but it is in itself already the perception of Chaos [*Chaos-Vernehmung*]." "Reason" is here the equivalent of Kant's "practical reason."[107]

In Heidegger's interpretation, Chaos not only is the principle of life, but possesses an inner law which we grasp in everyday life by executing the fundamentally evaluative acts of *praksis*. In order for this to occur, we must ourselves be already constituted as human beings who are active within the everyday world of *praksis*. It is true that Nietzsche refers in a fragment from 1888, already cited, to the fact that schematization occurs in accord with practical needs. But this passage cannot stand by itself as an account of Nietzsche's metaphysics. Nietzsche refers to *praksis* from a practical standpoint, that is, within the illusion. There is no analogy between this sense of *praksis* and the function of the term in either Plato or Kant, since we and the everyday world are already products of Chaos. In Plato, there is no constitution of the world but an apprehension of the cosmos, including therefore an apprehension of human being as the "place" (to employ an appropriate Heideggerian term) within which the cosmos is revealed. In Kant, practical reason does not constitute the world but rather the moral law by which we must live within a world that has already been constituted by theoretical reason.

In other words, from the standpoint of the Nietzschean philosopher, the projection by man of a horizon is itself an illusion; the true explanation of this illusion is that it is an epiphenomenon of the random disturbances of Chaos. Human beings accordingly "schematize" Chaos only in a secondary or instrumental sense, namely, as instruments of Chaos. This is what is meant by the assertion that the world is a work of art giving birth to itself. There is then no metaphysics of Chaos; there is instead a practico-productive doctrine of the human manifestations of Chaos, which always occur in accord with a rank-ordering that is itself not reducible to or comprehensible in terms of Chaos. Schematization occurs in accord with practical needs because there are no theoretical or metaphysical needs. Human beings are not literally gods who create worlds from the *nihil* of Chaos. They impose their wills onto already existing worlds. In this sense they are more like critics or hermeneuts than artists or creators; they give value to the self-producing world. But neither is there an inner law of Chaos, since this would be equivalent to an enduring metaphysical structure independent of human subjectivity or intentionality and to which acts of schematization would have to conform.

Nor is there any reference in Nietzsche to an inner law in Chaos. He makes it quite explicit that the reverse is the case. Regularity and form are imposed onto Chaos from within the illusion by powerful thinkers like Plato and Nietzsche himself, but in truth, this is merely one disturbance of Chaos canceling or rearranging another. To emphasize an earlier citation: Chaos as the eternal return is an "irrational necessity" (*unvernünftige Notwendigkeit*).[108] The "necessity" is not the function of a law, which would be rational; "necessity" here refers to the consequences of Chaos, which come independently of the human will as the perpetual recurrence of all possible organizations of matter, force, or energy. When Nietzsche speaks of *amor fati,* he means that the philosopher emulates Spinoza in accepting what occurs as the result neither of his own will nor intellect, and hence not of his or any other human perspective, but of nonhuman and (at least in Nietzsche's case) also nondivine necessity, which is thus synonymous with chance.

But the Nietzschean philosopher cannot emulate Spinoza in understanding the structure of necessity because no such structure exists. In one last formulation: all structures of Chaos are transient if recurring productions of that which has no structure. If the number of fundamental world-epochs is finite, then we might indeed be able to know the structure of the totality of the productions of Chaos. But this is not the structure of Chaos itself. If Chaos possessed a structure, it would no longer be Chaos or Becoming but a quasi-Platonist Being. However, Nietzsche does not say that Chaos is Being; he says instead that Being, that is, what we take for Being, is Chaos. To this one may add the following remark: Chaos is the ancestor of Heidegger's understanding of Being as a process of emergence. To attribute a structure to Chaos is equivalent to attributing a structure to Heideggerian Being and thereby to rationalizing or reifying it.

To come back now to the first stage of what Heidegger calls the history of Platonism, we have seen that Nietzsche's identification of this stage with Plato is rooted in his concern with philosophy as a way of life, and one in which the will predominates in the form of a projection of the self as a world-order. In order to identify Nietzsche's thought as the last stage of Platonism, it is also necessary to maintain the converse of this thesis: that Plato's thought is the first stage of Nietzscheanism. One could perhaps say, on the basis of the first stage of Nietzsche's discussion of the destiny of the true world, that he himself in fact takes Plato in this way. But Heidegger is careful to deny that Plato is a Platonist; he also denies that Plato is an explicit or intentional Nietzschean.[109] The link between Plato and Nietzsche is for Heidegger not conscious or intentional but lies in the destiny of Being itself or in what Heidegger calls elsewhere the "gift" by Being of itself in a concealed form.

Plato initiates Platonism, not Nietzscheanism. There is no doctrine in Plato of the will to power or Chaos, but only of a turning away from the original Greek conception of *phusis* and the coordinate notion of *alētheia* as a combination of concealment and disclosure.[110] One could say that Nietzscheanism is somehow latent within the "fall" from *alētheia* to propositional discourse about looks. But the transition from Plato to Nietzsche requires in addition the crucial step of Cartesian subjectivity as the radicalization of the Christian and Roman doctrines of will and truth as *rectitudo*.[111] There is then a certain tension if not an outright inconsistency in claiming that Plato is not a Nietzschean, but that Nietzsche is a Platonist. "Platonism" is thus transformed into a middle term that itself undergoes an essential metamorphosis at several points, and in such a way as to detach its originator from the culmination of what he ostensibly engendered.

Heidegger nevertheless insists that the "total history" of Western philosophy is Platonism.[112] The question therefore arises: if Plato himself is not a Nietzschean, in what sense is Nietzsche a Platonist? We have already elicited Heidegger's answer to this question: Nietzsche remains a Platonist by reversing the main terms of Platonism. But this in turn means that the main terms of Platonism are so to speak "ontological," or in other words *phusis* and *ousia* in the sense of the *idea* of the *on*. Whereas for Plato what endures as present and visible is the product of the emergence-process, rather than the shining forth of that process itself, what endures in presence for Nietzsche (the eternal return) is the emergence-process (will to power). This requires us to accept Heidegger's interpretation of the will to power as "the constancy of becoming in presence" (*die Beständigung des Werdens in die Anwesenheit*)[113] and of the eternal return as "most constant constancy of the coming to be of the constant."[114] In sum, the eternal or enduring in Plato is intelligible structure; according to Heidegger, the eternal or enduring in Nietzsche is the perpetual absence of intelligible structure or the perpetual presence of the "absenting" of presence. But this contradicts the Heideggerian thesis of an inner law in Chaos.

The will to power is "the what" of Being; it thus replaces the *ousia*, or Idea, of Platonism. In chapter 1, I pointed out that the equation of *idea* with *ousia* is a conflation of Plato with Aristotle. The same is true of Heidegger's reference to the eternal return as "the that." Is there an equivalent in Plato to the that or the given as given? In Aristotle it refers to the entities of genesis or nature, which are however for him already embodiments of *eidos*. The equivalent term in Plato would be *ta phainomena*. In order to bring this term as close as possible to the Heideggerian interpretation, I translate it as "the showing-forth from itself of that which shows itself."[115] This translation also allows us to be faithful to the double aspect of the visible as an image of an original, but therefore as a presentation, however concealed, of the original itself.

The term "presence" (*parousia*) as applied to Plato refers, if to anything, to the Ideas. It is the presence of the Ideas, themselves illuminated by the Good, that "light up" or make visible *ta phainomena* in the sense of the given entities of genesis or nature. To what in Nietzsche does "presence" refer? Certainly not to Platonic Ideas. Heidegger says that the will to power endures in presence. But what does this mean? Is presence something separate from the will to power, a medium in which it is accessible as visible? This is out of the question, since the will to power is the last fact, with the ambiguous exception of Chaos, which is "present" only as the absenting of presence. As to the eternal return, it is constancy, not presence: the constancy of the will to power. Since the will to power schematizes Chaos, and thereby establishes a world, through the practical efficacy of a perspective, "presence" in Nietzsche can refer only to the process by which Chaos diversifies itself into a viewer and a view, namely, an agent and a product of the will to power. This diversification is into conjoint processes, each of which is an illusory unification, by means unexplained, of the points of force out of which the will to power is itself constituted. "Presence" is there-fore *Schein* not in the sense of the pointing-itself-out from within itself of the Ideas or natural products of the emergence-process of *phusis,* but as the illusion of human existence, manifested as this or that perspective of Chaos onto itself.

Hence the central importance of the perspective, together with the coordinate term "interpretation" (*Auslegung*). Being is not the presence of that which is to be clarified or explained; it is the presence of a horizon or perspective of interpretation. And *Auslegung,* as we saw previously, is not *Erklärung,* or explanation. In what sense can this be called reversed Platonism? Nietzsche transforms understanding in the sense of the contemplation of what requires clarification and expla-nation into interpretation in the sense of bestowing order and value onto a world that is itself a perturbation of Chaos. In so doing, he transforms the interpreter into an irrational agent of the necessity of Chaos. Everything comes down to this: for Heidegger's Nietzsche the only permanence or constancy is the permanence of impermanence. The eternal return of the same is the eternal return of perspectival sche-matizations of Chaos by Chaos. There is then no "presence" in the Platonic sense as understood by Heidegger himself, but only *absence.* Or as one could also put it, presence in Heidegger's Nietzsche is the present absenting itself. One has the feeling that Heidegger's attempt to transform Nietzsche into the last of the Platonists is undercut by an equally strong tendency to see himself in Nietzsche.[116]

To come back now to the fable of the true world, in the first stage, Nietzsche says that the true world is a paraphrase of the statement "I, Plato, am the truth." Heidegger comments,

> Here the "true world" is not yet "Platonist" [*Platonisches*], i.e. not yet unachievable, not yet merely wished for, no mere "Ideal." Plato himself is who he is on the strength of this, that he unquestioningly and straightforwardly acts out of this world of Ideas as the nature [*Wesen*] of Being. The supersensible is *idea.* ... The thinking of the Ideas and the interpretation of Being attached to it are in themselves and out of themselves creative. Plato's work is not yet Platonism. The "true world" is not object of a doctrine, but the power of *Dasein,* that which illuminates by approaching [*das leuchtend Anwesende*], the pure shining without concealment.[117]

Heidegger's commentary is not exegetical in the sense of traditional philological scholarship. He is explaining Nietzsche's text on the basis of his own retrieval of what was left unthought, first by Plato and then by Nietzsche. Plato is considered not as the author of the dialogues from which is derived the "Platonist" doctrine of Ideas, but as actor rather than thinker, that is to say, as one whose thought is an active appropriation of the original gift of Being as *phusis,* namely, as the shining forth of that which discloses itself as present. "Das leuchtend Anwesende" here refers to the Idea, the look taken on by that which approaches, not to the process of approaching or presencing (in Heidegger's idiom). Plato as it were does not so much receive the gift of Being as bend it to his will, stamp it with the imprint of his perspective. Plato is presented as the creator of the perspective of Platonism rather than as its teacher. In this portrait, Heidegger changes Nietzsche's emphasis upon the wise man as pious and virtuous to an emphasis upon virtue as the production of a world through the "power of existence" or (as one may gloss this expression) the concentration of power within a perspective that is employed in the schematization of Chaos.

Nietzsche himself says nothing of the doctrine of Ideas, and he does not refer to "the shining of presencing." His statement is not metaphysical or ontological but moral; that is to say, it is an application of his thesis that each world-producing perspective is the expression of a rank-ordering or table of values. From this standpoint, when

Plato says, "I, Plato, am the truth," he is referring to the values, the *aretai* which he himself exemplifies and which he imposes onto his disciples as definitory of the way of life which constitutes "the true world" for those who can live in it. Perhaps Nietzsche is thinking of passages like the one in the *Republic* in which Socrates alludes to the city he is constructing with his young interlocutors as "a paradigm we have made in *logos* of a good city." It is the nature of things that *praksis* can get hold of truth less than *leksis*.[118] At the end of book 9, Socrates refers to the city in speech as a paradigm laid up in heaven for those who wish to see and dwell in it.[119] But this paradigm is not an Idea in the Heideggerian sense. It is not even a hypothesis in the sense of the *Phaedo* but "that which is wished for" (*tōi boulo-menōi*) by the "virtuous."

If one objects that the so-called just city cannot exist unless it is ruled by philosophers who practice dialectic, or the knowledge of the Ideas, the reply is that Nietzsche's silence on this point is supported by no less an authority than Aristotle, who, in summarizing the argument of the *Republic* in his *Politics*,[120] omits all mention of the central philosophical discussion, and so too of the doctrine of the Ideas. The philosophical views of the philosopher-kings are not a part of the political content of the *Republic;* Socrates himself refers to them as a "digression."[121] One way in which to understand this is that it hardly matters for the coming into existence of the city whether there exist Ideas or not, and so whether a science of dialectic is possible or not. All that is necessary is that the philosophers tell a noble lie to the effect that the Ideas do in fact exist and that their superiority as rulers is based upon their mastery of dialectic, now understood as rhetoric. Who in the city, given the education to which all are subjected from birth, will be in a position to contradict them?

In order to understand Nietzsche's text, which is brief but explicit, it is not necessary to adopt this radical hypothesis. Suffice it to say that Nietzsche treats the "true world" as an existential or ethico-political expression of Plato's will. If it is necessary or desirable to inculcate a belief in the hypothesis of the Ideas in order to strengthen the authority of the Platonist philosopher-kings, so be it. Note that this is entirely in accord with Nietzsche's previously cited assertion, according to which the schematizing of Chaos is carried out on the basis of "practical needs."[122] It is also in accord with Nietzsche's explanation of his task: to transform mankind via a new code of values[123] and thereby to enable man to master the great crisis of nihilism, a struggle that Nietzsche expounds and that is the history of the next two hundred years.[124]

Heidegger is no doubt correct in calling to our attention Nietzsche's conviction, mentioned for example in a letter to Carl Fuchs, that his work up to this point (approximately 1887) was a concluded stage in his life: "my total 'up to now' to be regarded as finished [*ad acta zu legen*]."[125] One week later Nietzsche writes to Carl von Gersdorff, "In a significant sense my life is at present in the fullness of midday: a door closes; another opens."[126] But the anticipated transvaluation of values is never detached from its "practical" or (in the Platonic sense) political dimension. The mastery of nihilism no more depends upon a doctrine of Being than does the establishment of the Platonic city upon the doctrine of Ideas. In both cases, what is required is the proper rhetoric. It is no doubt an oversimplification, but it surely points us in the right direction to say that Plato's rhetoric is designed to persuade his readers that they are philosophers, whereas Nietzsche's rhetoric is designed to persuade his readers that they are supermen or mouthpieces of prophets, if not themselves prophets, of new values.

I have lingered over the first stage of Nietzsche's fable in order to strengthen my account of the essence of Heidegger's interpretation of Nietzsche's Platonism. In order to preserve the force of the reference to reversed Platonism, Heidegger is required to "rationalize" Chaos or to invest it with metaphysical significance. But this in turn obliterates the difference between *Schein*, or human illusion, and the inner order of Becoming. The net result of Heidegger's interpretation is as it were to transform Nietzsche into Hegel. In fact, however, Nietzsche rejects the Hegelian thesis of an inner identity of *Schein* and *Wesen*. The absence of an ontological essence, together with the manifest intelligibility of the world as a self-producing (and so lawless or ungrounded) work of art, and so the manifest validity of the rank-ordering of human types and by extension of worlds, requires that we transfer the principles of order from Chaos into the illusion. Chaos is at most a negative condition of human freedom: it produces us haphazardly, but it is indifferent to our attempts to master what it has produced. Nietzsche is a dualist of *Schein* and *Wesen*; there can be no dialectical resolution of these two terms because necessity is unreasonable.

In sum, in the text under scrutiny, Nietzsche treats Plato as a Nietzschean, whereas Heidegger in his commentary treats Nietzsche as a Heideggerian. I turn now to the second stage of Nietzsche's "history of an error" (the subtitle to the passage). The first sentence reads, "The true world, unachievable for now, but promised to the wise, the pious, the virtuous ('for the sinners who atone')." In his parenthetical commentary, Nietzsche makes his meaning clear: the thesis of the true world "becomes finer, more insidious, more difficult to fix,—it becomes Woman, it becomes christian." We may think here of Nietzsche's famous remark that Christianity is Platonism for the folk.[127] But this does not mean that Christianity is a revised and popular version of the doctrine of Ideas. Nietzsche refers to the extension of accessibility to the true world of the virtuous to the believing Christian. Platonism in both its original form and this one is understood as a way of life, not a doctrine of Being.

In his commentary on this stage, Heidegger emphasizes the separation between the supersensible and the sensible; as a consequence, "in the essence and existence of mankind enters brokenness [*die Gebrochenheit*; cf. Hegel's *Zerrisenheit*], which at the same time permits ambiguity. The possibility of Yes and No, of 'as well as' begins."[128] This is helpful and to the point; but the point is blurred by the subsequent assertion: "Instead of Plato, Platonism now dominates." Heidegger explains this to mean that "the supersensible is no longer within the circumference of human existence and accessible [*anwesend*] to it as sensible"; the result is the split between the beyond (*Jenseits*) and the here and now (*Diesseitigen*). Heidegger implies that Platonism removes *Anwesenheit* entirely from this world to the next; he thus underlines Nietzsche's own distinction between Plato and all of Platonism.[129] But in this case, Plato must make no such distinction; accordingly the supersensible, by which Heidegger presumably means the Ideas, is accessible in this world, within everyday life. In stage 1, however, this accessibility was reserved for Plato himself and, by extension, for his philosophical disciples. In general, Heidegger takes the main point of this stage to concern human existence, not metaphysics, and to that extent his remarks deviate (for the better) from the ontological reading of the first stage.

I can give greater precision to Heidegger's approach by examining

Reversed Platonism

Nietzsche's central metaphor in stage 2. The shift from Plato to Christ, or the origin of Platonism, is equivalent to the transformation of the true world into a woman. Woman is "finer" and "more insidious" than man; in other words, Christian Platonism shifts from the warrior-philosopher to the family or private person: from the city to the hearth. This is a shift from what Plato calls the intellect and spiritedness to desire. In language closer to Nietzsche's, the shift is to the feelings and intuitions, to the "small perceptions" of everyday life. The ruling and active element of Platonism is replaced by the obedient and so passive element. The soul is subjected to the dissemination of a hypersensitivity to the nuances of personal existence that both refines and weakens it. The philosophical justice of Platonism is replaced by the effeminate compassion of Christianity: the shift in weight is from the few to the many. The refinement of female sensibility is thus the precursor of decadence.

Stage 3: "The true world, unachievable, unprovable, unspeakable, but already as thought a consolation, an obligation, an imperative." Nietzsche is thinking here primarily of Kant, as the parenthetical reference to "pale, nordic, königsbergish" makes plain. Heidegger of course recognizes this and comments accordingly. But a problem arises at this point. If Nietzsche's text contains an encapsulated history of metaphysics, what has happened to the seventeenth century? Heidegger normally places great emphasis upon Descartes and Leibniz in his analysis of the transformations of Platonism within the origins of modernity. But this analysis treats them fundamentally as thinkers of subjectivity, and so as stages toward the emergence of Kant as well as of German Idealism. Stated very broadly, Heidegger interprets the rise of modern science, at least in the pathbreaking work of the great philosophical thinkers, as a development of the subjective and reifying implications, as yet unthought by Plato, of the doctrine of Ideas. For him as for countless German academics, Descartes is primarily the thinker of the *ego cogitans;* the *cogito,* largely of interest to contemporary English-speaking scholars as a logical puzzle, is taken in the tradition which Heidegger both follows and stimulates as an anticipation or early ancestor of the Absolute Ego of Fichte and his immediate successors.

This approach is certainly not totally mistaken, and it is quite illuminating with respect to the development of the modern doctrine of subjectivity. But it hardly does justice to the origins of modernity or to the philosophical significance of modern science. To give only one example, I have argued elsewhere that the modern epoch, including its component of experimental science, has at least as much and perhaps fundamentally more to do with Plato's practico-productive doctrine of human activity as with his geometrical cosmology and emphasis upon mathematics as a propaedeutic to philosophy.[130] If this suggestion is sound, it lends further support to the claim that Nietzsche's Platonism is derived from the Platonic understanding of politics in the comprehensive sense of that term (what Nietzsche might call *die grosse Politik*) as a productive art. In Plato, there is no distinction between *praxis* and *poiēsis* (production); but there is a distinction between the practico-productive and the theoretical. By largely disregarding Plato's political thought, that is, his detailed interpretation of everyday human life; by detaching art from politics and linking it to the pursuit of theoretical truth and the Ideas; by reducing Eros to what could be called an ontological *nisus;* by insisting upon the ontological role of proto-subjectivity and perspectivism, Heidegger entirely distorts both Plato and Platonism. And this leads to his schematized, oversimplified, and unconvincing interpretation of the history of Western philosophy as metaphysical Platonism.

On the other hand, I agree with Heidegger that Kant was in many ways a Platonist. To spell this out in detail, however, would show that he was also an antiplatonist in a way that holds true of Plato himself.[131] I will add here only the following observation. The two Kantian worlds of the supersensible and the sensible are in the last analysis dimensions of thought (not of course of a self-conscious agent but of "the logical conditions for the possibility" of thinking a world like ours by beings like us). This dualism is the starting point for Hegel, and Hegel's articulation remains valid in Nietzsche, in however camouflaged a form. The eternal return of the same is Nietzsche's (no doubt unintended or "unthought") version of Hegel's circularity of the Concept, just as his will to power is his version of Hegel's *Bewegtheit,* or the negative albeit thereby productive excitation of Spirit. When Zarathustra says that to create is also to destroy, he is speaking like a Hegelian, although he does not carry through the tendency.

The modern philosopher-scientist transforms the Platonic war against human nature into war against cosmic or divine nature. In so doing, he reasserts masculine will to power over feminine refinement and insidiousness. Not only is the doctrine of the soul simplified and coarsened, but the soul is subordinated and eventually reduced to the body. Nietzsche attempts to unite feminine subtlety with masculine power, or in other words he attempts to preserve the doctrine of the hypersensitive soul even while interpreting the soul in physiological or materialist terms. The Platonic form, so to speak, of Nietzsche's *grosse Politik* is filled up with matter concocted from a synthesis of Christian spirituality and modern scientific brutality.

Nietzsche's failure to refer in the fable text to the seventeenth century, but also to British empiricism and in particular to Hobbes, who intersects the two spheres of scientific and empiricist philosophy, makes it impossible, even on Heideggerian grounds, to take seriously Heidegger's excessive praise for the fragment. I do not of course mean to deny that the fable is extraordinarily suggestive or that it tells us something true and important about the course of the history of philosophy. But it can hardly be regarded as the "great moment" that casts a new light on the whole domain of Nietzsche's thought;[132] or if it can, then it shows us the limitations of that domain. At the same time, Heidegger's response to the text shows us very well the limitations of his own understanding of Platonism as well as the ambiguous nature of his shift from referring to "Platonism" as a sketch of Plato's thought to regarding it as something quite distinct from that thought.

Stage 4 of Nietzsche's fable describes, as Heidegger puts it, the positivist consequences of Kant's denial that the supersensible is theoretically knowable.[133] Heidegger's commentary is quite interesting, but it leaves vague to the point of invisibility the connection with Platonism. The first sentence of the commentary reads as follows: "With this fourth section the *Gestalt* of Platonism is held onto historically, in that this abandons itself as a consequence of the previous Kantian philosophy, but without an original creative overcoming."[134] Perhaps this means that Platonism is present in the positivist consequences of the return to Kant following the death of Hegel, which in turn leads to the scientific Kantianism of the Marburg School (one thinks of Hermann Cohen and Paul Natorp); but Heidegger speaks instead of the pejorative reading given by Nietzsche to the great German thinkers from Leibniz to Schopenhauer. Nietzsche refers to these thinkers as *Schleiermacher,* that is, those who veil over things, in contrast to the Kantian denial of the knowability of the supersensible, which is the first dawning of honesty.

I find both Nietzsche's characterization of this period and Heidegger's analysis excessively opaque.

To mention only the critical point: the Neo-Kantians, as Heidegger of course knew very well, transformed the Platonic Ideas into Kantian concepts or discursive rules; in so doing, they anticipated and prepared the way for the British school of "predicationalists." To the extent that this has anything to do with Plato, it amounts to an interpretation of *logos,* as employed in the *Phaedo* passage we have already studied, as a discursive theory, whether transcendental or historico-empirical. One could say the same about many if not all of those whom Nietzsche refers to as "veil-weavers." We would have to distinguish the "Platonism" of the Neo-Kantian precursors to phenomenology from that of positivists in a sense closer to Comte, and of both from thinkers like Feuerbach and Marx. Some of these thinkers seem to fall into Nietzsche's fifth stage, in which the true world is rejected as no more binding or useful. Perhaps the best policy is to drop the strictly chronological approach to the fable and regard steps 4 and 5 as two different sides of the second half of the nineteenth century. In this epoch, thanks on the one hand to Kant's denial that the supersensible world is knowable, and on the other to the veil-weaving obscurantism of the German metaphysicians (apparently including Kant), the true world gradually loses its grip on the philosophical imagination and is finally repudiated altogether.

The nineteenth century is a baroque mixture of Idealist metaphysics, Romanticism, antimetaphysical and even antiphilosophical revolution, positivism, phenomenology—and of course, Nietzsche himself. It would be interesting to attempt to determine the sense in which each of these movements or tendencies is an expression, or contains elements, of Platonism. One could certainly infer from Nietzsche's text that the history of Platonism is a history of the gradual dilution and eventual disappearance of the doctrine of Ideas or the transformation of the supersensible world into the structure, transcendental or immanent, of the sensible world. But Nietzsche does not put the point in this way; he concentrates on the practical consequences of the evaporation of the Platonic projection of the accessibility of the true world as a place within which human beings can dwell. This evaporation coincides with the coming of the conditions that prepare Nietzsche himself and that he celebrates in *Human, All Too Human.* The fable reads, "Bright day;

Breakfast; return of *bon sens* and of serenity; Plato's blush; devil's cry of all free spirits"; this seems to describe the repudiation of Platonism in favor of a quasi-positivist, quasi-Voltairean liberation from metaphysics.

Heidegger rightly connects this fifth stage with Nietzsche's early development.[135] He also calls our attention to the fact that the "true world" is rejected "because it has become useless, superfluous." We must ourselves remember that even the late Nietzsche explains world-construction, or the schematizing of Chaos, as for the sake of practical needs. Heidegger does not make that point here; instead, he goes on to say, "Platonism is overcome insofar as the supersensible world as the true world has been abolished." But: "Despite the rejection of the supersensible world as the true world, there remains the empty space of this 'upper' [*Oberen*] and a building-sketch of an above and a below: Platonism."[136] The supersensible world has been rejected; but the retention of the sensible world as the true world remains within the circumference of Platonism because the truth of the world must still be distinguished from its sensibility. Differently stated, if the sensible world is the true world, then there is exactly one world: this one, which accordingly possesses or exhibits the structure of truth. There must be a "place" for that truth; but it is at the moment empty.

This is clearly implied by Nietzsche's formulation of the sixth stage: "We have abolished the true world: which world remains? the apparent [*scheinbare*] perhaps?...But no! *with the true world, we have also abolished the apparent world!* (Midday; moment of the shortest shadow; end of the longest error; highpoint of mankind; INCIPIT ZARATHUSTRA." The entrance of Zarathustra onto the stage of world history coincides with the repudiation of the "apparent" world in the sense of the residue of the "true" world. Heidegger refers to these two sides of what is at bottom the same world as "supersensible" and "sensible" because this makes it easier for him to connect the worlds to the Ideas, understood as genuine or true *Schein* and its associated sensuous illusion, or *Erscheinung*. For Nietzsche, however, "true" means "worthy of human habitation," according to Heidegger. The apparent world is the shadow of the true world because it prevents us from creating new worlds or from conceptualizing human existence as perpetual overcoming or decline. Nietzsche must then certainly reject the doctrine of the Ideas because they are the basis for the permanence of the structure of the given or everyday world, which is itself the presupposition for the world of traditional Platonism. He rejects them, however, not because they are false, but because they are useless.

"Falsehood" is from the present standpoint not a criterion for rejection; Nietzsche's own doctrines are also false or works of art. There is no true world because there is no truth about the world, other than the truth of practical necessity, namely, the necessity to invigorate the human race and to preserve it from nihilism. On the other hand, I entirely agree with Heidegger that for Nietzsche "at the end of Platonism stands the decision about the transformation of mankind."[137] I have been arguing throughout that this decision is practical or political, not in the usual senses of these words, but in keeping with the understanding of the philosopher as a prophet and lawgiver.[138] New laws or, as Nietzsche most frequently calls them, new values make a new breed of human being. Nietzsche's relatively early statement (1872/73) on the relation between philosophy and art continues to hold true throughout his mature thought and writings: "The philosopher ought to *know what is needed;* and the artist ought to *make* it."[139] This is Nietzsche's Platonism.

But it is also the heart of Plato's Platonism, and not its reversal. One must also question the thesis, attributed by Heidegger to Nietzsche but apparently accepted by him as well, that Platonism, as distinguished from Plato, rejects the sensible or apparent world. Would it not be more accurate to say that Platonism, for example in the case of Christianity, transfigures the sensible or apparent world, or in other words that Hegel is right to see in the figure of Christ the entrance of the Absolute into history, albeit in a still dualistic form, rather than the rejection of the sensible on behalf of the supersensible? In commenting on the fable text as a whole, Heidegger says, "Through the abolition of the sensible world the way is first opened for the affirmation of the sensible, and with it also the non-sensible world of spirit."[140] But it seems to me to be equally or more plausible to maintain that the destruction of the sensible world, which is a historical if not logical consequence of the destruction of the supersensible world, leads to the dissolution of the sensible into a *Gewühl* of sensations, and of the spiritual world into the kingdom of darkness, otherwise known as difference.

It would, says Heidegger, be a mere reversal of Platonism to give the sensible a higher rank than the supersensible. What Nietzsche requires is a new schema of rank-ordering that transforms the reversal of Platonism into its "switching off" (*Herausdrehen*). In the following chapters, I shall have to investigate, with Heidegger, the degree to which Nietzsche succeeds in this task. By way of a conclusion to this chapter, I suggest that Heidegger fails to articulate coherently and convincingly the difference on the one hand between Plato and Platonism and on the other between Nietzsche and Plato. The first failure leads to the transformation of the Ideas into a quasi-Aristotelian doctrine of being qua being. The second failure obscures the significance of "practical needs." In the case of Plato, the emphasis upon practical needs is in no way a denigration of theory; it rather reminds us of what Heidegger himself has often stated, namely, that theory is the highest form of practice. To theorize is to contemplate not some other world, but rather the nature of this world. In the case of Nietzsche, one cannot contemplate "this world" but only the residue of previous exertions of the will to power (or what contemporary philosophers of science call background theories). The philosopher is thus free to disregard the detritus of the past and so to return to the first stage of the fable by saying, "I, Nietzsche, am the truth."

The Spider and the Fly

For Heidegger, then, Platonism is fundamentally the doctrine of Ideas, understood in a quasi-Aristotelian sense as essences; as such, they are prototypes of the science of being qua being, and they underlie Heidegger's account of Western metaphysics as nihilism: "The essence of nihilism is the history in which no account is taken of Being."[1] In order to prepare for a consideration of Heidegger, I first attempted to understand the thinking that underlay Socrates' hypothesis of the Ideas. This investigation may be summarized in two points: (1) the copresence of presence and absence cannot be understood as a unified event or process in its own terms, that is, in terms derived not from what eventuates, occurs, or shows itself, but from eventuation, occurrence, and showing themselves. The attempt to speak of the lighting process leads to blindness, just as does looking directly into the sun. (2) We cannot, however, rectify the situation by turning directly to *ta onta,* or beings that show themselves; this is simply another way of attempting to view Being understood as the lighting process. The beings, viewed directly, are neither things nor "essences" (*ousiai*) but fluctuations in genesis. Physics, whether in its ancient or its modern form, reduces human life to illusion. Differently stated, even physics, as an *epistēmē*, requires measurement, which in turn is rooted in ratios of change; and these ratios must be captured by *logos*. Everything then turns upon the ontological status of *logos*.

This last point requires expansion. I shall begin with the distinction between deeds and speeches. We apprehend the fluctuations of genesis through our acts and our speeches. To act is to carry out an intention; to intend is already to qualify (one could even say "schematize") our prediscursive awareness of everydayness. By acting, we enter the domain of discursive thinking; and even if the two could be separated, intentionality would have the same consequences as discursive thinking, namely, the reification of genesis or the division of the seamless web of everyday life into units, whether events, things, or abstractions. In deeds and speeches, the web is preserved; but it is *articulated*. And this occurs as we move about the strands of the web, whether as a spider who has secreted these strands in the function of intentionality or as a being who has been thrust into the web, perhaps like the fly who is the initially unsuspecting quarry of the approaching spider.

No doubt the metaphor is inexact, but it does no harm, and it is illuminating, to conceive in a preliminary way of the fundamental philosophical distinction in terms of the spider and the fly. We must decide whether we have ourselves made the web or whether we fall into it. On the other hand, *both may be true:* we may be both the spider and the fly. In a more appetizing metaphor, the web of the everyday may be both acquired and produced by our perceptual and cognitive activity. This is crucial because it bears upon the question of the difference between theory and interpretation, or in other words on the truth of Nietzsche's injunction to speak of *Welt-Auslegung* rather than of *Welt-Erklärung*.

To connect this observation to my previous line of thought, the web is not itself given to us, whether from ourselves or through its own agency, as a lighting process. It is given as a web of fluctuations, to repeat the previous expression; that is to say, once we turn reflectively away from our everyday activity within the web to contemplate it, either as a whole or with respect to some particular section, the web resolves itself into events and things, the nodal points of our deeds and speeches. But when we focus our vision further on the nodal points and attempt to see them directly, as they are or show themselves rather than as we encounter and experience them, we detach them from the everyday, without detaching them from the web.

The web is now viewed not as the everyday, but as genesis, as *phusis,* or natural processes. We are therefore required to turn our gaze away from *ta onta* toward a reflective attempt to grasp not *phusis* as a comprehensive process, but the *phusis* of the being or beings with which we are concerned. This is what Socrates calls the turn to *logos,* which is the intermediate stage of his hypothesis of the Ideas. And this is the critical moment. Socrates maintains that the look made accessible within *logos* is the same as the look within the beings themselves. By this, of course, he means that the look is in both cases not a projection of human will, perception, or discursivity, but that which underlies, grounds, and thus opens the volitions, perceptions, and linguistic constructions that we generate with respect to that look. The most difficult aspect of this line of thought is the relation between the look (*idea*) and the perceptual shape (*morphē*) or image (*fantasma*). Socrates (or Plato) must contend that the look is accessible within, yet distinct from, the shape or image.

In other words, one cannot discriminate between theory and interpretation, between a viewing of the genuine looks of beings and the projection of perspectival constructions, unless we take everyday experience as regulative in the following sense. No hypothesis is secure or healthy if it contradicts everyday life or empties it of its significance and value by treating it as an illusion, beneath which there lies a true or genuine structure, such as the primary attributes of modern materialism, the equations of mathematical physics, the ontological categories of metaphysics, or the poetical constructions of postmetaphysics. I will give a familiar example of what this means. The shape or image of a cow is certainly relative to the nature of our perceptual organs; this image is accordingly a construction or interpretation (see the previously discussed account of perception in the *Philebus*). But the construction is also a function of the nature of the cow, not as relative to our perceptual organs, but in itself, as an *on ontōs on*, and the cow in this sense regulates our perceptual and discursive interpretations of it.

This regulatory process, however, is not carried out through some metaempirical cognition process of otherworldly Ideas; on the contrary, it is carried out within everyday life, from which there is in fact no escape. We carry out the regulatory process ourselves by attempting to explain the totality of our experience in a coherent, comprehensive manner. It is this attempt that constitutes the history of Western philosophy: the search for hypotheses by way of *logos*. The history of philosophy, contrary to Heidegger, never ends because there is no way in which to determine conclusively which hypothesis is the best. In order to do so, we would have to be able to step outside the totality of our experience or become a Hyperborean in an unqualified sense. In Heidegger's language, we would have to assume the standpoint of the origin; but this standpoint is no longer that of human existence, and it provides us with no regulatory assistance of any kind. Whether or not there is an origin, then, there is confirmation neither of Platonism, that is, of actual as opposed to illusory Platonism, nor of Kantianism or any other competent hypothesis. Philosophy never ends; instead, philosophers fail to appear or are not recognized, thanks to the general fatigue induced by the endlessness of the enterprise.

The renewal of Platonism is then not to be understood as a thoughtless reinstitution of some ancient orthodoxy; the renewal of Platonism is equivalent to the renewal of philosophy, not because Platonism is identical with all philosophical hypotheses, but because it is the attempt to account for the whole. To this extent, one can agree with Heidegger: if philosophy is thinking the whole, then the history of Western philosophy is Platonism. Heidegger's attempt to distinguish the thinking of the whole from the thinking of the origin is then not philosophy but theology; or rather, it is the attempt to replace *logos* with a new kind of thinking that conforms to the nonontic nature of the origin. Everything comes down to the question of whether such a thinking is possible and, if possible, whether it is desirable.

For the Platonist, this much is certain. We cannot begin with a pursuit of the origin. Such a pursuit deprives us of our bearings; it empties life of significance rather than enriching or illuminating it. Even the pursuit of the origin is an example of our actual beginning: the attempt to act for the best. Things may be an ever-changing congeries of what Nietzsche calls "points of force" or, in Heideggerian language, gifts of the originary Being-process. But in each of the various situations that arise from the encounters between humans and the beings of everyday life, there is something to be done, some decision to be reached, some line of action to take, some view to hold; and this means that there is a choice, however difficult to make, between better and worse. This is the point of contact between Socrates' story in the *Phaedo* and the reference to the Good, sometimes called the Idea of the Good, in the *Republic*. As the structure of the *Republic* makes clear, however, there must be an ascent from the needs of everyday life to the dialectical exercises, themselves preceded by mathematical purification, culminating in a vision of the Good. And even if this is an exoteric or political description of philosophy, contemplation of the Good is in terms of and with respect to the Ideas and, in that way, the wholeness of life. I shall consider this point more extensively in the next section.

Actual or genuine Platonism thus requires us to account for the distinction between better and worse hypotheses concerning all aspects of our lives. This in turn requires the preservation of everyday life, not the

The *Seinsfrage*

nihilistic reduction of everyday life to illusion. I should add here that, as I have already shown, there is another aspect to Nietzsche's thinking which coincides with genuine Platonism, a side that has little if anything to do with Heidegger's views on the difference between Being and the being of beings. This emerged from our examination of Heidegger's interpretation of Nietzsche's remark that his philosophy is reversed Platonism.

Nietzsche agrees with Plato concerning the central importance of the quarrel between philosophy and poetry, a quarrel, incidentally, which Heidegger almost accepts and yet obscures when he says that "all philosophical thinking and indeed the strictest and most prosaic is in itself poetic [*dichterisch*] and nevertheless never poetry [*Dichtkunst*]."[2] What Heidegger does not give sufficient weight is that just as this quarrel is based upon a prior agreement, so too are Plato and Nietzsche in agreement. I have already cited Nietzsche's remark that the philosopher determines what ought to be done, that is, what is best; the poet does it. Nietzsche is not at odds with Plato concerning the general nature of the best, but he sharply disagrees as to the nature of the hypothesis that is required to ensure the preservation of the best. Some of the substantive differences between Nietzsche and Plato are of course due to the different historical periods in which each lived. The decadence to which each is a response differs in content; but more important than this, I believe, is that the two thinkers differ on how to respond to decadence.

One last retrospective remark. The reader may be tempted to defend Nietzsche's doctrine of perspectivism on the grounds that there is no uniform or coherent pretheoretical understanding of everyday life. It is my contention that such a doctrine is in fact Platonic. But Plato draws quite different conclusions from this doctrine than does Nietzsche. I have emphasized, here and elsewhere, that Plato acknowledges the perspectival nature of human existence, and so the multiple interpretations of everyday life. There is of course no uniform or coherent pretheoretical understanding of everyday life; such an understanding would be a *theoretical* one, a *logos* or attempt to provide a basis for the adjudication of perspectives. This basis is for Plato the visibility of better and worse in human activity, not in a sense that requires ontological grounding but which provides the horizon, and so the limits, of ontological speculation. One can of course press the objection by insisting that "better" and "worse" are themselves perspectives or interpretations. To this, the only reply is to engage the objector in conversation in order to determine whether the objection itself conforms with our common experience as well as whether it is internally coherent.

And this is why Plato wrote dialogues: the origins are not subject to demonstration precisely because they originate demonstration. As Heidegger himself puts it, "The sayable word receives its determination out of the unsayable."[3] In listening to the speeches of the promulgators of radical perspectivism, we "see" what they are talking about; this is the first step in the refutation of radical perspectivism. It is also the link between speech and vision as mediated by *logos*. We can understand others only by sharing their perspective, by seeing things from their standpoint and thereby determining if what they see coincides with what we see. On many points, common experience will be enough to decide who is correct. But on many points it will not; and on some points, possibly the most important of all, there is no common experience. It is at this juncture that philosophy must supplement *logos* with poetic rhetoric.

So much for what has been considered thus far. In this chapter, I want to analyze the major step that leads to Heidegger's posing of the question of Being, namely, Kant's assertion that being is not a predicate and Husserl's development of that assertion. This will complement the discussion in chapter 1 of Heidegger's Aristotelian conception of Platonism. In the first chapter, we saw how Heidegger arrived at his understanding of the metaphysical approach to Being, namely, not as Being but as the being of beings. In this chapter, I shall study the crucial presupposition of the thesis of the ontological difference. This will be preparation to turn in chapter 6 to Heidegger's interpretation of the central doctrines of Nietzsche's reversed Platonism, doctrines in which Heidegger contends we are to find the culmination of metaphysics.

The Forgetting of Being

The simplest way in which to formulate Heidegger's central thesis is to say that, for him, the original manifestation of Being has been neglected or concealed, not merely by the negligence of Plato and the Platonists, but through a certain inevitable consequence of the nature of the manifestation itself. I find an ambiguity in this thesis, since it is never clear whether Plato's "fall" was necessitated by the veiling-over of Being through beings, or whether this fall might not have been averted through adherence to the doctrine of the pre-Socratic thinkers. Was the history of metaphysics necessary or contingent? Is Heidegger a quasi-Hegelian who maintains that it was required by the gift or gifts of Being itself that we move from error to error in the course of the devolution of Platonism? In this case, the "second coming" of the pre-Socratic revelation by Heidegger is presumably also necessitated, just as was Hegel's own concluding explanatory description of the totality of the manifestation of the Absolute.

The texts, especially but not exclusively those beginning with *Gelassenheit,* tend to support the interpretation of necessary "errance," that is, of a view of human error as fundamentally the "wandering" of Being. For example, the continuation of the text just cited concerning the unsayable reads as follows: "What is most the thinker's own is not his possession but the ownmost property of Being, the thrownness of which, thinking catches up in its project."[4] Again, in a passage that explains the genuine meaning of the term *Auseinandersetzung,* Heidegger says, "*Aus-einander-setzung* does not mean for us: a 'polemic' that knows better and idle 'critique.' *Aus-einander-setzung* means here reflection on the truth that is ready for a decision, a decision that is not made by us but rather is reached by the history of Being from within itself and falls into our history."[5]

On the other hand, although Heidegger speaks of the possibility of "another beginning," he is very far from guaranteeing that it will be made. As a representative passage, I cite the following:

> With this completion of the world-epoch of metaphysics [in Nietzsche] there defines itself at the same time in the distance [*in der Ferne*] a fundamental historical stance which, after the decision of that struggle [predicted by Nietzsche] concerning power over the earth itself, can no longer open and sustain the domain of a struggle. The fundamental stance in which the world-epoch of western metaphysics completes itself, is thus embraced for its part in a conflict of a totally different nature. This conflict is no longer the struggle over the mastery of beings [*Seienden*]. This latter points itself out and guides itself today in an entirely "metaphysical" manner, but always without the essential mastery of metaphysics. The conflict is the placing-apart from one another [*Aus-einander-*

setzung] of the power of beings and the truth of Being. To prepare this separating confrontation is the farthest goal of the reflection attempted here.[6]

Heidegger goes on to assure us that this "farthest" is in fact "closest," provided that "historical man listens to Being and its truth," and so on; hardly an assertion of necessity. One is reminded of the debate within Marxism concerning the end of history and whether the arrival of the classless society is necessary or contingent upon human decisions. The situation is also closely parallel to the ambiguity in Nietzsche concerning the relation between the doctrine of the eternal return and the exoteric invocation to late-European man to overcome the present decadent stage of existence by an act of creative destruction. Neither in *Zarathustra* nor in Heidegger's preferred Notebooks of post-Zarathustran vintage is there any reason to take the doctrine of the eternal return as advocating the possibility of a freely or spontaneously initiated creative revolution and coordinate transformation of human nature. I will look more closely in a subsequent section at the doctrine of eternal return. For the moment, I emphasize a fluctuation in Heidegger concerning the relation between man and Being.

If human beings are free to reject Heidegger's message, and it very much seems as if they are, then the attempt to place full or major responsibility for "errant" philosophical doctrines on Being itself loses much of its force. On the other hand, if Being dictates the course of human history, which is then not open to preparations for another beginning, we may be listed for a thousand-year-long engagement of the last men or, in Heidegger's terms, of the triumph of metaphysics as technology. In other words, either Being works its way on mortals, or else the history of Western philosophy is made up of a contingent series of interpretations. If we can take another path tomorrow, why could we not have taken it yesterday? In the former case, Heidegger is a mere mouthpiece for the current indeterminate period, a kind of *entr'acte* between what may be two acts of the world-epoch of metaphysics or a genuine pause before the initiation of the other beginning. In the latter case, his account of Being as a process of gift-giving is radically defective and perhaps even untenable.

By attributing the history of Being to an origin of which we are the consequence, Heidegger in effect identifies the errance of thinking with

The *Seinsfrage*

183

the errance of Being. As we shall see soon, this is also the doctrine he attributes to Nietzsche by insisting that the will to power and the eternal return say "the same." But Heidegger does not claim, as does Hegel, that the sameness of thinking and being is categorial. In Nietzsche's terms, the inner necessity of Being and hence too of world-projection or thinking is chaotic. The necessity of Chaos is not accessible to *logos* or *ratio;* in particular, we cannot predict what will come next. Philosophy, so to speak, is neither deductive nor inductive reasoning, but the prophetic play of possibilities.

But this formulation of the difficulty is only prefatory; the real problem concerns the intrinsic intelligibility of the attempt to think Being apart from beings, as must be attempted, given Heidegger's rejection of the Hegelian dialectico-speculative logic. In other words: how can we think Being apart from the *errance* of Being, that is, apart from the gifts of the Being-process, of which the most fundamental is thinking itself? I want to turn now to this problem. In the various Heideggerian analyses, the core of the matter is as follows. There are three elements or dimensions to be considered: (1) particular things like a piece of chalk, a blackboard, a tree, a stone, a star; (2) the being that is common to all of these things and that is exhibited in the verb "is" when we state that "this is a piece of chalk," "this is a tree," and so on; (3) the Being that presents us with things and so too with the common attributes or categorial structure by which we define the being of those things. Being in sense (3) is a process of making manifest, and so it is neither a thing nor the being of a thing. We have encountered the distinction between senses (3) and (2) previously in the distinction between "presencing" and that which presents itself as a consequence of the emergence-process. This is the distinction between *phusis* as process of emergence and *phusis* as *ousia, eidos,* or *on ontōs on.*

One could say that the investigation of the nature of items in the first group is carried out by the arts and crafts, which eventually evolve into the natural sciences. The being of the second dimension is studied by metaphysics, together with its offspring, logic. But the third dimension or sense is ignored by those whose attention is directed to the first and second dimensions. Why do we require the supplement of the third dimension? If the membership criterion for the first dimension is wide enough, we can classify not only things but events, powers, virtues, relations, and whatever is identifiable as a being of a particular kind.

Reversed Platonism

As a result, our categorial table will need to be sufficiently wide to include every property which must be present in order for anything whatsoever to exist, that is, to count as a being.

But a table of categories, even if adequate to its task, is a list of universal thing-predicates. As such, it has two deficiencies. We have noticed these difficulties before, but I want to restate them now from a Heideggerian perspective. First, a table of categories tells us what must be owned in order for the owner to count as a being; but it does not tell us what (or who) the owner is. If we try to rectify this omission by distinguishing between essential and accidental predicates, the problem arises again when we are asked to explain the criterion for the distinction. But obviously it is impossible to identify essential predicates, that is, those which ostensibly define the owner, unless one knows the owner independently of the essential predicates. If it is objected that there is no owner apart from the essential predicates, the reply is that the being of the essence must then be a pattern or way of being-together of the essential properties designated by the predicates, and this "pattern" or "way of being-together" is not itself a property that can be stated in predicative assertions: a set is not a member of itself. Second, categories define things, but the process by which things emerge into view is not itself a thing; hence the categories do not apply to, but are a second-level consequence of, that process.

The inner connection between these two deficiencies, when viewed from a Heideggerian perspective, is as follows. Until we can identify the owner of a set of properties, we must disregard the distinction between accidental and essential predicates. The mere listing of predicates, or names of properties that are normally found together, tells us nothing of the *being* that underlies that togetherness and transforms it from an empirical collocation into a unity and an identity, the former of which marks out the togetherness as constituting a being and the latter of which answers the question What is that being? We can identify dogs and cats empirically by observing the presence of a collocation of properties to which the name "dog" or "cat" is traditionally assigned. But we cannot state why or how the collocation succeeds in manifesting a dog or a cat, as the case may be, but not both, as in some random alternation of identities, and not something totally other, such as a giraffe or an aardvark (to restrict ourselves to other animals).

Our concentration upon dog-predicates or cat-predicates turns our attention away from the question of the being of the dog or cat in the sense just defined. At this point, a distinction is required. If we follow the Platonic-Aristotelian mode of analysis, the attempt to resolve the problem of locating the owner of properties or the subject of predicates leads us to the Idea or species-form. But this seems to be a specious solution, since it amounts to the assertion that the being of the dog or the cat is the look of the dog or cat. If one asks, "Which look is that?" one is told nothing in particular, not even a list of predicates that are useful for empirical identification, since our problem is not empirical but (let us say) metaphysical. If we follow the Heideggerian mode of analysis, we are told that the search for an owner is a mistake, induced by our beginning from properties, which define things, and which themselves lead us to the attempt to define the being of things in thinglike terms. An owner, in other words, is on this analysis just a hyper-thing, a meta-physical entity or *on:* an *ousia, idea,* or *eidos.* A look is the look of a thing, not a process by which looks are presented as the look of this or that thing.

Recourse to the look, in other words, no more explains the being of the thing than does a list of its properties or predicates. The look is just the configuration of properties associated with something, say a dog or a cat. But what constitutes the look as look? How do looks become visible to the eye of the soul, and how for that matter does the eye of the soul come to open itself in the presence of looks? What is the being of the soul, and in particular its eye, which has no look but is rather the *topos eidōn,* the place of forms, to adopt an Aristotelian expression for our own uses? As Heidegger says with respect to Plato, *"The interpretation of Being as eidos, presence in outlook, presupposes the interpretation of truth as alētheia, undissimulatedness."*[7] If truth is true or genuine being, that is, the Idea, this depends upon the openness of the Idea in its presence to the eye of the soul. But what "opens" or presents the Idea or look to the eye of the soul is not the look itself, not, in other words, the being of beings, but the emergence of the look into the light.

In order to formulate the Heideggerian thesis, it eventually becomes necessary to distinguish between "looks" or beings as visible and the process by which looks come to be visible. Is this a legitimate distinction? The first step in our present investigation requires an extended remark about Plato. Although there is considerable variation in the discussion of the Ideas within the dialogues, they are almost always portrayed as eternal beings that subsist independently of divine genesis or human cognition. There are, so far as I know, only two apparent exceptions to this rule, and both occur in the *Republic*. We have already studied the first of these two cases, namely, the Idea of the bed, as introduced in book 10. This passage, as we saw in chapter 1, figures prominently in Heidegger's attribution to Plato of a theory of Being as production. Entirely apart, however, from all questions about the context of the reference to an Idea of an artifact (namely, as part of a criticism of poets and artisans, and so of human producers), the art attributed in book 10 to God is that of the gardener, not of a demiurge or handicraftsman. This being so, it is strictly speaking false to say that God produces Ideas in a way analogous to the production of artifacts by the craftsman. Instead, God, whatever Socrates may mean by this expression, assists nature in the growth or (as Heidegger might put it) "emergence-process" of the Ideas. In other words, God represents here an aspect of the process by which looks come to be visible, but not the process as independent of the looks themselves. God does not grant but assists in the manifestation of the visibility of the visible.

The second apparent exception to the general rule is much more difficult to assess. We find it in book 6 as part of Socrates' account of what is variously called the Good, the Good itself, the Idea of the Good, and the state or condition (*heksis:* 509a5) of the Good. The variability in terminology is appropriate in view of Socrates' insistence that he cannot develop the topic adequately under the present circumstances (506d6ff., 509c8ff.). Socrates also implies that he himself lacks secure knowledge of "what kind of thing it is," although he can "divine" that it exists (505e1–506a3; a4–8). Heidegger is of course only one of countless interpreters of Plato who have disregarded Socrates' warnings in the attempt to discern in this text the highest principle of Plato's theoretical teaching. It is a mark of the striking force of the image of the sun that we normally forget its uniqueness. Nowhere else in the Platonic dialogues is there a reference to the Idea of the Good. The tradition according to which Plato announced a lecture on the Good and baffled his audience by speaking about geometry underlines the problematic status of this doctrine, if it is a doctrine.

Rather than to assume that we know or can readily determine exactly what Plato intended by the Idea of the Good, we do well to take Socrates at his word when he emphasizes that the language he employs in this context embodies a likeness, as it were the offspring of the Good (506e3–4). With this warning in mind, we can observe the main points of the presentation.

1.   The discussion of the Good is initiated in connection with a fresh consideration (*eks archēs*) of the training and establishment of the philosopher-kings (502c9ff.). It is therefore part of the explanation of why the just city depends for its existence upon the rule of philosophers. The peculiar claim is made that in order to be just, hence to give to each person his due, the philosopher must know the Ideas, of which the Good is the principle. This claim is peculiar, among other reasons, because it is never explained how perception of the Idea of justice will enable the ruler to discern which action is just in any particular situation. For our present purposes, this line of thought does not require to be pursued.

2.   In order to discern the Ideas, and hence to qualify as wise rulers, the philosopher must discern the Idea of the Good. Elsewhere Socrates denies that human beings may be wise; here, his hypothetical presentation of the science of dialectic, or knowledge of the Ideas (see especially 7, 533a1ff.), reinforces his hesitations about the Idea of the Good in such a way as to leave it highly unlikely, to say the least, that wisdom is possible. In this case, however, the just city must itself be impossible and not merely unlikely (7, 540d1ff.). This is because the possibility of the city does not rest upon the already unlikely chance of philosophers becoming kings, but rather upon the genuine impossibility that philosophers may be wise. If wisdom is not exhibited in the ruling class, then the entire argument on behalf of the justness of the city breaks down. At 506c2ff., Socrates says that it is not just to speak of what one does not know. He adds that whereas blind persons can sometimes take the right road "without understanding" (literally "intellect"), no one would wish "to see ugly, blind, and crooked things if it were possible to hear from others the shining and noble" (506c11ff.). Since Socrates is himself speaking by prophecy and in an accommodated form rather than by knowledge and with full explicitness, we are being given a myth or likeness about the Good, not the Good itself. The most we can hope to do then is to take the right road like a blind man without *nous*.

3. The previous point could also be understood to support the inference that it is not knowledge of the Good, but rather the belief among the nonphilosophical citizens that the philosopher-kings possess that knowledge upon which the authority of the rulers must rest. Such a belief could easily be inculcated among the citizenry by the stringent educational system, nor would it be likely to be exposed by the rulers themselves. This, I suspect, is why Socrates emphasizes the utility of the Idea of the Good, a utility that is not so much ontological as political. In a typical formulation, Socrates says that it is through the employment of the Idea of the Good that "just and other things become useful and beneficial" (505a2ff.). In the immediate sequel, Socrates emphasizes that in the absence of knowledge of the Good no possession or knowledge will be either beneficial or both noble and good (505a6-b4). The upshot of passages like these is that the Good is both useful and good. In other words, it is not possible to analyze or define the Good in an entirely noncircular way. As to utility, it is not necessary to invoke the radical hypothesis that the entire discussion is political rather than theoretical or ontological. As the first principle, the Good allows things to be what they are and thus to exercise their nature or capacity. The light makes things visible, the atmosphere allows creatures to breathe, plants sustain animal life, animals contribute to the welfare of human beings, and so on. This is not utilitarianism so much as the coherent functioning of the whole. It is not a concealment but rather a discovery of the natures of beings that they are useful to one another and, in particular, to human beings.

4. Socrates then summarizes the thesis of the Ideas as in each case a one over many, accessible to noetic perception rather than to vision or the senses, as are the many (507b5ff.). Each Idea is the "what it is" of the particulars in the corresponding many. This means that the answer to the question What is a horse is presumably not The Idea of the horse (since that answer would be false) but rather an account of the Idea of the horse. Since the Idea of the horse differs from the Idea of justice, each such What is X? question must receive a different reply. Even the question What is an Idea? will receive its own answer, albeit one that covers all Ideas. This raises the following difficulty. Whereas it may be necessary to know the Idea of the horse in order to know what a horse is, why is it necessary to know the Idea of the

Good in order to know the Idea of the horse? In keeping with Socrates' analogy, one must know what a horse is in order to identify a painting or photograph of a horse, and one can know a horse only if the horse is nurtured or (broadly speaking) illuminated by the sun; but it is not necessary to know what the sun is in order to know what a horse is. Grooms, veterinarians, and zoologists need not be astronomers in order to practice their sciences. In particular, reflections of this kind lead once more to the conclusion that knowledge of the Idea of the Good is not necessary for politics. All that is required is knowledge of the noble and the just things, and not even knowledge of the Ideas of nobility and justice.

5. At 508b12ff., Socrates says that the Good generates offspring that are analogous to itself. "As the Good is in the noetic place, with respect to *nous* and what is noetically perceived, so the sun is in the visual place with respect to the eye and the thing seen." The Good is not *nous,* or intellect, but it is accessible to the intellect apart from the senses. If this is true, then, as is also supported by the definition of dialectic, which proceeds exclusively by way of Ideas or via "a noetic melody" (532a1ff.), the "utilitarian" function of the Good is irrelevant to what one could call, following Heidegger, Platonic metaphysics. Dialectic proceeds exclusively via Ideas (511b3ff.); since Ideas are "beings" (*ousiai*), dialectic not only dispenses with sensuous particulars but cannot make use of the Good itself, which is "beyond being" (*epekeina tēs ousias:* 509b9). At 7, 534b3ff., Socrates says that the dialectician must give a *logos* of every *ousia,* but also of the Idea of the Good which he "abstracts" (*aphelon*) from all the other *ousiai.* If the Idea of the Good is beyond *ousia,* then the "abstraction" in question must be of the goodness bestowed upon *ousiai,* not of the Good itself. This would be like attempting to infer the sun from the visibility of what it illuminates or perhaps from the life of what it nurtures.

6. In the stretch of text running from 508e1 to 509b10, Socrates says that the Good furnishes to the Idea truth (and thus science to the dialectician), but also "its being and its beingness" (*to einai te kai tēn ousian:* 509b7–8). In contributing illumination or even nurture to the beings of the visible world, the sun does not transmit to them the nature of the sun itself. Our knowledge of the sun comes not from studying horses or human beings, but rather from direct or

instrument-mediated study of the sun. But the metaphor and its de-velopment provide us with no way in which to study the Good di-rectly. Furthermore, if the Good furnishes the Ideas with *alētheia, to einai,* and *ousia,* whereas the Ideas are eternally and independently subsisting entities, it is impossible that the Good should subsist in-dependently of the Ideas. To be "beyond" *ousia* must then mean not that the Good is a hyper-being, but rather that it is not a being at all. The Good is no more distinct from the goodness or visibility of the Ideas than is the god from the products of the ontological garden. The attempt to think through the fundamental properties of Socrates' exposition reveals that the metaphor of the sun is at bottom mis-leading. The sun is here a depersonalized version of the gardener-god in book 10; but we go entirely wrong if we take literally the separation of the sun from the beings that grow in the garden. At the same time, this metaphor is politically or pedagogically edifying: it is *useful* in the highest sense of the term for making Glaucon look up. The sun-image is the middle step for Glaucon between Apollo and the Ideas (509c1–2).

I am not the first to note that Heidegger entirely ignores the political context of the discussion of the Good in the *Republic.* My remarks were intended to bring out the significance of this context, but, more important, to show that it is impossible to derive a Platonist ontology from this ambiguous text. To the extent that one can discern the main implication, the text supports the thesis that the attempt to speak of the emergence-process in non-ontic language results in icons, myths, or poems that mislead from the outset because they are themselves inev-itably ontic. I note in passing that the identification of the Good with truth, being, and beingness underlies the distinction between philo-sophical and demotic virtue. Virtue in the genuine sense is intelligence, or the knowledge of beings. This in turn results in the doctrine that evil does not exist or, in other words, that it is a privation of being. I regard this as a fundamental defect of Platonism, but one which Heidegger, with his obsession for ontology, or the *Seinsfrage,* does nothing to rectify. If anything, he intensifies it, since he tells no salutary political myths.

To pass to another point, Heidegger, in attempting to confront Being rather than beings, shifts from his ostensible target, Being, to the sense or meaning (*Sinn*) of Being. At the beginning of the Nietzsche lectures, Heidegger defines the decisive question for the person "who actually still can and must question philosophically at the end of western philosophy" to be "no longer merely this, what fundamental character the existent [*das Seiende*] exhibits, how the Being of beings is characterized, but it is rather the question: what is this Being itself? It is the question concerning the 'sense of Being' [*Sinn des Seins*], not only about the Being of beings; and 'sense' is thereby delimited precisely in its concept as that from where and on the basis of which Being itself is capable of coming into the open and into the truth"[8]

The *Sinn* of Being, whether we define that term as "meaning," "sense," or "significance," is Heidegger's replacement for the Socratic *logos*. It is true that Heidegger, after *Being and Time,* defines *Sinn* as "openness for self-concealment, i.e. truth,"[9] or again, as the "openness of Being" and not as the sense of a word.[10] *Sinn* refers to the manifestation of Being and not to a proposition about Being or to a semantic entity independent from the manifestation. But genuine speech is still speech *about* Being, even if that speech consists of archaic etymologies and bad poetry. In other words, Heidegger, like Socrates, is unable to look Being directly in the face; and this is because *Being has no face.*

The shift from Being to the "sense" of Being, as I noted earlier, is in keeping with the shift in Kant from intellectual intuition to discursive intelligence. But Heidegger also does not wish to orient himself by the looks of beings; beings too are accessible only derivately as senses. The fundamental difference between the Socratic *logos* and the Heideggerian *Sinn* is that the former exhibits a look whereas the latter does not. And this is why Heidegger attempts to devise a new language or, as he calls it, a new way of thinking, which constitutes the other beginning for which he is preparing us, a way of thinking that is not bound to things, and so which does not employ predication in the Aristotelian sense (a sense that underlies modern functional logic) or say something of something, but which (if I may put it so) bespeaks the bewaying of Being.

The Surplus Theory of Being

The "bewaying" of Being is Heidegger's peculiar reinterpretation of a pre-predicative understanding of Being, the first hints of which we saw previously in Aristotle's conception of the nonpredicative nature of *ousia.* The "that" is so to speak the pre-predicative ground for the predicative figure of the "what." In general, one can say that underlying contemporary ontological doctrines is an apparently simple fact about predication. The predicate "exists" is evidently different in kind from predicates corresponding to properties of things. If existence is a property, it is one that does not enable us to identify its owner as a thing of such and such a kind. Perhaps we can say that "exists" lacks discriminatory power, of a sort that is possessed by predicates like "is a body" or "is colored blue." This fact has led to two quite different lines of argument. On the first approach, the question What is being?[11] is the illegitimate result of an error in syntax. Whatever we mean by "exists," so the argument goes, it does not correspond to a property "being" that is superadded as a kind of surplus onto the sum of properties of each existing thing. On the second approach, which seems to be related to the old doctrine of syncategorematic or transcendental terms, being is indeed regarded as a "surplus" of predication, to employ a term introduced by Husserl in his *Logical Investigations.* Whether or how we distinguish between being and existence varies from one representative to another of this second line of argumentation.

The first line of approach culminates in Fregean and post-Fregean logical theory, in which being is replaced by existence, as represented by the logical quantifier.[12] One could paraphrase this interpretation by saying that existence is synonymous with the instantiation of a concept. The second line of approach culminates in Heidegger's doctrine of the ontological difference or in other words of the difference between the being of existents (Aristotle's being qua being) and Being as the origin or ungrounded ground of beings. If we consider Husserl and Heidegger as the two most important recent representatives of the surplus theory of being, Heidegger distinguishes between being and existence whereas Husserl does not.

In this section, I shall be primarily concerned with the second line of approach, which I entitle "the surplus theory of Being."[13] My intention is to subject this theory to a critical analysis. I shall argue that if the surplus theorists are right, then nothing can be said about Being apart from discourse about or by way of beings. But first it is necessary to examine the fact of predication that gives rise to the two divergent theoretical approaches. This will require a certain amount of historical exegesis. For all practical purposes, I can begin with Kant's distinction

The *Seinsfrage*

in the *Critique of Pure Reason* between real and logical predicates. This will be followed by some remarks about Husserl and Heidegger.

Before I turn to Kant, however, I want to make a brief remark about the difference between Plato and Aristotle. The Platonic doctrine of the *koinōnia* or *sunousia* of eidetic elements, for example as it is described in the *Sophist* by the Eleatic Stranger, has nothing to do with predication, although it underlies the beginnings of a theory of predication. In the Eleatic Stranger's account, to be is to combine with the *genos,* or eidetic element *being,* whether as another *genos* or as a generated instance of an eidetic structure. To say that something is or, as we rather misleadingly express this in modern terminology, that something exists is to say that *being* is an element in its structure. What the Eleatic Stranger does not say, but which may be inferred from the discussion, is that the being of an eidetic structure, namely, of a *koinōnia* of *megista genē,* and so a fortiori of generated instances of such structures, is quite different from the being of the "alphabet" of *megista genē,* to apply the Stranger's own metaphor of spelling in an appropriate manner.

In other words, the letters of the eidetic alphabet, including *being,* must "be" in some way other than that of instances of their combination. But this way of being is concealed by the question of *koinōnia,* or combination, which is in turn disregarded when we are distracted by the question of language, or how it is that we can say something "of" something. This double concealment is accelerated by Aristotle's development of the doctrine of predication, which takes center stage, apparently in his own works but certainly in the tradition to which they give rise, a tradition which becomes the lens through which Plato himself is traditionally interpreted. Of course, the problem is hardly invisible in Aristotle, who insists that *pollachōs legetai to on.* I have already mentioned the problem of the difference between the predicates and the essence, or *ousia,* which cannot be a *koinōnia* of predicates, but which "owns" them in a way that neither Aristotle nor anyone else has ever explained.

This, stated as briefly as possible, is the origin of the fundamental problem in the history of Western philosophy, a problem that culminates in Heidegger's so-called discovery of the ontological difference, or the concealment of Being by beings. Heidegger was led to the desperate attempt to create a new way of speaking that would uncover Being from the double concealment of the doctrine of predication on the one hand and the being of eidetic structures or Platonic Ideas (not *genē*) on the other. In chapter 1 I showed that Heidegger collapses the difference between Plato and Aristotle in attempting to penetrate the veil that has been drawn over Being. But that is not my theme here. What I wish to contend instead is that by formulating the problem in terms of language, Heidegger made it impossible for himself to escape from the veil of predication. All that he managed to accomplish was to shift from prose to poetry, and, I am sorry to say, to bad poetry. Bad poetry is still predicational discourse; but so too is good poetry.

And now to Kant. In his frequently cited discussion of the ontological argument and the question of the difference between one hundred real and one hundred possible thalers, Kant makes a distinction between logical and real predicates.[14] Kant's general criticism of the ontological argument may be summarized as follows. To ask whether God exists is to consider the possibility of God, not his essential or defining properties. More precisely, it is to consider whether God is an actual element in our experience. Existence (which Kant uses throughout this text as synonymous with being), is not contained in the concept of God, whereas properties like "omnipotent," "omniscient," "eternal," and the like are so contained.

I note that by speaking of concepts and properties or predicates, Kant remains within the Aristotelian tradition, although by shifting from *ousiai* to concepts, a step that is required by his "Copernican" turn and the distinction between the noumenal and the phenomenal, he plays a crucial role in the development of what has come to be known as analytic philosophy. But the phantom of Being still hovers over the solid machinery of Kantian analysis, as can be easily indicated.

A concept may be instantiated or not without any change, whether of addition or subtraction, in its defining marks. In the statement "God exists," "exists" is a logical but not a real predicate. A real predicate is one which determines a concept by specifying its content. A logical predicate has nothing to do with content. Real predicates are thus the names of properties of *rès*, or things. Kant makes no distinction on this issue between God and one hundred thalers; for us, however, the main point is not God but the logical predicate "exists" or, more generally, "being." "Being [*Sein*]," he says, "is merely the position of a thing" (B626), by which he means the positing of an object by a subject within the network of rules that constitute (phenomenal) experience. To say that something exists is then to say nothing about its inner composition, but *also nothing about the inner nature of the positing subject.* Note that what exists is actual, not possible; hence the being or existence of the object of experience cannot be equated with the machinery of the transcendental ego. Being or existence is not merely position; it is also a relation, but a phantom relation.

I propose to expand on this contention by discussing some crucial aspects of Kant's doctrine of perception. It is my contention that Kant in fact has *no* doctrine or explanation of perception. Since Being is position and position is inseparable from perception, the lack of a doctrine of perception guarantees the lack of a doctrine of Being. Differently stated, Kant's inability to provide a transcendental source for the particularity, or *morphē,* of the perceived being is tantamount to the reduction of beings to subjective sensations on the one hand and of Being to an unspeakable and indeterminate emergence-process on the other. This is the ancestor of the Heideggerian adaptation of Husserl's pre-predicational approach to Being.

In order to demonstrate conclusively the defects of Kant's teaching, a separate monograph would be required. But I can indicate the pivotal points. Kant speaks regularly of an empirical concept that corresponds to each empirical object, such as a dog. I maintain that Kant provides no source from which to explain the origin of an empirical concept. The concepts of understanding cannot do so; they furnish us with the a priori structure of possible experience, not with the perceived *morphē* or *Gestalt* of actual objects like dogs or elephants. Neither can these *Gestalten* be derived from the pure forms of intuition, as scarcely needs to be argued. They cannot be furnished by schemata, which according to Kant furnish rules, not images, even though they are products of the imagination (B176ff.). If these shapes and hence the empirical concept could be derived from any source, it would be from sensation. But Kant insists upon the accidental or nonobjective nature of sensation as independent of the structuring activity of concepts of the understanding. Since this activity provides the a priori structure of a possible perception, it cannot also provide the empirical structure of an actual perception without obliterating the distinction between empirical and transcendental.

I have now exhausted the various origins of Kant's transcendental epistemo-ontology, to coin a phrase, without having identified any source for the empirical concept. Being or existence, namely, the object of perception, is *a phantom*. This peculiar situation, which I am about to document further, is no doubt repugnant to Kantians. But it should not surprise us because to say that Being is position is to say nothing about what is posited but rather about the relation of two variables, the subject variable and the predicate variable, as defined by a syntactical rule. The rule is transcendental but the interpretation of the variables is immanent or contingent. A being is then the empirical interpretation of a transcendental rule or statement in a linguistic model. Kant of course says that being or existence is determined by perception "in accordance with empirical laws," the *"universal conditions"* of "experience as a totality" (B628–29). But the laws, precisely as universal, define the structure of possible existence, not the nature, essence, or *Gestalt* of the actual content of that structure.

In the *Fundamental Problems of Phenomenology*,[15] Heidegger says that for Kant, existence is equivalent to perception, whether understood as the perceived *rès,* the act of perception, or as perceivedness (p. 65). Kant in fact says more than this, namely, that being or existence is determined by perception *in accord with empirical laws*. But empirical laws are not themselves established by perception independent of conceptual thinking. On the contrary, empirical laws already present us with an amalgam of concepts and perceptions. This is immediately obvious from the term "law," which refers to a necessary connection between concepts or in other words invokes the table of categories and the functions of understanding. Heidegger provides a much fuller and better account of Kant's doctrine in his paper *Kant's Thesis About Being* (1962).[16] He makes it perfectly explicit there that Being is for Kant "the objectivity of the object of experience" and so that Being must originate in the positioning function of the subject, since it is not a real predicate belonging to the object (pp. 289f., 291).

What Kant has in mind in the passage cited a moment ago (B628f.) is the need to distinguish between genuine perceptions on the one hand and illusions, fantasms, dreams, and the like on the other. But this distinction presupposes that perceptions arise from the application of the functions of conceptual thought onto sensations. The difference between a sensation and a perception, in other words, is not derivable from sensation or the stream of subjective representation alone; one must think the perceived thing as an object bound to the totality of experience as regulated by the laws of conceptual thought. Perception is the constitution, not the discovery, of objects of experience. We do not experience an independent reality that presents itself to perception; on the contrary, we *pose* or project experience.

It is therefore not precise enough to say that we shift from a possible to an actual object by supplementing thought with perception. To say this is to run the risk of confusing perception with sensation. Perception is in fact not possible apart from thinking; to perceive is to perceive an actual *object;* but an actual object is already constituted by thinking. It follows that there can be no false perceptions, since constituting an object by the conceptual and categorial functions of understanding is also knowing that object. We may, of course, think an object without perceiving it, but such objects will be mere *Gedankendinge;* that is, they will be either what Kant calls in the *Logic* logical essences[17] or else they will be products of the imagination in the Kantian sense of "fantasy." And in particular, they will neither "be" nor "exist."

We move from thinking (or imagining) to perceiving by combining a conceptual structure with sensations. Sensation, as it were, is the "surplus" that takes us from thinking to being or in other words from real to existential predication. But sensation in itself is a "rhapsody" (B195) or "confusion" (B123: *Verwirrung*), at best a collocation of quasi-objects regulated by the laws of psychological association of the British Empiricists (B119, B127–28). The associations of sensation cannot serve as proto-objects because they contain no objectivity; "quasi" is here a metaphor for private perspectivism. Nor could these perspectival associations be given the determination of actuality by laws defining the possibility of objects. As a "surplus," sensation is suspiciously reminiscent of pre-predicative presencing, or of what Being would be like if considered independently of the objects imposed onto it by predicative thinking.

The attribution of existence is distinct but not separate from the attribution of real predicates. What is perceived, exists; by our preceding analysis, there can be no false attributions of existence. Stated in another way, it is not satisfactory to say with the early Heidegger that for Kant (although he does not state it explicitly), being or existence is perceivedness. Heidegger means by this that being or existence is for Kant neither the act of perception, or subjectivity, nor the object perceived, or objectivity, but the "uncoveredness" of the object to the subject.[18]

But this uncoveredness is a "project" that manifests itself as a relation between subject and object. The unity of conceptual thinking and sensation produces objects of experience; to be or to exist is to be an object of experience. But the being or existence is not the object; it is the uncoveredness of the object to the subject. Uncoveredness is not the result of a discovered openness, but an artifactual consequence of the production of openness. On this fundamental point, Kant's doctrine is very close to that of the early Heidegger. Uncoveredness is the phantom of Being.

Being or existence is then better defined for Kant as experiencedness, that is, not simply as uncoveredness but as *uncovering* in the sense of producing. Openness (Heidegger's *Erschlossenheit*) is not the ground of uncovering but is rather produced by it. It makes good sense to attribute a "productive" doctrine of being and existence to Kant, regardless of whether Heidegger is right in attributing such a doctrine to Plato.

I want to make in passing another claim, difficult to summarize but an important consequence of Kant's Copernican turn. The attribution of existence cannot on Kantian grounds be a positioning of some object within an antecedently existing world of experience. We do not as it were simply encounter a new object of experience (and so of natural science) within an already existing world, since objects are posited, not encountered. But neither do we posit a new object in an already encountered world, and for the same reason. The world is not encountered but actualized by the specific act of perceptual cognition through which we think an object. To think an object of experience is to think, that is, to posit, the world of experience as the context of the object. This is the ancestor of the Husserlian and Heideggerian doctrine of the horizon.[19] But Kant's horizon is possible, not actual. How could the world, which is the totality of conditions for the positing of things, exist in advance of the thinking of an object? A possible world is not the world of our experience.

In other words, from the transcendental standpoint, the world must always actualize in the same way. But the world that actualizes is empirically changing with the advance of empirical knowledge. Even if we assume that Newtonian physics is eternally true, our knowledge of physical laws is also constantly being refined and extended. Whatever may be true of the transcendental domain of a priori conditions for the possibility of the world, what is the source for the continuous actuality of the empirical laws of phenomenal experience? They are supposed to exist as the actual context within which each object of perception is inserted. Yet they cannot be actual if they are not being thought, and they cannot be thought if there are no empirical concepts. This is another aspect of the phantom status of Being. Experience, understood as the positing by the subject in a world ruled by laws, and so as understanding of these laws, must be simultaneous with the cognition of an object. Without this simultaneity, there will be no world but only a rhapsody of fantasies. For Kant (and in truth), our experience of objects changes with the gradual accumulation of scientific knowledge. Let us assume that this is possible on Kantian grounds. But then each new cognition entails the constitution of a new world because the cognition of an object is the simultaneous actualization of the world of experience.

Despite the ostensibly eternal and uniform operations of the transcendental ego, and so the eternally valid conditions for the possibility of thinking a world at all, the world that we actually think is changing from one moment of increased empirical knowledge to another (B520–21, B755f.), as follows from Kant's fundamental distinction between pure a priori knowledge on the one hand and empirical knowledge on the other. But the particular empirical object that we perceive is both a transcendentally constituted object and a contingent empirical perception. As transcendentally constituted, the object must always be the same. As perceived empirically, it is not only contingent, but its nature, and hence its defining properties, as well as its *existence,* are relative to the current stage of scientific knowledge. By the argument just presented, the same must be true of the world. Not only, then, is existence not a real predicate, but *rēs* are artifacts of interpretation, just as is the world of experience. If there were empirical concepts, there would be determinate empirical objects. But then there could be no continuous scientific progress. Kant is thus surprisingly close to a hermeneutical doctrine of existence.

Here is another aspect of the same problem. The distinction between logical and real predicates disappears in the act of perception. To be or to exist is to be a perceivable thing, but to be a perceivable thing is to be a *rēs,* that is, sensation structured by concepts and categorial thinking. To exist, in short, is to be a *rēs.* What exactly then does it mean to say that existence is not a real predicate but is instead positioning via perception? We arrive at perception by the combination of thinking and sensation. There is no existing object already present in sensation and available for the scrutiny of conceptual or scientific thinking. Sensation cannot consist of preexisting paradigms of existing objects that serve to guide the activity of thinking. But neither is there an existing object present within thinking as independent of and antecedent to sensation. Preexistence in either of these senses would reinstitute Platonism or Aristotelianism; there would be transcendental objects rather than transcendental operations for the constitution of objects.

In fact, the arrival at perception is never explained by Kant, in the precise sense that there is no rule for the operation of perceiving. If there were such a rule, perception would be transformed into a transcendental function; otherwise stated, experience would be coextensive with necessity, and there would be no contingency. There is reason to believe, on the basis of the *Opus postumum*, that Kant's thought was moving in just this direction.[20] But no such doctrine is to be found in the First Critique. In the canonical doctrine, the contingency of existence is purchased at the price of the unintelligibility of the origin of existence, that is, of the combination of thinking and sensation that produces perceptible existence. Existence happens. We are reminded here of Heidegger's description of Being as *Ereignis,* or event.

To summarize, I have argued that Kant never explains the origin of empirical concepts, that he fails to explain the difference between sensation and perception, and that his conception of Being or existence reproduces in the distinction between logical and real predicates the same ambiguity, or "concealment" of Being, that one finds in Aristotle thanks to the doctrine of predication on the one hand and *ousia* on the other. "Positioning" is the opening of a phantom uncoveredness that is explained neither by logical nor by real predicates. The doctrine of predication pays dividends in our analysis of discourse but none in our effort to think Being.

Depending upon which aspect of this complex situation we emphasize, we may infer that being is a syntactical relation that manifests itself in predicative discourse, or we may search for Being as discovered (and also as covered or veiled) by the discursive power of cognition, which latter is not mere syntax but rather the synthesizing function that operates via discourse. In what follows, I shall pursue the second alternative, as represented by the early Husserl and Heidegger.

The *Seinsfrage*

I need to refer to Husserl's discussion of categorial intuition that occurs in number 6 of the *Logical Investigations*.[21] In paragraph 40, Husserl introduces his version of the Kantian distinction between real and logical predicates. The distinction remains within the Kantian horizon because it refers to intentionality or in other words to the act of consciousness that is directed toward an object which ostensibly transcends consciousness or exists in the natural world, just as Kant claims that his phenomenon or object is the thing in itself as it shows itself to the cognitive and perceptual processes of the transcendental ego. But Husserl is no more able to demonstrate the transcendence of intended objects than was Kant able to refute Idealism.

This aspect of the problem, however, is not my main concern. I am interested instead in the Husserlian distinction between sensuous matter and the categorially objective forms. This distinction corresponds in part to the Kantian distinction between sensation and concepts, but only in part. Husserl in fact means by sensation or sensuous content what Kant means by real predicates. In sensuous intuition, we perceive the properties that define what the intended object is; Husserl gives as an example a piece of white paper. The perception of the property "white" corresponds to the attribution of a real predicate to the object of perception. Husserl then says, "The intention of the word 'white' corresponds only partly with the color-moment of the appearing object; there remains a surplus [*Überschuss*] in the meaning [*Bedeutung*], a form that itself corresponds to nothing in the appearance by which it may be confirmed. *White,* that means white *existing* paper" (p. 131).

The surplus meaning "existent" (Husserl, like Kant, uses being and existence synonymously) is apprehended by categorial intuition. Categorial forms are then like Kant's logical predicates in the sense that they are "founded" in, that is, are accessible within, sensuous intuition; but they are unlike logical predicates in that they participate in the constitution of the object. To repeat, this mode of participation is not such as to "determine the concept" (as Kant would say) or to designate a perceived property in the object (ibid.). Being is not a real predicate. But it is also not a concept or judgment, that is, not a part of an inner psychic act.[22]

In these texts, being or existence is not the result of positing in the Kantian sense of producing the experienced object from sensuous and categorial matter. Categorial intuition is for Husserl no more productive than is sensuous intuition; to intuit is to see what lies before one, not to create. The seen object is given to us as composed of both sensuous and categorial properties. Being is therefore not a concept in the sense of an artifact of thinking. We can arrive at a concept of being, but not through reflection upon judgments or inner perceptions. "The origin of the concept 'fact' [Sachverhalt] and 'being' (in the sense of the copula) does not lie within reflection on judgments or rather in the fulfillment of judgments [i.e., the presence of a judgment to intuition]; it is not in these acts as objects, but in the objects of these acts that we find the foundation for abstraction leading to the realization of the aforementioned concepts" (pp. 140–41).

To say this in another way, objects are not produced by psychic acts; these acts instead "uncover" or disclose the objects that lie "open" before the mind's eye. Remember that Husserl insists upon the transcendence of the object or its existence independent of, but accessible through, the intentional activity of consciousness. The existence of the object is *given* by categorial intuition, not produced (as in Kant) by the positioning of the object within the totality of experience. And this givenness of being or existence is a property (or predicate) neither of the subject nor of the object; it is not a property of the object like "blue" or "mortal," but it is also not the creative activity of consciousness. The concept of being can arise only "when some being, actual or imaginary, is placed before our eyes" (p. 141).

This "placing before" (*vor Augen gestellt*) is not "positioning" in the Kantian sense. One could, however, say that it arises from the technical step of the transcendental *epochē*, or reduction, by which we are supposed to place the natural world and our involvement with its objects in brackets. But the technical status of reduced phenomena does not entail that they are produced by the transcendental reduction. The latter purifies and so intensifies; it does not create. There must then be an intuitive act that brings categorial *Bedeutung* before our eyes, just as sensuous perception does with material elements of meaning or signification. And this can be accomplished only by the act that brings the object of perception together with its categorial determinations before our eyes (pp. 142f.).

On the other hand, Husserl seems to contradict this line of argument when he speaks some thirty pages later of the categorial synthesis of sensuous objects, a synthesis which, he says, is not in the sensuous objects but "which *is grounded in the founding acts as such*" (pp. 173f.). I quote the following passage: "The categorial does not pertain to the representing sensuous contents but rather, and indeed necessarily, to the *objects* and thereby yet not to them in accord with their sensuous (real) content. This means: *the psychic character, in which the categorial forms constitute themselves, pertain phenomenologically to the acts, in which the objects constitute themselves*" (pp. 175f.). And again: it is in the categorial acts as founded within sensuous intuition "in which everything intellectual constitutes itself" (p. 176).

These rather heavy, not to say obscure, texts sing to my ear in a Kantian key; Husserl now attributes the production of the intuited object from what we may fairly call real and logical (= categorial) predicates to the *activity* of intuition. What is non-Kantian here is the substitution of intuition for sensation, perception, and conception. The Husserlian "evidence" of the object, that is, its full presence before the eye of the soul, and thus both its essence and its existence, is thus described inconsistently in the *Logical Investigations*.

The underlying problem does not seem difficult to identify. Husserl wishes to repudiate Idealism and solipsism, that is, to affirm the existence of things independent of consciousness. He sees that this cannot be done by beginning from the independence of subject and object. Accordingly, he claims that the conscious activity of the subject is already (as Heidegger puts it) directed toward objects or beings, by virtue of its intentional structure. But this accomplishes nothing, since intentionality is the structure of consciousness, not of the relation of the thinker to beings apart from consciousness. Instead, intentionality worsens the situation by detaching us from the "natural attitude" in which there is no question about the independence of beings from thought.

In the case of being or existence, the problem is as follows. Kant and Husserl both take their bearings by perception, but they are unable to distinguish between perceiving and thinking. Perception accordingly cannot traverse the separation of thought from beings or serve as a supplement to thought because perception is itself constituted by thought. We cannot move from nonperceptual to perceptual thinking by a preconceptual perception because there is no such perception but only sensation. Conceptual thinking is the most essential ingredient in perception, since it "constitutes" the object of perception. This constitution-activity is in Kant's case always and in Husserl's case sometimes referred to as synthesis.

In other words, abstracting from the differences between the two philosophers, it is impossible to move from thinking to being or existing by way of perception because thinking produces the object of perception. In order to be perceived, the object of perception must already exist.[23] But it is no transcendence of subjectivity to attribute existence to thinking. The object of perception comes into existence simultaneously with the act of perception. There is no detachment or distance between the presence of the object and the occurrence of the perception. Hence there is no "movement" from thinking to existence, but only the inexplicable application of thinking to sensation, of which perception, and so existence, is the result. Existence, so to speak, is a movement *within* thinking, not beyond it. And in Kantian terms, the surplus is sensation, not the category "Being." As pre-predicative, it is a turmoil or rhapsody, an emergence-process from which no thing, or *rēs*, emerges.

Being or existence, whether one calls it a category or a logical predicate, is now either a logical concept, that is, an artifact of abstraction that we employ in our effort to understand and so to explain the structure of our experience. Or else, if it is to be a Husserlian category, and so a mark of beings rather than an artifact of thinking, we can no longer sustain the distinction between real and logical predicates. The being or existence of a chair must be a property of the chair as much as its color, composition, and shape.

Husserl's "category" of being is not a logical abstraction, that is, an artifact of abstract thinking, but something ingredient in the thing itself. But to repeat, it is an ingredient of the existing thing. To call it a "surplus" added onto the real predicates is to say nothing more than that it is not a predicate of color, material, relation, or of some determination of the essence or eidetic structure of the object. It is not a predicate in the Aristotelian sense. But it is also not a logical predicate because it is not logic that grants being; being grants itself. Nor is being explained by the doctrine of categorial intuition; on the contrary, as we have seen, this doctrine dissolves on the one hand the distinction between thought and being by the doctrine of synthesis and on the other the distinction between being and the existing thing.

The *Seinsfrage*

If one considers a chair, it seems to be altogether evident that being is the property that permits us to say, "The chair is." It is a prejudice of dianoetic thinking to ask, "Is *what*?" In English we can avoid the problem by saying, "The chair exists." But Husserl no more than Kant distinguishes between being and existence; and in any case, we are left with the problem of explaining what it means to exist. To be some particular determination is neither to exist nor to be. But in order to be some property or another (thus replying to the dianoetic "what?"), the chair must first be. The problem arises from the fact that, as soon as we begin to explain or to analyze being (or existence), we slide necessarily into another modality, namely, that of predicates (including relations).

Certainly no one would say that being is a thing like a chair, but this is hardly a reason to maintain that being is a thought or a mere pronouncement (dressed up as a rule of syntax). Furthermore, to perceive or to intuit that a chair is or exists is not to intuit a category "being." It is instead to perceive the chair. Even if we did intuit a category "being," the properties of a category are not the properties of being and certainly not of the chair. On the contrary, being has no properties; it is *beings* that have properties, one of which is being or existence.

For these reasons, I am dubious about the Husserlian doctrine of the category of being or existence. But I agree with his thesis that being or existence belongs to the given objects. However, this contradicts the thesis according to which the object is constituted or synthesized by thought from the "thingish" material of the determined object together with the categories of intuition. It is here useful to add that existence is not synonymous in my lexicon with presence; a being does not cease to exist simply because of its absence. This difficulty may be avoided by a distinction between being and existence; I have touched upon this distinction previously and will add here just a few words. When one considers things like a chair, it is plain that there is a link between existence and perceptibility. But it is also plain that not all beings are apprehended via the senses. For example, neither for Kant nor for Husserl could one say this of concepts or categories. This is why Husserl speaks of categorial intuition. Unfortunately, he does not distinguish precisely enough between the intuition of the being of a sensuously perceptible thing and the thinking of the category of being.

In the Kantian doctrine, it is impossible to say that the categories "exist." But I believe that it is also impossible for Husserl. Categories "exist" only as founded in an object. That is to say that they exist only through combination with the category of existence (just as the Eleatic Stranger's *megista genē* other than being exist only through combination with being). Taken apart from this category, and so a fortiori from existing objects, they cannot be said to exist. But as founded within the structure of the existing thing, they "exist" only in a sense derivative from the function of the category of existence. And how could one say that the category of existence exists?

It is a platitude, and therefore it is true, to say that we conceptualize with concepts and categorize with categories. This is hardly surprising, since that is their respective work. But strictly speaking, it is impossible to decide whether concepts and categories exist or not, unless we make a distinction between being and existence in one way or another. Taking all the difficulties into consideration, I suggest that it is more convenient to say that concepts and categories "are" and that sensuously perceptible things "exist." It seems that Kant does not face the question of the being of the transcendental because he identifies being with actual existence. This problem becomes more explicit in mathematical logic when one quantifies over predicates.

All this is compatible with the recognition that existence is a special case of being. The distinction between the two terms is required when one wishes to distinguish between perceptible and cognitively accessible entities. But an existing chair also exhibits being: it *is* an existing thing. To come back to the main point, the Being of beings or existents "exceeds" real properties or predicates only in the sense that it does not determine the being or existent in any eidetic property. But this in itself is not surprising, since the analogous situation obtains for real or eidetic properties. The predicate "is brown," for example, does not determine the chair in any way except for its color. As is well known, the copula "is" in "is brown" may be eliminated without changing the sense of the predication. But even if this were not so and the "is" were implied by the notation of the expression that ostensibly eliminates it, this sense of "is" refers to the being of the chair and not to a Being in surplus of the being of the chair.

In short, one cannot replace the word "being" or "is" by the name of some other property. To do so would be like replacing the word "brown" in the description of a chair by the word "graceful." But one

The *Seinsfrage*

207

may construct concepts in the attempt to explain the contribution of being to a given entity. What we explain with these concepts is our understanding of being or of the relations through which we grasp the work (*energeia*) of being. But all this manifests itself in the language of predication, that is, in what is called by some surplus theorists the language of the reification of Being. If Being exceeds beings, and so too real predicates, this is because it exceeds language and hence logic; more generally, it exceeds *logos*.

For these reasons, I prefer the thesis that being is a real predicate to the rival contention that it is a logical predicate. The latter thesis reduces being to discourse, whereas the former at least makes clear that being is grounded in beings and not in rules governing speech about being, rules which are themselves speeches. As to human being, it is exactly the same as the being of a chair. Humans differ from chairs in many ways, but these ways are to be found in properties other than being.

By way of transition to the conclusion of this discussion, I repeat the principal thesis: We never grasp being or existence apart from something that is or exists. All concepts and categories are products of predicative discourse; all syntheses of thinking, whether labeled transcendental or immanent, issue in mental artifacts. These are or may be necessary for rational discussion of the being of beings. But they never give us access to a surplus Being.

I turn finally to a brief consideration of the thought of the young Heidegger and to his contention that the uncoveredness (*Entdecktheit*) of beings is grounded in the openness (*Erschlossenheit*) of Being. I put to one side the question of whether uncoveredness and openness are products of the constituting or intending activity of consciousness (or *Dasein*), as they are for Kant. We will assume that the beings are transcendent in the Husserlian sense that the intentionality of thinking is directed toward what is present before us, and so that disclosure or uncovering is the truth of the openness, that is, givenness, of Being. The distinction between uncovering and openness must then be explained as follows. Openness is truth (*a-lētheia*) that presents itself as concealed by the uncoveredness of beings. Therefore openness necessarily conceals itself, since it presents itself in the form of the uncoveredness of beings. By uncovering beings, Being covers itself. And yet this self-covering is precisely openness.

It follows that ontology in the sense of Aristotelian metaphysics concerns itself with the being of beings, namely, with the nature or structure of uncoveredness. This concern has the defect of concealing or covering over Being. In an alternative formulation, the presence of determinate beings covers over the openness of the presencing-process by which Being or openness presents us with beings. But concern with being as the structure of what it is to be a being is tantamount to concern with real predicates. Being is thereby reified or reduced to the status of a property of things.

Heidegger therefore directs us away from beings or, as one could express this, from real as well as logical predicates, but toward Being as the surplus of predication in a sense that is suggested by and originates within Husserl's surplus doctrine of being. According to Heidegger, Husserl, however, makes no attempt to give us the sense (*Sinn*) of Being; he is not concerned with the sense of intentionality that serves as the root of the four perspectives from which the determinations of being are derived, namely, immanent being, absolute givenness, the apriori in constitution, and the pure being of consciousness.[24] Differently stated, Husserl is concerned not with the being of consciousness but with how consciousness can become the possible object of an absolute science.[25]

This is Heidegger's original intention: to provide a fundamental ontology that is adequate to the sense of Being as the ground of the presentation of beings. In order to do this, he must go beyond the structure of beings qua beings or, as one could also say, he must go beyond the sense of being as a logical predicate superimposed onto real predicates. In Aristotelian language, he must go beyond the categories as the structure of a being qua being but also beyond the concept of the *ousia* as the way or configuration of the real predicates constituting the determinations of a particular being.[26]

So much for what Heidegger must transcend. But where does he arrive? Let us start with the notion of openness, or *Erschlossenheit*. We recall that uncoveredness is the presence of the being, or *rēs*. Beings are uncovered because of the openness of Being, which, so to speak, conceals nothing except itself. In another metaphor, openness is the surrogate of the *deus absconditus*. It is present only in the simulacrum of the uncoveredness of beings; and this uncoveredness, as I have tried to explain at some length, is itself inseparable from the real predicates or essence that is uncovered in each particular instance. Even in the case of ontic uncoveredness, there is no categorial structuration other than the specification of the real predicates of that which is uncovered. There are no properties of uncoveredness qua uncoveredness that are distinct from the properties of being qua being.

The situation, however, is even worse in the case of openness. Uncoveredness is always the uncoveredness of something, that is, of an *on* or *rēs;* and this in turn provides us with the possibility of "uncovering" another layer of structure, namely, the configuration of categories each of which must be instantiated in any being whatsoever. But openness is not the openness of something or other; one is tempted to call it openness qua openness. Furthermore, openness is itself accessible only as covered over by the uncovered beings; every attempt to give the sense of openness must apparently run the risk of decaying into a statement about the sense of *closure* or, in its exoteric identity, of uncoveredness.

It would be fatiguing to pursue the intricacies of the paradoxical situation in which Heidegger finds himself. Let me try to illustrate or make more vivid the peculiar assertions of his doctrine with a concrete example. I cannot carry out my search for the sense of Being by literally transcending, that is, disregarding, beings. I arrive at the insight or thought of Being as openness only by meditating upon beings as uncovered. I consider a chair, reflect upon my ability to consider it, and so discover (i.e., uncover) the chair as exemplificative of the openness of Being. The uncoveredness of the chair is not the same as the uncoveredness of the table; but both instances of uncoveredness are instances of the underlying openness.

I must not, however, say anything about the chair or the table if I am to approach the sense of openness. All statements about chairs and tables are real predications; they do not attain to the being of beings, let alone to Being. Furthermore, the uncoveredness or accessibility of the chair as chair and the table as table is not due to the chair or the table, that is, it is not due to the real properties corresponding to the predicates that determine their essences. This uncoveredness or accessibility is due to the openhandedness of the Being or presencing-process that "gives" us all beings and thereby withdraws behind the mask of its magnificent bounty.

It turns out that all that I can say about openness is that it conceals itself in the granting of uncoveredness. But this means that I cannot say anything positive or affirmative, that is, determinative, about openness. To do so would be to reify it, that is, to make real predications about it. Being qua openness is a surplus of beings qua uncovered, and so of the being of beings qua uncoveredness. But it is a vacuous or invisible surplus. Fundamental ontology, or its subsequent replacement, the recollective or rememorative meditating about Being, turns out to be very much like a poetic supplement to negative theology, not to say silence.

The journey from the distinction between real and logical predicates to the ontological difference and beyond is finally revealed as a progressive diminution of the sense of Being. In the case of the surplus theory of Being, more is less. But I must not be understood to say that Heidegger's central contention is an error. I say only that if one wishes to voyage beyond the beings, one is condemned to play the role of Don Quixote, the simulacrum of Odysseus. Heidegger would no doubt have preferred to be the Eleatic Stranger; but the father of the thinking of Being had no legitimate children. Each generation from the loins of Being is an image that falls into what the Stranger refers to in the *Statesman* as "the infinite sea of dissimilarity" (273d6f.).

According to Heidegger's interpretation of Nietzsche, Being in the traditional sense must be emptied of all substance in order to reinvigorate it in its residual form of becoming, alias the eternal return. In Heidegger's own thought, the eternal return is rarified by another turn of the ontological screw into the donative process of Being, of which one can say neither that it is eternal nor that it returns. The process shares the rhapsodic nature of Kantian sensation and Nietzschean Chaos. It is against this backdrop of silence wearing the mask of speech that we must consider Heidegger's interpretation of Nietzsche's metaphysics.

The Culmination of Metaphysics

6

The heart of Heidegger's interpretation of Nietzsche is to be found in his idiosyncratic explanation of three "thoughts": the will to power, the eternal return, and *Gerechtigkeit,* normally translated as justice, righteousness, or fairness. Stated in an introductory manner, the first two thoughts are said to combine as reversed Platonism, namely, the replacement of the Platonic Ideas by the permanence or constancy of Becoming. The third thought serves to install the thinker within Chaos and thereby to identify the activity of world making with the ostensible inner law of Chaos. What look like diverse and even inconsistent doctrines in Nietzsche's often fragmentary texts are thus shown to contain the initial expression of a unified metaphysical teaching. As we study the essential details of this general interpretation, three questions will be of paramount concern: Is Heidegger's interpretation sustained by the Nietzschean texts? Even assuming a favorable response to this question, is it plausible to refer to the resultant teaching as a reversal that is also the culmination of Platonism? And finally, is Heidegger justified in asserting that his own prophecy of Being as origin is distinguishable from the doctrine he attributes to Nietzsche?

One preliminary remark: for the purposes of exposition, I want to speak first of Heidegger's account of the will to power and the eternal return, and then of his interpretation of *Gerechtigkeit.* These two accounts are in my opinion not fully harmonious. The analysis of the will to power and the eternal return has the general implication that human being, and in the first instance thinking, as an expression of the will to power, is itself a product of the shaping force of Chaos. The interpretation of *Gerechtigkeit,* on the other hand, reverses this implication: human thinking is now treated as identical with the inner order and hidden law of Chaos. Throughout the first part of what follows, the reader should bear in mind that the discussion must be supplemented and modified by the second part.

According to Heidegger, the will to power and the eternal return constitute jointly the deepest expression of Nietzsche's "transformation of values," namely, a reversal of or countermovement with respect to Platonism.[1] The will to power is what Nietzsche refers to as "the last fact" or ultimate statement about the nature of Becoming, whereas the eternal return is "the thought of thoughts," an expression that Heidegger glosses as designating the manner of being of the totality of Becoming.[2] Heidegger claims to be the first to have understood the inner relation between these two doctrines because he is the first to think them together in the light of their metaphysical significance. The thesis of the will to power refers to the state or condition (*Verfassung*) of "the existent in its totality," whereas the eternal return expresses the manner of being (*seine Weise zu Sein*) of that totality.[3]

The What, the How, and the That

In a later discussion, Heidegger says that the will to power corresponds to the "what" and the eternal return to the "how" of the existent in its totality: "The will to power says *what* the existent 'is', i.e. as what it empowers (as power). The eternal return of the same names the *how*, in which the existent possesses such a what-character, its 'facticity' as a whole, its 'that it is.' Because Being as eternal return of the same constitutes the rendering constant of presence [*die Beständigung der Anwesenheit*], it is therefore the most constant: the unconditioned That."[4]

Heidegger's terminology makes clear that his understanding of reversed Platonism is constructed in accord with an Aristotelian model or in other words that he makes no distinction between the key metaphysical terms of Plato and of Aristotle. The "what" corresponds to *eidos* or *ousia* and the "how" to *aitia*. The reversal consists in the assimilation of *eidos* (the primary sense of *ousia* as well as of *aitia*) into the "that" or, in Aristotelian terminology, *to hoti*. As Heidegger himself puts it, "On the ground of this coherence of the that-being with the what-being (which is now the reverse of the original inclusion of the *estin* in the *einai* of the *ontōs on* as *idea*), will to power and eternal return of the same must not merely go together as determinations of Being; they must say *the same* [*dasselbe*]."[5]

In other words, whereas there is a separation between form and matter or factic existence in "Platonism," the two are unified in Nietzsche's metaphysics. Second, whereas form predominates or serves as the paradigm or essence of facticity in "Platonism," Nietzsche reverses the direction of assimilation. The "what" or the will to power does not furnish the Platonist attributes of constancy and identity; these are now derived from the eternal return. What is eternal or constantly present is not eidetic structure but genesis or Becoming, which Heidegger calls facticity or the that. Therefore, even though the will to power is "as essence the condition of the living nature of life (value) and in this stipulation at the same time the authentic and only That of the living, i.e. here of the existent in its totality,"[6] value understood as human activity, namely, as rank-ordering and world making, is assimilated into the cosmological process of Chaos. What is from the human standpoint the creation of a world by the projection of a table of values is intrinsically the self-organization of Chaos in accord with its inner law. Thus the assimilation of the what into the that amounts to a "devaluing" or "dehumanizing" of value, which must be understood here in the Nietzschean sense as quantum of power;[7] quantum of power is in turn "what" is constantly presented. What looks to human beings like a world order is "in fact" the facticity of Chaos. In an alternative formulation, value and life are transferred by Heidegger from human activity to the world-producing activity of Chaos.

One more citation from this context is required in order to establish firmly the aforementioned explanation of the ostensible reversal of Platonism in Nietzsche's unified doctrine. The will to power and the eternal return do not merely go together; they say *the same*. Heidegger expands on this as follows:

> The thought of the eternal return of the same [*des Gleichen*] expresses in the language of metaphysics and the end of history the same [*dasselbe*] as what the will to power, in the language of the end of modernity, says is the fundamental character of the beingness of the existent [*der Seiendheit des Seienden*]. The will to power is the self-surpassing in the possibilities for becoming of a self-managing command, which self-surpassing remains in its innermost core the rendering constant [*Beständigung*] of Becoming as such and, because it is foreign to and the enemy of all mere continuation into the endless, opposes itself to this.[8]

The "same" that is said by the two different formulations is the modern doctrine of the primacy of the will, or the projection of truth by subjectivity, but now in the final metaphysical version in which the activity of willing is attributed not to subjectivity, but to Becoming or Chaos. Plato's Ideas are prototypes of the categorial structures produced by the modern subject, within which intellect is subordinate to will. The will expresses itself for the sheer sake of expression: the will to will is in Nietzschean language the will to power. Whereas in previous modern thinkers like Descartes, Leibniz, and Kant "the beingness of the existent," that is, world order, is imposed onto primaeval Chaos,[9] in Nietzsche, the self-administering or intrinsically unrestricted function of the will is assimilated into and "shaped" or regulated by the circularity of the eternal return. To borrow an expression from Hegel, human thinking is *aufgehoben* into the cosmic processes of Chaos. What is "the same" in every world, previously understood as a project of the will of subjectivity, is not formal structure but *organized transience*. Differently stated, the surrogate of formal structure is the constancy of Becoming, or world making as a process. "Overcoming" or the expression of will does not continue endlessly as the increasing accumulation of force; this would result in the continuous erasure of every temporary quantum of power, and so would prevent any world whatsoever from appearing.

The reversal thus transforms Platonic forms into the self-shaping process of the accumulation and dissolution of points of force. Heidegger is silent on the issue, but the reversal also transforms the Platonic Eros, first into Dionysian intoxication, but then into the nonhuman fluctuations of Chaos. By insisting upon the fact that the will to power and the eternal return say *the same,* Heidegger carries out his intention of finding a unified metaphysical doctrine in Nietzsche, but at the price of rendering the human experience even less intelligible than it was in Nietzsche's own statements of his doctrines.

"For Nietzsche . . . 'Becoming' means the fulfilled content that discloses itself as the essence of the will to power . . . Becoming is the activity by which power transcends the current stage of power. Becoming means in Nietzsche's language the excitation, emerging to domination from itself, of the will to power as the fundamental character of the existent."[10] This leaves no room for modern subjectivity, and of course Nietzsche explicitly repudiates the stability of the subject, which he explains as a projection of the will to power. There is nevertheless an irreducible element of animism in Nietzsche's discussions of Becoming and Being, which Heidegger transfers to or incorporates within his interpretation of Chaos. This is the link to the later discussion of *Gerechtigkeit;* in that discussion, however, as we shall see, animism is "reversed," or in other words the emphasis shifts from the activity of Chaos to the shaping powers of human thinking.

Putting the aforementioned shift in emphasis to one side for the time being, our consideration of Heidegger's interpretation to this point warrants the assertion that his pursuit of Nietzsche's metaphysics leads him to disregard the human teaching or to explain it as only a general manifestation of the cosmological teaching. At first glance, Heidegger might seem to be more consistent than Nietzsche in carrying out Nietzsche's own thoughts. This appearance will alter when we come to the study of *Gerechtigkeit.* There we shall see how Heidegger, compelled by the inner incoherence of Nietzsche's doctrines, reverses the assimilation of the human into the cosmic. Meanwhile, we must admit that Nietzsche is an inconsistent rather than a coherent thinker and that he never succeeds in reconciling, let alone in unifying, his human and his cosmological doctrines. It may be this very inconsistency that gives greater weight to Nietzsche's human teaching. We now have to determine whether Heidegger is right on this crucial point.

In order to bring together the will to power and the eternal return into two expressions of the same doctrine, Heidegger must give precedence to the eternal return, which shapes and limits the nisus toward self-transcendence that characterizes the will to power. That is, apart from the eternal return, the will to power could not eventuate in the production of worlds. The "circularity" of the eternal return must refer to the process of world shaping, although Heidegger does not have much to say about how this world shaping is supposed to function. One has the impression, in reading Heidegger's expositions on this central topic, that all determinate order is replaced by or dissolved into process; that is to say, presence is replaced by presenting. Accordingly, presence is tacitly (or not so tacitly) understood as absenting. Presence is the presence of transience or the revelation of stability as illusion. This comes suspiciously close to Heidegger's own doctrine (or prophecy) of the Event, namely, of the emitting from a concealed origin the epochs of the history of Being, which come and go, possibly in obedience to the hidden inner law of the origin or in other words to what Heidegger attributes to Nietzsche in his interpretation of the ostensible inner law of Chaos.

Just as our attainment to the level of the recollecting of the question of Being affords us no assistance in understanding either the cause or the essence of what presents itself (temporarily), and of course no basis for evaluating the temporary world on any criterion other than that of its rendering accessible the aforementioned question of Being, so with Heidegger's version of Nietzschean metaphysics. Whether he speaks for Nietzsche or for himself, Heidegger has nothing to say of any value for our attempt to live a good life, other than to issue the injunction to listen to the voice of Being, which unfortunately does not seem to be saying anything in particular. Nietzsche himself, to the extent that he may be said to dabble in metaphysics (I prefer the term "cosmology"), has the marked tendency to reduce everything to Chaos. But I want to show now that Nietzsche never follows the implication of his own doctrine of Chaos, namely, to obliterate human existence by transforming it into "irrational necessity," which, as we saw in the previous chapter, is what he actually says about the working of Chaos.[11]

In other words, Nietzsche never refers to an "inner law" concealed within Chaos. It is true that his cosmological doctrine leads to the reduction of all human experience to an illusion or in other words to a perturbation on the surface of Chaos. But this reduction is not in accord with an inner law that identifies world making with the inner activity of Being (understood as Becoming). Very far from being a metaphysician, Nietzsche rules out all metaphysics as illusion. Metaphysics is rendered impossible by the irrational necessity of the Chaos that lies in the heart of all things. Chaos is indifferent to human wishes; it cannot be understood and accordingly it may be ignored. The irrationality of Chaos is precisely what allows us to carry out our human intentions, prominent among them Nietzsche's *grosse Politik* or revolutionary political Platonism. As to *amor fati,* or the doctrine that everything recurs perpetually, and so that whatever we do has been done and will be done an endless number of times, this corresponds to the necessity of Chaos. In a reversal of Spinozism, Nietzsche in effect teaches that we are necessitated to be free, not because of the inner order or *logos* of beings, but because necessity, as irrational, is indistinguishable from chance.

It is the fact that life makes no sense when viewed from a metaphysical or cosmological standpoint that gives weight to the intrinsically illusory but nevertheless present and enduring human experience. To the extent that Nietzsche attempts to argue for or to demonstrate the truth of the eternal return, he relies upon doctrines from nineteenth-century physics, of which the key premise is that time is infinite whereas matter is finite. There can then be only a finite number of combinations of the points of force that emanate from Chaos.[12] If this is so, then there can be only a finite number of recurring historical epochs or worlds; Nietzsche makes it clear in passages cited earlier that there are a finite number of human types, all of which he has understood. He can thus write, "I want to live through all of history in my own person, and make all power and authority my own."[13] Presumably Nietzsche sees no incompatibility between cosmological irrationality and human intelligibility, the common element of which is the circularity or finitude of the eternal return. If however the common element is transformed into sameness of law, then the distinction between the cosmological and the human disappears.

On balance, then, one must resist Heidegger's attempt to establish an inner unity in the two levels of Nietzsche's teaching. Nietzsche's own efforts to justify the eternal return on scientific grounds provide us with a crucial example of the intrinsic incompatibility of those two levels. We may grant that Nietzsche conceived of this doctrine, or at least recorded his thoughts about it, in 1881, "in the framework of physical and epistemological problems."[14] There is nevertheless, as the author just cited also admits, a shift in the later writings to discussion of the eternal return in the prophetic language of *Zarathustra*. The reason for this shift is in my opinion the contemporary emergence of Nietzsche's doctrine of interpretation. This view is expressed in conjunction with physics in *Beyond Good and Evil* (1886) as follows: "It is now dawning in perhaps five or six heads that physics is also only a world-interpretation and arrangement . . . and *not* a world-explanation."[15]

I must make this point in greater detail. Nietzsche claims over and over again that physics and epistemology, hence too mathematics and logic, and in general all structures of order are themselves interpretations or emanations of the will to power. If the eternal return is the "how" as well as the "that" of the "what" of the will to power, as Heidegger asserts, then it might be plausible to argue, as Heidegger does not, that physics is the inner law of Chaos. In fact, however, since physics, as an interpretation, is an expression of the will to power, the eternal return must be a hermeneutical project rather than the "how" of the will to power. Heidegger to one side, Nietzsche holds that "all our categories of reason are of sensualistic origin: read off from the empirical world"[16] and that the intelligibility of logic rests upon the will to sameness or in other words the will to power.[17] Necessity itself "is no fact, but an interpretation."[18] This passage, incidentally, supports my previous observation that the inner coherence of human interpretation is imposed onto, rather than that it is the same as or an expression of, the "inner law" of Chaos.

In sum, the epistemological and scientific "explanations" of the eternal return are themselves expressions of the will to power in its *human*, not its cosmological, manifestation: "Will to power as knowledge not 'knowing' but schematizing, an imposition onto Chaos of as much regularity and forms as suffice for our practical needs."[19] This is exactly how we must understand the doctrine of the eternal return: as a practically motivated prophecy. I note that Heidegger's own procedure is formally very similar. He dismisses the importance of the scientific justification of the eternal return not on the basis of any detailed argument, but simply by postponing a decision until such time as we have completed our coming to terms with all of Western philosophy.[20] Meanwhile, Heidegger connects the (for him) apparently scientific discussion of the eternal return to an interpretation of the world as Chaos. This line of thought culminates in his consideration of the problem of "anthropomorphizing" (*Vermenschung*) or interpretation.

Heidegger as it were both grants that the eternal return (and so implicitly the will to power) is a human interpretation of Chaos (which, let it be noted parenthetically, may itself also be an interpretation) and denies the vitiating consequences of this admission. According to Heidegger, the entire thrust of the doctrine of the eternal return is to overcome nihilism by giving a new value to each act of life as it is lived.[21] I think that this is correct, as far as it goes. But it must be added that the doctrine of the eternal return is also dangerous and even terrifying. Furthermore, these two aspects are clearly presented in *Zarathustra*, which Heidegger, citing an expression from one of Nietzsche's Letters, refers to as an "antechamber" of Nietzsche's final doctrine, possessing only the value of an edifying work of personal encouragement.[22] To this one could repeat a reference to a letter to Carl Fuchs, dated 14 December 1887, in which Nietzsche says, "My entire 'hitherto' is a closed book. Just about everything I am now doing is drawing a line underneath [the previous work]...Now, when I must go beyond to a new and higher form."[23] I take this to refer not to a repudiation of *Zarathustra,* but to the attempt to find a new form that will give a higher expression to the thoughts of his earlier work. Certainly this reading is sustained by Nietzsche's own extravagant assertions in *Ecce Homo* of the value of *Zarathustra.*[24]

In *Zarathustra,* Nietzsche introduces the eternal return in order to give weight to the decision to enter the gateway of the moment, that is, historical time, with the attendant commitment to a world or historical epoch, and in this way to reconcile oneself with the finitude and temporality of human existence. Eternal return is recompense for the deprivation of Christian immortality.[25] At the same time, it is a terrible doctrine, one which Nietzsche refers to in the *Nachlass* as "the most extreme form of nihilism: nothingness (the 'senseless') eternal!"[26] But how can redemption be the most extreme form of nihilism? Again we see clearly the incompatible nature of the two aspects of Nietzsche's teaching. From the Hyperborean standpoint of cosmology (or what Heidegger calls metaphysics), the rejection of Platonist metaphysics is necessary in order to liberate the will for its world-producing schematization of Chaos. But this reveals world-production to be nothing more than schematizing or "anthropomorphizing." In order to escape the debilitating effects of this revelation, one must depart from the Hyperborean stance and enter the gateway of time, which is then no longer visible as a gateway but is transformed into the world we have produced. Once we have seen the truth, we must forget it: Apollonian lucidity must give way to Dionysian intoxication.

This is hardly the stuff from which coherent metaphysical doctrines of Being are constructed. Heidegger is himself inconsistent in his interpretation of Nietzsche's anthropomorphic metaphysics. At one point in his lectures, Heidegger cites the following passage from *The Gay Science,* in which Nietzsche is arguing that the world is neither an organism nor a machine: "The total character of the world is rather for all eternity Chaos, not in the sense of lacking necessity, but of lacking order, structure, form, beauty, and everything as described by our aesthetic humanity."[27] After a reference to Heraclitus (as though this were the most direct route into Nietzsche's thought), Heidegger goes on to claim that the exclusion of unity and form from Chaos does not amount to its reduction to "an arbitrarily taken, contingent confusion and a universal world brew." Even though Chaos is said here by Nietzsche to lack order and law, Heidegger emphasizes that it retains necessity.[28] But some two hundred pages later (corresponding to a difference of two years), he asserts that Chaos is not an arbitrary *durcheinander* or *Gewühl,* a brew or swarm of sensations; it is rather "corporealizing life." He adds that it is not disorder but "that jostling, streaming excitation whose order is *hidden,* whose law we do not immediately know."[29] This passage is not supported by a reference to any Nietzschean text but begins with a reflection on Hesiod.

Heracleitus and Hesiod to one side, it is striking to see how Heidegger shifts in a space of two years from Nietzsche's attribution of necessity to Chaos to the entirely unsubstantiated attribution of a hidden inner order and law. This is the linchpin of Heidegger's attempted unification of Nietzsche's doctrines into a coherent metaphysics. Heidegger's version of the reconciliation of nihilism and the liberating effects of the eternal return, however, leads directly to the obliteration of the human or in other words to a metaphysical nihilism. And Heidegger is unaware of the difficulty: "The word 'Chaos' names in Nietzsche's lexicon of senses a preventative representation as a result of which nothing can be expressed about the totality of existents. The world-all thus becomes that which is fundamentally unaddressable and unsayable— an *arrhēton.*"[30]

To perceive this is presumably not to despair but to be liberated for the possibility of effectuating one's own interpretation. In a Hegelian play on the double sense of *meinen,* Heidegger observes that every such opinion ("one's own") is an anthropomorphizing of the totality of existents. But "anthropomorphizing ceases to be an essential endangering of truth to the degree that man occupies more originarily the standpoint of an essential corner [*Ecke*]," that is, viewpoint. This in turn is possible only if the totality of the existent is experienced and conceived with respect to Being.[31]

In short, Heidegger replaces Nietzsche's explanation of cosmological rank-ordering in accord with practical needs by the assurance that a metaphysics of the totality of the existent, that is, of the Being of beings, may be evaluated truly in accord with attentiveness to the voice of

The Culmination of Metaphysics

221

Being, or to what Heidegger calls "the origin." Heidegger does not infer, as I have, from the silence of the world-all that metaphysics is impossible. Instead, he implies, almost states, that the liberating consequence of Nietzsche's completion of Platonism or metaphysics is to free us not, as Nietzsche presumably believed, for the creation of our own metaphysics, but from metaphysics as a limiting condition or merely anthropomorphic perspective.

Nietzsche himself did not achieve this culminating realization: "Neither Nietzsche nor any other thinker before him—and in particular not even Hegel, who was the first, prior to Nietzsche, to think philosophically the history of philosophy—arrive at the originary origin [*in den anfänglichen Anfang*], but they see the origin continuously and only in the light of that which is already a fall away from the origin and the immobilising of the origin: in the light of the Platonic philosophy."[32]

What precisely is the difference between the Nietzsche of Heidegger's interpretation and Heidegger himself? In Heidegger's Nietzsche, the inner law of Chaos is the same as the world-creating will of the human thinker. Being is the same activity of interpretation that is exemplified in human existence. In Heidegger's own prophecy, the activity of interpretation emerges from an originary origin. The silence of the world-all is thus presumably replaced by the voice of origination. But what does that voice tell us? Nothing other than the worlds or gifts that it sends to us. The origin does not speak of itself as other than origin, for to do so would be to reify itself or to transform itself into a world, that is, into an anthropomorphic interpretation. There is, in other words, no inner law or necessity in the origin; law and necessity are gifts of the origin.

According to Heidegger's Nietzsche, Being is the self-legislating production of illusory because intrinsically chaotic worlds. We are therefore entitled to call it the self-concealment of Being within the gifts of worlds or beings. Being is self-presentation as absence or, perhaps better, as the activity of absencing. The inner law thus never reveals itself. For all practical purposes, there is no difference between Heidegger's Nietzsche and Heidegger himself. Both may be regarded as examples of a deteriorated Hegelianism, in which negative excitation is stripped of logical structure. In all three cases, what "accumulates" is the appearing or shining-forth of essence, but in the case of Nietzsche and Heidegger, the essence is nothing.

Reversed Platonism

Thus far I have shown how Heidegger moves from necessity to inner order and law. Now I want to demonstrate his shift from necessity to possibility. Nietzsche discusses the eternal return in the *Nachlass* of 1881 as perpetual circularity of motion: "The 'Chaos of the All' as exclusion of each purposeful activity is not in contradiction to the thought of circular motion: the latter is precisely an *irrational necessity,* without any formal, aesthetic aspect. The will [*das Belieben*] is absent, in the smallest respect and in the totality."[33]

Heidegger drops the "irrational," or rather cites the reference to necessity in *The Gay Science,* in which "irrational" is not mentioned explicitly but is clearly implied by the context. Necessity then is central to the interpretation of the eternal return contained in pages 355–64 of the first volume of Nietzsche lectures. Twenty-seven pages later (in the same lecture course from 1937), Heidegger explains the eternal return as a belief, in the sense of an act of the will, by which the believer stands fast in the truth.[34] I will allude to this text shortly when I turn more directly to the discussion of the will to power; for the moment, I note only what looks like a circle rather than a sameness. The eternal return explains the "how" of the "what" but is itself explained as a manifestation of the "what."

The issue of immediate concern, however, is visible in the following assertion one page later: "The thinking of the eternal return of the same *makes secure how* the nature of the world [*Weltwesen*] exists as Chaos of the necessity of enduring becoming."[35] This rather obscure assertion seems to mean that human beings, by thinking the eternal return in a way that is both willing and believing, themselves produce the world as a schematizing of Chaos and in so doing preserve that world as an expression of the necessity of the activity of preschematized Chaos. What precisely is necessary here? Heidegger seems to be saying that there is a sameness between what we think to be necessary (the eternal return) and the necessity of chaotic activity, that is, of world making. In old-fashioned terminology, there is a sameness of Being and Thinking, but with a slight preponderance in favor of Thinking, which *makes secure* the activity intrinsic to Chaos. And Heidegger goes on to say, "The thinking of this thought preserves itself in this way in the existent as a totality, so that for this thinking the eternal return of the same is valid [*gilt*] as the Being that defines all of the existent."[36]

Validity is evaluation, the basis of world making or schematizing of

The Culmination of Metaphysics

Chaos. The validity or value of the definition of Being depends upon the thinking of the eternal return; Heidegger does not say here that the validity of our thinking depends upon the independent or antecedent truth of the eternal return, since this would be a relapse into Platonism, not an expression of reversed Platonism. In other words, it would re-establish the dualism that I for my part find in Nietzsche, but which Heidegger is attempting to overcome. The eternal return, alias the necessity of Chaos, gives shape to the world that we will, thanks to our willing. Otherwise put, we arrive at the eternal return by a "leap" as the fulfillment of a project, and not, Heidegger tells us, by a proof grounded in the chain of facts constituting actual existence. "Accordingly, the thought contained in this process of thinking," that is, the eternal return, "is never given as a present individual actuality, but only as a possibility."[37]

Concomitant with the need to account for thinking or the human, and not merely to give a unified account of Nietzsche's cosmology or metaphysics, Heidegger is led to identify the eternal return as an anthropomorphizing or interpretation of Being, hence as an act of the will, and so as a leap rather than as a deductive argument from the independently existing evidence. The leap to necessity, however, need not be taken, since there can be no external compulsion on the project of the will. This leap is a *possibility*. As such, it corresponds to Heidegger's own definition of freedom, which I cite from a text dating back to 1929: "*The selfhood of the self that lies at the ground of all spontaneity rests however in transcendence.* The projective-overthrowing act by which the world is left to dominate, is freedom." It is the *Stiften*, or founding, that is a letting-be or opening up of the world for oneself.[38]

The necessity of Chaos functions only to provide the thinker with the matrix of a world, with the accumulation of points of force. But that any thinker will in fact think the world as the eternal return is only a possibility. To be sure, Heidegger claims (again echoing *Being and Time*) that possibility is more powerful than actuality.[39] He means by this that actuality restricts us, whereas possibility is like a gateway into the creative appropriation or shaping of future events.[40] The thinking of the eternal return, we are now told, changes "the existent as a totality"; it leads to "another history." This change is effected by the will of the individual thinker on the basis of his stance toward his own moment (*Augenblick*, the name of the gateway into time in *Zarathustra*), which stance is in fact all that he knows. Heidegger states the point in language that is unmistakably an echo of Zarathustra's rhetorical syntax: the decision arises "out of that which thou willest and canst will from thineself, the manner in which thou achievest thyself, in which thou becomest master over thyself, in which thou in essential willing taketh thyself into the willing and comest unto freedom. We are free only insofar as we become free, and we become free only through our wills." There follows a supportive citation from *Zarathustra*.[41]

I have now shown that Heidegger begins with a falsified reading of Nietzsche's discussion of Chaos in order to force onto the texts a unified metaphysical doctrine, but that this effort fails because of the inner incompatibility between Nietzsche's doctrine of the will to power on the one hand and of the eternal return on the other. The will to power tells us something about human being; the eternal return tells us something about Chaos. It is true that Nietzsche provides us with a cosmological interpretation of the will to power, but as we have now seen, he also provides us with a human interpretation of the eternal return. The cosmological interpretation of the will to power leads to the irrational necessity of Chaos, not to metaphysics. Conversely, the human interpretation of the eternal return makes impossible Heidegger's attempt to show that the will to power and the eternal return say the same thing. Underlying the incompatibility between the will to power and the eternal return is the incompatibility of Nietzsche's account of human existence on the one hand and of the nature of Becoming on the other.

Same or Other?

At first glance, the will to power and the eternal return are incompatible with one another, since the first sustains the doctrine of the creative freedom of the human being, whereas the second asserts determinism. One might wish to provide a quasi-Kantian solution to this problem by contending that the will spontaneously manifests itself in law and order, which is always the same and so may be said to recur eternally, namely, whenever the will attempts to create a world. But this is a purely formal solution to our problem; it casts no light on the specific content of any world in particular. The solution, like Kantianism, remains within the orbit of Platonism, since form and content are separated. Metaphysics is then restricted to the eternal return, or to the establishment of the laws by which points of force accumulate in a circular or finite manner, and to the explanation of why this is a necessary precondition for the appearance of any content whatsoever. The production of content, on the other hand, falls within the provenance of the free human will; it is matter shaped or produced by prophetic legislation, and in this sense it is a question of politics.

In any case, formal solutions cannot be attributed to Nietzsche, since form is according to his mature teaching an interpretation, or a consequence of the will to power. The practical upshot of this teaching is that the eternal return is not the same as, but rather a subordinate consequence of, the will to power. On the other hand, as I will now show, the doctrine of the will to power is itself identified by Nietzsche as "exoteric" rather than as the key to his metaphysics. To anticipate the main point, there are no wills, but only perturbations of Chaos, that is, the accumulating and discharging of points of force. Since these accumulations and discharges recur forever or, what comes to the same thing, are the underlying truth of whatever occurs, despite all (illusory) appearances to the contrary, the will to power turns out to be a subordinate consequence of the eternal return.

It is an elementary theorem of set theory that if A and B are two sets, such that A is a subset of B and B is a subset of A, then A = B. But the will to power and the eternal return are not sets; in the "logic" of metaphysics, if A is a consequence of B and B is a consequence of A, then we have established a circle according to which each term is the ground of the other. And this in turn is to say that A and B are both the same as and other than each other. But this is the underlying axiom of Hegelianism, not of Platonism.

We can distinguish the following three cases: (1) In Hegel, the identity of Being and Nothing generates a sequence of perturbations or appearances which are in a way like Nietzschean perspectives, not of human vision onto the whole but of the Absolute onto itself. These appearances in their totality are the same as essence appearing: the eternal return is the "how" and the Absolute is the "what," whereas their sameness is the "that." (2) In Heidegger's Nietzsche, the will to power replaces the Absolute; accordingly, the inner law of the "what" is chaotic rather than logical or conceptual. Appearances or perspectives are the appearance of essence only in the sense of a presentation of the absence of law and order: the eternal return is both dissolved and established by the will to power, which is to say that each is continuously being transformed into the other. (3) In Heidegger, there is a separation or otherness between the originary origin and that which originates or in other words between essence and appearance. This gap can never be closed because essence has no appearance. Accordingly, essence cannot be distinguished from appearance; otherwise put, essence "appears" only under the mask of appearance. Appearance is both the same as and other than essence. This is indistinguishable from case 2.

The question then arises whether case 2 is not a special case of case 1. Is not the Absolute the circular totality of the self-presentations and absences of appearance or in other words, essence in the process of appearing and disappearing as it appears, that is, as masked by each particular appearance? These reflections may strike some readers as metaphysical frivolity; others will be persuaded by the cunning of reason, which has its own irony, a reasonable approximation to frivolity. We return to the seriousness that is appropriate to our topic with the observation that the continuous transformation of the two terms, will to power and eternal return, into each other constitutes an erasure or cancelling of the independence of either, and in that way a springboard out of reversed Platonism. What we seem to have learned is that there can be no explanation of form in terms of genesis and that the only resolution to dualism is monism.

To come back to the concluding point of the previous section, as soon as Heidegger attempts to unify Nietzsche's doctrine of human being with that of his ostensible metaphysics, necessity is replaced by possibility and the eternal return is exposed as an interpretation or projection of the will. Human being is like the grain of sand in the oyster of Chaos. Without it, there would be no pearl of a world; but the grain of sand cannot be rendered the same as and is clearly alien to the oyster. In more prosaic terms, Nietzschean dualism cannot be overcome by metaphysics because metaphysics, precisely as understood by Heidegger, *is* dualism. More precisely, it is a multiplicity of dualisms, of which the most important are those of form and matter on the one hand and soul and body on the other. One could of course say that in the modern epoch, attempts to overcome Platonist dualism give rise to the apparently opposing metaphysical doctrines of Materialism and Idealism. But to say this is to grant that the history of metaphysics cannot be equated with Platonism.

Heidegger to one side, Platonism, as I have argued, can be called metaphysics only in the sense of an attempt to give an account of the totality of human experience. It takes its bearings from the everyday possibility of choosing between better and worse alternatives. The "world," to employ a modern term, in which these choices are accessible is the same as and cannot be reduced to or eliminated in favor of the world of theory or science. To the Platonist, Materialism and Idealism are absurdities because they falsify the experience they purport to explain. Experience is a seamless web of discontinuities. The web is woven from the differences between thought and action, body and soul, form and matter, and countless others. By attempting to remove those differences, we do not explain but rather dissolve the web. The quest for a single principle or underlying unity is a departure from Platonism, just as Heidegger's reduction of Platonism to an ontology or metaphysics of Ideas is a falsification.

If the will to power and the eternal return say the same thing, this is because each includes the other. As we have seen, this is not a sign of identity, but rather of their instability. They collapse into one another because of the unbearable pressure toward unification placed upon them by Heidegger. They cannot sustain this pressure or serve as a single principle of the whole because each is an impossible attempt to reconcile the human and the cosmological. Each is both an interpretation or anthropomorphism and a claim to speak the truth about Chaos. To say that truth is interpretation is simply to leave the dualism between man and Chaos intact. It makes no difference whether we claim that Chaos is an interpretation of man or that man is an interpretation of Chaos. In short, the concept of interpretation is too fragile to unify the dualism between man and Chaos. Interpretations emerge from Chaos through the mediation of human discourse. To say that man is the creature of interpretation is already to define human nature and thereby to establish the aforementioned dualism.

With these reflections in mind, let us now complete our earlier analysis of the eternal return by demonstrating the exoteric status of the doctrine of the will to power. We recall that Nietzsche regularly invokes the will to power as the reality underlying all manifestations of life: "There is nothing in life that has value, except for the degree of power—granted precisely that life itself is the will to power."[42] And again: "Diverse perspectival estimations of every event and experience emerge from each of our fundamental drives. . . . *Man as a multiplicity of 'wills to power': each with a multiplicity of means of expression and forms.*"[43]

The intellect, the will, sensations of perception, all depend upon our values. These in turn correspond to our fundamental drives and their conditions of existence. And our drives are in turn reducible to the will to power, the last fact.[44] It is a trivial corollary that philosophy, "this tyrannical drive," is also "the spiritual will to power, to 'the creation of the world,' to the *causa prima*."[45]

But even farther, Being is itself life: "We have no other representation of it than 'life.' "[46] "To estimate Being itself: but estimating is itself already this Being."[47] "By what is value measured objectively? Solely by the quantum of *increased* and *more organized power*."[48] Life, Being, value: all are expressions of the will to power. Every alteration in the nature of things is "an encroachment of power over power."[49] And again: "Every occurence in the organic world is an *overpowering, a coming to be master*."[50] "*This world is the will to power—and nothing beyond that.*"[51] Finally, truth is a name "for a will to overpowering that has no end in itself. . . . It is a name for the 'will to power.' "[52]

There can be no misunderstanding the comprehensive role assigned to the will to power by Nietzsche, nor is it difficult to understand why Heidegger equates it with the "what" or in traditional language with the essence of things; in other words, with the Nietzschean equivalent of being qua being. The will to power is the "origin of motion. . . . I require dispositions and centers of motion, from which the will extends its grasp."[53] The will replaces Plato's *archē kinēseōs*, or principle of change, which Socrates identifies in the *Phaedrus* with what is traditionally translated as "world soul" (*psuche pasa*: soul in its entirety: 245c5ff). However, in Plato, soul is one of two principles; or rather, it is distinguished from the many principles known collectively as the Ideas. It would be fair to say that the Ideas regulate or shape motion, a function that Heidegger says is assigned by Nietzsche to the eternal return. But according to Heidegger, the eternal return says the same as the will to power; it must therefore assign the regulation of motion to the principle of motion itself. But this is not reversed Platonism; it is the attempt to step outside of Platonism entirely. Heidegger's Nietzsche attempts to replace dualism by monism.

That the principle of motion cannot itself be an Idea is obvious from the fact that soul alone moves itself perpetually (*Phaedrus* 245d6ff). Apparently the personal or individual souls all share in this property of world soul (245e4ff). In the immediate sequel, Socrates does raise the question of the *idea* of the personal soul, but he states that to answer this question would require a divine and long discussion. On the other hand, it is a shorter and human affair to say what it is like (246a3ff). The likeness offered by Socrates is that of a charioteer, apparently without a chariot but driving a team of winged horses, one white and noble, the other black and base. For our purposes, the important point here is that the likeness is of moving entities. The ultimate goal of their motion is to rise to the roof of the cosmos, which is itself moving, and to stand on the roof or back or at least to extend the head of the charioteer up through the roof, in order to see the Ideas. The soul moves; the Ideas, referred to here as Hyperuranian beings, stand still, like the fixed stars (247c1ff). The term "idea," as applied here to the soul, cannot refer to a Hyperuranian being. There can be no question that in this myth, Socrates preserves the dualism of principles: soul and the Ideas. And the soul views the Ideas, that is to say, "genuine being" (*ousia ontōs ousa:* 247c3ff) "through time" (*dia chronou:* 247d3).

In order for Nietzsche to qualify as a Platonist, he must preserve the distinction between rest and motion, more precisely, between the principle of motion (soul) and the principle of form (Ideas). For his Platonism to be reversed, it is not satisfactory to collapse the distinction between motion and form; instead, motion must give order and value to form. But this is possible in only one way: if form is a product of motion. The doctrine that form, that is, order and value, is a product of motion is properly called Materialism. If the eternal return refers to the process by which motion is shaped and ordered and hence given value, then Nietzsche is a Materialist. But there is a further difference between Nietzsche and the reversed Platonism of Materialism. The Materialist as such does not deny that matter in motion gives rise to genuine form, and so to an order and even value that are not illusory but true and independent of human cognition. When this step is taken, the result is Idealism; in other words, Materialism inverts itself by referring to form, and so too to explanation, as the perspectival or anthropomorphic interpretation of Chaos. Matter, and so too motion as measurable, are themselves interpretations.

I have already suggested that Materialism and Idealism are unstable doctrines that continuously turn into each other or else return to Platonist dualism in order to state themselves coherently and consistently. Hegel is the (perhaps unique) paradigm of a philosopher who attempts to assert Materialism and Idealism simultaneously or to interpret their reciprocal transformations as the third principle, the notorious identity of identity and difference, or in other words the Absolute. In order to validate his doctrine, Hegel must (among other requirements) explain to us in an intelligible manner how the two monisms are reconciled by a third which is itself neither the one nor the other but exactly that process by which they pose and negate themselves. Heidegger's Nietzsche, as we have already seen, is not a Hegelian; but neither is he a Platonist or a reversed Platonist (i.e., a non-Idealist Materialist).

In fact, it is not possible to classify Nietzsche within any of the aforementioned rubrics, not because of his radical uniqueness, but because of the incoherence of his doctrines. Note that incoherence is not the same as instability. Materialism and Idealism are unstable but not incoherent; they succeed in saying something intelligible which is false. But Nietzsche's two teachings, which I have been calling merely for the sake of convenience the human and the cosmological, when taken jointly, cancel each other out. They do not succeed in making any statement that is capable of being called false. If Nietzsche's last word is the will to power, and the will to power is the accumulation and dissolution of points of force, then the will to power is indistinguishable from Chaos. All human manifestations of the will to power are meaningless perturbations on the surface of Chaos. Recourse to the eternal return accomplishes nothing: nothing of a scientific nature because science is an interpretation, and so an expression of the will to power, or in other words an excitation of Chaos; but also nothing of a metaphysical nature because the ostensible shaping contributed by eternal return to the accumulation and dissolution of points of force is nothing more than that accumulation and dissolution itself. In Heidegger's language, it is the constancy of Becoming in its presence.[54] "Presence" here refers to motion itself, not to the forms of motion.

If, on the other hand, the will to power, exactly like the eternal return, is an interpretation, then so too is Chaos. The identification of Being as Chaos serves the rhetorical function of repudiating all metaphysical doctrines, and so all cosmological restrictions on human productive activity. Chaos is Nietzsche's "Thing-in-itself," or *noumenon:* a word for the unknowable, for what can be thought only as necessary but as concealed by the spatio-temporal formations of genesis. The question then arises and overshadows all others touching upon Nietzsche's peculiar doctrines: what interprets? We cannot ask, "Who interprets?" in the traditional sense of that expression because Nietzsche denies the integrity of the *ego cogitans,* or subject, which is in fact explained as an illusory manifestation of the will to power. It would therefore seem that the answer to our question is that the will to power interprets. But how can an interpretation interpret?

At this point, it will be helpful to establish that Nietzsche himself regarded the thesis of the will to power as part of his "exoteric" teaching. As Nietzsche says in the *Twilight of the Idols,* "Today we know that ['will'] is a mere word."[55] The distinction between "esoteric" and "exoteric" is developed by Nietzsche at some length in his discussion of the philosophical nature in *Beyond Good and Evil.*[56] "In general and in brief, everything rare for the rare."[57] It is today widely supposed that esotericism could not have been practiced by genuine philosophers because it is a form of lying and hence beneath the moral rectitude of lovers of truth. I cannot explore this amusing subject in the detail it deserves, although I will not resist citing the following passage from Stendhal, inscribed by Nietzsche (on more than one occasion) into his Notebooks: "Une croyance presque instinctive chez moi c'est que tout homme puissant ment quand il parle, et à plus forte raison quand il écrit."[58]

The indispensable point for our purposes is that esotericism is not lying in the sense of simple concealment; instead, it is the method of saying both *A* and not-*A* in different contexts and frequency. Differently stated, the esotericist of the Nietzschean persuasion states quite openly his dangerous or sublime truths, but also their opposites; if he is competent, he will do so in such a way as to carry out distinct ends, by addressing distinct types of readers. In a passage from the Notebooks of 1886/87, Nietzsche distinguishes directly between his esoteric and his exoteric teachings, rather than describing the general method and its motivation. The example he cites of the exoteric doctrine is, "Everything is will against wills." The esoteric version is, "There are no wills."[59]

There is of course no reason for us to be shocked by this assertion, since its content follows immediately from the denial of the ego or of subjectivity: "The spontaneous mass of energy distinguishes human beings, not an individual-atom."[60] The will is a changing ratio of sub-wills, each in turn nothing more than an accumulation of points of force, each attempting to dominate the others. But let me be clear about this: if there are no subjects and hence no wills, there can be no will to power. In his esoteric teaching, Nietzsche does not reduce the human will to the will to power in the sense of deriving one type of will from another. His point is rather that the will to power is a mere slogan for Chaos: "Chaos works perpetually in our spirits: concepts, images, sensations are brought into proximity with one another *by chance*, scattered amidst each other by the throw of the dice."[61]

This text establishes unambiguously what it means to say, as I have of Nietzsche's doctrines, that by necessity he means chance. The world "is not an organism but Chaos."[62] Chaos, contrary to Heidegger, is disorder, lawlessness, random and irrational motion. Nevertheless, Nietzsche also maintains that law and order are a consequence of the will: "Will to power as knowledge [is] not knowing but schematizing, imposing onto Chaos as much regularity and form as suffices for the satisfaction of our practical needs."[63] This apparent contradiction may be resolved as follows: human being is that manifestation of Chaos which schematizes the remainder. But such a resolution merely shifts the problem back one step. For human being is itself an interpretation or schematizing of Chaos. In order to exist as human, man must already have been schematized by some hermeneutical agent. Chaos cannot produce order unless it has been organized. We may wish to say that order originates by chance, as a consequence of random, disorderly motion. But this is tantamount to asserting that human being is "natural" and not perspectival. The disorderly motion of Chaos must then have produced not an illusion or product of an antecedent act of the will, but the will itself. The will, or more precisely the human function of perspectival world making, exists by nature, not through some perspectival creation of illusory organization.

We thus arrive at A and not-A: the will is the last fact and the will is not the last fact. As this can also be expressed, either we take our bearings by Nietzsche's doctrine of our practical needs, and so by *praksis* in the Platonic sense of practico-production, or we try to reduce the various levels of Nietzsche's thinking to a unified metaphysics. The assertion that the will is the last fact does not support the latter alternative because will and Chaos are incommensurable forces. But neither is it compatible with the practical approach, unless we equate "will" with the human will and grant the dualism between human nature and Chaos. The metaphysical approach is best served by starting with the esoteric thesis that the will is not the last fact; but this leaves inexplicable the existence of human being. As will become still more evident when I turn to his analysis of *Gerechtigkeit*, Heidegger attempts to factor human being or thinking into the cosmological equation. The result is not unity or "the same" but a quasi-Hegelian *Gewühl* that is committed to an anthropomorphic interpretation of Chaos.

Gerechtigkeit

In his attempt to attribute an inner order and law to Nietzsche's Chaos, Heidegger appealed to Hesiod and Heracleitus. He traces Nietzsche's interest in *Gerechtigkeit* to his early studies of pre-Platonic metaphysics, in particular, of Heracleitus.[64] Whether or not this is true of Nietzsche, it is certainly true that, with respect to *Gerechtigkeit*, Heidegger was influenced decisively by his study of the pre-Socratic poets and thinkers. Heidegger admits that the importance he attributes to *Gerechtigkeit* is not directly visible in Nietzsche's texts; he says that he has discovered this importance by thinking through Nietzsche's doctrine of truth, a task accomplished by none of his predecessors, including Nietzsche himself.[65] In this connection, we should recall Heidegger's analysis in his lectures on Parmenides of the transformation of the Greek word *alētheia* into the Roman *veritas,* which is understood, in a confluence of Christian and Roman influences, as *rectitudo.* This etymological history is intended to show how the original sense of truth as openness is replaced by the notion of truth as correctness in the double sense of correspondence but also of doctrinal and legal righteousness or justice.[66] "The modern essence of truth is determined by certainty, rightness, being righteous [*Gerechtsein*], and *Gerechtigkeit.*"[67]

It follows from Heidegger's own account that the sense of truth in the metaphysical tradition is not merely theoretical but intrinsically practical. "Being is as righteousness [*dikē*] the key to the existent in its structure [*Gefüge*]."[68] On the other hand, Heidegger's explanation of the original or authentic sense of *dikē* in pre-Socratic thought, prior, in other words, to its corruption by Christian and Roman legal influences, is neither theoretical nor practical, terms he would associate with metaphysics. I would be inclined to characterize this explanation as the attempt, intentional or not, to unify thinking and being or, in the terms of our immediate interest, to identify the inner law of Chaos with that of the thinking of Being. Stated as simply as possible, genuine thinking is open to but also tends or cares for Being. Heidegger cites the injunction of Periander of Corinth, whom he calls the oldest thinker in the West: "Care for the all" (*meleta to pan*).[69] I note in passing that *meletē* and its associated verb-forms are used regularly by Plato to refer to the care of the cosmos by Zeus and the Olympians.[70] *Meletē* has a political connotation for the Greeks that is not present in Heidegger's account.

In addition to the Parmenides lectures, which were delivered in 1942/43, one should consult Heidegger's essay "The Saying of Anaximander," which dates from 1946, again within the decade that is of central significance for us.[71] This essay is devoted to the interpretation of the fragment attributed to Anaximander which speaks of the destruction of generated things as *dikēn didonai*, "paying the penalty." Heidegger explains this as the exercise of righteousness by beings toward one another in accordance with the order of time. That which is temporarily present sets things back into the groove and so removes the unrighteousness (*Unfug*) of destruction, or the disruption of the "groove" of genesis. Heidegger interprets *dikē* to mean "in the groove" and thereby connects righteousness (*Fug*) with structure (*Gefüge*).[72] In this way he transforms the political dimension in Anaximander's metaphor into an ontological or metaphysical concern, within which genesis shapes itself. This metaphysical sense is then applied to Nietzsche's doctrine of thinking as the shaping of genesis.

Heidegger does not mention Anaximander in his Nietzsche lectures. In the Anaximander essay, however, he discusses the young Nietzsche's translation of the fragment. The Greek reads, *didonai gar auta dikēn kai tisin allēlois*. In a standard English translation: "Then [the beings] must pay the penalty and be judged for their unrighteousness." Nietzsche renders the fragment as follows: "denn sie müssen Busse zahlen und für ihre Ungerechtigkeit gerichtet werden."[73] There can be no doubt of the connection in Heidegger's mind at this period between the earliest interpretation of genesis and Nietzsche's understanding of Chaos. But the last metaphysician has assimilated the modern doctrine of subjectivity; in his interpretation, Heidegger faces the task of reconciling the human teaching, or the doctrine of the will to power as it applies to mankind, to the cosmological teaching, or the will to power as shaped from within by the eternal return.

Accordingly, Heidegger explains Nietzsche's use of *Gerechtigkeit* to refer not to the cosmological process of genesis, but to human "producing and commanding" or the process by which man installs himself within Chaos.[74] It is the process in man that is coordinate to the inner order and law of Chaos, under which what presents itself as present acquires its limitation and definition as a particular manifestation of force or will to power. We note that postsubjectivist metaphysics remains subjectivist in the sense that the inner law by which genesis assumes the order of the cosmos must be the same as the will that defines human thinking. But this is not the same as to assimilate human thinking into the self-ordering process of genesis. The will to power, which is for Nietzsche exoteric, becomes for Heidegger the esoteric anthropomorphism or the standpoint within which the thinker obeys Periander's injunction to care for the whole. In sum, the interpretation that the will to power and the eternal return say the same leads to the assimilation of human thinking into the generative processes of Chaos. But the interpretation of *Gerechtigkeit* reverses this assimilation: the generative processes of Chaos are willed into being by human thinking.

If we look at Nietzsche's own use of the term *Gerechtigkeit,* we find no justification for attributing a cosmological or metaphysical significance to it. The following passage comes as close as any to linking *Gerechtigkeit* with Heidegger's favored terms: "In our greatest *Gerechtigkeit* and honesty is the will to power, to the infallibility of our person."[75] Nietzsche is here simply making a psychological observation about the concealed presence of the desire to dominate within our most virtuous actions. This typical Nietzschean usage can be illustrated at somewhat greater length by the following passage:

> Your Henrik Ibsen has become very clear to me. With all his "will to the truth," he has not attempted to free himself from moral illusion, which says "freedom" and will not admit what freedom

is; the second stage in the metamorphosis of "the will to power" from the side of those to whom it is lacking. In the first stage one demands *Gerechtigkeit* from those who have power. In the second stage one says "freedom" which is to say that one wishes to get loose from those who have power. In the third stage one says "equal rights" i.e. one wants, for so long as one does not have the upper hand to prevent one's competitor also from increasing in power.[76]

Heidegger ignores these passages and others like them and begins his interpretation with the assertion that truth for Nietzsche means "holding as true."[77] This is to say that truth is an activity of the will as much as of the intellect. Heidegger describes the activity as "the productive presupposition of a horizon of beingness [*Seiendheit*], of the unity of the categories as schemata."[78] This terminology reminds us immediately of Kant, but with a crucial difference. It sounds like a reference to the transcendental unity of apperception as a logical condition for the possibility of thinking a world. There is a crucial difference, to be sure; what is in Kant a logical condition becomes in Nietzsche an act of the will. But Heidegger is not referring here to the will of an individual or historical person; he is speaking of thinking as such, and in this sense he brings out, intentionally or otherwise, the Kantian flavor of Nietzsche's own doctrine. The real difference does not lie in Nietzsche's repudiation of the transcendental, which repudiation is contradicted by the status of the will to power; the difference lies in the fact that Kant's categories are necessary and "objective" in the sense that they and they alone account for the objectivity of the objects of phenomenal experience. Kant's categories are actualized by, but hold independently of, the action of the will. In this sense they are like Aristotle's species-forms. Nietzsche's categories are productions or poems, artifacts of the will.

As the making fast of that which will henceforward be called "beingness" (*Seiendheit*), *Gerechtigkeit* is a command; but it is an ontological rather than a political command. The question then arises: what is to prevent the command from lapsing into arbitrariness? "From whence does the giving of commands derive its standards?"[79] Since we have abolished the metaphysical distinction of truth in itself and so too the devaluation of illusion, the answer, Heidegger tells us, must be that the standard comes from the very act of "holding as true."[80] To say this in another way, according to this account of Nietzsche's teaching,

I will it to be true that truth is what I will to be true. Whether we take this at the individual or the transcendental level, the upshot is to reinstitute the primacy of Idealism over Materialism in Nietzsche's unstable teaching. In another vocabulary, it is no longer evident that *Gerechtigkeit* signifies what Anaximander is supposed to have meant by *dikē*.

Heidegger's Nietzsche, like Nietzsche himself, fluctuates between the two poles of man and Chaos. Man seems to be an interpretation of Chaos in both the subjective and objective senses of the genitive. Man "installs" himself in Chaos and hence must be initially independent of and dominant over it. But man, understood via *Gerechtigkeit,* must possess, and indeed he must *be* in the fullest sense, will to power. As such, it is man who produces not simply perspectival worlds, but Chaos itself, understood as the origin or substratum of creation. If the will to power and the eternal return taken together constitute the nature of Being, then Being is not simply man-made but the expression of humanity. But how can this be harmonized with Nietzsche's regular deconstruction of humanity into the will to power, understood not as the principle of subjectivity, but as Chaos?

I come now to the pivotal section of the Heideggerian passage that has guided our reflection on *Gerechtigkeit.* In this passage, Heidegger gives "the guiding, unexpressed and most universal metaphysical determination" of Nietzsche's conception of the essence of truth, as distinguished from what he actually says about that essence. This section is unfortunately extremely obscure and must be parsed sentence by sentence.[81] For the sake of convenient reference, I will number the sentences consecutively. Sentence 1: "The interpretation of truth as holding-as-true showed *pre*-positioning as the *positioning*-before of that which presses upon us, and thereby [as] the rendering stable of Chaos." The German term *Vorstellen,* translated here as "pre-positioning," has as its primary meanings representation and imagination. In both cases, the intellect performs a constructive act by which it either brings back into view something that was previously apprehended or else produces an image of the content of an antecedent apprehension. The intellect places or positions before itself what it cognizes. Heidegger brings out the Idealistic background of his terms by hyphenating *Vor-stellen* and italicizing first the prefix and then the main stem of the verb.

We may also paraphrase sentence 1 as follows: "The intellect projects in advance what it intends or wills to hold as true, and thereby imposes an imaginative representation of order onto Chaos." This is the completion, in the sense of rendering explicit the hidden meaning, of Platonic *noēsis,* which believes itself to contemplate the independent and eternal Ideas, but which instead serves as the lens through which the will projects a perspectival image of ostensibly genuine being. "Pre-positioning" is thus the self-positioning of the thinker, or the quasi-transcendental preparation of the horizon within which the thinker is about to project a world. Thinking is thought thinking itself; man has been transformed into the Aristotelian god. The "rendering stable of Chaos" is thus the human version of creation ex nihilo. It is not a consequence of the inner law of Chaos as the expression of a will to power independent of human being. To the contrary, Chaos is itself an interpretation of the *nihil* upon which the human will exercises itself.

Sentence 2: "That which is true in this holding-as-true secures Becoming, but thereby does *not* correspond to the Becoming-character of Chaos." The thinker, or the Nietzschean version of transcendental thought as brought to a focus within the individual agent, gives stability to Becoming in the act of willing a world. But this stability takes shape as the production of an illusion. The illusion is salutary for mankind, but health consists in the misperception of Chaos as order. Heidegger thus states explicitly that the production of illusion, by which Becoming is rendered secure for human existence, is not a product of the inner order and law of Chaos. A secure or orderly Becoming does *not* correspond to the insecure or disorderly nature of Chaos. Furthermore, security lies in the resolution of Chaos into Becoming, but not into Being. The stability of health is a precondition for the decline into sickness; security is orderly motion. It is therefore accumulation at the price of dissolution. In order to be healthy, we "pay the penalty" of the sickness unto death: hence the eternal return of same and other, order and disorder, genesis and destruction, Becoming and Chaos.

Sentence 3: "What is true in this truth is noncorrespondence, untruth, error, illusion." According to Heidegger, traditional Platonism holds to a correspondence-theory of truth, in which a proposition is said to be true if it exhibits the likeness (*homoiōsis*) of the order of beings to which it corresponds. But truth in Nietzsche is holding-as-true, that is, the projection of a salutary illusion or noble lie which does not correspond to the nature of Chaos; for Chaos has no nature. From this standpoint, to say that the world is a work of art giving birth to itself is to attribute the birth of the world not to Chaos, but to the process of world making as the expression of the will to power, understood now as the will of the thinker. The world is the expression of the table of values asserted by the thinker ("Thus shall it be!"), and these values are in turn expressions of power. But it is no longer possible to consider the mere expression of power as the last word. The expression of power is intentional or directed toward the creation of a world suitable for the dominance, and not just the existence, of the thinker.

Sentences 4 and 5 may be taken together: "However, this characterization of the true as a type of error is grounded in the assimilation of the pre-*positioned* to that which is to be made fast. Here too where the true of holding-as-true is grasped as the untrue, the most universal essence of truth is grounded in the sense of *homoiosis*." This passage appears to contradict my analysis of sentence 3. Heidegger wishes to establish that Nietzsche, as a reversed Platonist, must preserve a reverse version of the *homoiōsis*-doctrine of truth even in rejecting or attempting to reject Platonism. Platonism is rejected in the sense that there is no independent and stable order of beings to which our propositions are said to correspond. A true statement is not one that mirrors the formal structure of the world, if "formal structure" is understood to refer to Platonic Ideas or Aristotelian categories. But to say that truth is a type of error is to say that a true proposition mirrors or exhibits the likeness of an untruth. A true proposition is one that asserts an untruth, that is, a work of art, as opposed to some independent state of affairs that actually obtains, as in traditional Platonism. There is thus no contradiction with the previous interpretation.

True propositions are those which express knowledge. Knowledge is rooted in the stable world. But stability is secured by the will through the act of pre-positioning. Heidegger emphasizes the prefix when he wishes to focus upon the primacy of the will. He emphasizes the suffix when he is concerned primarily with the world as posited or secured. Knowledge is the act of the will with respect to the domination of the world as secured. Art is the act by which the will surpasses the limits positioned in and as knowledge. This is the transfiguration of knowledge into art. The collapse of the difference between the true and the apparent world establishes the *homoiōsis*-doctrine of truth in a sense that is the reverse of Platonism: the true world, and so too knowledge, is revealed as a work of art by which man installs himself and hence makes himself like Chaos.[82] This conclusion is reached in the two and a half paragraphs following our enumerated sentences.

What does Heidegger mean when he says that human life makes itself like and installs itself into Chaos? In the first place, *homoiōsis* is no longer a process of bringing propositions into accord with a fixed, in the sense of independently and eternally true, order. It is rather the process of accommodating human life to the absence of an independent and eternally true order. This accommodation is carried out through the process of world making, or *positioning*. But the positioned is a result of *pre*-positioning. Positioning makes possible knowledge, but pre-positioning is the ground for the transfiguration of knowledge into art and hence for self-overcoming, which is a mirroring of or rendering oneself like the fluctuations of Chaos. It could be said that Heidegger here emphasizes the accumulating function of Chaos and forgets the dissolving function. But death is the inner companion of life, which is not possible except as continuous growth, and so continuous destruction. I exist not simply by destroying others, but by continuously destroying my past. Conversely, others exist only by destroying me. I and others "pay the penalty" or set genesis back into the groove of its cyclical structure by coming into being and passing away.

A much more serious consequence of Heidegger's assertion, and in fact the crucial consequence, is that the inner order or law of Chaos is in effect identified as human life, more precisely, as the will to will, the truth of which is holding-as-true. The making of human life to be like Chaos "is not imitative and restoring adjustment to that which is present before us," not in other words the copying of an original, "but *commanding-poetic, perspectival-horizon-opening, secure-making transfiguration*."[83] Heidegger identifies this as the sense of *Gerechtigkeit*. In my own language, *Gerechtigkeit* is the "setting-straight" or ordering of Chaos. There is then no inner order or law in Chaos as independent of human willing and to which the latter accommodates itself or "makes itself like." The "making like" is rather an installing, in the sense of rendering Chaos secure for habitation, of that which imposes order by lawgiving. It is a making-like because human life is accumulation and dissolution of force.

But contrary to Heidegger's recreation of the "unstated" essence of Nietzsche's teaching, the installation of human life into Chaos is *not* a "making like" in the following crucial sense. Apart from its submission

The Culmination of Metaphysics

to the human will, Chaos is not alive, not intentional, not commanding or projective, not perspectival or horizon-opening. It is the unknown and unknowable thing-in-itself, the *nihil* or sheer possibility of creation. We see here once more the same problem that arose previously with respect to the will to power. Both Nietzsche and Heidegger fluctuate in their interpretation of will to power, understood as the last fact or principle of Being. Sometimes the will to power is clearly a pseudonym for Chaos, and at other times, such as in the text we have been studying, but also in Nietzsche's practico-political writings, it is the metaphorical expression of the human will. For Nietzsche, the will to power is an exoteric doctrine, but that does not resolve the contradiction between human life and Chaos. Heidegger takes seriously the will to power, but he is unable to resolve this deeper contradiction.

In fact, by taking seriously the will to power and by attempting to unite it with the equally rhetorical thesis of the eternal return in a unified metaphysics or doctrine of Being, Heidegger makes the task of understanding Nietzsche altogether more obscure than it need be. We do not need to take the extreme position of regarding the will to power and the eternal return as mere political slogans. Let them stand as expressions of Nietzsche's cosmological prophecy, namely, as doctrines that require belief if we are to be free of metaphysical doctrines that restrict the fecundity and so the health of human existence. Let us say that the human will is capable of imposing only a finite number of constantly recurring comprehensive or world-making perspectives onto Chaos. We are free because these worlds are our own creations; we can act with discrimination or evaluate, and so rank-order these worlds, because they are finite in number, which means that human beings come to exist in a finite number of ways, and so possess what for all practical purposes may be called a nature. Some worlds or lives or values are healthy; others are sick. If *Gerechtigkeit* is to be assigned an importance comparable to that given it by Heidegger, let us understand it as the process of setting straight the random motions of genesis in accord with the will to live, and so to transcend.

From this simplified (and so for some tastes less attractive) standpoint, Heidegger is right to say that *Gerechtigkeit* is a human thinking that builds a world by making decisions that separate measures and heights, that is, dimensions of quality and quantity within which the building can occur; and so too it is a negating of what has been previously constructed.[84] "The living core of life rests in nothing else than in that building, separating, negating thinking."[85] Heidegger goes on to say, "This pathbreaking, decisive, erecting grounding of a height that serves as a lookout post, is the ground for the capacity of thinking to designate the essential nature of producing and commanding, within which perspectives open and horizons construct themselves."[86]

Allow me to make explicit what Heidegger has left unstated (whether or not unthought) in this assertion. *Gerechtigkeit,* or human willing, has two dimensions, of which one is the world-making process we have been studying; the other, however, corresponds to what I have called previously the Hyperborean standpoint, albeit in a Fichtean rather than an Aristotelian mode of thinking thinking itself. But Fichte and Aristotle belong to that band of philosophers whose capacity to care for the whole depends upon their access to the "lookout post" that constitutes the genuine truth of Platonism.

Heidegger, needless to say, does not make a Platonic interpretation of the lookout post, which is for him itself a consequence of the building, separating, and negating thinking. Heidegger's lookout post, one could say, is precisely the installation within the heart of Chaos. But the passage he cites from Nietzsche in support of his interpretation also lends itself to a more Platonic reading: "*Gerechtigkeit* as a function of a power of looking about one for a far distance, one which looks out over the small perspectives of good and evil, and thus has a broader horizon of *advantage*—the intention of preserving something that is *more* than this or that person."[87] Heidegger says, "Looking about for a far distance is a *looking out over* the small perspectives, and so itself a genuine perspectivist looking, i.e. one that opens perspectives."[88] What he does not say is that it is the synoptic perspective that opens perspectives. Perspectivist looking is not the same as taking in the sense of restricting oneself to this or that perspective.

On the other hand, Heidegger in effect restates the Platonic understanding in Nietzschean language when he defines the nature of power as "a looking out that is a looking around for a far distance, in the outlook that, as looking over everything, is total domination [*Übermachtigung*]."[89] This is the basis for Heidegger's reply to the question, noted previously, about whether the doctrine of the will to power and the eternal return are themselves an anthropomorphizing (*Vermenschung*) of Being as the totality of the existent.[90] Heidegger first asserts

The Culmination of Metaphysics

that "the world totality and the thinking of the thinker cannot be detached from each other." In other words, the interpretation of *Gerechtigkeit* is the key to the interpretation of the will to power and the eternal return. Being is indeed a *Vermenschung,* which is to say that there is no inner order or law of Chaos independent of human will. Heidegger continues: the inseparability just cited "is the necessary relation of man as a being that has a standpoint in the midst of the beings as a totality," and it is the relation to this totality itself.[91] But this statement is rather obscure since it creates the impression that man and the totality of beings are initially separate but related by man's nature as the being that takes a standpoint.

I quote in full Heidegger's clarification of his own statement, which resonates with the language of *Being and Time:*

> The Being of man—and as far as we know *only* of man—is grounded in *Dasein;* the *Da* [there] is the possible place for the necessary standpoint of his Being. At the same time, we derive from this essential connection the insight: anthropomorphism [*die Vermenschung*] becomes all the less substantial [*wesenloser*] as a danger to truth, the more originarily man occupies the standpoint of an essential standpoint [*Ecke*], i.e. in so far as he knows and grounds *Da-sein* as such. The essentiality of the standpoint defines itself however from the originality and breadth in which the existent as a totality is experienced and conceived in accord with the only decisive respect, namely, that of Being.[92]

We have heard part of this citation previously. It applies only secondarily to Nietzsche as well as to his predecessors, but primarily to Heidegger. Interpretations of the All or whole are all perspectival or anthropomorphic, but they may be evaluated with respect to their openness toward Being. Nietzsche's standpoint is that of the installation of mankind into Chaos, which we may now understand as the prototype for Heidegger's origin. Just as the origin conceals itself within the disguise of its gifts, so too Chaos, the *nihil* or precondition of human creativity, is intrinsically inaccessible except *as* an interpretation. But Heidegger's origin is distinct from as well as the source of the will. The essentiality of *Dasein* thus differs in Nietzsche and in Heidegger. For Nietzsche, the *Da,* or possible place of human being, is human being itself. For Heidegger, it is the locus of openness to the origin of human being.

Nietzsche's doctrine is taken by Heidegger to be the culmination of metaphysics in the sense of caring for the All, which he explains as *Gerechtigkeit* in the sense of the schematizing of Chaos. But at the same time, Heidegger explains Nietzsche's doctrine as a metaphysics of Being, and more precisely of being qua being. These two interpretations are incompatible. The first account is predicated upon the exclusion of metaphysics; it comes much closer to genuine Platonism than does the so-called metaphysical doctrine that Heidegger finds in the will to power and the eternal return. The second account does not install man within Chaos but rather assimilates him into it, or treats man as a projection of Chaos.

Nihilism

7

European Nihilism

In chapter 6 I discussed the will to power, the eternal return, and *Gerechtigkeit,* three of the five terms that Heidegger deems central to Nietzsche's teaching. The two remaining terms are nihilism and the superman. I want next to study the difference between Nietzsche's understanding of nihilism and Heidegger's reappropriation of it as the history of metaphysics. I will turn shortly to a close analysis of a long fragment from Nietzsche's Notebooks, dated 10 June 1887 and entitled "European Nihilism."[1] This will provide the basis for a consideration of the very important section in volume II of Heidegger's *Nietzsche* lectures entitled "The *seinsgeschichtliche* Determination of Nihilism." The will to power and the eternal return are on the one hand an expression of nihilism and on the other a response to it. It is thus convenient to study nihilism first and then to consider the superman, who is intended by Nietzsche as a positive or active response to the destructive or reactive phenomenon of nihilism.

The will to power and the eternal return express the essence of nihilism because they deny a "sense" to the world, that is, to the existent as a totality, as Heidegger puts it. The world is reduced to Chaos. But the same doctrines are intended to provide the impetus for the creation of a new world out of the very same Chaos. Let me illustrate this dual sense of nihilism immediately with a citation from Nietzsche, in order to have the main point before our eyes when we immerse ourselves in the details of the doctrine: "What is a *belief*? How does it arise? Each belief is a *taking-as-true*. The most extreme form of nihilism would be: that *every* belief, each taking-as-true is necessarily false: *because there is no true world.* Therefore: *a perspectivist illusion,* the origin of which lies in us (insofar as we have continuous need of a narrower, abbreviated, simplified world)—that it is the *degree of force,* how much we can admit the illusoriness, the necessity of the lie, without being destroyed. *To that extent, as the denial of a true world, of Being, nihilism could be a divine mode of thought: - - -"*[2]

As a commentary to this text, one may consult a slightly later fragment of the same year, one in which Nietzsche distinguishes between active nihilism, or the intensified power of spirit, and passive nihilism, or the decline and retreat of the power of spirit.[3] The main point is that nihilism is not a gift of Being and not even a direct consequence of the will to power or the eternal return. It is a *belief* or condition of the human spirit, a belief with both negative and positive consequences. Only if one accepted Heidegger's extreme interpretation could one argue that beliefs and states of the human spirit are themselves manifestations of the identity between *Gerechtigkeit,* or human thinking, and the inner order of Chaos and in that sense a "gift" of Being. As we have seen, however, there is no inner order of Chaos for Nietzsche; what one could call the "belief" in Chaos serves effectively to liberate the will.

To say this in a slightly different way, the fundamental fact for Nietzsche is neither the will to power nor the eternal return and hence not Chaos, but rather the concrete historical problem of human existence within the epoch that extends from the archaic Greeks to Nietzsche's own time. Nietzsche takes his bearings by the cyclical intensification and dissipation of spiritual energy that defines human historical existence. The task he sets himself is the cultivation of a new race of superior human beings. The method he employs to carry out this task is the production of a set of diverse beliefs that will accelerate the destruction of a dying age from the dissipative effects of what it regards as its highest accomplishments. We may refer to this set of beliefs as Nietzsche's political rhetoric. This rhetoric is devised through the assimilation of the finite number of human types that appear in each cycle of history. Nietzsche is able to transform mankind because he has understood it as a totality.

The question arises whether Nietzsche intended to go beyond this finite circle of human manifestations, as is suggested by the doctrine of the superman, or whether he simply hoped to prepare the way for the recurrence of a higher type like the pre-Socratic Greeks or Renaissance Florentines. On balance, my own opinion is this. The extreme rhetoric of transcendence associated with the doctrine of the superman in *Zarathustra* is intended primarily to motivate the destruction of contemporay decadence by holding out the quasi-religious promise of a new incarnation. The concept of the superman plays no part in Nietzsche's writings after *Zarathustra*. More important, the theme of radical and continuous transcendence is in direct contradiction to Nietzsche's various statements on the finite number of human types or unchanging hierarchy of natures. It is in contradiction to the doctrine of the eternal return, as that doctrine is explained in *Zarathustra*.

As we have seen, the doctrine of the eternal return has as its primary role the reinstituting of weight or significance in a human existence that has been deprived of its Platonist and Christian foundations. It is thus both salutary and the most terrifying of doctrines. The terrifying nature of the doctrine is required by its salutary function. We cannot produce new values if we are bound by a permanent, immutable order. Creation, as Zarathustra insists, is also destruction. This continues to be true if the ostensibly immutable order is in fact undergoing a slow and paralyzing process of inner decay. The net practical effect of the two doctrines of the will to power and the eternal return is to teach that order is illusory, and so that we are free to create a new table of values. On my interpretation, the thesis of radical novelty is part of Nietzsche's exoteric doctrine; in the esoteric doctrine, the inner Chaos of Becoming sanctions transformations of order by the human will, but the number of possible transformations is limited. This interpretation is also required by the assumption, which Heidegger makes, that the will to power and the eternal return are metaphysical (or esoteric) doctrines.

To summarize this preliminary line of reflection: Chaos makes metaphysics impossible, except as a doctrine of the illusoriness of natural order. If we apply metaphysics to human nature, the result is destructive, reactive, or passive nihilism. Human existence is deprived of inner weight and dissipated into the accumulation and discharge of points of force. But it is necessary to expose humanity to the destructive nihilism as a purificatory preparation for rebirth. Just as destruction is an essential component of creation, so the terrifying nihilism is an essential component of the constructive, noble, or active nihilism: the denial of metaphysics, or the assertion of the metaphysics of Chaos, is transformed into a doctrine of liberation. The Holy Ghost is replaced by the human spirit; mankind is ready to create ex nihilo. The same conclusion may be expressed in Nietzsche's more poetic terminology as follows: Apollonian contemplation and understanding are transmitted via medicinal rhetoric into an enriched doctrine of Dionysian intoxication, in which a creative dimension is superimposed onto its intrinsically destructive mode of purification.

Destruction and creation as human acts are rooted in rank-ordering. Nietzsche never tires of informing us that the central thought in his teaching is rank-ordering. I give two paradigmatic passages:

1.   "My philosophy is directed toward rank-ordering: not to an individualistic morality. The sense [*Sinn*] of the herd ought to rule in the herd,—but not to extend beyond it: the leaders of the herd require a fundamentally different evaluation of their own activities, like those who are independent, or the 'beasts of prey' and so forth."[4]

2.   "What concerns me is the problem of rank-ordering within the species Man, in whose progress as a whole and in general I do not believe, the problem of rank-ordering between human types that have always existed and always will exist."[5]

One could of course object, in defense of the metaphysical thesis, that rank-ordering is itself the imposition of the will to power. Rank is assigned in terms of merit or value, and value in turn is measured as a quantum of power. But power is the accumulation of points of force; the will to power, as Nietzsche himself says, is an exoteric doctrine. He means by this that there are no wills, which could exist only in subjects, and Nietzsche reduces subjectivity to physiology, which in turn is an unexplained accumulation of points of force. This line of defense succeeds only in exposing rank-ordering as a manifestation of Chaos; and thus it makes a mockery of Nietzsche's most comprehensive human or politico-historical teaching.

Let me make it clear that I do not deny Nietzsche's belief in Chaos. My point is rather that Nietzsche's teaching is not perfectly coherent. It consists of two moments that are strictly speaking incompatible with one another. I referred to these in chapter 6 as the cosmological and the human moments. The cosmological belief in Chaos empties the human belief in rank-ordering of its significance. At the same time, Nietzsche employs the cosmological belief in the attempt not merely to liberate or purify mankind of decadence, but to deify it or to give weight and significance to the creative act of world making.[6] Nietzsche repeats over and over again how dangerous is this attempt; the danger is represented graphically in the distinction between the active and passive nihilism which we are now studying. Our salvation lies in our destruction. In this very vivid sense, Nietzsche is the theoretical precursor of the radical revolutionaries of the twentieth century who employ terrorism in the hope that the destruction of bourgeois society will be followed by a salutary creation ex nihilo. To link Nietzsche to revolutionary terrorism is of course not at all to associate him with liberalism, socialism, or egalitarianism, all of which he abominated.

The difference in rank is for Nietzsche not a matter of belief in the sense of a personal, subjective opinion. It is a fact of life, which we can explain metaphysically, in quasi-Democritean terms, as the human representation of the inclination of points of force to accumulate or to overwhelm lesser accumulations in their path. Rank-orderings or values are perspectives only in the human sense that they provide us with an intelligible organization of Chaos and thereby produce a world within which we can exist. But this existence is natural or "necessary" as the human expression of the quantity of force that constitutes our true "substance." The more we deviate from the human standpoint, the more our substance or personal identity dissolves into a congeries of interacting force-fields. Nietzsche can therefore assert his values and make his estimations of persons, doctrines, artworks, and broad historical movements with the confidence that derives not from valid argumentation or scientific knowledge, but from the strength of his own will. His values are sound to the extent that they dominate. And he is convinced that they will dominate because they incorporate the one truth, formulated exoterically as the will to power, which is true because Nietzsche *wills it to be true.*

One could therefore say that the perception of "the pathos of distance" is perspectival in the sense of an accommodation of cosmological truth to human vision. But it is no less true for the fact that it is manifested within the illusion of a world-order. "The pathos of distance, the feeling of rank-differentiation, lies in the last ground of all morality."[7] And morality is the last ground of the human representation of the will to power.[8] To insist upon reducing this fact of life into points of force and thereby to assimilate it into an edifying meditation on Being is of course partially justifiable by reference to Nietzsche's own reduction of life to physiology and of physiology to the will to power. But we have to resist this temptation to succumb to what is after all for Nietzsche a belief adopted *for the sake of life.* Or rather, we must pass through the terrifying aspect of this belief in order to reap its advantages for life.

The same problem surfaces in Nietzsche's doctrine of truth. On the one hand, Nietzsche celebrates the *amor fati,* or acceptance of the irrational necessity, at the heart of Chaos. On the other hand, as Heidegger himself calls to our attention, truth is a belief and so a possibility.[9] Possibility is more powerful than actuality;[10] but this is for Nietzsche a "practical," not a theoretical or metaphysical, fact. The irrational nature of necessity makes it indistinguishable from chance; it has no determinate bearing on human will, which is thus practically free. As Zarathustra says, in a passage cited by Heidegger, "Will frees: this is the true teaching of will and freedom."[11] The will cannot free us if we are patterns of force; it can do so only by employing the belief in patterns of force as an instrument of liberation.

The extended Notebook entry on "European Nihilism" is divided into sixteen paragraphs, the last of which consists of a single sentence, or rather a rhetorical question. In paragraph 1, Nietzsche lists three advantages accruing from the Christian hypothesis of morality: it gives to humankind an absolute worth in the face of the contingency of genesis; it allows us to attribute perfection to the world, including a sense to evil; it provides humankind with a knowledge concerning absolute values, and so adequate knowledge of the most important things. "In Summa, morality was the great *antidote* against practical and theoretical nihilism" (211). Accordingly, Christianity itself was originally a means for the preservation of life, and so it could not have been subject to the full force of the criticism that Nietzsche, in his more polemical moments, directs against it.

The problem with Christianity, even in its original form, is that it *preserved* life but did not enhance it. Humanity acquired stability through it, but at the price of limitation. Note that Nietzsche says nothing here, in listing the advantages of the Christian hypothesis of morality, of Jesus or salvation. It is not an advantage of Christian morality that it promises life everlasting in the next world, but only that it gives a basis for a finite existence in this world. As we are about to see, the stability of the Christian world contains the seeds of its own decay; but the otherworldly doctrine of salvation does not serve to liberate humankind from a decadent world by providing it with a healthy and powerful successor. This task of liberation is assigned, incidentally, to Zarathustra, who does not succeed in his own time and who thus prefigures Nietzsche's own self-assigned role as a "posthumous man." The cross, which is in one sense the sign of Christ's equivalent failure, is in another a sign of his success or departure on humankind's behalf from this world to the next, in order to make possible a similar transition for those who believe in him.

In *Zarathustra,* the gateway of the moment constitutes the Nietzschean reversal of the cross of Christianity. To enter into the symbol of the cross is to achieve salvation by dying to this world; to enter into the gateway is to achieve salvation in this world by abandoning immortality for the sake of the eternal return of the same temporal choice. The Hyperborean views the gateway from above, and so understands the temporal nature of human existence without being assimilated within one of its perspectives. But the Hyperborean stance is possible at all only for the happy few, and even they must pass through the gateway, thereby entering into time, and so accommodating themselves to a particular perspective. One could also say that for Nietzsche, salvation outside this world is impossible because the philosopher must forget his own doctrine in the very act of willing its truth. The death of Christ is a symbolic representation of the extinction of the transtemporal vision of the Hyperborean in the Dionysian affirmation of a world. This is what Nietzsche means when he says that he is prepared to sacrifice himself and his nearest of kin to the task of producing a being that is higher than the species "man."[12]

Paragraph 2 begins, "But among the forces that morality increased was *truthfulness:* this turned finally against morality, uncovered its *teleology,* its [self-]*interested* reflection, and now the insight into this long incorporated mendacity, which one despaired of removing, works rather as a stimulus. To nihilism." Morality produces truthfulness, which reveals the falsehood of morality. This has two principal implications. First, truthfulness is here not itself false, that is, not an illusion or a perspectivally conditioned interpretation. We see truly that what merely preserves life does so for its own reasons; these reasons are false in the sense noted above, that preservation is insufficient: we must go either forward or backward. There is no standing still in life.[13] Second, very far from understanding truth as the permanence of presence, Nietzsche implies that the true is the process of overcoming; and in this instance of the overcoming of permanence as it is manifested in the facts of human existence, not in the Being-process. What is permanent is the absenting of presence. The elements of Heidegger's own "post-metaphysical" thinking are already to be found within Nietzsche. I note further that the falsehood of morality does not make it less indispensable for life. The impetus toward nihilism consists not in the falseness of morality, but in our recognition of its falseness, that is, in our insistence upon truth.

In paragraph 3, Nietzsche points out that contemporary man does not have as great a need as did the early Christians for an antidote against "the first nihilism," since life is no longer so insecure and our self-estimation is quite high. And this in turn makes possible a reduction of the means of nourishment that gave such strength to the moral interpretation: " 'God' is much too extreme a hypothesis" (212). The expression "the first nihilism" refers to the decadent consequences of late pagan antiquity, against which early Christianity served as an antidote. The security and high self-estimation enjoyed by late-nineteenth-century Europeans protect them against the first nihilism but contain the seeds of what we may call the second nihilism. Late modern progress is to Nietzsche a sign of decay. It is a sign of the progress of rationalism to regard God as too extreme a hypothesis (remember Laplace's reply to Napoleon); but the diminution of the power of the founding hypothesis is a diminution in the power of the consequences of that hypothesis.

The first nihilism precedes Christianity; the second nihilism is a consequence of the gradual decay of European Christian civilization. This is why Nietzsche is silent about the interval between the beginning and the end of Christian morality. The decay between two transitional extremes is very gradual; Nietzsche must accordingly accelerate the decay and invoke a new crisis in order to make room for the possibility of a vigorous future, rather than to allow for the thousand-year-long decline of the "last men." "But extreme positions are not dissolved through moderate ones, but again by extreme, but reversed, positions" (par. 4, ibid.) The sequence of Nietzsche's thought is here initially obscure. Christian morality is no longer an extreme position; the hypothesis has been weakened. The extreme position against which we must guard ourselves is nihilism. "The most unwelcome of guests" is at the door.[14]

Nietzsche's extreme reversal is to invite nihilism into the parlor and to attempt to convert the ensuing terror and destruction into a creative sequel.

Nietzsche's account of his origins and intentions are "the history of the next two hundred years," a crisis that it is possible for humankind to master, presumably if the rhetorical weapons set into motion by Nietzsche have the desired effect.[15] On second thought, it is too moderate a formulation to say that Nietzsche opens the door and welcomes the guest into his home. Instead, he radicalizes the guest into an enemy and destroying angel. When Nietzsche then says that the consequence of the insupportability of a belief in God and an essentially moral order is "a belief in the absolute immorality of nature and in the purposelessness and senselessness of psychologically necessary *affect*," he is describing both the views of "enlightened" or "advanced" intellectuals of the day *and* his own philosophical teaching. The metaphysical equivalent to the senselessness of the psychologically necessary affect is the equivalence between irrational necessity and chance.

The difference between Nietzsche and these advanced thinkers is then that Nietzsche is more extreme than they. His "reversal" of Christianity is extreme or active nihilism; theirs is merely passive nihilism, and a nihilism that regards itself as progressive, liberal thinking. We must understand that Nietzsche does not appear on the historical stage ex nihilo. Modern science, intellectuals and artists, frequenters of salons, statesmen and journalists, liberals like Herzen and socialist and anarchical revolutionaries like Marx and Bakunin, the tolerance toward a pluralism of beliefs that is required by international commerce (a point forgotten by our own contemporary pluralists), progressive theological views and relaxed religious practices, democracy and egalitarianism: all these groups and movements prepared the way for Nietzsche. It was not his quest for Being but his rhetorical genius that united them into a mass movement, although it must be added at once that the consequences of this movement were quite different from what Nietzsche expected or at least hoped for.

This is not the place to discuss the "reversal" of Nietzscheanism that today marches backward into the future under his flag. I must continue with my analysis of his diagnosis of nihilism. Christianity and materialist atheism are extreme opposites, and in this sense the passage is coherent. But materialist atheism is passive nihilism, whereas what we require is active nihilism. This is tantamount to asserting that absolute immorality is precisely the morality required for life in the revolutionary transition to the new epoch. It is the passive nihilism that appears in the rubble of the "going to ground" of Christianity. Because Christianity appeared as *the* interpretation, it now seems that its demise leaves no sense at all in human existence, "as if everything were *for nothing*." This is the point of reversal from passive to active nihilism. Moral teleology is transformed into a meontic teleology; but if everything is for nothing, then everything is allowed, or, in other words, the most powerful will prevail.

In paragraph 5, Nietzsche notes that to live "for nothing" is "the *most crippling thought*." He then proposes in paragraph 6: "Let us think this thought in its most frightening form: life [*das Dasein*], just as it is, without sense and purpose, but unavoidably returning, without a finale in nothingness: 'the eternal return.' This is the most extreme form of nihilism: nothingness (the 'senseless') eternal!" (213).

The continuation of the paragraph connects the thought of the eternal return to science; in fact, Nietzsche claims that it is "the most scientific of hypotheses: We deny final purposes; if existence had such a purpose, it would necessarily have been achieved by now." But science and in particular cosmology is a product of the ostensible progress but inner deterioration of the Christian civilization. The eternal return is a rendering fully explicit of what is already to be found in natural science, the highest and proudest possession of late-modern humanity. Nineteenth-century Materialism is so to speak the exoteric version of Nietzsche's doctrine of Chaos and the illusory nature of human existence. What returns eternally is nothingness: this absence of a ground is itself the ground for the passive and the active forms of nihilism. Much the same answer will be given in paragraph 14 of the present text: "The *value* of such a crisis is that it purifies" (217).

The most extreme form of nihilism is the most extreme form of purification; it reduces life to a perpetuity not of presence, but of absence. The purity in question is not of the light, but of the absence of all illumination in total darkness. Not quite all, however, since even the nihilist must comprehend his situation, and this requires a degree of vision. One cannot see in total darkness; hence there must be a faint glow emanating from the horizon of the eternal return. But what does one see? Not the presence of values, and so not the basis for healthy life; a fortiori, not enough for knowledge of the most important things. What we witness is the absencing of absence as the inner truth of the presencing of presence. The latter is the illusory surface; the former is the hidden order of Chaos. As to the faint glow by which this most extreme form of nihilism is rendered visible, this is the residue of the intention that leads the philosopher to posit so extreme a hypothesis.

In paragraph 7, Nietzsche poses the following question: given the most extreme form of nihilism, it is only the moral God who is overcome. "Does it make any sense to think for oneself a God 'beyond good and evil'? Could a pantheism in *this* sense be possible? Do we remove the positing of a purpose from this process and nevertheless affirm this process?—That would be the case were something accomplished within each moment of this process—and always the same" (213f). Here Nietzsche seems to approach more closely than hitherto a number of the main themes in Heidegger's own meditation on the history of metaphysics: The gods have flown away from this parlous time. But can there be another coming, not simply of a new prophet, but of a new god or new gods? In fact, however, as Nietzsche explicitly indicates, he is thinking of Spinoza's pantheism of logical necessity. The affirmation of the eternal return, the most extreme form of nihilism, empties life of all merely human significance, and so too of Christian morality. But by affirming the eternal return, we deify it.

What is accomplished in each moment of eternally recurring logical necessity? Certainly not the Socratic *polis,* which grows and so moves like a circle, that is, in such a way that its *nomoi* never change.[16] The affirmation of the eternal return, understood as logical necessity, and so as the perpetual recurrence of the absence of *nomoi* or values, is a city in which *only* the philosopher can live, and even then not as a human being and not even as a superman; not, finally, as a resident of the land of the Hyperboreans. At this point, Nietzsche comes close to the unerotic paradigm of the philosopher, introduced by Socrates in conversation with mathematicians in the *Theaetetus,* a paradigm of total withdrawal from perception of and participation within the everyday life of human beings. This is geometrical, not erotic necessity; it is the geometry of Spinoza's *Ethics* and of Nietzsche's *amor fati.*

In sum, affirmation of the eternal return, the most extreme form of nihilism, purifies the historical cities of Europe of what we can call the nonphilosophers. But it also purifies these cities of the philosophers,

Reversed Platonism

who ascend to or are assimilated into Spinoza's logical pantheism. What is accomplished? Each moment is for the nonphilosopher a repetition of nothingness, whereas for the philosopher each moment is an affirmation, not of a God of the beyond, but of himself as a monad within the single divine substance, Chaos, a monad which is able to duplicate that divine antistructure in its own thinking. This is the substance that Hegel attempted to set back into motion by transforming it into the subject or, in less abstract terms, by reuniting it with history. It is thus not the speculative dialectician Hegel, but Nietzsche, the philosopher of history, the historicist version of Hegel, who speculates on philosophical salvation through the repudiation of history, albeit not the repudiation of time or circular motion.

But this is in no way Platonism, neither straightforward nor reversed. If Nietzsche speculates on a return to a Spinozist substance, this has nothing to do with *ousia* as *idea* or *eidos*. For Nietzsche does not endorse Spinoza's conceptual articulation of logical necessity: one monad is exactly the same as any other monad. We have returned to Eleatic monism, and not at all to the path of *doksa*. As the affirmation of a senseless world, the eternal return is a doctrine of senselessness, hence of silence, and so of an absence of significant thinking. In its place, presumably, is an *Erlebnis*, or experience of necessity, or what Nietzsche calls in paragraph 6 of the present text a "European form of Buddhism" (213). As we saw in the previous chapter, Heidegger also notes this aspect of Nietzsche's doctrine of the totality of things as an *arrhēton*.

In his articulation of the problem of nihilism, Nietzsche does not remain at this level of "purity"; Spinoza, he points out, was an isolated case (par. 8, 214). In general, human beings respond with approval to all moments of an existence that is stamped by the fundamental characteristic of their own natures. They call this characteristic "good, valuable, [and they] sense it with pleasure." This observation serves as a transition away from Spinozist austerity to historical existence. It also serves to reverse the Spinozist perspective; whereas Spinoza assimilates himself into the whole, Nietzsche derives that whole from Spinoza. Necessity is transformed into chance through the transformation of the *logos* of Spinoza's totality into the *arrhēton* of Chaos. Nietzsche's next comment is reminiscent of the Hegelian dialectic of master and slave. Morality preserves life "from despair and the leap into nothingness" among those who have been mastered and oppressed. The masters are equated with devils, "against whom the common man must be defended, i.e. to begin with, encouraged, made strong" (par. 9, 214). One may sense here an echo of Hegel: the Schellingian Absolute or the night in which all cows are black represents the "Buddhist" reversal of Spinoza's logical pantheism and serves as the content of the next moment of the dialectic. But this moment is Chaos rather than the Hegelian concept.

Hatred against oppression is disguised will to power and places the oppressed at the same rank-level as their oppressors. "There is nothing in life that has value, outside of the degree of power, it being granted in fact that life itself is will to power" (par. 10, 215). Life is affect, physiological drive, not simply the desire for self-preservation but the *nisus* to assimilate, to grow, and so to overcome. The emotional manifestation of this *nisus* is love toward what increases power and hatred toward what restricts or diminishes it. Spinoza's "intellectual love" is not directed toward the Christian God of morality but toward the whole, with which he identifies, thereby increasing his power to infinity. The hatred of the oppressed toward their oppressors is a coarse physiological version of reversed Spinozism. Their love is directed toward morality, which preserves them from nihilism; when the belief in morality "goes to ground," so too do the oppressed.

Nietzsche interprets the destruction of the oppressed as self-chosen; the will to destruction is a form of the deeper will to nothingness (par. 11, 215). He refers somewhat imprecisely to self-destructive acts of "self-vivisection, intoxication, Romanticism, and above all else the instinctive compulsion to acts with which they make the powerful into deadly enemies." Their nihilism, which leads them to transform the powerful into their executioners, is "the European form of Buddhism, do-nothingism, according to which existence has entirely lost its 'sense' " (par. 12, 216). This is the mirror image of Spinozist Buddhism, based upon a rejection of the whole. As such, it reflects the passivity of Eleatic nihilism.

In the next paragraph (13), Nietzsche makes a somewhat awkward transition from passive to active nihilism. He seems to imply that the passive nihilists continue to be insulated by morality from further deterioration, presumably because of their low degree of culture. Active nihilism, on the other hand, appears among "relatively more favorably formed circumstances. In order that morality be perceived as overcome, a tolerable degree of spiritual culture is presupposed." In this context,

Nietzsche observes that the teaching of the eternal return would have "learned presuppositions" just as did the teaching of Buddha. He thus seems to reverse himself by attributing active nihilism to his "cultivated" predecessors; this reversal is softened by understanding the cultivated nihilists to be suitable material for transformation by a rhetoric of active nihilism, as the uneducated lower classes are not. In other words, despite a number of similarities between Nietzsche and Marx, and Nietzsche's partial acceptance of the master-slave dialectic of Hegel, Nietzsche rejects the notion of the universal proletariat as the negative content of the revolutionary "second negation" that is to culminate in posthistorical affirmation. One sees here Nietzsche's separation from his postmodern disciples.

In paragraph 14, Nietzsche identifies the class of the oppressed by their physiological condition rather than by their political status. In this lowest stratum of nihilism, the belief in the eternal return would be perceived as a curse that drives them not to passive extinction, but to the active destruction of everything, in particular of the thought of the eternal return. In these last paragraphs, Nietzsche is clearly musing upon the possible effects of the introduction of his most difficult thought. He believes that it will initiate a crisis, but that the worth of this crisis is that it will purify by intensifying the destruction of the lower degrees of force and thus stimulate persons of opposing viewpoints to unite in deeds that will culminate in "*a rank-ordering of forces*, from the standpoint of health" (217). One may legitimately wonder whether, in this stage, the doctrine of the eternal return will still be advocated. In either case, it will continue to function at the cosmological level, since all accumulations of force inevitably dissipate.

In paragraph 15, Nietzsche asks, Who will show themselves to be the strongest as the result of this crisis? His answer is interesting: the moderate, who adhere to no extremes and can preserve their self-respect even while perceiving that their worth has been diminished. These persons are the richest in health because they have survived misfortune and do not fear it. They are secure in their power and represent with pride the level of force that humankind has achieved. In other words, the men of extremes will perish in the crisis invoked by the doctrine of the eternal return, which is the most extreme degree of nihilism. In this text, we see Nietzsche's political sobriety and his Machiavellian cunning: exactly the reverse of the Dionysian intoxication and endorsement of radical liberation that have so often been attributed to him by those who fall victim to his political rhetoric, that is, to the crisis which he initiated in order to destroy them. That they have survived and are even prospering in opposition to the moderate and healthy is a clear sign of the deficiencies in Nietzsche's political analysis, unless it is a less clear sign that the crisis continues and that the moderate and healthy persons have not yet emerged.

The text closes with a single question concerning the moderate person: "How would such a human being regard the eternal return?—" The dash that follows this unanswered question is a hint of what Nietzsche himself refers to on numerous occasions as the experimental nature of his thought: "An experimental philosophy, such as I live it, anticipates experimentally the possibility of fundamental nihilism."[17] Nietzsche adds that this is undertaken not as an act of naysaying, but rather for the sake of a Dionysian affirmation of life. We may conclude our study of Nietzsche's analysis of nihilism with the observation that he advocates Dionysian affirmation for the sake of moderation and moderation for the sake of Dionysian affirmation. This is the human form of the eternal return: a Machiavellian who seeks to intoxicate himself for prudential reasons; a Platonist who strives to abolish recollection by transforming eternity into the gateway of the present moment of time.

Nihilism as Metaphysics

Heidegger's interpretation of Nietzsche is in fact an interpretation of the history of Western metaphysics, alias Platonism. It must also be remembered that the collection of lectures in the two volumes entitled *Nietzsche* is not a single, coherent study but contains a series of seminars delivered by Heidegger over a period of five years: from 1936 to 1940, with an additional section of essays written between the years 1941 and 1946. We should therefore not be surprised to find some shifts in Heidegger's center of concentration, if not in the basic principles of his analysis. One apparent shift is in Heidegger's designation of the key terms of Nietzsche's planned major work and so of what Heidegger calls his metaphysics. In the 1936 seminar that opens the first volume, Heidegger, in commenting on a sketch for this projected work in Nietzsche's *Nachlass,* cites the eternal return, the will to power, and transvaluation as the three guiding terms of the entire enterprise.[18] In

1940, Heidegger, commenting on the same text, says that the five "fundamental terms" (*Grundwörte*) of Nietzsche's metaphysics are the will to power, nihilism, the eternal return of the same, the superman, and righteousness.[19]

In view of this apparent change of mind concerning the fundamental importance of nihilism, we might expect to find a corresponding shift in its interpretation. I believe that this is in fact the case. In the first volume of seminars, which dates from 1936 to 1939, relatively little time is devoted to nihilism in comparison with the extensive treatments of the will to power and the eternal return. In volume II, which stems from the period 1939–44, on the other hand, nihilism is discussed extensively. The seminar of 1940 is devoted to European nihilism; most important, however, is the essay from 1944/46 entitled *Die seinsgeschichtliche Bestimmung des Nihilismus* (The determination of nihilism in accord with the history of Being). The assignment of distinct topics to different dates is of course in itself inconclusive; Heidegger could easily have planned well in advance the order in which he would address himself to various themes. But the substantive difference is not to be explained in this way.

My point is not at all that Heidegger is discovered in some sort of contradiction or inconsistency. I am interested in the philosophical content of the shift in emphasis concerning nihilism. There may be a political corollary to this shift which is worth mentioning, but is for me of primary importance only as it affects Heidegger's thought. In 1937, commenting on a text from Nietzsche's *Zarathustra*, Heidegger says that nihilism must be overcome by its victim, namely, by the exertion of humankind itself, which is represented in *Zarathustra* as a shepherd who, in obedience to Zarathustra's shouted advice, bites off the head of a black snake that has entered his mouth and fastened its fangs within his throat. Three pages later, Heidegger explains that the shepherd is the man who thinks the eternal return but who does not think it in its essential dimension until the snake has entered his throat and he has bitten its head off: "The thought *is* only as that bite."[20]

In this text, Heidegger clearly places the initiative for the overcoming of nihilism in the *act* of thinking by the philosopher of the eternal return; he does so, of course, as a commentator on Nietzsche, and on a book which, according to him, is the "antechamber" to Nietzsche's main work rather than that work itself.[21] Both in the 1936 lecture and in the lectures and writings from the 1940s, Heidegger attributes to Nietzsche's last and decisive period the view that nihilism is "the fundamental character of what has happened in western history,"[22] although this is stated more sharply in the 1944/46 essay, where it appears in Heidegger's own terminology and in his own name. But there is an important difference. In the later essay, the responsibility for the arrival and also for the eventual departure of nihilism is attributed to Being, not to the thinker and, in particular, not to Heidegger himself.[23]

My political speculation concerning Heidegger's personal situation is that in 1936, he was still somewhat more optimistic about the power of philosophical thinking to overcome nihilism. By 1944, when it was obvious that Germany would be crushingly defeated, Heidegger seems to have reverted to a more passive stance before the gifts of Being. Nothing of any importance in my account of Heidegger's interpretation of nihilism turns upon the soundness of this speculation. It is at least equally plausible that the shift in emphasis is a sign not so much of Heidegger's changing mood, as of the difference between Heidegger and Nietzsche. Differently stated, Heidegger vastly preferred the fragments of the post-*Zarathustran* Notebooks to *Zarathustra* itself; perhaps he identified more closely with those fragments and thus read more of himself into his reconstruction of what Nietzsche had presumably left unthought.

In any case, I now want to concern myself with the question of nihilism and will make primary use of two passages contained in volume II of the *Nietzsche* lectures. On the safest hypothesis, these passages will provide us with the basis for distinguishing between Heidegger's own thought and his interpretation of Nietzsche; or alternatively they will assist us in distinguishing between a Heideggerianized Nietzsche and Nietzsche himself, as we have attempted to elicit him from Heidegger's preferred fragments. In the 1940 text, *Nietzsches Metaphysik*, Heidegger devotes eleven pages to an account of nihilism. A crucial introductory passage from these eleven pages begins, not unexpectedly, with a reference to Plato: "Plato, with whose thinking metaphysics begins, grasps the existent as such, i.e. the being of beings, as Idea."[24] The Ideas are the enduring and true in contrast to the changing and illusionary. From the standpoint of the "metaphysics" of the will to power, the Ideas are the highest values. And in fact, Plato "illuminates the essence of the Idea out of the *highest Idea,* the Idea of the Good [*agathon*]. 'Good' however means for the Greeks that which makes serviceable for doing something, and which makes this possible. The Ideas as Being make the existent thereby serviceable, visible, hence present, i.e. to be an existent." Henceforward, Being means for metaphysics the "condition for the possibility" of something to be."[25]

We have heard this story before, and I will not repeat what I have already said about the Good in previous chapters. I limit myself to a remark about utility. It is no concern of the beings that humans find them useful; this utility or serviceability is hardly surprising in a universe of things that interact upon one another and, in view of human nature, which consists of various modalities of response to elements within its environment. Heidegger seems to insinuate that in a post-Platonic, non-metaphysical epoch, human beings would no longer take advantage of the capacity of things to satisfy their desires or to enact their intentions. Even if we were to adopt the Heideggerian doctrine of Being as presencing, nothing would change with respect to the utility of things. And the presencing-process would continue to be "good," indeed, *the* Good, so far as human beings are concerned, because it would allow beings to emerge or present themselves. What could be more useful than that?

I understand very well that what Heidegger actually advises is a shift in attitude toward beings. But in allowing things to be, we are adopting a superfluous posture, one that simply masks our continuing need to make use of that which presents itself. Even worse, we cover with obscurantism the pressing need to modify these "presents," some of which are acceptable in their present form and many of which are not. In the not-so-long run, submission to the celebration of the eventing of the E-vent is more dangerous than the natural inclination to master and possess nature. Otherwise put, things will be what they are regardless of whether we contemplate Being or not. And our needs remain as they are and will be, regardless of our contemplative posture (or posturing).

In short, the utility of things has no bearing one way or the other on the nature of Being. Furthermore, whereas we cannot "use" directly the presencing-process or convert it into a tool, neither can we do this with the Platonic Ideas and certainly not with the Good. The sun shows us what it chooses to illuminate, not what we wish it to; but this does not make us less indebted to the utility of what is illuminated and hence to the sun as well. Had intelligent beings evolved in a universe of undulating waves or force-fields in which no things are present, some sinuous

Nihilism

Plato would have arisen with a theory of Ideas of wave-lengths or of patterns of distribution of points of force. Heidegger's criticism of utility in this context is itself rooted in a kind of caricature of Platonic contemplation or Aristotelian *noēsis tēs noēseōs* in which *nothing happens* but happening.

This is the place to insert an observation about Heidegger's analysis of technics as the culminating form of the last stage of metaphysics. Heidegger derives technics as a mode of presentation of beings from the initial Platonic turn away from the uncovering of beings to their utility as determinate looks. The Idea of the Good is thus the prototype or primaeval ancestor of the metaphysics of value as implemented by the will to power, which, in its final stage, is the will to will.[26] Instead of allowing Being to present itself as concealed by beings, modern man has turned progressively toward beings as useful in a way that Being (or the contemplation of the Being-process) is not, for the fulfillment of human intentions and the satisfaction of human desires. Hence the associated development of truth as correctness and precision and of the doctrine of subjectivity. The upshot is a new mode of "making" that differs from Greek *poiēsis* and *technē* by demanding and regulating what is to be manifested, instead of allowing or facilitating what *phusis* presents to us. Things are accordingly transformed into "stock" or "inventory," and the resultant manner of manifestation is called *Gestell*, by which Heidegger means "the gathering of that regulating by which mankind authorizes, i.e. challenges or provokes the actual to disclose itself in the manner of ordering as stock or inventory."[27]

In other words, humankind, acting not on its own initiative but once more in response to the uncovering of Being, has *covered over* Being with a framework of willful reification. This is not a very original or profound claim and scarcely requires the terminological heavy weather that Heidegger makes of it. We may nevertheless grant him part of the point: technics, if allowed to dominate human intentions and conduct, will transform the manner in which we view the manifestation of truth and being. Many of the consequences of this transformation will be harmful under any circumstances; if allowed to continue unchecked or in other words to serve as the basis for philosophy and political life, they will be disastrous. The serious issue, it seems to me, is how to respond to the challenge of technics. Differently stated, one must ask whether the issue is metaphysical or political.

Reversed Platonism

I do not mean by this that metaphysical reflections or for that matter authentic thinking have no bearing upon politics in the broad sense of the term. There is such a bearing, but it works in both directions. The accelerated development of technology is due not merely to changing theoretical views but to extraordinary discoveries in mathematics, physics, and technology itself. These discoveries make possible a reciprocal acceleration in the change of metaphysical doctrines. People tend to do what they are able to do, whether or not it is dangerous. This being so and given the impossibility of restricting technological development, as Heidegger would agree,[28] the prudent procedure is to respond to the danger of nihilism implicit in technics by acknowledging the desirability of mastering the environment not as an expression of the will to will, but for the good of humankind, on the basis of a doctrine, metaphysical or otherwise, that is capable of distinguishing between noble and base employment or "manifestation" of beings. One almost dares to suggest that more good comes from less profundity in cases of this sort. A repudiation of values is one thing; the disregard of the distinction between the noble and the base in favor of a meditative or poeticizing thinking on Being is something else again.

So far as our main theme is concerned, it is utter nonsense to accuse Plato of nihilism on the grounds that he neglects Being in favor of beings. The neglect of beings is in itself disastrous. But the attempt to derive the "genuine" or "original" response to beings from an immersion in a Being that has no value and no purposiveness, but simply happens, is absurd. Rather than discuss in detail Heidegger's account of technics, I shall restrict myself to studying the main points of the argument by which he uncovers the culmination of nihilism in Nietzsche's metaphysical Platonism. As a last general comment, I find it unjustified to derive a legitimation of unbridled technicity from Nietzsche's doctrine of the will to power, which, whatever else is wrong with it, is always directed toward the reinstitution of an aristocratic rank-ordering. There is no trace of evidence that Nietzsche accepted the modern doctrine of truth as certitude; *Gerechtigkeit* has for him nothing to do with *rectitudo* or *certitudo* but with seeing things as they are; it is not far removed from what Heidegger calls *Gelassenheit*. The philosopher views the whole from his Hyperborean vantage point; the precision he exercises is that of the philologist, not the mathematician. As to the nonphilosopher, exactness is itself a perspective or interpretation, not the measure of interpretations.

But this by the way. To make a further remark concerning the 1940 text on nihilism, it is true that the Platonic Idea is a condition for the possibility of the existence of things of that look. But it is the things that are possible, not the Ideas. The Ideas are *dunameis* in the sense of powers to effect something, not a possibility of something's occurring.[29] The *dunamis,* so to speak, must be actual in order that its effect be possible. The Aristotelian distinction between actuality and possibility is quite complicated, and no one has ever resolved all of the attendant ambiguities.[30] The crucial point is this: in order to preserve the distinction between *energeia* and *dunamis,* we must distinguish between two senses of the latter term: potentiality in the sense of potency or power and possibility in the sense of not yet existing, hence not yet possessing power, but not entirely prevented from existing. A *dunamis* in the former sense is in my opinion indistinguishable from an *energeia,* and that is the sense in which the Platonic dialogues speak of the *dunamis* of an Idea.

This is quite different from the Kantian situation, which Heidegger, in the text we are studying, compares to Plato and so assimilates into Platonism. In Kant, the conditions for the possibility of things coming into existence are not Ideas, and so they are not *energeiai* or *dunameis* in the sense of actually existing powers. The conditions are rules, and these rules are themselves possible, not potential in the sense of actually powerful; that is to say, they are actually powerful only when someone is thinking. The transcendental ego, which is Kant's somewhat anthropomorphic metaphor for the set of rules constituting the thinkability, and so the being, of anything at all as a resident in the world governed by Newtonian physics on the one hand and the human cognitive faculties on the other, is not an actually functioning emergence-process of thoughts and things; it is not the Absolute Ego. There are only finite egos, which sometimes think and sometimes do not. It is true that these finite egos could not think, according to Kant, unless the rules bundled together under the title "transcendental ego" were forever valid. But validity means precisely *possibility:* such and such is possible on the basis of such and such premises.

Valid inferences do not go about doing work unless someone applies an inference-pattern to the specific task of drawing a conclusion from premises. But even if some extreme Platonist (in the late-modern, mathematical sense of the term) were to insist that inference-patterns are Platonic Ideas, this would be Platonism, not Kantianism. For Kant, it is things that exist, not conditions for the existence of things. When Heidegger says that Kant gives to the Platonic notion of Being as "condition of possibility" "an interpretation defined from the standpoint of the subjectivity of the 'I think'," the most we could grant him is that Kant misinterprets the Platonic Ideas as rules. I doubt that this is what Kant did; he rather replaced Ideas by rules. It was the Neo-Kantians like Cohen and Natorp who attempted to identify the two.[31] Furthermore, as I have just noted, the subjectivity of the "I think" is one thing, the rules serving as the conditions for the possibility of thinking things is something else again.

Heidegger's next remark is certainly defensible: "Plato's concept of the Good, however, contains no thoughts of worth."[32] I pass by the use of "concept" (*Begriff*) with respect to the Good; Heidegger means that the Ideas are not projects of the will to power. If by "worth" or "value" is meant an estimation or measurement on the part of the thinker, then it is fair to say that values are properties of, or correlative with, objects as projects of subjects. Nietzsche, of course, denies the truth of the doctrine of subjectivity, but by attributing values to the will, that is, by interpreting them as projections designed to enhance power, he advocates a doctrine that is surprisingly close to the Kantian doctrine of the transcendental ego. On the other hand, one need not hesitate to say that the usefulness of beings is for Plato inseparable from their goodness. The element of utility enters into all of Socrates' discussions of the Good; for how could the Good be useless?[33] Heidegger's critique of utility cannot apply to thinkers like Plato for whom the source of the usefulness of beings is not the human will. I can make use of beings not because I conceive or project them in the image of my desires and intentions, but because my desires and intentions have been formed by nature in the image of the beings.

I do not mean by this last remark that there is a rigid natural teleology in Plato or that practical reason proceeds by consulting the order of the Ideas as embedded in a glassy essence. Human existence, including political life, is for Plato largely poetic, that is, practico-productive. But this is because of the indifference of beings to our needs, not because they are irrelevant to our welfare. A man may desire to be wealthy and even spend hours imagining that he is so, yet still be poor. The desire for wealth is in the first instance a desire for beings as things, but this desire has no direct effect on the things themselves. The man may be moved by his desire to take the necessary steps to become wealthy in fact, and he will use one set of beings as tools in order to accomplish his immediate goal, which is the acquisition of another set of beings. But none of this arises through the complicity of the beings themselves or from a natural teleology by which all mortals who desire to become wealthy will in fact succeed in their efforts to satisfy this desire.

Beings both yield and resist, they define our desires and frustrate them. They are useful, useless, and harmful, depending upon the circumstances. Accordingly, we may set a value on them relative to some particular intention, but there is no intrinsic value in beings, any more than there is an intrinsic utility. Beings are useful in general because without them nothing can be accomplished, including the search for the sense of Being. So too they are valuable in general because we never know when one of them will become useful for this or that purpose. There is thus a close tie, perhaps an identity, between value in the sense of a human projection and utility in the sense of applicability to the satisfaction of desire or the carrying out of intentions.

It is good for human beings to live in just and orderly cities. In order for this to occur, philosopher-kings are required. Philosophy is thus good for human beings, nonphilosophers as well as philosophers. But philosophy can take place if and only if there is a distinction between truth and opinion; otherwise, one opinion is as *good* as another, and disorder and injustice are as good as order and justice. The distinction between truth and opinion is rooted in the visibility of stable entities to the eye of the soul. Plato very reasonably has Socrates call these entities Ideas, the looks of things. Since philosophy depends upon them, such looks are good for human beings. Whether the visibility is intrinsic to the look or emerges from a separate principle, just as the sun is separate from the beings it lights up, is a question of interest to metaphysicians only. How we answer it does not affect the goodness of the visibility for all sane human beings.

To come back to Heidegger, it is for reasons like these that I am not much impressed by his reiterated thesis that metaphysics is nihilism. If the charge of nihilism is to be leveled at all, then it must be leveled against the presencers and eventers, since they seem to value nothing at all or, what comes to the same thing, since they replace the Idea of the Good with the facelessness of the event. In closing my brief commentary on the passage from the 1940 text, I want to repeat that Heidegger is officially expounding Nietzsche's metaphysics, not his own. But in this exposition, he clarifies Nietzsche's contentions by thinking what they leave unthought, and so by buttressing Nietzsche's judgments with his own understanding of Platonism.

European Buddhism

I turn now to an extended passage from the essay of 1944/46, one which we have had previous occasion to notice. This passage enables us to elicit and to comment on the general thrust of the argument of the essay as a whole. Heidegger's principal contention in this essay is that metaphysics is the history of the neglect or omission of the absence of Being.[34] That neglect, to repeat, is not a simple oversight on the part of philosophers. The history of metaphysics is the history of Being in the specific sense that this history occurs as the happening (*Geschehen*) of the absence of Being (375, 379). In yet another formulation, nihilism is that gift of Being in which Being promises itself in its openness but, as that promise, is covered over or absent (369). Thus Being is governing or carrying out its duties (*waltet*) within nihilism, which is not purely negative (365).

It is accordingly not "nihilistic" in the negative or destructive sense to counsel against the effort to overcome nihilism. To overcome is to cause something to submit, and so to put it behind one. Hence for humankind to overcome and to will to overcome nihilism means that "man goes up against Being in its absence from within his own resources" (*von sich aus:* ibid.) But it is beyond our powers to make Being submit to human domination. And the attempt sets man askew, since "our place consists in this, that Being itself, in whatever manner at all, even in its absence, lays claim to the essence of mankind, which essence is the lodging with which Being endows itself [*sich begabt*], in order to occur [*sich ... zu begeben*] as the arrival of uncoveredness within such a lodging" (365–66). The reader should notice the difference between Heidegger's interpretation here and my own. As I understand Nietzsche, the most frightening of guests is invited into the parlor; in other words, man is invited to overcome nihilism by submitting to it. This is

Nietzsche's reconciliation of freedom and necessity. He accomplishes it by excluding Being, not by forgetting it.

The difference between this text and Heidegger's interpretation of the *Zarathustra*-passage in 1936 is self-evident, despite the peculiarities in Heidegger's later terminology. Words like *Geschehen, sich begeben* and *Unterkunft* are obviously prototypes for *Ereignis, Erörterung*, and *topos*. But more important for us is the resignation or passivity of Heidegger's attitude here, in contrast with the activism of Zarathustra. The attempt to overcome nihilism is a dereliction from our essential nature. Heidegger uses the term *Auslassen* here, literally, an omission; the omission is active rather than passive because it results in our "not letting Being be" (*das Sein selbst nicht als das Sein gelassen*). *Auslassen* is thus tacitly contrasted with *Gelassenheit,* literally "composure" or "imperturbability" but used elsewhere by Heidegger to designate the acceptance of what Being sends us.

Heidegger used the term *Gelassenheit* in a lecture in 1955 which he published together with a "discussion" or (as some Heideggerians prefer to translate *Erörterung*) an "emplacing" of the term that dates from 1944/45, the same period as our essay. *Gelassenheit* is explained in the lecture as an attitude of acceptance and freedom with respect to the technical world (which is regularly taken to be the consequence of the will to power and the eternal return, that is, the essence of the last stage of metaphysics). "We are able to make use of technical objects, as indeed they must be used. But at the same time we can let these objects rest [*auf sich beruhen*] as something that does not affect us in our innermost, most genuine self."[35] This *Gelassenheit* toward things is coupled with an "openness for the mystery" (*Geheimnis*), in order to constitute Heidegger's recommendation concerning the attitude to be adopted toward the technical world.[36]

In the *Erörterung,* the discussion is presented as a dialogue in which Heidegger appears as an "investigator" (*Forscher*). He explains that *Gelassenheit* lies "outside the distinction between activity and passivity" and also outside willing.[37] The term is given the following summary exposition: "*Gelassenheit* is in fact self-releasement out of transcendental representation [*Vorstellen*] and so a disregard of [*absehen von*] the willing of the horizon. This disregard no longer comes out of a willing, unless it be that the occasion for one's entrance into membership in the *Gegnet* requires a stimulus of willing, which stimulus however dissipates into entrance and is completely extinguished in *Gelassenheit*."[38] The term *Gegnet* is "the tarrying with [or "farness": *Weite*] that, convening everything, opens itself, so that in it the open is supported continuously, thereby allowing each emergence in its resting."[39]

This passage reminds me of Hegel's remark in the introduction to the *Enzyklopädie* of 1830 that "it is the free act of thinking to place itself at the standpoint where it is for itself and thus itself produces its object and gives it to itself."[40] This free act is somewhere between Nietzsche's *Wollen* and Heidegger's *Gelassenheit*. Despite the emphasis upon the self-production and presentation of the objects of thought in the Hegelian text, it applies to Heidegger to the extent that he cannot dispense with a "free act" or in other words cannot simply rely upon Being to induct him into the *Gegnet*. One could also say that Heidegger's statement is not entirely different from Nietzsche's peculiar combination of complete lucidity and honesty about the truth of Chaos and the recommendation that life requires us to forget this truth and to step into the gateway of the Instant. What is forgetting or intoxication in Nietzsche is "dissipation" of the stimulus of willing in Heidegger.

Hegel and Nietzsche, however, direct us toward the production of a world, rational in Hegel's case and healthy or powerful in Nietzsche's. Heidegger directs us to avert our gaze away from the world toward the opening or clearing within which the world comes to presence. To come back to the *Nietzsche* essay, we are now in a better position to understand Heidegger's thought. It is not an overcoming but an enactment of nihilism to attempt to overcome nihilism by an act of the will, as Nietzsche recommends. What we must do instead is to "use" the artifacts of the nihilistic epoch without allowing them to determine our innermost core or nature. This in itself is both unobjectionable and trivial. But Heidegger's development of this reasonable triviality has the not-so-trivial consequence that human existence at any time, not simply in the epoch of nihilism, is a distraction from our true business, which, in the recent colloquial expression, is to go with the flow.

Otherwise stated, since human existence is by its nature thing- or being-centered, we will always be required to make use of things in such a way as to divert our gaze (or our ears) from the *Gegnet*. There is then no exit from nihilism, except in the purely nominal sense that all or some of us may remember the absence of Being as we participate in its continuation. I mean by this that so long as human existence continues, it will always be thing-centered. To decenter human attention to beings is to dissolve, not to deconstruct, our existence. The consequences of this decentering are very well expressed by a recent disciple of the late Heidegger who approaches him from the postmodern French standpoint: "To the question 'what ought we to do?' the answer is, then, the same as to the question 'How ought we to think?' Love the flux and thank its economic confluences."[41] "Economic" is used here in the sense of the *nomos* governing the house or space within the clearing in which we dwell. It is an adaptation of Heidegger's *Ort* in terms suggested by writers like Michel Foucault, Louis Althusser, and Jacques Derrida.

Heidegger, of course, is not a contemporary French anarchist. Let me instead note that in *Gelassenheit*, Heidegger advises us "to make use of" technical things. This advice brings him very close to Plato as he himself interprets Platonism, and specifically with respect to the utility of beings as a consequence of their determinateness through the reifying activity of perspectival looks, which is the unthought inner content of the doctrine of Ideas. Suppose we grant for the moment that all beings are technical things, as follows from Heidegger's full argument. Let us further assume that the principle of *technē* is the inner need to modify the emergent into tools for the satisfaction of our desires and fulfillment of our intentions. I will call this inner need the will to power. What is the genuine ground of the will to power?

On the Heideggerian position, it must be Being itself, understood as the history of its own concealment, that brings forth human beings to whom it shows itself *as* concealed, and so whom it produces, along with beings, by its own inner technicity, but for no purposes or reasons. The mystery of openness is that there is no mystery or still deeper ground underneath the presencing that occurs within the *Gegnet*. I am aware that Heidegger talks like a mystical theologian in the *Beiträge zur Philosophie*, regarded by his disciples as his most important work, a work that is roughly contemporaneous with the *Nietzsche* seminars. But even if we take the other beginning and find a new God awaiting us along the path, that God will be yet another emergent or being within the occurrences in the opening. In other words, either the next God will communicate with and have an effect upon the lives of mortals, in which case he (or she) will be exactly like the instrumental God whom Jews, Christians, and Muslims use for their own benefit. Or else this ostensible

God will be as indifferent to us as we must be open, calm, resigned, and accepting toward this indifference.

Whether we refer to Being or to some pseudonym from Heidegger's esoteric late terminology, the result is the same. Human existence, as a gift from Being, is nihilism. There is no way to deal with or to use things in accordance with releasement from their thinghood or utility. The only attitude we could take toward things that is a direct application of our releasement would be to let them happen, hence to take no stand whatsoever toward them, not even to love them, as is recommended by the commentator cited above. But by taking no stance toward them, by releasing them from our will, we would erase all projections of value, and so leave them without any rank-ordering. All would be on the same rank; and this is nihilism.

When Heidegger sanctions our making use of technical things, he of course means nothing so absurd as inviting us to love them or for that matter to remain indifferent to them. Why do we use technical things? Because they are necessary for our welfare. It is better to be healthy than to be sick, and so better to go to the surgeon if we have cancer than to be released toward Being. The surgery may of course fail, but if we ignore the surgeon and his technical instruments, we will be released without doubt, not toward the clearing but toward and into complete closure. Even Aristotle grants that *technē* completes nature. And he does so in a way that does not entail a radical separation between everyday life and the contemplation of Being by the sage. The sage, of course, abstracts himself from everyday life when in the midst of contemplation; but his use of beings and so his participation in everyday life is the necessary condition for contemplation, and not simply in a practical sense. Contemplation begins with the perception of the particular existing thing.

It has been a major contention of this study that Heidegger deviates most sharply from Plato by detaching philosophy, or genuine thinking, from everyday life. It now seems to be clear that this detachment is equivalent to a double nihilism: the nihilistic attitude toward the world of things and a nihilistic releasement toward the clearing and the emergence-process. Heidegger never succeeds in explaining why anyone would wish to engage in philosophical thinking. No doubt this is because he wishes to honor Aristotle's assertion that philosophy is not for the sake of anything else but only for its own sake. However, in saying this, Aristotle does not mean to imply that philosophy lacks the highest degree of nobility; he instead insists that the *bios theoretikos* is the highest form of human existence. Heidegger is not in a position to make this judgment; for him, it must be regarded as rank-ordering and so a version of the will to power, of anthropomorphism or humanism.

But even Heidegger observes from time to time that Being reveals itself, whether as concealed or open, to human being. It is human being, not the stars or the rocks, the plants or the brutes, that is open to Being. Man is the *Platzhalter* (place-holder) or shepherd of Being. Is this revelation void of significance? Is it not only without value, but also neither noble nor base? Is the sense of Being its senselessness, a tale told by an idiot, signifying nothing? If all this is so, would it not be infinitely better for human beings to forget the truth in a Dionysian intoxication of world-creation through the expression of the will to power? Or alternatively, would we not be well advised to immerse ourselves in the prudent use of beings for our own welfare, in accord with what we deem to be best?

According to Heidegger, Nietzsche intends to overcome nihilism "by the positing of new values out of the will to power." He is thereby the first to proclaim "genuine nihilism: that Being, which has become value, is not at all our concern."[42] A value, that is, a valuation, is the positing of a rank-ordering of ways of life, and so of interpretations of the utility of beings to increase one's health or power. But Being, as we have seen, has no value and is not a value. Nietzsche would agree with this, since what posits value is the will to power, not Being, that is, not Chaos, which is his surrogate for Being.

In a frequently cited passage,[43] Nietzsche writes in his Notebooks, "Recapitulation. To *imprint* the character of Being onto Becoming— *that is the highest will to power. Double falsification,* from the senses hither and from spirit hither, in order to preserve a world of beings, of the enduring, of what is equal in value, etc. That *everything returns,* is the most extreme *approach of a world of becoming to the* [world] *of Being—peak of contemplation.*"[44] Being as an imprint, namely, as a world of beings, is a double falsification. But the eternal return of the world as a result of the process of imprinting is a close approach to and therefore not the same as genuine or true Being. It is a close approach because of its eternality; there is always some world or other, and hence one may say that "worlding" is permanent. But it is not the same because what returns is an imprinting, that is, a continuously repeating exchange of a finite number of worlds, not the sameness of the one true world.

The general thrust of Heidegger's thought is to distinguish between two fundamental ways. One is the way of Western metaphysics, or the exchange of a finite number of worlds within a single cycle of *Seinsgeschichte;* the other, which so far as I can see plays the same role as the posthistorical utopia plays in Marxism and therefore which has the status, despite Heidegger's objections, of an Ideal, is the releasement from the world into the clearing or region of presencing. For Nietzsche, the valuelessness of the eternal return leaves room for human beings to project their own values onto Chaos; at least this is Nietzsche's exoteric or political, that is, philanthropic, teaching. But it is also his esoteric or philosophical, and so self-interested, teaching since he cannot bear to exist within a world of decadence, ugliness, and absence of rank-ordering.

One may doubt whether Socrates would care to live in his own city and thereby be forced to turn away from philosophy in order to rule the nonphilosophers. But Nietzsche does not construct any world in particular; he advocates a rank-ordering based upon the principle of nobility or power (however mistaken he may be to equate these) and is thus open to the creation of a variety of embodiments (or "enworldments") of that principle. There is the following difference between Socrates and Nietzsche: Socrates excludes disagreement among his philosopher-kings, whereas Nietzsche insists upon such disagreement by defining life, and so philosophy, as continuous overcoming, as the struggle for dominance between worldviews. One can easily imagine that Socratic uniformity is as impossible as Nietzschean difference; uniformity dissolves into difference through internal pressure, whereas a war of differences, especially when it is a war of differing degrees of power, leads invariably to the uniformity of tyranny.[45] Looked at in this light, there is no intrinsic difference in the practical outcome of Socratic and Nietzschean politics: both lead to or represent different stages within the eternal return.

If this is so, and I believe that it is so, can we say that Heidegger is superior to both Socrates and Nietzsche and by generalization to what we are now entitled to call the history of Platonism understood as metaphysics, namely, the averting of the gaze from Being to a world? I see no basis for such a judgment. Nietzsche's worlds, an expression that in the present carefully defined context applies to Plato as well, are transient attempts to make sense out of human life in the light of the perception of nobility, understood in the human rather than the cosmological sense; and I note that however different may be Nietzsche's account of the inner truth of nobility from Plato's, his concrete estimations of nobility and baseness are surprisingly (or not so surprisingly) Platonic. The world of Becoming is able to approach very near to the world of Being because the principle that guides the approach is that of the world; it is a *worldly* and indeed a political principle, not an ontological or postontological principle of releasement from the world. However—and this is crucial—only a *worldly* principle is true to Being because Being shows itself as and is only accessible via a world.

The converse of this statement is on the other hand entirely false. We learn nothing about the world and not even about "worlding" or world-construction from listening to the voice of Being or gazing upon what transpires as pure mittence or event. But that from which we can learn nothing is not true, just as that which is of no use to us whatsoever is not good. Heidegger's nihilism arises from his desire to jump over his own shadow or to see the dark side of the moon without technical instruments. The last fact thus turns out to be not entirely removed from what Nietzsche claimed it to be: let us call it reversed Nietzscheanism. The will to power is true and good to the extent that it is useful, not for domination or continuous overcoming, which we may reject as the fantasy of an invalid, but for the noble preservation of human life. In other words, it is true and good to the extent that it is not the will to power, but Eros, or the love of the Ideas, and so not simply Dionysus but Apollo as well. For we cannot love what is invisible to us. Heidegger's teaching thus turns out to be a version of what Nietzsche called European Buddhism.[46]

I conclude this section with a note on difference. Gianni Vattimo, in his valuable book *The Adventures of Difference*,[47] points out that Derrida rejects Heidegger's account of Nietzsche as the last metaphysician. Instead, Derrida says that Nietzsche thinks difference itself as Dionysus.[48] In the text under discussion, Derrida says,

> We should conclude, but the debate is interminable. The divergence, the *difference* between Dionysus and Apollo, between ardor

and structure, cannot be erased in history, for it is not *in* history. It too, in an unexpected sense, is an original structure: the opening of history, historicity itself. *Difference* does not simply belong either to history or to structure. If we must say, along with Schelling, that "all is but Dionysus," we must know—and this is to write— that Dionysus is worked by difference. He sees and lets himself be seen. And tears out (his) eyes. For all eternity, he has had a relationship to his exterior, to visible form, to structure, as he does to his death. This is how he appears (to himself).[49]

Vattimo explains that for Derrida and his students, the reference to Dionysus "places the discourse immediately in an area distinct from that of metaphysics."[50] He indicates that Derrida's reading of Nietzsche has been influenced by the existentialist doctrine of the finitude of human existence, and so that Derrida treats the eternal return as a repetition or reinstitution of differences, in the sense of a continuous reassertion of finitude. Vattimo cites Derrida's statement that the introduction of *différance,* that is, the eternal return as the differentiating of differences, is established by "a throw of the dice" and cannot be verified by reference to any state of affairs. In Derridean language, "In the play of the signifier, there occurs always once more the originary differentiation."[51]

To this interpretation, Vattimo makes two main objections. First, the assertion that "all is but Dionysus" is a metaphysical statement; that is, it attributes a defining property or nature to the whole. Second, for Nietzsche the eternal return is the "arch-structure that founds and opens history itself." Hence it is not compatible with repetition in the sense of the continuous reassertion of finitude. "The eternal return, far from being repetition and *mise en scène* of difference, is the end of history as the domination of difference."[52] To these objections I would add the following: It is Schelling, not Nietzsche, who says that "all is but Dionysus." The divergence between Apollo and Dionysus does not collapse into a suppression of difference via the continuous expression of differences. On the contrary, Derrida himself, in the passage cited above, refers to this difference as "an original structure" and "historicity itself." The "seeing" and "being seen" (but not the tearing out of his eyes) of Dionysus is effectuated by Apollo. In other words, historicity is constituted by the reciprocal activity of the Apollonian or Hyperborean vision of temporality and the Dionysian immersion within a historical epoch by stepping into the gateway of the moment.

Derrida refers to the establishment of *différance* by a throw of the dice, an expression also employed by Nietzsche to refer to the emanations of Chaos in accord with an "irrational necessity."[53] Derrida follows Heidegger in the assimilation of human life, and so too of the discovery and production of sense, into the perturbations of Chaos. But he does not establish the installation of human thinking in Chaos by *Gerechtigkeit,* except in the sense that the metaphor of the throw of the dice is already a human interpretation. Even here, however, the will to will, or the conception of truth as holding to be true, is dissolved into chance. In sum, Derrida subjects Nietzsche to the trivializing ministrations of his own doctrines. Nietzsche explains rank-ordering in terms of quantity of power; Derrida denatures quantity of power into the random combinations of the dice.

Vattimo himself refers, as I just noted, to the eternal return as an "arch-structure." But he seems to me to characterize the function of this arch-structure in two opposing ways. On the one hand, he says that it founds and opens history itself; this is virtually equivalent to Derrida's thesis about difference, except that for Vattimo the eternal return overcomes all differences or fractures between essence and existence, event and signification, whereas for Derrida it produces differences as irreconcilable.[54] On the other hand, Vattimo holds that the eternal return is the overcoming of history as the domination of difference. To be within history is accordingly to be within difference. But it is not clear to me from Vattimo's text whether this mode of being is within or outside of, that is, beyond, the eternal return. Differently stated, is it the positing of the eternal return by Zarathustra, who himself observes rather than enters the gateway of the moment, or the circle of time, or is it the circular motion of the eternal return itself, as prophesied by Zarathustra, that liberates us from history?

The second of these alternatives makes no sense since it equates liberation from difference with domination by difference. But the first alternative requires that we live beyond history and time as well as beyond metaphysics, difference, and so the ontological difference. This is apparently Vattimo's understanding of Nietzsche, since he makes essentially this point as a criticism of Heidegger. Nietzsche, he says, wishes to surpass metaphysics and hence the difference between Being and beings. In other words, Nietzsche wishes to surpass Being. Heidegger, on the other hand, wishes to recollect or to remember the ontological difference between Being and beings because it is only thus that Being is accessible. But this requires us to remember and thus to remain within history or metaphysics. To the extent that Heidegger also wishes to surpass metaphysics, he too is committed to a forgetting of difference, and so of the difference between Being and beings, that is, of Being.

Vattimo infers from this that Being as eventuality (*Ereignis*), and hence difference, cannot be an arch-structure that is valid for every possible history; one thinks here of the late Heidegger's attempt to replace "Being" with a variety of alternatives.[55] To problematize Being as eventuality, one must surpass the horizon of metaphysics (and thus the eternal return as closure) and so too human nature. But this is possible only for Nietzsche's superman, who thus becomes, on Vattimo's interpretation, an authentic Heiddegerian. The statement that God is dead means that the epoch of metaphysics and difference is over; but it will take time for humankind to realize this. Heidegger's thought takes place within the interval of time required.[56]

To conclude, I take Vattimo to be saying that the eternal return, or Derridean difference, founds not *all* history, but the history of metaphysics. But this seems to be incompatible with his assertion that for Nietzsche the eternal return is the arch-structure that founds history itself. This apart, Vattimo's interesting analysis establishes the validity of the distinction between the Hyperborean and the historical standpoint on a theoretical basis that is quite different from mine. Even if we grant that there will be no end of historical epochs, it will always be necessary for man, or the superman, to rise above the level of humankind achieved within the epoch that is coming to a close, in order to see what the future holds in store. Schelling was therefore mistaken to hold that "all is but Dionysus."

The Superman

Whether or not one attributes a metaphysical doctrine to Nietzsche, it is unmistakable that his teaching is intended as a call to action. "My challenge: to produce beings [*Wesen*] that stand out as superior to the entire species 'Man': and for this goal to sacrifice myself and those who are 'closest' to me."[57] It is also plain that this challenge is in the first instance directed toward himself: "I have always composed my writings with my entire body and life: I do not know what 'purely spiritual' problems are."[58] And again: "I want to live through all of history in my own person and make all power and authority my own."[59] The connection between the personal and the public intentions is well captured by a juxtaposition of the following two Notebook entries: (1) "I write for myself alone."[60] (2) "I write for a species of human beings that is not yet present: for the 'masters of the earth.' "[61]

By "masters of the earth," Nietzsche means beings who are neither simply "human" nor merely brutes, but "supermen" who combine the pride of the eagle with the cunning of the serpent. The serpent is not only an echo of the biblical figure who tempts humankind to acquire the knowledge of good and evil that will make human beings like the gods or, in Descartes' statement, "like masters and possessors of nature." The serpent is the symbol of wisdom that is transformed into cunning by a return to the earth. "My task: the dehumanization of nature and then the naturalizing of mankind, after it has acquired the pure concept 'nature.' "[62] The return to the earth is not simply a metaphysical repudiation of the Hyperuranian domain of Platonic Ideas. It is an expression of Nietzsche's Machiavellianism or, more accurately, of his Thucydideanism: "Thucydides is the type who is closest to me."[63] In the *Götzen-Dämmerung,* in the section entitled "What I owe to the Ancients," Nietzsche says, "My recreation, my preference, my *cure* from all Platonism, was always *Thucydides.* Thucydides and, perhaps, the *principe* of Machiavelli are most closely related to me through the unlimited will not to fool themselves, and to see reason [*Vernunft*] in *reality,* not in 'reason,' still less in 'morality.' "[64]

The intention to dehumanize nature is clarified by the following fragment: "Most important viewpoint: to attain to the *innocence* of becoming, in order that one thereby exclude *purposes* [*Zwecke*]."[65] This is in turn required in order to allow humankind or, rather, the superman to establish through his own will the purposes of a new epoch. But behind the mask of the superman is his prophet, Zarathustra; and behind Zarathustra is the philosopher: "*The genuine philosophers are commanders and lawgivers:* they say, 'Thus it shall be!' "[66] In sum, the philosopher must prepare himself for the production of a new species by a lifetime of solitary study and reflection which centers around the assimilation of the entire history of the human species, not in the philological but in the psychological or spiritual sense of "history." Self-preparation is self-transformation, self-dehumanization: "In order to live alone, one must be a beast or a god—says Aristotle. This omits the third case: one must be both—Philosopher."[67]

That the philosopher is not the superman, or that there is a fundamental distinction between the two roles, is plain from the fact that, in order to assimilate the entire spiritual history of the human race into oneself, one must *recollect;* whereas, in order to act or to create, one must *forget.*[68] This is expressed by Nietzsche in a wide variety of ways, which we may summarize in the paradigm-case of Dionysus, the god of creative frenzy or intoxication. The following fragment should also be considered in this connection: "Man is the unbeast and the super-beast; the higher man is the unman and the superman; thus these go together. With each growth of man in greatness and height, he grows also in depths and the terrifying."[69] In the *Genealogy of Morals,* Nietzsche refers to "Napoleon, this synthesis of unman and super-man."[70] He does not refer to Plato, Protagoras, Descartes—or to himself—in these terms.

The superman cannot live alone; the prophet Zarathustra must himself come down from his cave on the mountaintop and into the marketplace of the city called "the Motley Cow" in order to announce to the assembled people: "Where is the lightning that will lick you with its tongue? Where is the madness with which you must be inoculated? Look; I teach you the superman: he is this lightning, he is this madness!"[71] The meaning of this text is perfectly clear—to us, not to the crowd, who take Zarathustra's speech to be an introduction of the rope-dancer. Zarathustra says that the superman is not the philosopher but the lightning and the madness with which the philosopher must inoculate human beings in order to transform them into a higher species.

From all these passages, which could easily be multiplied, it is evident that the superman is the extreme symbol or expression of the practico-productive core of Nietzsche's teaching. And by "practico-productive" I mean *political,* not metaphysical, praxis. In Heidegger's interpretation, the political dimension is entirely submerged in the account of the metaphysical doctrine of subjectivity. My objection is not at all to the general thesis of this account, namely, that Nietzsche, and so too the superman, is a late form, perhaps the latest, of the modern transformation of thinking into subjectivity, with the correlative association between the intellect and the will.[72] I object to the collapse of the separation between the philosopher and the superman, and so to the transformation of Nietzsche's political program into a metaphysical expression of nihilism or the forgetting of the absence of Being.

To say this in another way, I object to Heidegger's complete disregard for the *Platonic* implications of Nietzsche's turn from Plato to Thucydides. Most important, I object to this disregard because it renders invisible a difference between Nietzsche's Platonic or Hyperborean synoptic vision and his anti-Platonist attack on the supersensible world. This difference makes it impossible to understand Nietzsche through the exclusive use of the paradigm of modern subjectivity as "a hidden consequence of the veiled *relation* of Being itself to the *nature* [*Wesen*] of man."[73] Heidegger's account of modern subjectivity is inextricably rooted in an interpretation of Descartes, repeated many times in his writings, that takes its bearings by the *cogito* or *ego cogitans*.[74] I note that the *cogito* theme figures rarely in Descartes' corpus, and that even in the *Meditations* it is connected to a doctrine of the *lumen naturale* or the direct apprehension of geometrical form which has nothing to do with modern subjectivity and is a continuation of the Greek doctrine of *noēsis*. This is all that I can say here about Descartes.[75]

There is no doubt that the modern emphasis on subjectivity is closely connected to the emancipation of the will. Whether this is a metaphysical or a political "project" is another story. Heidegger's verdict on this project, namely, that it has its roots in a transformation within the history of metaphysics, understood as the forgetting of the absence of Being, is itself based upon the assumption that such a history has actually occurred. Heidegger assumes, or talks as if he assumes, that technicism and cyberneticism, that is, the abuse of technology and cybernetics, are the necessary outcome of the modern attempt to free humankind from God and nature. Nietzsche's superman is in his interpretation the metaphysical radicalization for the paradigm of human existence that underlies this disastrous outcome. This paradigm is reached in two main steps. In the first step, the subject or will becomes not merely the judge but the lawgiver.[76] In the second step, the subject or will gives not merely the law, but itself.[77] Step two, which is taken with Nietzsche, eventuates in the superman: "*The completed subjectivity of the will*

Reversed Platonism

to power is the metaphysical origin of the essential necessity of the 'superman.'"[78]

Man thus replaces God or wills the superman as the creator of the world ex nihilo. But the world thus created is itself, since it is a pure extension of human—or superhuman—will, mere flux or Chaos. The dehumanizing of nature is the basis for the understanding of nature as Chaos—"Chaos sive natura: *of the dehumanizing of nature*"—Heidegger himself cites this fragment from an early sketch of the teaching of the eternal return.[79] But the dehumanizing of nature in the previously noted sense of rejecting all natural purposes is "the humanizing through the supermen" (ibid.) or transformation of the world into a project of the superhuman will.

Heidegger summarizes the outcome of this process as follows: "The superman is the blow of that humanity that first *wills* itself *as* blow and strikes this blow itself."[80] In order to strike this blow, however, the superman has need of a hammer, and this hammer is the teaching of the eternal return.[81] We may grant all that is true in this formulation and still make a distinction between what I have been calling the theoretical and the practico-productive. The hammer of the eternal return is forged in the smithy of the philosopher and wielded by the superman. But as an artifact produced by philosophy, the hammer of the eternal return is not a truth but an edifying or noble lie. As a "metaphysical" truth, to employ Heidegger's term, the doctrine of the eternal return expresses the chaotic nature of becoming: *Chaos sive natura* is of course a radical revision of Spinoza's *deus sive natura*. The superman is able to replace God because Chaos has no inner or hidden order; it is open to whatever interpretation we choose to impose upon it; that is to say, it is open to any possible interpretation. For the "absolute necessity" of the eternal return means only that "the impossible is not possible."[82]

Exactly the same must be said of the teaching of the eternal return. It means what we will it to mean: "Thus shall it be!" To the philosopher, it means that there are no natural purposes; there is no natural order other than the perpetual reoccurrence of the finite number of combinations of points of force. This in turn leads to the *amor fati*, or recognition that human activity, *and so too human will*, is an illusion: what is, must have been; what will be, must be. The fundamental question is then, How can this teaching serve as a hammer or stimulus to creative action? I think that the answer is plain. The teaching, as just presented, *cannot* move us to act; its consequences, as Nietzsche himself recognized, can be only those of passive nihilism. One must therefore change the interpretation. Nietzsche the political rhetorician must emphasize the liberating dimension of the eternal return; it purifies through destruction and concentrates the energies of the human race for the creative act of the transvaluation of values. This interpretation in no way follows from Heidegger's attempt to identify the *Gerechtigkeit* of the thinker with the hidden inner order of Chaos. Such an identification makes *Gerechtigkeit* a pseudonym for *amor fati;* what seems to be free creation is an illusion for the necessity of chance, that is, of what happens.

This comes close to Heidegger's preferred understanding of the e-vent of Being as a happening in which nothing happens. Unfortunately, it also reduces human activity, and so the creation of a world through the transvaluation of values, into a perturbation on the surface of nothingness. In other words, Heidegger's transformation of Nietzsche's doctrine of the eternal return into a metaphysical or concealed version of the e-venting of the event has the result of transforming Nietzsche into a passive nihilist. And it does this by transmitting Heidegger's own passive nihilism into the Nietzschean texts. If we put Heidegger to one side and think hard about Nietzsche, we are forced to recognize that it is impossible to "reconcile" the two interpretations of the eternal return, activist and passive, in one fundamental and systematic metaphysical doctrine. Either the doctrine of the eternal return is a noble lie; or else, if it is a terrible truth, then the philosopher must lie about its significance. But none of this concerns or is carried out by the superman, who, far from making use of a hammer, is himself the hammer made use of by the philosopher.

This leads me to make an observation about Heidegger's own political activity. In my opinion Heidegger's disgrace of 1933 stems from the fundamental error of failing to distinguish between the philosopher and the superman. The philosopher must prepare for the revolution; he cannot lead it or become its spokesman. In the older tradition the philosopher acted, or attempted to act, as the counselor to the king or prince, whose own views were entirely conventional. Twentieth-century philosophers like Lukács, Heidegger, and Alexandre Kojève acted, or attempted to act, as kings or princes by combining the articulation of the new revolutionary doctrine with direct political action. But this is

Reversed Platonism

impossible, as Plato learned in Syracuse. Heidegger's Platonism amounts to his disregard of Plato's advice. The *vulgus* cannot be moved by philosophical rhetoric. In order to transform a society, one requires intellectuals and ideologues who mediate the philosophical rhetoric by debasing it into a form that is accessible to the crowd. Strictly speaking, for a philosophical revolution a superman is unnecessary and even dangerous. What one requires is loyal disciples. Nietzsche understood only part of this political truth; Heidegger apparently understood none of it.

On the other hand, I do not wish to deny that a defense could be made for Heidegger's political behavior on purely political grounds. Needless to say, this remark is not intended to suggest that the Nazi regime was arguably legitimate or philosophically defensible. The question of the proper relation between the philosopher and the tyrant has been discussed since antiquity, and I do not believe that the issue is definitively settled. But this is because the terms of the issue have nothing to do with metaphysics, ontology, or deconstruction. When and how the philosopher is entitled to make the attempt to modify tyrannical behavior for the good of the community, is a question of *phronēsis:* namely, of the assessment by practical intelligence of the variables of the given situation. Whatever may be true of Heidegger's character, his ontological posturing is indistinguishable in its practical consequences from European Buddhism. Although I disagree with the details of the activist doctrine of *Sein und Zeit,* I am more sympathetic to that doctrine than to the succeeding recommendation to *Gelassenheit,* with its admixture of orientalist kitsch and Gothic etymologizing.

To go to the heart of the matter, the only serious defense of Heidegger the thinker (as distinguished from Heidegger the political actor) is one which claims that we cannot effectively construct a political community or try to resolve the practical problems of everyday life until we have clarified our thoughts on Being. This would be a reasonable defense if it were possible to achieve clarity, or greater clarity, about Being and thereby to see beings, including political beings, in a new and more focused light. I have explained at sufficient length why I believe that this is impossible. It remains to add that a similar point must be made with respect to Plato. The difference between the philosopher and the superman can be brought out by a reflection on the doctrine of Ideas and its actual political role. To begin with, a continuous viewing of, or attempt to view, the Ideas does not lead to the just city but to the extinction of the philosopher's humanity. But what is perhaps more important, even if we could regularly turn our gaze from the Ideas to the city and back again, not much if anything of benefit would follow for the resolution of political affairs.

I will illustrate this point by way of the Idea of Justice. The Idea of the Cow, let us admit for the moment, enables us to recognize certain animals as cows. This is possible because cows are always cows, regardless of the context within which we encounter them or the perspective from which we view them. But the vision of the Idea of Justice does not in itself permit us to identify acts as just because what counts as just depends upon the circumstances. To see the Idea of Justice is not to see a picture of just conduct that is universally valid; perhaps it is something that is much closer to a general definition of justice. There is no picture that will cover every just act in the full variety of its circumstances. But unfortunately the same is true of a definition. For example, suppose that the definition is "mind your own business." As the *Republic,* if not our common sense, makes clear, we now have to determine what *is* our own business, and this will vary depending upon the situation in which we find ourselves.

It may very well be that the Idea of Justice corresponds neither to a picture nor to a definition. Perhaps it is like a Hyperuranian bell that rings whenever we encounter a just act—but why multiply absurdities? The fact is that we do recognize certain acts and persons as well as just. But we do this by perceiving the justice of the particular act or of the particular person's character, not by catching a glimpse of the Idea of Justice. When we say that we have access to an Idea of Justice, we mean that we draw an inference from a multiplicity of what we recognize to be just acts or persons, to some set of general properties that is common to every just act or person. But which properties? How could we define the properties of justice unless we first knew what justice is, that is, how could we understand that the Idea of Justice *is* in fact the Idea of *Justice* unless we first understand what justice is?

Unless we can explain what justice is, we cannot rely upon the Idea of Justice, since we will never know whether we are merely hallucinating or actually seeing some genuine being. And even assuming that we are seeing some genuine being, *what is it that we are seeing*? The Idea of Justice cannot explain itself, since it is not a voice or a speech, not a set of written instructions, and not a universally applicable picture. Are we to say that it is a feeling of righteousness? How is it to be distinguished from self-righteousness or pharisaism? It would thus be no help from a political standpoint if as a matter of fact the philosopher *could* see the Idea of Justice within certain acts or persons and thereby know for certain that these acts and persons are just. It would still remain for him to explain to the nonphilosopher, and even to the dissident philosopher or anti-Platonist whose Hyperuranian vision is cloudy, in what the justice of the given act or person consists.

Let me not be misunderstood here. I am not denying the existence of justice. My claim is that we see the justice of acts and persons not by consulting the Idea of Justice, but by seeing that this or that is just in such and such a case. This may sound as if I am admitting that we see the Idea of Justice as the one-in-many or that which is the unity within the diversity of instances of justice. But that is precisely *not* what I am saying. I hold rather that we see this or that instance of justice *and nothing more than that*. At this point and only at this point the "ontological" side of the doctrine of Ideas enters into the discussion.

It may well be that, underlying and somehow illuminating the multiple instances of justice that I have seen, there is an Idea of Justice, which I do not and, as a human being, cannot see, just as there are atoms underlying the visual appearance of the table which I, as a human being, and without the assistance of powerful microscopes, will never see and which, if I could see them, would look nothing like the table. I am even willing to entertain the possibility that the Idea of Justice may become visible to me in a fit of erotic madness. Furthermore, this vision may have a tonic effect on my character and inspire me to become just, as I previously was not. But it will tell me nothing whatsoever about how to be just, about what decisions to make in any particular case. It is superfluous to look away from the act or person toward the Idea because what we would see would be neither a just act or person nor a paradigmatic picture or identifying definition but what we may call an ontological entity. Knowledge of the Idea of Justice would not be knowledge of justice, but only of the ontological foundation for justice.

So it comes back to *phronēsis*, as even Plato admits in the *Statesman*. If we postpone the active assumption of our political responsibilities on the grounds that we are waiting for a clarification of the sense, truth, or *topos* of Being, then we are waiting (literally) for nothing. By Heidegger's own account of things, nothing is going to happen that will shed any light on the question What is to be done? Now I can easily understand someone refusing to engage in political life because it bores him or because it takes too much time away from metaphysics or even from listening for news about the e-venting of the e-vent. I can also understand someone's becoming a Nazi or a Stalinist or for that matter the secretary of state of the United States or foreign policy adviser to the president on the grounds that, by so doing, one will mitigate otherwise disastrous and immoral policies. But abstention in one case and intervention in the other is a practical decision about what it is best to do. It has nothing to do with Being.

My remarks in this section have had more than one purpose, but not the least of these is to support the contention that Heidegger's interpretation of Nietzschean nihilism is unsound. If Nietzsche, as a political thinker, forgot about the absence of Being, he was well advised to do so. As a matter of fact, the nihilism of the nineteenth century and by extension of the twentieth century had and has nothing to do with either the forgetting or the remembering of the absence of Being. It arose for the reasons given in detail by Nietzsche in a passage from the Notebooks for 1887 that deserves to be quoted at length:

> Causes of *nihilism*: (1) the *higher* species is absent, i.e. the one whose inexhaustible fertility and power of belief in Man keeps him upright (one thinks of what one owes to Napoleon: virtually all the higher hopes of this century) (2) the *lower species* "Herd" "Masses" "Society" forgets modesty and puffs up its needs into cosmic and metaphysical values. In this way all of human existence [*Dasein*] is vulgarized: insofar namely as the *Masses* rule, they tyrannize the *exceptions,* so that these lose their belief in themselves and become nihilists[.] All attempts *to devise higher types fail . . . Opposition* to the higher type as result. *Decline and insecurity of every higher type;* the struggle against genius ("Folk-poetry" etc)[.] Compassion for the inferior as *measuring rod* for the *heights of the soul*[.] The *philosopher is lacking,* the interpreter of the deed, *not* only the reproducer.[83]

The steady decline in fertility and self-confidence among the intellectual leaders of European civilization during the nineteenth century has often been attributed to the Enlightenment. From the Heideggerian standpoint, the Enlightenment is one stage in the development of subjectivity, and so of the emancipation of the will, that is, the development of the will to power, with the steady reifying or mechanizing of human existence, accompanied by a flattening and vulgarizing of spiritual standards. It could be argued that Nietzsche's view is, if not identical, quite similar. But there is one important difference. Nietzsche advocates the revolutionary attempt to transform the values of the Enlightenment, or their nineteenth-century vulgarization, by an extraordinary intensification of subjectivity as the will to power.

For Nietzsche, as I noted previously, Christianity, which underlies modern socialism and compassion for the inferior, is Platonism for the people. Perhaps one could say in his voice that modern science is, at least initially, Platonism for the few, although its consequences are by Nietzsche's standards spiritually disastrous. The reversal of Platonism requires compassion for the few and the replacement of physics by philology as the paradigm of the scientific worldview. I do not of course mean by this that Nietzsche advocated a return to the pre-Galilean dark ages; let me quote again an important passage from *The Twilight of the Idols:* "Spoken into the ear of a conservative—What one did not know previously, what one knows today, could know—a rebuilding of the past [*eine Rückbildung*], a return in any sense and degree whatsoever is entirely impossible.... No one is free today to be a crab"—that is, to walk backward.[84]

Nietzsche was very harsh on the peculiar nature of the professional philologist, but this is irrelevant for the present point. In order to see what is meant by replacing physics with philology as the paradigm of science, one should read paragraph 52 of *The Antichrist,*[85] in which Nietzsche criticizes theologians for their philological incapacity. "By philology should be understood here in a very general sense the art of reading correctly—to be able to read facts, *without* falsifying them through interpretations, without losing caution, patience, subtlety [*Feinheit*] in the desire for understanding." Physics, like all of natural science, is for Nietzsche an interpretation; the task of the philologist is to regulate or keep in check interpretation—"Philology as *ephexis* in interpretation"—and to do so with what August Boeckh called *subtilitas legendi.* In other words, physics must be subordinated to the "text" of human existence as it is interpreted by those who know how to read, by the reader of refinement, by the philosopher. Philology is the same as the *philologia* of Socrates in the *Phaedrus* (236e4f).

Those who know how to read the text of life (something quite different from attempting to reduce life to a text) will understand the fundamental danger in Nietzsche's experiment. The attempt to create the superman results all too frequently in the production of intellectuals and ideologues. And these masters of vulgar rhetoric will always triumph over the philosopher in the public arena. The truth of history is that one cannot intentionally create a superman: Napoleon was born, not made.

The History of Being

8

Looking Backward

It is now time to bring this book to a close. But I prefer not to assemble a summary list of established or defended theses. To do so would be to trivialize a long and complex investigation. I offer instead in this section an extended remark that follows from the content of the preceding pages and that will prepare the way for a final consideration of a crucial Heideggerian text, one that has been chosen as appropriate for a conclusion. It should go without undue emphasis, but not without saying, that conclusions to labors of the sort that have occupied us here are always invitations to another beginning. Heidegger is never more Platonic than when he emphasizes that he is *unterwegs;* in a favorite Socratic expression, *palin eks archēs.* "Once more from the beginning"; but the beginning is the whole.

And now to my remark. Heidegger is the most influential as well as the most ambiguous of the twentieth-century generals in what Socrates, speaking in the *Theaetetus,* refers to as Homer's army. Socrates says that this army consists of all the philosophers except Parmenides as well as of the most prominent poets, whether comedians like Epicharmus or tragedians like Homer himself. The unifying thesis of this army, which Socrates ironically identifies with the secret or private teaching of Protagoras, is that "it is out of movement and change and mixture with each other that are generated all those things which by an incorrect appellation we say to be (*einai*). For nothing ever is (*esti*) but is always coming to be" (152c8ff). Heidegger's version of Protagoreanism could easily be mistaken by the unwary for an unusually garrulous and pedantic version of Eleaticism, so often and with such forceful obscurity does it speak of Being. As we have learned, however, Being is for Heidegger neither an entity nor a ground. Contrary to the instructions of father Parmenides, Heidegger says the thing that is not; even worse, like Hegel, he identifies Being and Nothing. Being is neither this nor that, but instead an event or process by which things come to be. But contrary to Hegel, the process has no permanent, definite structure which may be elicited from its total manifestation.

On a related point of great importance, Heidegger is sufficiently close to Hegel to make a contrast between the two thinkers illuminating. With all respect for their doctrinal differences, one may nevertheless say that both attribute a history to Being. There is for Hegel not merely a development of the categorial structure of the Absolute, but a development that is isomorphic with the major epochs of world history. This comprehensive structure integrates pagan *logos* and Judaeo-Christian spirituality, together with Rousseau's and Montesquieu's history of the development of humankind and a further synthesis of the two dimensions, noumenal and phenomenal, of Kant's transcendental philosophy, in such a way as to make immanent or human history the mirror of its transcendental ground. Hegel masters contingency by transforming it into a logical category. Nietzsche, so to speak, reverses Hegelianism by transforming logic into a category of contingency.

Both Hegel and Nietzsche offer us a circular totality that rotates on the axis of spirit. Nietzsche is in his own way as much a transcendental philosopher as Hegel, since the hypothesis of the eternal return is the necessary condition for the possibility of the synoptic or Hyperborean vision that preserves the doctrine of perspectivism or interpretation from dissolution into what is today called *différance*. For Hegel, what recurs is the logical structure of absolute spirit; for Nietzsche, it is the rank-ordering of human types. Finally, what Hegel calls negative excitation is in Nietzsche's doctrine known as Chaos. In what is the fundamental difference between the two thinkers, Hegel explains the transition from negative excitation to an orderly world as the necessary consequence of the positive accumulation of successive sequences of negations. Stated in a non-Hegelian but, I believe, illuminating way, random motion accumulates into order. I add parenthetically that it would not be difficult to show the inner identity between Hegel's baroque logic and the dominant philosophical basis of modern science.

Hegel, however, identifies excitation and spirit. Nietzsche returns to Kantian dualism by distinguishing between the excitation of spirit and that of Chaos. In simple or exoteric language, Nietzsche denies the classical doctrine of the cosmos; he denies order, purpose, and so value to the random concatenations of points of force. In a more esoteric vocabulary, and contrary to Heidegger's interpretation, there is no identity between the human will and the inner order of Chaos; this is because there is no inner order of Chaos. It therefore follows that the eternal return must be no less an exoteric hypothesis than the will to power. It is Chaos that is eternal; what recurs is Chaos, interpreted as a historical perspective or epoch. Nietzsche's understanding of human experience is thus a radicalized version of Dilthey's professorial attempt to develop a critical philosophy of historicity.

I do not mean to suggest that Nietzsche was directly influenced by Dilthey, whom, so far as I know, he never mentions. But Dilthey represents the dominant current in nineteenth-century philosophy, namely, the attempt to reconcile Kant and Hegel in a positivist or quasi-scientific framework. We arrive at Nietzsche if we think through the consequences of the combination of the following statements by Dilthey: (1) "The world exists nowhere else but in the representations [of human beings]"; (2) "Nature is alien to us. It is a mere exterior for us without any inner life. Society is our world"; (3) "Everything brought about by men in this socio-historical reality happens by means of the mainspring of the will. . . . Even the sense of justice is not a fact of cognition but rather a fact of the will."[1]

This is the background against which one has to understand Heidegger's peculiar return, by way of Augustinian anthropology and Scholastic metaphysics on the one hand and Kant and Husserl on the other, to the Greek thinkers and in particular to the pre-Socratics or, in short, to Homer's army. We have to distinguish what Heidegger has assimilated from what he repudiates in the process of articulating his own interrogative path. I am not concerned with the details of this assimilation. For my purposes, what counts is the general observation that the repudiation of modern subjectivity is conditioned, at first by the acceptance of modern, transcendental subjectivity under the designation of *Dasein,* and then, after the so-called *Kehre* ("turn"), by the transference of the locus of subjectivity from *Dasein* to the departed gods who maintain an ambiguous relation to the veiled and apparently inaccessible "origin" from which all ways, Heidegger's version of what were for Hegel and Nietzsche historical epochs, emerge. The critic of onto-theo-logy is himself transformed into a quasi-Zarathustran prophet of Being and the pagan gods of the Germanic folk.

In the long stretches of European history, with its epochal campaigns for the conquest of the human spirit, Homer's army assimilates bar-

The History of Being

barians into its originally Greek squadrons. For those to whom war (and hence change) is the father of all things, the distinction between Greek and barbarian is no more substantial than the difference between two simulacra of the "trace" of postmodern deconstructionists. Nor can Heidegger, with all his philological *Spitzfindigkeit* and obsessive musing over the Greek texts, purge himself of the incense of barbarian gods. Heidegger transforms the Greek *historiē* into a secularized version of Judaeo-Christian historicity according to which the Germans are the chosen or metaphysical people; *Geschichtlichkeit* in turn becomes the donation of the history of Being, not in the Hegelian sense of the unfolding Concept nor even in the Nietzschean sense of an eternal return, but as the unexpected event: and not as this or that event, but as sheer eventuation, as *Er-eignis*. The empirical priority of the that to the what is in Aristotle itself subordinated to the essential or eidetic priority of the what to the that. Heidegger abolishes this priority; this is his own acquiescence in positivism or, more precisely, in an edifying positivism.

The idiosyncratic nature of Heidegger's Homericism resides finally in the positivity of the event. Heidegger restates the dialectic of motion and rest in the poetical language of manifestation and hiddenness, disclosure and concealment, presentation and withdrawal. In Hegel, there is finally no separation between essence and appearance; in Heidegger, nothing is what it seems to be. This last phrase could also be read positively: *nothing* is what it seems to be or, conversely, what *seems* to be is nothing, namely, Being. In straightforward language, the celebration of the donative process of Being empties the gifts themselves of significance. The attribution of significance or, in Nietzsche's expression, value to the gifts is for Heidegger tantamount to the reification and hence forgetting of Being.

It is my suspicion that Heidegger's positivism, as I call it, is due to an inability to rid himself of the influence of the Husserlian orientation by perception.[2] In the *Logical Investigations,* with which the young Heidegger occupied himself intensively as student and teacher, Husserl develops his doctrine of intentionality as dependent not upon anticipation but upon fulfillment (40).[3] "In fulfillment we experience [*erleben*] as it were a *that is it itself,*" via more and less direct perceptions (65). In other words, fulfillment is the direct self-givenness to our intuition (*Veranschaulichung*) of the content of perception, whether this content be a sensuous object or some abstract category founded in sensuous objects (73). The content of perception must stand before the very eye of the soul, as it were (81). The last foundation of all intentional acts is *Vorstellung* or *Repräsentation,* that is, the pure intuition of the fully given content of perception (94–95, 98). In sum, fulfillment is finally "the object itself, as it is in itself," and this in turn leads to the *adaequatio rei et intellectus,* or truth (118). Husserl also calls this full givenness of the object *Evidenz* (121f). In Evidence, we live (*erleben*) truth as the complete correspondence between the intended and the given as such (122).

In a term that Heidegger himself would eventually apply to Kant, Being is for Husserl perceivedness or, as one could also say, the presence of the That. But the attribution of significance to the content of a perception depends upon a detachment from that perception in order to place its content within a hierarchy of concepts and categories. Briefly expressed, to say "this is significant" or "that is good" is not the same as to have before one in full evidence the "that" of perception. Values are themselves for Husserl perceptual structures, that is, objects of pure intuition founded in sensuously perceived objects. But to perceive a value as founded in an object of perception is not the same as to evaluate an object of perception. Like other representatives of the scientific Enlightenment, Husserl defined truth on the basis of sense-perception and thereby inevitably reduced the difference between values and significations or meanings on the one hand and real essences on the other to that between two species of intuition.

The same point can be illustrated from a late work, the *Crisis of the European Sciences,* in such a way as to distinguish between Husserl's doctrine of the lifeworld and the Platonic understanding of everyday life as developed in chapters 2 and 3 above. The lifeworld is for Husserl "the forgotten foundation of meaning of natural science" (48).[4] It is the world of praxis and prudence that has been covered over by "the garment of symbols" devised by modern, Galilean mathematical physics (51, note). Husserl goes so far as to identify the lifeworld with the Greek *doksa;* but he immediately separates himself from the Greeks by asserting that his is the first attempt to transform *doksa* into the foundation of *epistēmē* (158). That is, Husserl intends to propound a *science* of the lifeworld by rising above the subjective-relative level of *doksa* to the scientific level of an objective description of the structures of the lifeworld (135, 142). This is equivalent to the analysis of the structure

The History of Being

of intersubjectivity (170, 175). The lifeworld of praxis and culture is grounded in subjectivity as a continuous change of relativities (which Husserl explicitly refers to in an earlier text as Heracleitean flux, the style of which he wishes to grasp: 159); despite this change, the lifeworld "contains its essentially regulative typic, to which all life and so all science, whose 'basis' it is, remains bound. So the lifeworld also has an ontology that is to be produced out of pure evidence" (176).

In order to arrive at the structure of premathematicized intersubjectivity, and so to reach the ultimate level of intentionality, from which the meaning of science is produced, we undergo a transcendental *epochē,* or detachment, from the lifeworld, except to the extent that it is the object of perception, given to pure, in the sense of impersonal, intuition: "I stand *over* the world, which has become for me now in an entirely peculiar sense a *phenomenon*" (154). But even though the lifeworld is centered in the ego-pole, subjectivity itself is what it is only in intersubjectivity, that is, in the intersubjectively identical lifeworld of the I-Thou-We (174–75). The main characteristic of this impersonal subjective perception of the structures of the lifeworld is detachment or neutralization: "Naturally we have in the present thematic sphere no share in all the interests that any human praxis brings into play" (159). We change from the natural attitude of interested participant in the lifeworld to "the uninterested observer" (178) and in this way achieve with respect to the lifeworld the level of philosophy as universal objective science which remains blind to the "full concreteness" of Being and life (179).

In the lifeworld, we live and move and have our being. But to the phenomenologist, the lifeworld is a pure perception or object of intuition. The point of phenomenological description is not at all to distinguish the worse from the better, but to bring to full presence before "the eye of the soul" (in Aristotle's expression) the structures by which residents of the lifeworld fulfill their intentions. And here again, despite all reference to the determination of signification or meaning, "intentionality" is understood primarily in terms of the object of sense-perception. This arises from the *Geltungsepochē,* or bracketing of validities, hence of evaluations (239), by which we detach ourselves from all interested participation in the lifeworld and so "take no position" with respect to anything that transpires therein (241–43). Now this kind of detachment from the lifeworld, if it is possible at all, can succeed only in rendering alien the phenomenon of life from the fulfillment of intentions. In my opinion, it is in fact impossible and leads rather to the unconscious imposition of prejudices derived from the ideal of scientific objectivity onto the domain of the everyday. One cannot "perceive" the genealogy of human signification except by participating in the prudential, deliberative, and so evaluative process that permeates it. Without such participation, there is no inner grasping of what becomes instead a sequence of pictures.

Phenomenology is thus at bottom positivism rooted in the paradigm of perception. But it is also historicism, the inner sense of what Heidegger calls the eventing of the E-vent. The Heideggerian thinker stands to the E-vent of Being as the Husserlian phenomenologist stands to the flow of purified essences. There is, however, this fundamental difference between the two. The Heideggerian has no access to the origination of the E-vent but must receive what occurs through it. The Husserlian, on the contrary, is perceiving the content of his own stream of consciousness, which he deludes himself into defining as the impersonal domain of intersubjectivity. The desedimentation of history, or the extricating of the structures of the lifeworld from beneath its raiment of symbols, is in fact the purification of memory, or a subjective version of what Plato calls "recollection" (*anamnēsis*).

Husserl wishes to avoid historicism and insists that, whereas "history is the living excitation of the interaction of originary sense [*Sinn*] formation and sedimentation," the *Sinn* is an objective ideality when fully formed. History or sense-formation thus possesses a "dominant structural a priori" (380). In his development of this crucial point, Husserl says that there is a general a priori structure of each epoch of history. But this structure is itself a historical construction of meanings; the series of constructions is derived finally from *Urevidenz*, which, Husserl adds in a crucial footnote (381), is determined by cultivated persons "who pose new questions, new historical questions" belonging both to the outer domain of the sociohistorical world and to the inner world, the "dimension of depth."

In sum, Husserl insists that history has an a priori and apodictic *Evidenz* (381ff), and so that there is an apodictic essence of the lifeworld with which the geometer (= the Galilean) is concerned. Historical analysis of the origin of geometrical truth thus leads us back to the "invariant or absolute a priori" presupposed by all historical facts (382–85). But this structure is geometrical; it is the basis

The History of Being

of the history of geometry and thus of mathematical physics, not the basis for judging the difference between the noble and the base, the better and the worse, and so, the very significance or meaning of science for which Husserl is himself searching. Even, however, if one insists that the phenomenological method applies to all structures of the lifeworld, including those of morality and what Husserl calls "culture" (*Bildung*), the same criticism applies. The perception or intuition of structure is not the same—in fact it is explicitly separated from—the prudential assessment of, through interested participation in, culture. And perhaps most important, the entire descriptive process is directed not toward life, but to the individual phenomenologist's inner perception of life. The result is not even intersubjectivity but the phenomenon or, as I would put it, the image of intersubjectivity as accessible to the solipsist.[5]

Phenomenology begins with perception, the basic apprehension of material bodies,[6] and shifts to intuition, or the contemplation of the modality of consciousness that corresponds to the real content of the perception. The extension of intuition to nonsensuous properties and relations of perceived bodies does not result in rank-ordering or the determination of the significance of regions of modes of consciousness for the totality of my life, or for that matter of the life of the human race, but in *description* of that which is present as the fulfillment of an intentional act of consciousness. This transcendental solipsism is further characterized by radical temporality; there is no last perception of an object but rather unending variations of presentation; Husserl goes so far as to refer to the actual world as a special case of possible worlds.[7] Even the ideal thing that is constituted from the flow of *Erlebnisse* presents itself "in the *necessary 'form' of time*."[8] This leads in turn to the doctrine of transcendental subjectivity as the constitution of temporality, and so, whether as anticipation or through reciprocal influence, to Heidegger's doctrine of temporality as the aperture (my word) through which Being is accessible, whether as a project of *Dasein* or as a gift from an unseen benefactor.

In sum, the ostensibly a priori structures of transcendental subjectivity can no more escape their temporary status than can the existentials of *Being and Time*. Phenomenology is the description of the temporary organization of intersubjective time, as it is accessible in the private subjectivity of the phenomenologist. Being, nonbeing, and their modal inflections (= predicates) refer not to the so-called external object but to the intended as intended, to "objective sense," and thus to the cogito.[9] Everything that exists for the pure ego is constituted within it. It is senseless to think of the universe of true Being as standing outside the universe of possible consciousness. Beings are a concrete unity "within the single absolute concretion of transcendental subjectivity."[10] And subjectivity is the self-organizing activity of ceaseless temporal flow. Phenomenology is the attempt to describe fully the structure of the object of perception as presented fully to the intentionality that generates it. It is thus a species of historicist positivism masking itself as the pursuit of apodictic certainty.

It is of course true that Husserl and Heidegger both refer to the concept of the world as the horizon of phenomena and their senses. To restrict ourselves now to Heidegger, it is also true, however, that the world gradually assumes for him the role of that which is gathered together within the clearing of Being or in other words the role of the surrogate for the phenomenon in the Husserlian sense. The truth of Being as disclosure of the interplay of coveredness and uncoveredness replaces the self-manifestation of the phenomenon; but this means that disclosure replaces self-manifestation.

Disclosure has a more complex inner structure than self-manifestation, but the orientation of the thinker toward disclosure (*Entbergung*) is the analogue of the phenomenological orientation toward the intentional content of the cognitive perception. Whereas the Husserlian phenomenologist begins by contemplating the essence of his own intentional act of consciousness, Heidegger begins by *attempting to contemplate* Being. Husserl is thing-oriented (i.e., he gazes upon the "what" of consciousness) as Heidegger tries not to be (i.e., he meditates or recollects Being, not beings). Nevertheless, Heideggerianism is reversed Husserlianism: thinking remains oriented toward the open and visible, of which the audible can only be derivative. It remains *theoretical* in the literal sense of disregarding or bracketing all considerations other than the meditating of Being. This is the obvious consequence of the enforcement of the ontological distinction. Even the force of the distinction between Husserlian subjectivity and Heidegger's insistence that openness is a property of beings, and so a result of Being, is undercut by Heidegger's insistence that Being requires humankind in order to manifest itself.

The History of Being

So much for my general remark, which is intended in lieu of a summary of my critique of Heidegger's interpretation of metaphysics. I want to close this study by considering a fundamental Heideggerian text, but to do so in such a way that sublates what has preceded into an open horizon. As I indicated at the outset of this chapter, there is no last word in philosophy. I turn now to a section from volume II of the *Nietzsche* volumes, entitled *Entwürfe zur Geschichte des Seins als Metaphysik* (Sketches toward a history of being as metaphysics) and dated 1941. This text itself looks both backward and forward, since the history of Being as metaphysics is intended by Heidegger as a prelude to another beginning in the unceasing flow of human history. The section I shall discuss is called "The Completion of Metaphysics."

Heidegger begins with his familiar assertion that the completion of metaphysics establishes the existent (*das Seiende*) in the abandonment of Being (*Seinsverlassenheit*).[11] The assertion is familar, but what precisely does it say? The existent is the totality of everything that exists: *Seienden* or the Greek *onta*. "Existence" does not here bear the technical meaning of the mode of Being of *Dasein*. We can however make use of the etymology for our own purpose by noting that an *on* "stands out" from the process of emergence not as the flower emerges from the soil, but as the flower and the soil take their stand in opposition to one another by an appearance or self-presentation that deflects our attention from the underlying process of presencing. In a subsequent paragraph of the section we are studying, Heidegger says, "Existence [*Existenz*]: the coming to be manifest [or "disclosed"], bringing itself to itself, being itself in coming to be itself, with respect and contrary to the ground."[12]

This statement is made in conjunction with a remark about Schelling: "Becoming in itself 'contradictory' (Schelling)"; but it expresses a thought that is independently useful. Let me try to state very generally the experience that underlies the two remarks about *Seinsverlassenheit* and *Existenz*. It is plain that Heidegger's general approach, despite the idiosyncrasy of his language, has to do in one sense or another with the phenomena, that is, with what appears as it appears; and by "appears" I mean "shows" or "manifests" itself, in a sense that is prior to the distinction between appearance or illusion and reality or actuality. Now it is of course questionable whether we are able in fact to arrive at this fundamental level of apprehension. Without being excessively concerned about the details of Husserl's phenomenological method, we can nevertheless assert that this method stands or falls upon the ability of the observer to attain to a clear and distinct, that is, accurate, and so indubitable, apprehension of what appears.

In other words, the phenomenologist assumes that, by a series of "reductions" or purifications, he can arrive at the naked phenomenon, as it were, at that which not only appears, but which shows itself to be exactly that which appears. This assumption is in turn grounded in a prior assumption, namely, that although a phenomenon is what shows itself *to me* as observer, I can arrive at the phenomenon itself by discarding the various perspectival distortions within my own consciousness, distortions that could interfere with the direct grasping of the phenomenon. This prior assumption is problematical, not to say dubious, for the following reason: Just as one could say on behalf of Kant that we can think only what we can think, so with respect to Husserlian phenomenology we must point out that we can see only what we can see. These platitudes, which are intended by their proponents to establish the centrality of consciousness, or of what is called the Kantian Copernican Revolution, at the same time restrict what we see or what we contemplate by a kind of inner or reflexive gazing upon what we see. At each stage of viewing, we are restricted by what presents itself to us. But this means that unless the initial presentation is indubitable and thus serves as the standard for all subsequent purifications, there is no way in which to carry out the various phenomenological reductions. In order to arrive at the purified phenomenon, we must be guided by an initial apprehension of the purified phenomenon.

Let me compare the problem with the one that Plato faces with respect to the original and image. In the case of Husserl, it must be held that I cannot be mistaken about the fulfillment of the intentionality of my own act of consciousness. If I take myself to be viewing a rose, then it cannot be something else. But this is not quite right because Husserl also talks about the phenomenological purification of the content of consciousness, that is, of a shift from the initially given intuition (as we may call it) to the *Wesen* or the genuine being of the intuition. The process of purification is entirely interior to consciousness, since there is obviously no possibility of checking the accuracy of my intuitions by stepping outside of my consciousness and taking a look at the "things themselves." Therefore the process of purification itself proceeds by means of intuitions. Furthermore, it must be the case that the initially given rose is not indubitably what it *seems* to show itself to be. For if it were, no purification would be required. There must be a gap between the "seeming" and the "showing." But there is no way in which to fill that gap, except with other seemings, each of which is in the same situation as the initial member of the series.

This is precisely the problem of original and image in Plato. Plato distinguishes between accurate and inaccurate images, with the additional complication that accurate images provide us with inaccurate views of the original, whereas some inaccurate images, namely, those which are accommodated to human perspective, provide us with accurate views. For our purposes we can simplify the Platonic problem radically. If our access to the original is by way of images, how can we distinguish between an accurate image, in the sense of an image that gives us an accurate view of the original, and inaccurate images, unless we are able to compare them both to an independent vision of the original? And if we possess this independent vision, why do we need images? But if we do not possess this independent vision, then there are no images at all, but all views are originals. There is then no difference between "accurate" and "inaccurate." There are only *differences* of perspective.

To return to the phenomenon, it is plausible to claim that what shows itself to us at any moment is the only original to which we have access. Every attempt to purify the initial show is based on nothing other than this initial show together with subsequent shows. But subsequent shows, even those which we take to be the same in content with the initial show, are literally *subsequent,* and so distinct from the initial show. How can we be sure that we remember the initial show (which now assumes the status of original) with sufficient accuracy to identify its successors as contentually the same? Furthermore, if they are the same, then no phenomenological reduction is needed or possible. But if they are different, then how can we call them "purifications" of the initial show? How do we know that they are not rather distortions? Or presentations of *new* content?

It is obvious that we cannot go outside our consciousness for confirmation by a process of comparing our visions or viewings with how things are in themselves; there is no outside access to things except by way of the views we acquire of what shows itself. Therefore, since we have to remain within our consciousness, we have no other recourse but (1) to assume that we remember the initial show, and (2) to proceed not simply to compare subsequent shows with the initial one, but to arrange these subsequent shows or to consider them in their order of presentation, in conjunction with other sequences of shows, and thereby to arrive at a determination of the nature or essence of the initial show by the criteria of coherence, completeness, and so on. In other words, we employ logical or categorial criteria by which to perform the phenomenological reductions of the phenomenon or show itself. And this means that the show itself does *not* show itself as it is, where "as it is" means "as we determine it to be with precision" and where "with precision" means "on the basis of categories that seem self-evident to us." To this I add that the process of arriving at the essential appearance includes the technique of imaginative variation of the content of the initial appearance. The "essence" is to this extent an artifact of the imagination, something that Heidegger mistakenly attributes to Plato when he interprets the passage in book 10 of the *Republic* about the Idea of the bed.

A variation on this problem goes as follows. If the initial "seeming" of, say, a rose is not in itself veridical, we are not going to arrive at a purified version of the essence of this seeming by examining subsequent seemings or intuitions, as has just been stated, unless, of course, we have access to the "Idea" of the rose as independent of the intuitions. "Independent" here means not outside of consciousness, but rather separate from the intuitions themselves. It must be the case that the initial view of what seems to be a rose is modified through subsequent seemings, not on the basis of those seemings, all of which are as dubious as the initial member of the series, but by access to an independently accessible paradigm of what the seeming must be a seeming *of*. Intuition, in other words, or the viewing of the ostensible fulfillment of the intentionality of consciousness, must stimulate a process very much like the Platonic recollection of the Idea that is suggested to us by our perception of generated instances. But in Husserl, the closest we come to recollection is imagination. That is to say, the imaginative variation on the content of the actual perception or phenomenon in a sense produces an original that is independent of and inferred from the fragmentary or unpurified images of initial presentation.

The History of Being

303

The introduction of categories leads to problems in its own right, problems which suggest that Husserl was mistaken to believe that his later work superseded the *Logical Investigations*. But to stay with the phenomenon as show for a moment, that is, as the show of a determinate content of an *on* or *Seiendes,* this phenomenon has been assigned contradictory roles. This is because Husserl is in fact not a Platonist and cannot maintain that we correct our intuitions or fulfillments of intentionality by means of an independently acquired Idea; on the contrary, he claims that we arrive at the Idea through the process of purification of the contents of our consciousness, or what I am calling intuitions. On the one hand, what is initially given is said to require purification in order for us to be able to establish it in itself, independent of all distorting perspectives. On the other hand, the initial show must serve as the criterion for all subsequent shows, including those which are ostensibly steps in the purification procedure. We can therefore say with Schelling that Becoming is contradictory in itself. It is not simply the case that the phenomenon, or the *Seiendes* that shows itself, conceals the presencing-process of Being; even worse, the phenomenon conceals itself, precisely in the act of showing itself.

Take a simple analogy from sense-perception. We can never be 100 percent certain that our initial perception of an object is veridical. In all cases, even the most obvious, if our criterion is sense-perception, we have to acquire additional perceptions; and this is insufficient in itself, since we must employ categories of ordering and relating, the application of which do not themselves *produce* the original from the perceptions, but either refer back to some original that is somehow accessible to us via perception or else which is imposed onto the perceptions by cognition. The first of these alternatives is the Platonic approach; the second is the Kantian. In his concentration upon the concealment of Being, has Heidegger forgotten or overlooked the self-concealment of the *on* as phenomenon?

Although I know of no passage in the Heideggerian corpus in which he discusses this problem in the precise terms that I am now employing, it is implicit in the "dialectic" (my term) of disclosure and concealment within *Entbergung.* Furthermore, in *Being and Time,* Heidegger, with all his talk of the phenomenological method, does in fact go beyond consciousness and the Husserlian *Wesensschau* (viewing of essences) with his key notion of "Being in the world." This notion replaces the

Husserlian doctrine of intentionality by placing primary emphasis not on the object of perception, but on the web of relations emanating from the everyday activity of *Dasein* by which phenomena are connected, whether as tools or as things, into a world. The *Kehre* in Heidegger's thinking after *Being and Time* does not affect this central point. As is plain from the texts we have been studying throughout this investigation, the notion of world continues to play a prominent role; only now, the world is not an emanation of *Dasein* but a gift or project of Being. This shift is equivalent to Heidegger's criticism of Nietzsche's doctrine of the will and, more extensively, of the central role of the will in modern philosophy.[13]

By giving central prominence to the projection of a world, Heidegger deviates from Husserlian phenomenology, with its concentration upon the object of perception; he also offers a solution to the problem of solipsism from which Husserl was never able to free himself. What is called *Dasein* in the period of *Being and Time* and "the thinker" in the subsequent period is always a being for whom the "opening" of thought, and so too of the viewing of what shows itself, is simultaneous with the opening of a world. Furthermore, Heidegger does not quite take his bearings by the phenomenon as what shows itself; instead, he takes his bearings by the *Seinsfrage,* that is, by the distinction between Being and beings, and so by the distinction between what shows itself and what is concealed by that showing.

One could therefore say on his behalf that the contradictory nature of the phenomenon, namely, as that which both shows itself and conceals or covers over its own showing, is assimilated into the distinction between beings and Being. In my "Platonic" terminology, the original is the ground or presencing-process; the phenomenon is an image in two senses. First, as an emergent thing, it images the emergence-process or ground. Second, as a phenomenon, for example, a flower or a tree, it is also an image of the world-process, that is, of the categorial process of relating and ordering that gives to the phenomenon *in* the world its precise sense. Note that this is true whether we take a scientific or rationalist approach to the structure of the world or a Nietzschean approach according to which a world is founded by an evaluation or rank-ordering.

My present concern is not philological; I want to make plausible the basic experience of thinking that underlies Heidegger's approach. And in so doing, I am entitled to think the unthought, to repeat a familiar expression, if indeed Heidegger did leave this issue unthought. Heidegger's problem is thus the reverse of that of Husserl. The problem is now to establish the genuineness or reliability of the apprehension of Being as regulative of our meditation on beings. It turns out, in other words, that on Heideggerian grounds what shows itself is not the flower as flower, but the world as world within which the flower is perceived as a flower and hence as undergoing various determinations, themselves ultimately defined or attuned by the particular manifestation of the sense- or truth-giving process that I have called previously the "worlding" of worlds. So Heidegger must explain how we have access to the Being that serves in his thinking the role played by the purified phenomenon in Husserl and the Ideas in Plato. We cannot get this access from the beings because they conceal or divert our gaze away from Being. It would therefore seem to be necessary that we have this access "in advance." But in advance of what, and in what sense? How can we be in advance of the beings, which are given to us by the same "thrownness" or (in the later terminology) openness or clearing by which the world is given? And it certainly is implausible to maintain that both are given at once, that is, separately, whereas we put them together by some kind of posterior synthesis that retains a memory of the separately presented Being.

Husserl does not claim that we have a pregiven perception of an object, say a rose, that serves to guide the process of bringing to full phenomenological purity the givenness in and to consciousness of the rose. To speak of "pre-predicative" awareness, for example, is to continue to refer to what is given as present in and to consciousness, if as prior to the articulation by discursive or predicative speech of the categorial structure that makes this given content thinkable. But Heidegger must claim that we have a preawareness of Being that allows us to distinguish between Being and beings. And entirely apart from whatever Heidegger may claim, this is required by the terms of his doctrine if he is to avoid a problem analogous to the one that I have indicated in the cases of Plato and Husserl.

What shows itself as a rose, a tree, or a person does so not in isolation, like a picture flashed upon a pitch-black backdrop, as one might polemically characterize the situation in Husserl, but as occurring in a *place* that is itself opened or provided by the world. It is the world that shows us the rose, whether a something at hand, to be enjoyed, smelled, given to one's beloved, used as a decoration, and so on, or as a thing that is open for inspection, whether by the science of horticulture or as the content of perception from the standpoint of the neurophysiologist or psychologist. What Heidegger in *Being and Time* calls *Zuhandenheit* (tools) and *Vorhandenheit* (things) are types of being in the world. The world does not have to be inferred or constructed from our reflections on the phenomena understood as objects; on the contrary, it is the objectivity of the phenomena presented by the world that must be inferred from that broader, indeed, comprehensive presentation.

On the other hand, it must be admitted that we do not initially focus upon the world, but instead upon what it shows us, whether in the case of individual entities or as what one could call a region of the continuum of being in the world. The direct presence of the world is something like Husserl's pre-predicative experience. When I look out of my window in an idle moment, not to see something in particular but merely because my face is turned toward the window, I see a four-dimensional continuum (since time is present in the changes that the scene undergoes), not, of course, *as* a four-dimensional continuum, but as a seamless web of things, persons, and events, and all of this prior to my establishing the relations and orders by which the web is articulated into the presentation of identifiable and usually already identified beings.

The fact is that my look out of the window comes to a reflective focus in my recognition not of the world as a presencing of beings within a concealed order of relations and senses, but in a perception of a landscape, with or without figures, but containing trees, bushes, flowers, lampposts, telephone wires, glimpses of the sky, clouds, and so on. This is not to return to the Husserlian situation of isolated phenomena within the gaze of consciousness. I am indeed in the world, but my being in the world is precisely nonreflective; what I reflect upon is the scene; and I do this by virtue of apprehending its elements. In addition to what has been said from the perceptual standpoint, one must of course add the factors of enjoyment, boredom, beauty, ugliness, anticipation of the utility of what I see, such as the rose, or of the impending decay of a bush and the associated feeling of melancholy, and so on.

In short, the seamless web is not itself the world but a representation of the world, a testament to its presence rather than its presence in the sense of what shows itself to me. The fact that it is a trivial step from the perception of a rose to the reflection that the rose is in the world does not alter the fact that a step separates the two. The world, in presenting itself to me by way of its elements, absents or conceals itself. I must find it. And as soon as I begin to look for the world, the triviality of the step that sets me onto the trail dissolves into complexity, ambiguity, and even mystery. This is the analogy to the problem in Plato and Husserl. How do I find the very world that is given to me in the direct manifestation of beings in the world? On the one hand, I am aware of the fact that it is the world that shows me the rose, not vice versa; and I do not show it to myself. On the other hand, my awareness is itself grounded in the rose, that is, in what shows itself as this or that, not as a showing or presencing.

In stating this problem, I have abstracted from the difference between world and Being or world-presentation in order to simplify my exposition. It is at least plausible to maintain that the underlying and encompassing "worlding" process is itself the same as the process by which this world is constituted or presented. In other words, we may distinguish between the specific values, rank-ordering, or epochal gift of truth that defines the worldliness of this particular world from the general operations of constituting a world from one or another table of values, rank-ordering, set of categories, and so forth. One world is very much, qua world, like another, however different may be the truth embodied in each. In any case, the problem of the accessibility of Being is fairly represented by the practically equivalent problem of the accessibility of the world.

This said, what our various examples of perception and psychic responses to perception show us is that the world presents itself to us by way of the beings in the world; but conversely, the beings in the world present themselves to us by way of the world. "Becoming is contradictory" in the sense that whichever starting point we select is immediately contradicted by its opposite. Another way to say this is that Becoming is circular. Once we move from the everyday level of perception and reflection and attempt to delineate the sense or truth of the everyday, we are required to distinguish between the rose and the world, or between beings and Being. But this distinction can be drawn only by appeal to the distinction itself; we must know in advance the difference between the rose and the world, between beings and Being. The process by which we articulate this difference is thus analogous to what is called recollection in the Platonic dialogues.

In other words, human apprehension of the phenomena is not at all of what shows itself as it shows itself, but rather of what shows itself as other than itself. The rose shows itself as a rose by virtue of its ability to show itself as a being in the world and thus to show us not itself, that is, not the rose, but the world. This is the difference between Heidegger and Husserl. In Husserl, the world never succeeds in showing itself; at least not prior to the *Crisis* and perhaps not even then, since the *Lebenswelt* is itself the result of a phenomenological reduction, not of being in the world. In Heidegger, the world shows itself at the outset, not immediately as what shows itself as it shows itself, as a self-pointing-out, but as an anticipation or "recollection" that allows us to infer the world from the otherness of the phenomenon. If perception were nothing but the apprehension of, say, a rose, there would be no way to arrive at the world from this beginning. And, as I noted a moment ago, Husserl never arrives there, at least not without a departure from the methods of the phenomenology of the *Ideas*.

I understand that Husserlian essences are not restricted to roses, but that they include spiritual attributes, social and political structures, and so on. But to seek the "essence" of a human type or even of a city or nation in the depths of consciousness is to proceed with respect to these exactly as if they were isolated upon a black backdrop within consciousness and exposed to the eye of the intellect. The "essence" of the world, even if it were accessible to consciousness, is not itself a world nor is it a being in the world. Here I think Heidegger is right to deny the appropriateness of the term "essence" to his sense of "world" or "Being."

I have now said all that is here required about Husserl. The second sentence in "The Completion of Metaphysics" reads as follows: "The abandonment of the Being of the existent [*des Seienden*] is the last reflection [*Widerschein*] of Being as the concealment of unconcealment, in which any existent of any type is able to appear as such." In other words, awareness of the Being of the existent (e.g., of being qua being in the Aristotelian sense) is itself a kind of unreflective anticipation of Being itself; so long as we are concerned with the being of beings, we are at least asking the question *ti to on?* or What is Being? even if we have not rightly or fully understood what it is that we are asking. But in Nietzsche, the process of inquiring about the being of beings is itself abandoned at the conscious level; for Nietzsche, beings have no being other than Chaos or the eternal return of the will to power. The closest we come to Being is in the eternality of the eternally returning presence of the worlds constituted by the will to power. But Nietzsche does not take this approximation to be a kind of reinstituting of the being of beings; he does not understand (according to Heidegger) that his reversed Platonism is still Platonism. What he means by the approximation is that Platonism has been abandoned by his reversal. There is no Being, only Becoming.

Heidegger, for reasons that we do not now need to repeat, elicits a hidden Platonism from this thesis. But Nietzsche's conscious rejection of the Being of the existent is finally the same as Plato's abandonment of Being on behalf of the being of the existent. Plato abandons Being for the Ideas; Nietzsche abandons the Ideas for interpretations. But Nietzschean interpretations are projections of the will to power, which, since it eternally returns, reestablishes the process of return as the being of the existent and in that sense continues to be an abandonment of Being. Nietzsche's doctrine is a reflection of Platonism; remember that in mirror images, the original is reversed. The last reflection of Being as the concealment of unconcealment is reversed Platonism, namely, a Platonism in which Becoming is the replacement for Being. Being is thus concealed by Becoming.

Why does Heidegger use the expression "abandonment of Being"? Not to designate the ingratitude or carelessness of human beings or of thinkers like Plato and Nietzsche; on the contrary, it is Being that abandons humankind. This abandonment does not occur out of anger or vengeance; it is intrinsic to the way in which Being offers itself. Being can offer itself *only in a concealed manner,* namely, through beings. As I have argued throughout this book, this fundamental necessity will never change, so long as intelligent creatures exist, because the gift of a pure presencing-process that presents us with nothing is a gift that is intrinsically impossible for intelligence to receive. It is not the forgetfulness of Being that enforces this necessity, but the nature of thinking.

We cannot think except by thinking something; to think a process, such as the presencing of Being, is itself to think something: this particular process, as opposed to what is presented by that process. We cross the barrier of the "opposed to," which I called above the "otherness" of the phenomenon, by way of the phenomena themselves. And we arrive at the phenomena, the starting point for our voyage of crossing over, by virtue of the process through which they stand apart from and in opposition to one another, hence as perceptible or viewable and yet as related to one another, and so to our thinking or consciousness, by what we can call a fluent, and so flexible or changing, categorial structure, a structure that must change as the phenomena themselves change, in order to be true to these changes. Heidegger calls these categories *Existentialen* in *Being and Time* and other names in his later thought, for example, *das Geviert* and *das Gestell*. This categorial structure is the sense, truth, openness, or emplacement of Being as a world. In the *Nietzsche* volumes, the equivalent passage is to be found at I, 173f., where Heidegger says that the essence (*Wesen*) of truth can change, even though that which has changed remains the essence for the same domain of cases. The essence remains the essence; what is unchanged or (in Heidegger's jargon) what *west* (third person singular of *wesen*) is the function of essence played by the two different contents.

Heidegger goes on to say, in "The Completion of Metaphysics,"[14] that the abandonment of Being contains "the undecided," namely, "whether the unconcealment of this concealment, and so the more original origin [*der anfänglichere Anfang*], illuminates itself in it as an extreme of the concealment of Being." The more original origin is what Heidegger calls elsewhere "the other beginning." He means by this a return to the original manifestation of Being in *phusis* and *alētheia,* not as that manifestation is developed by Greek thinkers, but as the beginning of a meditative or memorial thinking that appropriates Being from its very concealment. The unconcealment of concealment is the extreme form of concealment. In other words, total unconcealment is intrinsically impossible. There is no "self-pointing-out" of Being as unconcealment because what points itself out is the phenomenon, the being; and it points itself out not as what it is, but as that whose "what" or essence is to be, in the genuine sense of "to be," presented by the presencing of the world; and so the phenomenon shows itself in its otherness as what it genuinely is, namely, by showing itself as what it is not.

Heidegger's backward look at the history of metaphysics is thus a forward look at the possibility of another beginning. I want now to illustrate the connection between looking backward and looking forward with a reference to the last section of the second volume of *Nietzsche,* entitled *Die Erinnerung in die Metaphysik* (Recollection in metaphysics). Some translate *Erinnerung* as "remembrance" in order to distinguish it from Platonic "recollection," but the two acts fulfill analogous functions. In Plato, we "recollect" the Ideas. Nietzsche transforms the Ideas into perspectives, of which the most fundamental are the finite number of world-producing evaluations; it is this finitude that permits the will to power to recur eternally. In Heidegger, we "remember" the epochs of that finite stretch of the history of Being that is called "metaphysics." Each epoch is a gift of Being, and "gift" is Heidegger's replacement for Nietzsche's world-producing perspective or evaluation. There is thus an analogy, not complete but significant, between Heideggerian remembrance and Platonic recollection. Whereas Plato recollects the Ideas in order to understand the beings, or what Heidegger would call the Being of the existent, Heidgger himself recollects the epochs of the history of metaphysics in order to approach (not to "understand") Being by a memorial deconstruction and reconstruction of those gifts. This approach by way of recollection is also the approach to another beginning.

The analogy between Heidegger and Plato is limited because no one can say what will come next, and in particular after what Heidegger calls the other beginning. Still, we can say that the epochs of metaphysics are Heideggerian Ideas. If Being could speak, it would say, "By my gifts shall ye know me." As Heidegger himself expresses this point, "The remembrance of the history of Being expects of historical humankind to become aware of this; that *before* all dependence of mankind on powers and forces, providences and orders, the nature of the human is admitted into the truth of Being."[15] We must remember or recollect the truth of Being, that is, Being, not from our viewing of the phenomenon as it shows itself, but from the review, the appropriative recollection of the epochs or gifts constituting the history of that Being; and the portion of that history with which we have been concerned, namely, the portion extending from the pre-Socratics through Nietzsche, is the history of metaphysics.

But how do we know that the history of metaphysics is the history of Being? What is it that turned Heidegger to the study of that history? Obviously enough, we must distinguish between the period of his conventional studies and the period following his basic apprehension of the difference between Being and beings. Even this, however, is too superficial. Just as Heidegger did not enroll in the gymnasium or university in order to become aware of Being, so too there was no particular course or book or conversation which set him straight. Books like Franz Brentano's study of the senses of being in Aristotle no doubt stimulated him to consider the question, but they could not have given him the answer; if they had, Heidegger would have become a disciple of Brentano or of some other author. Heidegger was set straight, as he explains it in the cryptic language of the *Nietzsche* volumes, by Being itself, that is, by the history of Being, and by this thanks to his existence within historical humankind (*dem geschichtlichen Menschentum*).

Stated with all the concreteness that Heidegger himself requires of us, he was directed to the history of Being by virtue of living within the last stage, or the direct consequences of the last stage, of metaphysics and by being a German, hence a member of the metaphysical people who have been given the gift of one of the two genuinely philosophical languages. Before we laugh at this naive patriotism (as I myself am often inclined to do), we should at least consider that Plato no doubt felt very much the same about his Greekness, except that for him, history in the Heideggerian sense was irrelevant and in fact nonexistent. But what Plato could also undoubtedly agree upon, were he alive in our century, is Heidegger's conviction that after Nietzsche, and indeed, as prepared to a decisive degree by Nietzsche, the human race is mired in the swamp of nihilism, a nihilism intended by Nietzsche as a purification and concentration of energy for the creation of a new, aristocratic world-producing evaluation, but which Heidegger sees as the intensification of the abandonment or forgetting of Being. If human beings no longer remember that Being is concealed, then they fall out of their very humanity and become machines. We enter the age of cybernetics.

It is of less importance to decide whether cybernetics is the last expression of metaphysics than it is to see that philosophy is over when human beings can no longer distinguish between themselves and machines. The reason is this: it makes no difference what machines do or what they think, except to the extent that they are used by human beings for human purposes. It is a laughable hypocrisy to anthropomorphize machines by endowing them with human emotions, feelings, and evaluations. In so doing, our hyper-cyberneticists simply transform human beings into their own adolescent version of the Nietzschean superman. If machines become human, then philosophy will begin again, not perhaps as the "other beginning," but at least as the beginning that is made fully present, not as the phenomenon, but as the perpetually human attempt to act for the best.

The attempt to appropriate or enter the experience underlying Heidegger's journey toward Being leads to the following conclusion. We may agree with Heidegger's motivating perception of the concealed presentation of Being within beings. Equally plausible is his substitution of Being-in-the-world for Husserlian intentionality. But we should not be swayed by his longing to avert the human gaze from beings to Being. Heidegger himself gives a perfectly explicit account of why this is impossible: "What happens in the history of Being? We cannot ask the question in this way, because then there would be a [process of] happening and that which happens. But happening itself is the only event [*Geschehnis*]. Being alone is. What happens? Nothing happens, if we are pursuing that which happens in happening. Nothing happens, *event e-vents* [*das Ereignis er-eignet*]."[16]

I stated previously that Heidegger never discusses nobility. I can underline this point by citing from the same passage, a few lines later, the following assertion: "The eventing origin is honor [or "dignity": *die Würde*] as the truth itself as that which towers in its absence. Honor is the noble [*das Edle*] that e-vents, without requiring to produce effects [*ohne des Wirkens zu bedürfen*]."[17] It follows that the effects or events of the e-venting of Being are themselves dishonorable or ignoble at worst and void of merit at best. Despite Heidegger's continuous assertion—or implication when he is not asserting—that the quest for Being will illuminate our experience of beings, I believe that the opposite is the case. The more we meditate on Being, the less we see of beings.

On the other hand, the more carefully we inspect beings, the more clarity we achieve about Being. This clarity may be analytical and it may be mythical. But it is clarity about Being, not about some inferior construct called "the Being of the existent" or the being of beings. This is because there is no difference between the Being of beings (as distinguished from being qua being) and Being. On Heidegger's own testimony, the event of Being is an e-venting in which nothing happens. Even on Heideggerian grounds, the event (or the e-vent) is the worlding of a world; and Being is the process by which worlds come to be, not some process in addition to this by which nothing comes to be. What, then, is metaphysics? Metaphysics goes beyond *ta phusika* or *onta* in thinking the whole. But this thinking, as it is found in Plato, is not a science of being qua being. It is the attempt to understand the implications of our capacity to do what we believe to be best. One such implication may well be that we are required to consider being qua being. But the more important question is the place of such an investigation within the totality of human existence and therefore of my existence because "human existence" does not itself exist except as a derivative of the existence of you and me. And there is not some other world to which we aspire as metaphysicians, but only a better version of this world. We conclude, as we begin, not in the hermeneutical circle, but in the circle of the everyday, which resists all our attempts to transform it into a derivative not of the will to power, but of the decadence of the emancipated will. The last stage of European history, which is of course last only in the sense that it is our stage, is not the will to will, but the illusion of the spontaneity of the imagination. The clarification of this illusion is the next task that is posed by the question of Being.

Appendix

As the present book was being prepared for publication, I received a copy of Heidegger's 1924–25 lectures, recently issued for the first time, on Plato's *Sophist*.[1] The volume consists of 610 pages of Heideggerian text, in addition to various appendices. Of the main text, the first 226 pages are devoted largely to a synoptic account of Aristotle's doctrine of the modes of *alētheuein* or (as Heidegger would translate it) "unconcealing," that is, in the usual translation, "speaking the truth." The remaining 374 pages contain a very detailed (but not exhaustive) analysis of the Platonic dialogue *Sophist*. This is by far the longest study of Plato in the Heideggerian corpus, as it is presently constituted. It is therefore of considerable interest as evidence of Heidegger's relatively early approach to Plato.

I can say without hesitation that the analysis of the *Sophist* is entirely superior to any subsequent Heideggerian interpretation of Plato known to me. Heidegger's procedure is nevertheless idiosyncratic in certain decisive ways, and this qualifies, although it by no means erases, the power and detailed interest of his commentary. The most serious restriction is visible immediately (p. 11) in Heidegger's reiterated assertion that we are to approach Plato by way of Aristotle. The most extreme statement of Heidegger's position is to be found on page 189. After remarking that the long introduction to Aristotle was a *"preparation"* for the understanding of a Platonic *scientific* [*wissenschaftlichen*] dialogue, Heidegger goes on to say that *"there is no scientific understanding, i.e., no historical return to Plato without going through Aristotle."*

In general, Heidegger insists that it is self-explanatory to say that we always approach earlier thinkers from later ones; more particularly, he claims that "Aristotle saw the immanent limits of [Plato's] dialectic because he philosophized more radically" (p. 189). That is to say, his philosophy is a more radical development of the inner presuppositions of Plato's thought, as well as a superior revision of such key Platonic doctrines as those of dialectic and the account of nonbeing. Aristotle thus makes intelligible what is undeveloped and even inadequately understood in Plato.

The deficiencies of this contention are evident from Heidegger's own interpretations of the pre-Socratics, which (however idiosyncratic in their own right) always insist upon the need to recreate the thought of the earlier thinkers by a reappropriation of their own words, not through the medium of Aristotle's (or for that matter Plato's) account of them. If Heidegger's contention were to be adopted, we would presumably have to turn to Derrida in order to understand Heidegger himself. In the immediate case, Heidegger simply assumes that Plato was engaged in the attempt to propound a "scientific" doctrine of Being and that his failure was rectified (within the limits of Greek ontology) by Aristotle.

One can express Heidegger's deficiency by saying that he fails to take into account the difference between a Platonic dialogue and an Aristotelian treatise. This is no doubt partly due to a misinterpretation of the relation between dialectic and rhetoric in Plato. Despite his attention to the positive discussion of rhetoric in the *Phaedrus* (pp. 308–52), Heidegger concludes that rhetoric as the *psychagogia* of the soul is entirely subordinate to dialectic, "the sole fundamental *Wissenschaft*" (338), in which the *logos* of "self-expression, clarification, communication, publication" is grounded (337). Dialectic is "the primary art of the existent itself" (ibid).

In other words, Heidegger tends to assimilate the rhetorical nature of the Platonic dialogue into dialectic, understood as the attempt to articulate an ontology, albeit an attempt that fails because of Plato's indifference to the distinction between the ontological and the ontic (pp. 449, 453). As I see it, he takes too seriously Plato's rhetorical endorsements of dialectic and fails to appreciate the sense in which the dialogue form is an implicit restriction on those endorsements. Heidegger writes as though the statement of the regulative Ideal (if I may employ a Kantian expression) of dialectic in the *Republic* is in fact carried out in the *Sophist*. He therefore does not reflect with sufficient care upon the difference between the account of the Ideas by Socrates in dialogues like the *Republic* and the Eleatic Stranger's discussion of the greatest kinds in the *Sophist*. This is evident, for example, in Heidegger's treatment of the use by the Stranger of *eidos* and *genos* as apparently interchangeable terms (pp. 524ff, 547ff).

The second defect in Heidegger's approach follows directly from the first. Despite his awareness that the intention of the *Sophist* is to explore two kinds of human life, namely, that of the sophist and the philosopher, and that the dialogue, despite its ostensibly "scientific" character, is not an exercise in scholasticism (see especially pp. 573f.), Heidegger understands the underlying theme in the light of his own "phenomenology of *Dasein*" (pp. 62, 396ff). I mention in passing that the long introduction on Aristotle is of special interest because it shows how the *Daseinsanalyse* of *Being and Time* was decisively shaped by Heidegger's study of the *Nicomachean Ethics* as well as of the *Rhetoric*.

The account of the sophist as a human type and the parallel investigation of the nature of the philosopher are tacitly assimilated by Heidegger into ontology, just as his own analysis of the everyday life of *Dasein* is intended as the introductory step in the pursuit of the sense of Being. In a passage that is italicized in the original to indicate its importance, Heidegger says, "For the Greeks, reflection on human existence is purely oriented to the sense of Being itself" and not toward "ethics" in the modern sense (p. 178). There is a good bit of truth in this observation, but in Heidegger's own interpretation, it hinders us from understanding the Platonic distinction between human life and what Heidegger calls "ontology" and most scholars refer to as the "theory of Ideas."

There is no doubt that Plato regarded philosophy as the highest form of human existence; but there is considerable doubt as to Plato's views on the possibility of a "theory" of Ideas. Still more precisely, Heidegger makes it impossible to consider the evidence, which I have discussed at length in the present book, that Plato's diverse portraits of the philosophical life are intended to exclude the possibility and desirability of a distinction, in Heidegger's terms, between the ontological and the ontic. Very far from being indifferent to this distinction, Plato could be said to have repudiated it, as I have tried to show at length. From this standpoint, even the late dialogues are closer to tragic comedies or comic tragedies than to *Wissenschaft* or dialectic in Heidegger's sense.[2]

Despite the great care that Heidegger exerts to think through the exact words of the Eleatic Stranger, and hence his genuinely splendid analysis of many passages, notably the seven definitions of the sophist in the first part of the dialogue, he reads those words through the lenses of the fundamental ontologist. With all of his perspicuity and attention to detail, Heidegger soon forgets, and tempts us to forget, that we are reading a drama about someone who is neither Socrates nor Plato and who presents a technical doctrine that cannot be immediately attributed

Appendix

319

to Plato. The limits of Heidegger's appreciation of Platonic rhetoric is clear from his assertion that the dialogue form is a response to "an inner need to arrive through *logos* as chatter [*Gerede*] at a true *logos*" (p. 195).

The phenomenological method seems to be deaf to the ironical presence of a silent Socrates throughout the interrogation of Theaetetus by the Eleatic Stranger. Unfortunately Heidegger does not give us the announced interpretation of the *Philebus,* which might have directed his attention to the problem of the shift in principal spokesmen in the late dialogues between the Stranger and Socrates. From a remark about *Philebus* 51c6f (pp. 544f.), I infer that Heidegger would regard Socrates' imperfect late ontology as identical with that of the Stranger. The remark, incidentally, makes the very good point that in both dialogues attention is drawn to *pros ti* ("with respect to something") as an essential ingredient in the structure of intelligibility, but that in neither place is it adequately explained.

At the level of technical detail, one sees in these lectures an early version of Heidegger's most characteristic interpretations of Platonism and of Greek philosophy, yet always in a less dogmatic manner than is evident in the later works and with occasional qualifications that deepen the approach. For example, Heidegger attributes to the Greeks in general and to Plato in particular a doctrine of the sense of Being as presence (*Anwesenheit*) and of *ousia* as "standing ready for disposal" as that which is produced (*Hergestelltsein:* see pp. 269ff. and 398 in particular). He thus places special emphasis upon the role of production (*poiein*) in the *Sophist* (e.g., pp. 271ff.) and, although regularly alert to the Stranger's doctrine of the "greatest kinds" as *aei on,* Heidegger insists upon the temporal origin of the Platonic doctrine of Being as *parousia* (see, for example, the discussion of *Anwesenheit* on p. 225 and the affixed *Zusatz* on the Greek interpretation of the sense of Being "aus der Zeit": p. 632; for *parousia,* see p. 486).

I will restrict myself to one further extended comment about this most interesting interpretation of the *Sophist.* Heidegger regularly emphasizes that the underlying theme of the dialogue is *logos* understood as dialectic, or in other words the question of "the correct discursive account of non-being" (*orthologia tou me ontos:* p. 419) as well as the correlative question, "What do you intend to point out [*sēmainein*] when you say 'being' [*on*]?" (pp. 446ff.; the reference is to *Sophist* 244a4ff). He also observes that the discussion of the greatest kinds, which discussion he styles as dialectical (i.e., as Plato's primitive version of ontology), does not move in the domain of *logos,* and so must be supplemented by the discussion of the true and false (or, in Heidegger's useful translations, revealing and deceiving) assertions (p. 575). Heidegger very reasonably notes that the dialectical section is then the basis for the analysis of *logos.* But this is inconsistent with his explanation of dialectic as itself rooted in *logos.* The inconsistency is mitigated if not entirely removed by Heidegger's additional claim (in my opinion a correct one) that underlying discourse in dialectic is vision, that is, the noetic perception of the pure eidetic forms (pp. 349, 410; cf. 504f.). But this (correct) contention seems to point toward the thesis that the fundamental problem of the *Sophist* is not the discursive question of what we mean when we say "being" or "nonbeing," but rather the question of the discontinuity between vision and discourse, or *noēsis* and *logos.* In my opinion, reflection on this question leads us toward the "second sailing" described by Socrates and analyzed by me in chapter 2 above.

To conclude, Heidegger takes Plato, in the persona of the Eleatic Stranger, to define the sense of Being as "presence of the power of communion" (*parousia dunameōs koinōnias*; p. 486). He thereby combines the definition of Being as *dunamis,* attributed by the Stranger at *Sophist* 247d8ff. to an improved version of materialism, with the doctrine, enunciated by the Stranger in his own voice, of the communion of the greatest kinds or fundamental elements of intelligibility. This is a defensible but far from certain reading of the dialogue, and one that raises grave problems for the coherence of the Stranger's revision of Eleaticism. I have discussed these difficulties elsewhere and cannot repeat them here.[3]

Essential as this topic may be to the understanding of the *Sophist,* and so of Plato, it is quite striking to note that it contributes very little to the account of Platonism as developed by Heidegger in the period following *Being and Time,* which has been my principal concern in the preceding pages. Heidegger, despite the criticisms I have recorded, is much closer to the Platonic text in 1924 than he was ever to be again. One could well wish that at least in this respect, the extraordinary virtues of the early Heidegger had not been submerged by the consequences of the shipwreck of *Being and Time*. As a token of my appreciation of Heidegger's genius, I close this study with the following words from the lectures on the *Sophist:* "Only when we are historical [*geschichtlich*] will we understand history; and when history [*Geschichte*] is understood, it is *ēo ipso* overcome" (p. 257).

Appendix

Notes

Introduction

1 The standard English work of this sort continues to be W. J. Richardson, *Heidegger: Through Phenomenology to Thought* (The Hague: M. Nijhoff, 1963). See also two quite different studies, both of which cover the full scope of Heidegger's career: Arion Kelkel: *La legende de l'être* (Paris: J. Vrin, 1980); Dieter Thomä, *Die Zeit des Selbst und die Zeit danach: zur Kritik der Textgeschichte Martin Heideggers 1910–1976* (Frankfurt: Suhrkamp, 1990).

2 See my *Nihilism* (New Haven and London: Yale University Press, 1969).

3 On this topic, see Franco Volpi, *Heidegger e Aristotele* (Padua: Daphne Editrice, 1984).

4 For the history of the term "metaphysics," see Pierre Aubenque, *Le problème de l'être chez Aristote* (Paris: Presses Universitaires de France, 1962); André de Muralt, *Comment dire l'être?* (Paris: J. Vrin, 1985); J. F. Courtine, *Suarez et le système de la métaphysique* (Paris: Presses Universitaires de France, 1990).

5 *Einführung in die Metaphysik* (Tübingen: Max Niemeyer Verlag, 1953), p. 10 (hereafter cited as *Einführung*).

6 One of the most detailed and forceful series of etymological analyses in the entire Heideggerian corpus is devoted to the encrustation or blockage of *alētheia* by the Roman and Christian senses of *falsum*, *verum*, and *rectitudo*. See *Parmenides* in *Gesamtausgabe, Bd.* 54(Frankfurt: Vittorio Klostermann, 1982), which contains a lecture course given at Freiburg University in 1942–43. All citations from the *Gesamtausgabe* will be given henceforth by the title of the individual volume, and, in an initial citation, by the volume number and the date of publication.

7 See for example *Heraklit* (Seminars from 1943/44), *Gesamtausgabe, Bd.* 55 (1987), p. 17.

8 *Einführung*, p. 11. I translate *das Seiende* here as "the thing." The terms "being" or "entity" are too cumbersome for the present context. Elsewhere I shall also make use of the expression "the existent" to render *das Seiende* in contrast to *Sein*.

9 Ibid.

10 *Heraklit*, p. 139. It is perhaps true, as Werner Marx asserts in the reappraisal to his 1961 study *Heidegger and the Tradition* (Evanston: Northwestern University Press, 1971), that in the early Heidegger, "the realm of light" and "the realm of darkness" are equal partners, whereas in the later Heidegger, concealment is more important than disclosure (xl). But Marx may not have seen the Heracleitus lectures, which were unpublished when he wrote his study and which certainly suggest that disclosure occurs within a horizon of concealment. For a more detailed defense of the thesis put forward by Marx, see Ernst Tugendhat's discussion of *Entborgenheit* in his *Der*

Wahrheitsbegriff bei Husserl und Heidegger (Berlin: Walter de Gruyter, 1970), esp. p. 389.

11 *Beiträge zur Philosophie, Gesamtausgabe, Bd. 65* (1989), pp. 208ff. (hereafter cited as *Beiträge*); *Einführung,* pp. 138f.

12 *Einführung,* pp. 49ff.

13 *Brief über den "Humanismus,"* in *Wegmarken* (Frankfurt: Vittorio Klostermann, 1967), p. 145.

14 *Einführung,* p. 11.

15 "Die Frage nach der Technik," in *Vorträge und Aufsätze* (Pfullingen: Günther Neske, 1954), p. 25. In the German, the verbs *entsprechen* (to correspond to) and *zusprechen* (to award) contain the verb "to speak" (*sprechen*), which must be brought out in the translation to make Heidegger's point.

16 *Einführung,* p. 98.

17 Ibid., p. 100. Heidegger is discussing Heracleitus here as the thinker who expresses the genuine or original senses of the terms that become pivotal for philosophy.

18 Ibid., p. 136.

19 "Wissenschaft und Besinnung," in *Vorträge und Aufsätze,* p. 48.

20 *Nietzsche* II (Pfullingen: Günther Neske, 1961), p. 484 (I will cite this two-volume edition henceforth as *N* I and *N* II). This was the publication that had a decisive influence on a generation of readers, and not the *Vorlesungen,* published subsequently in the *Gesamtausgabe.*

21 *Einführung,* p. 134.

22 Cf. *Sein und Zeit* (Tübingen: Max Niemeyer Verlag, 1977), pp. 158ff. (hereafter cited as *SZ*).

23 *Beiträge,* p. 3.

24 See the *Nachwort* by F. W. von Hermann to the *Beiträge,* p. 512.

25 *Beiträge,* p. 7. This passage renders dubious or imprecise the statement on p. 129 of the excellent study by Marlène Zarader, *Heidegger et les paroles de l'origine* (Paris: J. Vrin, 1986): *Ereignis* is not a new qualification of Being "mais une tentative d'accès au territoire originel auquel appartient l'être lui-même ... et où il se trouve ainsi essentiellement 'repris.' " In the course of his career, Heidegger uses a variety of terms as apparent replacements for the standard *Sein*. This becomes important only when Heidegger wishes to distinguish his terminology from that of the metaphysical tradition, and in particular, when he alludes to the "other way" that lies beyond the Greek tradition of which we continue to be a part. The other way is concerned not with Being but with the "origin" from which Being, as both present and absent, constitutes the history of metaphysics.

26 See again Zarader, *op. cit.,* p. 282.

27 Cf. the previously cited study by W. Marx, *Heidegger and the Tradition,* p. 9.

28 On this point, there is a sharp difference between *echt* Heideggerianism and the French deconstructors led by Jacques Derrida, for whom 1968 was evidently a ghostly "reprise" of 1830 and 1848.

29 At all periods of Heidegger's thought, one finds the constant assertion of the radical inferiority of the modern epoch, and in particular of the twentieth century, to Greek

antiquity, and in particular to pre-Socratic antiquity. I cite a passage from a Freiburg University seminar of 1931/32 as a fair example: "Was da bei Platon schon im Gang ist, das Schwinden der Grunderfahrung, d.h. einer bestimmten Grund*stellung* des Menschen zum Seienden, und das Machtloswerden des Wortes *alētheia* in seiner Grundbedeutung, das ist nur der Anfang jener Geschichte, durch die der abendländische Mensch als ein existierender den Boden verlor, um in der heutigen Bodenlosigkeit an ein ende zu kommen" (*Vom Wesen der Wahrheit, Gesamtausgabe, Bd.* 34 [1988], p. 120).

30 *Einführung,* p. 28 ("dieselbe trostlose Raserei der entfesselten Technik und der bodenlosen Organisation des Normal-menschen"); consider also the remarks about the inner truth and greatness of National Socialism: 29, 38, 96, 152. On the topic of Heidegger's Nazism, which is important in its own right but peripheral to the theme of the present study, one may now cite, in addition to Hugo Ott, *Martin Heidegger: Unterwegs zu seiner Biographie* (Frankfurt and New York: Campus, 1988), the extremely useful book by Tom Rockmore, *On Heidegger's Nazism and Philosophy* (Berkeley: University of California Press, 1992). Still indispensable: Karl Löwith, *Heidegger, Denker in dürftiger Zeit* (Göttingen: Vandenhoeck und Ruprecht, 1960).

31 *Gesamtausgabe, Bd.* 39 (1976), p. 121.

32 Ibid., p. 144.

33 Ibid., p. 214.

34 *Gelassenheit* (Pfullingen: Günther Neske, 1959), pp. 40ff.

35 The most learned of the anarchists is Reiner Schürmann; see his *Heidegger. On Being and Acting: From Principles to Anarchy* (Bloomington: Indiana University Press, 1990). Schürmann is certainly correct when he says of *Ereignis,* "What bequeaths the historical epochs and their principles, the 'event,' is itself nothing, neither a human nor a divine subject, nor an available or analyzable object" (p. 57). From this, Schürmann infers that there is no normative discourse at the end of modernity. "We *think* by complying with the economic mutations of presencing. We *act* in the same way" (p. 78).

36 A careful student of Heidegger observes in a recent essay that "it is incorrect to claim that Heidegger can do no more than *await* the unpredictable irruption of a new epoch: all changes are *prepared,* and the turning point lies actually in a 'free relationship to the technological world' " (the inner quote is from Heidegger's *Spiegel* interview). Yet this author asserts in the continuation of the passage just cited that "thought can protect us from the worst by simply keeping open the range of the possible." To call this a "minimalist" political task for thought, as does the author, is obviously to indulge in euphemism. Michel Haar, "The Ambivalent Unthought of the Overman and the Duality of Heidegger's Political Thinking," in *Heidegger and the Political, Graduate Faculty Philosophy Journal* 14/15 (1991): 132.

37 These remarks are addressed to Heidegger's thinking after the *Kehre.* All questions of Heidegger's character and behavior to one side, one finds different political implications at different periods of his life; the implications of the rhetoric of *Sein und Zeit* are not the same as those of the Hölderlin lectures of the mid-thirties, and these differ again from the essays and lectures of the postwar period. By and large, after

he resigned from the post of chancellor of the University of Freiburg, Heidegger emphasized that mankind must await the gift of Being, and that the thinker is not responsible for what Being gives him to think. This is the view that I am criticizing. The best presentation I have seen of the fluctuations in Heidegger's thought, and in particular of his thought as influenced by political considerations, is in Thomä, op. cit.

38 This observation is the basis of a fine doctoral dissertation by my student Paul Gallagher. In his previously cited work, Dieter Thomä documents the influence of Hegel (and Dilthey) on the young Heidegger (pp. 68ff.). That influence can be indirectly inferred from the work of Heidegger's most daring student, Heribert Boeder; see his *Topologie der Metaphysik* (Freiburg/München: Verlag Karl Alber, 1980).

39 "Das Ende der Philosophie und die Aufgabe des Denkens," in *Zur Sache des Denkens* (Tübingen: Max Niemeyer Verlag, 1969), p. 63. Elsewhere (in the *Nietzsche* lectures) Heidegger mentions Hegel in conjunction with Nietzsche rather than Marx. There is apparently some ambiguity concerning the precise manifestation of the end of philosophy. On this point, it is also worth consulting Alexandre Kojève, *Introduction à la lecture de Hegel* (Paris: Gallimard, 1947).

1 Platonism Is Aristotelianism

1 *Heidegger et Platon* (Paris: Presses Universitaires de France, 1987), p. 40. See also J. F. Courtine, "Le platonisme de Heidegger," in *Heidegger et la phénoménologie* (Paris: J. Vrin, 1990), pp. 129–60, and my own earlier discussions: (1) "Heidegger's Interpretation of Plato," reprinted in *The Quarrel between Philosophy and Poetry* (New York and London: Routledge, 1988), chap. 8; (2) *Nihilism*, esp. chap. 5.

2 *Heidegger et Platon*, pp. 149ff.

3 *Beiträge*, pp. 208f.

4 *Platons Lehre von der Wahrheit*, in *Wegmarken*, p. 131; cf. *Einführung*, pp. 138f.

5 Ibid., p. 131.

6 Ibid., pp. 136f.

7 N II, p. 226.

8 *Beiträge*, p. 72.

9 *Die Grundprobleme der Phänomenologie*, in *Gesamtausgabe*, Bd. 24 (1975) (cited hereafter as *Grundprobleme*).

10 Paragraph 11, part (b), pp. 149ff.

11 P. 149 (until otherwise indicated, citations are from *Grundprobleme*).

12 Ibid.

13 P. 150.

14 Ibid.

15 Ibid.

16 A 1, 980a25–27.

17 Pp. 150f.

18 P. 151.

19 P. 152.

20 This was called to my attention by my student Alfredo Ferrarin.

21 Ibid.: "zur Herstellbarkeit eines Hergestellten überhaupt."

22 P. 153.

23 Ibid.

24 P. 213.

25 *Einführung*, pp. 48–56.

26 See for example "Vom Wesen und Begriff der *Phusis*. Aristoteles' *Physik* B, 1," in *Wegmarken*, p. 345.

27 N I, pp. 198–217. The section is entitled "Platons Staat: Der Abstand der Kunst (Mimesis) von der Wahrheit (Idee)." It is part of a seminar presented at the University of Freiburg in 1936/37. Until otherwise indicated, citations are from this volume.

28 In her previously cited work, *Heidegger et les paroles de l'origine*, M. Zarader says (p. 75) that from 1946 on, "truth" (*alētheia*) replaces "Being" (*Sein*) as the primary term in Heidegger's thought. This seems dubious for more than one reason; what could be said is that talk about "truth" in the sense of the unconcealment or unveiling of Being replaces talk about the "sense" (*Sinn*) of Being. Truth also exhibits the same dual structure of hiddenness and disclosure that characterizes Being.

29 "Die Frage nach dem Technik," in *Vorträge und Aufsätze*, p. 19. The interpretation of *technē* as *wissen* is related to this; see *Einführung*, p. 132: "Das Werk der Kunst ist in erster Linie nicht Werk, sofern es gewirkt, gemacht ist, sondern weil es das Sein in einem Seienden erwirkt." The conception of *technē* as "menschliches Wissen" (N I, p. 96), is more general.

30 N I, p. 199. Citations are once more from this volume until otherwise indicated.

31 P. 199.

32 P. 200.

33 P. 201.

34 P. 213.

35 P. 203.

36 Pp. 204–06.

37 P. 207.

38 Ibid.; in the first case, Heidegger says *das sich Zeigende*, and in the second, he says that the same look manifests itself (*im sich Zeigen*) in the mirror and in the constructed house (*sich zeigend*).

39 Cited on p. 208.

40 For a more extended discussion of this point, see my *Plato's Sophist: The Drama of Original and Image* (New Haven and London: Yale University Press, 1983).

41 See *Heraklit*, p. 140: "Nach Platon ist das 'Wesen der Dinge', d.h. die *idea* schwer zu erblicken, weil das Auge des Menschen getrübt ist, nicht aber weil das Wesen der Dinge sich versteckt. Dieses versteckt sich ganz und gar nicht, sondern ist das eigentlich Leuchtende und Scheinende."

42 P. 199.

43 P. 212: "So ist hier auf der Spitze der Platonischen Auslegung des Seins des Seienden als *Idea*."

44 P. 211.

45 P. 213.

46 Pp. 214f.

47 P. 216.

48 *Grundprobleme*, pp. 30f.

49 *SZ*, p. 3. The citation of Aristotle is from *Metaphysics B* 4, 1001a21.

50 Heidegger here follows the Thomist understanding of Aristotle's *pros hen legome-non*, the dubious status of which cannot be discussed here.

51 *SZ*, p. 3.

52 See for example *Beiträge*, p. 209, where the Idea as *Seiendheit* is said to be "*das 'Generellste'*" determination of Being.

53 Ibid., 191.

54 *Einführung*, p. 144.

55 *Einleitung* of 1949 to "Was ist Metaphysik," in *Wegmarken*, p. 207.

56 "Vom Wesen und Begriff der *Phusis*," p. 373.

57 *Heraklit*, p. 255: "Wohl dagegen erkennen Platon und Aristoteles, jener ahnend, dieser deutlicher, dass im jedem *logos* im Sinne der gewöhnlichen Aussage die *ka-tēgoria* waltet."

58 *Einführung*, pp. 60ff.

59 On this point, see Heidegger's remark on p. 345 of "Vom Wesen und Begriff der *Phusis*" concerning the mode of access of the Aristotelian *eidos*. Heidegger argues here that the *morphē* is the same as the *eidos* in this ontological context. I will contend later that these two terms are not the same in Plato's teaching about the Ideas.

60 See Thomä, op. cit., pp. 516–18, and Gerold Prauss, *Erkennen und Handeln in Heidegger's "Sein und Zeit"* (Freiburg: Alber, 1977), pp. 94f., 101. As these authors point out, there is a shift from the "subjectivist" projection of the sense of Being in *Sein und Zeit* to an "Aristotelian" receptivity of the givenness of Being in the middle and later texts. But Being hides behind produced beings; the gift is so to speak retracted as it is given.

61 Thomä (op. cit.) is very helpful in his discussion of the rejection by Heidegger after *Sein und Zeit* of the ontological centrality of *Zeitlichkeit* (p. 452) and the new importance of the *Augenblick* as related to *Erschlossenheit* (p. 306). But the epochal gifts of *Sein* (or its surrogates) are unmistakably part of Heidegger's unacknowledged retention of the Hegelian doctrine of the isomorphism between human history and the self-presentation of the various categorial stages of the Absolute.

62 See for example the two essays "Was ist Metaphysik?" and "Vom Wesen des Grundes" in *Wegmarken*, esp. pp. 7, 52.

63 See my essay "Much Ado About Nothing," in *The Quarrel between Philosophy and Poetry*.

64 See my previously cited essay "Heidegger's Interpretation of Plato."

65 See *Phaedo* 100a3 and *Philebus* 16d1.

66 *Metaphysics, Gamma* 2, 1003a33.

67 *Posterior Analytics, B* 3, 90b33.

68 *Metaphysics, Z* 8, 1034a6; 12, 1038a33.

69 19, 100b7. See also *Nicomachean Ethics,* VI, 1040b31ff.

70 VI, 1040b31ff.

71 *Metaphysics,* 1, 981b27–29; 2, 982b7–9.

72 *A,* 73b26ff.

73 In particular, in chapter 13 of Z. See the commentary on this passage by M. Frede and G. Patzig in their edition of *Metaphysics Z* (Munich: C. H. Beck Verlag, 1988), Bd. 2, p. 241.

74 Note here a similar point made by Heidegger in *Einführung,* p. 67: the "Wesen des Seins" is not a "Wortbedeutung." Hence the "Sinn des Seins" refers to the openness of Being (p. 64), not to a discursive concept. Unfortunately, this bears directly upon the impossibility of saying anything definite about Being.

2 Socrates' Hypothesis

1 E.g., in *N* II, pp. 72ff.

2 *Phaedo* 84d8, 115c5. There is a good deal of laughing throughout the dialogue, as is made plain at the outset (59a8). According to Brandwood's *Index,* Socrates does not laugh in any other dialogue. By way of contrast, cf. Heidegger's extensive remarks in *Die Grundbegriffe der Metaphysik, Gesamtausgabe,* Bd. 29/30, on melancholy (*Schwermut*) as the *Grundstimmung* of philosophy (pp. 270 ff.). Heidegger cites Aristotle's *Problēmata* on the *melancholia* of Socrates and Plato. If this observation is accurate (I am not denying it), it raises the question as to why there is no trace of melancholy in the dialogues themselves (to say nothing of Aristotle's treatises).

3 *Critique of Pure Reason* B180. See my paper "Squaring the Hermeneutical Circle," in *Review of Metaphysics* (June 1991): 707–28.

4 The other is at *Lysis* 217e7.

3 Presence and Absence

1 E.g., *N* I, p. 377; "Was ist Metaphysik?" in *Wegmarken,* p. 1; "Vom Wesen und Begriff der *Phusis*" in *Wegmarken,* p. 311, *Einführung,* p. 14.

2 *Beiträge,* p. 426.

3 "Was ist Metaphysik?" p. 7; *Einleitung* to "Was ist Metaphysik?" p. 207.

4 *N* I, p. 535.

5 *Was ist das—die Philosophie?* (Pfullingen: Neske Verlag, 1956), p. 24: the particular reference is to Heracleitus and Parmenides, who were not philosophers because they were greater thinkers.

6 *Unterwegs zur Sprache* (Pfullingen: Neske Verlag, 1959), p. 180 (hereafter cited as *Unterwegs*).

7 Ibid., p. 193. For the sense of *Wesen,* see p. 201: "Das Wort 'Wesen' meint aber jetzt nicht mehr das, was etwas ist. 'Wesen' hören wir als Zeitwort, wesend wie anwesend und abwesend. 'Wesen' besagt währen, weilen."

8 Ibid., p. 200.

9   Hölderlin, Gesamtausgabe, Bd. 39 (1976), pp. 30, 33, 79, 140, 251.

10 N II, p. 484.

11 Heraklit, pp. 55ff.

12 Ibid., p. 278: Logos is "das Sein selbst, worin alles Seiende west."

13 See "Was ist Metaphysik?" pp. 7, 19, and "Vom Wesen des Grundes," p. 39, both in Wegmarken.

14 N I, p. 277.

15 Gorgias 508a3; Theaetetus 203e1ff.; Sophist 244d14ff. and 245b7-c10 (this text brings out the difference between the all and the whole); Philebus 28d5ff. For the difference between the whole and the all, see Aristotle, Metaphysics Delta, 1024a3.

16 Republic 6, 486a4–7.

17 Ibid., 5, 475b4–10.

18 Phaedrus 246a3ff.

19 Symposium 203d5ff.

20 Phaedrus 229e4ff; Apology 20e6ff.

21 SZ, p. 73.

22 The Limits of Analysis (New Haven and London: Yale University Press, 1985).

23 Metaphysics A 2, 982b24ff.; Nicomachean Ethics Z 5, 1140b4ff.

24 Politics A 1, 1252b27ff, esp. a25–29.

25 E.g., Politics, H 3, 1325b16ff.

26 A 2, 982b2ff.

27 Sophist 219a4ff. For the following discussion on the division of the arts and sciences in Plato, see my Plato's Sophist, pp. 91ff.

28 Politics A 2, 1252a24ff: ei de tis eks archēs ta pragmata phuomena blepseien ...

29 4, 420b4ff. It is not clear how a city can be happy, whether or not its citizens are happy, but especially if they are not.

30 See Phaedrus 271d8: en tais praksesin onta te kai prattomena; Republic 5, 473a1ff: phusin echei praksin lekseōs hētton.

31 Republic 2, 374a5 (eplattomen tēn polin), 377b6 and c3; III, 395b9f (the guardians are restricted to being dēmiourgous eleutherias tēs poleōs); 5, 466e6 (the guardians are dēmiourgoi of war); 6, 500d4–8 (the philosopher makes [plattein] for the city himself, but also sumpasēs tēs dēmotikes aretēs as copies of the Ideas); 5, 500e2–4 (we are zōgraphoi who draw the city) together with 501a1-c3; 501e4 (hē politeia hēn mutholgoumen logōi); for further citations and discussion, see my The Quarrel between Philosophy and Poetry, pp. 1–26, esp. p. 5.

32 Ibid., 9, 592b2–5.

33 The citation is from 61b11ff; the metaphor of mixing and blending the good life occurs throughout 61c9–64b4. It is derived from the introduction of to meikton, "the mixed," as a blend of the unlimited and the limit, at 25b5ff.

34 E.g., Gorgias 450c7ff; Charmides 165c10ff; Republic 7, 521c10ff.; Sophist 219a4ff.; Statesman 258d3–5.

35 For extended discussion, see my Plato's Sophist, pp. 245ff., esp. 252ff.

36 See Jacob Klein, Greek Mathematical Thought and the Origins of Algebra, tr. Eva Brann (Cambridge: MIT Press, 1968).

37 *Republic* 6, 500d4–8: the philosopher makes temperance, justice (*kai sumpasēs tēs demotikēs aretēs*); 7, 518d9ff: virtues other than that of intelligence (*hē de tou phronēsai*), i.e., what are called virtues are *produced* (*empoieisthai*) by habit and exercise (*ethesi kai askēsesin*).

38 *Statesman* 258e4–5, 261b4–12, 267c4, 311b7.

39 *Republic* 7, 537c7: *ho men gar sunoptikos dialektikos.*

40 *Sophist* 253d1–4.

41 *Republic* 6, 522b3ff.; 7, 531d7ff.

42 See also the important passage at *Republic* 7, 533b6ff: mathematics dreams about being; cf. 5, 476b6ff. for a distinction between philosophers who are awake and the dreaming non-philosophers, who must be soothed by the founders of the wished-for city. At 7, 540d1, Socrates says that "we have not altogether been giving speech to our wishes" (*kat' euchas*); i.e., the speech about the city is not altogether a daydream; but it is so in part. Socrates himself is not fully awake in the *Republic*, which takes place all through the night, under artificial light: the perfect medium for an artificial and nocturnal dreaming out loud.

4 Nietzsche's Platonism

1 *Sämtliche Werke. Kritische Studienausgabe,* ed. G. Colli and M. Montinari, 15 *Bände* (Berlin: Walter de Gruyter, 1980), VII, p. 199 [7 (156)]. All citations from Nietzsche, unless otherwise indicated, will be from this edition. Reference will be by volume, page, section, or (for unpublished texts) Notebook number and (in the latter case) year of entry.

2 *N* I, p. 233.

3 *N* II, p. 201.

4 II, p. 666 [II.2, no. 265].

5 XIV, p. 437.

6 Ibid., pp. 413, 415.

7 VI, p. 169.

8 VI, p. 11.

9 Ibid., p. 170.

10 Ibid., p. 174.

11 7, 540e5ff.

12 XII, 39 [1 (120)], 1885/86.

13 2, 376d9-e1.

14 4, 420c4–5.

15 5, 478d8-e2.

16 10, 592b2–5.

17 5, 473a1–4.

18 2, 378e4ff.

19 3, 395b9-c1.

20 3, 401b1-d4.

21 5, 462a9-b3.

22 4, 431d9ff.

23 4, 443b1–2.

24 4, 428d8; 429a5–7.

25 4, 428a11ff.

26 7, 519e1–520a4.

27 2, 412b1ff.

28 2, 414b8ff.

29 3, 382b9-c6; 415a1; 5, 459c2–7.

30 3, 382b1-c5.

31 4, 421c1–2.

32 7, 817b1ff.

33 5, p. 79 [61].

34 Ibid., p. 151 [214].

35 Ibid., p. 145 [212].

36 VII, p. 199 [7 (156)]; 1870/71.

37 IX, p. 666 [17 (4)]; 1882.

38 *Jenseits von Gut und Böse* in V, p. 57 [40] (cited hereafter as *Jenseits*).

39 In *Pythian* 2, 72, Pindar says, "Become what thou art by understanding" (*genoi hoios essi mathōn*). Nietzsche gives this a Platonic interpretation; in contemporary discussions, *mathōn* is overlooked.

40 X, p. 340 [8 (15)]; 1883. Cf. VII, p. 199 [7 (156)]; 1870/71 and *Sämtliche Briefe, 8 Bände, KSA*, 1986; VII, p. 449 (22 Oct. 1883) on "wie sehr Zarathustra *platonizei*." Letters are cited from the Colli-Montinari edition by volume, page, and date of composition.

41 *Jenseits*, in V, p. 217 [263].

42 Ibid., p. 233 [287].

43 VII, p. 70 [3. 36]; 1869/70.

44 I, pp. 62, 72, 103, 141.

45 XII, p. 116 [2 (110)]; 1885/86.

46 XII, p. 116 [2 (110)]; 1885/86.

47 VIII, p. 463 [23 (159)]; 1876/77.

48 IX, p. 620 [13 (12)]; 1881.

49 X, p. 244 [7 (21)]; 1883.

50 III, p. 59 [3].

51 229e4–230a6.

52 N I, p. 231ff.

53 XIII, p. 227 [14 (21)]; 1887/88.

54 XIII, p. 194 [11 (415)]; 1887/88; cf. *Götzen-Dämmerung* in VI, p. 127 [*Streifzüge* 24]; 1889.

55 In V, p. 18 [4]; 1886.

56 XII, p. 41 [1 (128)]; 1885/86. Cf. p. 114 [2 (108)].

57 *Briefe*, VIII, p. 196. Cf. the previous citation from Heidegger on philosophical *Schwermut*.

58 *Briefe*, VIII, p. 214 [20 December 1887].

59 E.g., *Jenseits*, in V, p. 33 [283]; p. 34 [289].

60 IX, p. 577 [12 (8)]; 1881.

61 X, p. 109 [4 (2)]; 1882/83.

62 X, p. 341 [8 (20)]; 1883. See also XII, p. 450 [9 (188)]; 1887.

63 *Götzen-Dämmerung*, in VI, p. 61.

64 XI, p. 134 [25 (454)]; 1884.

65 *Briefe*, VIII, p. 24 [13 February 1887]; see also *Götzen-Dämmerung*, in *Werke*, VI, p. 147.

66 XII, p. 153 [2 (172)]; 1885/86.

67 *Zur Genealogie der Moral*, in V, p. 279 [1 (13)] (cited hereafter as *Genealogie*).

68 IX, p. 212 [6 (70)]; 1880. Cf. p. 263 [6 (52)]; XI, p. 434 [34 (46)]; 1885.

69 XI, p. 654 [40 (53)]; 1885.

70 XI, p. 661 [40 (61)]; 1885.

71 XII, p. 25 [1 (58)]; 1885/86.

72 IX, p. 528 [11 (225)]; 1881.

73 XIII, p. 37 [11 (74)]; 1887/88.

74 XIII, p. 333 [14 (152)].

75 X, p. 210 [5 (1) 106]; 1882/83. Cf. XII, p. 385 [9 (91)]; 1887.

76 VII, p. 111 {34 (33)]; 1870/71.

77 XII, p. 119 [2 (114)]; 1885/86.

78 XIII, p. 18 [11 (31)]; 1887/88.

79 "*Amor fati:* das ist meine innerste Natur": *Nietzsche Contra Wagner, Epilog* in VI, p. 436 [1]. Cf. *Briefe*, VI, p. 111 (30 July 1881).

80 Cited from *Friedrich Nietzsche. Werke in drei Bände*, ed. K. Schlechta (Munich: Hanser Verlag, 1956), Bd. 3, p. 834.

81 XII, p. 116 [2 (110)]; 1885/86.

82 *Also sprach Zarathustra*, in IV, p. 75 (*Von Tausend und einem Ziel*) (cited hereafter as *Zarathustra*).

83 IX, p. 620 [13 (12)]; 1881.

84 IX, p. 582 [12 (34)]; 1881.

85 X, p. 244 [7 (21)]; 1883.

86 XI, p. 544 [35 (76)].

87 V, p. 344.

88 VIII, p. 43 [23 (159)].

89 XIII, p. 226 [14 (24)].

90 N I, p. 226.

91 Ibid., p. 195.

92 Ibid., p. 226.

93 Ibid., p. 247.

94 Ibid.

95 XII, p. 39 [1 (120)].

96 XII, p. 114 [2 (108)]; 1885/86.

97 X, p. 243 [7 (18)].

98 N I, p. 132.

99   *Jenseits,* in V, p. 21 [I (9)].

100   *N* I, p. 90f.

101   Ibid., pp. 231ff.

102   VI, pp. 80ff.

103   VII, p. 803 [34 (33)]; 1874.

104   XI, p. 611 [38 (12)]; 1885.

105   *N* I, p. 566.

106   Ibid., p. 575.

107   Ibid., p. 576.

108   IX, p. 528 [11 (225)]; 1881.

109   E.g., *N* II, pp. 217, 273.

110   The best discussion of this point is to be found in the Freiburg University seminar of 1931/32 entitled *Vom Wesen der Wahrheit* in *Gesamtausgabe, Bd.* 34 (1988).

111   See the *Parmenides* seminar of 1942/43 in *Gesamtausgabe, Bd.* 54.

112   *N* I, p. 433.

113   Ibid., p. 656.

114   *N* II, p. 14.

115   See *N* I, p. 604.

116   See Jacques Taminiaux, *Heidegger and the Project of Fundamental Ontology* (Albany: SUNY, 1991), tr. M. Gendre, p. xxii: "Finally, there is the acerbic remark [Heidegger] made in front of Gadamer during their last meeting, 'Nietzsche destroyed me.' "

117   *N* I, pp. 235f.

118   5, 472d9ff.

119   592b2–5.

120   B1, 1261a4.

121   8, 543c4; cf. 5, 449a7ff.

122   XIII, p. 333 [14 (152)]; 1888.

123   E.g. IX, p. 525 [11 (211)]; 1881; and X, p. 244 [7 (21)]; 1883.

124   XIII, pp. 56f. [11 (119)]; 1887/88.

125   *Briefe,* VIII, p. 209 (14 December 1887).

126   *Briefe* VIII, p. 214; see also the letter of 2 September 1886 to his sister and brother-in-law in VII, p. 241.

127   *Jenseits,* in *KSA* V, p. 12.

128   *N* I, p. 236.

129   Ibid., pp. 236–37.

130   "*Technē* and the Origins of Modernity," forthcoming.

131   See my "Antiplatonism: A Case Study," in *The Ancients and the Moderns: Rethinking Modernity* (New Haven: Yale University Press, 1989), chap. 3.

132   *N* I, p. 234.

133   Ibid., p. 238.

134   Ibid.

135   Ibid., p. 239.

136   Ibid., p. 240.

137 Ibid., p. 240.

138 *Jenseits,* in V, pp. 142 f. See also XI, pp. 611 f. [38 (13)]; 1885.

139 VII, p. 423 [19 (23)].

140 Ibid., p. 242.

5 The *Seinsfrage*

1 N II, p. 338.

2 N I, p. 329.

3 N II, p. 484.

4 Ibid.

5 Ibid., p. 98.

6 Ibid., pp. 261f.

7 N I, p. 212.

8 Ibid., p. 26.

9 *Beiträge,* p. 11.

10 *Einführung,* pp. 64, 67.

11 I remind the reader that I distinguish "Being" in Heidegger's sense from "being" in the traditional or (as he would call it) metaphysical sense. In some cases it is difficult to decide which spelling to employ; on these occasions I shall write "Being."

12 This is not to say that the distinction between being and existence does not occur in the analytical tradition; it is made by Moore and Russell at the turn of the century, but not as representatives of the standard analytical doctrine. For discussion, see Peter Hylton, *Russell, Idealism and the Emergence of Analytic Philosophy* (Oxford: Clarendon Press, 1992).

13 See also Jacques Taminiaux, "Heidegger and Husserl's *Logical Investigations:* In Remembrance of Heidegger's Last Seminar," in *Dialectic and Difference* (Atlantic Highlands, N.J.: Humanities Press, 1985), pp. 91–114.

14 *Kritik der reinen Vernunft* B625ff.

15 Previously cited as *Grundprobleme* (*Gesamtausgabe,* Bd. 24).

16 *Kants These über das Sein,* in *Wegmarken,* pp. 273–308.

17 *Logic (Jäsche),* tr. Hartmann and Schwartz (New York: Dover Press, 1974), p. 67.

18 *Grundprobleme,* pp. 64ff.

19 When Heidegger gives up the concept of horizon, he shifts his attention from beings as constituted by the intentional activity of *Dasein* to the "Greek" notion of the givenness of Being. But what is given is suspiciously like the pre-predicative sensation noticed above.

20 See Vittorio Mathieu, *Kants Opus postumum* (Frankfurt: Vittorio Klostermann, 1989).

21 *Logische Untersuchungen* (Tübingen: Max Niemeyer Verlag, 1968); Bd. II/I.

22 "Der Gedanke *Urteil* erfüllt sich in der inneren Anschauung eines aktuellen Urteils; aber nicht erfüllt sich darin der Gedanke des *ist.* Das Sein ist kein Urteil und kein reales Bestandstück eines Urteils" (p. 139).

23 As Heidegger notes in *Grundprobleme,* p. 66.

24 *History of the Concept of Time,* tr. Theodore Kisiel (Bloomington: Indiana University Press, 1985), p. 116.

25 Ibid., p. 107.

26 This configuration or way is the Aristotelian equivalent to the surplus being of Husserl's doctrine of intuition.

6 The Culmination of Metaphysics

1 *N* I, pp. 433ff.

2 *N* II, p. 417.

3 *N* I, pp. 463f.

4 *N* II, p. 16.

5 Ibid., p. 17.

6 Ibid.

7 *N* II, p. 270.

8 Ibid.

9 See *N* II, pp. 164ff, for an especially good discussion of this familiar Heideggerian thesis.

10 *N* II, p. 268.

11 IX, p. 528 [11 (225)]; 1881.

12 IX, p. 523 [11 (202)]; 1881. Cf. Heidegger's discussion at *N* I, pp. 341ff. and XII, p. 205 [5 (54)]; 1886/87. The standard secondary work on the doctrine of will to power as force is W. Müller-Lauter's *Nietzsche: Seine Philosophie der Gegensätze und die Gegensätze Seiner Philosophie* (Berlin: Walter de Gruyter, 1971). Also worth reading are his two articles "Nietzsches Lehre vom Willen zur Macht," in *Nietzsche Studien, Bd.* 3, 1974, pp. 1–60, and "Der Willenswesen und der Übermensch. Ein Beitrag zu Heideggers Nietzsche-Interpretation," in *Nietzsche Studien, Bd.* 10/11, 1981/82, pp. 132–77.

13 IX, p. 666 [17 (4)]; 1882.

14 Gunter Abel, *Nietzsche* (Berlin and New York: Walter de Gruyter, 1984), p. 189. Abel tries to justify the scientific cogency of the doctrine of the eternal return. Although I regard this effort as misguided, Abel's book is very helpful. For Nietzsche's texts, see IX, pp. 494f. [11 (141)]; 502 [11 (157)] and 523 [11 (202)].

15 V, p. 28; I. 14.

16 XII, p. 391 [9 (98)]; 1887.

17 XII, p. 106 [2 (90)]; 1885/86.

18 XII, p. 383 [9 (91)]; 1887.

19 XIII, p. 333 [14 (152)]; 1888.

20 *N* I, p. 340.

21 Ibid., pp. 408f.

22 *Briefe,* VI, p. 496 [7 April 1884, to Franz Overbeck]. Cf. *N* I, pp. 20f.

23 *Briefe,* VIII, p. 209.

24 But also in his correspondence: "Von meinem Zarathustra glaube ich ungefähr, dass es das tiefste Werk ist, das in deutscher Sprache existirt, auch das sprachlich voll-

kommenste"(*Briefe* VIII, p. 340 [21 June 1888; to Karl Knortz]). This is a representative text.

25 See especially part II, section 20, "Von der Erlösung" in IV, pp. 179f.

26 XII, p. 213 [5 (71)]; 1886/87.

27 *N* I, p. 349; III, p. 468 [109].

28 *N* I, pp. 350, 354.

29 *N* I, p. 566.

30 *N* I, p. 353.

31 *N* I, p. 381.

32 *N* I, p. 469.

33 IX, p. 528 [11 (225)]; 1881. This is one of a sequence of texts about the eternal return; see also pp. 498 [11 (148)], 502 [11 (157)], 560–62 [11 (311)], [11 (313)].

34 *N* I, p. 391.

35 Ibid., p. 392.

36 Ibid.

37 Ibid.

38 "Vom Wesen des Grundes," in *Wegmarken,* pp. 60f. In order to see how Heidegger modifies this "Nietzschean" conception of freedom in his later years, the passage just cited should be compared with "Die Frage nach dem Ding" (1953) in *Vorträge und Ausätze,* pp. 32f. The main difference is the detachment of freedom from the will and the accompanying replacement of world-projection by the process of clearing that is also a concealing; the locus of action is now in Being, but no longer understood as eternal return.

39 *N* I, p. 393.

40 Ibid., p. 392.

41 Ibid., p. 400.

42 XII, p. 215 [5 (71)]; 1886/87.

43 XII, p. 25 [1 (58)]; 1885/86.

44 XI, p. 661 [40 (61)]; 1885.

45 *Jenseits* [1. 9] in V, p. 22.

46 XII, p. 153 [2 (172)]; 1885/86.

47 XIII, p. 45 [11 (96)]; 1887/88.

48 Quoted by Heidegger in *N* II, p. 270.

49 XIII, p. 260 [14 (81)]; 1888.

50 *Genealogie* [II, 12] in V, pp. 313f.

51 XI, p. 611 [38 (12)]; 1885.

52 XII, p. 385 [9 (91)]; 1887.

53 XIII, p. 274 [14 (98)]; 1888.

54 *N* I, p. 656.

55 VI, p. 77.

56 V, pt. II., pars. 26–30, esp. par. 30, 40.

57 *Jenseits,* II. 43 in V, p. 60.

58 XIII, p. 19 [11 (33)]; 1887/88. For critical statements on esotericism by modern

philosophers, which recognize the widespread nature of the phenomenon, see Francis Bacon, *Advancement of Learning,* in Spedding, Ellis, and Heath, vol. 6, pp. 290f., and Immanuel Kant, *Kritik der reinen Vernunft* B776.

59 XII, p. 187 [5 (9)]. Cf. the discussion by G. Colli in the *Nachwort* to *KSA* XIII, pp. 651ff. To my knowledge Heidegger never mentions the crucial distinction between the esoteric and the exoteric in Nietzsche.

60 IX, p. 263 [6 (252)]; 1880. I purposely cite a relatively early text in order to show that this view was held by Nietzsche long before his final period.

61 IX, p. 484 [11 (121)]; 1881.

62 XIII, p. 37 [11 (74)]; 1887/88.

63 XIII, p. 33 [14 (52)]; 1888.

64 N I, pp. 632ff.

65 Ibid., p. 632.

66 *Parmenides,* pp. 69ff.

67 Ibid., p. 76.

68 *Einführung,* p. 127.

69 N I, p. 475.

70 See *Phaedrus* 246e4ff: Zeus drives a winged chariot round the cosmos, at the head of the Olympian choirs, *diakosmōn panta kai epimeloumenos.* The word plays an especially important role in the *Statesman,* e.g., at 267d8, 271d4, 276b2 and 7, etc.

71 In *Holzwege* (Frankfurt: Klostermann, 1952), pp. 296–343.

72 See esp. pp. 327, 332.

73 Ibid., p. 296.

74 N I, pp. 642–45.

75 IX, p. 229 [6 (129)]; 1880.

76 XII, p. 495 [10 (66)]; 1887.

77 N I, p. 634.

78 Ibid.

79 Ibid.

80 Ibid., pp. 634f.

81 Ibid., pp. 635ff.

82 Ibid., p. 636.

83 Ibid.

84 Ibid., p. 642.

85 Ibid.

86 Ibid.

87 Ibid., p. 645.

88 Ibid.

89 Ibid., p. 651. Cf. N II, p. 326.

90 N I, p. 364.

91 N I, p. 381.

92 Ibid.

7 Nihilism

1 XII, pp. 211–17 [5 (71)] (hereafter pages of citations from this section appear in the text).

2 XII, p. 354 [9 (41)]; 1887.

3 XII, p. 350 [9 (35)].

4 XII, p. 280 [7 (6)]; 1886/87.

5 XIII, p. 481 [15 (120)]; 1888.

6 I thus agree, although with different emphasis, with Pierre Klossowski, according to whom the heart of Nietzsche's effort "est de combattre l'attrait irresistible qu'exerce sur lui le chaos." Thus the thought of Nietzsche describes simultaneously two divergent movements: "la notion de lucidité ne vaut que dans la mesure ou l'obscurité totale ne cesse d'être envisagée, donc affirmée." In *Nietzsche et le cercle vicieux* (Paris: Mercure de France, 1978), pp. 12f.

7 XII, p. 13 [1 (10)]; 1885/86.

8 This requires amplification. According to Nietzsche, "Philosophy since Plato has been under the mastery of morality": XII, p. 259 [7 (4)]; 1886/87. Cf *Jenseits*, par. 191. Hitherto, moral problems have been the most fundamental. But there are still more fundamental problems which come into view when one has put one's moral prejudices behind one: XII, p. 220 [5 (80)]. These more fundamental problems are cosmological or treat of Chaos as the backdrop against which we attempt to produce a morality that is beyond good and evil, i.e., beyond Platonism and Christianity.

9 *N* I, p. 391.

10 Ibid., p. 393.

11 Ibid., p. 400.

12 X, p. 244 [7 (21)]; 1883.

13 Cf. *Götzen-Dämmerung*, par. 43, in VI, p. 144.

14 XII, p. 125 [2 (127)]; 1885/86.

15 XIII, p. 56 [11 (119)]; 1887/88.

16 *Republic* 4, 424a5: *hōsper kyklos auksanomenē.*

17 XIII, p. 492 [16 (32)]; 1888.

18 *N* I, p. 25.

19 *N* II, p. 259.

20 *N* I, pp. 442, 445.

21 Ibid. p. 12.

22 Ibid., p. 35.

23 E.g., *N* II, pp. 375, 379.

24 *N* II, p. 272.

25 Ibid., p. 273.

26 In addition to the two *Nietzsche* volumes, one may consult "Die Frage nach der Technik" and "Überwindung der Metaphysik," in *Vorträge und Aufsätze*, and "Die Zeit des Weltbildes," in *Holzwege*.

27 "Die Frage nach dem Ding," in *Vorträge und Aufsätze*, p. 28.

28 Ibid., p. 13.
29 Consider *Republic* 5, 477c1-d6. At 6, 508b6, Socrates speaks of the *dunamis* of the sun or the Good. Perhaps the most important occurrence of *dunamis* in an ontological sense is at *Sophist* 247d5ff.
30 For some discussion, see my essay "Much Ado About Nothing," in *The Quarrel between Philosophy and Poetry.*
31 See Paul Natorp, *Platos Ideenlehre, Eine Einführung in den Idealismus* (Darmstadt: Wissenschaftliche Buchgesellschaft, 1961), pp. x, 29, 74f.
32 N II, p. 273.
33 See my *Nihilism,* chap. 5, pp. 168ff.
34 N II, p. 360. Numbers in parentheses in the text of this section refer to pages in this volume.
35 (Pfullingen: Neske Verlag, 1959), p. 24.
36 Ibid., p. 26.
37 Ibid., p. 35.
38 Ibid., p. 59.
39 Ibid., p. 42.
40 Par. 17, p. 50 (Hamburg: Felix Meiner, 1969).
41 Reiner Schürmann, op. cit., p. 81.
42 N II, p. 340.
43 Ibid., p. 288.
44 XII, p. 312 [7 (54)]; 1886/87.
45 This reflection lends some support to Gilles Deleuze's observation that the noble and the base are not in Nietzsche values but "the differential element from which the value of values themselves derives." See *Nietzsche and Philosophy,* tr. Hugh Tomlinson (New York: Columbia University Press, 1983), p. 2. But this observation is based upon what Heidegger calls Nietzsche's metaphysics, and what I call his cosmological doctrines. Deleuze's statement cannot be reconciled with Nietzsche's human or political teaching, for reasons which I have explained at length.
46 XII, p. 213 [5 (71)]; 1887.
47 *Le Avventure della Differenza* (Milan: Garzanti, 1988).
48 Ibid., p. 76f.
49 "Force and signification," in *Writing and Difference,* tr. Alan Bass (Chicago: University of Chicago Press, 1978), pp. 28f.
50 Vattimo, op. cit., p. 82.
51 Ibid., pp. 80–82.
52 Ibid., pp. 79, 85.
53 IX, p. 528 [11 (225)]; 1881.
54 Vattimo, op. cit., p. 85.
55 Ibid., pp. 89f.
56 Ibid., pp. 91f.
57 X, p. 244 [7 (21)]; 1883.
58 IX, p. 170 [4 (285)]; 1880.

59 IX, p. 666 [17 (4)]; 1882.

60 X, p. 341 [8 (20)]; 1883.

61 XI, p. 50 [25 {137}]; 1884.

62 IX, p. 25 [11 (211)]; 1881.

63 IX, p. 296 [6 (383)]; 1880.

64 VI, p. 156.

65 X, p. 245 [7 (21)]; 1883.

66 *Jenseits,* in V, pp. 144f.

67 *Götzen-Dämmerung,* in VI, p. 59.

68 VII, p. 706 [29 (180)]; 1873. This is indicated in *Zarathustra* in the first speech of part 1, "On the Three Metamorphoses": "Neue Werthe schaffen - das vermag auch der Löwe noch nicht: aber Freiheit sich schaffen zu neuem Schaffen - das vermag die Macht des Löwen." Such creation is reserved for the child or third metamorphosis: "was vermag noch das Kind, das auch der Löwe nicht vermöchte? ... Unschuld ist das Kind und Vergessen, ein Neubeginnen, ein Spiel, ein aus sich rollendes Rad, eine erste Bewegung, ein heiliges Jasagen": IV, 30f. The child represents the creation of a new epoch in the cycle of the eternal return.

69 XII, p. 426 [9 (154)]; 1887.

70 V, p. 28.

71 *Zarathustra,* in IV, p. 16.

72 N II, pp. 291ff.

73 Ibid.

74 See N II, p. 63, for the link between the *cogito* and the superman.

75 For further discussion, see my "A Central Ambiguity in Descartes," in *The Ancients and the Moderns.*

76 N II, p. 296.

77 Ibid., p. 302.

78 Ibid.

79 N II, p. 307. The sketch is of book I of Zarathustra: IX, pp. 519f [11 (197)]; 1881.

80 N II, p. 312.

81 Ibid.

82 XII, p. 536 [10 (138)]; 1887.

83 XII, pp. 357f. [9 (44)].

84 VI, p. 144.

85 VI, pp. 232ff.

8 The History of Being

1 *Introduction to the Human Sciences, Wilhelm Dilthey, Selected Works,* ed. Rudolf A. Makkreel and Frithjof Rodi (Princeton: Princeton University Press, 1989), vol. 1, pp. 81, 88, 103, 105.

2 With the following discussion, cf. Ernst Tugendhat, op. cit, pp. 255ff.

3 Until otherwise stated, numbers in parentheses in the text refer to pages from the Sixth *Untersuchung* (op. cit).

4 *Die Krisis der europäische Wissenschaften und die transzendentale Phänomenologie* (The Hague: Martinus Nijhoff, 1954). Until otherwise stated, numbers in parentheses in the text refer to pages in the *Krisis*.

5 For further discussion of this whole topic, see the valuable study by David Carr, *Phenomenology and the Problem of History* (Evanston, Ill.: Northwestern University Press, 1974). Carr points out with respect to the *Krisis* as well as to *Erfahrung und Urteil*, that in order to recapture the lifeworld from history, we must already be resident within and determined by a particular historical epoch (230, 232). In an alternative formulation, "if the natural attitude is really essential to consciousness, how can phenomenology succeed in overcoming that attitude?" (268).

6 See, for example, *Ideen zu einer reinen Phänomenologie I* (The Hague: Martinus Nijhoff, 1950), pp. 57ff., on the natural attitude, in which one finds oneself in an extended world of perceived bodies, by which one orients oneself for all subsequent phenomenological procedures.

7 *Ideen I*, p. 111.

8 Ibid., p. 367.

9 *Cartesianische Meditationen und Pariser Vortrag* (The Hague: Martinus Nijhoff, 1963), p. 91.

10 Ibid., p. 117.

11 *N II*, p. 471.

12 Ibid., p. 473.

13 *N I*, pp. 44ff; *N II*, p. 467: "Der Wille wird in der actualitas erst dort wesentlich, wo das ens actu durch das agere als cogitare bestimmt wird, da dieses cogito me cogitare ist ... "

14 *N II*, p. 471.

15 Ibid., p. 482.

16 Ibid., p. 485.

17 Ibid.

Appendix

1 *Platon: Sophistes, Herausg.* Ingrid Schüssler, Bd. 19, *Gesamtausgabe* (Frankfurt: Klostermann, 1992). For details concerning the manuscripts and stenographic copies of students' notes from which the published text was assembled, see the editor's *Nachwort*, pp. 654ff. The coherence of the published text is of a very high order.

2 See also my article "The Golden Apple" in *Arion* (Winter 1990): 187–207.

3 See my *Plato's Sophist* (New Haven and London: Yale University Press, 1983), pp. 217ff., 281ff.

Index

The Abbey Company at Synge's cottage on Inis Meáin, the Aran Islands, *c.1967*.
Photograph: Peter Dorney. By Courtesy of the National Library of Ireland (R*29,361*).

THE ABBEY THEATRE
1899–1999

THE ABBEY THEATRE
1899–1999

Form and Pressure

ROBERT WELCH

OXFORD

UNIVERSITY PRESS

OXFORD
UNIVERSITY PRESS

Great Clarendon Street, Oxford OX2 6DP

Oxford University Press is a department of the University of Oxford
and furthers the University's aim of excellence in research, scholarship,
and education by publishing worldwide in

Oxford New York

Athens Auckland Bangkok Bogotá Buenos Aires Calcutta
Cape Town Chennai Dar es Salaam Delhi Florence Hong Kong Istanbul
Karachi Kuala Lumpur Madrid Melbourne Mexico City Mumbai
Nairobi Paris São Paulo Singapore Taipei Tokyo Toronto Warsaw

with associated companies in Berlin Ibadan

Oxford is a trade mark of Oxford University Press
in the UK and in certain other countries

Published in the United States
by Oxford University Press Inc., New York

British Library Cataloguing in Publication Data

Data available

Library of Congress Cataloging in Publication Data
Data available
ISBN–0–19–812187–3

1 3 5 7 9 10 8 6 4 2

Typeset in Sabon
by Alliance Phototypesetters, Pondicherry, India
Printed in Great Britain
on acid-free paper by
Biddles Ltd,
Guildford and King's Lynn

For
SHIVAUN O'CASEY
and in memory of
TOMÁS Ó MURCHADHA
and
LIAM LYNCH

Prologue

This is a history of the Abbey Theatre and its plays. It begins with the foundation of the Irish Literary Theatre, and its inaugural performances in 1899, because those days in May of that year witnessed the first stirrings of the movement which led to the establishment of the Abbey Theatre in 1904.

It is *a* history, and a very condensed one at that. There could be, and there should be, other kinds of history, but my focus here has been on the Abbey as an arena in which the latent forces, and energies, and pressures of modern Irish consciousness manifest themselves; and on the plays in which these pressures are given imaginative form.

Ireland in the twentieth century, the period covered in this history, has been a country(?), a territory(?), an island which has experienced cataclysmic change and utter transformation: revolution, independence, partition, neutrality in the Second World War, a complete alteration in land ownership, economic subsistence, economic boom, the Troubles, civil war, the Troubles again, the breakdown of government in Northern Ireland, paramilitary violence, no-go areas, the decline and revival of the national language, the relaxation of the controls exercised by the Catholic church, and so on. No culture, no country, this century has a monopoly of suffering, hardship, terror: indeed in comparison with many territories (and it would be indecent to name in this context some of the more brutalized civilizations of this last remorseless century) Ireland has enjoyed a hundred years of relative calm. Nevertheless, there have been outrages, injustices, bestialities; and there have also been accords, generosities, acts of reparation and kindness.

In all of this the Abbey, and its predecessors, has functioned as all real theatre must function: as a laboratory for testing the prejudices of the mind, the nature of emotion, the value of the spirit. Through its playwrights, directors, and actors, it has been a space in which public attitudes and private concerns have been subjected to the kind of experiential, that is to say moral, analysis only theatre can provide for society. The Abbey has been the conscience of modern Ireland, a responsibility any national theatre must discharge. The Abbey has, in the words of Patrick Mason, done the 'work', the labour of showing (in the phrase Hamlet uses to the Players at Elsinore) the 'very age and body of the time his form and pressure'. This phrase is the third wave of the thought that opens with the comment about the purpose of playing being as 'as 'twere to hold the mirror up to nature'. As ever in Shakespeare, the second phase of the thinking strikes deeper, because, Hamlet says, acting shows 'virtue her own feature, scorn her own image'. And now a third phase drives to the core, into the form theatre gives to the pressures that build up in the individual psyche and in society in general.

Shakespeare's phrase, one which has haunted me for years, gave me the subtitle for this book. As I wrote I found myself continually returning to a relationship between the forms theatre creates to shape and give vent to personal and collective pressures, and the form or forms of representation and government that would accommodate the different inheritances and inbuilt divisions of Irish history and society. In theatre, as in all the arts, artistic form strives to shape that which resists, most strenuously, being brought to book; yet without this attempt to harness the pressures that drive society, those voices that are most crucial to our well-being, the ones that speak of tragedy and joy, cannot be heard. This is Patrick Mason's 'work': it involves order and emotion, form and pressure. Form arises from (amongst other things) judgement and morality; pressure builds out of emotion and pity and fear. The body of the time is embodied in the physical presence of the actors on the stage. In the twentieth century Ireland discovered its dramatic identity: the Fays, Máire Nic Shiubhlaigh, F. J. McCormick, Barry Fitzgerald, Siobhán McKenna, are, all of them, physical realizations of an Ireland present to itself, ready to absorb the mystery and awe of its reality, for the first time shown to itself by itself. In a seminar once at Coleraine Frank McGuinness described the extraordinary success of eighteenth-century Irish playwrights and actors in London as the Irish finding in Drury Lane and elsewhere an opportunity for saying 'we're here; we exist'.

In the twentieth century the Abbey was one of the crucial spaces in which the Irish said to themselves, and to each other: 'we're here; we exist. This is how we talk; this is what we do. This is how terrible we are. This is also our gentleness, our hurt. These are our memories, our shame, our delight.' The world listened, because what was being voiced and embodied in Dublin was powerful; it sprang from the inner life, the emotions, the collective pressures, of a people.

I have often thought that I must have some kind of self-punishing instinct in the tasks I set myself as a writer, as a researcher. Or maybe there is some obscure impulse of self-justification. My first book was a study, not of a nineteenth-century novelist or poet, but of Irish poetry in English of the nineteenth century; my second was a history of verse translation from the Irish, not a study of an aspect, or a theme, or an author; my third was a study of the body of literature in Ireland in the twentieth-century; and then there was the *Oxford Companion to Irish Literature* (1996), which took all of Irish literature, in all its languages, as its field.

And here is 'the Abbey'. I realize now that what I do, for better or for worse, is groundwork. This is the title of my last novel (*Groundwork*, 1997), itself an attempt to uncover the genealogies of Irish feeling. I try to open ground.

So much work remains to be done on the Abbey, Ireland's national theatre: there need to be histories of the actors, the performance methods, the personalities and motivations of the directors, of design, of language, and of the reception of the plays. This book is a beginning in what I sincerely hope may become a network of interrelated undertakings on the Abbey's history, in time, perhaps, for the 2004 celebration of the opening of the theatre in the old Mechanics Institute.

R. W.

Cúl Raithin
Nollaig 1998

Acknowledgements

My deepest dept of gratitude is recorded in the dedication. One evening in Portstewart, on the north Derry coast, east of the Bann, I was telling Shivaun O'Casey, the playwright's beloved daughter, of the way in which the Abbey patent was transferred to Lady Gregory when Miss Annie Horniman withdrew her patronage. In conversation Shivaun asked why I wasn't writing a history of the Abbey. I replied that, not being a theatre person, I wouldn't have the nerve; her response to this was typical: I was told to go ahead and do it. Here it is, the best I could manage for a great subject. I am deeply grateful for that fortifying imprimatur, given in advance, and therefore an act of faith.

It is a pleasure to record my gratitude to the British Academy which, once more, has eased the burden by graciously awarding me a personal research grant: their generosity allowed five weeks' uninterrupted work at the Manuscript Rooms of the National Library of Ireland. I thank my colleagues at the University of Ulster: the Dean, Professor Terence O'Keeffe; my Head of School, Professor Richard York; the Head of our Research School, Dr John Gillespie; our Pro-Vice-Chancellor (Research) Professor Gerry McKenna. Practical and moral support was never withheld by: Professor Lord Smith of Clifton and Mountsandel, Kt. (Vice-Chancellor, UU); Professor Fabian Monds (Magee College); Professor A. N. Jeffares, University of Stirling (Emeritus); Professor Terence Brown (TCD); Professor Brendan Kennelly (TCD); Professor Pádraig Breatnach (UCD); Professor Declan Kiberd (UCD); Professor Alan Titley (St Patrick's, Drumcondra); Dr Patricia Noone (Claremorris); Anthony Cronin (Dublin); Professor Brian Walker (QUB); Dr Patrick Maume (QUB); Dr Patrick Walsh (QUB); Professor John Cronin (QUB); Dr Sophie Hillan King (QUB); Dr Allan Blackstock (QUB); Dr Jim Doan (Nova University, Florida); Declan Molloy (Leamagowra, Donegal); Brian and Denise Ferran (Belfast and Donegal); Robert MacLiam Wilson (Belfast); Glenn Patterson (Belfast); Ciaran Carson (Belfast); Medbh McGuckian (Belfast and Ballycastle); Michael and Edna Longley (Belfast and Mayo); John F. Deane (Dublin); Pádraig Ó Snodaigh (Dublin); Seán Hutton (British Association for Irish Studies); Jack Gamble (Belfast); Greg Delanty (St Michael's College, Vermont); Professor Seamus Deane (Notre Dame University); Dr Seán Mac Réamoinn (Dublin); Professor Seán Ó Tuama (UCC); Fred Johnston (Galway); Professor Colin Smythe (Gerrards Cross and UU); Ann Haverty (Dublin); John Behan (Galway); Thomas Kilroy (Mayo); Professor Hiroko Mikami (UU and Waseda University, Tokyo); Professor Joseph O'Leary (Sofia University, Tokyo); Professor Toshio Akai (Kobe University); Dr Fethi Hassaine (Aix-en-Provence); Dr Britta Olinder (Göteborg University); Professor

Heinz Kosok (Wuppertal University); Seán MacCarthy (Cork); Professor Seán Lucy (Chicago); Gerard Kenny (Galway); Seamus Heaney (Dublin); Brian Friel (Donegal); D.E.S. Maxwell (Belfast); John Hunter and Patricia Farren (Portstewart); Professor John Pitcher (St John's College, Oxford); and Professor Terry Eagleton (St Catherine's College, Oxford).

I am very grateful for the kindness and tolerance of my colleagues at the Centre for Irish Literature and Bibliography at the University of Ulster, Dr Anne McCartney, Dr Frank Sewell, Mrs Wendy Taulbutt, and Mr David Vauls. Mrs Taulbutt, as our Project Assistant, went way beyond the call of duty to produce a typescript from writings and library over-writings in what was a very taxing endeavour. I wish also to thank my colleagues at UU, especially the following: Mr Felix Agnew; Dr Ronnie Bailie; Professor Richard Bradford; Miss Kathleen Devine; Dr David Gilligan; Dr Art Hughes; Mr Jim Hunter; Dr Jan Jedrzejewski; Dr Elmer Kennedy-Andrews; Ms Bernie Leacock; Professor Gerry MacCarthy; Professor Séamus Mac Mathúna; Professor Joseph McMinn; Mr. Brian Devine; Mr Alan Peacock; Mr Philip Tilling.

Mr Patrick Mason, between commitments on two continents, gave me the favour of a personal interview; and Mr Tomás Mac Anna, with no little trouble to himself, gave the time to answer a series of written questions in a scrupulous and superbly informative manner. Ms Máiréad Delaney, the Abbey Archivist, responded most efficiently and with professional rigour, to my enquiries, as did the manager, Martin Fahy.

I thank the staff of the library of the University of Ulster at Coleraine, especially Ms Kay Ballantine, Mr Joseph McLaughlin, Ms Jean Dunlop, and Mr Frank Reynolds for unremitting support and assistance. The National Library of Ireland was a pleasure to work in: Noel Kissane, Librarian in charge of the Manuscripts section, was understanding and ready always to assist, going to great lengths one evening in November 1998 to track down an especially recalcitrant reference.

As will be all too evident to the reader of this book, anyone working on modern Irish theatre is profoundly indebted to the labours of one scholar in particular, who, over the past thirty years, has done more than anyone else to record the diversity of Ireland's theatrical heritage. I mean Robert Hogan, who, with various assistants, produced the extraordinary six-volume documentary history of Modern Irish Theatre, from 1899 to 1926, published by Dolmen and latterly by Colin Smythe. The Herculean nature of this task is borne out by the fact that no one has followed his example to provide the documentary history from 1926 onwards. This six-volume history Robert Hogan supplemented with other editorial and critical endeavours, all testifying to the excellence and strenuousness of his work. Compiling the Bibliography I was struck, yet again, by the debt which scholarship owes to one publisher beyond all others: Colin Smythe, whose industry, since the inauguration of the Coole edition of Lady Gregory, has been as powerful as his generosity is deep. John Kelly's superb edition of Yeats's *Letters* makes the task of any researcher of Yeats's life and work immeasurably easier; and Roy Foster's biography of Yeats is remarkable for many reasons, but in this context chiefly for its detail and exemplary scrupulousness.

I thank my editors at Oxford University Press, in particular Frances Whistler, Sophie Goldsworthy, and Jason Freeman; and the copy-editor, Jackie Pritchard.

I have worked on the principle of fair dealing in relation to permissions for the quoting of published work, and I thank the many authors whose works are quoted in this account of the Abbey Theatre. If any author wishes for further clarification on this point can I ask him or her to get in touch with me or with the publishers? Every effort has been made to gain permission to quote from unpublished materials, and I thank the following: the Estates of Frank and William Fay, Máire Nic Shiubhlaigh, Siobhán McKenna, John McCann, T. C. Murray, Bryan MacMahon, and Liam Lynch; Francis Stuart; and Antoine Ó Flatharta.

I want to mention the two other dedicatees of this book, friends who are dead, who taught me about the theatre and about the kind of thinking that happens in its space: Tomás Ó Murchadha, who directed *Soldier*, and Liam Lynch, who wrote it.

Contents

[O]nly two topics can be of the least interest to a serious and studious mind—sex and the dead.

(W. B. Yeats to Olivia Shakespear, October 1927)

[T]hat's the terrible thing. To be always remembering.

(Brinsley MacNamara, *Margaret Gillan* 17 July 1933)

1899–1902
'Four Green Fields'

Florimand Comte de Basterot was a French count who had a summer house at Duras, beyond Kinvara in Co. Clare. Lady Gregory and her husband Sir William used to visit him at Duras and bring their children there with them to spend long summer days idling in the seaside garden, where lavender and carnations grew profusely and there were plums along the walls. This was strange, because outside the walled garden there were bare rock-strewn fields, swept by the fierce Atlantic winds. The Comte appears to have been an interesting character: Lady Gregory tells us that he believed that all human activity and custom came down to racial origin; and she also recalled how, in the early years of his visits to Ireland, horsemen rode naked into the sea at Duras on one Sunday during the summer.[1] On a visit in summer 1897 W. B. Yeats arrived at the house with Edward Martyn, Lady Gregory's Catholic neighbour of Tillyra Castle; they had lunch, during which Lady Gregory and Yeats renewed a friendship begun in meetings in 1894 and 1896. In 1896 Yeats had stayed with Martyn, a wealthy landowner, interested in art and especially the music of Palestrina, and urged Lady Gregory to collect the folk tales and poems of the countryside, thereby encouraging her to make use of her somewhat limited knowledge of Irish, a language she had been interested in since childhood. Now in 1897 she and Yeats were on the verge of a great friendship, one in which his creativity and energy were perfectly matched by her kindness and intelligence.

That afternoon at Duras she sensed, she tells us, that the Comte wanted to speak privately to Edward Martyn, and it being too wet and blustery to go out she and Yeats retired to the steward's office where they started to talk about theatre. Yeats declared that he had always dreamed of an Irish theatre, where his plays and those by Edward Martyn (who had, she learned, completed two) could be performed, but that such a thing seemed impossible as theatre of the kind he and Martyn wished to write could not pay its way in an Irish context where playgoers in Dublin wanted to see Dan Lowry's variety shows, Shakespeare as given by visiting English companies, or the Irish productions by J. W. Whitbread at the Queen's Theatre. As they talked, it seemed as if it might not be as impossible a task as first envisaged: they agreed that their best prospect was to raise practical support in advance for the idea by getting friends to guarantee financial backing. Lady Gregory herself offered to put up £25, a sum in today's money equivalent to *c.*£2,500.

A few days later Yeats came to stay with her at her house at Coole—the first of many extended summer visits—and there she typed up (on a Remington typewriter given to her by Lady Enid Layard, sometime wife of the British Ambassador at Constantinople) their proposal and request for assistance. Outlining their plans, they said they wished to perform every spring certain Celtic and Irish plays (the 'Celtic' inserted for the benefit of the mysterious 'Fiona Macleod', pseudonym of the Scottish Celtophile and poet William Sharp whose unactable plays they never, in fact, performed); they hoped to find an audience in Ireland ready to listen to eloquent language by virtue of its appreciation of oratory; they aimed to correct false and demeaning stereotypes of Irish character and Irish sentiment; and they declared that they would steer clear of all political factionalism. This last avowal reflected Yeat's anxieties concerning his recent involvement in radical politics through Maud Gonne's influence, and his worry that activism which could and did lead to violence was, as he put it later, 'wasteful'.

In an *Autobiography* which remained unpublished until 1972 Yeats describes the harrowing Jubilee Riots of 22 June 1897, and Maud Gonne's exhilarated nationalist subversion and demagoguery that stoked passions as old Fenians and republicans prepared to celebrate the centenary of the 1798 rebellion.

The 22nd was Queen Victoria's birthday and Maud Gonne had been prevented from decorating the graves of the United Irishmen John and Henry Sheares and William Orr in St Michan's Church. In Dame Street, before a large crowd, Yeats heard her say slowly in a low voice: 'must the graves of our dead go undecorated because Victoria has her Jubilee?', at which the crowd went wild.[2] That night there were riots, the police baton-charged a crowd at Rutland (now Parnell) Square, injuring 200 people and killing an old woman, a Mrs Fitzsimons. It is not surprising that Yeats hoped that what he described as an Irish appreciation of oratory could, by a theatrical movement, be turned towards more peaceful outcomes.

Moreover, apart from his fixation with Maud Gonne (what he described as 'a miserable love affair'[3]) there were other reasons why a change of direction and the relaxing atmosphere of Coole Park beckoned. He was exhausted, physically and emotionally. His occult researches, all part of an attempt to break into new forms of illumination that were necessary, he believed, in order to renew a tired and lacklustre European society, were taking him into strange and difficult paths. MacGregor Mathers, a weird magician and a member, like Yeats of the esoteric society the Order of the Golden Dawn, was going mad. Mathers believed that he was in continuous contact with otherworld beings, and that a universal war was shortly to take place, for which reason he had his wife learn ambulance work so that they might prove useful to the roving bands that would follow the apocalypse. He was in charge of the Paris temple of the order, known as the Athanoor, whence he controlled the Temple of Isis Urania in London. Mathers, who later adopted the wild and powerful mage Aleister Crowley as an acolyte, was greatly disliked by Maud Gonne, although at this stage he was still advising Yeats on the rituals appropriate for the Order of Celtic Mysteries which Yeats hoped to establish in Ireland along with his old colleague in occult studies, George Russell ('Æ'), a project in which Gonne was also interested. And to top it all, a sexual liaison with Olivia Shakespear, which had brought some release from the sexual tension he suffered because of his frustrated love, ended in early 1897 because she knew there was, so she put it during the final emotional break, 'someone else in your heart'.[4]

By that wet afternoon during which he and Lady Gregory had their first conversation about a theatre, he was in that state he himself diagnosed as 'the leprosy of the modern'—'tepid emotion and many aims'.[5] Occult preoccupations increased anxiety about a coming apocalypse; unrequited love led to sexual stress which he relieved by masturbating, leaving him guilty and exhausted; political activism, into which he was drawn by Maud Gonne, could erupt into criminal violence, as he had seen in Parnell Square in June; and meanwhile, also, his London friends, the poets Lionel Johnson and Ernest Dowson, were sinking into drink and the delirium of unfocused lives driven only by appetite or addiction. Lady Gregory's air of dignity, a virtue she cultivated; the relaxed air of her house at Coole, with its centuries-old books bound in leather and vellum; and the attraction of a tangible ideal in the form of an Irish theatre—all these were compelling to someone whose romantic personality drew him to forms of mystical idealism or extremism at the expense of reality and practical objects.

Lady Gregory's letter went out to all her friends and her appeal won support from such as Aubrey de Vere, the Wordsworthian poet who lived at Curragh Chase, Co. Limerick, and who had, many years before, written movingly of the Famine; J. P. Mahaffy at Trinity, mentor and tutor of Oscar Wilde; W. H. Lecky, the historian of the Anglo-Irish of the eighteenth century; and many others, including Douglas Hyde, the president of the Gaelic League, John Redmond, leader of the Irish Parliamentary Party, John O'Leary, the old Fenian, and Emily Lawless, the poet and novelist. Lecky proved practically useful to the new movement. He was a member of Parliament at Westminster for Trinity College and drafted a clause for a Local Government (Ireland) Bill which went through the House in July 1898, whereby an old Act of Parliament from the reign of George III prohibiting theatrical performances, except for charity, in buildings other than those licensed by royal patent was amended. Lecky's amendment allowed for performances which would aid science, literature, or the fine arts 'exclusively'. Hence, the Irish *Literary* Theatre, which was what the new grouping was called.

It was not as if there was no Irish theatre in Dublin at the time. There were the productions of J. W. Whitbread at the Queen's Theatre, which mixed patriotism, melodrama, and spectacle. Reading the accounts of these by Joseph Holloway, the architect and theatre-enthusiast (whose theatrical recollections run to hundreds of volumes in the National Library of Ireland), one is struck by how exciting and thrilling these productions at the Queen's must have been. Whitbread mounted and acted in revivals of Boucicault, as, for example, in a production of *Arrah-na-Pogue* in September 1898. Holloway says that 'the Queen's is the home of Irish drama', and that the audience at such shows 'knows every line of the text and every bit of by-play in the various parts, [and] it sees that it gets the full value for its money, or lets those on the stage know why'.[6] The Holloway accounts also reveal how the popular theatre of this period often strained to create theatrical effects which would be as spectacular as possible. In *Arrah-na-Pogue*, for instance, the wedding scene was staged by opening the gates at the rear of the theatre, to allow the audience to see the walls of Trinity College and an actual laneway, up which the wedding party came on horses and carts. This search for verisimilitude and gripping effects reveals a stagecraft longing for the fluidity and realism of film. Whitbread, an English actor-manager, also himself wrote popular plays on patriotic themes, such as his *Wolfe Tone* which ran for four weeks in early 1898, or *The Irishman*, later that year. But there was also Max Goldberg's *The Secrets of the Harem* (1898) which, Holloway tells us, featured an English officer nobly defending a Christian maiden by wrapping her in the Union Jack and defying the infidels to violate it.

There were Irish plays, therefore, alongside rival pieces designed to appeal to British or Imperial patriotism; but what Dublin did not have was a living theatre reflecting the literary and artistic developments of the day, such as Jack Thomas Grein's Independent Theatre Club in London (founded 1891), which championed Ibsen and first staged G. B. Shaw; or the Théâtre Libre of André Antoine, founded in 1887 in Paris.

Edward Martyn, the Comte de Basterot's neighbour, was a student of Irish, and a committed cultural nationalist. As well as being interested in Gaelic culture, he combined a devout Catholicism with a cultivated and knowledgeable literary sensibility; and he also thought that theatre should, as in Ibsen, address psychological and social issues. Although his literary and artistic tastes were, in many respects, antithetical to those of Yeats, nevertheless he agreed to become a founding member of the Irish Literary Theatre and to give his Ibsenite study of landlordism, *The Heather Field*, to the new company, to be staged in tandem with Yeats's *The Countess Cathleen*.

Enter George Moore. Moore was Martyn's cousin, and, like him and Lady Gregory, a landowner, with a family estate in Co. Mayo. Moore had left the estate in the charge of his brother Maurice while he pursued a literary career first in Paris, then in London. He had had some considerable success, in particular with *Esther Waters* (1893), a realistic novel portraying the fortitude and steadfastness of the heroine, who has an illegitimate son, and who survives a disastrous marriage to an alcoholic and a gambler. His study of her quiet resolve in the face of the compulsions of addiction owes something to Émile Zola, whom Moore knew in France and greatly admired. But for some years now Moore had lost artistic direction and was struggling with an almost pathological revulsion against England and what he thought of as English imperialist acquisitiveness greed. He had even grown sick of the English language, which he had come to think of as exhausted by overuse and decadence, describing it in a characteristically Mooreish exaggeration as a 'woolly language without a verbal system'.[7] This revulsion he transmuted into an enthusiasm for the Irish literary movement and the Irish language, and he describes in *Ave*, the first volume of *Hail and Farewell*, his auto-biographical reminiscence of his involvement in the Irish Literary Revival, how Yeats's evocations of Ireland's artistic and spiritual destiny in a world grown over-sophisticated and remote from primal energies entranced him during long conversations in Arthur Symons's rooms in London. Strangely, Moore the arch-realist, and one-time detractor of Ireland and all things Irish (as in *Parnell and his Island*, 1887), had become susceptible to Yeats's cultural nationalism and idealistic symbolism. He once, he tells us in *Ave*, actually saw what he believed to be an emanation of the female spirit of Ireland, Cathleen Ni Houlihan, during a visit to the Burren in Co. Clare.[8]

Yeats said that Martyn and Moore were 'bound one to the other by mutual contempt'[9], but one must make allowance here for Yeats's own later antagonism towards Moore. Martyn invited his cousin to rehearsals of *The Heather Field* but Moore did not miss the opportunity of poking his nose into the rehearsals of *The Countess Cathleen* as well. He relished, mischievously, the eccentricities of the production style of the director Florence Farr. She was an actress in London and a well-known, even notorious social figure, a 'New Woman' who had played the female lead in Shaw's *Widowers' Houses* (1892), and she became the playwright's mistress for a time. Shaw remarked that 'she attached no more importance to what you call love-affairs than Casanova or Frank Harris'.[10] She had also produced Yeats's *Land of Heart's Desire* (1894) at the Avenue Theatre in London, financed by Miss Annie Horniman, later to become the patron of the Abbey Theatre. All three were in the Order of the Golden Dawn. Yeats and Florence Farr had a love affair in 1904, and he later told his wife Georgie Hyde-Lees that Farr was someone to whom he could tell everything. A photograph of her, kept in the University of Reading theatre archive, shows her reclining in a hammock in a fluted Grecian dress, loosely flowing round her long legs, her hair up in a braid in a classic Hellenic style. The languorousness of this pose is not much in evidence in Moore's account of her surprising technique while directing *The Countess Cathleen*:

[an] actress walked up the stage and stood there looking contemptuously at Miss [Farr], who laid herself down on the floor and began speaking through the chinks. Her dramatic intention was so obscure that perforce I had to ask her what it was, and learnt that she was evoking hell.

The reason for this was that two of the characters in the play are devils disguised as merchants, so she was, presumably, trying to create an authentic demonic atmosphere. Moore was unimpressed and said to her (according to his account): 'But the audience will think you are trying to catch cockroaches.'[11]

Meanwhile Edward Martyn had asked a friend of his (a 'friar' according to Moore) to vet Yeats's play for its theological accuracy. This succeeded in stirring up a hornets' nest. Although Yeats gained the approval of a Fr. William Barry of

Wallingford (he compared the play to Calderón), and eventually managed to pacify the two cousins who seemed intent on having a row about principles of freedom and orthodoxy, the word went out that there was something heretical about the play that the Irish Literary Theatre were to mount on 8 May 1899 at the Antient Concert Rooms in Great Brunswick (now Pearse) Street.

Frank Hugh O'Donnell, an opponent of Yeats's from way back (he once, during a political meeting, threw a chair at Yeats's old friend and mentor, the Fenian John O'Leary), wrote a pamphlet, *Souls for Gold*, which misrepresented the arguments of the demon tempters in the play as Yeats's own. It also attacked Yeats's depiction of the peasantry of Ireland 'of the old days' as being 'like a sordid tribe of black devil-worshippers and fetish-worshippers on the Congo or the Niger'— this presumably representing the greatest insult O'Donnell could imagine being thrown at 'holy' Ireland. The pamphlet (the text of two letters by O'Donnell attacking the play as a slur upon Irish probity) was circulated all over Dublin and put through people's letter-boxes. This ensured maximum publicity for the opening night but also made it inevitable that there would be trouble. Yeats, aware from his first-hand experience of the Jubilee Riots of the ease with which public disorder could erupt in Dublin, asked for (and got) protection from the Dublin Metropolitan Police.

Moore did not attend the opening night but arrived from London the following day, when he was shocked to discover that Yeats had brought in some native Irish speakers from Galway, to make a realistic *caoine* (keen) or death-wail over the body of the Countess at the end of the play. Moore, typically, is very caustic about this. In his account the hecklers in the gallery, incited by O'Donnell's pamphlet, shouted at the actors, while, for the first time ever in Irish cultural history, a *caoine* was being staged using singers from the Gaeltacht. The uproar, Moore says, made him 'really frightened'; but it must also have been hilarious.[12] Among those in the gallery, not taking part in the heckling, was James Joyce.

The following night, 9 May, Martyn's play was staged. This was a complete contrast to the mythological and moralistic dreamscape of Yeats's miracle play, although the theme of self-sacrifice is evident in both works. In *The Heather Field* Carden Tyrrell has an overwhelming obsession with his land. Grace, his wife, longs to see him adjust himself to worldly concerns and material advancement, whereas he wants to devote his energies to the reclamation of an infertile heather field. The mood and tenor of the play is grim; Tyrrell's resoluteness and dedication have an iron fatality about them. The sense of character as a fated set of reactions unable to cope with necessity is Ibsen-like in its stern focus, and this materialist realism had a readier appeal to the audience than did Yeats's romantic evocations of the soul and the forces that seek to entrap it. Holloway's diary records his and the audience's excitement at *The Heather Field*'s immediacy: he calls it 'a work of real dramatic grit'.[13]

The National Literary Society, of which the Irish Literary Theatre was a strategic offshoot, published a journal, *Beltaine* (meaning May and referring to the old Irish festival of Bealtaine marking the spring), which mixed Yeatsian ideals with discussion of the more immediately contemporary concerns of Ibsen and the kind of modern theatre gaining recognition amongst urban European audiences. Yeats, who edited the journal, wrote, in a piece entitled 'The Theatre', that modern drama (and here he is thinking of Ibsen) arouses a 'sympathy of the nerves', whereas the only thing that will restore the stage to its 'greatness' is ritual which will recall 'words to their ancient sovereignty'.[14] What Yeats wanted from the stage was spiritual energy: at a dinner at the Shelbourne Hotel on 11 May, hosted by the *Daily Express*'s editor T. P. Gill, he said that he and his friends wished to 'spiritualize the patriotism and drama of [his] country'.[15] This he wanted to do through powerful speech rather than grim analysis in the manner of Ibsen. The 'Theatre' essay speaks of the red-haired orator John F. Taylor repeating some mediocre political verses, but doing so in 'a voice that went through one like flame'.[16] This fire and energy, united with subtle thought and a respect for traditional myth, legend, and folklore, was what he hoped would materialize in the Irish Literary Theatre. Even at this stage, however, Yeats is aware that it is unlikely his kind of theatre will prevail. In 'Plans and Methods' in *Beltaine*, for example, he says that if his writers appeal to those in the audience who remember the songs of J. J. Callanan and Edward Walsh (two translators of Irish folk song), Gaelic legend, or to those who love good literature from any country, then the writers will not mind if other people 'are bored'.[17] Not exactly a recipe for popular success, and signalling, at the very outset, Yeats's awareness that the kind of theatre he wanted was what he would later call the antithesis, or 'anti-self', of the Ireland of his time. His national theatre, even then, involved a defiance of at least a considerable portion of the nation it sought to animate.

Martyn was being proclaimed, in Dublin, as a great dramatist, but when *The Heather Field* was staged at Edward Terry's Theatre in London on 6 June it met with a very cool reception: 'a drama of drainage' according to the *Daily Telegraph*.[18] Plans were being laid for the second season which was to put on two plays by Martyn, *Maeve* and *The Tale of a Town*, along with Alice Milligan's *The Last Feast of the Fianna*. In a mood of increasing confidence the Gaiety Theatre was booked for 19–20 February 1900. But there were problems with *The Tale of a Town*, which Martyn completed before his trip to Bayreuth to attend performances of Wagner's *The Ring* with Moore in the summer of 1899. When he had finished he sent the script to Moore, whose reaction was unambiguous. He wrote back to Martyn from London: 'There is not one act in the five you have sent me which, in my opinion, could interest any audience—Irish, English or Esquimaux.'[19] After writing this to his cousin, Moore was, by his own account, seized with remorse, but when he joined Martyn at Victoria Station to set off on the first leg of their journey to Bayreuth, he found him quite serene, and, apparently, not at all put out by his cousin's gibe: 'huge and puffy, his back to the engine, his belly curling splendidly between his short fat thighs, his straw hat perched on the top of his head.'[20] Attempts by Moore on the journey to get Martyn to discuss the play failed to disturb his cousin's enjoyment of the continental landscape, Martyn being more interested in the scenes that inspired Hobbema and Ruysdael than in the structure of *The Tale of a Town*.

After the Bayreuth trip Moore (again according to his account) parted company with Martyn in Antwerp to continue into Holland with two women artists whom he calls 'Florence' (Ethel Walker) and 'Stella' (Clara Christian), arranging to return to Tillyra in a month to work on *The Tale of a Town*. When he did return Yeats was staying at Coole with Lady Gregory. Yeats visited Tillyra, and read them his complex symbolic play *The Shadowy Waters*, which he had been working on for years. Moore describes it as being 'laden to the gunnel with Fomorians', symbols of indeterminacy and threat, and tells us he offered to help Yeats to 'redeem it' from its mythological tangle. But this collaboration was doomed, because Moore was unable to sympathize with the poet's inadequately realized symbolic system, describing Yeats's mind as being like the wheel of a carriage when it is being washed: lifted off the ground it spins at the smallest touch of the mop because, Moore says wickedly, it is not 'turning anything'.[21]

There is no doubt but that here, between Yeats and Moore, we have a relationship in which each individual was, at this stage, strenuously attempting to find grounds for mutuality: Moore because he had grown tired of the pattern of his life in England, Yeats because he thought Moore's consequence as a writer would bring added prestige to the literary movement in Ireland, now entering its new, theatrical, phase. It is obvious from their later commentaries that there was a profound antagonism between them (Moore even saying that Yeats and his cousin Martyn were alike in being 'subaltern souls'[22]) so that they could never accomplish jointly anything of lasting worth. But they tried, and when the complicated meanings of *The Shadowy Waters* proved impervious to Moore's attempts at structural reshaping, they turned, in a kind of relief, to the work of a third party, Martyn's *The Tale of a Town*, which Yeats tells us he and Lady Gregory found 'crude', 'childish', and 'ridiculous'.[23]

Yeats told Martyn, bluntly, that the play was 'entirely impossible', Moore later confessing that his own behaviour was like that of a literary inquisitor. Martyn washed his hands of the whole thing and told them they could do what they liked with the play; they began work immediately. Moore's enthusiasm and dogged energy as they worked exhausted Yeats, and he would often have to lie down to rest. Ironically, Yeats stayed at Tillyra, Martyn's home, and he and Moore remodelled the play over a few days, changing the title to *The Bending of the Bough*.

The second season of the Irish Literary Theatre opened on 19 February 1900 at the Gaiety Theatre with Martyn's *Maeve* (published in 1899) and Alice Milligan's *The Last Feast of the Fianna*, the latter a narrative recitation in different voices about the mood of the Fianna after Fionn Mac Cumhail has allowed Diarmuid to die, and taken his love Grania back as his consort.

Alice Milligan's recited verse tale had considerable impact: here was the first theatrical representation of Irish legendary figures for a Dublin audience, the whole thing sonorously declaimed to Gaelic music composed by the author's sister, Mrs C. Milligan-Fox. Alice Milligan had, in fact, acted in a performance of an anonymous play, *The Passing of Conall*, at a Gaelic festival in Letterkenny, Co. Donegal, on 18 November 1898 which included a scene of St Patrick at Tara trans-lated into Irish by Patrick O'Byrne of Killybegs. This scene must be the first (recorded) instance of the staging of a dramatic piece in Irish. The recitation at the Gaiety is also notable in that it featured the old Fenian John O'Leary as one of Fiann's band at the banquet.[24]

Martyn's *Maeve* mixed the social and psychological realism of Ibsen with Yeatsian symbolism. One of the characters, Peg Inerney, a vagrant, was created by Martyn after he had heard Yeats and Lady Gregory talk of women they had met while collecting folklore in Galway and Clare, who have the capacity to cross over into the otherworld of the *sí* (or fairyland) while asleep. Peg persuades the heroine, Maeve O'Heynes, to choose the world of the *sí* rather than marry an Englishman. Some of the audience, from Holloway's account, found the whole thing hilarious: Maeve's wistful longing for the otherworld caused 'irreverent mirth', one old playgoer remarking as he left the theatre that they 'ought to have clapped that one in an asylum'.[25]

The following night saw the production of Martyn's rewritten *The Tale of a Town*, with Moore credited as author. In the Yeats–Moore rewrite the setting was shifted from the west of Ireland to Scotland, and the conflict is now between two competing borough councils rather than between Irish and English interests, as Martyn had first written it. If anything, the distancing effect heightened the im-pact on an audience sensitized to Anglo-Irish conflicts and differences. Holloway wryly remarked that 'Northhaven' and 'Southhaven' were evidently representa-tive of 'poor Ireland's struggle against mighty England' and that 'this construc-tion was to be put on the actions and sayings of the various characters and [the audience] applauded many of the passages right heartily on this account, as they discovered clever home thrusts in them'.[26] The 'home thrusts' were most likely from Yeats's pen, as amongst the reasons for the fatigue he experienced in the col-laboration were the endless explanations necessary for Moore about contempor-ary Irish politics. The plot seemed to refer to recent negotiations within the Irish Parliamentary Party under its leader John Redmond. Yeats himself acknow-ledged the 'political epigrams' in the play were his, as well as 'certain bitter sen-tences' in a speech by the young firebrand Jasper Dean at the opening of the play.[27] Yeats and Moore modelled Dean's mentor, Ralf Kirwan, on Standish James O'Grady, the antiquarian, novelist, and political activist, who, at this time, was extolling Ireland's legendary past as a prophecy of a dynamic energy awakening in the modern world. Years later, in the poem 'Beautiful Lofty Things', Yeats re-called a drunken speech of O'Grady at this time, during which he declaimed 'high nonsensical words'.[28]

At a celebratory luncheon in the Shelbourne Hotel after the run, hosted by the National Literary Society, Douglas Hyde, president of the Gaelic League, who was devoted to the 'de-Anglicization' of Ireland and the restoration of the Irish language, gave the encomium. He enthused about the Irish Literary Theatre, saying that it was trying, like many other agencies of the time (he was thinking of the Gaelic League), to 'embody and perpetuate Irish feeling, genius, and modes of thought'. It was, he declared, a *national* theatre (echoing the ideals and sentiments of Yeats and Lady Gregory at that meeting in Duras House in 1897), and he went on to clarify what he meant by that term: 'By national I mean something absolutely uncontentious, non-political, and non-sectarian.'[29] These sentiments aroused a chorus of approbation. Hyde clearly felt that the country was on the verge of a new 'national' (in the specialized sense he used it) breakthrough and associated the three plays they had seen that week with the recent speech by Robert F. Starkie, a member of the Board of National Education, advocating the inclusion of Irish as an examined subject in the curriculum in the teeth of ignorant opposition from J. P. Mahaffy and Robert Atkinson of Trinity College. Hyde's speech was followed by one from Moore, which expressed his enthusiasm for the Irish language (while also saying that he was too old and too busy actually to learn it), and giving notice that the following season would include another play, like *The Last Feast of the Fianna*, based on the Fionn cycle of tales; and, significantly, a play in Irish, a translation of Yeats's *The Land of Heart's Desire*. This last project never came to fruition.

Martyn also spoke at this luncheon and said, rather ominously, that he was proud to be associated in the programme with Alice Milligan, and then sat down. Sometime thereafter, when Yeats broached the question of funding for the 1901 season with Martyn, the reply he got was decisive: 'Henceforth I will pay for nobody's plays but my own.'[30] Yeats had foreseen that there probably would be difficulty in retaining Martyn's financial support, given the fact that his play had been so ruthlessly transformed for the 1900 season. However, Yeats lost no time in seeking other sources of money: in a letter to Lady Gregory dated 31 January he had already identified Miss Annie Horniman as a potential patron.[31]

Miss Horniman was a Manchester tea-heiress and a Quaker by upbringing, but this did not prevent her from pursuing fashionable occult interests. She was, along with Yeats and Maud Gonne, a member of the Order of the Golden Dawn and had disapproved of MacGregor Mathers. In 1900 her judgement seemed to be vindicated when Mathers broke into open conflict with the London branch of the Order, sending the young Aleister Crowley (then involved in a homosexual scandal) as his emissary from Paris to Hammersmith to take over the Isis Urania Temple at 36 Blythe Road. He was successfully repulsed by Yeats and another occultist, Edmund Hunter (who was also, usefully, a trained boxer), and they suspended Mathers from the Order at a meeting on 21 April.[32] Yeats and Horniman became colleagues in the reform of the Order, but a problem arose in that Florence Farr and Yeats's potential patron hated each other, Horniman accusing the actress who had played the poet Aleel in *The Countess Cathleen* in 1899 of dangerous occult proclivities, revealed in her wish to incorporate rituals into the Order from the Egyptian *Book of the Dead*.[33]

In the summer Yeats returned to Coole and in the autumn worked on *Diarmuid and Grania* with Moore, Lady Gregory placing a seat under a weeping ash in the walled garden where the collaborators could sit. She, wisely, tried to get them to work separately, as they found it difficult to agree over the most basic matters, such as the style the play should be written in. Yeats wanted dialect, in order to create a peasant Grania, but Moore, even more preposterously, thought they should use the language of the Bible. At one stage they seriously contemplated having Moore write the play in French, a language he knew colloquially, then getting Lady Gregory to translate the French into English; Tadhg Ó Donnchadha would then turn this into Irish; Lady Gregory would translate this third version back into English; and Yeats would complete the process by 'putting style' on the whole thing. Yeats woke Moore up one night at Coole to reveal this brainstorm.[34]

These technicalities about the process and style are comic, with hindsight, but they reveal how concerned were Yeats, Lady Gregory, and indeed Moore too, to find a style adequate for the representation on the Irish stage of a legend from the Irish past, something never attempted hitherto. There was a concern that a commodious and indigenous form of language should be created in order to translate images from Ireland's mystic past into terms that would evoke those images in the shared mind of an immediate present. This proposed translation across three languages was animated by some instinct that, were it feasible to find the right language, something intrinsically Irish, national, personal, and ancestral would be expressed. Each one saw this in his own way, Moore, characteristically, in a sex-obsessed manner. These were his thoughts (or so he said later) on the train to Coole to start work with Yeats: 'Athlone came into sight, and I looked upon the Shannon with a strange and new tenderness, thinking that it might have been in a curtain bed of rushes that Grania lifted her kirtle, the sweetness of her legs blighting in Diarmuid all memory of his oath of fealty to Finn.'[35] However, it was not long before Moore grew tired of the way in which Lady Gregory fussed over Yeats at Coole; in any case, his habit of speaking unabashedly about his sexual conquests made him a difficult house guest. He decided to leave Yeats and Lady Gregory to the collection of folklore which had become a regular feature of life during their summers, and went to Paris to draft the first act of the play, in French. So, in spite of the jocular tone in which he recounts the linguistic arabesques in later years, he does seem to have fallen in with the first part of the plan, at least.

The play was nearing completion by October 1900, leaving Maud Gonne 'breathless with excitement' when she read it.[36] Moore and Yeats wanted a great actress to play Grania, and on 26 October they went to see Mrs Patrick Campbell in her dressing room at the Royalty Theatre in London, where she was starring in Frank Harris's *Mr and Mrs Daventry*. She was very enthusiastic about the play, but after some complicated negotiations on the Dublin and London runs and how they should be timed, Moore fell out with her during a brief illness of Yeats's.

This manœuvre may have been staged in order to draw Yeats into the kind of 'surreal public confrontation' (in Roy Foster's words[37]) that Moore enjoyed, but whatever the motivation, the collaborators toiled on, though fractiously. Meanwhile Martyn grew increasingly anxious about the morality of the play. Moore had reworked the legend to draw in very contemporary issues: psychology, sexual freedom, and women's rights. However, Miss Horniman, setting aside possible disapproval from her Quaker relations, guaranteed the next season of the Literary Theatre against loss, thus relieving Yeats of financial worries.

Frank Benson's company, known for their Shakespearean productions at Stratford and London, were engaged to act the play and the Gaiety Theatre was again booked for the 1901 season, this time for the autumn. There was an agreement that Mrs Campbell would act in a London production, but that was never to be. The rehearsals for the Dublin production took place in Birmingham, the English actors finding enormous difficulty with the Gaelic names of the characters. Grania was being pronounced 'Grainyar' or 'Grawnia'; but the real challenge was Caoilte, variously attempted as 'Kaoltay', 'Wheelsher' (the latter apparently Yeats's phonetic suggestion), 'Wheelchair', 'Coldtea', or 'Quilty'.[38] Moore, disastrously, had a hand in the direction.

The play was given on 21 October, followed by *Casadh an tSúgáin*, a Gaelic play by Douglas Hyde from a scenario by Yeats, and performed by the Keating Branch of the Gaelic League in Dublin.

The main play was a complete flop, not helped by the fact that Benson, who was playing Diarmuid, had formed the idea that he could increase verisimilitude by bringing a live sheep on stage during a shearing scene. He was persuaded by Moore to use a kid-goat instead, but it too proved troublesome, at one point eating the ivy off the scenery. Also, some of the dialogue, perhaps because of a desire on the part of the collaborators to create an ideal mythological atmosphere which would also have psychological and emotional immediacy, offered hostages to the fortune of common sense. When Diarmuid said to Grania, 'The fools are laughing at us', they brought the house down. Grania was described by the reviewer in the *Evening Herald* 'as being like someone with an M.A. degree from Boston, while Diarmuid seemed as if he'd read Herbert Spencer'.[39] Violet Martin, who attended the play, writing to her cousin Edith Somerville in Cork, described Laban, an old druidess, as 'a stout lady in a teagown and conversational English accent . . . [prophesying] out of her spinning wheel'.[40]

The second, brief, play, in Irish was, however, an unqualified success, with Hyde himself playing the part of the wandering poet Hanrahan. Luckily, the original idea, that Benson's company should be trained to speak Gaelic phonetically, was abandoned.

This evening was, as it turned out, the last evening of the Irish Literary Theatre. It represented a deliberate attempt at bringing Gaelic mythology, folklore, and language onto the Dublin stage. In spite of the mirth inadvertently aroused by *Diarmuid and Grania*, a group of young Gaelic Leaguers, all nationalists from the gods, wanted to unyoke the carriage Yeats and Maud Gonne were taking to a supper party afterwards, and pull them through the streets.

As in the previous seasons, Yeats edited a journal to appear in conjunction with the productions, calling it *Samhain* this time (the Irish festival at the beginning of winter) seeing as the plays were produced in the autumn. His essay, 'Windlestraws', mentions a number of Gaelic plays that have been written in the recent past, and then concludes on a valedictory note, saying that the Irish Literary Theatre has come to an end 'in its present shape'.[41]

As the curtain fell on the production of *Diarmuid and Grania* at the Gaiety a specially commissioned funeral dirge by Elgar was played. Amongst the listeners was John Millington Synge. Yeats had met him in Paris as far back as December 1896, and advised him then or later to cease writing criticism of French literature and go and live on the Aran Islands where he would find a life that had yet to receive literary expression in English. Synge's family, a Church of Ireland one, had links with the islands through clerical appointments, but he seems to have been inspired by Yeats's advice and began spending his summers on Aran from 1898. By the time he came to Dublin to see the Irish Literary Theatre's plays in autumn 1901, he had written much of his prose work *The Aran Islands*, though it remained unpublished until 1907. At least one publisher, Alfred Routh, was put off by what he regarded as its 'formlessness'.[42]

Synge, in an article in *L'Européen* on 31 May 1902, gave an account of the 1901 performances of the Irish Literary Theatre at the Gaiety. He described *Casadh an tSúgáin* as 'une petite pièce charmante', but also remarked on the striking effect created by the singing of Irish songs from the gods during the interval. The plot of *Casadh* on *tSúgáin*, in which the poet Hanrahan is ejected from a closed, tight community, by the device of getting him to back out the door twisting a hay-rope, is an anticipation of the way Christy Mahon is treated by the 'fools' of Mayo in Synge's *Playboy*.

In the *Samhain* for 1901 Yeats makes mention of a Mr Fay, who 'has got together an excellent little company which plays both in Gaelic and English'.[43] This was William G. Fay, who along with his brother Frank had extensive experience of the fit-up companies which toured Ireland in the late nineteenth century. At one time William Fay had been in *Uncle Tom's Cabin* with an American black actor called R. Lewis. In the 1890s the Fays formed a number of touring ensembles, such as 'W. G. Fay's Comedy Combination', and employed actors such as Dudley Digges and Sara Allgood, later to be players with the Abbey Theatre. In autumn 1900 William Fay directed a play in Irish for a new radical organization for Irish women, Inghinidhe na hÉireann (Daughters of Ireland), which Maud Gonne had founded and of which she became president. The play was *An Tobar Draoidheachta* by Pádraig S. Ó. Duinnín, the Jesuit and brilliant lexicographer. So that when George Moore found himself nonplussed trying to direct the Gaelic League actors in *Casadh an tSúgáin*, for the 1901 performances of the Literary Theatre, William Fay was called in to take over.

His brother Frank, a theatre critic for the *United Irishman*, found the acting in *Diarmuid and Grania* 'execrable', 'vulgar', and 'worse than useless' because the players were English, their accents and style making them incongruous in the parts they tried to play; a point of view, incidentally, not remote from that taken by Violet Martin in her letter to her cousin. But Hyde in *Casadh an tSúgáin* Fay thought 'in great form', and 'irresistible'. Nevertheless, there was a hiatus; a break of some kind seemed necessary. Moore was growing ever more intractable and (to Yeats) maddening. His baffling waywardness was in evidence when, in an interview in the *Freeman's Journal* (13 November 1901), he called for clerical censorship of the Irish theatre in order that it might free itself from the vulgar tyranny of popular opinions, and proclaimed that the Irish theatre was badly in need of new plays by Catholic priests. If this was a joke, Yeats did not get it, or chose not to. On 14 November the paper carried a statement by Yeats that Moore makes his 'proposal on his own authority'.[44] There would be no more collaborations and mutual suspicion would deepen into steadfast hate.

As James Flannery argues in *W. B. Yeats and the Idea of a Theatre* (1976) the ideal of a 'national' theatre was in the air at this time. The Gaelic League was extraordinarily popular: no more than seven years after its establishment in 1893 there were hundreds of branches throughout the country and An tOireachtas, a national festival of Gaelic art, was inaugurated in 1897. In 1901–2 more than twelve plays in Irish were presented, according to Pádraig Pearse, the future leader of the 1916 Rising. The *Leader*, founded by the nationalist firebrand D. P. Moran (a model for Joyce's Citizen in the Cyclops episode of *Ulysses*) furiously argued for an 'Irish Ireland' and against 'West-British shoneenism' (i.e. little John Bullery). Moran advocated using Irish homespun, while Arthur Griffith's *United Irishman* (founded 1899) attacked Irish businessmen who advertised in Britain for senior positions in their firms. Writing in Griffith's *United Irishman* on 1 May 1901 Frank Fay attacked the Irish Literary Theatre on grounds which Moran or Griffith would have approved:

Let Mr. Yeats give us a play in verse or prose that will rouse this sleeping land. There is a herd of Saxon and other swine fattening on us. They must be swept into the sea along with the pestilent crowd of West-Britons with which we are troubled . . . This land is ours, but we have ceased to realise the fact. We want a drama that will make us realise it.[45]

This hit the mark, and Yeats responded to this crude nationalism with surprising alacrity. He and Lady Gregory set to work on *Cathleen Ni Houlihan* that summer in Coole. In the event the play was mostly Lady Gregory's.

In August 1901 Maud Gonne's Inghinidhe na hÉireann commissioned W. G. Fay's latest ensemble, the Ormond Dramatic Society, to stage *The Deliverance of Red Hugh* by Alice Milligan at the Antient Concert Rooms, along with *Eilís agus an Bhean Déirce*, by P. T. McGinley, as part of a pan-Celtic festival. The *Freeman's Journal* reports that there were six encores.

All these elements—politics, cultural nationalism, personal inclinations, Yeats's continuing wish to take a leading role in the development of an Irish drama and to create a distinctive Irish literary culture—constellated around the Fays. Yeats went to the Fay production at the Antient Concert Rooms, and came away, he later wrote, with his 'head on fire'; in particular the careful direction of the delivery, using the actual speech inflections of the actors, but making them more emphatic and deliberate, made him wish to see his own plays so performed.[46]

In later years the Fay brothers themselves and George Russell claimed that Yeats and Lady Gregory took too much of the credit for the formation of an Irish 'national' theatre; and Maud Gonne in 1903, in an angry letter to Yeats, asserted that the real originators of the modern Irish drama were Inghinidhe na hÉireann.[47] James Cousins, a Belfast-born theosophist, even claimed that it was at a meeting that he arranged between Russell and the Fays, to discuss a possible production of a play Russell had started on the Deirdre theme, that the national theatre was really begun. It is perfectly clear, however, amidst this buzz of claims and counterclaims, that while the origins of any development of real human or artistic significance are difficult to trace exactly, it is entirely reasonable to say that the chief energy for the establishment of an Irish national theatre was Yeats's, and that he was sustained in this, selflessly, by Lady Gregory. She even allowed him, not without misgivings, to take the credit for the play she really had written and which was to be the great success of these early years, *Cathleen Ni Houlihan*. In a memorandum Yeats prepared for the patent inquiry in 1904, when Miss Horniman financed the Abbey, Yeats summarized this development of 1902: 'we started afresh with a company of Irish actors.'[48] And this of course was crucial: with the Fays Yeats began a theatre with actors who had Irish accents (and Irish temperaments), and who would be less likely to pronounce 'Caoilte' as 'Wheelchair'.

The first act of a play by Russell on the Deirdre story had appeared in the Christmas journal for 1901 for the Irish Agricultural Organization Society, which he edited. This subject, mythological, legendary, and treated by a poet admired for his Celtic mysticism, appealed to the Fays, who got his permission to perform a completed version at the meeting which James Cousins arranged. And meanwhile Lady Gregory's Cathleen theme united folklore and patriotism in a heady brew. Early in 1902 Maud Gonne agreed to act the main part, but this owed as much to William Fay's involvement with Inghinidhe na hÉireann as it did to her friendship with Yeats.[49] Fay, as well as directing their performances for the pan-Celtic festival in August, had given acting classes to members of the society.

'W. G. Fay's National Dramatic Company' staged the two plays in St Teresa's Hall, owned by the Carmelites of the nearby church, in Clarendon Street, opening on 2 April 1902. Russell's *Deirdre*, atmospheric and poetic, was acted behind a thin gauze to create an ethereal effect. Russell himself designed the costumes which were run up by Inghinidhe na hÉireann, and he painted the scenery in his luminous flowing colours. It was, according to Yeats, writing a few days later to

Lady Gregory at Coole, 'thin and faint', like 'wall decoration', but he liked it on the whole, 'strange to say'. The other play, his and Lady Gregory's *Cathleen Ni Houlihan*, evinced a wholly different response from him: Maud Gonne was 'magnificent', exhibiting a 'weird power' in the tragic main part.[50] Máire Nic Shiubhlaigh, who played Lavarcam, Deirdre's foster-mother, wrote in a manuscript lecture (probably that given in Galway in March 1948): 'it was all played behind a green gauze which gave a very weird effect we behind it couldn't see anyone in front which was an advantage for we were all very nervous.'[51]

This tiny play could not be simpler in its plot: an old woman comes to the Gillane household; it is 1796, the time of revolution; the young man of the household, Michael Gillane (played by Dudley Digges), is getting married but when he hears the old woman talking of her 'four green fields' that have been taken from her and of the sacrifices young men have made for her across the ages he is stirred; she leaves; news comes that the French have arrived in Killala harbour; and the young man goes to fight for Ireland. The old woman is seen leaving, but she is changed into a young girl, with the 'walk of a queen'. The play is, still, extraordinarily powerful, even on the page; in the theatre in 1902, when nationalist Ireland was like a powder-keg, it must have been devastating. Stephen Gwynn, a sober and urbane man of letters, was deeply disturbed and left the theatre wondering, he tells us, 'if such plays should be produced unless one was prepared for people to go out to shoot and be shot'[52], words echoed by Yeats in 1938 in 'The Man and the Echo':

> Did that play of mine send out
> Certain men the English shot?[53]

The play derived its power from its immediate and direct political message, but also because it drew upon a symbol or an archetype in Gaelic and nationalist tradition: that of Ireland imaged as an old woman who can be made young again by sacrifice and devotion to the cause of Irish freedom. The 'sean-bhean bhocht', the poor old woman, becomes the 'spéir-bhean' or goddess of Irish sovereignty in the Gregory/Yeats play as she had done in Gaelic *'aisling'* or vision poetry from the seventeenth century down. What was enacted on stage was a scene of transformation; what the play accomplished was also an act of translation, whereby emblems and figures out of the Irish cultural memory were carried over into the twentieth century and given immediate and shocking relevance. Modern Irish theatre begins here, with this performance of a play, of mostly psuedonymous authorship, written by two products of Anglo-Ireland, with a revolutionary feminist in the title role.

The sensibilities of Yeats and Lady Gregory had been opened to Gaelic tradition. Lady Gregory had the advantage of knowing a certain amount of Irish (she had been studying it, on and off, since her teenage years), but Yeats had an intuitive understanding of the structures and emotional significance of Gaelic folklore, mythology, and, even *sean-nós*—the native form of Irish singing which is highly dramatic and intensely declamatory. When he heard it at a Gaelic *feis* near Coole in June 1902 he said that the rhythm and intonation had planted themselves in his 'nerves and mind'.[54] *Cathleen ni Houlihan* showed that Lady Gregory and Yeats were in touch with reservoirs of feeling, imagery which they were capable of translating onto the stage, in shockingly realized form.

On 21 April 1902, writing from London, Yeats outlined his newly revised plans to Fay, making it plain that, from his point of view at least, Fay's 'National Dramatic Company' was a continuation of the Irish Literary Theatre:

> I want to make people understand the importance of the St. Theresa's Hall experiment, and to prepare them for future work. You might join in if you see a chance . . . I think we must [get] all the good plays we can from Cousins and Russell and anybody else, but carrying out our theories of the stage as rigorously as possible.[55]

Frank Fay and his brother offered to Yeats the possibility of creating something which the Irish Literary Theatre had failed to realize: a poetic drama, based upon Irish speech, that would work upon the nerves in the way Irish singing did. Frank Fay responded with enthusiasm to Yeats's intense interest in declamation and in reciting to the psaltery. This letter also intimates that there is a rich friend who is interested in his plans, and who would also subsidize a theatre which would advance Yeats's theories into practice. Although this friend is referred to as a 'he', it was in fact Miss Horniman. In an earlier letter (12 April) Yeats promises a new *Samhain*, so he is quite clearly thinking of any new venture as a development from where he began.

Fay's 'National Dramatic Company', fired by the success of their April performances, and encouraged by Yeats, met on a number of occasions and, after some discussion as to whether Russell or Yeats should be offered the presidency of the company, they decided to approach Russell, who declined, then offered it to Yeats, who was elected on 9 August 1902, at an inaugural meeting of the 'Irish National Theatre Society', as it now styled itself. The meeting took place at a small hall in Camden Street, its new base. The founding members were: the Fays, Dudley Digges, P. J. Kelly, Máire Nic Shiubhlaigh (Mary Walker), Máire T. Quinn, Helen Laird, Fred Ryan, James Starkey, and George Roberts. Russell, Maud Gonne, and Douglas Hyde were appointed vice-presidents; Edward Martyn was offered a vice-presidency, but declined. At this meeting the following were nominated as members of the Society: James Cousins, Frank Walker, Thomas Keohler, H. Norman, J. M. Synge, Padraic Colum, and Sara Allgood. Only at a later meeting was Lady Gregory elected, along with Udolphus Wright and Mary Garvey. The vice-presidencies of Maud Gonne and Douglas Hyde sustained vital connections between the Society and Inghinidhe na hÉireann and the Gaelic League.

Yeats himself, while becoming less revolutionary in politics, was growing more nationalist in spirit: at a dinner in London in May 1903 with some English colonial administrators, when asked what Britain should do in Ireland he replied: 'Nothing simpler, clear out.'

1902–1910
'Screeching in a straightened waistcoat'

Exit George Moore. Although he settled in Dublin in 1901, in order the more effectively to participate in the intellectual, cultural, and linguistic movement he believed to be under way in Ireland, his association with Yeats and Lady Gregory
was soon to end. Relentless in his enthusiasm, which he always seems to have
prosecuted with an undercurrent of mischief, he arranged for a performance, in
his garden in Upper Ely Place, of a play in Irish, *An Tincéar agus an tSídheóg*, on
19 May 1902. Directed by himself, it had Douglas Hyde its author in the leading
part, and Sinéad Ní Fhlannagáin (later Eamon de Valera's wife) was also in the
cast. W. B. Yeats was there, and his father John B. Yeats, as well as Russell, Edward
Martyn, and Alice Milligan. Yeats's father described the scene: there had been
a storm in the morning, but fortunately rain held off until nearly the end of the
play when umbrellas went up amidst the large crowd of perhaps two hundred
people.[1]

Around this time Yeats and Moore, strangely enough, given their difficult
working relationship on *Diarmuid and Grania*, discussed another collaboration,
this time on a theme to do with a religious zealot who rejects ordinary life, tries to
reform the practices of belief, and is eventually rejected by his society. Moore and
Yeats met at the *feis* near Coole at which Yeats was overwhelmed by the *sean-nós*
singer, who influenced his thinking about declamation and the psaltery. By now he
had accepted the presidency of the Irish National Dramatic Society at the request
of its secretary, Fred Ryan, and told Moore that he had to commit himself to the
furtherance of its interests and that his own development as a dramatist was crucial to this responsibility. Soon after this meeting Moore seems to have sent a
telegram to Yeats saying that he would get an injunction against him if Yeats
made use of the plot about the problems of belief which Moore claimed he had
devised. Angered and keen to protect his interests, as he saw them, Yeats with
Lady Gregory's help wrote *Where There is Nothing* in a fortnight at Coole, and
published it as a supplement to Arthur Griffith's *United Irishman*, thinking that
Moore would not dare to prosecute a nationalist newspaper, for fear he would get
his windows smashed. Afterwards John Quinn, an American lawyer friend of
Yeats's, and Arthur Symons, the London man of letters, tried to bring Moore and
Yeats together again, but Yeats walked out of Symons's flat, refusing to shake
Moore's hand. Moore took his revenge later, in *Hail and Farewell*, Yeats answering

in turn in *Autobiographies* and in the concluding verses of the volume *Responsibilities* (1914).

The Fays now took centre stage. William Fay had played the part of the young Michael Gillane in *Cathleen Ni Houlihan*, and Frank, his brother, the treacherous High King of Ulster, Concobar, in Russell's *Deirdre*. They were preparing for an autumn season in 1902, and Yeats, true to his word, was compiling the issue of *Samhain* he had promised them. Once again here there is mention of the *feis* near Coole that summer where he told Moore that he was now committed to the new phase of the movement the Fays had opened for him: 'the Irish Literary Theatre has given place to a company of Irish actors.'[2] He mentions a folk story told in Irish by a young girl, and goes on to argue that 'everything' must come back to the 'spoken word'; this gives the only true 'literary quality', which is the 'breath of men's mouths'.

Much fun has been made of Yeats's experiments with chanting, and with the psaltery he got Arnold Dolmetsch to make for Florence Farr and himself. In fact he was trying to create a radical orality in dramatic speech; this immediacy, if ordered and deliberate, would unite folk energy and the profundity of meditative chant. He was looking for 'abundance', 'extravagance', and 'imaginative acting' that can envision human nature free of 'arbitrary conditions'.[3] These high claims are not 'traditional' in any narrowly conceived sense of that term: rather is Yeats looking for a theatre of 'danger' (as he was later to call it[4]) but which would draw its energy from the vitality of speech, a feature which (he correctly divined) was a crucial element in traditional Irish singing. The autumn season of 1902 opened at the Antient Concert Rooms on 27 October with songs and stories (some translated from the Irish by Lady Gregory), reflecting Yeats's desire to recreate the vitality of oral tradition and its immediacy, qualities which he thought her *Cuchulain of Muirthemne*, published in May, had achieved on the page. These were followed by Florence Farr reciting some poems by Yeats and others to the psaltery; Yeats then lectured on this new rediscovery of the power of chant, a tradition of oral presentation of emotion which he traced back to Greece and Irish bardic tradition.

Instead of belittling these experiments (the usual response to Yeats's attempts to develop radical new voicings in the theatre) we might try to think through what Yeats was attempting to achieve: a theatrical experience in which words were released from their ordinariness and foregrounded as elements in a potential force-field of realization and energy. His essay on 'Magic', first published in 1901, was built upon the founding idea that the entire field of existence formed an occult unity, a cohesion hidden from all but those who have retained or recovered simplicity, or who have studied hard, imposing upon themselves the strictest discipline. This unity of being can be evoked by images and by the careful deployment of language: hence the moral significance of poetry and the social relevance of a theatre dedicated to the reconstruction of an ancient integrity. Yeats's idea of theatre originated in one of the governing principles of Platonic thought, expressed in the

Timaeus, where it is argued that it is possible to rebuild the damaged circuits in the human brain by thinking on the inherent unity in all being. Yeats's theatre was to be an arena where the broken circuits of Irish life and culture, connections dislocated by the disruptions of political and social disaster over hundreds of years, could again rebuild themselves. He was giving everything he could to this purpose, and he was attracted to the Fays because they, it seemed to him (and he was right), were instinctively closer to the broad flow of ordinary Irish life than he or Lady Gregory could be. He delighted in the way in which the Fays allowed their Dublin speech to inflect their declamations; the orthodoxy on the English (and Irish) stage was to expunge any trace of regional language other than for comic effect. The Fays, by contrast, drew energy for their cadences from the innate inflections of their own speech patterns. This was the source of their strength, and the reason Yeats was attracted to them. That this recognition by Yeats of their power was not a local obsession is borne out in their subsequent careers as working actors in the touring fit-ups in England, where they were valued by William Poel, William Archer, and others.

The flow of life Yeats recognized in the Fays, in its speech, habits of thought and feeling, carried within it deep memory-currents of Gaelic culture, a source Yeats knew he had to tap if the circuits were to repair themselves. Hence the singing, the psaltery (which looked like an Irish harp), the maximization of the force of the word. For Yeats, as Christopher Murray says, 'theatre was no idle business but the moulder of the people's very souls'.[5]

In 1902 Yeats's *Cathleen Ni Houlihan* was staged again, as was Russell's *Deirdre*, and there were new plays by James Cousins (*The Sleep of the King* and *The Racing Lug*), Fred Ryan (*The Laying of the Foundations*), P. T. McGinley (*Eilís agus an Bhean Déirce*), and a further collaboration between Yeats and Lady Gregory (*The Pot of Broth*). The programme opened on 27 October.

Cousins's *The Sleep of the King* was based on the early Irish tale *Echtra Conlai* (*The Adventure of Conlai*), a story recounted to the Belfast theosophist by Frank Fay when the Fay brothers visited the author earlier in the year, asking him to join the company. Cousins had already written *The Racing Lug*, a short play (in prose) based on a drowning in his mother's family in Carrickfergus. The Fays liked this play but wanted a verse drama to go with it, and Cousins obliged, quickly writing *The Sleep of the King* from Frank Fay's scenario. The latter's mythological theme, in which the oppression of reality is relaxed in order that the otherworld can exercise its allure, reflected Cousin's occult interests and the influence of Russell and Yeats. *The Racing Lug* was realistic, and made a strong emotional impact, with its depiction of the effect of a tragic death on a small, closely knit community. Fred Ryan's play, of which only one act has survived, dealt with corruption in municipal politics, and took an Ibsenite view of power-brokering in the Irish context, although the treatment was light-hearted and satirical rather than sombre.

There was now a new-found confidence in the theatre movement, in part deriving from the Fays' commitment, but also from Yeats's endorsement. These were

Irish actors, with Irish speech patterns, offering (if they could be trained) new exciting inflections, a dramatic power that would make poetic theatre come alive for ordinary people. Frank Fay wrote to Joseph Holloway on 6 November that the new company, with its headquarters at 34 Lower Camden Street (which the actors had refurbished themselves), if it could focus its energies, would rediscover a dramatic energy in Irish literature: 'it is only Irishmen who can write good plays in English. If you put aside *The Cenci* and Browning's plays, there have been no good plays written from Sheridan and Goldsmith to Oscar Wilde and Shaw, in English, in my opinion.'[6]

Although entrance to the Camden Street Theatre was through a narrow passageway often obstructed by egg-crates and beef carcasses, there was undoubtedly a sense of renewed beginnings, with Yeats relishing the challenge and pleasure of leadership and the enthusiasm of people quite different from those he knew in London or in the circles in which he moved in Ireland. Máire Nic Shiubhlaigh, in her memoir *The Splendid Years*, recalls this time. She describes the Camden Street Theatre as the first Irish theatre, where the 'foundations were laid'.[7] After these productions of Yeats, Cousins, Fred Ryan, and P. T. McGinley there was a short run of previously staged plays from 4 to 7 December, but it soon became apparent that the physical limitations of the hall were unsuitable for anything other than small-scale productions and rehearsals.

In December 1902 Yeats told Lady Gregory that James Cousins was 'hopeless', and that the sooner he had him as an enemy the better.[8] William Fay wanted to produce a new play by Cousins, a farce entitled *Sold*, but Yeats found it vulgar, threatening to resign his presidency if they went ahead. Fay gave in. Yeats obviously recognized a natural opponent in the northerner; and in any case he was now looking out for potential writers in the theatre movement that was forming around him, who would respond to the radical ideals he longed to realize. Cousins was a George Russell protégé and Yeats, in spite of their long friendship, distrusted Russell's democratic tendencies and his inclination to overvalue talent he had encouraged. It is a remarkable feature of Yeats's personality that he was utterly decisive in his assessment of people: once he formed a view of someone's spiritual and moral nature, he rarely changed it, and he was always on the lookout, not for disciples, as has often been averred, but for traitors or backsliders. The trouble one has, writing a history of this sort, where one is exposed to the fulminations and bitterness people have left behind them on paper, is how accurate Yeats often was in his appraisal of people, and in his detection of treacherous instincts. A more immediate reason for distrust of anyone emanating from Russell's circle had recently presented itself. Russell printed some early Yeats poems in the *Irish Homestead*, the journal he edited, without consulting him, and the poet's misgivings about Russell, and by extension his acolytes, intensified.

Yeats had need of allies: there were problems over a new play by Padraic Colum, another of Russell's protégés, whom he described as 'a rough jewel . . . but a real one. I prophesy about him.'[9] Fay agreed to put on Colum's *The Saxon*

Shillin', a patriotic play about recruitment into the British army, along with a new play by Yeats, *The Hour Glass*. Some revisions were required of the Colum piece by Fay, on apparently artistic grounds, but these were opposed by Maud Gonne and Arthur Griffith. Meanwhile Yeats was in London. The argument rumbled on, Maud Gonne claiming that she spoke for Cumann na nGaedheal, a nationalist grouping with which Inghinidhe na hÉireann were in association, and accusing Fay of bullying Colum because he lacked the guts to stage the play as it was. Russell now stepped in and, true to his democratic and bureaucratic leanings, drew up a set of rules and procedures for play selection.

The underlying tension here, of which Yeats remained in ignorance until February 1903, was the fact that Maud Gonne had been secretly engaged since the summer of 1902 to Major John MacBride, a nationalist who commanded the Irish Brigade in the Boer War on the rebel side. The theatre society was in some confusion as it sought to find some degree of consensus over who should do what; and it also now needed to define its relationship with Cumann na nGaedheal and Inghinidhe na hÉireann. It decided to reconstitute itself as a co-operative venture rather than a commercial undertaking, to be known as the Irish National Theatre Society (INTS), on 15 February 1903, relinquishing former designations as 'W. G. Fay's National Dramatic Society', or the 'Irish National Dramatic Company'. Yeats was re-elected president with Maud Gonne, Russell, and Douglas Hyde remaining as vice-presidents; William Fay became stage manager and Fred Ryan secretary. A reading committee was set up on 2 June to include Yeats, Russell, Colum, and the Fay brothers. This device, instituted in order to allow some degree of democratic decision-making (a play was accepted if it got three-quarters of the votes), was abandoned in the summer when Cousins's *Sold* was reconsidered. Yeats overruled the reading committee, much to the dismay of its members, and eventually Maud Gonne and Hyde left the Society when their opposition to another new play, this time Synge's *In the Shadow of the Glen*, was ignored. Yeats's actions in these matters have been widely criticized, and there is no doubt that he was temperamentally intolerant of democracy or the notion that others' opinions could be as valid as his or those of his chosen friends. But Yeats wanted a theatre which would truly challenge orthodoxies, including nationalist ones, and create an 'unruly' audience, which would, he wrote, include 'zealous bricklayers' and the 'odd corner boy or two'.[10] His nationalist friends often seemed to him to be timorous and respectable, and under the sway of a fearful Catholic church, one essentially conciliatory towards British authority. He was appalled when he learned that Maud Gonne was becoming a Catholic, in preparation for her marriage to MacBride, and reminded her of how the church had exhorted its flock against Fenianism.[11]

However, Yeats's *The Hour Glass*, performed by the INTS with Lady Gregory's *Twenty-Five* at the Molesworth Hall on 14 March 1903, was a play which had, at least as part of its intention, a wish to reconcile some elements of clerical opposition. The Wise Man (played by the intense nationalist Dudley Digges) is shown to be an arid materialist, guilty of propagating his godlessness amongst unthinking followers. An angel comes to tell him his life is running out and that he is destined for hell, 'the place for those who deny',[12] unless he can find someone who believes. Having infected everyone with his own poisonous scepticism the Wise Man is in despair until he finds that the Fool (played by Frank Fay) does believe. The Wise Man kneels before the Fool and does penance, obtaining a release from hell. This ending was later changed and the transformation occurred in the Wise Man's own perception and vision, but in 1903 the powerful image of modern materialist thought bowing to tradition seemed to extend a gesture of sympathetic understanding to conventional patterns of belief and to Catholicism in particular. Indeed on 18 April 1902 he had written to Lady Gregory that this play might 'propitiate Holy Church'.[13]

Twenty-Five was Lady Gregory's first play to be performed. It had been blocked the previous autumn by Maud Gonne, on the grounds that in it the returned emigrant is the hero at the expense of the Irish at home. After an act of selfless generosity Christie Henderson returns to America in good spirits, leaving behind him his lethargic neighbours. This theme, that of leaving a close-knit, perhaps somewhat claustrophobic community after an act of daring or generosity or heroism, is one that surfaces time and again in Irish literature and drama, and reflects a set of continuing social conditions in twentieth-century Ireland which many artists and writers perceived to be inhibiting. The hearth and the village and the known environs of a city have their attractions, but these are often seen as impediments to the necessary energy which the personality needs to unleash if it is to attain scope and freedom. The theme of exile and freedom is the core-subject of George Moore's short stories *The Untilled Field* (1903) and the related novel *The Lake* (1905), which he was at this time deeply engaged in after his rupture with Yeats. And about now Joyce was preparing his first stories for publication in Russell's the *Irish Homestead* which would expand into extensive and manifold variations on the theme. But on 20 January 1903 Synge read, in Lady Gregory's London flat, his shocking treatment of a close-knit community on the Aran Islands, and the virtual impossibility of escape from its iron necessities: this was *Riders to the Sea*. On 3 March Synge again read this play at Lady Gregory's, along with *In the Shadow of the Glen*, which is a play about the shadow of routine and the countervailing attraction of the open road, recklessness, freedom.

In May 1903 the INTS, at the invitation of the critic Stephen Gwynn, secretary to the London Irish Literary Society, performed five plays from its repertoire at the Queen's Gate Hall in South Kensington. The reaction was extremely favourable, Yeats and Lady Gregory having made sure that influential figures from the English literary and theatrical scene (such as William Archer the Ibsenite, Wilfrid Scawen Blunt, man of letters and one-time lover of Lady Gregory, Henry James, and, crucially, Miss Annie Horniman) were in attendance. Arthur Walkley in *The Times* praised 'first and foremost . . . the pleasure of the ear'[14] he got from the musicality and poetry of the speech of the Irish actors, far removed from the stage-Irishry familiar to English readers from the pages of nineteenth-century fictional purveyors of the stage-Irishman—Thackeray, Lever, Trollope, and others. He waxed lyrical about the touch of melancholy Irish accents gave to English, describing it as an aural minor key. There is no doubt but that the success the INTS had in London was a proving-ground for Dublin opinion. If London critics were impressed, then this new venture could be something worth paying attention to.

However, when Yeats returned to Dublin, he had to face acrimonious discussions with Russell and Maud Gonne MacBride (she married Major John MacBride on 21 February) over James Cousins's *Sold*, Russell being keen to advance the younger writer. He also attended, in June, performances of Martyn's *The Heather Field* and Ibsen's *A Doll's House* staged at the Queen's Theatre by the Players' Club, a company which had been in existence since the 1890s, but now used by Martyn presumably to remind Dublin audiences of his importance in the theatre movement. He got Moore to direct. Yeats declared himself indifferent to their attempt at rivalry, and went on to Coole to work on *The King's Threshold*, a play which asserted the supremacy of art over politics and morality. The tensions between the conflicting claims of national interest, morality, and a 'cause', and the freedom of the artist to create his or her own bid for self-expression, were to explode in the controversy over Synge's *In the Shadow of the Glen* when it was staged in the autumn.

In August 1903 Arthur Griffith founded Sinn Féin, a party dedicated to realizing, in political terms, the cultural nationalism enshrined in Hyde's Gaelic League. As the summer wore on Maud Gonne MacBride grew ever more hostile to the Irish National Theatre Society and her growing disenchantment with Yeats's change of attitude from that expressed in *Cathleen Ni Houlihan* was shared by some of the Society's actors, Dudley Digges amongst them. As the Society went into rehearsals for the autumn season, Dudley Digges and Máire Quinn (whom he later married), supported by Maud Gonne, set up a rival company, calling itself the Cumann na nGaedheal Theatre Company. It put into rehearsal Cousins's *The Sword of Dermot*, a play about a love affair between Thomas Costello and Una Bhán, famous in Gaelic folklore; a skit on Edward VII's recent visit to Ireland (*A Twinkle in Ireland's Eye*); and a send-up of Trinity College's ill-informed prejudice about the Irish language by Hyde entitled *Pléusgadh na Bulgóide* (*The Bursting of the Bubble*). This new rival company was calling its season the Samhain Festival, a depressing attempt to try to discredit the INTS as pretenders to Gaelic probity, as well as a deliberate ploy to confuse Dublin audiences. Fay even wrote to Yeats suggesting that he change the name of the INTS journal, which he was editing as usual for the autumn season, from *Samhain* 'to something else'. The rancour evident in correspondence between all parties at this time (William Fay saying, 'I know Mr Digges after five years; where there's the most honour there will be Digges'[15]) ensured that when *In the Shadow of the Glen* and *The King's Threshold* opened at the Molesworth Hall on 8 October there was every likelihood that there would be a violent reaction. Arthur

Griffith, Maud Gonne (calling her company the Cumann na nGaedheal National Theatre)[16], Cousins, Russell, some of the actors still in the INTS, D. P. Moran (editor of the *Leader*, a nationalist newspaper established in 1900), Hyde, Martyn—all believed, in their different ways, that Irish theatre should project a positive and progressive view of the character of the Irish people (whatever that was), and advance national self-esteem. These two plays seemed to turn aside from any form of Irish civic responsibility. *The King's Threshold*, with the hauteur of its hunger-striking poet, disdaining duty and the pressure to conform, was bad enough; but Synge's play, with its (then) shockingly frank depiction of adultery, greed, and moral cowardice amongst Irish country people, was seen as a calculated insult. Its reputation preceded it, word having got out from the various readings the play received before rehearsal. Maud Gonne thought it was 'horrid' before she read it.[17]

As a matter of fact her (premature) evaluation, though obviously wrong-headed, does register something of the play's shocking authenticity. 'Authenticity' is a word that can be (and has been) loosely used to refer to a kind of art or writing closely attuned to a certain type of nationalist *pietas* or allegiance, but Synge's authenticity is of an entirely different kind. It is a form of super-realism, or, as he termed it, 'transfigured realism', where the elements of a situation or a mood or a set of human atmospheres are presented in all their surprising (and sometimes brutally divergent) diversity. This is the energy that animates Synge's drama; it is completely and utterly Irish (as Daniel Corkery later realized) but entirely remote from any comfortable idea of 'Irishness'.[18] Yeats recognized immediately that here, with Synge, was the real thing. Here, in the strong and hurtling speech, the passionate exchanges, the frankness, was the kind of thing he admired in *seannós* singing, and which he thought he might recreate, artistically, through the psaltery. Synge's suddenness of realization and harshness of outline were qualities he would try to emulate in his own art, and he succeeded in doing so. Although *In the Shadow of the Glen* may not be 'horrid' (in Maud Gonne's term), it is quite horrifying, in a compelling way.

The young, recently widowed Nora (Máire Nic Shivbhlaigh) goes out into the black night, leaving the Tramp behind with the corpse (as she believes) of her aged husband, and whistles for her lover, Michael Dara. Dan, the supposed corpse, says: 'Did you ever hear another woman could whistle the like of that with two fingers in her mouth?'[19] Did you ever, the audience is being asked in the Molesworth Hall, see an Ireland 'the like of that' on stage or in books where women of the mountains whistle for their lovers? And, they are being asked, don't you know that that is the way it is? This was no 'cracked looking-glass of a servant' in Joyce's phrase; this was the 'reality', purged of sentiment, piety, morals, optimism, benevolence, idealism. It was (and still is, despite the liberalism of the late twentieth century) shocking enough to make the hair stand on end, 'horrid'. It is exactly the world Marina Carr, the playwright of the midlands, has brought back in the 1990s, revealing that Irish country life has, in some ways, hardly changed at all in close on a hundred years. Towards the close of Synge's tiny play

the old man throws Nora out, enjoying every second of his rage and verbal violence, as he condemns her to a wasted old age, wandering the roads, until 'they
find her stretched like a dead sheep with the frost on her, or the big spiders maybe,
and they putting thin webs on her, in the butt of a ditch'. And then Synge introduces an entirely different tonality, from the Tramp (William Fay) who has wandered into this Irish family romance. The old husband has, gleefully, challenged
Michael Dara, the lover, to be daring enough to take her on, and he evades the moment of choice. Now the old man, loving his anger, asks the Tramp to take her.
When he speaks it is with tenderness and humanity, the tone indicating that the
two of them would be well shut of a house full of pretence, rage, and miserliness:
'We'll be going now, lady of the house; the rain is falling, but the air is kind, and
maybe it'll be a grand morning, by the grace of God.' They are heading off into
sin and freedom, 'by the grace of God'. The age-old tension between pagan and
Christian in Irish life and culture is reactivated, but only to indicate that the sober
life of the formally Christian may be less worthy than the gladly accepted world
of nature, paganism, and adultery. Indeed, God's own grace may be more in evidence on the wild paths of the night than in a house darkened by the shadows of
custom, anger, and meanness.

There was outrage. Not only was there a secession from the board of the INTS
and by some of the actors, there were protests in the newspapers in advance of
opening night. Yeats in his *Samhain* for the 1903 season enunciated a set of principles and convictions about theatre which to some degree Synge's play had
fortified and his own *The King's Threshold* had expressed. He advocated a theatre
that would be a place of 'intellectual excitement'[20], and that would value considerations of artistic integrity over political or moral expediency (or correctness).

These were the '*Samhain* principles' that Miss Horniman would refer to again
and again, as she sought to keep Yeats and the Abbey Theatre she funded un-
tainted by nationalist politics. The principles were four in number. The other
three were: the Irish theatre should be one which: (*a*) gave speech the vitality of
poetry; (*b*) simplified acting style; (*c*) simplified scenery. To many, especially to
Arthur Griffith of Sinn Féin and the *United Irishman*, this looked like an about-
turn from the attitudes expressed in *The Heather Field, The Hour Glass*, and especially the nerve-tingling republicanism of *Cathleen Ni Houlihan*. Something
like a change of direction was definitely taking place, but it would be impossible
to disentangle a single motive for this alteration from the welter of impressions,
feelings, and ideas Yeats had been experiencing over the last year or so: the un-
reliability of emotional people; the betrayal of those whom he had thought allies;
his own intolerance and anger (at Maud Gonne's marriage and conversion); and
the revelation of energy that was Synge's art.

The *Irish Times* found *In the Shadow of the Glen* 'distasteful'. Thomas Kettle,
a young economist and a moderate nationalist, attacked Yeats's *Samhain* principles, warning him that 'a philosophy, like an animal, can maintain itself only as
long as it abides in harmony with its environment . . . his reading of life may

diverge so widely from ours that all his fine artistry will not save his work from au-tomatic extinction'.[21] Yeats's father, John B. Yeats, came to Synge's defence in Griffith's *United Irishman*, and superbly described the play's suddenness and ex-citement: 'every incident (and every incident is a surprise) conveys a deep mourn-fulness.'[22] But Griffith himself, and Maud Gonne, attacked Yeats and Synge for failing to depict accurately the real Ireland. Although Synge may speak Irish and live part of every year in Aran he is a stranger to the Irish character. 'Nationality', Griffith declared, 'is the breath of art'; while Maud Gonne accused Yeats of falling under 'foreign influence'.[23] Eventually Griffith gave his support to the plays under rehearsal by the 'Cumann na nGaedheal National Theatre Company' for their rival 'Samhain Festival'. Molly Allgood (stage name Máire O'Neill) joined the company for the production of *The King's Threshold* from Inghinidhe na hÉireann. She and Synge were to fall in love.

Griffith published in the *United Irishman* a send-up of Synge's play entitled *In a Real Wicklow Glen*, in which Nora, now an old woman, has had many children by her ancient husband; and Michael Dara, the young man, has made nothing of his life. This, Griffith is saying, is what Irish life is really like.

In 1903 Miss Horniman sent Yeats a series of Tarot readings, related to the es-tablishment of the Abbey, his part in it, the currents of energy he had to negotiate, and the forces that would oppose him or come to his aid. On 1 March she wrote: 'Gain of further force governs the whole.' On 1 May she asked the cards how the following day's performance would affect him. Fay ('a dark man') is worried, but he and Yeats will work together 'though they are not harmonious characters'. On 13 September she writes, ominously, 'disappointment in friendship crowns all'. On 9 October she asks what is the right thing for her to do. She writes: 'I am so anxious to help effectually as best I may and it seems as if it were already ordained . . . Do you realize that you have given me the right to call myself "artist"? How I thank you.'[24]

Annie Horniman had come over for the performances in the Molesworth Hall, and had, in fact, designed the costumes for *The King's Threshold*, hence her com-ment about Yeats making her an artist. On the night of 10 October Yeats went on stage after the performances to attack his critics and proclaim the kind of intel-lectual freedom and excitement he believed his theatre should realize. That same evening Annie Horniman offered to back him in the establishment of a profes-sional Irish theatre so he could realize these ideals, and implement the principles enunciated in *Samhain* for 1903. Hence came into being the Abbey Theatre.

In November Yeats went to America on a lecture tour arranged by the New York Irish-American lawyer John Quinn, which was to last until March 1904. In his lectures there he more or less conveyed the impression that the Irish National Theatre Society was his creation, downplaying not only Inghinidhe na hÉireann but also the Fays.

On 3 December *Broken Soil* (later *The Fiddler's House*), the first play by Column to be produced by the INTS, was staged at the Molesworth Hall. Colum, from the midlands (he was born in Longford, and grew up there and in Dublin), was 22 at this date, and many, including Yeats, expected great things of him. Like *In the Shadow of the Glen*, *Broken Soil* dealt with a tramp, a wandering musician in this case, but in Colum this figure does not represent an imaginative freedom (as he does in Synge); here he is a man ruined by the vanity of genius, who brings great sorrow to the daughters who are devoted to him. Colum's realism is not of the 'transfigured' kind, as Synge's was; it presents the actuality of situations and people with a steadfast and sombre focus.

There is more than a trace of Ibsen in the way in which Colum portrays Maire (played by Máire Nic Shiubhlaigh): she is half in love with the wild horse-trader Brian McConnell, but fears his energy and masterful power. When he comes to woo her, and promises to build a fine white house for her, she remembers seeing him taming a stallion: 'I was afeard of you when I saw you that time. Sure I thought it was you and not the horse that would trample us all down! I wanted to be where you couldn't see me.'[25] She thinks he is trying to tame her in the same way. Her sister Anne is prepared to accept the quietness of a life based on marriage to a strong father, but she is, in some obscure way, timorous of men and their power to control nature. This is why she refuses the horse-trader and joins her father Conn (played by Frank Fay) on the open road, signing over the family house to her sister. The father loves the free life of the wandering artist, but he is feckless and unsteady. He cannot resist the love of music, or of the public house, or of the accolades he can easily win from admirers. The play is not a simple affair of the allure of wildness set against the cultivation of the domestic virtues (although that is amongst its themes): there is a sense of the darkness of impulse, that the imagination may involve a kind of ruin.

Cousins reviewed the play for Griffith's *United Irishman* under the pen-name 'Spealadóir' ('The Reaper') and summed it up as leaving an impression of 'immature inadequacy'. Oliver St John Gogarty defended Colum in the same paper the following week, praising the exactness of his treatment of Irish life. From Cousins's critique there is the unmistakably acid whiff of sour grapes. Yeats, in New York, was overjoyed at the success of *Broken Soil*, writing to Frank Fay on 29 December: 'Please tell Colm [*sic*] how delighted I am at his success and please set him to work at a new play if you can.'[26]

On 14 January 1904 the INTS produced Yeats's *The Shadowy Waters*, the symbolic play he had been working on for years. Its dense storyline, involving an impossible love affair, conflict with otherworld evil forces, a voyage into cold unknown seas, and druidic music and enchantment, proved baffling to most of the audience, Synge tartly describing the reaction in the theatre as 'the most disturbing failure the mind can imagine,—a half-empty room, with growling men and tittering females'.[27]

The play is an extraordinarily atmospheric evocation of longing and frustration. Its plot is, actually, very simple: Forgael, an Irish pirate, is seeking his 'heart's desire' on the misty seas of the northern waters. He and his crew encounter a

Viking ship and capture it. They kill the Viking king on board, and bring his wife to Forgael. She wants to return to her country, but Forgael's music enchants her; she and the pirate commune in the realm of spirit; they then part, mournfully. The play, the most extreme venture into symbolism in Irish literature, has its own remote, even inhuman beauty. Like *The Wanderings of Oisin* or 'The Tower' it is one of the crucial works in Yeats's canon. Its allure is perhaps more effective now than it was in 1904, but its strangeness and eerie power had little impact on its original audience. Forgael, as his men kill their victims on the Viking ship, sees their souls flying up through the masts:

> A grey bird has flown by. He has flown upward.
> He hovers above the mast and waits his kind;
> When all gather they will fly upon their way.
> I shall find out if I have lost my way
> Among these misty waters. Two! Now four!
> Now four together! I shall hear their words
> If I go nearer to the windward side,
> For there are sudden voices in my ears.
> Two hover there together, and one says,
> 'How light we are now we are changed to birds!'[28]

This idea, of the souls of the dead turning to birds immediately they enter the afterlife, is one Yeats returned to in 'Cuchulain Comforted' in 1939, one of his last poems; and in *The Death of Cuchulain*, his last play.

This play shared the bill with a much more directly appealing piece, Seamus MacManus's *The Townland of Tamney*. From Mountcharles in Donegal MacManus drew upon his knowledge of folklore to create a play mixing Gaelic storytelling with a plot about the inheritance of land. However Synge thought that the actors relaxed too much in the MacManus piece, creating a great deal of hyperactive business to amuse an audience somewhat taxed by what Holloway called 'the not wholly disagreeable dreariness' of Yeats's symbolic drama.[29]

Synge's *Riders to the Sea* was produced on 25 February at the same venue, the Molesworth Hall, with Sara Allgood, Molly Allgood's sister, playing Cathleen, Maurya's daughter. Synge himself directed the piece, and it was played along with a revival of Russell's *Deirdre*. The critics hated it, but with some exceptions the audience were profoundly moved by the starkness and unremittingly bleak force of Synge's tragedy. Holloway tells us that on 26 February the audience responded to the curtain with total silence. However, the *Irish Times* (27 February) objected to the bringing on stage of Bartley's corpse after his drowning—'a cheap trick of the Transpontine dramatists'—and the same paper went on to say, callowly, that 'the East wind does not always blow on the Irish soul, and there is mirth still in Erin. Up till now our stage has not been remarkable for diffusing sunshine around, and we need sunshine badly.'

This embarrassingly knowing cheerfulness and worldly wisdom, so clearly an attitude assumed in Dublin literary and artistic circles in these years, is flawlessly captured, in all its fawning obsequiousness and self-aggrandizing moralizing, in Gabriel Conroy's after-dinner speech in James Joyce's 'The Dead', written in 1907.

Synge's play is a masterpiece of concentration and structure. Its language, with its strong emphasis on the particularity and physicality of the island world this play evokes, has the felt reality of concrete experience. Synge achieves this strength through an adaptation into English of features of Gaelic grammar and syntax, filtered through his accurate ear for Hiberno-English speech. This language, often parodied and frequently misunderstood, is a perfect dramatic vehicle for registering shocks of realization, horror, grief. When Maurya, the mother who loses the last of her men in the course of the play, comes back after trying to bless her boy at the well, she says: 'I seen the fearfulest thing.' Cathleen, her daughter, leaves her spinning wheel to look out the door of the cottage, which in the play is surrounded by the noise and terror of the sea, and the dark forces of malignant fate and grim necessity. She looks out, and sees her brother: 'God forgive you; he's riding the mare now over the green head, and the grey pony behind him.' The grey pony has a rider, however. Cathleen cannot see him, but the rider is Michael, the dead brother, whose corpse has been washed ashore in the far north, in Donegal:

Maurya (*starts, so that her shawl falls back from her head and shows her white tossed hair. With a frightened voice*) The grey pony behind him?
Cathleen (*coming to the fire*) What's it ails you at all?
Maurya (*speaking very slowly*). I've seen the fearfulest thing any person has seen since the day Bride Dara seen the dead man with the child in his arms.

The two daughters do not speak at this; they utter a groan, 'Uah', and crouch down in front of their mother, stricken by the thought of anything that could be worse than what Bride Dara saw. She tells them; she saw the riders to the sea:

Maurya. I went down to the spring well, and I stood there saying a prayer to myself. Then Bartley came along, and he riding on the red mare with the grey pony behind him. The Son of God spare us, Nora!
Cathleen. What's it you saw?
Maurya. I saw Michael himself.[30]

'The red mare', 'the grey pony', 'to myself', 'himself': all these usages (the definite article profusely employed, the reflexive emphatic pronoun) drawn from Irish and Hiberno-English serve to intensify the audience's receptivity to the series of shocks that this perfectly constructed tragedy administers. The terrible primal horror of folk tale is united with the spare artistry of tragic writing at its finest. This was, undoubtedly, the Abbey's first masterpiece; Yeats's dramatist had arrived. The company returned to London on 26 March, and performed *The King's Threshold* and *Riders to the Sea* at the Royalty Theatre. The notices of Synge's play were markedly different from those received in Dublin, Max Beerbohm finding in its simplicity evidence of a 'Keltic' spirituality.[31]

While Yeats was still in America (where he remained until 8 March 1904, re-turning in time for the London performances of Synge's and his own plays) the INTS was approached by James A. Reardon, a representative of an international trade fair to be held in St Louis, Missouri, requesting it to perform some of its bet-ter-known plays. Realizing they would have to give up their jobs the actors, al-though at first very keen, reluctantly declined the invitation. But Reardon now had an approach from the actors who had seceded from the INTS. Dudley Digges and his wife Máire Quinn indicated their willingness to go to St Louis. From the INTS the actor P. J. Kelly also agreed to take part. These players approached Russell to release his *Deirdre*, which he did. Yeats was furious. He wanted the INTS to tour the USA and here Russell was supporting a group who would be pre-pared to exploit any confusion in America as to who they were and what the Irish National Theatre Society was. Yeats told Russell he should not release *Deirdre* for performance without the Society's permission, and that in doing so he had acted disloyally. Yeats, in a letter to John Quinn in New York, said that he believed that Russell did not quite understand what he was getting himself into. The Society ex-pelled P. J. Kelly for engaging himself elsewhere without first gaining permission. William Fay was unbending and demanded the expulsion; and Kelly was sent out through the door of Camden Street Hall, his colleagues gazing silently on his shame.[32]

In the middle of this acrimony between Russell, Digges, and Yeats, Miss Horniman was proving as good as her word. On 8 April Yeats sent Russell, as vice-president, her proposal, that she buy the Mechanics Institute in Abbey Street, along with a disused morgue in adjoining Marlborough Street, which, after suit-able refurbishment, would become the home of the company of the Irish National Theatre Society. Yeats moved quickly: on 10 April Annie Horniman in-vited Joseph Holloway, the theatre diarist whose day job was as an architect, to her hotel, the Standard in Harcourt Street, to discuss renovations. On 11 April they went to the morgue but were refused entrance to the Mechanics Institute by the irate existing tenant, a music-hall entrepreneur. They returned later, in the af-ternoon, this time with Yeats along as well. The music-hall man remained angry, shouting 'land-grabbers' at them, and as they left cursed them: 'May you and your morgue have luck.' Holloway's comment on this outburst, 'distinctly droll', hardly seems apposite.[33] By the end of the month, as Yeats was negotiating a patent for the theatre—hitherto it had been licensed only to stage one-act plays, and was mostly used as a nationalist meeting room for lectures or political meet-ings—Russell had effectively resigned. He could no longer tolerate the force of Yeats's outraged rebukes.[34]

Miss Horniman hired William Fay to oversee the renovations of the Mechanics Institute, and Yeats advised on fittings: Sarah Purser, the stained-glass artist, was employed to create the windows; Lily, Yeats's sister, hung embroidered work in the lobby; and there were paintings by John B. Yeats of the directors and Miss Horniman. Yeats wanted to keep their plans secret for as long as possible, knowing that other theatres would oppose the renewal and extension of patent to the Institute. The application was, in fact, opposed by the Royal, the Gaiety, and the Queen's theatres. When the patent was granted, after much lobbying, to Lady Gregory—Miss Horniman being ineligible as a grantee as she was not resident in Ireland—restrictions were imposed: only plays in Irish or English by Irish writers on Irish themes, or foreign work of the highest quality, were allowed, leaving what the competitors (rightly) judged would be the most popular plays to them. The patent was granted on 20 August. A week previously, on 13 August, the *United Irishman* reminded the INTS that they were taking over ground which was hallowed to nationalists—Young Ireland had convened there, John Mitchel had incited to rebellion, Thomas Francis Meaghar ('of the Sword') had inflamed patriotic feeling; and the body of the Fenian John O'Mahony, shipped back from America, had lain in state there when the Catholic pro-cathedral had refused to accept it.[35]

As ever, preparations were being made up to the last minute. There was, for example, a problem with the last urinal, the contractor for the plumbing writing to Holloway, the architect, on 3 December: 'I beg to say I am writing to Twyford's to see if I can get another top piece with back to fit the last urinal.'[36]

On 27 December 1904 the Abbey Theatre opened its doors. The opening night featured Yeats's first Cuchulain play *On Baile's Strand* and Lady Gregory's *Spreading the News*, a comedy about the contagion of rumour in a small community, the latter a theme not irrelevant to the fraught dissensions in Irish literary life that surrounded the Abbey's inauguration. George Roberts's *Minute Book* of 1904 reveals that on 10 August the Society had agreed to open with Lady Gregory's *Kincora* and a play by Hyde in Irish; also that W. G. Fay tried (unsuccessfully) to get the Society to agree to a charity performance for the unemployed.[37]

On Baile's Strand tells how Cuchulain, at the command of the High King Conchobor, kills his son who comes from Aoife, his mother in Scotland, to challenge the warriors of Ulster. There is a kind of choric antistrophe to the main action, involving a Blind Man and a Fool, who mock the heroic ideals that animate the competing champions. The play's symbolism is complex, but interwoven into its texture of old love and betrayal, of violence and antagonism supplanting affection and fellowship, there is a strand relating to the conflicts Yeats experienced in establishing a theatre in the teeth of uncomprehending opposition, mistrust, and internal dissension. Cuchulain fighting the waves at the end as the Fool and Blind Man steal food, and the indifference of those in whom the future of the territory is invested, is not unconnected to Yeats's own expense of spirit as others took advantage of and undermined his unremitting energy.

The other plays for this season included Synge's *In the Shadow of the Glen*, *Cathleen Ni Houlihan*, and Lady Gregory's *Spreading the News*. George Moore was gone, as was Edward Martyn; Dudley Digges had left, P. J. Kelly was expelled from the company for his collaboration with the St Louis performances (which were, in fact, a failure), and George Russell had resigned—though Yeats continued to make use of his diplomatic skills to traverse tricky constitutional passes in the company. But now, with the Fays behind him, flanked by Lady Gregory and Synge (who was not yet a director), and backed by Annie Horniman's money drawn from income off her shares in the Hudson Bay Trading Company, he had a theatre in Dublin.

The next play at the new Abbey was to be Synge's *The Well of the Saints*. This was not the play Yeats and Lady Gregory had been considering in the autumn of 1904, Shaw's extraordinary inversion of Irish and English cultural stereotypes, *John Bull's Other Island*. Shaw had promised a play for the INTS as far back as 1900. Synge, now on the Reading Committee, liked Shaw's new play and wanted the Abbey to do it, but Yeats was uneasy with its relaxed brilliance and detached mockery, and gladly accepted the excuse that the part of Broadbent, the English idealist, posed seemingly intractable casting difficulties. It was eventually staged at the Abbey in September 1916.

Predictably, the reactions of the Dublin papers to *The Well of the Saints* when it was produced on 4 February 1905 were hostile. Arthur Griffith attacked the play, which dealt with the gap between actuality and the stories people concoct about it, as being 'harsh, unsympathetic, and at the same time, sensual'. Not inaccurately, he detected 'a note of utter hopelessness' in the work, which is relentless in its stripping away of the comforts of illusion to reveal a human dynamics of self-seeking and self-aggrandizement.[38] William Fay, writing to Holloway, who had attended rehearsals, and who was concerned about the 'nastiness' of the play, shows that he understood Synge's tragic vision as one that cuts through sentimentality to get at a rough and energetic reality.[39] Synge's plot is simplicity itself: Mary and Martin Doul, two blind tramps, are given their sight back by holy water from a saint's well. Now sighted, they discover that they have maintained a mutual illusion in their blindness that they are both beautiful. They are brought face to face with reality; Martin is put to working at the forge, helping the smith hammer out the implements of everyday existence. As the miracle wears off they welcome the return of blindness, because it allows them to reinvent their own world, a world of mutual happiness. When the saint offers permanently to restore their sight, they leave the place of their miserable illumination (set in Wicklow) and head for the south. Martin Doul says to his wife

Martin Doul. Come along now and we'll be walking to the south, for we've seen too much of everyone in this place, and it's a small joy we'd have living near them, or hearing the lie they do be telling from the gray of dawn till the night.
Mary Doul (despondingly). That's the truth, surely; and we'd have a right to be gone, if it's a long way itself, on I've heard them say, where you do have to be walking with a slough of wet on one side and a slough of wet on the other, and you going a stony path with a north wind blowing behind.
Jimmy. There's a power of deep rivers with floods in them where you do have to be lepping the stones and you going to the South.

This is a sombre and delicate mix of emotion. The two blind people must negotiate the tricky path of life, in a state of continual alertness far surpassing the trivial awareness of the life they are leaving, and which they have seen enough of. Their new way of going, propelled by the despondency of facing reality, and driven by the relentless pressure of necessity, is a way of tension; but it is alert. Here we have sober, wide-awake recognition of the way things are on this bitch of an earth, as Pozzo declaims, much later, in Beckett's *Waiting for Godot*. Beckett of course recognized the indebtedness.

Throughout 1905, Yeats fought to establish control of the Abbey, vest it in a small committee of three (himself, Lady Gregory, and Synge), and end pretence of democracy in the theatre. He had been reading Nietzsche, who seemed to authorize powerful action, and he was backed financially by Miss Horniman. The irony was that he enlisted Russell's help in bringing about these changes, even though Russell had resigned in 1904, probably because he thought that his one-time friend's credibility with the actors would assist in implementing the changes he wanted. He got him to write a constitution whereby the new society would be a society of authors and other nominated individuals. The actors would not, crucially, be members of the society and would have no voting rights. They were, by this rearrangement, meant to be 'freed' to concentrate on theatre work.⁴⁰ Meanwhile the Abbey became a public limited company, with the three directors (Yeats, Lady Gregory, and now Synge as well) holding the vast majority of shares. The actors were offered contracts specifying their newly defined duties. One of them, Máire Nic Shiubhlaigh, was fiercely bullied by Yeats to accept her new contract, he adding insult to injury by offering to increase her stipend if she agreed to become wardrobe mistress. A curious series of events unfolded in which she fled for sympathy to Yeats's sisters in Churchtown, with their father John B. Yeats taking the actress's side in the dispute. Fissures were opening everywhere, however, as Yeats tried to impose order. On 3 June 1905 Colum wrote to Yeats: 'I voted for the establishment of a limited liability in order to save the Society from a disastrous split. I come back to Dublin and find the Society hopelessly shattered . . . I appeal to you . . . to take steps to re-unite the groups.'⁴¹

In early January 1906 all the dissension arising from Yeats's reorganization of he Society came to a head when one of the most schismatic ruptures in the history of the Abbey took place: there was a walkout by the actors George Roberts, James Starkey, Helen Laird, and Frank Walker (brother of Máire Nic Shiubhlaigh), followed soon after by Padraic Colum, in spite of Lady Gregory's best efforts to persuade him to stay. The grounds for this protest were many—that the 'new' Abbey would not be national enough, that the seats were too expensive —but the real reason for the protest was a sense (far from being unjustified) that the actors were not accorded sufficient respect by the directors, especially Yeats himself, whose temper and manner were getting worse, although he was not above being calculating in his outbursts. In any case the seceders claimed that *they* were the real Irish National Theatre Society, and that the remaining group at the

Abbey were impostors. On 10 March 1906 Arthur Griffith's *United Irishman* quoted a letter from one of the seceders making exactly this claim.

During all these conflicts Lady Gregory strenuously exercised herself on Yeats's behalf, acting as his confidante and frequently intervening in eloquent and persuasive letters to Russell and others in order to explain and defend Yeats's vision of what the Irish theatre should be. Entirely sympathetic and partial to his view, she worried about the strain and tension he was suffering from as a result of the bickering and politicking in the theatre as he strove to counter assertions and rumours of anti-nationalism and West-Britonism. Adding to his difficulty was the fact that Miss Horniman was becoming more and more anti-nationalist in her attitudes, insisting that the Abbey steer clear of political affiliations. These pressures reveal themselves in Yeats's contribution to *Samhain* in 1905, where he quotes the poet Coventry Patmore's dictum, 'the end of art is peace', in order to defend a theatre not immediately preoccupied with causes or politics but concentrated upon what he describes as 'attention'. He will not, he says, allow 'those friends of ours who are ever urging us to attack the priests or the English' to dictate policy.[42] However Miss Horniman was ready to dictate; after all, she was in a position to do so. She put it bluntly in a telegram to Yeats: 'NO POLITICS'.[43]

At the end of the 1905 *Samhain* essay he tells us that he has written the piece quickly, allowing the first draft to remain with, he says, all its slackness of 'phrase and rhythm'. He worries that he may have to give up the hope of developing a fine prose style, because of pressure of work, but offers for excuse the fact that he has been busy with a 'practical project', none other than the transformation of the Abbey Theatre from a society, where the actors felt they should be offered some parity, to a company, where they were to become employees. Yeats has often been criticized for his alliance of Nietzschean philosophy and capitalism in these manœuvres, but he did have a point: how could the actors remain on the executive if they were salaried? How, in other words, could they be their own employers? On 22 September, at a general meeting of the INTS, Russell put forward a resolution for the dissolving of the Society and the formation of the Irish National Theatre Society Limited. The motion was carried by fourteen votes to one.

As well as being Yeats's moral and emotional support in this turmoil, Lady Gregory had two full-length plays produced in 1905: *Kincora* (25 March) and *The White Cockade* (9 December). These interesting works provide an example of how theatre very frequently can arise (in part) from circumstances and situations amongst theatre people themselves. In *Kincora* Brian Boru is striving to unite a country riven by political spite, quarrelsomeness, and hate. In the prologue, Aoibhell (Sara Allgood), goddess of Munster, comes to Brian seeking to win him away from continual strife amongst his enemies. She says that it is the fate of those who serve Ireland that they who 'should be most their friends turn to be most their enemies, till the heart grows dry with bitterness, dry as the heads of the mountains under the summer heat'.[44] Brian refuses conflict, and in the play his heart does not grow brutal with the fare of bitterness. At the end of Act II, before

Clontarf where he is to face Ireland's enemies, Brian declares: 'It was my heart's desire to mend that torn fleece [of Ireland, ravaged by the wolves and foxes of dissension]; to gather up that ragged wool; to weave it into a border fit for the cloak of the King of Heaven. I made a peace. I thought to fill Ireland with joy.'[45] Much of the discord of the play proceeds from the sexual and emotional manipulations of Queen Gormleith, wife first to Maelmora of Leinster, then Malachi the High King, then Brian; she also has a dalliance with Olaf, one of the Danes. She was played by Máire Nic Shiubhlaigh and her character draws, remotely, upon Maud Gonne, Miss Horniman, Florence Farr, and Nic Shiubhlaigh herself. Brian was played by Frank Fay, who remained loyal to the directorate, for the time being. Another conflict that the play explores is that between Yeats and D. P. Moran, and, as Bernie Leacock has shown, the character 'Morann' in the play is deeply implicated in the themes of personal and cultural hostility.[46]

The White Cockade is concerned with the dereliction of authority. King James (Arthur Sinclair) after the Boyne thinks only of getting out of Ireland, a 'detestable' country; Patrick Sarsfield (Frank Fay) wants to retrieve the situation and attempts to awaken the King's courage but to no avail. Sarsfield has true leadership and energy, the King confessing that: 'when he begins drawing maps with a flourish of his sword (*Mimics Sarsfield*), or talking as if he were giving out the Holy Scriptures, there is something—a something—that takes away my strength, that leaves me bustled, marrowless, uncertain.'[47]

When Lady Gregory wrote to Padraic Colum on 7 January 1906, seeking to persuade him not to join the secession, she appealed to his loyalty and tried to awaken what she felt should be his integrity, because she was worried he would weaken and be led away from his true path—which in her view was, needless to say, to follow Yeats: 'It is hard to hold one's own against those one is living amongst. I have found that, and I have found that peace comes not from trying to please one's neighbours, but in making up one's own mind what is the right path and in then keeping to it.' And again she had loyalty in mind when she wrote to Synge three days later complaining that Russell was much to blame for the mess:

he undertook to settle the whole matter in the summer . . . and left us worse than before. Yeats wrote to him the other day, and only received a letter full of all the disagreeable things and personalities he found possible to say, and the real cause comes at the end 'you went about sneering at Deirdre and saying it was a sad and popular play'! I am sure he never said it was popular! I don't think Russell will be any use to help us now, but if we find he would be of use, I would not let him off to save him trouble.[48]

On 6 June 1906 the seceders formed the Theatre of Ireland, with Edward Martyn as president and Padraic Colum as secretary.

In spite of the upheavals of 1905 it was a year in which the new Abbey enjoyed a considerable degree of success with the public and the critics. Lady Gregory's two historical plays had enthusiastic receptions; William Boyle's caustic play of provincial realism, *The Building Fund* (25 April), was a success; and Colum's *The*

Land (9 June), which remained with the Abbey in spite of the rancour, was hailed as a development of the realism of *Broken Soil*.

The Building Fund is an odd, nasty little play. Mrs Grogan (played by Emma Vernon) is an old miser, whose meanness is only outdone by her son Shan (William Fay). Local parishioners have set up a building fund to raise a new church, but the Grogans refuse to subscribe. Sheila O'Dwyer (Sara Allgood) arrives on the scene: she is Mrs Grogan's granddaughter, is poor, and is seeking a position in service. She and the old woman begin to grow close, but Mrs Grogan dies before she has time to become more humane, although not before she makes a will. In the third act it is revealed that she has left everything to the church in order to ensure her place in heaven. There were brief flickers of an attraction between Sheila and the young farmer MacSweeney but he is really only after her money. And in any case, Sheila says at the end that she saw through him:

Sheila. . . . I guessed it; I knew he was in debt and wanted money. I never meant to marry such a beggar.
O'Callaghan. Ah! I see you are a girl as well able to look after number one as all your family.[49]

Looking 'after number one' is the dominant theme of the play; this is what the dying Mrs Grogan does also, and it is the motivation that draws Sheila and Shan together at the end, uniting in self-interest because 'he knows how to make money'.

The consciousness of the power of money, its domination over all other impulses, whether of passion or belief or fellowship, is clearly registered in this play by Boyle. A concern with the nature of money, related to issues of property, the land, inheritance, and marriage, is one that preoccupies Irish theatre from its beginnings in the Irish Literary Theatre. Indeed Martyn's *The Heather Field* introduces it, but this play by Boyle's isolates the way in which obsession with the gaining and losing of money turns life into a sterile sequence of financial contracts, triumphs, or failures. Only Russian theatre has anything comparable to the Irish obsession with money and the land; and there are, of course, very good reasons why these two societies developed theatrical traditions so transfixed with banks, mortgages, dispossessions, and clever buying where the vendor is at a disadvantage. This latter is known as land-grabbing in Ireland, the malediction flung at Yeats and Miss Horniman by the previous tenant of the Abbey.

Padraic Colum's *The Land* deals with an issue of great contemporary relevance, and one closely linked to the themes explored in Boyle's sour comedy. It is not often recognized, but the transfer of ownership of the land in Ireland from landlords and landed gentry to tenants that took place in the twenty years or so between 1885 and the 1900s was due to one of the most remarkable economic transformations that occurred in nineteenth-century Europe. It was also notable in that in spite of considerable agitation in the early Land League days, the transfer of property took place in a relatively quiet and peaceful manner, aided by government loan schemes to facilitate tenant ownership. Colum's play is an attempt at presenting this great theme, and also tries to show how land ownership and land hunger affected the emotional lives and aspirations of the young.

Murtagh Cosgar (played by William Fay) is a weathered old farmer, finally taking over his own land, which he has slaved at all his life, from the landlord. His neighbour Martin Douras (played by Frank Fay) has not yet realized this ambition; he has been in prison for unnamed political activities (there is more than a suggestion of Fenianism) but he has acquired a taste for reading and the things of the mind. This has left him poor, so that old Murtagh will not consent to a match between his son Matt and Martin's daughter Ellen, who will have no dowry with her. Murtagh says to Matt: 'Boy, your father built this house. He got these lands together. He has a right to see that you and your generation are in the way of keeping them together.'⁵⁰ Meanwhile, as some of the farmers are settling on the agreements that will allow them to buy out their land, young men and women are leaving for America, glad to be getting away from the wearisome toil and endless effort of farming. Ellen, though she loves Matt, also wants her freedom. In the middle of Act II she and Matt agree to emigrate, but then he suddenly loses courage and tries to convince her that he should conciliate the old man. She will not accept this, and they separate.

Colum is trying to register the effect upon emotional life of the seismic economic changes taking place, and Matt's failure of nerve is meant to show how property can overwhelm personal feelings, but the writing is not up to the challenge. Ellen says, imagining their life in America: 'You can offer me the sights of fine towns, and the fine manners, and the fine life.' And now, at the crucial moment of the play, Colum cannot find a way of conveying what it is that pulls Matt back from this. Lamely, he says, drawing away from her: 'It's not me that could offer the like of that. I never had anything to my hand but a spade.'⁵¹ Matt goes on to talk about a man's name and its importance, but the rift is there between them. Dramatically, it fails to convince. And when they agree to go off together again, in Act III, there is a sense of Colum's imperfect grasp of human impulse and drive. In a sense one has to wait for John B. Keane's *The Field* before we encounter any Irish play adequate to this powerful obsession with land. Oddly enough, Colum thought in 1963 when he wrote an introduction to a selection of his plays that the theme was out of date, and that the play was of historical interest only. It is more likely that he realized that it had failed to register the force of his theme.

In 1906 William Fay married Brigid O'Dempsey in Glasgow and he later described that year as the most successful in his life to that point.⁵² It was a year of continuing strain and tension at the Abbey, in spite of the haemorrhage of actors in the January secession. The players went on tour during the summer, performing in Wales, England, and Scotland. Miss Horniman accompanied them and was shocked at what she regarded as their vulgarity and their high spirits. From a letter of 12 June to Yeats from Edinburgh it is quite clear that she and William Fay were clashing badly: 'I refused to send [£50] to Fay to have it dribbled away with-out(?) any account being rendered to me.' And on 16 June she wrote to Yeats again: 'Every bitter thing I have said about Ireland has been put into my mind by my experiences among your people.'[53] She was outraged when, at the Trevelyan Hotel in Leeds, the actors kept on running in and out of each other's rooms until 2.00 a.m., one of them blowing a tin trumpet. The same tin trumpet had also fea-tured on the train journey from Cardiff, this time played by Brigid O'Dempsey. Arthur Sinclair, who had recently joined the company, became roaring drunk on at least one occasion. Her antagonism to William Fay continued to deepen, and the all-too-evident affection between him and O'Dempsey did not help. Fay, she insisted, in a letter of 21 June to Yeats, '*must* be brought to his senses'. And, she says, Fay 'blarneys' Yeats by 'using big terms and philosophical phrases'.[54] Her mounting detestation of Fay and the Irish actors seethes through the letters she bombarded Yeats with during the tour. Even Synge, who was with them, and who was falling in love with Molly Allgood—which also disgusted her—she accuses, frantically, in a letter of assumed artificial eloquence, as being guilty of a mixture of 'impudence' and 'cowardice'.[55] In August she summed up her feelings about the tour (and about Ireland), saying that she is '*thankful* to feel it is all over. I hope that it will be a long long time before I am obliged to go to Dublin again, to be snubbed and affronted by snarlers and sulkers and always fearing the insult of being forced into George Moore's presence.'[56] This last comment was calculated to appeal to Yeats's anger against Moore, now a clear enemy.

The plays of the 1906 autumn season included *The Mineral Workers* by William Boyle, a realistic play, concerning an Irish-American mining engineer who wants to smelt ore in rural Ireland to the discomfiture of the local commu-nity who resent the disruption of the settled habits of their lives. Its uncompli-cated subject-matter and its realistic mode found favour with the Dublin critics, a response which Yeats's *Deirdre* (24 November) did not enjoy.

Through Miss Horniman's offices Yeats engaged Florence Laetitia Darragh, a well-known London actress who had played in Oscar Wilde's *Salomé* with Florence Farr, for the part of Deirdre, much to the annoyance of Fay who wanted to control the casting, and to Lady Gregory's disquiet, who distrusted Darragh's gossipy ways. The reviewer in the journal *Sinn Féin* found *Deirdre* undramatic and compared Florence Darragh unfavourably to Máire Nic Shiubhlaigh in Russell's play on the same theme. It is fairly evident now why contemporary audi-ences found the play melancholy and unsettling: it is an intensely focused play, full of a sense of emotional irreconcilability between men and women, and between men when passion and loyalty create conflicting demands. Until the end, when Deirdre kills herself, the audience is left unsure as to whether or not she will go over to Conchubar. At one point she exclaims:

> Although we are so delicately made,
> There's something brutal in us; and we are won
> By those who can shed blood.[57]

The play failed miserably on the stage. It is deeply influenced by Yeats's disastrous relationship with Maud Gonne. Her choice of MacBride, the man of ostensible power and action, is refracted through the sadness and indecision of Deirdre, whose instincts remain inscrutable. However, on 2 December Yeats dictated a long memorandum to Lady Gregory for her eyes and those of Synge only at this time, in which he appraised the company's achievements so far and outlined the problems. His interpretations were not uninfluenced by the failure of *Deirdre* and Miss Horniman's antagonism towards William Fay. 'My work', the memorandum ruefully acknowledges, 'will not draw large audiences for a considerable time.' The company needs, he argues, someone different from William Fay, good though he is as a comic actor, to train players in a tragic style of acting, one which would have a less ostensibly Irish approach; the company also needs more capital to accomplish these objectives, and Miss Horniman may be induced to oblige. William Fay should concentrate on his artistic work and give up his responsibilities as stage manager (this recommendation surely owing something to an incident at Edinburgh when Fay drove Miss Horniman out of the dressing room as she tried to interfere in the making-up); and a new managing director should be engaged. These thoughts were given added urgency by the fact that Miss Horniman had let Yeats know that she would, under certain circumstances, part with £25,000 for redevelopment. The pressures Yeats was under in trying to deal with Miss Horniman are revealed in the crudity and banal sexual jealousy of her letters, as when, for example, she expresses amazement at John B. Yeats's admiration 'for Māire Nic Shivbhlaigh's (non-existent) figure, especially her (invisible) shoulders'. She goes on to generalize this detestation into a racial slur about 'the natural slothfulness of the players', a 'want of life and vitality [which] is naturalistic and true to Irish life'. Which is why, she snidely says, Irish people of any spirit 'long for America'. On 17 December she wrote to Yeats before leaving to holiday in Algeria that as long as the new stage manager was 'fairly young, of good manners and such a temper as will make the position possible for him' she would pledge the money.[58]

Synge responded to Yeats's memorandum in a letter to Lady Gregory on 13 December, from Byfleet in Surrey. He is against Yeats's ideas for Europeanizing the theatre, and insists that there is now a recognized Abbey style, which should be strengthened, using Fay's skills. In an undated memorandum, also responding to Yeats's ideas, he declares that Yeats should be allowed to do what he can to improve the staging of his own work; and that Fay must continue to direct all '*dialect* plays, peasant or not'.[59] Lady Gregory agreed with Synge that the Fays should not be 'forced out'.[60] On 19 December Miss Horniman wrote to Lady Gregory offering to fund the post of managing director, with Fay remaining in charge of the production of peasant plays. They were asked to make up their minds by 21 January. Meanwhile she was continuing to try to undermine Synge and Fay, as revealed in a private letter of 31 December to Yeats from Algiers: 'My dear Demon [a version of Yeats's secret name in the Golden Dawn], Mr Synge wants Fay to run the show, is too lazy to care about anything except his own plays and too cowardly to fight for the whole. You must work for a larger World than that in which something run under Fay can reign.' She also, in an undated fragment, states that Synge told her that he 'only gets his own way with Fay by humouring him'.[61]

Synge's *The Playboy of the Western World* was by now in rehearsal. This was a play the writing of which had driven Synge to distraction; he went about the task with extraordinary care and scruple. Fay read it for the directors in November; and Synge wanted Fay to direct it, not some newcomer brought in through Miss Horniman's influence. This new manager, an English vegetarian ('Bernard Shaw says that vegetables are good for the temper', wrote Yeats in a letter to Lady Gregory[62]) called Ben Iden Payne, was appointed in January, Synge and Lady Gregory imposing a six-month trial period. Meanwhile William Fay retained responsibility for directing the *Playboy*, also playing the title role. In a letter of 9 January 1907 to Yeats Synge pleaded with him not to bring Payne over until the *Playboy* had been performed: 'it is absolutely essential that Fay should be undisturbed till he has got through this big part.'[63]

They were expecting trouble. For once, Joseph Holloway was banned from rehearsals, where he was a frequent visitor, Fay and Synge surmising that he would find the content shocking. There was considerable anxiety over the impact the language, the theme of parricide, and the glorification of physical violence would have. And, in any case, nationalist Dublin was intensely suspicious of the author of *In the Shadow of the Glen*, confidently known to be a 'French decadent', and suspect, to Catholic nationalists, for his Anglo-Irish and clerical background.

On 29 January, a Saturday, the audience remained quiet enough during the first two acts, but they became increasingly vocal as the third act progressed. Christy's violent attack on his father, making good his word that he had killed his 'da', was the catalyst, and shouting and catcalls were heard—including 'Sinn Féin for ever'—until total disorder erupted at Christy's declaration that he'd prefer Pegeen, even if the Widow Quin would bring him 'a drift of chosen females, standing in their shifts itself'.[64] Yeats was in Scotland this evening, staying at the house of Professor Herbert Grierson in Aberdeen—editor and exponent of John Donne and the metaphysical poets—where he received a telegram from Lady Gregory: 'Audience broke up in disorder at the word shift.' Yeats returned for the second night, the following Monday; this time Sinn Féin protesters and other members of the audience booed and shouted from the start. William Fay, playing Christy, tried to remonstrate with the audience, on the odd grounds that he, as a man of Mayo extraction, took no offence at a play which was supposed to calumniate his county, but he was shouted down. Police were called in, but their presence only made matters worse and they were asked to leave.

Tuesday was even rowdier, the situation not being helped by a nephew of Lady Gregory's, who, turning up drunk with a group of Trinity College men, proceeded to sing 'God Save the King'. Yeats took the stage himself and asked that the play be given a hearing, to a mixture of claps and jeers, but to no avail: the performance was continuously interrupted and a number of arrests were made. The most frequent shout of outrage was: 'That's not the West.' When the play was over the nationalists and Sinn Féin members refused to leave and sang patriotic songs until the police cleared the building. And so it continued throughout the week, the newspapers reporting, in detail, on the disruptions and the consequent hearings for disorderly behaviour, at which Yeats himself appeared as a witness. The father of Padraic Colum (also Patrick) was fined 46s. (or a month in jail) for disorderly behaviour. Amongst other condemnation in the papers, *Sinn Féin*'s was typical, describing it as a 'vile and inhuman story told in the foulest language'.[65]

At a meeting of the Boyle, Co. Roscommon, branch of the Gaelic League on 3 February a motion was unanimously agreed where the branch entered their

protests against the so-called picture of western life. the objectional characters have been drawn so outrageous that we can only come to the conclusion that the alleged play has been prepared and is produced not for the sake of arts but with a purpose.[66]

That purpose being the defamation of the west. More than anything else this inchoate and semi-literate objection gives an idea of how the *Playboy* was received as an insult by many Irish people. The Boyle committee had not, of course, seen the play.

On Monday, 4 February, there was a public discussion of the play at the theatre, chaired by the critic P. D. Kenny of the *Irish Times* who, of all the reviewers, saw more clearly than any of his fellow-journalists what Synge was trying to do. Russell had been asked to chair the meeting but declined, even going so far as to publish a satire on Synge and Yeats in Griffith's *Sinn Féin*.

At the meeting Yeats reminded the audience of his nationalist credentials: he had been president of the Wolfe Tone Association; and he had praised the Irish when in America as an 'imaginative and animated people'. Francis Cruise O'Brien was against the play, for no very clear reason to judge by the reports; Piaras Béaslaí declared it was a shame that Yeats knew no Irish; and John B. Yeats stood up to declare that Ireland was an island of saints, but of 'plaster saints'. On 9 February *An Claidheamh Soluis*, the organ of the Gaelic League, accused Synge and the Abbey of propagating 'the monstrous gospel of animalism', and announced that the *Playboy* was 'the beginning of the end'. A silly piece of doggerel in the *Mail* (9 February) encapsulates Dublin's mixture of complacency and outrage:

> 'The Blushes of Ireland'
>
> Allusions to a flannel shirt
> (Young man, remember this, I urge 'ee)
> Afflict with agonising hurt
> Our patriot clergy.
>
> You come sir with your English ways,
> Your morals of the Cockney cabby,
> Corrupting with unseemly phrase
> The Abbey babby.[67]

In protest the realist playwright William Boyle withdrew his work from the repertory, and the Abbey was attacked by the Gaelic scholar and translator George
Sigerson and by Alice Milligan, the poet and writer of tableaux.

It was not, simply, the theme of parricide and the depiction of Mayo people as
feckless drunks and ineffectuals that outraged nationalist opinion. There is a
sense in which the Sinn Féin supporters and the readers of the *Leader* (the advanced nationalist paper edited by D. P. Moran) very accurately discerned the implications of Synge's play. The *Playboy* is about the attraction of physical violence
and heroic rebellious action against oppression, and Synge was depicting, ruthlessly, this human actuality. When Christy tells the *story* of his killing his da he is
heroized, but when he attacks him in the 'actuality' of the play's action, it is a different matter. Synge, in other words, is presenting his audience with the in-
tractabilities of an actual moral dilemma which nationalists had to (and would)
face when it came to a choice for (or against) action against the British crown.
This moral focus provides the imaginative dynamism that drives the play's furious
action and its searingly concrete linguistic energy. It is a deeply troubling and profoundly daring play, qualities very evident to the first audiences, and they did not
like them. The play's production history is curious, because through a kind of
sentimental obfuscation, there developed a performance style in the Abbey which
blunted this play's lethal edge, turning it into a hobbledehoy extravaganza, di-
verting attention from the work's brilliantly realized moral core, thereby crippling its energy. There are, in this play, layers of political and moral implications,
but these complexities are carried by the urgency of Synge's language, his commitment to bringing onto the Abbey stage the thrilling danger and strangeness of
actual people in the west, people he knew well, and admired, and whom he had
studied as an artist studies his subjects, weighing them, feeling with them, sharing their world view. Old Mahon (played by Ambrose Power), for example, leaps
straight out of life, the kind of life visually portrayed in the paintings and draw-
ings of Jack B. Yeats, his companion on many of his Irish travels. Here he is talking to the Widow Quin (Sara Allgood), protesting his sanity when she suggests he
may be driven mad by his gaping brain-pan:

Mahon. I never went mad to this day, and I not three weeks with the Limerick girls drinking myself silly and parlatic from the dark to dawn . . . Is my visage astray?
Widow Quin. It is, then. You're a sniggering maniac, a child could see.
Mahon (getting up, more cheerfully). Then I'd best be going to the union beyond, and
there'll be a welcome before me I tell you (*with great pride*), and I a terrible and fearful
case, the way that there I was one time, screeching in a straightened waistcoat, with
seven doctors writing out my sayings in a printed book.[68]

Hard stuff indeed for the likes of D. P. Moran or Arthur Griffith to take. The fact
of the matter was that they, unlike Synge, did not know the west of Ireland, or
rural Ireland at all, or at least not in the way that Synge did. He knew its wildness,
knew that there were nights on Aran or in Kenmare or Killybegs when it was not
at all infrequent to hear people talking like Old Mahon, or to hear a man boasting

that he had killed another. There are still such nights, and such places, but today's equivalents of Moran would not be seen dead in them.

Ben Iden Payne did not last long. Miss Horniman's insistent campaign against William Fay meant that after an initially calm period, the Dubliner and the Englishman ended up in a state of open conflict. Payne resigned in June and Miss Horniman put him in charge of her new venture, to which her interests were transferring, the Gaiety Theatre in Manchester. To Yeats she wrote, trying to persuade him to abandon the Abbey, 'you are being made a slave'.[69]

On 9 March Lady Gregory's one-acter *The Rising of the Moon* was produced, with William Fay playing the part of the rebel ballad-singer who is allowed to escape when he awakens a policeman's patriotism by singing the stirring song 'The Rising of the Moon'. Miss Horniman would not have approved and the *Irish Times* fulminated at the affront to the RIC: 'If there is one body in the country which more than another Irishmen of all classes feel a just pride in it is the Royal Irish Constabulary, and any attempt to hold up its members as cowards and traitors is certain to be bitterly resented.'[70] A noteworthy event on the 30 March was the staging, at the Abbey, of two plays from the Ulster Literary Theatre, *The Pagan* by Lewis Purcell, a comedy set in sixth-century Belfast, and *The Turn of the Road* by Rutherford Mayne, a realistic drama of northern rural life. The Ulster Literary Theatre was initially founded in 1902 in emulation of the achievements of the Irish Literary Theatre. At the year end, on 26 December, the Ulster group performed, in Belfast, *Suzanne and the Sovereigns* by Lewis Purcell and Gerald MacNamara, a farcical extravaganza on the Williamite Wars, and an interesting contrast to Lady Gregory's *The White Cockade*. Meanwhile the Theatre of Ireland, under Martyn, was producing a new play by Seumas O'Kelly, *The Matchmakers*, and a revival of Colum's *Broken Soil* as *The Fiddler's House*. On 18 March the National Players (who were linked with Inghinidhe na hÉireann) performed James Cousins's comedy of Co. Down life *Sold*, which had already been staged in late 1906 by a group calling itself the Cork National Theatre, and which had originally been rejected by the Abbey.

The Abbey had a success in the autumn with *The Country Dressmaker* (3 October 1907) by George Fitzmaurice, a playwright from near Listowel in north Kerry. Fitzmaurice wrote in the peasant idiom of Synge and Lady Gregory, but his scenes and characters have a kind of grim and harsh bucolic realism. Yeats did not like this play but audiences enjoyed its depiction of country people animated by common sense and the need for security in a precarious existence on the land. The story concerns a returned Yank who finally, and very unromantically, wins back the girl at home he has all but lost. Yeats thought it calumniated the Irish even more completely than did the *Playboy*, and he was right. In its own way Fitzmaurice's piece is as strange and disturbing as anything Synge wrote. Fitzmaurice was the first in a line of dramatist-writers from the Listowel area of north Kerry; the others include Bryan MacMahon, John B. Keane, and Brendan Kennelly. Fitzmaurice and his successors all mix realism with a wild fantastic streak, but their imaginative strangeness is not a concocted or otherworldly affair: it is rooted in the surprising twists and turns of human character and social behaviour.

Synge's wildness is driven by a delight in what is rare and unique in human individuality, and most frequently his talkers and storytellers are at odds with their environment. In Fitzmaurice the environment and the people therein are registered with an uncompromising fidelity, so that we are shocked into the realization that this is how people really behave when they are exposed to certain situations of crisis or uncertainty. Fitzmaurice is, in this respect, almost like a precursor of Brecht, in that his theatre is a space of thinking and contemplation rather than reverie or identification.

The Country Dressmaker is a sombre and reflective drama, which takes an entirely surprising and unsentimental view of marriage, matchmaking, and love. Julia Shea (played by Sara Allgood) has waited ten years for her 'Yank' to come home from America to marry her, as promised. Meanwhile her Yank, Pats Connor (played by a new recruit to the company, J. M. Kerrigan), has, we learn, been married to a heavy-drinking German who has died from alcoholism, and there have been other women too. Luke Quilter, the brilliantly realized matchmaker (played by William Fay), takes up the challenge of making a marriage between Julia and Edmund Normyle, a respectable farmer from the hills. Julia gives in to his persuasions, and agrees to marry Normyle if Pats does not return in the next three months. He does, of course, and he is immediately set upon by the desperate and greedy Clohesys, whose outward show conceals penury, bad management, and bad luck. However, they are foiled by Luke Quilter and by their own impatience. Although Luke and his mother Norry (played by William's wife Brigid O'Dempsey) have tried to keep Pats's history from her, Julia hears of it, and a 'black frost' comes on her heart. She almost manages to intercept Normyle, who is on his way to his wedding to another girl, but she is thwarted in her attempt; Pats is almost nabbed by the Clohesys a second time; and eventually Luke concludes the match. The mood at the end is resigned and joyless. This is how Julia finally accepts Pats's suit: 'The spring of life is broken in me, but if it is your wish entirely, then I am willing to make the best of it.' Luke, ruefully, remarks on the business, in disappointment and, to some degree, in sadness:

It's the most timorous job I ever put of me. But it's a happy couple they'll make with their troubles behind them. I have the name of being a jolly man with no trouble on me, but for the day that's in it. That's all as I roved out, and its only a way I have for shaping through a mournful world. With all my talk it's many a time I had to make the best of it with each of my two first wives and even with the dead-alive thing I have now itself.[71]

The language is based on north Kerry English, itself deeply influenced by Irish; the sentiments are those of the wide-awake countryman, with a sure grip on reality, without the slightest trace of illusion, or self-deceit.

In the summer of 1907 Miss Horniman made it clear that the £25,000 capital she was holding (a legacy from her father) was to go to Manchester, along with

Ben Iden Payne. Lady Gregory wrote to Synge on 29 June 1907 saying that, even though there would be no further money from their patron when the current patent ran out in 1910, nevertheless, she was 'in good spirits on the whole, being I think really far from Miss H. and further foreign invasions'.[72] These feelings went into the writing of her one-act play about Dervorgilla, the mistress of Dermot MacMurragh and wife of Tiernan O'Rourke. MacMurragh's abduction of O'Rourke's wife was part of a dynastic struggle which was to lead to the Norman Invasion in 1169. In Lady Gregory's play *Dervorgilla* (31 October 1907), the hero-ine (played by Sara Allgood) is an old woman, living in remorse in Mellifont Abbey. She is conscience-stricken at the bloodshed she has caused but she hopes that 'those were wrong who said the English would always bring trouble on us'.[73] No one knows who she is, save that she is generous, and dispenses gifts and prizes to the young who are taking part in a sports-day, organized by the English sol-diers. A singer arrives and, to her horror, sings of the perfidy of Dermot and the guilt of Dervorgilla:

> The rat in the larder, the fire in the thatch,
> The guest to be fattening, the children famished;
> If 't was Diarmuid's call that brought in the Gall,
> Let the weight of it fall upon Dervorgilla.

She is now terrified that her secret will out and sends her servant Flann to pay the singer to leave Ireland, but he is killed by a drunken English bowman. In her grief Flann's wife reveals who Dervorgilla is, and the young, to whom she has been gen-erous, turn away, and she experiences their 'swift, unflinching, terrible judgement'.

As Adrian Frazier has argued, Abbey politics are the play's 'motive, not its meaning'. It grapples with the issues of power, money, betrayal, and loyalty that were deeply implicated in Miss Horniman's relations with the Abbey, its actors and directors. Frazier also argues that the privilege (not just Miss Horniman's financial assets but Lady Gregory's own status also) 'that makes it possible to make gifts compromises those gifts and leads to further domination'.[74] Even the Abbey's high ideals and the effort that went into their realization can have bitter consequences. People do not always react generously to generosity; and as the play's complex of meanings implies, selflessness can sometimes be an attempt at expiation of guilt, and the recipients of gifts can sometimes suspect the motive be-hind the giving. However to lump Lady Gregory and Miss Horniman together, as conjoint wielders of a privilege that exposes them to accusation, fails, to some de-gree, to register the difference between Lady Gregory's scruple and Miss Horniman's moral crudity. Although the patent did not run out until 1910, and even though she continued her subsidies, from the summer of 1907 Miss Horniman had no commitment to the Abbey; however that did not stop her from offering (mostly unwelcome) advice.

From correspondence between William Fay to Yeats and Lady Gregory in the summer of 1907 it is perfectly clear that Fay was becoming harassed, anxious, and confused. In one letter, perhaps with some justification, he attacks Yeats and Lady Gregory for issuing contradictory instructions within days of each other; in another (22 August) he complains about an amateur actor who has demanded payment, having heard that others in similar positions in the company have received money:

You see its got round town we are paying people and that we did well on tour, so that every sundowner that turns up expects to be paid. And its perfectly absurd. The cheek they have. They can't speak King's English walk or do a thing unless one has to begin at the very beginning with each of them and waste the time of our own people . . . The actor Power. your Lady Gregory put in a word for him with *Brice* Chief Secretary. he done a lot of work for us.

This is a man who is harried and overworked. Another letter to Lady Gregory tells her he has no money to pay the actors the following week. Intriguingly, the bound manuscript volume in the National Library of Ireland which contains these (carbon-copied) letters also contains, at the back, some pages of an unfinished story in Fay's hand written from the end in, on the dangers of hashish.[75]

Now, however, William Fay sought to assert his authority over the company, with disastrous results, leading to the Fays themselves joining the other secessionists. On 1 December 1907 he wrote to the directors, demanding that he be given complete control of the engaging and contracting of actors; and that the company be released from their existing informal terms of employment, and be re-engaged by him. Fay himself claimed that his position was made untenable by the fact that actors who were aggrieved by anything he said or did went along to the directors who then overruled him.[76] The directors would not agree to these conditions, and in any case a number of company members disliked Fay, who had a foul temper and his own prima donna ways. Yeats wrote to Synge on Christmas Day 1907 briefly outlining his plan to get rid of Fay while making it seem that it was the company which wanted him out: 'I am very certain that Fay is going out but I am anxious not to seem to push him out. I want the pushing to come from the company. The Allgoods etc. should at once ask for a directors meeting or put their case in writing.'[77]

From a letter of Frank Fay's to W. G. Lawrence written at Queenstown (Cobh) on 24 May 1907 the depth of the animosity between Yeats and Lady Gregory, on the one hand, and the Fays on the other, becomes painfully evident:

[Henderson] tells me, by the way, that Synge is seriously ill. I hope he exaggerates, because if anything happened to him, it would give the whole movement into the hands of two selfish children that would then be cocks of the walk . . . Yeats has brought effeminate artistry into Ireland and it will not have a healthy family.[78]

William Fay, his wife Brigid O'Dempsey, and Frank Fay resigned on 10 February 1908, when they returned from a tour in Scotland. It was a sad ending, and the Fays' careers did not prosper thereafter, in spite of the caretaker's prophecy as he said goodbye to William: 'You'll be owner of this theatre yet.'

In 1908 the Fays went to New York to make some money. They allowed themselves to be described as the Irish National Theatre Co. from Dublin, much to the
annoyance of Yeats, who was told by John Quinn what they were doing. Dudley
Digges appeared with them in *The Rising of the Moon*: 'the old crowd is coming
together again', Fay wrote to W. J. Lawrence on 19 February 1908. On St Patrick's
Day, 17 March 1908, Frank Fay describes Yeats as 'selfish' and 'crooked'. The bitterness had gone very deep. On 18 March the Fays were suspended from membership of the Society; Frank Fay protested to Lawrence that they had resigned from
the Abbey not the Society, but the argument is disingenuous.[79]

F. Norreys Connell (pen name of the Dublin writer Conal Holmes Connell
O'Riordan) had his short play *The Piper* in rehearsal in December 1907, and there
were arguments amongst the players about its theme, William Fay himself dislik-
ing it intensely. When it opened on 13 February there was some of the usual disruption in the theatre at its subject: Yeats defended it, tendentiously, as an
allegory on the inertia in Irish political life since the death of Parnell. However,
the play is a bitter critique of nationalism, the rhetoric of opportunistic hatred,
and the inhumanity of war. A band of croppies in the United Irishmen rebellion
of 1798 are in retreat with a prisoner they have taken into custody, a Captain
Talbot of the Warwick Fencibles. Larry the Talker blathers on about the 'gloori-
ous victhry' he has led them to, but Black Mike insists on pointing out that the
croppies were 'bate'. The croppies want to hang Talbot, who remains stoically indifferent to his fate, but points out that if they do so they will be committing a
crime:

Larry (with real passion). Is it crime ye talk of? You spawn of hell! What about England's
    crimes?
Talbot. Sir, I do not endeavour to justify England anymore than a Bow Street runner en-
    deavours to justify the law. I am merely an English gentleman paid to cut throats in
    Ireland.
Larry. Ye'd have done well to cut them somewhere else.
Talbot. Two years ago I was cutting them in India.[80]

Connell's acid and somewhat Shavian rationality was bound to cause outrage. He
came to the Abbey with a background in the theatre—he appeared in Ibsen's
Ghosts in 1894—and with a reputation as a writer of serious and searching novels
about army life, such as *The Pity of War* (1906). His depiction of the cowardice of
the croppies, who flee when fired upon by the militia, is set against the courage of
the Piper, who, little more than a boy, raises the green flag against the fusillade of
English musketry from below the hill on which he proudly holds the rebel banner
aloft. Talbot gives him a soldier's burial, and insists on the flag being put in the
grave with him as a mark of honour, even though an Ensign wants to take it as a
trophy of victory.

On 8 October 1908 the Abbey produced a first play by a new Cork dramatist, S.
L. (Lennox) Robinson. Then in his early twenties, Robinson had been stimulated
to write drama by a visit of the Abbey to the Cork Opera House the year before,

where he saw the company play *Cathleen Ni Houlihan* and *The Rising of the Moon*. Their mixture of nationalism and realism inspired him to approach the life he knew, in the south, with a sharp but sympathetic eye. His first play, however, *The Clancy Name*, dealing with an attempt to cover up a rural murder to keep the Clancy name from blemish, was lambasted by the critics, although George Fitzmaurice was greatly impressed by it.

The following week, on 15 October, Thomas MacDonagh's *When the Dawn is Come* was produced, directed by MacDonagh himself. MacDonagh was, at this time, teaching at Pádraig Pearse's school, St Enda's, in Rathfarnham, and he was to be one of the signatories of the Proclamation of the Republic in 1916, and was executed for his part in the Easter Rising. That Yeats accepted his play, subtitled 'a Sinn Féin drama', reveals him, with the Fays gone, seeking to re-establish a common ground between the advanced nationalists and his theatre, for a time at least. This *rapprochement* had not a little to do with the fact that he and Maud Gonne were once more reconciled, now that she had separated from MacBride. In fact, some form of mystical marriage took place between them in the summer of this year, and there may have been a physical union.

MacDonagh's play is set fifty years in the future, and Irish nationalists are at war with Britain. They win in the end but the hero, an intellectual, loses his life and continually behaves 'like one seeking death'. The boys at St Enda's, who were brought to see the play, returned from the performance they saw 'yearning for rifles', as recorded in the school journal. Maud Gonne sat with Yeats at the 17 October performance, but Yeats did not like the play.

Early in the year, in January, Synge's *The Tinker's Wedding* was published but, significantly, not performed by the Abbey. There is no doubt but that its goliardic characterization of the venal priest, and the pagan energy of the tinkers, would have outraged Catholic nationalist opinion. Holloway, in his diary for 26 January, described how he came upon a newspaper poster, as he was walking round the town, which declared: 'The writer of *The Playboy of the Western World* insults the priesthood.'[81] The article in the newspaper described the play as 'abominable' and 'scurrilous'. Meanwhile Synge's health was deteriorating. He had Hodgkin's disease, but he was never told what the diagnosis was. On 5 May Sir Charles Ball operated on him in the Elpis Nursing Home for a lump in his side and found an inoperable tumour. The day before he wrote to Lady Gregory asking her to do what she could for Molly Allgood: they had planned to marry at Easter, but he had said nothing 'to avoid gossip or advice.'[82] It took until July for the wound to close over sufficiently for him to be discharged. When Lady Gregory invited him to Coole he told her that the scar would not stay closed, opening one day and closing the next, and that he would have to go to some 'very bracing place'.[83] In October he went to Koblenz to stay with a family he had known since student days in Germany in the 1890s. All through an autumn and winter of failing convalescence he was working on *Deirdre of the Sorrows*. On 3 January 1909 he wrote to Lady Gregory saying that the first act had to be rewritten because of changes he had made in later scenes, but also telling her that he could only work a little every day because of digestive disorders.[84] In February Lady Gregory became seriously ill and suffered a cerebral haemorrhage, while Yeats, too, had some kind of breakdown and was stricken by a severe attack of rheumatism while visiting Miss Horniman in Manchester.

On 23 March Synge sent a message to Yeats through Molly Allgood asking him to come and talk over arrangements after his death (Yeats had agreed to be adviser to the executor in the summer) but he died in the early hours of 24 March. He said to the nurse: 'It is no use fighting death anymore' and turned over and died.[85] That night Yeats gave a memorial speech in his honour at the United Arts Club on Stephen's Green, where Count Casimir Dumier-Markievicz (Constance Gore-Booth's husband) surprised Yeats by praising the way he had assisted Synge: Markievicz had first thrown in his lot with the Theatre of Ireland before establishing his own Independent Dramatic Company in 1908. A few days later Thomas MacDonagh (for whom Yeats had acted as referee in a post he had applied for—successfully—at the National University) wrote of Synge in *T.P.'s Weekly* that his work had 'the rich power of real life and the elemental'.

Early in April 1909 Norreys Connell was appointed salaried managing director, taking over the working of the theatre, a tenure that lasted until 2 July when he resigned. He had annoyed the actors intensely when, on a visit to Cork, he drafted a letter to the company which he insisted on having read aloud to them, saying that they often failed to speak clearly, and advising them to read the English novelist Galsworthy to each other to improve their diction. Connell also irritated Miss Horniman who flew into a rage when Sara Allgood took part in a reading organized by Mrs Patrick Campbell in London on behalf of the Women's Movement. Miss Horniman felt that Connell should have prevented the actress from joining in what was a political meeting, or so she argued; but in effect, she was making it clear that she wanted finally to withdraw from the Abbey, now that it had become plain that her campaign to woo Yeats to her designs was not going to succeed. Norreys Connell's rueful comment, written retrospectively to an old Dublin friend, from London in 1937, is probably an accurate account of his predicament. He writes on old Abbey paper he has found amidst his effects:

it dates from that period just eight and twenty years ago when I was theoretically managing the Abbey company with Lady Gregory on the one hand and Miss Horniman on the other doing their best to bedevil me, in order to vent their spite on one another, while Maire O'Neill kicked me from behind.[86]

A pathetic and sad letter of 8 July reveals Miss Horniman to be hopelessly in love with Yeats and trying to cope with emotions which mix self-abasement, anger, and her consciousness of the power of money:

If you get those guarantors together and they object to paying me £500 for freeholds costing £1,500, I'll take less; even a 'slave' can avoid being greedy . . . You have chosen your own course and I *accept* fully that you have a full right to it, in contradistinction to your contention that we poor 'slaves' should *bow* to everything said by a superman.[87]

The patent granted in 1904 was to expire in December 1910 and money had to be raised to replace her endowments as well as to buy out her interest. Lady Gregory, during an Abbey run at the Royal Court Theatre in London, joined George Bernard Shaw and his wife Charlotte in their box, whence began a correspondence and friendship that lasted for the rest of her life. Hoping that Shaw might assist financially and being well aware of his standing in international theatre, she asked him to replace Synge as one of the triumvirate of directors. He declined the invitation, on the grounds that he would find it difficult to give the Abbey sufficient time, nor could he assist with funds, having recently lost a £6,000 investment on productions by Harley Granville-Barker and J. E. Vedrenne at the Royal Court. However, he did offer *The Shewing-up of Blanco Posnet*, written for Herbert Beerbohn Tree's After Noon Theatre, but banned by the Lord Chamberlain's office on the grounds of blasphemy: the English system of licensing plays from this office did not apply in Ireland where authority derived from the letters patent of the crown. The Abbey agreed to stage the play, Lady Gregory and Yeats resisting pressure from Dublin Castle to have it stopped. When it opened on 25 August 1909 there was a packed house, the Horse Show week crowds hoping for something a little improper or titillating. James Joyce, who was there reporting for the Triestine *Piccolo della sera*, was mightily unimpressed by this tale of the surprising action of grace set in the American Wild West. Blanco Posnet is a ne'er-do-well in a town at the back of nowhere, which once had mushroomed when there were rumours of gold deposits in the area. Now the main diversions are drinking, whoring, and lynching, and a special enjoyment is the shooting of the corpse after it has been hanged. Posnet is being tried by the Sheriff for stealing a horse; the jury is eager to get to the hanging; and everyone is ready to proceed with all dispatch, including Feemy the whore, who is only too eager to swear that Posnet is guilty. He is, but towards the end of the play the trial is interrupted by a woman who 'shews up' Blanco: she tells the court that Blanco gave her the horse, so she could ride to a doctor to save the life of her child who is dying of a croup attack. The child dies, but Blanco has been assailed by kindness; to her own surprise Feemy is also, and she lies to save him, swearing that she did not see him with the horse. The play expounds, in fairly blunt terms, Shaw's relativist view of good and evil, and his attitude towards instinct, which can impel to charity as well as to selflessness. The individual's own volition is seen to operate within strict confines, and general conceptions of God are unthinking sentimentality. Blanco explodes, as follows, at the piousness of his brother, who has 'got religion':

What do you know about Him? You that always talk as if He never did anything without asking your rotten leave first. Why did the child die? Tell me that if you can. He can't have wanted to kill the child. Why did He make me go soft on the child if He was going hard on it Himself? . . . Why did I go soft myself? Why did the Sheriff go soft?[88]

Yeats wrote to Herbert Grierson on 12 October, telling him that the Abbey's stand on the Shaw had enhanced their reputation with nationalists, and also announcing that they were planning to produce *Oedipus* in the New Year, a play also banned by the Lord Chamberlain's office, on the grounds that it dealt with incest.[89] Meanwhile Shaw was advising Lady Gregory to deal firmly with Miss Horniman, assuring her that she was something of a lady, 'in spite of her perverse delight in assuring the world that she is nothing but a commercial traveller'.[90]

George Moore, writing in retrospect in *Vale* (1914), said, characteristically, 'Synge's death seems to have done him a great deal of good';[91] a collected edition of his writings was planned, and *The Playboy* was revived on 27 May, to a much more enthusiastic set of notices in the Dublin papers. The revival was comically described by director Norreys Connell in his semi-autobiographical *Adam in Dublin* (1920) through the eyes of an inebriated playgoer: 'half a dozen men were holding another down that had his teeth buried in yet another's calf, and a young girl was trying to get at one or other of them with a pair of red-hot tongs. Mr Macfadden clapped his hands: he had never seen anything half so good on the stage before.'[92] Sadly the Fays were by now entirely bitter and deeply estranged from the Abbey, Frank (who played Shawn Keogh in the first production) writing to Máire Garvey on 6 March that 'Lady Gregory's dialogue used to make my teeth ache by a sort of bread and milk quality in it . . . when will someone with "guts" and without pose arise in Ireland?'[93] However, the frustrated bravado of this is put into context when it is recalled that early the following year, after the success of Synge's *Deirdre of the Sorrows*, Frank Fay asked to be brought back into the company only to be refused.

On 26 November 1909 the Ulster Literary Theatre opened at the Abbey, with the premier of Gerald MacNamara's one-acter *The Mist that Does Be on the Bog* and a revised version of Rutherford Mayne's *The Drone*. MacNamara (pseudonym of Henry C. Morrow) had written *Suzanne and the Sovereigns* (1907), a farcial treatment of Irish history, and in *The Mist* he parodied the Abbey style of peasant play. In it a group of middle-class urban folk, with cultured tastes, motor to the west of Ireland in order to acquire an authentic brogue. There they encounter another seeker after the purity of peasant speech, a playwright, who is a caricature of Synge and Colum. The 'mist' is the confusion that enshrouds this group of cultural revivalists.

Meanwhile, in Cork, Daniel Corkery was inaugurating the Cork Dramatic Society, founded in May 1909, with productions of his plays *Embers* (6 May), which deals with the ways in which Fenianism can be reactivated to fan the flames of contemporary nationalism, and *The Hermit and the King* (2 December), weighing the claims of the spiritual and the actual life. This pre-Christmas run in Cork at 'The Dún' in Queen Street also featured a new play by Lennox Robinson, *The Lesson of his Life*, and T. C. Murray's first play, *The Wheel of Fortune*. Murray, Robinson, and Corkery, along with R. J. Ray, were later to be known as the 'Cork realists'. Murray, from Macroom, was teaching in Cork at this time, and he was a member of the Dramatic Society. Among the co-founders of the

Cork Dramatic Society was Terence MacSwiney, later a revolutionary, who died on hunger strike in 1920.

As 1909 drew to a close Yeats was receiving what can only be described as manic letters from Miss Horniman, offering complicated financial arrangements, buy-outs, loans, and the promise of freedom from her influence. On Christmas Day she wrote: 'Long ago I warned you that supermen cannot prevent a revolt of slaves.'[94] Yeats, showing a not inconsiderable business sense, had the theatre valued at much less than Miss Horniman anticipated and based an offer for purchase on this figure. Lady Gregory was the one who had to face Miss Horniman with these terms, a meeting which she described to Yeats in a letter of January 1910 as 'dreadful'. Shaw had suggested to Miss Horniman that the Abbey directors were trying to 'beat her down'. The experience of watching her ranting and raving was, Lady Gregory said, 'like looking at some malignant growth'.[95] By February the price was agreed: Miss Horniman would receive £1,000 and she would pay out the subsidies for 1910 amounting to £400.

Synge's *Deirdre of the Sorrows* was produced on 13 January 1910, with Molly Allgood, Synge's fiancée (under the stage-name Máire O'Neill), playing the main part. It is a sombre and harrowing play, full of the conditionality of life, and darkened by a sense of the futility of human endeavour. Bravery, energy, and beauty are seen to be pathetic; the intensity of passion is qualified by the open grave which awaits the lovers behind a curtain in the place they have been lured to by the wiliness of power and authority. There were mixed reviews, but on the whole the reception was respectful and awed. The legend of Synge had begun to build, but nevertheless the spell cast by this play about death and violence, written by a man coping with a fatal illness, could not fail to move many people, even in Dublin.

On 10 February a revision of W. B. Yeats's 1908 play *The Golden Helmet* was staged under the title *The Green Helmet*. A 'heroic farce', it dealt with a challenge offered by an otherworld creature to the warriors of Ireland which none meets except Cuchulain, who offers his head on a block to the Red Man from the sea. Padraic Colum (whose *Thomas Muskerry* was scheduled for production in May) wrote enthusiastically about Yeats's play, describing it as 'thrilling in its rapidity, its suggestion, its triumphant verse'.[96] This well describes the play's impetuous force, and it was, probably, Yeats's most accomplished piece of dramatic writing so far. Its cold and swift energy convinces, as the crammed action moves to a climax in which Cuchulain is prepared to die to honour a promise made. The mixture of quarrelsomeness, cowardice, and dishonour amongst the other Ulster warriors stands out in sharp relief to Cuchulain's concentrated simplicity of character. Clearly Yeats is here sketching the lineaments of his Cuchulain mask: heroism isolated by a selfless act when others fail in nerve and honour. The Nietzschean strain, so mocked by Miss Horniman, is in evidence. Cuchulain, turning away from Emer's pleas that he should save his skin, says:

> Would you stay the great barnacle-goose
> When its eyes are turned to the sea and its beak to the salt of the air?[97]

The squabbling for precedence and the faithless caving in of Cuchulain's comrades when issued with an unremitting challenge reflects Yeats's experiences in the Abbey through the past years: Miss Horniman's demands, Russell's two-facedness, the Fays' estrangement, the howling of the nationalist press, the condescension of the British. Naturally enough, the Red Man gives the green helmet, symbol of authority, to Cuchulain.

During this month Yeats wrote to Lennox Robinson in Cork, asking him to come to an interview. He appointed him manager, although Robinson was only 22, explaining to the young man that Ibsen had been appointed to the Norwegian theatre in Bergen at a similarly early age, having previously worked behind the counter in a pharmacy. Yeats sent him off to London to study direction at the Duke of York's Theatre, where he was captivated by Harley Granville-Barker's method of planning stage movements: he painted chessboard squares on the stage and got his actors to make knight's diagonals or bishop's swoops, the whole thing inscribing a set of orchestrated stage manœuvres. When Robinson told him of this Yeats was delighted, urging him to adopt this method on the grounds that it would help the youthful manager terrify the seasoned actors into submission. Robinson spent six weeks in London, studying under Dion Boucicault (the nineteenth-century playwright's second son), as well as with Shaw, whose *Misalliance* was in rehearsal. When Robinson returned he started rehearsing Colum's new play, *Thomas Muskerry*.

This opened on 5 May. The play's sombre dwelling on the egoism of old age in the character of Muskerry, a workhouse master, and his undoing by an unscrupulous but harried daughter, drew forth comparisons with *King Lear* and Balzac's *Old Goriot*. Muskerry has been swindled by a sharp operator in the midlands town where the workhouse is; he has signed certificates for a quantity of coal, and only half the amount has been delivered. The fraudster has gone to America, having tricked Muskerry's son-in-law Crilly and his daughter Marianne out of £400 as well. Muskerry is persuaded to resign to allow Scollard, the man his granddaughter plans to marry, to take his place. When Anna, the granddaughter, discovers that her parents too have been tricked she insists on having her dowry, backed up by the ambitious and cold practicality of the new workhouse master. Muskerry wants to pay back to the Guardians the amount he is responsible for, but when he tries to reclaim investments in his son-in-law's shop he discovers that the bank have foreclosed on all credit. There is nothing left. Muskerry ends up in the workhouse himself; his final dream of a little cottage with a half an acre is snatched from him on a bureaucratic technicality; he has a stroke and dies.

The play captures, very effectively, the relationship between money, authority, and freedom. Muskerry is stripped of his dignity and has to bear the offence of having an upstart underling mock him to his face when his fortune changes. Even his own flesh and blood, intent on their own concerns, show no loyalty or consideration, and he has to rely on the good nature of strangers, paupers, a blind piper, and an old friend, also disgraced and in a similar position. The play's force derives not so much from the pathos of the old man stripped of his authority, but from Colum's clear understanding of the way money controls society, particularly the Irish rural one, with its memories of famine and starvation. Foolishness with money can be a matter of life and death as revealed in Muskerry's outburst to his daughter when it is revealed her husband has lost £400 in the bad guarantee: 'And do you think, Marianne Crilly, there can be luck or grace in a house where such a thing could happen? There could be no good prayers in a house like this. I'll go out of this house and I'll never put foot into it again.'[98]

This play about the dissolution of authority was matched by a piece of public theatre on the same theme (with farcical subplots) on the following day, Friday, 6 May. Edward VII died during the night. In the morning W. A. Henderson, the Abbey secretary, came around to Lennox Robinson's house to see if the performance scheduled for the afternoon should go ahead: all the other theatres were closing as a mark of respect. Robinson telegrammed Lady Gregory who sent back the message, 'should close through courtesy', but the telegraph boy delayed on the way back to the post office in Gort so that the message arrived too late for Robinson to cancel. Miss Horniman erupted into fury and demanded an apology through the Dublin papers, threatening to withdraw the remaining subsidy. Yeats and Lady Gregory did not comply on the grounds that no one was at fault, but Miss Horniman remained unmollified, and lawyers were engaged to wrest from her the subsidy which, it was now being argued, was being unlawfully withheld. The case went to arbitration under Charles Prestwick Scott of the *Manchester Guardian* who found in favour of the theatre, in May 1911. Miss Horniman telegrammed to Yeats: 'You have shown me that I do not matter in your eyes the money is paid supermen cannot associate with slaves may time reawaken your sense of honour then you may find your friend again but repentance must come first.'[99] By now Yeats and Lady Gregory had, through fund-raising, put the theatre on a reasonably secure footing and told their erstwhile patron they did not want the money, at which she promptly paid up.

Yeats gave public lectures in order to raise funds, and one of these, to become the essay 'J. M. Synge and the Ireland of his Time', developed an argument which both praised what he regarded as Synge's aloof detachment and attacked the kind of personality stimulated into passion by abstraction, politics, and ideology, whether nationalism, unionism, or imperialism. He had seen what this had done in the Abbey's first ten years, and how it had ruined the lives of, amongst others, Maud Gonne and Miss Horniman. Such minds and personalities are, he says,

preoccupied with the nation's future, with heroes, poets, soldiers . . . while a secret feeling that what is so unreal needs continued defence makes them bitter and restless . . . A[n] attitude of defence, of continual apology . . . makes the mind barren because it kills intellectual innocence . . . the mere drifting hither and thither that must come before all true thought and emotion.[100]

The year 1910 was one in which 'realism' came to the fore, beginning with Colum's *Thomas Muskerry* and continuing with Robinson's own *Harvest* (19

May), R. J. Ray's *The Casting out of Martin Whelan* (29 September), T. C. Murray's *Birthright* (27 October), and Seumas O'Kelly's *The Shuiler's Child* (24 November). O'Kelly's play had previously been staged by Martyn's Theatre of Ireland, and when it came to the Abbey it brought with it back into the company the estranged Máire Nic Shiubhlaigh (Mary Walker).

Ray's *The Casting out of Martin Whelan* is a blueprint of what became known as PQ—'peasant quality'—a convention of grim rural naturalism in which issues of land ownership, religion, nationalist politics, and familial guilt are both analysed and satirized. This play concerns a returned émigré Irishman, an election, a hanging, an informer, and the conflict between youthful idealism and crabbed bitterness: the kind of combination of elements that proved very durable on the Abbey stage.

Murray's *Birthright* also deals with land ownership, but with a grim and surprising ferocity. A tightly written, intense play, directed by Murray himself, who had now moved to Dublin, it deals with an arbitrarily cruel and violent father, and his sudden decision to disinherit his elder son in favour of the younger, who is more dutiful and more attentive to the farm. At the end the brothers fight and the elder son is killed. The writing captures some of the ferocity and brutal forthrightness of west Cork speech. In the following extract Hugh, the elder brother (played by the recently recruited Fred O'Donovan), is slightly tipsy, having been to a party celebrating his team's victory in a hurling match:

Bat. Yes look at him!—look at the cut of him!
Maura. Wisha, Bat.
Bat. Wisha, Bat. . . Ah, Maura, Maura, 'tis you have the good right to be speaking for him—him that has the great love for you keeping you up in the bitter night till near cock-crow. . .
Maura. No, no, Bat, you're wronging him. . .
Bat (thunderingly). Hush your mouth, you![101]

It would not be a misrepresentation of the Abbey's history to say that from the appointment of Lennox Robinson onwards the theatre's style and ethos changed considerably. These Cork realist plays were popular (the finances improved markedly, Yeats announcing in *The Times* for 14 June that, unlike the Moscow Arts Theatre, they would soon be solvent) and they and Colum's *Thomas Muskerry*, his last play for the Abbey, depict an Ireland more immediately alive to the pressures of necessity and cash than Yeats's heroic world, Lady Gregory's Kiltartan, or Synge's strange and violent west.

The original patent ran out in December 1910. Yeats and Lady Gregory applied for its renewal, but their claim was contested by Martyn's Theatre of Ireland (supported by Russell), who argued that they should have concessionary rights at the Abbey on the grounds that they had inherited some of the original spirit of the old Irish National Theatre Society. The Bill of Costs, held in the National Library, reveals the extent of the complex correspondence between all parties as Miss Horniman was legally released from the patent, and the Theatre of Ireland's attempted coup resisted. The legal wrangle went on from 17 February 1910 to 23 December 1912, and the final costs were £180. The matter was in effect finally settled by Winston Churchill, then Home Secretary, who granted sole patent to Lady Gregory and Yeats for twenty-one years. Yeats had secured the theatre, and when asked by his sister Lily how things were at the Abbey, replied: 'The usual quarrelling. But then the founder of the Christian religion had the same trouble with his company, and had to invent parables to keep them in good humour.'[102]

3

1911–1925
'O Absalom, my son'

With Horniman's departure from the scene, and Synge dead, the theatre now virtually belonged to Yeats and Lady Gregory. They had, Yeats said in an interview in the *Pall Mall Gazette* (13 January 1911), 'begun with the peasantry', but he went on to say that they did not intend to stop there. He referred to a new play from the north, 'a study of artisan life in Belfast' (this was St John Ervine's *A Mixed Marriage*) which they could place alongside the series of plays from the Cork realists Robinson, Ray, and Murray. Here he saw evidence of a new impetus, coming from the cities and small country towns, to set alongside the drama of Lady Gregory, Synge, Colum, and Fitzmaurice. In the same interview he said that the Abbey wanted to 'touch all Irish life'; he acknowledged, implicitly, that his own work—imaginative, symbolic, and poetic drama—would continue to appeal only to a relatively small audience, but nevertheless that would be catered for too, 'from time to time'.[1] Clearly, Yeats understood that the popularity of the new kind of realistic writing, with its avid observation of the minutiae of family life, and the pressures wrought upon it by money, property, and sex, would bring in audiences more readily than would evocations of moods and states of feeling. Yeats was far from being unappreciative of the toughness and bite of the new realism, and its edgy modernity got into his own style and indeed into the way he looked at men and women in his verse, but also in his plays. The psychological realism of plays like *The Only Jealousy of Emer* (printed 1919, but not performed until 1922 in Holland) owed not a little to the work of Robinson, Murray, and Ervine.

Edward Gordon Craig, the famous stage-designer, created a set of screens for the Abbey, first used on 12 January 1911 for the staging of a revival of Yeats's *The Hour Glass* and Lady Gregory's one-acter *The Deliverer*. These were to be used to create atmospheric effects and to throw the actor and the language into relief. There were a number of gibes about the screens and their uses in relation to *The Deliverer*, which was set in ancient Egypt at the time of the exodus of the Jews. The solemn theme and the starkly symbolic background seemed incongruous when the characters spoke in Lady Gregory's Kiltartan. On 26 January, the writer-aristocrat Lord Dunsany (a supporter of the Abbey during its process of disentanglement from Miss Horniman) had a play staged with the Craig sets: *King Argimenes and the Unknown Warrior*. This play had an eastern setting and characters with names like Zarb, Cahafru, and Atharlia, reflecting Lord

Dunsany's taste for fantasy and the bizarre. It occasioned, however, some un-intended hilarity.

St John Ervine's *Mixed Marriage* opened on 30 March 1911. Ervine, a disciple of Shaw, came from Protestant east Belfast and was the son of deaf mutes. His first play tackled the problem of sectarian division in Belfast. John Rainey is a Protestant worker whose son Hugh is engaged to Nora, a Catholic. This pro-posed union, and the united strike action between Protestant and Catholic work-ers, outrages the father. Their house is attacked by rioters and Nora is shot. It is a grim evocation of deeply entrenched hatreds.

While visiting England Yeats saw at Norwich a production of *The Countess Cathleen* by Nugent Monck, a disciple of William Poel, and, like Poel, a cam-paigner for the revival of medieval English drama: early twentieth-century England witnessed a renewal of interest in native English traditions, a fashion owing something to the influence of William Morris and the Arts and Crafts Movement. Monck, it seemed possible, might be the person to bring grace, vigour, and poetry to the Abbey, to counter the social realism that seemed to have its own momentum under Robinson, and Yeats invited him to take a position as a manager and to establish an acting school in the theatre. He admired the stateli-ness of Monck's realization of *The Countess Cathleen*, describing it as 'like the page of a missal' in a letter to his sister Lily.[2] The company was scheduled to tour for the first time in the USA from September through to March 1912, and Monck would be free to experiment and develop his school while the leading actors were away. In effect he was put in charge of a second company in the Abbey, specially funded from a source neither Yeats nor Lady Gregory ever revealed.[3] A notice ap-peared in Dublin papers on 30 September announcing the beginning of classes at the Abbey in acting, elocution, gesture, and deportment. Máire Nic Shiubhlaigh did not go with the company, staying behind, ostensibly to assist Monck, but in fact Yeats and Lady Gregory had decided that she had exhausted her acting talent.

Monck's first presentation, by the 'Abbey School of Acting', was *The Interlude of Youth (Mundus et Infans)* (23 November 1912), a medieval morality play, which shared the bill with *The Marriage* (a translation from the Irish of Douglas Hyde by Lady Gregory), a folk morality, in which the ghost of Raftery transforms the dismal marriage of a poverty-stricken couple into a celebration of community and human generosity. *The Second Shepherd's Play* (23 November) from the Wakefield Cycle of mystery plays was also directed by Monck, with A. Patrick Wilson taking the part of Mac the sheep-stealer, who is drawn into the drama of the incarnation. Monck also produced Rutherford Mayne's bitterly realistic *Red Turf* (7 December), dealing with the malice and violence of land disputes.

Yeats travelled to the USA with the main Abbey company, embarking at Queenstown on 13 September. He knew there was going to be a fight, and *The Playboy* was certain to cause trouble, but the agents Lieber & Co. insisted that the play be in the repertoire. He carefully prepared the ground for the reception of the plays in a lecture to the Drama League in Boston, where he described Synge's shocking originality, comparing him to Cervantes, paid tribute to Lady Gregory, and explained the new school of realism (Robinson, Murray, and Ervine) as a re-action to his own emphasis on poetry and symbol. He openly attacked Irish-American sentimentalism, accusing it of being out of touch with Irish actualities, which were accurately reflected in Synge's work and in that of Lady Gregory. *The Playboy* opened in Boston on 16 October and was, on the whole, well received. Yeats returned to Ireland, leaving Lady Gregory in charge for the New York run. Here matters were quite different, and the stage was actually mobbed by an out-raged audience on 27 November. She responded by trying to address them from the stage. The situation got worse, and Foster quotes from a 'poisoned pen' letter she received on 17 December, which maliciously referred to the fact that Yeats had recently had a Civil List pension from the British government: 'I seen ye where [*sic*] got slated in New York. How is the Pensioner? Yours, Mike.'[4] On 18 January 1912 the District Attorney, egged on by Irish-American nationalists, arrested the actors for 'sacrilegious and immoral' behaviour.[5] They were successfully de-fended by John Quinn, the Irish-American lawyer and friend of Yeats and the Abbey, who became Lady Gregory's lover during her stay in the USA.

Meanwhile back in Dublin Monck continued to train the second company, and staged two further mystery plays *The Annunciation* and *The Flight into Egypt* (4 January 1912). Around this time there took place an odd tangle of sexual mis-conceptions, which Yeats related to Lady Gregory, still in New York. A young man, calling himself Carter, joined the school of acting and confided to Monck that he was a transvestite, telling him also that his family had sent him off to sea in an attempt to make a man of him. Now they had accepted his effeminacy and agreed that he become an actor. He was disliked intensely by Monck, Yeats con-fessing that the young man made him uneasy, though he was sorry for 'the pathos of the poor boy's life', always trying to ingratiate himself with everybody. Eventually a member of the School met an aunt of 'Carter's', who remarked on what a pleasant time her niece had had with the company. One female student was particularly outraged at discovering that 'Carter' was a girl, as 'he' had once tried to embrace her.[6] On 15 February Monck directed the first new production of a play in Irish at the Abbey, *An Tincéar agus an tSídheóg* by Hyde, with Michael Conniffe, a native speaker from Tawin Island in Galway Bay, as the tinker. This was the play Moore had produced at his Gaelic League lawn party in Upper Ely Place in the summer of 1902. Monck, however, was suffering from a nervous dis-ability, and on 1 March announced his intention to resign. The company returned triumphant from their success and legal victory in the USA on 12 March. They had, while on tour, been rehearsing Lennox Robinson's new play *Patriots*, which was staged on 11 April 1912, the day on which the third Home Rule Bill was in-troduced in the House of Commons at Westminster.

James Nugent, a 'physical force' patriot, and a Fenian, comes home from prison and wishes to continue the work of republican organizing and training. He is opposed, however, by those who wish to adopt a more constitutional approach;

and he is bitterly disappointed by the apathy and self-seeking he finds dominating people's interests. It is a play of ideas, which tackles a difficult subject, but it was received enthusiastically by receptive audiences, who clapped Fred O'Donovan in the leading role throughout the play. The actress Kathleen Drago joined the company for this production. Although constitutional nationalism was still the broadly accepted strategy for the attainment of a degree of independence in Ireland, sympathies and attitudes were, as early as 1912, beginning to harden, Pearse (with others) founding the Irish Volunteers the following year.

At the end of April the Abbey went on a long tour in Britain, which would draw to an end with a première of a new T. C. Murray play at the Royal Court in London. The play was *Maurice Harte* (20 June). These London shows (which included a new one-act comedy by Lady Gregory, *The Bogie Man*, 4 July 1912) were enthusiastically reviewed and did excellent business: the Abbey had become a fashionable cult in London, and Lloyd George, the Prime Minister, went to see them twice.

Maurice Harte is a powerful portrayal of a poor farming family near Macroom in west Cork. Maurice (played by Fred O'Donovan), the hope of the family, is shortly to be ordained while the other son, Owen (played by J. A. O'Rourke), will marry well, two events which will release the family from the depths of debt to which they have sunk in sending the boy to Maynooth. However, briskly and brutally, it is revealed that Maurice has no vocation and he pleads with his parents to release him from the sacrifice of falsely taking his ordination vows. But they compel him to return by revealing how much they have spent on him, and Mrs Harte tells him that it will kill her if he does not go through with the ordination. He bows to her will, but as the play draws to a close the cost to the young man is made plain when he returns a year later broken in mind. The play is entirely convincing in the way it shows how impossible it is for Maurice, in his circumstances, not to bow to his mother's will, even though it is the ruin of him.

On 20 December 1912 the Abbey went on a second American tour, accompanied by Lady Gregory, and they remained in the USA until 21 April 1913. Nugent Monck went with them, still in his position, while Robinson stayed behind to train the 'second' Abbey company. This second long tour provoked heated exchanges in the *Irish Times* in December, the critic Ernest A. Boyd attacking the National Theatre for failing to discharge its patriotic responsibilities and, inaccurately, for staging very little new work. These charges were answered by Robinson and the Abbey was, interestingly, supported by Countess Markievicz.

On 20 February the Abbey's second company produced a translation of Gerhardt Hauptmann's *Hannele* and on 6 March a version of August Strindberg's *There are Crimes and there are Crimes*, to a certain amount of bafflement and disappointment: the critics were expecting racy and daring plays when in fact they encountered serious moral lessons and meditations. Later in March a first play by John Guinan from near Birr in Co. Offaly was staged, called *The Cuckoo's Nest* (13 March), a rambling piece which concentrated on the comic effects of peasant speech. An unusually productive season continued with a new play by two Cork women, Suzanne R. Day and Geraldine Cummins, *Broken Faith* (24 April). These two feminist women were active in the Munster Women's Franchise League and they also showed an interest in spiritualism and psychical research. *Broken Faith* deals with a wife who, for the sake of her children, admits to a crime committed by her useless husband. She anticipates that her man will give their offspring a new life in America. When he refuses to take responsibility for them she throws him over and seizes freedom for herself and her children but he is arrested for his crime. Suzanne Day and Geraldine Cummins went on to write another play for the Abbey, *Fox and Geese* (1917), despite a lukewarm reception for *Broken Faith*. Lennox Robinson directed *Broken Faith* and he was also responsible for the staging of the play that shared the bill with this two-acter: this was George Fitzmaurice's extraordinary one-act black farce *The Magic Glasses*. Since *The Country Dressmaker* (1907) he had had another one-acter staged, *The Pie-Dish* (19 March 1908), directed by William Fay. With *The Pie-Dish* Fitzmaurice's strange grim humour and disruptive energy returned to the Abbey stage. *The Magic Glasses* continued in this style. Jaymoney Shanahan (played by Charles Power), suspected of being a changeling, is 38 years of age; he has retired to the loft, where he plays weird music and stares into magic glasses sold to him by a 'brown woman' in a wood. Mr Quille, a faith healer (played by Philip Guiry), is summoned to cure him and fails. Jaymoney returns to his loft, seems, to his family, to turn into the devil, then the loft collapses, killing the changeling, whose legs stick up out of the debris. It is a fierce, cruel, and angry play; and its core theme is the destruction wrought by sexual frustration. This indeed was Fitzmaurice's central preoccupation, and maybe was the reason Yeats and Lady Gregory were less than enthusiastic about his work. His dramatic language has a vitality which derives from the accuracy with which it registers the shocks of fear, emotion, or despair. Here is Padden describing, in terror, the power of Quille the faith healer, in his curing of Looney Carroll, who had an obsession with going around every tree in his path; and of Josie Patt, the idiot:

another man was eye-witness the way he managed Looney Carroll, chasing him through a wood in the dead hour of the night till the fool ran up again a tree unbeknownst, was flung back on his back, the blood of a pig spouting out of his nostrils, and, signs by, the fool won't go around a tree since. . . A queerer thing itself he did on Josie Patt. Hit him on the head with a mallet, I hear, when the big tongue was out and the teeth coming together— the Lord save us, half the big tongue fell down on the ground![7]

Since 1910 Yeats had been championing the Bengali writer Rabindranath Tagore, and helped him in the translation of his poetry and plays. When *Gitanjali* (1913) was published it became an international success and Tagore won the Nobel prize for literature. Yeats lectured on Tagore in Dublin in March 1913, while the Abbey was preparing to produce his play *The Post Office* (17 May), which Yeats hailed as a masterpiece. Tagore's work, bringing together a pacific Indian wisdom and elements of aristocratic and peasant life, chimed with Yeats's own desire to rebuke an Ireland that was proving to be penny-pinching in responding to Hugh Lane's gift of his collection of French impressionists on condition that an appropriate gallery be built to house them. Furthermore, he was attracted by Tagore's Vishnuism, a branch of Hinduism which stressed the individual's yearning to know and experience the godhead directly, and laid no great stress on doctrinal orthodoxy. Yeats's lecture on Tagore was, he said in a letter to Lady Gregory (12 April 1913), 'an attempt to free myself from the need of religious diplomacy'.[8]

Tagore's play, as Yeats said, is a little masterpiece. It is set in an Indian village, where an orphaned boy, Amal (played by Lilian Jago), is dying. He is confined indoors, out of the wind and the sun, because the doctor's medical texts prescribe it for his condition. In spite of his confined state, the boy has an extraordinary power to imagine reality in such a way as to restore a freshness and receptivity to those for whom the world has grown stale with familiarity. A new post office has opened in the village and Amal is told that its function is to dispense the King's letters and do his will. He is led to believe that the King will send him a letter and he longs to be a postman, like the one he vividly imagines:

the King's postman coming down the hillside alone, a lantern in his left hand and on his back a bag of letters; climbing down for ever so long, for days and nights, and at the foot of the mountain where the waterfall becomes a stream, he takes to the path and walks on through the rye then comes the sugar-cane field, and he disappears into the narrow lane cutting through the tall stems.[9]

At the end the King's physician comes to prepare the boy for his master's arrival, a visit which is entirely unforeseen. The royal doctor throws open the doors of the house to let the air in. But the boy dies, and a village flower-girl strews him with flowers as they await the King. The King is the Lord Vishnu coming directly to assume Amal into the godhead; the post office is an image for the traffic of the world all of which will, eventually, lead to God.

The play was directed by Lennox Robinson. It is an oddity of Irish theatre history that *The Post Office* shared the bill on 17 May 1913 with a play by Pádraig Pearse, staged by the pupils of St Enda's, called *An Rí* (*The King*), in which the hero accepts his own death as a sacrifice for the good of his kingdom, if such is demanded of him. It is strange that Tagore's play should have had the title it had, when it is considered where Pearse's revolutionary drama was to be staged in 1916, and how the post office Pearse occupied came to symbolize a choice between a reality of rationality and authority as against imagination and rebellion. Another curious fact in this connection is that Yeats gave the takings from these performances as a benefit for St Enda's.

In May 1913, James Cousins left for India with his wife Margaret, recently released from Tullamore Jail for her involvement in suffragette activities. Cousins was to devote his life to education and self-development in Madras. Colum made the valedictory speech at the Hardwicke Street Theatre, home of Martyn's Theatre of Ireland, in which he praised Cousins as a philosopher rather than a poet, comparing him to Eriugena.

In summer 1913, as they had done the year before, the Abbey company performed for a season at the Royal Court Theatre in London. They sought to repeat the previous year's success with *Maurice Harte* by staging another 'Cork realist' play, R. J. Ray's *The Gombeen Man*. It was directed by Robinson. The play had been with the Abbey since 1911, and it had gone through extensive revision, Yeats himself advising closely on the rewriting. It was a dark, melodramatic piece, which attempted to create a rural world without any of the wild grandeur of Synge, the dark energy of Fitzmaurice, or the pressure of tragic necessity in Murray. This is a world animated by greed, hate, and mean-spiritedness, projecting a view of Irish society not too dissimilar from that in Yeats's 'September, 1913':

> What need you, being come to sense,
> But fumble in the greasy till
> And add the ha'pence to the pence
> Add prayer to shivering prayer, until
> You have dried the marrow from the bone.[10]

In Ray's drama Stephen Kiniry, the gombeen man (a Hiberno-English term used to describe small grocers, hucksters, or moneylenders, who profit from others' misfortunes during times of shortage), uses his power and money to terrify people. Kiniry (played by Arthur Sinclair) tries to drive his young wife (played by Sara Allgood) to suicide by playing upon her sensitive and susceptible nature. A kind of expressionist psychologization of Boucicault, this work of Ray's remains unpublished.

In some respects Ray's play derives from the economic realism of Martyn's *The Heather Field*; however, Ray moves closer to his subjects, making questions of money, mortgages, foreclosures, and borrowing matters of life and death, as indeed they so often were in Ireland after the Land Acts. This period, when a large proportion of the population were, for the first time, owners of their holdings, with all the anxiety and responsibility that involved, was one in which many families went into spirals of debt, victims to their own lack of prudence and the opportunism of moneylenders such as Stephen Kiniry. Roger Connors, a property-less man, ruined by Kiniry, describes the ruin easy borrowing can create: 'I've noticed what I might call an epidemic of mortgages, and after a bit, what there'd be no mistake in calling an epidemic of auctions of houses and farms for sale.'[11] The farmers of the area are without control of their own affairs, for economic reasons, but this victimage extends to other areas as well. Kiniry has married a widowed girl because he has been able to force her father to his will with the mortgage he holds on his farm. And she, now, cannot control her feelings. She fears death and madness: 'it isn't the dark roads of Curtanmore is in my mind at all now, but there's the mortgage . . . It's my tongue is always running away with me, and the queer feeling is here, always here now.'[12] But Kiniry himself is out of control: he wants to destroy his wife, and terrifies her by reminding her of the darkness she fears: 'it's the big black river will be calling for you always!' In the end Mrs Kiniry goes mad, but in her madness reveals she is pregnant. The gombeen man now has his wish fulfilled but he must face the prospect of a deranged child.

The play has a strong emotional impact. It depicts a society profoundly repressed; money and harsh necessity impose iron constraints which lead to lives of snarling vituperation, hatred, and pure malice.

There were some attacks this year on the Abbey during its London season. St John Ervine defended the company and its plays in the *Evening Herald* for 11 August 1913 from the charge that they had become monotonous and predictable. In doing so he provides an admirable characterization of the different strains of recent Abbey theatre:

We are a scattered band, we Irish dramatists, working entirely in our own fashion, and using only the materials we find lying about us. My play (Mixed Marriage) deals with the Ulster people, the Orangemen from whom I come, while Mr. Robinson deals with the people of Cork, Lady Gregory's peasants belong to Galway, Mr. Colum's to the midlands of Ireland, and Mr. Yeats's people live in the past and in the imagination. Each of us tried to do what no English dramatist does, write out of our experience and knowledge. This is true of Irish drama, as it is untrue of English drama, that each person in the plays is a living being, observed and understood. If you ask me what is the dominant note of Irish drama, I reply in one word: sincerity.[13]

On 20 November St John Ervine's *Mixed Marriage* was revived; introducing it, there was staged a skit on Dublin enemies of the Abbey, also by Ervine, entitled *The Critics*. Set in the Abbey vestibule, the critics chatter on ignorantly about *Hamlet*, the play to be performed that evening. The level of uncomprehending stupidity which the Abbey had often to deal with is made painfully clear in the *Evening Herald* review of this squib, where Jack Point lugubriously pointed out 'to Mr Ervine that *Hamlet* is not recognized as perhaps the greatest of plays on account of certain language used by the distracted Ophelia', than which, for sheer fatuousness, there can be few comments more exemplary.

On 18 December the company produced Seumas O'Kelly's *The Bribe*. O'Kelly had had a success in 1910 with his one-acter *The Shuiler's Child* (24 November) previously seen acted by Martyn's Theatre of Ireland in 1909. O'Kelly, from Loughrea, Co. Galway, evoked a nostalgic rural Ireland in most of his drama and fiction, but *The Bribe* was an Ibsenite study in small-town corruption.

At this time Yeats was spending his first winter at Stone Cottage near Coleman's Hatch in Sussex, with Ezra Pound, the young American poet and aesthete, acting as his amanuensis. While there he discovered, through Pound, Ernest Fenollosa's translations of Japanese Noh plays, which were to have a profound influence on Yeats's own dramatic practice and thinking. In the New Year of 1914 Yeats went on a lecture tour of the USA once again (earning enough to repay a long-standing debt to Lady Gregory) and a third Abbey tour coincided with part of this visit. The company sailed on 5 February on board the *Oceanic* and had a dreadful crossing, Arthur Sinclair ruefully noting in a diary he sent to a friend that the captain of the boat was a brother of the Captain Smith who went down with the *Titanic*. Robinson was managing this tour, but it did not prove a financial success, as the previous ones had. Lady Gregory was inclined to hold Robinson responsible, and he, in any case, was growing restless and fearful that his work as manager was distracting him from his writing. (A letter of 12 June 1914 from London to Yeats announced his formal resignation as he headed off to Paris.[14]) In September a new manager, A. Patrick Wilson, was appointed, and one of his first tasks was to give Yeats a full explanation as to why the Abbey gave in to police pressure to take *The Playboy* off the stage at the Liverpool Repertory Theatre after rioting broke out in late November 1913: apparently the local theatre management caved in after being visited by the Chief Constable.

Although Robinson was gone, for the time being, he returned to direct a new play by one of the lesser-known Cork realists, John Bernard MacCarthy, *The Supplanter* (3 September 1914). MacCarthy (1888–1979) came from Crosshaven, Co. Cork. He contributed three other plays to the Abbey between 1914 and 1923, *Kinship* (2 April 1914), *Crusaders* (1918), and *Gurranabraher* (1923). He wrote in a popular melodramatic style, and his plays enjoyed some success at the Abbey, but especially in the amateur theatre movement. *The Supplanter* is a strong piece about John O'Connor (Sidney J. Morgan), a good-for-nothing who contrives to marry a comfortable widow, Mrs Keegan (Eileen O'Doherty), thereby supplanting her admirable and hard-working son Phil. The son is in love with Ellie Cassidy (Eithne Magee), but she loves another, Pad Saunders (Philip Guiry). Phil knows, that in the old days, Saunders's people ruined Ellie's, but for love of her he keeps it from her. O'Connor takes to the drink as soon as he gets his feet under the table, and steals the money Phil has saved for his passage to America. Enraged, Phil runs out and kills the man who has ruined his mother, and who has made his life a misery. The play combines three persistent themes in those Abbey plays written in a realistic mode: the land, money, and rage. Drink is a curse because it consumes property and releases the destroying anger of self-hate and accusation. Crudely, but effectively, O'Connor reveals his true colours after he has been to the fair and spent the money on drink or lost it in gambling:

John O'Connor. Whin I married yeh I thought I was marryin' a wife and not a woman who'd be houldin' up a model of a son to me all life long...
Mrs Keegan. No, 'twas to make life a misery to me, an' yeh have succeeded. Oh, John O'Connor, it was the sad day you married me. Why did you do it?...
John O'Connor. I married yeh for the farm of course. What else would I marry yeh for? Another man's lavin's.[15]

The land is fiercely contested in the play. Young Phil is enraged at O'Connor's deliberate wastefulness, not simply because his mother has been maltreated, but because the fruits of his own labours on the farm—digging drains, building walls, ploughing—are being quickly dissipated in the momentary pleasure of drink.

In 1914 A. Patrick Wilson directed a number of plays, including a version of Richard Brinsley Sheridan's *The Critic*, and also his own *The Slough* (3 November), a grim study of Dublin tenement life set during the Dublin lockout of 1913, when an employers' cartel locked out members of trade unions. An anticipation of O'Casey's *The Plough and the Stars* in some respects, it features a feckless father, pre-marital sex, and a prostitute, all depicted in sordid settings. Curiously enough, given its theme, the play was very popular with Dublin audiences and reviewers.

Wilson directed *Shanwalla* (8 April 1915) by Lady Gregory, with Kathleen Drago in the part of the young wife, Bride Scarry, who is murdered in Act I. Her husband Lawrence Scarry (played by H. E. Hutchinson) is the trusted stablehand of Hubert Davey. Shanwalla is the name of a superb horse, cared for by Scarry. Two villains, O'Malley and Brogan (played by Fred O'Donovan and Arthur Sinclair), try to poison the horse, so they can bet against him in the Inchy races, but Brogan is caught red-handed by Bride. They try to talk Scarry into taking revenge on his master in Act II, but his wife's ghost appears and brings him back from temptation. When, in Act III, Davey as magistrate investigates the poisoning of his horse, Scarry is almost sentenced to be hanged, but for another apparition by Bride to the blind beggar Owen Conary, who brings to light the evidence that exonerates the accused. The play is over-fulsome in its plot and language, but it is an interesting experiment in attempting to unite melodramatic effects with Irish folklore about ghosts who come back to resolve complexities they have left behind and which trouble the living. Owen Conary, terrified at hearing her voice, is told by the ghost why she has come back:

My heart is living, Conary. I have not passed the mering of the world. It is to serve Lawrence I am come and to give him a warning—to save him from bad handling and from harm, to save him from doing a great wrong. Question me, question me![16]

Wilson appears to have acted independently and against the interests of the Abbey during the spring of 1915. He did not rehearse Synge's *Deirdre of the Sorrows* which was intended for the summer run in London. There was a quarrel and a heated meeting between Yeats, Lady Gregory, and himself, after which, on 14 May, he wrote a letter of resignation which was quickly accepted. He was, however, still acting as manager in July and Yeats summarily dismissed him, alleging that he had stirred the actors up against their employers, the directors, and that he had made private contracts with them, so they could act in a play of his own. This was regarded as an act of outright effrontery and the directors appointed Udolphus Wright as acting manager protem. He was succeeded by St John Ervine, who took up his duties on 29 October. Ervine had capably defended the Abbey against its detractors in 1913 and now he was given his reward. He was a unionist and also an admirer of Shaw, whose iconoclastic distrust of all pieties, especially those espoused by nationalists, he relished. When he became manager he gave an interview to the *Weekly Freeman* (30 October 1915) indicating that he would like to broaden the repertoire from its perceived concentration on 'peasant plays', and giving notice that the planned production of *O'Flaherty V. C.* by Shaw would set a tone which would excite and stimulate audiences. The First World War was now in progress (Robinson had tried to enlist but was rejected because of his poor eyesight), and Shaw's play was stopped by the military authorities, not so much because the play was an anti-recruiting piece (which it was not—Shaw's irony cannot be so easily simplified), but because it would be seen to be, and would cause disturbances—an assessment which was probably not inaccurate, and which persuaded the directors, and even Ervine himself, not to go ahead with the play. Writing to Yeats on 8 November 1915 Shaw revealed that he was, in any case, uneasy about the suitability of the actor J. M. Kerrigan for the O'Flaherty part. He also went on to confess an anxiety over Ervine's attempts to impose 'Ulster discipline' on the company. Shaw's view was that Ervine's rule that actors with no specific reason for being there should clear out of the green room would drive them into the public house, and 'he will curse the day . . . if he carries his plan out'.[17]

Ervine's own play, a tragedy of northern Presbyterianism called *John Ferguson*, was in production, and he decided to concentrate first on this and return to the Shaw later, at his leisure. *John Ferguson* (30 November 1915) is set in rural Co. Down; old John Ferguson is a devout, Bible-reading man, whose fortunes have declined. His house and land are mortgaged to the brutal Henry Witherow, and the family's only chance of survival is a marriage of convenience between their daughter Hannah and the bitter, pusillanimous local shopkeeper, Jimmy Caesar. Witherow rapes Hannah, and Jimmy swears to kill him, but in fact it is the dreamy young son Andrew who murders his sister's assailant, although Jimmy is imprisoned for it. At the end, Andrew confesses his crime and the family is broken. John and his wife Sarah are left alone on stage at the end, when Andrew, accompanied by his sister, goes to the police to give himself up. The writing is powerful in its unrelenting bleakness and terrible fortitude:

Sarah Ferguson. He's my only son and I'm an old woman. You had no call to be sending him away.

John Ferguson: Isn't he the only son I have too? Is it any easier for a father to give up his son nor it is for a mother? . . . Is it women only can feel hurt? Woman, woman, your sorrow is nor more nor mine, and mine nor more nor yours. We're just stricken together. Come here, Sarah! . . . God's been good to us and He's been bitter hard. But whatever it was we've bore it together, haven't we? . . . Listen to God's Word, Sarah, and that'll strengthen you. 'And the king said unto Cushi, Is the young man Absalom safe? And Cushi answered, The enemies of my lord the king, and all that rise against thee to do thee hurt, be as that young man is. And the king was much moved, and went up to the chamber over the gate, and wept: and as he went, thus he said, O my son Absalom, my son, my son Absalom! Would God I had died for thee, O, Absalom, my son . . . my son (*His voice ends in a sob . . . There is a low moan from his wife.*)[18]

The theatre burst into tumult. Ervine was twice called onto the stage.

John Ferguson is not only a study in grim northern resolve pitted against necessity; it is also shadowed by the war raging in Europe. Ferguson's son Andrew is

sacrificing himself to the ineluctable demands of duty, and his departure to encounter his fate resonates with an experience deeply familiar to many families of
the time whose sons were heading off to the trenches of Flanders. The play's stern
prescience and intense humanity reflect Ervine's deep northern sensibility and his
unionist principles. Memorably, he wrote to Yeats, as he was working on this play
(12 January 1914), that true 'tragedy is as bare as the branches in winter'.[19]

In a lecture to the Dublin Literary Society on 11 February 1916, entitled 'Some
Disjointed Remarks on Drama', and reported in the *Irish Times* the following day,
Ervine declared that the Abbey was 'now quite safe', Rathmines having discovered it at last. Defending the theatre against its attackers who accused it of disparaging Ireland, Ervine said that 'there must be something in this country that
was wrong, or the dramatists would not be so angry about it'. He was bound to
annoy people with this kind of outspokenness, not helping himself either by his
assertion that Belfast people could take criticism better than Dubliners. He called
for rationality and reason, arguing that the current situation was one in which
men could not talk about Ireland for ten minutes without losing their tempers.

Ervine produced revivals and what proved to be popular satirical comedies by
Bernard Duffy (*Fraternity*, 4 January) and John Guinan (*The Plough-Lifters*, 28
March). After the financial mess which Wilson had left behind Ervine brought
business acumen to his management responsibilities and on 6 March he was given
a bonus of £50 in recognition of his prudence and effectiveness. A reduction in the
actors' salaries had been negotiated prior to his taking office which contributed in
no small way not only to the theatre's improved financial position but also to a rift
opening up, once again, between actors and the management.

A new play by T. H. Nally called *The Spancel of Death*, dealing with black
magic in eighteenth-century Co. Mayo, was scheduled for Easter week 1916, but
all the theatres in Dublin closed during the rebellion, which lasted from Monday,
24, to Saturday, 29 April, and the play was not performed. A typescript of it is,
however, preserved in the National Library. In May the Abbey were on tour in
Limerick where they were also rehearsing revivals of William Boyle's *The Mineral
Workers* and *The Playboy*. The players, angry at Ervine's political attitudes towards the Rising and his insistence on working them hard on tour, refused to comply with his demands; meanwhile he sought the permission of the directors to
have virtually the entire company put on notice of dismissal. Notices were given,
but the actors, now back in Dublin, threatened Ervine with the sack, on the
grounds that they understood themselves to have shares in the theatre. Ervine
wanted to bring William Fay back, and to get rid of Arthur Sinclair, Sidney
Morgan, Kathleen Drago, and others. He telegraphed Fay, offering him the job,
without clearing it with Yeats and Lady Gregory, and Fay had the satisfaction of
turning the offer down. It was a mess. The company was given notice of dismissal
on 27 May, and then refused to work their week's notice.[20] On 29 May *The Playboy*
was to be performed, but patrons arriving at the theatre were handed a slip of
paper which read: 'The players regret to disappoint their public this week as they

cannot appear under the present manager, Mr. St. John Ervine; full particulars
will appear in the press.' There was insubordination and bad feeling on the actors'
side; but Ervine too was cantankerous and inconsistent, sometimes not turning
up for rehearsals which he had insisted upon. In June the actors, led by Sinclair,
left the theatre and formed a company called the Irish Players, under which name
they toured in Britain and Ireland, retaining A. Patrick Wilson as manager. Ervine
was, in any case, now eager to enlist in the army (although he did submit his own
wishes to Yeats's authority) and eventually on 14 July the directors released him.
In a kindly, if somewhat rueful, letter of thanks and discharge, Yeats described the
Abbey as in 'a fine state of commotion', while recognizing that Ervine had 'the
impatient temperament of the imaginative man'. Yeats has to acknowledge that
Ervine has annoyed everyone, but offers the consolatory thought that 'Your fire,
your moral zeal unfits you, I suspect, for the management of players'.[21] The harsh
reality was that Yeats and Lady Gregory had, once more, to take up the reins.
Yeats was inclined towards Robinson, but Lady Gregory resisted him. Joseph
Augustus Keogh was engaged as Ervine's replacement (Keogh in fact had offered
his services), and began his work with the Abbey with the first production there,
at last, of Shaw's *John Bull's Other Island* (25 September). Keogh, a Dubliner, had
worked with Miss Horniman's Gaiety Theatre in Manchester, in opera, and in
pantomime. Immediately before returning to Dublin he had been stage manager
at the Royalty Theatre in London. At the meeting of 14 July which appointed
Keogh, Robinson's reappointment was also broached but Keogh was engaged initially for a six-month period.[22] A devoted Shavian, he produced, with his own
company, a summer season at the Abbey comprising *Widowers' Houses* and
Candida before formally assuming his duties. He brought back Fred O'Donovan
and J. M. Kerrigan to the Abbey for these productions: they had joined a newly
formed Irish Film Company. To complete this deluge of deferred Shavianism at
the Abbey *Arms and the Man* opened on 16 October. This 'autumn season of
G.B.S.' was enthusiastically supported by Lady Gregory.[23]

    John Bull's Other Island was, of course, written for the Abbey in 1904. It had
had a number of productions in Dublin before Keogh's revival of 1916, the first at
the Royal Theatre as early as November 1907. The production at the Abbey was
an outstanding success. Shaw's reputation amongst nationalists was very high at
the time; he had bitterly criticized the British government's execution of the
Easter revolutionaries, and referred to it as a 'Terrorist' administration. The play
is deeply critical of Irish 'dreaming': the Irishman Larry Doyle is driven to exas-
peration by the thought of it, and by the readiness of his English colleague, Tom
Broadbent, to yield to its allurements. But as the play develops, and when Doyle
and Broadbent return to Ireland, Shaw makes it quite clear that English pragma-
tism and opportunism can reside in the same personality as a readiness to sentiment. Broadbent wins Nora, the Irish girl who had remained true to Doyle's
memory, by the end of the play, and he has begun (with Doyle's weary collaboration) a new phase of exploitation of the Irish small farmers by means of

economic manœuvring and trickery. The play showed that it had retained the
power to shock and to entertain, not least because of Shaw's powerful analysis of
Anglo-Irish tensions in emotion and attitude, under which lie factors of money,
the control of labour, and the burdens and anxieties ownership of land can bring.
There is a bitter anger at the heartlessness of capital, which, Shaw is saying, is
often English capital in Ireland. Keegan the ex-priest attacks Doyle and
Broadbent, whose efficiency and money will bleed the country dry:

you will foreclose your mortgages most efficiently [*his rebuking forefinger goes up in spite
of himself*]; you will drive Haffigan to America very efficiently; you will find a use for
Barney Doran's foul mouth and bullying temper by employing him to slave-drive your
labourers very efficiently; and [*low and bitter*] when at last this poor desolate countryside
becomes a busy mint in which we shall all live to make money for you, with our Polytechnic
to teach us how to do it efficiently, and our library to fuddle the few imaginations your dis-
tilleries will spare, and our repaired Round Tower with admission sixpence, and refresh-
ments and penny-in-the-slot mutoscopes to make it interesting, then no doubt your
English and American shareholders will spend all the money we make for them very
efficiently in shooting and hunting, in operations for cancer and appendicitis, in gluttony
and gambling; and you will devote what they save to fresh land development schemes. For
four wicked centuries the world has dreamed this foolish dream of efficiency; and the end
is not yet. But the end will come.[24]

On 13 December Keogh directed Lennox Robinson's *The White-Headed Boy*, the
playwright's first full-length comedy. Robinson wrote it, he tells us, in a week and
rewrote it the week following. It was accepted by Yeats, but without enthusiasm;
however Lady Gregory said of it, years later, that Robinson had 'waded through
blood' to write it.

    Reading the play today, one is struck by its assured technical mastery, its inte-
gration of structure and plot, and its extremely bold use of a narrator who sets the
scene, like a voice from *Ulysses*. Here is part of the opening stage direction,
spoken to the audience:

You're admiring the furniture? 'Twas got five years ago at the Major's auction. A big price
they had to pay for it too, George didn't want to buy it but the mother's heart was set on it.
They got new horse-hair put on the arm chair, the Major had it wore to the wood sitting all
day over the fire, cursing the Government and drinking whiskey.[25]

This is an intensified realism where voice and impressions entirely collaborate
and it is completely new. It has an extraordinarily effective and very simple advantage: this technique of ironic and comic narration across the events reproduces a storytelling feel while also introducing that element of distance from
emotion crucial to comedy, and to laughter. The family, headed by a widowed
mother (played by Eileen O'Doherty), is in financial difficulties trying to keep
Denis (played by Fred O'Doherty), is in financial difficulties trying to keep Denis
(played by Fred O'Donovan), the white-headed boy or pet, at Trinity College
where he has failed his medical exams three times, and taken to gambling.
George, the eldest, is worn out trying to provide for Denis and his four brothers

and sisters, all of whom are held back by their mother's indulgence towards the boy. Now at the end of his patience he tells Denis he must emigrate to Canada and fend for himself. Denis calls off his engagement to Delia Duffy and the first act ends with him petulantly refusing a piece of toast that has been made for him:

Denis. . . . You can keep your bally toast. *But*, says the narrator, *he's taking the piece his mother holds out to him*.[26]

Robinson said that the play was political from beginning to end, and definitely there is a deep comic reflection of the events of 1916 at work: George (played by Breffni O'Rourke) is the irate authority, Denis the devil-may-care indifferent, who only ever made some semblance of applying himself to his duties because it was expected of him, and because he will comply with forces that seem stronger than he. George is not called that by accident, and Denis Geoghegan closely resembles an earlier Hibernian feckless type, William Carleton's Denis O'Shaughnessy. But the resonances of this comedy ramify well beyond simple allegory: Denis's family (for which we may read the entire complex of kinship between Ireland and England) make all kinds of demands on him according to the whims of whatever necessity, financial or emotional, arises. Aunt Ellen, his (eventual) benefactress, asks:

Aunt Ellen. In the name of God what do you want?
Denis. I want to be let make my own life in my own way. I want to be let alone and not bothered. (*He's going towards the door*.).[27]

One of the attractive features of this semi-allegorical resonance the play has is that in being a comedy it allows for the twists and turns of surprise, the accidentality of life, to take a turn towards happiness and comfort, giving the play a warm flow of human sympathy, and a kind of generous detached wisdom. This maturity emerges in the autumnal love-match between the irascible widower Mr Duffy and the frantically hyperactive spinster Aunt Ellen.

Amongst the Abbey actors were many dedicated nationalists who saw action during the Easter Rising: Sean Connolly, who had been an officer in James Connolly's Irish Citizen Army, was shot on Easter Monday; Arthur Shields and Máire Nic Shiubhlaigh were arrested; Nellie Bushell, an usherette, carried messages to and from the Post Office, the revolutionary headquarters; and the press on which the proclamation of the Republic was printed was hidden in the theatre.

J. Augustus Keogh, though inspired by Shavian idealism and Fabianism, also had an instinct for what was popular. 'Cork realism' was now well recognized as a literary and theatrical convention, and one that exercised some attraction for audiences in Dublin, if less so in Cork itself. In 1917 Keogh produced two new plays from Cork at the Abbey: J. Bernard MacCarthy's *Crusaders* (19 January) and Suzanne Day and Geraldine Cummins's *Fox and Geese* (2 February). MacCarthy's *The Supplanter* had been a success in 1914, directed by Robinson. *Crusaders* dealt, comically, with the crusade of a temperance priest, who finds to his horror, when he visits his native town, that his parents have taken over a pub.

A surprising member of the cast list was Frank Fay, in the small part of Thade Mulligan, a drunk. He had a number of other parts in 1917 at the Abbey and taught elocution there and at the Jesuit Belvedere College. But his return ended in disillusion and disappointment: by all accounts it would seem that his years in English touring companies had turned his style into an inflated mannerism and overemphatic bravura. *Fox and Geese* had been accepted by Ervine, who was unaware that Yeats had already rejected it; however Yeats agreed that Keogh put it on, knowing also that its tomfoolery and farcical Hiberno-English would prove popular.

Nevertheless there were problems with Keogh. Ominously, in a journal entry for 23 December 1916 Lady Gregory wrote; 'Went to Dublin and did business; helped in the eviction of Keogh's two brothers from the Abbey.'[28] Keogh was something of an entrepreneur; he continued to run his own theatre company at the Tivoli and elsewhere, and the directors were worried that his loyalties were divided, and that his energies were being dispersed. When it came to Shaw, however, he was indefatigable: on 26 February he staged *Man and Superman* (first produced in 1901) at the Abbey, then in March *The Inca of Perusalem*. *The Doctor's Dilemma* (26 March) received its Dublin première at Keogh's hands, but Holloway had enough, and in his diary for 25 March wrote:

Mr. Keogh, like all stage folk, is full of his own importance and thinks himself the last word in stage producers, etc., etc. His fetish is Shaw; all other dramatists are nought. . . . and when I chanced to remark, 'We have had far too much Shaw of late at the Abbey. . .' he nearly had a fit and rushed away from us.[29]

On Wednesday, 9 May, Holloway wrote to the critic W. J. Lawrence, who had been an acerbic reviewer of Abbey plays, telling him that Keogh had 'got his walking papers' on the grounds of his Shaw fetish and his 'hatred' of the Irish drama: 'Keogh from the first wanted to make it a sort of Shaw playhouse, and not caring a tinker's curse for the traditions of the little theatre . . . As an Irish theatre, the Abbey reached its lowest ebb under the reign of Keogh.'[30] In fact Keogh's relations were also a problem, in that his brothers, who were part of the private company Keogh was managing at the same time in the Tivoli and elsewhere, spent a good deal of time in the Abbey (hence Lady Gregory's 'eviction'). Furthermore, he was enticing Abbey actors into his own enterprise, on lucrative short-term contracts. When he was dismissed he established a theatrical agency and mounted touring productions. He set up a Shaw company, then emigrated to the USA, where he became head of the New York Irish Repertory Theatre.

Fred O'Donovan the actor, who had joined the company in 1908, became manager on 25 May when the keys of the theatre were taken from Keogh in the office of Fred Harris, the Society's accountant, and handed to the new man.[31] O'Donovan first appeared at the Abbey in W. F. Casey's *The Man Who Missed the Tide* (13 February 1908), and had been a favourite with Dublin audiences since that time. He took the company to London for a summer season in August, and opened the autumn season with a new play by Seumas O'Kelly, *The Parnellite*, dealing with the tragedy of a follower of Parnell who stands up to pressure from his parish priest and stays loyal to his leader, only to meet his death at the hands of an anti-Parnellite mob. O'Donovan himself played the part of Stephen O'Moore, the Parnellite. On 4 December he produced *Blight: The Tragedy of Dublin*, a new play jointly authored by Oliver St John Gogarty and Joseph O'Connor. O'Connor was a journalist, and Gogarty, at this stage, an established Dublin surgeon, with a reputation for writing scatological poems and songs, and for a ready and iconoclastic wit. Written pseudonymously (by 'Alpha' and 'Omega'), *Blight* was the first real 'slum' play of the Abbey, apart, perhaps, from Wilson's *The Slough* and Shaw's *Widowers' Houses* (9 October 1916), although Shaw's setting was London and the Home Counties, and the theme was concerned with capital and economics. *Blight* is an 'exposition' (so called in the subtitle) of the causes and effects of exiguous living in subhuman housing. There is much speechifying and argumentation but there is a world of difference between *Blight* and O'Casey's *Juno and the Paycock*, to which it has sometimes been compared.

In the cast of the Gogarty play was the young Michael Mac Liammóir, then aged 18, who had made a profound impression on Joseph Holloway when he called on him the previous April, carrying a portfolio of art work influenced by Jack B. Yeats. There were also two characters, Medical Dick and Medical Davy, who turn up in Joyce's mocking burlesque of Gogarty's obscene wit in *Ulysses* (1922).

Holloway's *Diary* for 1918 tells us that Frank Fay left Dublin again early in that year, a bitter and estranged man. 'Dublin', Fay wrote, 'is and I fear will remain largely an amateur city. One can only learn from people who know more than you do, and I can honestly say there's no-one in Dublin who knows more acting than me.'[32]

Lennox Robinson was at this time working as an organizing librarian for the Carnegie Trust in Limerick and Kerry, a post to which he was appointed by Sir Horace Plunkett, the social reformer and founder of the Irish Agricultural Organization Society. Plunkett also secured for him an appointment as secretary to one of the committees serving Lloyd George's Home Rule Convention when it met in Dublin under Plunkett's own chairmanship. This close encounter with the complexities of political life, combined with his own nationalist commitment, led to his writing *The Lost Leader*, which opened at the Abbey on 19 February 1918. In this play Robinson artfully plays with the notion that Parnell may not be dead, and that he is living as the hotel owner-manager Lucius Lenihan in a remote corner of the west of Ireland. The audience is kept guessing and it is never made absolutely clear whether or not Lenihan is suffering from delusion. Robinson ends the play with a call for the renewed resurrection of the spirit of the nation, now that the time has come for a radical new development with the return of the 'lost leader'. Lenihan says: 'It's the great moment that comes but once or twice in a nation's history, it's when the water stirs, it's when the mind of a nation is broken up, is ready to be moulded, is soft clay, warm wax. That moment has come now.'[33] This ambiguous but inspirational figure is (bathetically) killed by a blow from a hurley, meant for somebody else. Yeats wrote to Robinson from Oxford, having read the play, that it was 'probably the best work you have done'.[34]

From the beginning not just at the Abbey, but at the Irish Literary Theatre, Yeats had wanted the National Theatre to stage European and international masterpieces, ancient and modern, as part of his aim to broaden Irish literary culture by providing the best models and exemplars from all over the world. This international scope would, he believed, assist in defining and refining the Irish national theatre's own sense of purpose. In 1913 Robinson had directed Hauptmann, Strindberg, and Tagore at the Abbey and there had been the experiments in medievalism of Nugent Monck. But on the whole, with very few exceptions, the Abbey staged Irish plays and Dublin audiences expected as much. There were, of course, Lady Gregory's sustained efforts to adapt Molière to the Kiltartan dialect, but if anything, the Abbey's repertoire had narrowed to a focus on rural realism, with the fantastic and legendary initiatives of earlier years failing to sustain themselves beyond occasional revivals of plays already tried and tested. To remedy this Robinson, along with James Stephens, Ernest Boyd the critic, and Yeats himself, established the Dublin Drama League in the autumn of 1918, with a public meeting called for 10 October.[35] At this meeting Yeats was elected president. The League set itself the object of producing the best contemporary world theatre within the precincts of the Abbey, and under the aegis of the National Theatre Society. It should not be forgotten, however, that Martyn's Theatre of Ireland in Hardwicke Street was discharging objectives very similar to those of the Drama League; but Yeats wanted the Abbey to have within itself the stimulus of diversity.

Fred O'Donovan was getting restless, and in any case relations between him and the directors were becoming strained. He was looking for more money, his ambitions fuelled, perhaps, by the hugely popular success of a film he had made of Knocknagow, Charles J. Kickham's novel about landlords and tenants in nineteenth-century Tipperary. This film, released in the summer of 1918, included an 8-year-old Cyril Cusack in the credits. O'Donovan left the theatre and Robinson was invited to return as manager, though not without some considerable unease on Lady Gregory's part; she remained anxious about his ability to be efficient and decisive. For Yeats Robinson's loyalty and the fact that he was a man of educated tastes were deciding factors. In any case they were colleagues in the new venture in international theatre, the Dublin Drama League, the first production of which opened at the Abbey on 9 February 1919. The play, The Liberators by the Bulgarian Sugjan Tvcic, was an anti-war tract, directed by Robinson himself. It was a strange choice at a time when the Anglo-Irish War was in its opening phases: on 21 January two police officers were shot by republicans when they were escorting a shipment of gelignite in Co. Tipperary. As the year progressed the war was to increase in ferocity, a mood captured by Yeats in the poem 'Nineteen Hundred and Nineteen'.

A production reflecting the nationalist and patriotic mood of these months was that by Máire Nic Shiubhlaigh of Pádraig Pearse's *The Singer*, a frankly revolutionary drama, staged at the Abbey on 25 May. Mac Dara, the singer, who composes songs of rebellion and defiance, offers his life for Ireland's freedom. Pearse himself had intended producing the play just before the Easter Rising in 1916 but decided against it on the grounds that its obvious message would provide the authorities with an excuse for interning the participants.

There was now yet another exodus of actors, this time with Fred O'Donovan, and Lennox Robinson had the task of rebuilding the Abbey company once again. Barry Fitzgerald (William Shields, brother of the long-standing Abbey actor Arthur, who did not leave with O'Donovan) joined the Abbey and played the part of the King in Lady Gregory's 'wonder play' *The Dragon* (21 April 1919). Fitzgerald was to have an illustrious career which took him to Hollywood and international fame as a comic actor in films. Other notable new recruits to the company for *The Dragon* were F. J. McCormick, who was to be a favourite with Dublin audiences for years, and Maureen Delany. A character-actress who excelled in portraying a particular kind of knowing mischief, she brought this quality to parts such as the Widow Quin in *The Playboy* and Aunt Ellen in *The White-Headed Boy*.

Robinson's next plays were *The Saint* by Desmond Fitzgerald (2 September), father of the statesman Garrett Fitzgerald—a fervent and by all accounts perfervid meditation on sin and repentance—and Daniel Corkery's first piece for the Abbey, *The Labour Leader* (30 September). Corkery's play, inspired by the Easter Rising and Pearse's charismatic personality, shows a revolutionary idealism being translated into labour activism, reflecting Corkery's own political views and social concerns.

Yeats's drama, after long absence, returned to the Abbey on 9 December 1919 with Lennox Robinson's production of *The Player Queen*, a play that he had been reworking since 1908, and which was first staged on 27 May at the King's Head in Covent Garden (with a young Edith Evans in the part of Nora).

Although a recurrent feature of Yeats's artistic life was his capacity to reinvent himself, nevertheless, at this time he had gone through the profound spiritual and emotional transformations that would make him a great poet, as distinct from an influential man of letters and cultural activist. He married Georgie Hyde-Lees in 1917, and a few days after he discovered that his wife, who was also a member of the Order of the Golden Dawn, was capable of making contact with the 'instructors', spirit guides who came to give him metaphors for his poetry and his plays, and who revealed a complex system of forms that, he and his wife were convinced, determined all the apparent accidents of history and of human interaction. He had bought, in 1917, Thoor Ballylee near Lady Gregory's Coole, a Norman tower which symbolized his own desire for remoteness, power, and order. Furthermore, through the influence of Pound, he had, with great excitement, found that he could adapt his form and style so as to carry the weight and stress of twentieth-century actuality in all its savagery and terror. This scope and urgency give a new authority and flexibility to his verse and a density to his dramatic writing.

In 'Nineteen Hundred and Nineteen' he wrote, possibly thinking of Lady Gregory's *The Dragon* and of the Anglo-Irish War:

> Now days are dragon-ridden, the nightmare
> Rides upon sleep: a drunken soldiery
> Can leave the mother, murdered at her door,
> To crawl in human blood, and go scot-free;
> The night can sweat with terror as before
> We pieced our thoughts into philosophy,
> And planned to bring the world under a rule,
> Who are but weasels fighting in a hole.[36]

The Player Queen, a strange mixture of symbolism, allegory, and politics, is an attempt to convey the psychological and emotional disruptions caused by the violent conflict of the Anglo-Irish War in the aftermath of the horrors of the 1914–18 conflict. The player Queen, Decima, is a harlot who, it is darkly implied at the play's end, will mate with the Unicorn to produce a new era of cold savagery. The mood of the play is fierce and troubled, and its meaning obscure and baffling. It is a tragic farce with a desperate and sardonic edge, a strange return for Yeats to the Abbey stage. The *Evening Telegraph* reviewer said of it, describing the silence that greeted the play's final curtain in most of the house: 'A great many people, it was clear, were conscious of an unpleasant taste in the mouth.'[37]

The chaos and confusion of this play reflect the mounting violence in the streets of the towns and in the countryside: houses were being raided and vandalized; the Black and Tans were frequently engaged in punitive reprisals of appalling savagery and brutality; and the British government seemed to be carrying out a policy of deliberate exacerbation. Lady Gregory's *The Golden Apple*, a 'wonder play', opened on 6 January 1920: it had a prince, a giant, a scenario that shifted all over the world, witches' caves, and much fanciful invention. On 11 January Lady Gregory entertained Douglas Hyde's and James Stephens's families, along with Iseult Gonne, Maud Gonne's daughter, to tea and lemonade and cakes: a charming occasion, charmingly recorded in her journal. But two days before she had been to see George Russell, who told her he had it on totally reliable authority that the British War Office had issued orders to the increased military presence in Ireland 'to make the most of every disturbance, and then use the most violent means of oppression'.[38] The aim of this policy was to create enough antagonism and hate to provoke outright rebellion.

The remainder of 1920 was a relatively undistinguished period for the Abbey. St John Ervine had a one-acter produced on 20 October called *The Island of Saints, and How to Get out of It*, attacking Irish intolerance, north and south; and on 30 November Brinsley MacNamara's *The Land for the People* was staged. From Delvin, in Westmeath, MacNamara had joined the Abbey as an actor in 1909, after which he had settled in the USA for a time, before returning to write his well-known novel *The Valley of the Squinting Windows* (1918), an attack on small-town values, and on the literary idealization of rural life. *The Land for the People* deals with a theme very familiar to Irish literature, dramatic or otherwise: the taking over and holding of land—how it may or may not be done, the consequences of dispossession, and the anxiety and trouble of ownership. The play may also be seen as reflecting contemporary concerns in relation to how territory may be governed justly, and the breakdowns that ensue when responsibility is not exercised.

On 21 January 1921 Lady Gregory wrote to John Quinn in New York, describing the atrocities of the continuing Anglo-Irish War. A local man had gone to his family doctor and told him that he and his son 'had been held by the Black and Tans against a wall, while in his presence others of them attempted to violate (and the doctor is certain they succeeded) his daughters . . . I wrote to Bernard Shaw to come over, but he did not think it advisable. Yeats is too settled in England.'[39] In effect the Abbey was now in the hands of Lennox Robinson, with Lady Gregory functioning as the more accessible of the two directors, Yeats intervening in the resolution of difficult cases especially in matters such as choice of play.

In Dublin a curfew extending from 10.00 p.m. to 5.00 a.m. was in place from the latter part of 1920 to 4 March 1921, when it was put back to 9.00 p.m., and then, later in the month, to 8.00 p.m. The mayhem encroached upon the Abbey itself. The *Irish Independent* for 23 March described an occurrence during rehearsal for a rerun of Terence MacSwiney's play *The Revolutionist*. Men armed with revolvers surrounded the theatre; a number went inside declaring they were looking for a photographer from the *Daily Sketch* who, they said, had faked some pictures for the British secret service. They did find a hapless individual, backstage, who admitted he was a photographer, but swore he was not the man they were looking for; the paramilitaries departed, apparently satisfied.

MacSwiney, head of the Cork brigade of the IRA, had become Lord Mayor of the city in March 1920. Arrested in August, he went on hunger strike and died after a seventy-four-day fast. Robinson was being very provocative in staging MacSwiney's play (24 February 1921) but it was an extraordinary success, the audience breaking into cheers when the hero, Hugh O'Neill (played by F. J. McCormick), attacks the priest Fr. O'Connor for meddling in politics. MacSwiney's widow came to the performance and Lady Gregory told her the Abbey was proud to have performed the play 'for the first time, that we felt we were laying a wreath upon the grave'.[40]

George Shiels, from Ballymoney in Co. Antrim, had his first play at the Abbey, *Bedmates*, staged on 6 January 1921. At the end of the year, on 13 December, Lennox Robinson directed Shiel's *Insurance Money*. He was to become a staple provider of rural Ulster comedies for the Abbey, and this play announced his favourite situations: trickery and double-dealing animated by greed; love and good nature winning through in spite of all.

In November the directors considered a play called *The Crimson in the Tricolour*, submitted by Sean O'Casey, and rejected it, Lady Gregory with some reluctance, Yeats emphatically. Lady Gregory was sympathetic because she thought O'Casey might learn how to improve his technique by seeing it staged. At this point he had written *The Story of the Irish Citizen Army* (1919), an organization of which he had been a member but from which he resigned when James Connolly moved it closer to revolutionary socialism in 1914.

The Troubles had the effect, naturally enough, of diminishing the Abbey's income, and Yeats gave a fund-raising lecture in London in May 1921. He had some Shavian-style fun at the expense of nationalist enthusiasms in Ireland, and of official policy. Recalling *The Rising of the Moon*, Lady Gregory's patriotic one-acter in which an RIC man lets a Fenian go free, he told how the actors refused to play it on the grounds that a policeman should not be depicted as having patriotic instincts; Dublin Castle, however, when they did play it again, refused thereafter to give them old police uniforms. There had better, Yeats said, be Home Rule, 'because there are so many police in our plays'.[41] He went on, in a more serious vein, to admit that, for the foreseeable future, the theatre would continue in the social realist style of Robinson, Murray, and Ervine, and also argued that this would serve a pragmatic function in a newly settled Ireland, that of explaining one faction to another, and party to party.

During this time the theatre was closed, because of the curfew. It reopened on 2 August after a truce was declared between Ireland and Britain on 10 July. Following the cessation of hostilities there were protracted discussions in London, Michael Collins leading the Irish delegation. A treaty was signed on 6 December, under which twenty-six counties of Ireland acquired 'dominion' status as an Irish Free State, six northern counties remaining within the United Kingdom, a manœuvre reflecting unionist pressure. On 7 January Dáil Éireann ratified the Treaty, but the President, Eamon de Valera, led a walkout of republicans, and those who went with him formed the republican leadership in the Civil War which followed. Rory O'Connor occupied the Four Courts in Dublin on 13 April with an IRA division. Although they were bombarded and driven out in June the republican cause spread throughout the country. Michael Collins, the leader of the pro-Treaty side, was shot on 22 August. St John Ervine wrote to the old Abbey actor Dudley Digges, long settled in New York: 'Ask Whitford Kane [an Irish-American actor sympathetic to the republicans] what he thinks of that damned dago de Valera now? . . . what's the use of writing about Ireland? It's a cursed country.'[42]

Yeats, however, now settled in Ireland. Up to this time he had divided his time more or less equally between London and Ireland, but he, like his brother the painter Jack Yeats, deliberately threw in his lot with the new state. His wife bought a house at 82 Merrion Square, and a couple of rooms were nearly ready at Thoor Ballylee, providing him with both town and country residences. Yeats was appointed to the Senate of the new Irish government, an honour which greatly pleased him. This, however, made him a target for the anti-Treaty side, and he had an armed guard assigned to him. T. C. Murray had a new play opening on

10 January 1922. This was *Aftermath*, a sombre study of the emotional consequences of matchmaking when the feelings of the young are overruled. Myles O'Regan (played by P. J. Carolan) comes back from teacher-training college in Dublin, submits to his mother's will, and marries Mary Hogan. He breaks with Grace Sheridan, the local schoolmistress whom he really loves, but after six years leaves his wife and makes off into the night never to return. Lennox Robinson directed this play, as he did his own *The Round Table*, a 'comic-tragedy', which opened on 31 January. This play had some thematic resemblances to *Aftermath*, in that the main character, Daisy Drennan, has to choose between familial duty, the expectations of her fiancé Christopher Pegum, and the urgings of her own soul. The 'Round Table' in Daisy's bedroom, which she polishes every day, is meant to represent the daily 'round' from which she seeks to break free. The figure of the mysterious strange woman who advises Daisy created some confusion amongst contemporary critics, who could not decide if she was meant to be real or not. This figure reflects Robinson's own interest in spiritualism and occult psychology. At the end the heroine leaves all her known surroundings and embarks on the adventures which she is called to by the 'strange woman'. Daisy was played by Eileen Crowe and her brother De Courcy by Barry Fitzgerald.

Two nights prior to *The Round Table* the Abbey staged a production by the Dublin Drama League of a translation of Arthur Schnitzler's *The Festival of Bacchus*, directed by Thomas McGreevey. McGreevey, a poet from Kerry who had served as an artillery officer in the First World War, was then working as a critic and reviewer. He was to become director of the National Gallery in 1950.

On 3 October George Shiels's new comedy *Paul Twyning* opened, with Barry Fitzgerald in the title role. Twyning, a migrant plasterer from Dublin, comes to work for James Deegan (Gabriel Fallon), a litigious farmer in Co. Antrim. Twyning, who is an inveterate matchmaker, urges the mild and timorous son Dan (Michael J. Dolan) to make love to Rose McGothigan, whose father and Deegan are sworn enemies. The father bullies Dan into denying any interest in Rose and attempts to divert his attention to Daisy Mullen, newly (and apparently richly) returned from America. But the father himself pays court to her, assisted by Twyning's emollient skills. Now the farcical plot goes into overdrive, with breach of promise accusations, Daisy turning out not to be what she seemed, wills and legacies discovered, Rose and Dan getting together, and Twyning and Daisy heading off, at the end, to America together. There were songs and boxing matches, meditations and orations, and topical references to the occupation of the Four Courts.

On 14 November was staged Lennox Robinson's sparkling one-acter *Crabbed Youth and Age*, in which the middle-aged Mrs Swan (played by Helena Molony, and supposedly modelled on the artist Sarah Purser, to whom it was dedicated) outshines unintentionally her three rueful, slightly crabbed, daughters. All the young men dance attendance on Mrs Swan because of her vitality and love of life.

A curious production on 3 December by the Dublin Drama League at the Abbey was a version of Robert Browning's verse play *A Blot on the Scutcheon*, abridged from the ponderous original of 1843 by Lennox Robinson, and produced by Frank Fay. Indeed in 1922 Fay returned to the Abbey to act in some of his old roles, the Wise Man in Yeats's *The Hour Glass*, for example; and the old farmer Michael O'Callaghan in William Boyle's *The Building Fund*, first staged in 1905.

From correspondence in the National Library of Ireland, and from the Fay papers lodged there, it is very clear that Frank Fay's fortunes as an actor were precarious after leaving the Abbey. Although he was esteemed as a performer of style and consequence, working with, among others, the Shakespearean actor-manager William Poel (who emerges from the papers as a crafty and tight-fisted businessman), nevertheless the demands of making a living as a jobbing actor took their toll. He had grown used to playing for broad effect; and his ego expanded as his fortunes declined. As Yeats and Lady Gregory surrendered most day-to-day responsibility to Robinson, on whom drink was beginning to take hold at this stage, the Abbey players started to grow more and more wilful and less disciplined. Around this time the practice of 'gagging' began, in which the actors work the audience for laughter and applause, however inappropriate these might be to the play. This behaviour coarsened the actors' craft and the receptivity of the audience, although the Dublin theatregoers loved the hamming. The playwrights, of course, hated it. Udolphus Wright, for example, would, in his small parts, contrive to mention the names of people in the audience. And Sara Allgood on 26 August 1922, on a return appearance to play Aunt Ellen in *The White-Headed Boy*, tripped over a rug in Act I, only to say, much to the audience's delight, 'I enjoyed the trip very much'.[43] This practice became a feature of the way in which Abbey audiences reacted to their favourite actors: no matter what part Harry Brogan played in the 1950s and 1960s, for example, he always milked it for laughs, the audience exploding into hilarity at his first entrance, determined to laugh at all costs.

At this time the Abbey actors were engaged, mostly, on an entirely informal basis: for example, on 24 April 1922 Robinson wrote to Yeats underlining the fact that on that date there was only one member of the company permanently engaged. The theatre was in dire financial straits, and the realization was growing that it was becoming necessary to acquire state subsidy. There were expectations that the new Ireland coming into being would be favourably disposed to placing the Abbey on a secure footing as the Irish National Theatre. Over the next months Robinson prepared a statement for submission to the Irish government which was corrected and amended by Yeats and Lady Gregory. The statement reviewed the theatre's past, stating that it came into being as the Irish Literary Theatre in 1899; briefly rehearsed its achievements; indicated the nature of current problems; pointed out that every 'civilized' government except that of England and its colonies, the USA, and Venezuela endowed a national theatre; expressed a wish to develop a theatre in Irish; and asked for money. This was to be a long campaign, concluding in 1925 when the government voted a subsidy of £850 for the following year.

In April 1923, in the course of meetings with Eoin McNeill, the Gaelic scholar and historian and Minister of Education in the government, the directors broached the possibility that the state take over the theatre, much to McNeill's chagrin, whose view was that the last thing the government needed was the headache of running and paying for a national theatre. Their financial position was now so desperate that the bank was dishonouring cheques, and Lady Gregory was certain that a businesslike approach to planning and finance was required; she was never convinced that Robinson had these talents, and, on the evidence, it looks as if she was correct in her assessment of his deficiencies in practical matters. A formal offer to hand over the theatre to the government was made in summer 1923 but the President, W. T. Cosgrave, had no interest in the Abbey and, according to Ernest Blythe, the northern ex-revolutionary who was Minister of Commerce, Finance, and Posts and Telegraph in the government, boasted that he had never been inside its doors. Ernest Blythe was of the view that the offer to hand over the theatre in its entirety to the state was tactical, but it seems not to have been so: Yeats and Lady Gregory were tired of the continual harassment and quarrelsomeness it involved.

As from 1 December 1923 Lennox Robinson resigned as manager, to be replaced by Michael J. Dolan, an actor with the Abbey, who had already produced some plays. On 15 April 1924 Robinson was appointed a director, filling, after long absence, the post left vacant after Synge's death. On 22 November 1912 the total shareholding of the company had been agreed as follows: Yeats (188), Lady Gregory (188), Sara Allgood (4), Robinson (2), Wright (2), W. F. Bailey (2), Philip Hanson (2). Now Yeats and Lady Gregory transferred to Robinson 49 shares each, giving him 98, while they retained 139 apiece.[44] They hoped that Robinson would now carry some of the burden of responsibility which continually fell to them. However, his inferior status in the directorate was made evident in that he had to be reappointed annually at the Society's general meeting, a practice that continued up to his death in 1958. At the same meeting at which Robinson was made a director it was formally agreed that the Society ask the state for a subsidy of £1,000 per annum. On 21 November 1924 Lady Gregory records in her journal that they have now sold off all the Abbey's investments and repaid all debts, leaving £500 in the bank in credit. She then goes on to say she has been to see Blythe the day before

at 11 o'c. He was very encouraging, had spoken to the executive Council about helping the Abbey and they incline to it. I told him our need, our actors underpaid, our actor Manager (Dolan) getting only £6–£7 a week; our building so shaky and wanting repair . . . He asked how much we want to keep going, and I asked for £1,000 a year, and £1,000 down for repairs. He will go into figures.[45]

Blythe was himself on the Executive Council of the government, as were Eoin McNeill and Desmond Fitzgerald, Minister of External Affairs, and all were sympathetic to the Abbey Theatre. In the government meetings to decide grant allocations in 1925 a sum of £850 was voted to the theatre, reflecting the accepted view that the Abbey had a national role to play in the formation of theatrical and cultural taste in the new state. Announcing the endowment from the stage on 8 August Yeats praised the government for 'this new manifestation of their courage and intelligence'. A condition of the grant was that the directorate be expanded to include a government nominee, the first of these being Professor George O'Brien, an economist at University College, Dublin. Within the relatively short space of two years the Abbey had achieved national theatre status, recognized by subsidy, while, at the same time, managing to retain a good deal of its autonomy.

Back in early 1923 the Civil War was still being waged and amongst the outrages committed was the destruction of the houses of the Anglo-Irish gentry by the IRA: the Earl of Mayo's Palmerston was burned on 29 January; Horace Plunkett's Kilteragh at Foxrock was bombed on 30 January; Moore Hall, George Moore's house, in Co. Mayo was destroyed in early February; and on 19 February Renvyle, Oliver St John Gogarty's house in Connemara, was gutted, he himself, a Free State Senator, having narrowly escaped being killed at the hands of IRA gunmen in Dublin on 20 January by jumping into the Liffey and swimming to safety. A bullet crashed through the window of the café at the Abbey on 19 February. In March the theatre, along with all other places of entertainment in Dublin, received a letter from Pádraig Ó Ruitléis, Minister for Home Affairs in the provisional government of the 'Republic of Ireland'—in other words a shadow government claiming to be the true authority as distinct from the supposedly bogus one in Merrion Square—ordering all theatres to close as a gesture of mourning in view of the acceptance of the Treaty by the Free State. The government (in Merrion Square) ordered they be kept open, but police protection became necessary. Lady Gregory's journals record that when she dined with Yeats on an evening in early April she was let into his house in Merrion Square by a Civic Guard in uniform. Yeats told her that he had been threatened because he was in touch with Maud Gonne, widow of John MacBride, one of those executed after the Easter Rising, presumably because, as a Free State Senator, he should not be in contact with the widow of a republican icon. She and her daughter Iseult, now married to the IRA man and writer Francis Stuart, were interned on 10 April in Kilmainham Jail. Maud Gonne went on hunger strike and was released on 24 April.

It was in this atmosphere of civil war, incendiaries, shootings, snipers, shadow government, threats, orders, counter-orders, police protection, guns, bombs, and hunger strikes that Sean O'Casey's *The Shadow of a Gunman* opened on 12 April, with the theatre still under armed guard.

O'Casey had sent plays to the Abbey before this one: after *The Crimson in the Tricolour, Profit and Loss* is entered in the play logbook in the Abbey archive marked simply 'returned'. Another play, *The Frost in Flower*, now lost, was submitted in 1919 and returned marked 'Not far from being a good play'.

Directed by Lennox Robinson, *The Shadow of a Gunman* had Arthur Shields playing Donal Davoren, the 'gunman', F. J. McCormick as Seumas Shields, a pedlar, and Michael J. Dolan as Tommy Owens, who idealizes republican violence. The play is set during the Anglo-Irish War of no more than a year or two before the actual date of performance. Davoren is believed to be a gunman on the run by the tenants of the huge Dublin tenement where he lives, when in fact he is an aimless dreamer and a sentimental would-be poet. Shields professes a devout Catholicism, Davoren a philosophical Stoicism, creeds that offer no antidote to the fear aroused by the shootings that take place off stage. Maguire, an IRA bomber, leaves a cache of bombs in the room shared by Davoren and Shields. There is a Black and Tan raid, and Minnie Powell, to save Davoren who she, like everyone else, thinks is on the run, takes the sack to her room where it is discovered. She is shot through the chest trying to escape from the Black and Tan lorry when it is ambushed by the IRA. Meanwhile the tenement-dwellers are either trying to reassemble their dignity by reconstructing their self-delusions (like the Orangeman Mr Grigson pretending he was not frightened and denying that he was made to sing a hymn by the Tans); or, as with Davoren, they abase themselves in shame and self-pity. Davoren says, before Minnie Powell is shot: '(*sitting down on the bed and covering his face with his hands*) We'll never again be able to lift up our heads if anything happens to Minnie.' Shields responds: 'For God's sake keep quiet or somebody'll hear you.'[46] The strange impact of the play, its frightening immediacy and relevance, is underlined by an anecdote Lady Gregory recorded in her journals. She found one of the Free State armed guard in the green room putting finishing touches to the uniform of Tony Quinn, who played the Black and Tan, and 'showing him how to hold his revolver' like a professional. P. S. O'Hegarty, the historian from Co. Cork, writing of the play in Russell's *Irish Statesman* on 7 June 1924, tersely described it as one of 'disillusion for people who have been disillusioned'.[47] O'Casey's next outing on the Abbey stage was a one-acter called *Cathleen Listens In*, an unsuccessful farce attacking nationalist pretensions and divisions.

In James Joyce's story 'The Dead' in *Dubliners* (1914) a Miss Ivors berates the gauche yet overweening journalist-cum-writer Gabriel Conroy for his lack of interest in the Irish language and in Gaelic culture. The model for Miss Ivors's not entirely unsympathetic character (given Gabriel's embarrassing superficiality) was Kathleen Sheehy, the daughter of David Sheehy, a nationalist MP. She also informs the characterization of Kathleen Kearney, in Joyce's 'A Mother' from the same collection, another pained but vicious study of nationalist hypocrisy and calculated enthusiasm. Kathleen Sheehy became Kathleen Cruise O'Brien on her marriage; one of her children was Conor Cruise O'Brien, the controversial statesman and author, indeed future Abbey playwright. Kathleen Sheehy was also a writer, and on 3 September 1924 a one-acter of hers, *Apartments*, under the pseudonym Fand O'Grady, was directed by Lennox Robinson, with Sara Allgood in the lead role of Mrs McCarthy, who owns the boarding house where the play is set. It is a slight piece; nevertheless the boarding house is intended as an image of Irish society, with Mrs McCarthy energetically trying to keep the lives of all her tenants economically viable by pawning and redeeming successively the possessions of her charges. The farce is intended to be an exercise in the futility of necessitous economics, reflecting perhaps the fact that Kathleen's sister Mary had married the economist Thomas Kettle, who died in action in the First World War, and who was an advocate of welfare measures. It would seem that this implication of the play escaped the notice of contemporary reviewers.

Brinsley MacNamara, the ex-Abbey actor and dramatist, and also novelist of some considerable achievement at this stage, entered the news in 1923. His novel *The Valley of the Squinting Windows*, set in his native Delvin, Co. Westmeath, had been published in 1918, but now the viciousness and vindictiveness of some elements in an Irish Free State which was quickly becoming repressive emerged in a boycott against MacNamara's father James Weldon, a local teacher. Local people were outraged at the unflattering treatment of themselves in MacNamara's novel. Weldon issued a writ against his parish priest and a handful of parishioners, but lost the case.

Meanwhile his son on 27 November had a three-act comedy *The Glorious Uncertainty* produced at the Abbey. It is set in the fictitious Ballycomoyle, and centred on the local 'Grand National'. The play had Barry Fitzgerald and F. J. McCormick in the character roles of Sam Price and Andy Whelehan. On one level the play attempts to create a spirit of carnival and festivity in celebration of the variety and colour of ordinary Irish life, where, as this play presents it, there is considerable interest in drink, gambling, laughter, and having fun. The action is set in Cuneen's Railway Hotel, and there is a not unsuccessful attempt at creating the dramatic equivalent of a Jack Yeats painting of characters and of people drawn together in communal activity. There is a darker side, in that there is skulduggery afoot, but the play is an interesting exercise in depicting a middle Ireland (the play's action takes place in the midlands where MacNamara came from) teeming with life and persisting in its vitality in spite of cheating, chicanery, and bad faith. In the end the finances of the hotel, depleted by the gambling of its owner, are saved by the fortuitous marriage of his daughter to a decent but unsuspecting Englishman, who remains unaware that there is a conspiracy to fleece him. The girl, Suzie Cuneen, while not entirely innocent, is nevertheless unaware of the full nature of the deceit being practised.

On 12 November 1923 a triple bill of one-act plays in Irish was performed by the Gaelic Players. These were the acting company of a new formation, An Comhar Drámaíochta, established by Piaras Béaslaí, Gearóid Ó Lochlainn, and others to promote drama in Irish, which had been almost entirely neglected by the Abbey since its inception. Béaslaí, born in Liverpool to Irish parents, and a revolutionary who fought in the Easter Rising, supported the government during the Civil War, and coined the term 'irregulars' for the anti-Treaty or IRA side. As director of propaganda he rose to the rank of general in the Free State army. One of his own plays *Fear an Sgéilín Ghrinn* was on the bill on 12 November, along with a translation of *In the Shadow of the Glen (Uaigneas an Ghleanna)* by 'Fiachra Éilgeach' (Risteárd Ó Foghlugha).

An Comhar Drámaíochta was established to bring together all those who were interested in drama in Irish, both in Dublin and also throughout the country. They modelled their organization on the Dublin Drama League; like the League, An Comhar was to be an in-house production company at the Abbey, engaging actors as needed for their plays. However, because Béaslaí was closely involved in An Comhar, many republicans would have nothing to do with the organization. An application for government assistance for drama in Irish was successful, and from the end of 1924 An Comhar was in receipt of an annual grant of £600. From November 1923 to May 1930 (when they removed for a time to the Gate Theatre) An Comhar staged a monthly bill of plays during winter and spring. In the 1924/5 season they staged a few original plays, such as *Éirghe Anairde* (5 May 1924) by Tadhg Ó Scanaill, and translations, such as a version of Chekov's *The Bear* (10 March 1924) by Risteárd Ó Foghlugha.[48]

On 24 May 1923 de Valera issued an order to the 'Rearguard of the Republic', the IRA, to cease hostilities, and an uneasy and truculent peace began to settle. At the end of the year the Abbey staged Lady Gregory's verse monologue *The Old Woman Remembers*, in which Sara Allgood, as Mother Ireland, recalls all the Irish heroes, lighting a candle for each in turn. Donall O'Brien, King of Munster, Art Mac Murrough, Shane O'Neill, Patrick Sarsfield—all are recalled, along with others—the men who fought in Easter week, and Terence MacSwiney, who died on hunger strike:

> Terence, who waned, while moons grown old
> Thrice gazed on an unconquered man.

This piece, Lady Gregory wrote, was a 'rosary of praise' for the heroic dead, and a prayer for 'lasting peace'.[49]

On 10 December 1923 Yeats went to Stockholm to collect the Nobel prize for literature, and, in his address responding to the honour, spoke of the Irish theatre. He recalled Synge and invoked the presence of Lady Gregory, thinking, as he spoke, how 'deep down we have gone, below all that is individual, modern and restless, seeking foundations for an Ireland than can only come into existence in a Europe that is still but a dream'.[50] Lady Gregory was, of course, very pleased, and also because she felt her trust in him had been vindicated. Writing to John Quinn in New York on 28 November she recalled how her neighbours and relations disapproved of his presence at Coole, convinced he was a republican activist. They 'lamented my folly and obstinacy in housing him and other writers in the house instead of the ordinary "country house parties". Now . . . [they] are much impressed.'[51]

On 5 December Edward Martyn died. By now the Abbey had seriously begun to fulfil one of the objectives Martyn had initially argued for at the founding stages of the Irish Literary Theatre: the development of a repertoire of continental plays. The Dublin Drama League, affiliated to and using actors from the company, carried forward this Europeanization of the theatre's provision. In 1923 to 1924, for example, there were productions of plays by Gregorio Martinez Sierra from the Spanish, Paul Claudel from the French (*The Hostage*, translated by Bryan Cooper), and Henri Lenormand (*Time is a Dream*, translated by Thomas McGreevey). Luigi Pirandello's *Henry IV*, translated by Edward Storer, was played on 27 April 1924, directed by Arthur Shields, and featuring Lennox Robinson in the leading role, a performance which has achieved legendary status as one of the finest ever on the Abbey stage.

In 1924 it became apparent that a new master had arisen in the Irish theatre, to join the other established talents: O'Casey now took his place alongside Yeats, Synge, Lady Gregory, T. C. Murray, Lennox Robinson, and St John Ervine. The manuscript of a new play, *Juno and the Paycock*, was handed in on 3 January 1924, and it opened on 3 March. O'Casey's methods, now revealed in their full maturity, were closest to those of Synge, and not just because they each brought a dramatic intelligence to bear upon the use of Hiberno-English in the theatre; they also shared a view of character, reality, and the language people use to express themselves which was profoundly sceptical as well as comic. Samuel Beckett put his finger on this core element of O'Casey's dramatic vision when he described him as a 'master of knockabout [farce] in this very serious and honourable sense—that he discerns the principle of disintegration in even the most compla-cent solidities, and activates it to their explosion. This is the energy of his theatre . . . mind and world come asunder in irreparable dissociation.'[52] This 'dissocia-tion' is also at the centre of Synge's dramatic practice in that his theatre special-izes in depicting the yawning chasms between what a person sees and hopes and believes, and what is revealed to be the case. This revelation is at the heart of drama, and is as old as Sophocles; it was first described, critically, by Aristotle, and Synge's forceful and experiential recovery of its import is what truly ener-gized Irish theatre. By 1924 Yeats has turned to the Noh theatre of Japan as a tech-nical manœuvre to create a fully realized scene that will encompass the theatrical energy released when drama does its work of registering the gap between illusion and actuality; *The Player Queen* captured only imperfectly his insights into psy-chological stress and political conflict. O'Casey, however, returned to Synge's model but sited his depictions of discontinuity and trouble in the inner-city tene-ments that he knew, their sordid squabbles and unquenchable human animation being the antithesis of Synge's fractious and voluble countrymen and women.

The Shadow of a Gunman was set during the Anglo-Irish War; *Juno and the Paycock* comes forward in time to the Civil War which had ended only the year be-fore the play was produced. When it opened the players were cast in parts that might have been created with the actors' distinctive personalities in mind: Barry Fitzgerald as Captain Boyle, Sara Allgood as Juno, Arthur Shields as Johnny Boyle, F. J. McCormick as Joxer Daly, Maureen Delaney as Mrs Madigan. The play was directed by Michael J. Dolan, who also played 'Needle' Nugent.

During rehearsals it became apparent that with this play the Abbey had found another masterpiece. Gabriel Fallon, who played the schoolteacher and ineffectual lawyer Bentham who gets Mary Doyle pregnant, records how he watched the third act in dress rehearsal on 2 March, sitting two seats behind O'Casey. He gazed, entranced, as Sara Allgood's tragic genius revealed itself in her pacing, control, and timing. He described how, as Juno, she was able to 'pin down' the laughter caused by Fitzgerald's and McCormick's uproariously funny exchanges as Boyle and Joxer, and quieten the atmosphere to 'freezing point'. He continues:

When Juno returns from the doctor with Mary the author's simple directions are: 'Mrs Boyle enters; it is apparent from the serious look on her face that something has happened. She takes off her hat and coat without a word and puts them by. She then sits down near the fire, and there's a few moments' pause'. That is all. Yet Sara Allgood's entrance in this scene will never be forgotten by those who saw it. Not a word was spoken: she did not even sigh: her movements were few and simply confined to the author's directions. She seemed to have shrunken from the Juno we saw in Acts 1 and 2 as if reduced by the catalytic effect of her inner consciousness.

We watched the act move on, the furniture removers come and go, the ominous entry of the I.R.A. men, the dragging of Johnny to summary execution, the stilted scene between Jerry Devine and Mary Boyle, and then as with the ensnaring impetus of a ninth great wave Allgood's tragic genius rose to an unforgettable climax and drowned the stage in sorrow. Here truly was the very butt and sea-mark of tragedy! But suddenly the curtain rises again: are Fitzgerald and McCormick fooling, letting off steam after the strain of rehearsal? Nothing of the kind, for we in the stalls are made to freeze in our seats as a note beyond tragedy, a blistering flannel-mouthed irony sears its maudlin way across the stage and slowly drops an exhausted curtain on a world disintegrating in 'chassis'.[53]

As a description of the visceral impact of artistic shock, the jolts and shudders of realization that come thick and fast in a dramatic structure that is as focused as it is mobile, this account by Gabriel Fallon could not be bettered. The pity and terror of this play are made only the more affecting by the comic or sentimental grotesquerie that accompanies them in the dramatic unfolding. W. J. Lawrence, in a brilliant review in the *Irish Statesman* (15 March), described O'Casey as 'at once iconoclast and neo-Elizabethan', and tells how moments in this play 'transcend all theatricality and thrill me to the marrow like matters of personal suffering'.[54]

Lady Gregory, now old and ailing, was enthralled at the success of *Juno*, which played to packed audiences in an extended run that came at an opportune time in the negotiating process for a subsidy with the government. She notes in her journal that she said to Yeats: 'This is one of the evenings at the Abbey that makes me glad to have been born.' That was on 8 March. On 11 March 1924 Yeats told her that he was most impressed by her new play, *The Story Brought by Brigit*, and that it should go on before the end of Lent. However, he depressed her when he showed her the typed version of his Nobel lecture which he had delivered in December 1923, where he somewhat unfeelingly described her as 'an old woman sinking into the infirmities of age'—'not even fighting against them', as she ruefully remarked privately in her journal. Lennox Robinson agreed with her that this description would 'send down my market value, and be considered to mean I had gone silly'. Yeats agreed to take it out but confessed he had already sent a copy to the Dáil and that it might be too late to have it stopped.[55] It was.

The Story Brought by Brigit was in rehearsal, directed by Michael J. Dolan, with John Lyle Donaghy, a young poet then at Trinity, playing Christ. It was produced on 15 April, and met with considerable success. Maud Gonne, accurately, remarked on its 'republican' element, and, certainly its treatment of the Christ story emphasizes the revolutionary import of the gospel. The scribes of Caiaphas regard the Nazarene, with his gospel of love and integrity, as a threat to their authority, and though they resent the Roman imperial presence, nevertheless use it to protect their own position. As Marcus, a sergeant in Pilate's guard, says to one of the scribes: 'You are always calling out against the Roman government, and the minute you have a quarrel with some of your own people you come calling and craving for our help.'[56] The targets here are those of the Irish who had wished to retain the British presence in order to keep a grip on their authority and power which was sponsored by Westminster; and also contemporary politicians reluctant to achieve the nationalist aim of a thirty-two-county Republic.

The play makes use of Irish folklore concerning Brigit, according to which Mary took her son to Ireland rather than to Egypt during the time of Herod's persecution of the Innocents. Now, Brigit has a vision in which she sees the body of the child she once sheltered, grown into a man, covered in wounds in Jerusalem. She travels to the Holy Land to be at the Crucifixion. At the end of the play, when John comes in to tell the women that Christ has died, she leads them in a keen. It is a powerful and arresting play and had a profound impact on Lennox Robinson and on the poet Thomas McGreevey, who told her he had cried all through the last act. Hyde considered it the best thing she had ever done. Lady Gregory, in the second act, makes much of the story of Pilate's wife, and her dream of premonition, in which she sees her husband trying to wipe blood off his hands. Jack B. Yeats, who sat near Lady Gregory on the second night, 16 April, liked the play very much, and it is no coincidence that one of his greatest and most enigmatic canvases is 'The Dish in Which Pilate Washed his Hands', painted some ten years or so later.

In June 1924 the Abbey company went to Cork with *Juno* under Sara Allgood's management. They were taking advantage of a concession whereby, during the summer months, the actors could work independently for their own advantage, a freedom they were happy to exploit given the sporadic and uncertain nature of the contractual arrangements with the company. To the players' horror the Opera House management insisted that references to Mary's pregnancy be omitted, and that her diagnosis at the doctor's be changed to tuberculosis. This edict was issued between the first and second houses on the opening night and Sara Allgood had to try to improvise changes in the dialogue. It didn't work. Gabriel Fallon describes the embarrassment:

Fitzgerald as Boyle was standing still and apprehensive, holding up his moleskin trousers as he asked her what the doctor had to say about Mary. Allgood sat down and tapped the table with nervous fingers saying 'Oh, Jack, Jack . . .' which was rather far off script. Something in Fitzgerald's manner made the house titter. Suddenly to my utter amazement I heard Allgood quickly say: 'Oh, Jack, Jack; d'ye know what Bentham's after doing to Mary?' This was capped by the loudest laugh I have ever heard in a theatre.[57]

In August *Juno* returned for a further run in the Abbey and Holloway records Padraic Colum's reactions on 13 August: 'he became so excited during the events in the second act that he kept unconsciously jumping up and down in his seat, and even went over to the stage front and placed his elbows on the stage ledge as he gazed intently at what was taking place thereon.'[58] We also learn from Holloway's diary entry on 23 August that O'Casey was still trying to find work as a labourer, and queued for an hour and a half at the Labour Exchange to get to the hatch to which he had to report, but eventually, feeling faint in the huge throng of men, pushed his way out.

On 12 May George Shiels's comedy *The Retrievers* was directed by Michael J. Dolan. The *Irish Times* on the following day described it as a 'Wild West farce in a border setting' and the play deals with land disputes, robbery, sectarianism, revenge, in a grotesque and energetic way.[59] The play is intricate, its hurtling power catching the confusion and startling unpredictability of the Civil War period, in which it is set. Since 1915 T. C. Murray had been a Dublin resident, having moved from Rathduff in Co. Cork to the post of headmaster at Inchicore Model School. On 8 September Michael J. Dolan produced his masterpiece, *Autumn Fire*, with himself in the leading part of Owen Keegan.

In a letter to Frank Hugh O'Donnell of 10 November 1924, Murray himself makes it clear, in his modest way, that he is aware that he has written something of real power, and that he is fully aware of how the play accumulates its 'impact slowly': 'I think it is fairly good stuff particularly in the third act. The other two amble along quietly enough but there is sufficient in them to carry the argument through logically, and they have gleams of quiet comedy not infrequently.'[60] Keegan is a middle-aged widower who remains fresh and vigorous and full of animation and life. Encountering young Nance Desmond (played by Eileen Crowe) who has come back to Tobarnabrosna to look after her ageing mother, he cannot stop himself from telling her that she is 'lovely'. Responding to the young woman's compliments he boasts: 'Show me another man, east or west, that plunges into the river in October and runs around the field naked to the sky in the dew o'the morning.'[61] Unbeknown to his mild son Michael (played by Arthur Shields) and his dark and emotional daughter Ellen (played by Sara Allgood), Owen courts Nance, and marries her to Ellen's horror and Michael's distress. Michael has loved Nance for years, but his yielding nature is no match for his father's Herculean force: Murray did conceive Owen along heroic lines. Owen's brother Morgan (Barry Fitzgerald), who arrives when Owen is bedridden after a fall from an untrained pony, says that 'he was ever doing strange things—but sure the life of a man is his will'. Ellen, however, counters this by pointing out: 'That's all very well if having your will isn't the ruination of other people. There's Michael and myself and we often spending a good share of our lives here and we don't know no more than the dead how we would stand if anything happened this minute.' to which Morgan replies, reassuringly: 'I wouldn't be troubling about that. He'd not be wronging his own I'm sure.'[62]

However, when Morgan and Owen discuss the making of the latter's will, on the doctor's advice, we find that he does, indeed, intend leaving virtually everything to his young wife, on condition that she will not remarry. 'Spancelled, she is Morgan, though there's little need for it.' However, Morgan, who disapproves of this wilfulness and control, hints that it may be difficult to control the young, advising his brother that he should not leave his young wife and son too much alone together. Furious, Owen smashes a whiskey glass into the fireplace, while Morgan tries to undo the trouble he has broached, but to no avail. And later, when Ellen returns, she too cannot help making a similar insinuation. The tragic secret, which Owen at first cannot accept as being conceivable, has begun its unavoidable emergence. Nance and Michael come back from the fair; they are caught out in a lie attempting to cover up the fact that they dawdled on the way home; and eventually it is revealed that they actually kissed the previous night. Nance implores Michael to leave and he begs one last kiss. The father comes down the stairs and sees them in their passionate embrace. Everything is ruined; Owen throws his son out of the house and commands his wife to submit to his will. Nance accepts her humiliation and sorrow: 'I'll—I'll listen and no word o' complaint you'll hear from my lips. To live is to suffer, and I'm satisfied.'[63]

And so the play closes in the bleak iron sadness of lives that have been destroyed by an old man's wilfulness and all-too-human bitterness. Murray's writing is spare and superbly honed to give the feel of the sharp hurt of sorrow as it cuts into ordinary people's lives. Restrained and powerfully structured, the events unfold up to the last tragic scenes against the background of a warm summer evening, with the bees droning, and a road visible from the window winding through hawthorn and low hills. As the young lovers come back from the fair Ellen sees the 'puce' in Nance's hat through the gaps in the furze, and hears them laughing.

Curiously, this play, which was submitted to the Tailteann Games—a national cultural and sporting festival—lost out to a one-acter by Kenneth Sarr (pseudonym of Kenneth Reddin) entitled *The Passing*. The judges, who included Lennox Robinson, found *Autumn Fire* somewhat 'verbose', a quite astounding adjudication. Sarr's play was performed at the Abbey on 9 December 1924. It dealt with Dublin slum life, in which a dying whore gets her retarded son to throw her money into the river. Sarr, a district judge who had been imprisoned for republican activities, was also a novelist.

By this time, and no doubt partly influenced by the campaign to have the theatre subsidized by the state, plays in Irish were a regular monthly feature in the Abbey programmes. On 17 November new plays by Pádraic Ó Conaire and

Pádraig Ó Siochfhradha ('An Seabhac') were performed by Aisteoirí Átha Cliath under the auspices of An Comhar Drámaíochta. The piece by 'An Seabhac', *Dáil na mBan*, drew upon the comic tradition of parliaments convened by women and set it in a contemporary context. On 16 February 1925 *An Saoghal Eile* was by Liam S. Gógan, the Dublin-born scholar and keeper of antiquities in the National Museum. Gógan's play was a discussion piece, between university students, on the nature of reality, and on the possibility of an afterlife. Later in the year (14 December) T. C. Murray's *Aftermath* was performed in a translation by Mícheál Ó Siochfhradha.

After the extraordinary flourishing of 1924, in which two plays of outstanding quality were first performed, O'Casey's *Juno* and Murray's *Autumn Fire*, the following year proved somewhat lacklustre by comparison, although there were productions of Lennox Robinson's *Portrait* (31 March), a version of Strindberg's *Ghost Sonata*, titled *The Spook Sonata* (19 April), Shaw's *Fanny's First Play* (21 April), George Shiels's *Professor Tim* (14 September), and Robinson's *The White Blackbird* (12 October).

There is a Strindbergian mood of ennui, gloom, and a kind of tragic gaiety in Robinson's *Portrait*. Robinson, an admirer of Strindberg, played the part of Auchenholz in *The Spook Sonata* under his acting name, Paul Ruttledge, itself taken from Yeats's *Where there is Nothing*. Lady Gregory noted, in her journals, that Robinson had a tendency to 'gloom', and *Portrait* is a study in disappointment. Peter Barnado (Arthur Shields) is a shy and unaggressive man who is spurned by his fiancée Maggie (Sara Allgood) in favour of the pushier and more competitive Tom Hughes (P. J. Carolan). Towards the end of the play, in a fit of drunken bravado mixed with despair, Peter shoots himself. When Maggie's parents look in, disturbed by the report of the gun, Maggie dances with her dead fiancé in her arms to the music of a victrola playing jazz. Sara Allgood was, as Maggie, a fairly matronly Dublin flapper. Dublin audiences were somewhat taken aback by this experimental play dealing with the urgings of passion, violence, and brutally indifferent whim, although Susan Mitchell in the *Irish Statesman* declared it 'the strongest of Mr. Lennox Robinson's plays'.[64]

After Robinson's *Portrait* the Abbey closed for a time during which the Strindberg *Ghost Sonata* was rehearsed: audiences had been declining, and the state subsidy, while in the offing, was not yet secured; that was not in place until August 1925 so it was more economical, at this stage, to keep the theatre 'dark'.

George Shiels had been writing for the Abbey since 1921, with his one-acter *Bedmates*, and had a success with *Paul Twyning* in 1922. *Professor Tim* was written to provide a good night's entertainment. Yeats liked it and he and Lady Gregory suggested detailed revisions to the first version submitted in May, which Shiels carefully worked in, redrafting in pencil before retyping the whole play.

Professor Tim returns to Ballykennedy to his sister's family in the guise of a drunken sailor and con-man, who pretends he has been on such a bender that he cannot remember the past few months. His niece Peggy is in love with young Hugh

O'Cahan (P. J. Carolan), who has a reputation for extravagant living; now the bank has foreclosed on his loans and he must sell Rush Hill, the family home. Peggy, however, in a strategy very familiar in Irish theatre, is matched with Joseph Kilroy, a useless coward; and Kilroy's father James plans to buy Rush Hill for his son, but only through getting Peggy's father, the blunt and forthright John Scally, to go guarantor for money which he does not have. This tangle of deceit is all resolved at the end with Professor Tim turning out to be a man of means after all: as a benign *deus ex machina* he restores O'Cahan to his house, saves him and Peggy from poverty and the elopement they have planned, brings Mrs Scally down to earth, and even manages to reconcile the Kilroys with the Scallys. It is far from being the slight piece of entertainment it is frequently dismissed as: there is a flexible and impulsive comic energy running through the action, and it creates a world of nervous and alert kindness shining through the classic set of reconciliations at the end, which is alive with hope and good nature. Through it all there is a deep affection for Irish country people. This play, by a mostly house-bound invalid from Ballymoney in Co. Antrim, is a moving tribute to what Shiels regarded as permanent formations of trust and good feeling in Irish society which still survive in spite of the Anglo-Irish and Civil Wars. Furthermore, Shiels's ear for dialogue is impeccable; forceful and salty, he captures the flow and rush of ordinary speech as people try to talk their way through life's dilemmas and surprises. In the following extract John Scally and O'Cahan realize that they each value Peggy as much as the other, one as her loving father, the other as the man who wants to marry her:

John. I'm proud of Peggy . . . Hugh O'Cahan, you don't know what you're getting. It's not because she's my daughter I say this: no man in the world is good enough for Peggy Scally to clean her feet on.

O'Cahan. I didn't think you knew that, John.

John. But she's going with you, and I won't stop her . . . [Blinking] But, Lord, I wish you were staying at home, . . . But here's a fair offer: stay here another week and get married proper, and I'll give Peggy her fortune.

O'Cahan. Peggy's all the fortune I want, John. I'm going to throw off my coat and vest and work.[65]

Mrs Scally, the shrewish wife, was played by Sara Allgood, although her well-known inability or reluctance to learn lines was much in evidence, with the prompter being heard throughout the theatre in the performances. F. J. McCormick played the supposedly drunken Professor Tim, who had a fine old time hamming things up; while Barry Fitzgerald played Joseph, the timorous son of the land-grabber Kilroy.

By now the government subsidy was agreed and at the public announcement on 8 August 1925 Yeats boasted that in the Abbey there had been created 'an assembly where we can discuss our own problems and our own life', and praised the government and the vision of Ernest Blythe in bringing forward a state subsidy. Yeats wanted to acknowledge what he regarded as a most enlightened act publicly and on 12 July wrote to Blythe outlining his plans for the evening of

8 August: there would be public thanks from the stage, then the Minister and Mrs Blythe would be given supper on the stage. Robinson would write an article for the *Observer*. He wrote: 'You have created the best endowed theatre in any English-speaking country.'[66] George O'Brien was the government nominee on the (slightly) expanded Abbey board. He was pleased to be involved although a little worried at the prospect of having to defend his and the board's decisions against an increasingly pious set of public opinions on morality, sex, and belief which had formed very quickly after the foundation of the Free State, as if in reaction to the anarchy of revolution and its aftermath. Also on 8 August, the day on which the government subsidy was announced, a memorandum was sent to Blythe from Brinsley MacNamara outlining policies and strategies for the new directorate. The contents of this had, in part at least, been the subject of previous discussion between the correspondent and the recipient. MacNamara's memo argued for a press officer, a manager, and a director of plays. Blythe passed it to O'Brien, who passed it to Yeats, who replied to Blythe saying that it was 'thoughtful', but that 'every suggestion would greatly increase the expense of running the theatre'. He assured Blythe, however, that they were 'filing the document for future reference': a steady response to a clumsy (and bureaucratic) manœuvre.[67]

O'Brien's nervousness manifested itself immediately over Robinson's next play at the Abbey, *The White Blackbird* (12 October 1925), when it was considered by the board of directors. In the play William, played by F. J. McCormick, expresses an inclination to marry his half-sister Bella, the liveliest of his mother's second family, the Naynoes. The play also features a prostitute who unsuccessfully tries to seduce this kindly but timorous young man. O'Brien took advice about its content from legal friends of his at the Kingstown Club, a move which outraged Robinson. Eventually O'Brien agreed to allow the play to go on, for fear of raising suspicions of over-zealous government interference at so early a stage in the new arrangements.

On 27 December 1925 the Abbey held a gala night to celebrate its first twenty-one years in the building. The plays put on that evening were Yeats's *The Hour Glass* with Frank Fay invited back again to play his old role as the Wise Man; Lady Gregory's *Hyacinth Halvey* with Arthur Shields as Hyacinth; and Synge's *In the Shadow of the Glen*. Lady Gregory gave a closing speech in which she thanked, above all, the audience, especially the pit, because they and the Abbey had had 'some lovers' quarrels together'. She spoke, too, and very movingly, of how the players loved the theatre itself, the actual physical space, and praised the day-to-day creative life and collaborative work that took place within the building.[68]

Trouble was, however, looming, trouble that would lead to the biggest row the Abbey had ever seen; and which would eventually culminate in the exile of one of the theatre's greatest dramatists and possibly the destruction of his dramatic energies. The trouble was, of course, the storm of anger and protest that broke over the production of O'Casey's *The Plough and the Stars* on 11 February 1926.

Yeats, however, in a famous speech of rebuke to the Dublin audience, declared that O'Casey's fame was born that night, that the trouble was his 'apotheosis'.

There were problems from the outset: on 1 September 1925 Michael J. Dolan, an enemy of O'Casey, wrote to Lady Gregory warning her that they should think twice before having anything to do with the play; George O'Brien, while generally admiring it, wanted Yeats to agree to various cuts, especially in the early part of Rosie Redmond, the prostitute in Act II, arguing that her 'professional side is unduly emphasized', advice firmly declined. A directors' meeting was called on 24 September at which a compromise was struck, some cuts being made, but the prostitute scene was retained. Yet another compromise was needed, this time between the author and the actors. On 10 January 1926 O'Casey wrote to Lennox Robinson, who was directing, withdrawing his work on the grounds that the 'impudent fear' of the actors was threatening to usurp 'quiet courage'. Eileen Crowe, who originally was cast for the talkative Mrs Gogan, was worried at the looseness of some of her lines, and even considered checking with her priest if she should act at all. Eventually accommodations were made, and the play opened to packed and enthusiastic houses on 8 February. Reviews were extremely good, and in the *Irish Times* Ria Mooney was praised as Rosie Redmond, the whore, for representing Dublin life as 'it is lived'. Barry Fitzgerald as the alcoholic Fluther, Maureen Delaney as Bessie Burgess, Michael J. Dolan as the Covey—all were singled out for praise. But on 9 February there was some ominous hissing during Act II, and the sister of Kevin Barry, the young martyr of the Anglo-Irish War, protested at the republican flag being brought into the pub.[69]

This mounting outrage may be accounted for by the gradual absorption on the part of Dublin audiences of what this play was actually communicating about the struggle for Irish independence in 1915–16, and the foundational event of the Easter Rising itself, already hallowed in nationalist memory and emotion. Acts I and II take place in the autumn of 1915 while III and IV are set during Easter week. During Act II the ferocious idealism of Pearse (The Man) is set against human frailty as the sacrificial rhetoric Pearse deployed in late 1915 to inflame rebellion and fortify republican sentiment is set against Rosie's transparent silk stockings and Fluther's grateful return to drink after three days' (alleged) sobriety. Pearse's great speech at the grave of O'Donovan Rossa in August 1915 is powerfully juxtaposed against human venality; sacrificial bloodshed is contrasted with the traffic in human flesh. Fluther's excuse for his return to drink is that to do anything else after hearing words like 'bloodshed is a cleansing and a sanctifying thing' would be unworthy. Bloodthirsty speechifying leads, it is implied, to other kinds of thirsts and cravings. Gogarty told Holloway that the play would give 'the smug-minded something to think about'. It certainly did.

This radical and extremely dramatic juxtapositioning represented a profoundly anti-idealistic and, indeed, anti-republican and anti-patriotic critique of the founding icons of the Irish Free State. We are not surprised to find that Dan Breen, the guerrilla fighter from Cork, and Mrs Margaret Pearse, Pádraig Pearse's mother, Mrs Tom Clarke, and Mrs Frances Sheehy-Skeffington were shocked and distressed at what they regarded as an unfeeling and scandalous betrayal of what Pearse, Connolly, Plunkett, MacDonagh, and all the other men and women of 1916 stood for. These were their menfolk that O'Casey was subjecting to intense criticism, even mockery. We should recall, for instance, that Pearse's mother had asked him, in his death-cell at Kilmainham, to write her 'a little poem which would seem to be said by you about me'. This was 'A Mother Speaks':

> Dear Mary, that didst see thy first-born son
> Go forth to die amid the scorn of men
> For whom He died,
> Receive my first-born into thy arms.[70]

This was the emotional background to the anger and outrage that greeted O'Casey's play. The events it seemed to many to demean were not yet ten years in the past. To many this play was not just an affront; it was a betrayal and a calculated insult. Although *The Plough* is often characterized as a 'woman's play', in that in it women have to carry the burdens laid on them by heroism and rhetoric, it was nevertheless women, the women of the men of 1916, who spoke out most vehemently against what they saw as O'Casey's apostasy. Frances Sheehy-Skeffington wrote on 23 February as follows: 'The women of Easter Week, as we know them, are typified rather as the mother of Padraic Pearse, that valiant woman who gave both her sons for freedom. Such breathe the spirit of Volumnia, of the Mother of the Gracchi.'[71]

There was uproar on 11 February as Act II began and Ria Mooney was booed and catcalled. The demonstration, in which the women played a leading role, continued throughout the act. At the beginning of Act III Bessie Burgess, a Protestant street vendor, shouts abuse at the republicans from her window, while news comes of Pearse's stand in the Post Office. Nora Clitheroe has been out looking for her husband Jack who has joined the fighting, and she relates, in terrified weariness, how she saw the fear in the eyes of the insurgents, and a body in North King Street its 'face . . . jammed again th'stones, an' his arm was twisted round his back'. At this point or near it a dozen or so women got up on stage, and were followed by young men. A fight broke out amongst the players and the demonstrators. A man struck Maureen Delaney, who was playing Bessie Burgess; Barry Fitzgerald knocked him sprawling into the wings. The curtain was lowered, the screaming women taken off stage, and Yeats came on to try to shout down the clamour in the auditorium. Police were brought in, and gradually a semblance of order was restored. The play continued, with further interruptions, to the close.

On 13 February, a Saturday and the last day of the play, three young men armed with revolvers tried to kidnap Barry Fitzgerald. They arrived at his mother's house at Seafield Road in Clontarf, where he was not in fact living at the time, and declared that they wanted to stop him playing that night. Fitzgerald was not there, though he was registered at the address, and the men, nervous and fidgety, left in a car. Liam O'Flaherty, notably, attacked Yeats and O'Casey in the *Irish Statesman* on 20 February: 'I bow down before the courage of Pearse and Connolly and their comrades. I did not have the honour to fight with them. But I am "cut to the bone" [Yeats had said O'Casey's play had cut the Irish to the bone] because an Irish writer did not, unfortunately, do them justice.'[72] On 6 March O'Casey left Ireland for London and many were glad to see him go. Now he was widely regarded as insincere, hypocritical, and selfish, and the Dublin gossip-machine cranked itself into action.

4

1926–1951

'The birth of a nation is no immaculate conception'

It is sometimes said that a period of assimilation is required before an artist can cope with the immediacy of turbulent events. For example, the so-called 'Troubles' of 1968 to 1998 in Northern Ireland are often said to have induced a jejune sensationalism in the work written during that extended period. But it would seem that while there may be some temptation to cheap exploitation of the rawness of immediate event, nevertheless it cannot be denied that the thirty years from 1968 have seen a new vigour in all aspects of creative activity in Ireland, north and south, and that this quickening of impulse has a great deal to do with the emotional and intellectual destabilization brought about by violent conflicts. Not only that, it was not unusual during this period to witness some of the finest literary achievements—such as Seamus Heaney's *North* (1975) or Brian Friel's *Translations* (1980)—arise directly out of a sense of crisis created by the piling up of specific atrocities, injustices, lies, humiliations.

Such was the case with the Abbey in the years to 1926. O'Casey's plays register the shock of seismic transformation in people's minds and attitudes as the country goes through a convulsion from which it will emerge utterly changed. The Dublin trilogy—the *Gunman, Juno*, and *The Plough*—responds in complex and devastating ways, a compound of emotional readiness and superbly alert dramatic technique, to the shifts and turns of public and private feelings and persuasions.

In the autumn and winter of 1926 T. C. Murray gave a series of lectures on the Irish Theatre for the Catholic Writers Guild. These lectures are preserved amongst the Murray papers in the National Library of Ireland, and make interesting reading as the expression of a strong, conservative, and intensely Catholic intellectual. In 'Catholics and the Theatre' he begins by attacking a comment by the critic Ernest Boyd that 'the task of fostering thought and education in Ireland has naturally fallen to Protestants, Catholics being puritanical and unartistic'. He reminds his audience that very many of best dramatists in the Abbey have been Catholic, and notes that 'our own National Theatre has preserved on the whole a singularly healthy tone far above any standard which obtains elsewhere. This is directly due to the fact that it derives its inspiration from the life and thought of the most Catholic nation in the world today.' In the lecture on 'The Irish National

Theatre: The First Phase—Poetical and Idealistic', he brilliantly evokes the technique developed in the early plays of Yeats and Synge. Restrained and deliberate, the style the Fays evolved had depth and impact: 'In a world of things overdone, like the stage, where quietude has the value of epigram, [it was] like a thing soberly said in a newspaper.' In 'The Second Phase: The Trend to Realism', he describes, superbly, with a dramatist's understanding of mood and economy of effect, the 'solemn beauty' of Synge's *Riders to the Sea*: 'it impresses like the movement of a nocturne heard when day is passing and the shadows begin to gather'. Murray argues that Synge, along with Padraic Colum and William Boyle, brought to the Abbey a vitality which, while not exactly realistic, nevertheless brought more of the roughage of experience into the theatre, a toughness and alertness, not noticeably advanced since Martyn.

In 'The School of Realism' Murray goes on to describe the naturalness and ease of Robinson as well as responding to his more experimental edge; he admires Seumas O'Kelly's intensity, the precision of St John Ervine, and the sheer originality of O'Casey (although he is critical of O'Casey's handling of structure, saying he has little sense of 'craftsmanship'). On *The Plough*, he says that it cannot stand comparison with the plays that went before it.

'The Evolution of the National Theatre' (dated 1 January 1927) is a synoptic lecture incorporating material from the three already given on the history of the Abbey. The first, on 'Catholics and the Theatre' is mostly left aside, but its thinking permeates the overview as it does the more detailed historical lectures. Murray's analyses are interesting in themselves, for their clarity and calm and measured appraisal of material that was still, to a considerable degree, contemporary.

But they are also of value in that they reveal, in 1926–7, a clear sense that the National Theatre, as founded by Yeats and diversified by other talents, already represents a cultural institution of profound value to the new state. This pride in an established achievement gains all the more authority for being expressed by one of the country's leading Catholic intellectuals, which is what Murray, it is now very evident, was. In the New Year lecture of 1927 he writes that the Abbey's story is itself a drama: 'the drama of a nation's consciousness awakening to its potential genius in a field of art which probably she alone of European nations left unexplored.'[1] Before the end of 1926 there were two further new plays at the Abbey which, in their very differing ways, offer reactions to the turbulent events of the ten years from 1916 onwards: these are Lennox Robinson's *The Big House* (6 September) and Yeats's *Oedipus the King* (6 December).

Robinson had been not a little discomfited by O'Casey's startling successes at the Abbey, and *The Big House* is, in part, the projection of a less moralistic and perhaps less humanitarian view of conflict than O'Casey's in the trilogy. It is also a meditation on the decline of the Anglo-Irish ascendancy, here typified in the Alcock family at Ballydonal House in Co. Cork. But it advances, in its closing scenes, an important role for that class, so long as it does not relinquish its uniqueness and its difference from the so-called 'native' Irish.

St Leger Alcock and his English wife have lost a son in the First World War. In the opening scene, set on Armistice Day in 1918, they are celebrating the end of hostilities and awaiting the return from the Front of their other boy Ulick. But as the bell which marks the armistice tolls out at 11 o'clock, news arrives that Ulick too has been killed. This devastates the Alcocks, and especially Kate, the daughter, who has hoped to provide leadership and resolve, along with her brother, for the ideal community of which she has dreamed: she wants to join in the work of revitalizing Ireland by learning Irish, joining co-operative schemes, and learning new and more productive methods of farming. The scene now shifts to 1921, and the Anglo-Irish War is raging, with the Black and Tans committing atrocities in response to IRA guerrilla activity. Innocent people are shot, and villages are being set on fire. Captain Despard, an old friend of Kate's eldest brother who proposed (unsuccessfully) to her in the first scene, now returns as a Black and Tan officer to search the house. He is drunk, and attempts to force his attentions on her; when St Leger, her father, comes in, he tries to bully them into submission but fails, Alcock reacting with a mixture of insouciance and contemptuous rage. Strangely, the ghost of Ulick speaks to Despard as the scene closes, and the English officer shoots at this emanation of the house and of Anglo-Ireland. The next scene is set during the Civil War in 1923 two years later. Kate has been in London but has become sick of the émigré Irish gentry milking English sympathy; she has also grown impatient of her own overreaction to the banalities (as she finds them) of the complacency of English life.

I insulted the émigrés, I loathed their long, gloomy, Protestant faces, their whiskey and their appetite for luncheons; I insulted the English, I told them it was none of their business what we did with our own country, and anyway, as we'd beaten them it would be more becoming if they kept their mouths shut. I made myself thoroughly objectionable to everyone, and then I suddenly realized that I was behaving like any Irish girl in a tenth-rate novelette written by some horrible Colonial, that I was being 'so Irish', as mother calls me.[2]

However three representatives of her 'own country' now arrive; they are 'Irregulars', republicans, fighting Cosgrave's Free State government, and are on a mission to burn down Ballydonal House as a symbol of English oppression. Many such houses were set on fire in the Civil War; some members of the old ascendancy had made a swift accommodation with the Free State authorities.

The closing scene takes place in the summerhouse as some furniture and other effects are saved from the fire. Kate is resolved to stay on at the big house but will no longer try to erase her difference from the Irish; rather she will assert the distance between her own people and those now in power, and thereby enhance the quality of life in the new order of things: 'We are formidable if we care to make ourselves so, if we give up our poor attempt to pretend we're not different. We must glory in our difference, be as proud of it as they are of theirs.'[3] The play closes with another vision of her dead brother Ulick being vouchsafed to Kate.

This play, in its cool, even-tempered appraisal of the turbulence of life in Ireland during the years when the country was in the process of achieving a measure of independence from the British government, presents a quite different Ireland from that evident in O'Casey's plays. It is not just that Robinson deals with Anglo-Ireland, whereas O'Casey creates an underprivileged slum environment; Robinson accepts the inevitability of conflict, and this sturdy resignation, while it prevents any avowals of humanitarian passion, nevertheless allows a dramatic realization to unfold which shows that people put up with life as best they can, and that remorse and pity may, in the face of the harshness of events, be redundant emotions. Robinson's cold appraising eye has yet to receive its due acknowledgement in Irish theatre history. The ghostly presence of Ulick would seem to be an attempt to indicate that longing and persistence never die, and that loyalty to one's place may extend beyond the limits of a single individual personality. As a dramatic effect it is risky, and sorts ill with the realist style of the play; however, Robinson was always a complex realist, ready to question too complacent an assumption that life is what it normally seems.

F. J. McCormick played Captain Despard in Robinson's play; on 6 December he played Oedipus the King in Yeats's version of Sophocles' tragedy to considerable acclaim, many remarking that someone regarded as a great comic actor had displayed considerable prowess and authority in this hugely demanding part. Yeats had been working on a version of *Oedipus* since 1904, when Oliver St John Gogarty furnished him with a literal translation of the Greek. Now he returned to it, because he thought the relentlessness and rigour of its plot would provide a framework for the exposition of the tangles of private and public emotion in modern Irish society. The theme, of course, is one which is relevant to any society that discovers a rottenness at its heart. While this tragedy is universal in its resonances relating to guilt and wrong committed in the heat and press of events, nevertheless it spoke pointedly to a deep sense of trouble about the nature of Irish society in the aftermath of independence. A son kills a father, and extends this calamity through a marriage contracted as a consequence of an apparent triumph of bravery and intelligence: Oedipus answers the riddle of the oppressive sphinx only to find himself all the more completely entangled in a fate that is ineluctable. The Irish, it would appear, had found some kind of release from the dominion of England, only to realize also that the freedom gained was a kind of plague, a torment of impossible choices, treacherous alliances, moral recrimination, and murder. Yeats here raised questions as to what consequences may flow from violent acts, even if those acts are committed in impetuous good faith or on understandable impulse. The play's terrible last lines deepen a national crisis into a tragic and personally registered realization:

> Call no man fortunate that is not dead.
> The dead are free from pain.[4]

In November 1926 the long-anticipated experimental and teaching theatre, which would act as a testing-ground for new ideas and techniques, was realized. Premises attached to the Abbey which had previously been let to a college for the teaching of Irish were renovated for these purposes. The architect of this new complex, known as the Peacock, was a young part-time Abbey player called Michael Scott, later to design the new Abbey which opened in 1966.

Liam O'Flaherty, from Inishmore in the Aran Islands, was by now the well-known author of a number of successful works, including *The Informer* (1925), one of his finest. He had also written some short stories in Irish, and An Comhar Drámaíochta approached him for a play in Irish for their monthly Abbey play. He wrote *Dorchadas* (1 March 1926), a dark tragedy of island life which caused a certain amount of disquiet and protest in the theatre: word had gone forth that a native Aran man was here traducing his own people in a manner reminiscent of though more reprehensible than Synge, he being of the islands himself. The Guards were called in once again.[5]

The Peacock's first production was of a German expressionist play by Georg Kaiser, *From Morn to Midnight* (13 November 1927), and it was directed by Denis Johnston, then becoming involved in Dublin drama circles and, in particular, Robinson's Dublin Drama League.

Early in 1927 a new government representative was appointed to the board as a replacement for George O'Brien. He was Walter Starkie, nominated to the directors by Ernest Blythe because he was a Catholic, as well as being a relatively young professor of Romance languages at Trinity. In her journal for 10 January Lady Gregory tells how she and Yeats favoured Starkie above the other Blythe nominees, T. C. Murray and Daniel Corkery, for his scholarship and distinction, but also because 'he is very tractable and wouldn't give us any trouble'. She also remarks that he is not a very good Catholic, adding, extracting from her letter to Blythe, 'we must have someone we can talk freely to and before'.[6]

The state subsidy for the financial year 1926–7 had been increased from £850 to £1,000, thereby allowing the actors' wages to be fixed for the first time. Existing full-time actors were paid £7 10s. a week, and they received half that amount during non-playing periods. Part-timers were paid according to the size of the part, and Lennox Robinson, as play-director, received £400 a year.[7]

Lady Gregory's two last plays, *Sancho's Master* (14 March) and *Dave* (9 May), were produced in 1927. *Sancho's Master*, adapted from Cervantes's *Don Quixote*, was based on a theme very close to Lady Gregory's heart, as indeed it was to Yeats's: that of the idealist dreaming of betterment in a world only too ready to scoff at his visions. In Lady Gregory's own copy of the play, she wrote: 'the world is not yet free of the dreamer seeking to realize the perfect in a community not ready for its Millennium, and where he may meet with anger or ridicule that scorches or have the name thrown at him that Festus flung at St. Paul.'[8] The play was directed by Lennox Robinson, and had F. J. McCormick in the role of Don Quixote, with P. J. Carolan as Sancho. Although it does deal with the perennial theme of the tribulations experienced by idealists in a world motivated by avarice and envy, the play also has certain contemporary references. In the first act, for example, Carasco the notary gets Sancho to burn the Don's books; the priest, he tells the housekeeper, has ordered this, because the reading of anything other than devotional works conduces only to vanity, self-delusion, and objectless desire. Carasco says: 'There is only one way to make an end of them—that is by fire . . . The priest laid down they should be burned by fire the same as if they were written by heretics.'[9] At a time when the Irish Free State was consolidating itself as a deeply conservative Catholic entity, united by a shared set of beliefs and practices that originated in an antimodernist ideology promulgated by the Vatican, books and the ideas and the feelings they may inspire came under suspicion. As Austin Clarke put it in the poem 'Tenebrae' from *Night and Morning* (1938):

> An open mind disturbs the soul.[10]

This was the era of tightening censorship as the majority of the Irish people identified ever more closely with the Catholic church and its anti-modernist values, in an attempt to create a stable society after a century of disaster, upheaval, violence, and hunger.

In Lady Gregory's play Don Quixote and Sancho became the butt of everyone's jokes, with the last act making use of an elaborate stagecraft to suggest to the two gullible creatures that they can fly and that Sancho has been made governor of an island. At the end, Don Quixote, exhausted, seeks to return to his native countryside of Toboso; his adventures and the tricks played upon him by a flighty Duke and Duchess have tired him out. When the Duchess relents and promises him comfort and ease, he responds as follows: 'Freedom's best. It is one of the best gifts heaven has bestowed upon men. The treasures that the earth encloses or the sea covers are not to be compared with it. Life may and ought to be risked for liberty as much as honour.'[11] That last line is the product of a tough and uncompromising mind and temperament.

Dave (9 May, 1927) is a miracle play. The title-character is a foundling hired by the O'Cahan family as a *spailpín*, or itinerant labourer. The crooked old serving man (played by P. J. Carolan) Timothy Loughlin never has a good word to say about the young hireling. When O'Cahan and his young wife Kate are away Loughlin tries to rob him, and Dave and he fall to arguing and fighting. The O'Cahans return unexpectedly and, finding Dave apparently ready to set fire to the house, knock him senseless and tie him up. O'Cahan and Loughlin now leave Kate in charge and try to contact the police. While they are away Kate, who has always had a soft spot for the boy, unties him; as she does so strange music is heard and Dave envisions a paradise where his brother calls to him. He resolves to go and work for the poor and famine-struck in Connemara, about whom a wandering preacher has been speaking.

It is a strange, poignant, affecting play, which encapsulates many of the Abbey themes and concerns: idealism, and the trouble of life that subverts it; a mean-minded peasant, who is contrasted with a noble one in touch with the other world; a young wife dreaming of freedom, and her older man who is locked into the past; the allure of wild places; the feeling for the people of Ireland; but most of all, the sense that this world and the next are not necessarily separable entities. There is also the preoccupation with the Famine, which is such a central feature in much of Lady Gregory's writing, giving a sombre back-colouring to her vivid evocations of feasting, drink, and community itself. This is Dave describing how he will dedicate himself to the people of Connemara as he takes up his spade and hat:

If it should fail me to earn a handful of meal to keep the life in them, I can show service to the dead. Those that die on the roadside I will not leave to be dragged by a dog, or swallowed down in a boghole. If I cannot make out a couple of boards to put around them, I will weave a straw mat with my hands. If the dead-bells do not ring for them, I will waste a white candle for their wake![12]

On 31 December 1926 Lady Gregory recorded in her journal that Yeats had written to her saying that he was making good progress with *Oedipus at Colonus*, and that he 'would be much more content with [his] work for the Abbey when this play is finished'.[13] In early February 1927 he told her, with typical Yeatsian modesty, that with her help he had made *Oedipus* 'a masterpiece of English prose'.[14]

Yeats returned to the Oedipus story because its concern with the consequences of actions, whether deliberate or not, fascinated him. This story has, amongst its many implications, an exploration of what constitutes correct action, loyalty, and behaviour that runs true to what fate has ordained. The first Oedipus tragedy deals with the misery that may befall a man as a consequence of his (even unwitting) actions; its sequel, humanized to some degree by the gentleness and love of the daughters Antigone and Ismene, considers the possibility that a man or woman may behave with integrity and resist the attractions of anger or the enticements of opportunistic revenge. Oedipus, fortified by the support of Theseus, King of Athens, shows qualities of loyalty and steadfastness, and for this reason is subsumed into the earth and stone and trees of the sacred groves of Colonus. Theseus is a figure of complete humanity and ordinary goodness, a true hero. When he meets Oedipus, in exile from Thebes, he says: 'I myself have been in exile, nor has any living man been in greater peril of his life than I. Never will I reject such a wanderer; what am I but a man, and I may suffer to-morrow what you suffer to-day.'[15] At present, in the play, Thebes and Athens are at peace, but Oedipus lets Theseus know that the oracle has decreed that unless his bones be buried in Theban soil the city will be conquered by the Athenians. Creon, brother-in-law of Oedipus, comes from Thebes to try to cajole him back, a blandishment which fails; then the emissary uses deceit and force, abducting the blind man's daughters in order to compel Oedipus to his will. Theseus intervenes on behalf of the man he has vowed to protect, restores Antigone and Ismene to him, and sends Creon back to Thebes. Now Polyneices, one of Oedipus's sons, seeks audience with his father/brother, the man he had, years back, while living in Thebes, cast into exile. He, it turns out, has in turn been the victim of a coup by his brother Eteocles, who now reigns over the city. Meanwhile Polyneices has been to Argos and married the king's daughter; with Argive support he and six others plan to attack Thebes but the oracles have said that their endeavour will fail without the support of Oedipus. Oedipus submits to Antigone's pleas that he listen to Polyneices: 'think of all the evils that have come upon you through your own father and mother; think what you did in your anger against your own father and against your own sight. What good ever came of intemperate anger?'[16] But Oedipus is appalled at what Polyneices asks; that he support his disloyal and murderous attack on his own country and against his own kin. He rejects both Antigone and his son, leaving them to destroy themselves, which he knows they will:

you and your brother are strangers and no sons of mine. Therefore the eye of God has seen you; punishment has begun, but it shall not ruin you utterly until your army marches upon Thebes. You shall not overthrow that city. No, but you shall fall and your brother fall, each drowned in the other's blood.[17]

It is hard not to read these driving sorrow-riddled sentences without thinking of the war and strife and heartbreak that are the central concerns of O'Casey's great trilogy also, the violence and bloodshed in which the modern Irish state broke into existence. Oedipus' capacity to come through his anger and misery, to survive them by suffering them to the limit, offers not hope, but a kind of exultant triumph: the implication, carried by some of the last lines of the chorus, is that suffering through life's 'entanglements', without giving in or completely losing control, is what the human spirit may achieve. It is a bleak victory, but strangely blessed; these lines carry the strange joy of Yeatsian tragedy, an energy that derives from a mixture of moral, philosophical, historical, and civic elements. Oedipus is dead, and the chorus imagines death singing his elegy, an elegy welcoming him to Hades after he has completed his fate:

> Nor may the hundred-headed dog give tongue
> Until the daughter of Earth and Tartarus
> That even bloodless shades call Death has sung
> The travel-broken shade of Oedipus
> Through triumph of completed destiny
> Into eternal sleep, if such there be.[18]

Yeats believed that these plays were haunted. In a letter of October 1927 to Olivia Shakespear, his one-time mistress, he wrote that during the performance of *Oedipus at Colonus* there was heard the loud barking of a dog in the gallery. There were, it turned out, dogs in the house but the two owners heard the barking from different places. The actors thought it was the ghost of a dog who had starved to death in the theatre once when it was closed for the summer.[19]

Yeats was right to realize he had written a great drama, in which the Irish context continually surfaces as the narrative shocks of the plot are realized in the spare and bleak language. Lennox Robinson directed this play, which opened on 12 September 1927, with F. J. McCormick as Oedipus again; Shelah Richards playing Antigone; and Barry Fitzgerald as Creon.

Still, however, Yeats had no suitable actors for the intensely evocative verse plays he had been writing since 1913, influenced by the Japanese Noh drama, and by Ezra Pound; nor indeed had the Abbey players much sympathy for these densely packed, subtle, and intricate meditations on personality and fate. The Oedipus play, though complex, had a raw human power, but Yeats's symbolic purity in pieces such as *The Only Jealousy of Emer* required an absorbed dreamlike deliberateness, as well as skills of dancing and incantation.

In November 1927 Ninette de Valois (subsequently founder of Sadlers Wells Ballet, later to become the Royal Ballet) established a school of ballet at the Peacock, to be part of the acting school re-established the previous year: Nugent Monck had been given this responsibility when he was appointed in 1911. One of the objects of this development was the training of dancers capable of performing in Yeats's plays, or in plays like his.

On 10 January 1928 Lady Gregory had a letter from Sean O'Casey, from London, saying he hoped to have his new play, *The Silver Tassie*, ready by the end of March. By the beginning of March he was writing: 'Personally I think it is the best work I have yet done. I have certainly put my best into it, and have written the work solely because of love and a deep feeling that what I have written should be written.'[20] There had been, in Dublin, some gossip to the effect that O'Casey was not going to give the new play to the Abbey, rumours that he had had visits seeking reassurance from an anxious Robinson and an agitated Yeats that the new play was destined for the Abbey. There seems to have been some truth in this gossip because O'Casey, in his autobiography *Rose and Crown*, does say that the play was under consideration by the London producer C. B. Cochran while it was being read at the Abbey.[21] Robinson, when he read it, thought that the play was broken-backed: he liked the first two acts, but thought that thereafter it fell into 'rowdiness'. Lady Gregory agreed, and Robinson was relieved: 'If you had disagreed with me I should have suspected myself of all sorts of horrid sub-conscious feelings.'[22] Both he and Lady Gregory held off from giving their opinion until Yeats and Starkie, the government-appointed director, had time to consider the play. The affair was giving Lady Gregory a great deal of anguish, all the more so because O'Casey, not mentioning the play, was writing her warm and affectionate letters. When Yeats's criticism came to Coole, she sent the reports to O'Casey, who was, at the time, correcting the proofs of *The Silver Tassie* for publication by Macmillan; she hoped that he might revise the play, or hold it back for further work. In her journal Lady Gregory wrote: 'I had a bad night, or early morning, thinking of the disappointment and shock he will feel.'[23] She was not wrong.

The letter arrived on the morning O'Casey's son Brian was born, and, unable to resist opening the large envelope from the Abbey, he tore through its contents before going upstairs to see the mother and child: 'Curse o'god on them! His anger grew at every line,' O'Casey wrote.[24] He quotes Yeats's withering attacks. The play deals with the First World War, and its terrible carnage. Yeats wrote:

'You are not interested in the Great War; you never stood on its battlefields, never walked its hospitals, and so write out of your opinions . . . Among the things that dramatic action must burn up are the author's opinions.'[25] O'Casey was especially incensed by Yeats's suggestion that he withdraw the play and say that he himself had become dissatisfied with it; the plan was then that the directors would keep silent so as to save face all round. But O'Casey, tormented by the thought of his poverty and the needs of his new family, resolved that the only way to deal with this 'blow to the heart' was to fight, and to make the fight as public as he possibly could.

He sent the letters (not all of them, he kept back Lady Gregory's note agreeing with Yeats's and Robinson's judgements) first to Russell's the *Irish Statesman*, who (correctly) refused to publish private correspondence. He then sent them to St John Ervine who had them published in the London *Observer* on Sunday, 3 June 1928. The following day they were copied in the *Irish Times*.

The acrimony deepened and Yeats threatened to sue for breach of copyright in regard to his private letters. Shaw came in on the side of O'Casey, and wrote consolingly to him on 19 June, saying of Yeats that all his cleverness deserts him 'when you expect him to be equal to the occasion. [He] is not a man of this world; and when you hurl an enormous chunk of it at him, he dodges it, small blame to him . . . Cheerio, Titan.'[26] Lady Gregory saw C. B. Cochran's London production at the Apollo Theatre, with the very English Charles Laughton incongruously playing the part of Harry Heegan, the Dublin labourer who wins for his girl the silver tassie (cup) in a football match. In her journal she wrote that they should have put it on at the Abbey, and said as much in a letter to Yeats, which she copied to O'Casey. It was, in Lady Gregory's own words, a painful business, and meant that O'Casey was now at odds with the Abbey, and indeed with Ireland.[27]

New developments were in train. The Dublin Drama League had been performing plays by Serafín and Joaquín Quintero, the 'Quintero Brothers', Pirandello, Strindberg, and others, including Denis Johnston's production of Kaiser. Johnston, a Dubliner of northern extraction (his father had dabbled in liberal politics for a time), had studied law in Cambridge and Harvard, but while in the USA had become obsessed with the theatre. When he returned to Dublin he took some briefs in a desultory way, but his real passion continued to be plays and players. He was interested in extending the emotional, intellectual, and technical range of the Irish theatre, and studied the German expressionism of Kaiser and Ernst Toller. He adopted the Teutonic-looking pseudonym 'E. W. Tocher' for the programme-note of *From Morn to Midnight*. In 1928 he married the Abbey actress Shelah Richards, and in that year also he submitted *Rhapsody in Green* to the Abbey. The typescript was returned with, it is said, '*The Old Lady Says "No"*' written across it, a purported reference to Lady Gregory's judgement of the play. However, it would appear that Johnston may have perpetrated this story and written the indictment himself.

Yeats was impressed by the young man, and he was given the opportunity of directing *King Lear* with the Abbey company (26 November 1928). A deal was done between Johnston, Yeats, and Robinson, and Lady Gregory confided to her journal that she had never been told that *Lear* was being put on: 'I fancy it was given to him to make up for the rejection of his impossible Emmet play', the play that was to be eventually staged by the Gate Theatre, as *The Old Lady says 'No!'*[28]

The Gate Theatre was founded by Mícheál Mac Liammóir and Hilton Edwards in 1928, and its first home was in the Peacock, the Abbey's experimental annexe. The name seems to have come from Peter Godfrey's Gate Studio in London, where Johnston and O'Casey saw expressionist work in 1926. It opened on 14 October 1928, as the Dublin Gate Theatre Studio, with Ibsen's *Peer Gynt*, followed by a production of Wilde's *Salomé*, and on 3 July 1929 Johnston's *The Old Lady Says 'No!'*, directed by Hilton Edwards. Yeats and Robinson guaranteed this production against loss to the sum of £50, Yeats claiming, to Lady Gregory's bafflement, that this subvention had been agreed at a meeting of the Abbey board.

Johnston's *Lear* was the first Shakespeare produced at the Abbey and F. J. McCormick had a triumph (despite initial nervousness, notwithstanding the tragic range he had revealed in Yeats's Sophocles adaptations) in the most demanding role on the English stage. Lady Gregory attended on 30 November and was irritated at a farcical delay at the end when Lear carries the dead Cordelia in his arms: there was a 'scrimmage' behind the curtain, calls, and scuffles, and then they appeared. Shelah Richards, as Cordelia, had apparently sloped off to have a cigarette, and was nowhere to be found. Lady Gregory's comment was: 'I wish she would leave us altogether.'[29]

The Old Lady Says 'No!' features an actor playing Robert Emmet in a nationalist play; the actor becomes concussed, having been knocked to the ground by soldiers. A doctor is called for from the stage (this shock realism was so novel in Dublin at the time that members of the audience rushed forward to help), and it is announced that the actor has been badly injured. There follows a series of dream-scenes in which the dazed actor encounters icons of nationalist idealism in a Dublin far removed from such traditional aspirations. The play violently opposes the static idealizations of nationalism with the sordid reality of materialistic Dublin. These oppositions had, at this time, the virtue of novelty. The part of the actor was played by the young and brilliant Mícheál Mac Liammóir. At a deeper level the play explores the ways in which reality is shaped, and one of the chief means by which this is done is language. Irish theatre, and the Abbey in particular, had been, and was for many years to continue to be, a theatre of words. Here Johnston, in a deliberate critique of Abbey methods and practices, subjects language to a series of subversive strategies, as he shows how people are controlled by the language they speak and the clichés they mouth and are expected to mouth. There is in Johnston (and this quality stayed with him throughout his writing career) a brave insouciance and a willingness to use the theatre to get his audience to question their own versions of reality. It was a pity that the Abbey could not accommodate this subversive talent, both for the theatre, and for Johnston himself.

In 1929 Yeats rewrote *The Only Jealousy of Emer* for the Abbey in a simplified prose version to which he gave the title *Fighting the Waves*, no doubt inspired by the talent of Ninette de Valois, who was responsible for directing the short-lived ballet school at the Peacock. *The Only Jealousy of Emer* was part of Yeat's Cuchulain cycle of plays based on Ulster saga and modelled on the severe style of the Japanese Noh he had studied and meditated upon since first encountering this tradition in the writings of Ernest Fenollosa. Ninette de Valois was the stage name of Edris Stannis, born in Co. Wicklow in 1898, later to become extremely influential in the development of British ballet. *The Only Jealousy* is a difficult play based on saga material which Yeats adapts to express his own view of human psychology as an arena of conflict between ordinary reality and the otherworld. It was produced by Albert van Dalsum in Amsterdam in 1922. *Fighting the Waves* strips the poetic and rhetorical effects bare, to reveal the essential elements in the plot, and to foreground the play's dance sequences, which were led by Ninette de Valois herself, playing the wordless part of Fand, the Woman of the Sidhe, who seeks to entice the Ghost of Cuchulain to the other world. He is pulled back by Emer's self-sacrifice, although in renouncing his love she knows she will lose him for ever to the younger Eithne Inguba and his own remorse. The play ends with Fand's dance expressing her grief at the loss of Cuchulain. Neither the living nor the dead have peace.

It would be tiresome to politicize so allusive and inscrutable a work, but there is little doubt that part of this tiny play's force is owed to Yeats's sense of the never-ceasing conflict in modern Ireland between the authority of the dead and the harsh need of the living for human comfort and understanding. It is precisely the moral dilemma O'Casey tackles, except that Yeats does it in his own arcane, but no less passionate way. He was very excited by the production and he wrote to Olivia Shakespear on 24 August 1929 declaring that he had 'discovered a new form by this combination of dance, speech, and music', and that everyone was as convinced as he was that he had made some kind of theatrical breakthrough.[30] Lady Gregory went to see it with him, and described it as 'wild, beautiful . . . We might all have been at the bottom of the sea'.[31]

In 1930 in George Shiels's *The New Gossoon* Peter Carey, uncle to the 'new gossoon' of the title, exclaims: 'This country's going to hell at a hundred miles an hour! Petrol and pictures and potheen and jazz and doles and buses and bare legs and all sorts of foreign rascalities.'[32] Uncle Peter has been called in to help put Luke Carey, the 'new gossoon' who has been swept up in these rascalities, straight. His widowed mother Ellen is distracted at what she has reared, 'a lazy, selfish, headstrong rascal, and about half-wise', who spends his time and his mother's money on a motor-bike, greyhounds, and running around the countryside.

However the conventional comic oppositions between wise old age and reckless youth ('Forty hates twenty-five, sixty hates forty. And seventy hates everybody,' as Luke puts it) are not that simple in Shiels. Ellen has made 'an outrageous promise' to her dying husband that she would never remarry, and denied the love that has grown between herself and Ned Shay over the years; Peter, the supposedly wise uncle, turns out to be incapable of behaving firmly and authoritatively; and Sally Hamil, the poacher's daughter who wears short skirts and smokes cigarettes, turns out to be the real organizing intelligence in the whole play. She resolves all the difficulties, takes Luke in hand and agrees to marry him, and also gets Ellen and Ned to face up to the way they feel about each other. There is a comic exuberance in the play, but also a delight in the way that character escapes categorization. The young bring changes, but Ned says that they may be all for the better. New 'gossoons' demand 'new treatment'. There is a marked fluidity of judgement in this play, as in much of the later Shiels, a strong reluctance to submit his comedic energy to given moral rules. Sally Hamil was played by Eileen Crowe, Luke by Denis O'Dea, and the redoubtable F. J. McCormick played Robit Hamil, Sally's father, with Arthur Shields directing. The play opened on 19 April.

This frank, non-judgemental modernism did not, on the whole, appeal to Yeats: of Shiels's 1927 comedy *Cartney and Kevney* (29 November) he wrote, 'it displayed a series of base actions without anything to show that its author disapproved or expected us to do so'. D. E. S. Maxwell acutely comments on this and on Shiels's comic world: 'we need not share Yeats's uneasiness to allow the justice of his comment.'[33] And indeed *The New Gossoon* is a kind of extended critique of Yeats's idealism, famously expressed in the opening lines of 'Sailing to Byzantium' in *The Tower* (1928):

That is no country for old men.[34]

Luke says of Ireland, as he longs to break free of it: 'It's an ideal country for growing old men. They can live on a diet of legends about Brian Boru and the Big Wind.'[35] It would, of course, be fatuous simply to categorize Yeats as a purveyor of legend or a nostalgist for orders of decency now gone from a declining earth. His concept of history and his view of how character can be made or unmade, while it does have mythical elements, is nevertheless far from simple, and those mythical elements themselves are closely related to Yeats's complex formulations with regard to the interactions between history and individual identity. These concerns of his were forcefully enacted in a play, directed by Robinson, that formed part of the autumn season in the same year as *The New Gossoon* was produced, *The Words upon the Windowpane* (17 November 1930).

This play, and the introductory essay he wrote for it, present Yeats's mature estimation of Swift, Anglo-Ireland, freedom, the nature of government, and the labyrinth of personality. The prose of the introduction is crammed with thought, some of it unruly and problematic; while the play brilliantly dramatizes the shock of the utterly strange and mysterious. Swift, he writes in the introduction: 'haunts me; he is always just around the next corner . . . This instinct for what is real and yet hidden is in reality a return to the sources of our power and therefore a claim made upon the future.' Whatever this thinking is seeking to realize, it remains open, anxious, probing.

No simplification of emotion is involved here. He goes on:

Thought seems more true, emotion more deep, spoken by someone [Swift] who touches my pride . . . who seems to make me a part of some national mythology, nor is mythology mere ostentation, mere vanity if it draws one onward to the unknown; another turn of the gyre and myth is wisdom, pride, discipline. I remember the shudder in my spine when Mrs Patrick Campbell said, speaking words Hofmansthal put into the mouth of Electra 'I too am of that ancient race.'[36]

And then he quotes his famous translation of Swift's epitaph, 'Swift has sailed into his rest'. The intellectual core of the essay, and the dramatic nature of the play itself, derive from Yeats's powerful reading of Swift's 'one philosophical work', his *Discourse of the Contents and Discussions between the Nobles and Commons in Athens and Rome* (1703). Summarizing abruptly, Yeats (not inaccurately) sees Swift as foretelling the dominance of the Many against the One (the absolute executive authority in a state) and the Few (an aristocracy with admixtures of those who rise by merit). The Many, in a surprising twist, affect a 'singularity; but set them to the work of the State and every man Jack is "listed in a party", becomes the fanatical follower of men of whose characters he knows next to nothing, and from that day on sets nothing into his mouth that some other man has not already chewed and digested'.

The sickening implications of this metaphor are a measure of Yeats's disgust at democracy, a revulsion he also identifies in Swift. Yeats now turns to the question of Swift's love life, his reputed celibacy, and the accusations sometimes levelled at him that he treated Stella and Vanessa badly. He relates Swift's personal behaviour to his philosophy, and maintains that Swift remained celibate because he feared not death but life, 'what might happen next';[37] Yeats puts this thought into the mind of John Corbet (played by Arthur Shields) in the play, who voices Swift's attitude thus: 'Am I to add another to the healthy rascaldom and knavery of the world?'

John Corbet is a Cambridge student who joins a seance at the Dublin Spiritualists' Association. They hold their meetings in an old house where a few lines of a poem by Stella to Swift are cut into the windowpane. Mrs Henderson (played by May Craig, a recent addition), a famous London medium (whose 'control' or spirit guide is a little girl called Lulu), has already given a couple of seances, but they have been disrupted by a strange presence, which turns out to be Swift. Again, this time, Swift invades the seance, save that on this occasion Hester Vanhomrigh (Vanessa) is present also, both spirits speaking through the medium. Stella also arrives in the spirit-world, and Swift speaks tenderly to her, but he rejects sexual love with them both, because, Corbet suggests to the medium when her trance is over, 'he must have dreaded the future'. Mrs Henderson, of course, knows nothing of what has happened. When the young man, the last to leave, departs, she begins to make tea when, once again, she is invaded by the presence of Swift.

Swift haunted Yeats, not only because he seemed to represent the intellect free from the requirements of submissive belief, but also because he seemed to be released from any sentimentality about the individual. He believed, but not as 'cranks' or 'sectarians' believed; about such things, Yeats said, a man should 'think his own thoughts in silence'. He also detested the 'Many', and hated (in Yeats's interpretation) democracy. These formulations about Swift reflect Yeats's own tragic sense of the dereliction of man's condition in the twentieth century but they also draw upon the never-ceasing arguments in the Abbey Theatre itself about the need for greater democracy and accountability and the role the theatre should have in promoting various forms of sanitized cultural values. There is little doubt but that the Abbey often wore Yeats out, and that the individuals involved frequently drove him not to his wit's end, exactly, but to the kind of ferocious anger the thinking in his Swift play reveals.

The following year, on 27 April 1931, Lennox Robinson's production of Denis Johnston's *The Moon in the Yellow River* opened. In *The Words upon the Windowpane* Yeats wrote of the 'singularity' affected by the Many when really they submit their characters to the domination of others, mimicking the ideas and feelings of those they imagine to be of consequence. Johnston's play, while one would not wish to push the link too far, is a kind of meditation on 'singularity', the individual, power, and modernity in Free State Ireland.

The play is a kind of intellectual farce, but animated by a grim and unrelenting scepticism. The central set of themes, which revolve around the complexity of human motives and the difficulty in forming clear judgement, are presented in a dramatic action that is shocking and casual at once: Johnston is portraying a society that coolly, and in a kind of resolved steadiness, is harsh and brutal and where romanticism and patriotism breed mayhem and confusion.

Set in the west of Ireland, the play deals with the destruction of a new hydroelectric plant situated near a big house, inhabited by entirely 'singular' remnants of the aristocracy. Dobelle (played by F. J. McCormick), a retired engineer, presides over this disorderly house, plays with his large toy train-set, neglects his daughter, and allows his sister, Aunt Columba (Eileen Crowe), to indulge her whimsicality, rudeness, and eccentricity to her heart's content. Terrible events occur: an IRA gunman arrives, intending to blow up the powerhouse, but he turns out to be the housekeeper's son, who tells him she will 'lam [him] with the flat of [her] fist' if he does not leave them alone. His IRA commanding officer, Donnell Blake (Denis O'Dea), arrives; appropriately bearing a romantic name, he mirrors the waywardness of the Dobelle household, and Blanaid (Shelah Richards) the daughter is infatuated with him. Blake and Tausch (Fred Johnson), the German engineer at the works, get drunk and have an altercation, farcically presented as a mockery of a trial scene, debating the merits of modernization against the attractions of a more rooted life in a traditional community. The playfulness and wit of this set piece is devastatingly exploded when the Free State soldier and ex-IRA gunman Lanigan (P. J. Carolan) abruptly shoots Blake dead. Dobelle reacts to this by recalling a memory of childhood:

I was driving with my uncle in one of those old-fashioned high dog-carts. We were coming back from duck-shooting and a rabbit ran across the road directly in front of us. My uncle rose in the seat, took a careful aim, and shot the horse through the head. It was a most surprising incident at the time.[38]

Meanwhile Aunt Columba is searching for her ice-skates: she has 'a championship to defend'. This is 'singularity' all right, but one which is a fuddled state of protective neurosis, a 'satiric neurosis', that anaesthetizes experience, as alcohol may do, or romanticism. Johnston's drama of ideas, which owes much to Shaw, reveals a world in which people are compelled to back away from a reality that is all but ungovernable and utterly strange: the melodramatic effects, such as Lanigan's shooting of Blake, are theatrically effective in their abrupt suddenness and terror. As Thomas Kilroy says: 'dottiness . . . is a way of surviving when all the power has passed to the brutally efficient, the engineers and the gunmen.'[39] Lanigan explains his motives, such as they are: 'I'm a physical-force man born and bred in the movement. I'm only doing my job—the job I'm able to do—the job that always seems to deliver the goods.'[40] And slightly earlier: 'If I don't get what's coming to me for this business, I suppose I'll be plugged sooner or later by somebody.' Dobelle, echoing O'Casey's 'hearts of stone' speech, says: 'take away this cursed gift of laughter and give us tears instead'; although O'Casey's humanitarian outrage is kept well at bay, Dobelle ruefully commenting: 'The birth of a nation is no immaculate conception.'[41]

The play's ending moves, surprisingly, to an extraordinary moment of human closeness between Dobelle, the widowed father, and the daughter whom he scarcely knows, as if to say: the drunk Chinese poet (Li Po) who tried to embrace the moon in the yellow river is not just a figure of fun but of human loneliness and the desire to end suffering and cruelty.

A masterly play, its surprising and dynamic structure is entirely adequate to the realization of the terror that is the play's core, the terror (which is also at the heart of Yeats's Swift play) that human society may have gone beyond the point where it may be redeemable. These two bleak plays of 1930 and 1931 are masterpieces of modern (world) theatre in a period when it is commonly believed the Abbey was in steep decline.

The Abbey directors themselves were convinced that there was, at this time, a shortage of good new plays, and they mounted a competition in 1931 to encourage new writing. The prize was shared between Paul Vincent Carroll, for *The Bed of Procrustes*, later changed to *Things that Are Caesar's*, and Teresa Deevy's *Temporal Powers*. Carroll had had a one-acter in the Peacock Theatre in 1930, *The Watched Pot* (17 November); while Deevy had already had two plays produced at the Abbey: *The Reapers* (18 March 1930) and *A Disciple* (24 August 1931).

Carroll, from Dundalk in Co. Louth, had trained as a teacher at St Patrick's College, Drumcondra, from 1916. During his college years he saw the Easter Rising and experienced the disruption of life in Dublin during the Anglo-Irish War of Independence. He haunted the Abbey Theatre, which became, he wrote, his 'spiritual home'. In 1921 he went to live and work in Glasgow, where he began to write.

Things that Are Caesar's (15 August 1932), like the plays of T. C. Murray (with whom he corresponded and to whom he sent drafts of his work), deals with small-town, rural Irish life, and the oppressive effects of family and religion. Eilish Hardy, an Ibsenite heroine, has a manipulative conventional mother, Julia, and an indulgent if idealistic father, Peter. Julia connives with the orthodox, conventional, and dogmatic Fr. Duffy to ensnare Eilish into a marriage with Phil Noonan, a mediocre but fairly wealthy local farmer. Her father is unhappy with this arrangement, but he dies in Act II, leaving Eilish at the mercy of her money-grubbing and snobbish mother, and the priest whose estimate of human possibility is so low that the best option for people, in his view, is unthinking compliance to necessity: 'render unto Caesar the things that are Caesar's.' In the 1932 version Eilish surrenders her spirit, but in 1944 she leaves her marriage, defies Fr. Duffy, and emigrates to America.

Lady Gregory died on Monday, 23 May 1932. Yeats stayed with her at Coole almost continually during her last year. She was suffering from cancer and was in terrible pain a good deal of the time, especially during the last months. In October 1931 she paid her final visit to the Abbey, and said farewell to the actors in the green room. Yeats, at Coole, was, in her own words, happily and peacefully working on *A Vision*, while she tried to keep from him the agony she confessed to her journal.

In 1933 Lennox Robinson, with *Drama at Inish*, began a series of four plays set in the small seaside town of 'Inish', with its hotel, the Seaview, its boarding houses, its close-knit community, and its rival tourist attraction, Shangarry Strand. The other plays in the series were *Bird's Nest* (1938), *Forget Me Not* (1941), and *The Lucky Finger* (1948). *Drama at Inish* (6 February) was written while Robinson was on holiday at a place not unlike the seaside town where it is set, and at his usual cracking if not manic pace, completing it in a week.

The bibulous John Twohig (played by William O'Gorman), who owns the Seaview, has invited the highfalutin De La Mare Repertory Theatre company for a summer season to Inish; he is hoping that their continental and intellectual plays (echoes of the Dublin Drama League and the Gate) will prove more attractive to the summer visitors than the last season's offering, a low revue performed by a fit-up called the Comicalities. Hector De La Mare (Paul Farrell) and his wife Constance Constantia (Elizabeth Potter), oblique if affectionate caricatures of Hilton Edwards and Mícheál Mac Liammóir, have a vision of theatre as a mission to revolutionize people's souls. He declares: 'I am myself a convert.' To which John Twohig responds: 'Do you mean you used to be a Protestant?'[42] But Hector explains that though he is not speaking in the 'strictly religious sense', some form of conversion did take place at the Cork Opera House twenty years ago. Octavia Kenmore's repertory theatre performed plays that revealed the illusory nature of Cork life: 'I could translate every play in terms of the South Mall or Montenotte or Sunday's Well.' This last epiphanic revelation he now seeks to recreate in Inish, with disastrous consequences. Robinson is having fun at, to some degree, his own expense as well as that of the Gate: he, like the De La Mares, was an enthusiast for Russian and Scandinavian plays; and he, too, experienced a conversion in the Cork Opera House as a young man. The second part of Act I is a hilarious burlesque of a Chekovian crisis in the form of a rehearsal by the De La Mares at Seaview, to try to get the 'vibrations' right.

It seems, indeed, that they get the vibrations all too right. In Act II it is revealed that the company is doing well, but only because the denizens of Inish are taking the plays all too seriously. Someone has attempted suicide; Lizzie, Twohig's sister, seeing in her life a Chekovian dreariness, is getting depressed; while Twohig himself is taking to the drink. Eddie Twohig (played at the Abbey by the young Joseph Linnane) has also been infected by melancholy and meanwhile over at Shangarry Strand a young couple have tried to gas themselves but the penny-in-the-slot meter 'gev out'.[43]

However, in Act III life reasserts itself. The gloom and sadness of art and artifice are dispelled, and there is a series of recoveries and discoveries. For example, it turns out that the aloof but beautiful accountant Eddie has courted in vain for years loves him after all, something she realizes only after he is nearly drowned in a mood of lethargic despondency. A circus is hired and the end of the play fills with light and energy.

It is a strange piece and resonates with implications relating to art, freedom, the dangers of the imagination, and communal responsibility. It shows the firmness of Robinson's grip on reality and his distrust of the phantasms that may arise from excessive self-awareness or self-examination.

Francis Stuart, the novelist from Co. Antrim, who married Iseult Gonne in 1920, had *Men Crowd Me Round* (15 March 1933) produced to a deeply unenthusiastic reception. Based upon his experiences in the IRA during the Civil War, the play's rawness and blunt language affronted the audience, Holloway recording how stony and unreceptive it was.

Brinsley MacNamara returned to the Abbey stage with *Margaret Gillan* (17 July), a fierce and emotional domestic tragedy. Directed by Arthur Shields, the play had Barry Fitzgerald and F. J. McCormick in the leading roles of Master Growney and John Briody. It is an amalgamation of an Ibsenite theme of family remorse and malice with a Freudian drama of misapprehension and repression. It is probably one of the most psychologically complex plays ever staged at the

Abbey, and very nearly a masterpiece. Margaret Gillan (played by May Craig) is the young widow of her aged husband Peter, who has 'spancelled' her in a will designed to entrap her; a will brilliantly drawn up by the dead man and the sinister Master Growney, who can foresee every move she will try to make to break free of their web, a web based on their complete understanding of her nature. Gillan has appointed John Briody, the man whom Margaret loved, to be his executor; he leaves the house and shop to her until their daughter Esther (Kate Curling) comes of age, as long as she remains unmarried; if she marries the property goes to Esther, with Briody holding it in trust for her until she is 21: if, however, the daughter marries and leaves the property, it reverts to her mother, as long as she herself is still a widow. A release from this tangle of injunctions seems possible when it looks as if Briody, who also owns a shop and is very successful, is renewing his suit to Margaret; but in fact it is Esther he wants to marry. Esther accepts this offer, because of her love for her mother, thinking she is freeing Margaret from the spancel of the will, when, in fact they are all ensnaring themselves ever more completely in the dead man's web: Esther repeats the error her mother made, Briody repeats Gillan's mistake. The new marriage, like the old one, is a misery, and Briody, who moves in with the Gillans, fails in business, while Margaret thrives. Esther dies in childbirth, and by the shock of a new set of arrangements Margaret proposes to try to escape the past: these are that she marry Michael Taaffe, her servant (played by Denis O'Dea), and relinquish the property to Briody and Esther in return for Briody's shop which she plans to build up again. Margaret and Briody are distraught after Esther's death, even contemplating going away together, but she concludes the whole tangled mess by killing the man she loves.

The play's strength and sombre power comes from the sense that the plot, which is a tangle of emotional confusion and distress, is all caused by the legacy of the dead man, and the malicious and delighted connivance of his henchman Growney, who describes the will as 'a magnificent piece of work, Mr. Gillan! Why it's like somebody's death warrant, it's so complete. . . (*John Briody appears in the doorway. . .*)'. He is the man whose death warrant the will is designed to be. Master Growney knows just when the emotional tangle has reached a point where the victims will try to find a way of breaking through what is ordained, and he is there to assist them, only for them to discover that the more they try to break free the more entrapped they become:

Master. Do you think I don't know what you're going to do?
Margaret. I wonder. Oh, I wonder!. . . Hateful as you are. . . evil as you are. . .
Master. You'll always do what I want you to do. That is Peter Gillan's will.[44]

The theme of the dead controlling the affairs of the living broadens into a complex network of concerns which embrace the philosophical and moral concepts of necessity and freedom, and political implications to do with tradition, fidelity to the dead, and the legacy of the past. These political, social, and moral influences are all the more effective for being subtly implicated in the emotional intricacies of domestic conflict and unhappiness.

In the summer of 1934 two extraordinary new plays by Yeats were performed: *The King of the Great Clock Tower* (30 June), with Ninette de Valois in the non-speaking part of the Queen who comes from the other world; and *The Resurrection* (30 July). In *The King of the Great Clock Tower*, a strolling poet (Denis O'Dea) comes to the palace and announces that the Queen will dance for him and that she will kiss him. The King (F. J. McCormick) has his head cut off and brought on stage, and then the Queen, Salome-like, dances for it before picking it up and kissing it. The lips of the severed head, to the King's horror, start to move, and its mouth sings. Other players, two attendants, sing for the head and for the Queen. The Queen's voice intones:

> Nobody knows what may befall;
> *Said the wicked, crooked hawthorn tree.*
> I have stood so long by a gap in the wall
> May be I shall not die at all.[45]

This play, in its forbidding strangeness and cold intensity, unites the psychological mysticism of Yeats's conception of personality with folklore, myth, and symbolism. The 'gap in the wall' is remembered from the love song 'Dónal Óg' translated by Lady Gregory. But the dramatic excitement of the play derives from the stark confrontation between mortal and immortal longing: the Stroller and the Queen from the other world experience a mutual and unsubduable passion. As he wrote in a letter of October 1927 to Olivia Shakespear: 'only two topics can be of the least interest to a serious and studious mind—sex and the dead.'[46]

The Resurrection deals with the same theme, except in more extreme terms. The 'Notes' Yeats wrote for the play when it was published the following year carry, in terse, enigmatic, and even baffling form, much of Yeats's mature thinking on history, human personality, sex, and the soul. In an extraordinary phrase, he summarizes his vision and a central artistic and philosophic principle, one which had led to the establishment of the Irish Literary Theatre in 1899 with his dead friend Lady Gregory. It is this: 'I am satisfied, the Platonic year in my head, to find but drama.'[47] The Platonic year is the time it takes the precession of the equinoxes to complete its movement; they move at the rate of one degree every hundred years, so the Platonic year is 36,000 earth-years in duration. All forms, human and divine, wax and wane in the course of this huge precession, this great turn of the wheel. All there is is the drama of everything returning back to itself having sojourned through all possible difference: that unfolding (symbolized in the unfolding of the cloth in Yeatsian Noh—this play is dedicated to the Japanese Junzo Sato who gave Yeats his ancient sword) is the process of time; the folding back is the process completing, as the precession of the 'equinoctial sun' concludes its lengthy circuit. Yeats believed what Ptolemy the astrologer and geographer thought: that around the time of Christ the Platonic year ended. What happens in the play is that mortal and immortal fuse; material reality ceases to be capricious and becomes animate with spirit.

A Greek and a Hebrew stand guard outside the upper room in Jerusalem where the eleven apostles wait, in terror and confusion, for some message, some instruction. A Syrian has been sent to the tomb where Christ is buried, but returns to tell them, in horror and exultation, that the tomb is empty. He speaks wildly:

The Syrian. . . . another Argo seeks another fleece, another Troy is sacked.
The Greek. Why are you laughing?
The Syrian. What is human knowledge?
The Greek. The knowledge that keeps the road from here to Persia free from robbers, that has built the beautiful humane cities, that has made the modern world, that stands between us and the barbarian.
The Syrian. But what if there is something it cannot explain, something more important than anything else?
The Greek. You talk as if you wanted the barbarian back.
The Syrian. What if there is always something that lies outside knowledge, outside order? . . .
The Hebrew. Stop laughing.
The Syrian. What if the irrational return? What if the circle begins again?[48]

The play opens these questions; it does not answer them. And Yeats would maintain that the work of poetry and theatre is precisely this; to lead to an enlargement of thinking whereby human and eternal are seen as involved in a mutual interanimation. Christ comes into the house to appear to the apostles; the sceptical Greek touches him, believing it to be a phantom, and arguing that Christ was an illusion all along, in true doctrinaire Platonic style, following Plato's concept of idea and shadow. But to his horror (he screams) he finds the phantom's heart beating when he puts his hand on Christ's side.

When the play was performed there was a strike in Dublin, which prevented publication of newspapers and reviews, otherwise, Yeats believed, surely correctly, there would have been outrage at the play's heresy. Not only that, as the apostles wait, the Dionysian revels are taking place on the streets outside; the Greek describes a man and woman having sex in the open, because the woman believes there is a chance that, in the flurry of the cycle starting all over again, she may become pregnant with the reborn deity. Despite the arcanity of some of its materials, the play is an extraordinary piece uniting theatrical and philosophical daring, a play illustrating that 'danger' years called for right at the outset of his theatre.

Since the death of Lady Gregory the day-to-day running of the Abbey had fallen to Lennox Robinson. Yeats, ever watchful, however, realized that the company was again in need of some fresh impulse, and engaged, for a short season, Bladon Peake, trained by the old Abbey producer Nugent Monck at the Maddermarket Theatre in Norwich, and therefore imbued with Monck's ideas on reconciling traditional theatre with technical innovation. Peake's production of Molière's *School for Wives* and Pirandello's *Six Characters in Search of an Author* were admired for their innovatory stage technique and stark design.

Yeats gave an interview to the London *Daily Express* (31 December 1934) in which he declared that the Abbey had to make a 'fresh start'. On 31 January of the following year Yeats called a board meeting to which he presented a memorandum, addressed to him, under the title 'Proposals to the Board of the National Theatre Company Ltd'. This memorandum argued that new insights and fresh thinking were required in the theatre, especially in view of the fact that the Gate Theatre of Hilton Edwards and Mícheál Mac Liammóir, which had begun operations under the aegis of the Abbey, was now thriving in its own premises at the Rotunda. The memo coyly says: 'drama enticing to the intellect and to the eye is now found on another stage.' The proposals, which were the work of Brinsley MacNamara and the young poet F. R. Higgins, both writing with Yeats's encouragement, went on to advocate the establishment of an advisory committee to the board which would make recommendations on all matters relating to management and policy. The board members, at the time, were Yeats himself, Walter Starkie, Richard Hayes, the new government nominee, and Lennox Robinson. De Valera's government refused to reappoint Starkie but he was retained as a director, even though Hayes was the new official government representative.[49] Hayes was (from 1940) chief librarian of the National Library of Ireland and the man responsible for the compilation of the great *Manuscript Sources for the History of Irish Civilization*. Robinson was at this time in the USA, where he had joined the Abbey's main company, which was making one of its lucrative lengthy tours. The objective of the advisory committee was, as Hugh Hunt correctly stated, the removal of control from Robinson, to whom Yeats was loyal, but who he realized had lost control of the company.[50] The proposed strategy would have been clumsy and probably contestable. In any case Richard Hayes's more bureaucratic solution prevailed: that the board be enlarged. At an extraordinary general meeting on 22 March 1935 it was agreed that in addition to the four allowed in the articles of the Society, further directors could be appointed to a maximum of four. The new directors were confirmed on 9 August, but they were at work before that date. Yeats brought onto the board the young, ambitious, and 'pugnacious'[51] (to use Frank O'Connor's adjective) F. R. Higgins, a neo-romantic poet from Co. Mayo, whose work was marked by updated Celticism and a remote energy, along with the acerbic but, in his own way, devoutly Catholic Brinsley MacNamara. The third new addition was the man who, more than any other, was to manipulate and direct artistic policy over the next three decades, the ex-revolutionary and Protestant nationalist from Lisburn, Co. Antrim, Ernest Blythe, or Earnán de Blaghd, as he preferred. Blythe was an old friend of the Abbey, and had assisted in securing the subsidy; and, as an ex-Minister for Finance, it was thought that he would bring financial stability to a company £2,500 in debt at the time. He looked, O'Connor wrote, 'like a Buddha in grey plaster, and spent most of his time doodling on his pad', yet he was the one who would outlast them all.[52]

The new board now sought to make amends to O'Casey (even though MacNamara would later reveal a fierce antagonism to him) and they agreed to stage *The Silver Tassie* (12 August 1935). The play was directed by Arthur Shields. It caused a public outcry. Dublin working-class women are depicted as anxious to get their men back to the Front, being only too aware that overstaying leave can have serious consequences, and not just for the soldier. Mrs Heegan, Harry's mother, is very keen to make sure that he is on the boat at the next tide:

Mrs Heegan. He's overstayed his leave a lot, an' if he misses now the tide that's waitin', he skulks behind desertion from the colours.
Susie. On active service that means death.
Mrs Heegan. An' any governmental money grant would stop at once.
Susie. That would gratify Miss Jessie Taite, because you put her weddin' off with Harry till after the duration of the war, an' cut her out of the allowance.[53]

Violence, wife-beating, and bullying follow as Teddy Foran terrifies his wife upstairs because she has been singing to herself in great good humour now that he must return to the Front, and she can continue to have a care- (and husband-) free time. Act I ends with Mrs Heegan, Harry's mother, saying: 'Thanks be to Christ that we're after managin' to get the three of them away safely.'[54] Harry has won the 'silver tassie' for his football club, and has had a few drinks, but he leaves in time for his boat, through his mother's insistence, spurred on by his father.

Although Act I was bad enough, with the greed and selfishness of the Dublin women unsparingly depicted, and with Harry, in his exaltation, lifting Jessie's skirt to show off her legs, Act II appalled the Dublin audiences. The scene moves to the trenches; Barney Bagnal, a friend of Harry's, is tied to the gunwheel in punishment for stealing a cock; and in the background, looming symbolically, is a ruined monastery. From the broken nave there comes the sound of the chanted mass, which mixes with the profanity and human bleakness of jaded and dispirited soldiers. Their lot is harshly but effectively contrasted with that of the 'staff-wallahs':

> His last view of the front-line sinking
> Into the white-flesh'd breasts of a judy.[55]

These lines are sung by the unnamed men (they are called by their numbers only) in plainchant, an anti-chorale to the Latin of the sung mass. The scene concludes with the men psalming to the big howitzer to which Barney (the only named man) is strapped; and their god is swung round and a shell loaded into the breech. Vivid flashes indicate the detonations; 'no noise is heard', as the stage-direction says.

In Act III the men are convalescing, having been maimed or crippled or shell-shocked in Flanders. Harry Heegan has lost the use of his legs and is to have an operation on his spine, but the surgeon is keener on flirting with the nurse than in discharging his duties. The men's spouses and sweethearts arrive, but Jessie, Harry's girl, will not come up to the ward to see him, staying below with Barney

Bagnal, Harry's friend, and the man who rescued his maimed comrades, sustaining remarkably little injury himself.

The last act unleashes the full ferocity of a confrontation between Harry, who has lost everything—his health, energy, idealism, and his woman—and those who take from him, Jessie and the hero Barney Bagnal, who has been given the Victoria Cross. In a daring and, for its time, shocking piece of stagecraft, the crippled Harry watches as Bagnal half-undresses Jessie; Harry cannot keep silence and explodes in rage: 'So you'd make merry over my helplessness in front of my face. . . Hurt her breast pulling your hand quick out of her bodice, did you?' When he rages against her for doing with Barney what he did with her she denies it:

Jessie. He's a liar, he's a liar, Barney! he often tried it on with coaxing first and temper afterwards, but it always ended in a halt that left him where it started.
Harry. If I had my hands on your white neck I'd leave marks there that crowds of kisses from your Barney wouldn't moisten away.
Barney. You half-baked Lazarus, I've put up with you all evening, so don't force me now to rough-handle the bit of life that Jessie left you as a souvenir.

And indeed when Harry insults him again Barney does attack him.

The act draws to a conclusion which, as the hale partners team up to dance the night away, underlines the cruelty of life which determines that those who survive often care nothing for those who suffer. It is a brilliantly effective piece of theatre, driven by humanitarian rage, and a sense of bafflement as to why people treat each other so viciously. It is exactly the kind of humane sorrow that was bound to create an aversion in Yeats, even though he finally overcame his distaste for the play ten years after its first submission to the Abbey. Not that Yeats was inhuman; it was just that his perception was that suffering was inevitable and had to be endured, whereas O'Casey's emotional nature longed for social improvement. Yeats believed this was impossible, and that the theatre should turn from the accidents of fortune to the mysteriousness of man's fate.

The silver tassie of the title is symbolic of all that men and women value in themselves and others: Harry wins it in Act I and in Act IV dashes it to the ground as a thing rendered meaningless by those who want only to stay ahead in life's game. It is a tragic vision presented in harsh theatrical juxtapositions that were meant to startle and shock the audience into new realizations of the hidden cruelty of society's institutions: these include the forms of church and state and the codes they imply—honour, bravery, morality, fidelity. This is a play with deeply anarchic impulses, which were immediately recognized by Dublin audiences; the Catholic church was especially appalled, not least because of O'Casey's deliberate travesty of the mass. The Irish Catholic (7 September) said O'Casey's plays should be banned outright; and P. T. McGinley, president of the Gaelic League and erstwhile author of Eilís agus an Bhean Déirce demanded in the Irish Independent that the Abbey itself should be closed down.

One of the most vocal of all the play's critics was the recently appointed director on the expanded board, and author of one of the most powerful plays since

O'Casey, *Margaret Gillan* (1933): Brinsley MacNamara. He attacked what he regarded as the blasphemy of the play in a two-column cannonade in the *Irish Independent* (29 August), describing O'Casey's work as 'vulgar and worthless'. MacNamara was asked to resign and refused, arguing that he was acting for the good of the theatre; the board set up an interim committee to conduct operations until MacNamara could be got rid of, an objective Yeats achieved. MacNamara's vacancy was filled by Frank O'Connor, the short-story writer from Cork, who was appointed to the board on 9 October 1935.

O'Connor's arrival coincided with that of Hugh Hunt, a young English producer appointed on the advice of John Masefield, the poet laureate; Hunt was yet another protégé of Nugent Monck's at the Maddermarket Theatre in Norwich. It was hoped that he, as an outsider, would impose more discipline in rehearsal and restrain a company which by now had developed many bad habits, among them a tendency to ham parts up and play for laughs to an audience often only too ready to indulge the players' vanity. O'Connor described the theatre as being like a garden where all the weeds had grown so tall it was impossible to see anything. The actors frequently rehearsed themselves, and often they chose the plays from the repertoire to be staged. As well as introducing some much-needed discipline, Hunt's job remit included a recommendation that he produce foreign plays, which the Gate Theatre had shown there was some demand for. Hunt's request that the board engage the brilliant designer Tanya Moiseiwitsch was agreed. On Hunt's own admission he was 'totally ignorant of . . . the traditions of the Abbey. I was twenty-four and spoke with an Oxford accent. A more unlikely candidate for the task of directing a distinguished company of Irish players it would be hard to find.'[56] Nevertheless he and O'Connor hit it off immediately. O'Connor provided dynamism and ideas, while Hunt's stagecraft and dramatic intelligence responded with alacrity to the daunting challenges he faced. There was a creative as well as a pragmatic alliance.

Hunt's first productions were Shaw's *A Village Wooing* and *Candida* (both 20 September), which were followed by plays which attempted to compete with the Gate's stagings of non-Irish drama: André Obey's *Noah* (11 November), Shakespeare's *Coriolanus* (13 January 1936), and James Elroy Flecker's *Hassan* (1 June). Yeats wanted to stage a blue-shirted *Coriolanus*, reflecting his brief flirtation with General Eoin O'Duffy's Blueshirts, a high Catholic movement supportive of the doctrine of corporatism, and opposed to the version of republicanism advocated by de Valera's Fianna Fáil. It is strange to think that Yeats's ideas about how *Coriolanus* should be staged (which were successfully resisted) carried some very oblique connection with the complicated origins of the modern political party known as Fine Gael. However, these foreign plays did not win back to any appreciable extent audiences that had been attracted to the Gate. O'Connor set about getting rid of what he believed to be the utterly misguided scheme for competing with Edwards and Mac Liammóir.[57] He was convinced that the Abbey should stick to its chief original aim of fostering Irish dramatic talent, pointing out that if the theatre failed in this respect young or new Irish dramatists would have no chance of getting their work performed.

In December 1935 Hunt was appointed manager as well as producer, and with O'Connor's support began to change the style of acting and delivery, introducing a new deliberateness which mixed realism and poetic effect: O'Connor described it as 'delicate, precise and poetic in its own realistic way', with Cyril Cusack being a representative of this innovatory method.[58] This thoughtful approach to acting and voice-work shows that Hunt had quickly begun to create an atmosphere of discipline and work within a company that had grown careless and lazy.

From now on Robinson was sidelined more and more. He was drinking heavily and a morbid streak that Lady Gregory had discerned in his make-up very early on took hold. He was monosyllabic at board meetings. O'Connor's account of a difficult meeting with him, in which it became clear to O'Connor that Robinson was a broken but complex man, is devastating.

Houses improved and the debt was being reduced. St John Ervine returned to the Abbey with a new play that turned out to be the very popular *Boyd's Shop* (24 February), directed by Hunt with Cusack playing alongside the great senior co-medians from the company, F. J. McCormick and Barry Fitzgerald. Strangely enough an entirely different production opened first in Liverpool at the Play-House on 19 February, with the young Michael Redgrave in the cast. By now Ervine had established himself as a well-known (and somewhat feared) drama critic, writing for the *Observer* and contributing to the *New York World*; he wrote for the West End, and became 'professor of dramatic literature' at the Royal Society of Literature (1933–6). Though based in Devon, in a house called Honey Ditches (a 'mellifluous name' as John Cronin tartly remarks[59]), in the 1930s he re-turned to Ulster themes, beginning with *Boyd's Shop*.

This play has acquired a kind of classic status in Northern Irish amateur the-atre. Its appeal is understandable: it evokes a good, solid Ulster background, where hefty teas of corned ox-tongue and hot barmbrack dripping with butter are consumed on Sunday afternoons with the Presbyterian minister and his young as-sistant visiting the decent parlour behind Boyd's grocer's shop. Andrew Boyd's people have run the business in Donaghreagh for a hundred years. Opposite him, a new shop is opened by the pushy but decent John Haslett. Another ambitious young man, Dunwoody (played by F. J. McCormick), is helping the old minister, Patterson, with his duties, while putting it about that the old man is about to re-tire. Dunwoody is courting Agnes, Boyd's daughter, whom Haslett also loves. Dunwoody's star rises while Haslett's declines, even though old Boyd has his doubts: '[Dunwoody] has a queer habit of thinkin' that things are goin' to happen because he's here. . . There's times when I think he'll bounce into heaven an' ex-pect the whole place to turn upside down because he's arrived.'[60] Old Andrew confides this to John Haslett, with whom he has a natural rapport, and as the ac-tion develops old Boyd comes to John's rescue when things go against him. At the end, Haslett's shop goes up in flames, and Dunwoody reveals his bumptiousness, bad-mindedness, and guile when he lets it slip how fortunate it is that a bankrupt shop has caught fire. This idea spreads (a technique of insidious rumour that Dunwoody has also used to get rid of Patterson), but it eventually comes to light that the suggestion began with him. Agnes now rejects Dunwoody and Ervine pulls out all the emotional stops connected to family and communal feeling in the last moments of the play. Agnes writes 'Boyd & Son' on the price blackboard, and the play concludes with the close knitting together of family and romantic affections. It is an oddly powerful piece, partly because it draws on feelings of communality in Ulster and Irish life that evoke a traditional past; but also because it projects, in defiance of worsening economic circumstances in Ireland, north and south, an idealized vision of simplicity, goodness, and honest dealing, which survives in spite of chicanery and cant. It is interesting to reflect that the device of rumour spreading in a community, and altering that community's perception of itself, was originally used in Lady Gregory's *Spreading the News*.

Barry Fitzgerald played the small cameo part of William Henry Doak, a big farmer keen on drink, and in Teresa Deevy's *Katie Roche* (16 March 1936) he played his last role at the Abbey, the kindly family friend Frank Lawlor. In the summer of 1936 John Ford contracted some Abbey players for the film of *The Plough and the Stars*, among them Fitzgerald. From this time onwards he lived in the USA and starred in many Hollywood movies, among them *Going my Way* (1944) with Bing Crosby.

Teresa Deevy came from Waterford, of a middle-class, nationalist family, the youngest of thirteen children. While a student at UCD she contracted Meniere's Disease which left her totally deaf. Abandoning her studies she turned to writing and had her first play, *The Reapers*, produced at the Abbey by Lennox Robinson (30 March 1930). The prize-winning *Temporal Powers* (12 September 1935) dealt with a theme that preoccupied her, the balancing of temperaments and needs that takes place in families and how these are reflections of broader pressures in society at large. Teresa Deevy is the only serious woman dramatist of the Abbey, apart from Lady Gregory, until comparatively recent times. There are many and complex reasons for this vacuum that have to do with the nature of Irish society from the Land War to the 1960s and 1970s and the attitudes to women that the Catholic church and the Irish state both reflected and fostered. But this is not the context to ruminate on such matters: it is more appropriate, here, to recognize Teresa Deevy's special achievements in the 1930s.

The King of Spain's Daughter (29 April 1935) is an utterly surprising one-acter, which had Cyril Cusack in the part of Jim Harris, a road-labourer who longs to marry the wilful Annie Kinsella, who was played by Ria Mooney. This is a play which astonishes in its swift and brutal energy; the young woman, Annie, is a kind of rural Miss Julie, whose insatiable appetite for life leaves her dissatisfied with the few roles open to her: wife, or factory-worker in the nearby town. She flirts with any man she fancies and although her father Peter beats her, he cannot subjugate her spirit. Mrs Marks, who arrives at the somewhat Beckettian scene in which the play is set—a roadway of broken stones where the labourers are quarrying—warns young Jim to have nothing to do with Annie, and advises him to settle down with his sisters, or get a sensible girl. Love, romance, sex—these are illusions, better done without: a sentiment unerringly capturing the ethos of rural Ireland in the 1930s when it was often decided to avoid economic uncertainty by not marrying. Marriage tempted fate and children offered hostages to fortune. Annie herself later on says that she 'dreads' the prospect of children, and the possibility that having them might have the effect of compelling resignation to a loveless marriage. On the other side Jim is told by the Pozzo-like Mrs Marks that he should toughen himself and become impervious to compassion: 'The hard man wins.'[61] The ending of the play remains open: the audience thinks that Annie will probably marry Jim after all; and she is drawn to him, not out of love or affection, but because his determination impresses her and she thinks, excitedly, that he might be 'a man might cut your throat'.[62] This is a far cry from Synge's ironic questioning of a society that admires the idea of violence; here there is a sense that a repressive society built on anger and intolerance loves the violence that it may need to use from time to time against transgressors. Annie likes the idea of a violent man and, unlike Pegeen, does seem really to want one to take the place of her brutal father. It is a bleak, powerful, and compelling play that opens up a complex tangle of emotion and social psychosis which remained, to a large extent, unexplored in theatre until the work of Samuel Beckett, in French, in the 1950s.

Teresa Deevy's next play, *Katie Roche* (16 March 1936), was directed by Hugh Hunt and designed by Tanya Moiseiwitsch. It takes up the conventions of rural drama, as developed in various ways by Murray, Ervine, and Shiels, but, as would be guessed from the originality of the depiction of country life in *The King of Spain's Daughter*, she handles these tried and tested forms and types in new and quite troubling ways, as Judy Friel discovered when she directed a revival at the Abbey in 1994.

Deevy was deeply influenced by Ibsen, and Katie Roche is an Ibsenite heroine: indeed her next play, *The Wild Goose* (9 November 1936), gestures towards him. But in some respects her true antecedent is Strindberg, with his wild, unpredictable surges of wilfulness and passion. Katie Roche is, as someone describes her in the play, 'vagarious', 'she varies off and on'. In Act I it is revealed that she is illegitimate, that her mother was a great beauty, and that her father, who was married when she was conceived, disappeared. She is toying with joining a convent, but enjoys being courted by Michael Maguire (played by Arthur Shields). She also receives a precipitate proposal of marriage from Stanislaus Gregg, the brother of Amelia, for whom she keeps house. They get married, but in Act II she throws herself at Michael, regretting now her impulsive acceptance of Stanislaus's offer. At the centre of the play, an old wandering holy man, Reuben, reveals that he is her father, but this occurs after he has struck her with a stick for leading young Maguire on. This discovery comes after a brittle and nerve-racking set of exchanges between Katie, Stanislaus, Michael, and Amelia, where the ordinary politenesses of Irish small-town living are clung to (making scones, visiting neighbours, offering a drink) while in reality an entire family is cracking up. The sudden outbursts, the physical violence, the sexual tension, and the deep anxious silences are like nothing else in Irish theatre up to this point. Reuben finds Katie in Michael's lap, where she has flung herself in a mood of sexual euphoria and indifferent bravado:

Reuben. You'd better go now.
Michael. I've done no wrong, Reuben.
Reuben. Go on now, and don't come to this house again.
Michael. She called me to come in. I was passing the door. I didn't ask her arms round me. . .
Katie. Isn't he the grand fellow! Now if you were Mr. Gregg—

Mr Gregg is Stanislaus, her husband, to whom she is being unfaithful:

Michael (furious). And if I were I'd teach you something! (*Reuben holds up a warning hand.*)[63]

Michael is about to strike her, but he is stopped by Reuben's presence. Katie taunts Michael, saying, 'There's the real rough,' comparing the man she has just been teasing unfavourably with her husband. Later in the scene, after Michael leaves, when she taunts Reuben, mocking his advice as he (her father, it will be revealed) counsels her to value the man she has, he hits her, full force, across her shoulders with his stick. The abrupt surprises continue: Michael, on his mother's instructions, tells Stanislaus that his wife made love to him, at which Stanislaus leaves the house, angry, saddened, vindictive, and, in a curious way, pleased with himself for his nobility and capacity for solitary anger. In the final act set a year later, Stanislaus comes back (having returned a few times already) to discover his wife still carrying on with Michael, in an aimless, arbitrary, experimental kind of way. Amelia, Stanislaus's sister, receives a proposal of marriage from Frank Lawlor (which she will probably accept, but it is left open) while Stanislaus orders Katie to leave with him, so he can keep an eye on her. This act, like the others, is riddled with deep silences, in which emotions kindle and die only to flame up again, and yet again go nowhere. This edgy theatre is utterly new and original and stands halfway between the emotional shocks of Strindberg and the icy abstract detachment from feeling encountered in Pinter and in some of Beckett. Indeed, there is a sense of menace in Deevy's writing, often breaking into actual physical violence. Katie's submission to her husband's will at the end has embarrassed feminist writers, but the play's sense of the trouble of human personality is such that the feeling is conveyed that it may be better to accept rules, however arid, than venture too far into the realms of violence and emotion.

The weakness of the play is one of structure: the sudden abrupt actions and impulses do not flow from a sense of inevitable onward impetus. This flaw, an understandable one, given the focus of the play upon the dereliction caused by the unpredictability of human motive, Deevy sought to remedy in her next play, *The Wild Goose* (9 November 1936), of which Lennox Robinson, who acted as her mentor, remarked: 'The hazelnut in October, a masterpiece of construction.'[64] Martin Shea, the wild goose, is the focus of the play, which is set in the aftermath of the Battle of the Boyne and the Treaty of Limerick. He rebels against the constraints of the Catholic church, only to defend Fr. Ryan against the English soldiery. He then decides for the priesthood himself to follow the patriotic example of the priest, but returns, unpriested, and marries Eileen Connolly. In a matter of weeks he is away again to fight for France as one of the 'wild geese'. These sudden reversals point not only to the central Deevy preoccupation—the instability of human motive—but also to a political context for emotional un-certainties. Public duty and the codes by which people find they must live can ex-haust the personality and suck it dry: it is not for nothing that Stanislaus's sister in *Katie Roche* is married to a man called Drybone. *The Wild Goose* was directed by Hunt, and had Fred Johnson as Martin Shea and Ria Mooney as Eileen Connolly.

Evidently 1936 was a year of remarkable productivity for Teresa Deevy, and in-deed she was for a few months recognized as a major force in Irish theatre. However, that force did not continue to find an outlet; and it was not until 1948 that the Abbey, at the Peacock, staged another play of hers, *Light Falling* (25 October). Some diminishment of energy did take place: her discontent is here as immediately present as a wound that aches, but hers seems to have been a talent not satisfied with the neurotic probing of social and personal malaise: it sought sharper and more dangerous expression, something not possible for a woman (or perhaps for anyone) in the Ireland of her time. When she submitted her next major play, *Wife to James Whelan*, to the Abbey in 1942 it was rejected by Ernest Blythe, who claimed that the characters were uninspiring. The Gate rejected it also. These reactions may have owed something to the fact that Deevy was an out-spoken critic of the Irish Censorship Board, had written to the newspapers on the subject, and featured in the notorious Senate debate on *The Tailor and Ansty*, Eric Cross's book on the broad storytelling of Timothy Buckley, a tailor from Gougane Barra, Co. Cork, and his equally outspoken wife Ansty.

Between the two productions of the Deevy three-acters in 1936 Hunt had put on a summer season and gave *The Playboy of the Western World* (27 July) and Yeats's *Deirdre* (10 August). Both productions, although commercial successes, sparked off internal quarrels and boardroom politicking. Cyril Cusack played Christy Mahon in his own inimitable twinkling style, which, Hunt being away at the time, brought the wrath of Higgins down upon him. The director stormed into Cusack's dressing room and made a scene. Yeats, likewise, was furious at Hunt's realistic treatment of *Deirdre*, with Mícheál Mac Liammóir playing Naisi, and was first out of the theatre on 10 August 'bellowing with fury'. A board meeting was called at which Hunt was debarred from producing any of the clas-sic repertoire, and Higgins given the job of placating the shade of Synge in a production which, by all accounts, was hilarious in its hyper-rustification, Higgins going for what Frank O'Connor called 'porthery'.[65]

With *Blind Man's Buff* (26 December 1936) Denis Johnston returned to the Abbey. This play, an adaptation of Ernst Toller's expressionist *Die blinde Göttin*, was a court-room drama, directed by Hunt, and was to be rewritten as *Strange Occurrence on Ireland's Eye* (1956). Meanwhile Paul Vincent Carroll submitted from Glasgow a new play to the Abbey, *Shadow and Substance* (25 January 1937). Set in Co. Louth, at the foot of the southern slopes of the mountains of Mourne, the play takes place around the feast of St Brigid, celebrated on the first of February.

The Canon, Thomas Skerritt, is a sophisticated, well-educated man, who leads a leisured and cultured life. His curates, by contrast, are hot-faced enthusiasts of the new school of Irish Catholicism, involved in social, pietistic, and devotional activities, from football-playing to sodalities and confraternities. His house-keeper-servant Brigid is a simple girl with a history of mental illness, whose faith and mental instability combine in visions she believes she has of St Brigid. The Canon has a private and very intense devotional life which only Brigid under-stands, while he, for his part, has a deep regard for her goodness and emotional honesty. These two intense souls are surrounded by job-seekers and puritans, who constantly connive to recruit the Canon's authority for their own interests. Meanwhile, a headstrong and independent schoolmaster, Dermot O'Flingsley (played by Cyril Cusack), as well as writing a thinly veiled and pseudonymous at-tack on the Canon, confronts his boss over Skerritt's discharge of his duties as manager of the local education system. O'Flingsley is eventually destroyed, but between them, the Canon and he cause the death of Brigid. Ever more deranged as the action proceeds, because the Canon resists her desire to become a nun and give her life totally to the spirit, she goes to rescue O'Flingsley at the end of the play from a mob throwing stones at his house. She is struck, sustaining the disfigurement St Brigid inflicted upon herself so she would be less attractive to men, and then she dies.

Clearly there is a serious and intense substratum to this play, which engages with censorship, clericalism, clientism, jobbery, and the embarrassments of Irish society in the 1930s as it sought to develop a cohesive sense of identity, in which process the Catholic church played a crucial role. Catholicism, in its Irish version, provided models for behaviour; it created jobs, and gave leadership; but mostly it provided a moral and emotional structure upon which modern Ireland leaned after the turmoil of the founding revolution, and the aftermath of Civil War. Such a structure, needless to say, often failed those people who cultivated an intense life (such as the Canon) or who were condemned to personalities they could not fathom (as with Brigid) and this meant that desperate tragedy and breakdown was a daily possibility. The poems in Austin Clarke's *Night and Morning* (1938), a volume of poems deeply racked by these impacted tensions, show a tempera-ment subsiding under just such pressures:

This is the hour that we must mourn
With tallows on the black triangle,
Night has a napkin deep in fold
To keep the cup; yet who dare pray
If all in reason should be lost,
The agony of man betrayed
At every station of the cross?[66]

Carroll's play, however, acquires its strange brio from the nightmare comedy that flashes across these depths, with the Canon relishing every chance he gets of putting his horny-handed curates in their places. In Act I, after Fr. Corr has been trying to defend his attempts at cultivating popularity, the Canon rebukes both him and the other curate:

Canon. . . . these popular heroics of yours are not, canonically speaking, the duties of a
    Catholic curate.
Father Corr (blushing and abashed). I—I was only trying to be kind Canon.
Canon. I call it hunting after popular glory—an Irish clerical disease,
Father Corr (rising with fire). I'm a farmer's son, Canon, and I'm not ashamed of it.
Canon. I am not interested in your antecedents. I am interested instead in the behaviour of
    my curate. You may be seated.
(Father Corr sits down, crushed. Father Kirwan shifts uneasily in his seat, with
one eye on the Canon, who presently regards him with calm brutality.)
Canon (with slight cough). Father Kirwan, may I ask if it is the custom in your part of the
    country for the curate to don football regalia and—er—kick ball?
Father Kirwan. Sure, it's quite common down in Ballyedminstown Canon. The curate in
    my father's place is a very noted centre-half.
Canon (cruelly, leading him on, hand to ear). I didn't quite catch that word, Father Kirwan.
    Centre—what?[67]

Carroll has, throughout the play, perfect pitch for dialogue and, continuously, the scenes depicted have a sure and steady focus, rendering the psychological and social tragedy that is unfolding behind the comic surface all the more devastating. In 1937 Arthur Shields played the Canon, and the young Phyllis Ryan the ethereal yet forceful Brigid.

Lennox Robinson returned to the theme of his 1926 play *The Big House* in 1937 with *Killycreggs in Twilight* (19 April). The 'twilight' is that of the Anglo-Irish ascendancy, sadly lingering in their ancestral homes. Judith de Lury, the more realistic of the two de Lury sisters, is going to marry Francis Morgan and convert to Catholicism, much to the horror of the snobbish Kit:

Kit (utter horror in her voice). You're 'turning'?
Judith. Darling, I think I'll go on saying my two or three old Protestant prayers night and
    morning and read the Bible father gave me on the day I was confirmed.[68]

Later, Judith says, in explanation: 'I wish we'd been burned out in the Troubles; I wish all our sort had been burned out. I wouldn't have behaved like that fool-girl in the play, *The Big House*,' a reference to Kate Alcock who hoped to retain a role for their class in a modern Ireland. Here, Robinson seems to be acknowledging that the old days are gone and the play concludes in a melancholy longing mixed with an attempt at gaiety. The last act of the play was written with Robinson's customary rapidity in one day while he was a guest of the American novelist Edith Wharton at her French chateau at Hyères, and this hospitality was recalled in the dedication.

The play was directed by Hugh Hunt, and from the beginning of this year, 1937, until his departure in October 1938 he produced sixteen new plays in all. This energy and commitment reflected the influence of Frank O'Connor, who was proving to be a dynamic force on the Abbey board; and it suited Hunt to immerse himself in creative work while the politicking of Higgins, Hayes, Blythe, and O'Connor himself went on behind the scenes. O'Connor and Hunt formed a writing partnership, the latter adapting O'Connor's short story *In the Train* for the stage (31 May 1937), before they went on to co-author *The Invincibles* (18 October 1937) and *Moses' Rock* (28 February 1938). Hunt's and O'Connor's domination of the Abbey's activities in 1937 and into 1938 owed not a little to the fact that Higgins, whom O'Connor distrusted, was away in the USA on tour with the first Abbey company from September to May. At a farewell luncheon for the company O'Connor praised Carroll's *Shadow and Substance* as introducing a new drift in Irish theatre towards tragedy and realistic satire.

The Invincibles dealt with the Phoenix Park murders of 1882, in which the newly appointed Chief Secretary for Ireland, Lord Frederick Cavendish, and his assistant T. H. Burke were knifed by an extreme nationalist secret society known as 'The Invincibles'. Joe Brady, one of the assassins, says: 'What did Parnell and the rest want if 'twasn't murder? Why did they talk to us of our wrongs?'[69] On the opening night Robinson took part in a debate at the Gate Theatre about the play and denounced it as being disloyal and hurtful to the memories of the men who were hanged by the British. Richard Hayes called for Robinson's dismissal from the board. His behaviour, in part no doubt due to drink, had become inexplicable and erratic; he had advised O'Connor on matters of style and construction, and he had given his approval for performance as a board member. A special meeting was called at which Yeats, defending his old friend, said: 'Every member of this Board realizes that Lennox Robinson is no longer responsible for his actions,' an apology which Robinson allowed to be offered on his behalf in crestfallen, despondent silence.[70]

With O'Connor's encouragement his fellow Corkman Sean O'Faolain wrote his only play *She Had to Do Something* (27 December 1937), which had in the leading female role the young Welsh actress Evelyn Bowen, wife of the English actor Robert Speaight. She and O'Connor fell in love, and went to live together in Co. Wicklow, before getting married in 1939 when she was divorced.

O'Faolain's play is set in a small provincial city, on the seaboard. It is a farce of middle-class life, where people with artistic aspirations are compelled to lead a trammelled existence, subject to the puritanical dictates of an ignorant and obsessive clergy. The humour is broad and, at times, a little seedy in its knowing use of double entendres unintentionally made by pompous clerics. Here is Canon Kane expatiating on how all occasions, even beautiful ones, can become occasions of sin as he looks out the window over the river Lee (for this is Cork, where else?) and listens to the sound of someone playing the piccolo (yes, the piccolo) to his girl on the river:

Those boys and girls, rowing down among the crannies and rocks of the Harbour Mouth, if they are not well protected by their religion, what will happen there before the night is out? Yes, they play on their piccolo, now, but what tune will they play in nine months' time? (*Bangs the window*).[71]

There is a plot involving a Russian ballet dancer, and the indefatigable curiosity and energy of the arty Maxine Arnold, who is French, loves art, and loves life in a kind of Lawrentian enthusiastic haze of cigarette smoke and emotion. She successfully resists the threats of an ex-IRA man, who has redeployed his commitment to the Catholic sodalities of his parish, but still wears his trench coat. It is an amusing farrago, full of O'Faolain's impatient contempt for the provincial Irish Catholicism from which he came.

Moses' Rock returns once more to the figure of Parnell and the fact that the issue of Ireland's self-determination had not been fully resolved with the establishment of the Irish Free State in 1922. Parnell's legacy was one of failure: Home Rule was not accomplished in the 1890s; his party had split because of a scandal involving adultery and a divorce case; and a great leader had been destroyed.

Hunt provided O'Connor with advice on dialogue and scene arrangement in the writing, but plot and character were O'Connor's own, and for these he drew extensively on his familiarity with Cork life, where the play is set. Ned Hegarty, a poet and a Parnell activist, has just been released from prison, and he and his friend the lawyer Jer Coughlan, who defended him at his trial, where he flamboyantly threw his papers in the judge's face, turn out to be rivals for the hand of the heroine Joan O'Leary. When the Irish Parliamentary Party splits Hegarty remains loyal to Parnell, while Coughlan opportunistically shifts his ground. Joan, sick of the pair of them and of the 'mangy' watchful city, throws both of them over and runs off with Fortescue, a British army officer, even though, like Parnell, he has been involved in a divorce case. She is weary of Irish politics, and of the ways in which men exploit their ideologies in order to indulge their own emotional meanness and spite. When Coughlan, defending himself, says: 'I didn't ask for the split.' She replies:

Of course you asked for it. You and Ned and all the others. All the pretence is broken down at last, and you can indulge all the weakness of your mean little souls, spitting in your neighbour's face, stealing his trade, plotting and intriguing against him, and all in the name of Ireland and religion.[72]

The rock the nation hopes to found itself upon is a Moses' rock, and it splits, much (O'Connor is implying) to the satisfaction of the many who have their own private agendas, or their own anxiety to seize or retain power.

When Higgins returned he discovered that Robinson, during his absence, had been assuming a directorial role in the theatre, instead of confining his activities to the school of acting, which was what had been agreed after the *Invincibles* debacle. On 23 June 1938 Yeats wrote to Blythe urging that when Hunt departed in November Higgins be made salaried manager, on the grounds that someone was needed, day to day, to be in charge of the detailed business of what was now a large organization. This Blythe agreed to.[73]

Theatre has a curious habit of reflecting, in its own inner society, stresses and strains operating at large. The microcosm, at times painfully, re-enacts the tensions and torsions of the macrocosm. As *Moses' Rock* was being rehearsed and staged (with Cyril Cusack playing the devoted Parnellite Hegarty) the Abbey itself was going through a series of convulsions that would result in another split, reflecting an irreconcilable conflict between those, like O'Connor, who wanted a more open and free-spirited approach to social and moral concerns in the theatre, and others, such as F. R. Higgins and Ernest Blythe, who wanted to introduce a new uniformity in compliance with a deepening conservatism. These wrangles over points of principle and policy were reflected in the choice of plays and in the psychological and moral atmosphere generated in the theatre. This growing and radical desire for uniformity, corporatism, mass values, and communal feeling were everywhere in evidence, in Europe and in Ireland itself. There was an attraction towards the ethos of the group, the tribe, the state; and away from the individual and any stubborn insistence on uniqueness. Blythe gained his confidence not from any tyranny latent in his nature, necessarily, but because people at this time were attracted to strong men, with charisma, capable of silent resolve, who seemed to know what was what. Of course such qualities always attract disciples, but in the 1930s, when the full implications of the uncertainties of modern capitalism and the insolencies of doctrinaire socialism were making themselves felt, authoritative individuals were cultivated as icons to set against an overwhelming sense of powerlessness. And so it was with the Abbey. In the play Joan's (theatrically unconvincing) sudden departure is an expression, on one level, of O'Connor's disillusion with de Valera's post-Treaty Ireland, but on another level he is giving vent to his own frustration with the shenanigans in the Abbey itself, the off-stage Parnell standing in for a Yeats who, increasingly ill, was no longer able to impose his will on a fractious and quarrelsome directorate. Blythe was a Stalin to Yeats's Lenin, but Lenin had not finished yet.

The Abbey Board rejected Yeats's *The Herne's Egg* in 1938 on the grounds of obscenity, although Ernest Blythe commented that it was so obscure no one would know if it was obscene or not. Yeats was furious at this decision, and attacked O'Connor for not having insisted that the play be produced when he had, so Higgins had told Yeats, a majority of the board behind him. When Yeats told him this, O'Connor realized that Yeats's version of that evening had come from Higgins, who had omitted to say that O'Connor was in the minority, with only Blythe supporting him, while Higgins was the most vocal in his opposition to the play. Yeats, however, while he was incensed that his own board should reject him, was also relieved; he knew that had the theatre gone ahead there would have been another public outcry. In 1938, also, the company decided to inaugurate an Abbey Theatre Festival, to run from 8 to 20 August, following the Dublin Horse Show, a period when the theatre had often done well in the past, with Dublin full of visitors seeking entertainment in the evenings. As part of the Abbey Festival there were morning lectures in the Gresham Hotel, and the evening performances at the Abbey were meant to be representative of its achievements, past and present. To indicate new directions in the theatre, while at the same time venerating the only surviving founding member of the Irish Literary Theatre, it staged Yeats's second last work of drama, *Purgatory* (10 August 1938), directed by Hugh Hunt.

This play is one of Yeats's grimmest and most powerful writings, and not exactly the kind of thing to appeal to the horsy set in Dublin during Horse Show Week. An old pedlar (played by Michael J. Dolan) and his son (Liam Redmond) return to the big house where the father was conceived. He tells the boy how his mother married a drunken stablehand who ruined her life, and burned the house down. The pedlar then informs the boy that he killed his father with the knife he is now going to use on him, to stop the consequence of his father's pollution. He murders his child, only to discover that the ghosts of his father and mother begin to relive again, in the ruined house, the lust that spawned him. The bleak determinism of the play, the complex view of the helpless inevitability of human brutality, the blind act of instinct: all of these made the title, *Purgatory*, seem incongruous, blasphemous even, to an Ireland where ideas of the afterlife were pretty clearly defined. Higgins had the misfortune of lecturing on Yeats at the Gresham the morning after the production, and was asked by an American Jesuit what the play was about. Questioned thus, Higgins had to admit that he was not sure. Lennox Robinson, who was in the chair, said that only Yeats knew the answer to the question. (It should be said, in fairness, that this is an extraordinarily condensed piece of dramatic action, and that the thought moves at great speed, making it a piece that would tax any audience's powers of immediate response and comprehension.) But the Jesuit battled on, not to be put off by Robinson's invocation of Yeats's mage-like inscrutability, saying that he could not understand what the plot was meant to symbolize. Inevitably, letters mushroomed in the *Irish Times* and elsewhere in the next few days, a John Lucy commenting on 15 August as follows: '[this] grim play has a definite Catholic flavour, which to one quietly thinking about it smacks of perversion.'[74]

There is little doubt that in this play we see Yeats breaking taboos: a father kills a son; a woman throws away her self-respect for her lust; a child looks upon his parents having sex; and there is a hatred of life. The Senecan side of Yeats, and the

Sophoclean iron of *Oedipus Rex*, is to the fore in this play: there is nothing to be
done; there is no point in praying or imploring mercy; life is what it is and will do
to you what it is ordained to do irrespective of your wishes. This is the harsh and
terrible Yeats, the iron sorrow of what cannot be endured must be suffered through
anyway. It is Yeats's most contemporary play, and is already in touch with realities
in Germany and elsewhere, where certain unavoidable consequences flowed from
accidents of birth. To his dead parents the old man says, after killing his boy:

> . . . you are in the light because
> I finished all that consequence.
> I killed that lad because had he grown up
> He would have struck a woman's fancy,
> Begot, and passed pollution on.[75]

But he fails. The whole thing starts all over again. The heartbeats thunder again
and the dead parents rise to relive their orgasms.

The Abbey board rejected Paul Vincent Carroll's next play, *The White Steed*, on
the grounds that it was anticlerical, even though, as a piece of social criticism, it
is a great deal less disturbing than *Purgatory*, Hugh Hunt, disillusioned with the
bickering and infighting that was increasing at the theatre, and thoroughly fed up
with Higgins's domineering style as the newly appointed managing director as
from 1 September (a post created by Yeats in the mistaken belief that Higgins
would maintain the principles of the original founders), left the Abbey in
November 1938. He went to New York to direct Carroll's *The White Steed* on
Broadway, with Barry Fitzgerald, Liam Redmond (who had played the boy in
Purgatory), and the American actress Jessica Tandy.

There were other movements afoot: in January 1937 Blythe had approached the
then Minister of Finance, Seán McEntee, with a view to rebuilding the Abbey on
the old site but making it big enough to accommodate not only the Abbey and the
Peacock's activities, but also those of An Comhar Drámaíochta. On 18 May 1938
a memorandum from the Department of Finance to the board welcomed the proposed association of An Comhar with the Abbey: 'It seems desirable that the
Comhar Drámaíochta should be brought into as close association as possible
with the Abbey Theatre so that their productions would benefit by the experience
and traditions of the Abbey.'[76] Blythe was manœuvring not only to bring the
Irish-language players under the control of a national theatre; he wanted to house
the Gate as well, thinking that it could discharge the Peacock's role within the
new, manifold, Abbey.[77] On 25 November 1938 a meeting took place in the theatre
in which this scheme was agreed, and a submission made to the government to
fund it. By then, however, the Second World War had been declared; the Minister,
Seán T. Ó Ceallaigh, stated on 14 November 1940 that nothing could be done
while the conflict continued, but that the scheme would be acted upon eighteen
months after hostilities ceased. And there matters appeared to rest; however,
Blythe was, all the time, working to get the government grant to drama in Irish

absorbed into the Abbey subsidy, a piece of intrigue which the members of An Comhar knew nothing about until 1942, when it was too late.

O'Connor's next play, *Time's Pocket* (26 December 1938), was directed by Frank Dermody, who had been trained at the Taibhdhearc, a Gaelic theatre in Galway founded in 1928, and was regarded favourably by Blythe, whose greatest ambition was to promote theatre in Irish at the Abbey. Dermody had, in fact, directed the first newly composed play in Irish for the Abbey stage, *Baintighearna an Ghorta* (12 December) a one-acter by Séamus Wilmot. Dermody's career was to be a long and distinguished one in the Abbey. O'Connor wanted Hunt to be succeeded as manager by Denis Johnston, a suggestion pooh-poohed by the board on the grounds that 'he would want to have his own way'.[78] Louis D'Alton, a playwright from Dublin whose play about the poet James Clarence Mangan, *The Man in the Cloak* (27 September 1937), had had some success, was preferred. However, D'Alton resigned in May 1939 and in his place Dermody was appointed, a manager who would be useful to Blythe in his attempt to realize a living Gaelic theatre in the capital of the Free State. Of course, Dermody's appointment was also strategic: here was a professional, trained in the Gaelic theatre in Galway, directing new work in Irish on the Abbey stage. That the post of Abbey producer-manager had gone to an Irish speaker showed An Comhar how serious Blythe was about Gaelic theatre; how could they oppose his devouring of their grant?

Meanwhile Yeats was wintering (and dying) at Cap Martin in the south of France. Towards the end he had a premonition that dreadful things were happening at the Abbey (how right he was), and he wrote to O'Connor, full of anxiety, asking him to wire him in France if he thought he should return and begin a complete reconstruction of the management and policy of the Abbey. O'Connor tells us he wrote a 'soothing reply' from Chester, where he was at the time, and on his way to post the letter bought the *Daily Telegraph* on which was the headline: 'Death of W. B. Yeats'. It was 29 January 1939, and Yeats had died the day before.[79]

Now the machinations began to get rid of O'Connor. Certainly a major factor in the antagonism towards him was his adultery. Richard Hayes led the move to ostracize him, but eventually, finding O'Connor obdurate and able to fight his corner, they changed the articles of association to give themselves the power to dismiss a fellow-director. There were a number of calculated insults and affronts: Hayes, for example, had a resolution passed that a planned reissue of Yeats's theatre journal the *Arrow* with an introduction by O'Connor be submitted to Robinson for his approval; and he was deliberately omitted from the guest-list of a farewell dinner for the designer Tanya Moiseiwitsch. A special resolution was passed on 18 August 1939 dismissing O'Connor on the grounds that he supported divorce. After further battles, in which the company tried to compel O'Connor to return the shares he held as a director, the board eventually forced his resignation on 2 May 1940.

This vacancy was filled by Roibeárd Ó Faracháin, a close ally of Blythe's. Ó Faracháin was a poet and critic, and at that time director of talks on Radio Éireann, the Irish government radio station. A Dubliner, Ó Faracháin (also known as Robert Farren) wrote in Irish as well as English, and he, along with Austin Clarke, another Dublin poet and critic, were practitioners of a type of Irish verse in English which sought to make it distinctive and national by importing (often somewhat woodenly) the devices of Irish prosody from the bardic classical tradition. Now Farren's experiments in this line seem dated and cumbersome; Clarke's have worn somewhat better. But at the time there were many who regarded their disruptions of poetic syntax by using adaptations of Gaelic metric forms as a unique blend of tradition and modernity, creating a mood of spontaneity and improvisation on old patterns. With Farren and Dermody at his side Blythe hoped to modernize cultural nationalism, and to create a theatre fully alive to the relevance of Gaelic tradition in the modern world. In Michael J. Dolan's papers in the National Library there is a spoof ballad sending up this policy of Gaelicization, obviously penned by one of the actors, perhaps Dolan himself:

> And then me darling Bob goes on to speak about the men
> Who, he blazons out quite proudly, spoke the Erse (well—now and then!)
> And then he gets up again and tells us some fairy tales,
> To convince us that the Abbey was always run by Gaels
> An Gawd help the poor auld Gaels. . .
> For they have a new Defender, bould Roibeard, the Prince of Wails.[80]

While managing director of the theatre O'Connor made funds available to Anne Yeats, Yeats's daughter, to enable her to study stage design in Paris, even though her father was anxious about how a young girl would fare in a risqué and cosmopolitan city. She designed the sets for a production of *Fohnam the Sculptor* (28 August 1939) by Daniel Corkery. Corkery, a brilliant critic of Irish and Anglo-Irish literature, was by this time professor of English at University College, Cork, having defeated the most distinguished of the other candidates, his old protégé and fellow Corkman Sean O'Faolain, in one of the most invidious contests imaginable for a university position. Corkery's reputation as a critic was based upon a superb study of the Gaelic poetry of eighteenth-century Munster, *The Hidden Ireland* (1924), and a thoughtful, challenging, and controversial study of Synge, *Synge and Anglo-Irish Literature* (1931). He had also written a grim novel of provincial life, *The Threshold of Quiet* (1917), which has a brooding Russian intensity, and many collections of short stories. *Fohnam the Sculptor* was first written as *Israel's Incense* and produced in 1912 by the Cork Dramatic Society, a group which had amongst its members and associates Terence MacSwiney and T. C. Murray.

Corkery was an unapologetic supporter of the idea of a literature that would embrace the life and feelings of ordinary Irish people, and he was a fierce and thoughtful critic of the dangers of Yeatsian aestheticism (as he saw it) and Dublin pseudo-sophistication. There is no doubt but that Blythe and Dermody welcomed a revision of a play that Corkery had been seeking to get right for more than thirty years, and from someone committed to promoting a traditional and Gaelic cultural ethos for modern Ireland. In the play Fohnam represents Corkery's own dilemma, and one that he never resolved artistically: how can a person be an artist, and therefore live a life dedicated to the cultivation of the creative imagination, and at the same time be responsible to a community? It was the same dilemma that Yeats and Russell rehearsed in their different ways, the one solving it by continuously opening the question for himself; the other failing to resolve it by imagining that the issue was less important than ultimate spiritual development. Corkery's play is troubled and 'incoherent', as Patrick Maume says.[81] The reason it is inchoate is because the storyline and the characterization embody many different impulses and convictions in Corkery's personality and beliefs, and very few of them connect with one another. Fohnam lives in the woods with an old sailor, Connud, where he makes strange and furious forms out of stone stained with the blood of the quarrymen; the King, Tethra, asks him to come back to civilization to build him a great city, which Fohnam does, partly because he is lured by one of the women of the court, Eeving. Fohnam makes a fine old mess of the city's architecture, completing nothing, and degenerating into a sadistic entertainer. He now seduces Alova, Tethra's Queen, and Eeving kills herself. They plan to leave from the sordid quays of the city, where hundreds of people emigrate or enjoy the stews where there are women with 'mouths like soldiers'. Abruptly she changes her mind, and refuses to leave her native shore and desert her husband. Not only that, she decides to humiliate herself publicly for her faithlessness: now a mob, who have been incensed by Fohnam, kill her in a riot; when he learns of this he goes mad, and is cut down by the King's bugler. Tethra throws his body into the gutter. The Abbey production by Dermody failed, and Corkery, while partly blaming the actors (Fred Johnson played Fohnam and Phyllis Ryan Eeving, the woman he destroys), admitted that the play was out of date. However, it is an absorbing study in the responsibility of government and the role of art. Corkery is deeply suspicious of art, and imagines that its freedom is all too easily converted into licence, wilfulness, and self-indulgence: there is little doubt but that Fohnam is, in part, a study of Yeats but he is also a version of part of Corkery himself: his irresolution, and his lack of focus because he lives between two worlds— the woods and the court—map out aspects of Corkery's self-doubt and an anxiety born out of a sharp consciousness that he is not English or Anglo-Irish; but neither is he Gaelic. He cannot write, he cannot *be*, in Irish. Fohman's disgrace and his ignominious non-burial are the fate of a man who is a victim, a victim of power outside him and of his own impulses, neither of which he can control. This play is a study in the shame of having been colonized.

Paul Vincent Carroll returned to the Abbey with *Kindred* (25 September 1939), a play dealing, as did Corkery's *Fohnam the Sculptor*, with the dangers of artistic freedom and yet also, like Corkery's play, acknowledging the attractions of the imagination, and relishing a defiance of necessity. This conflict, between the liberty of invention and the drastic actuality of contemporary life, was a common theme in the literature and art of the period, an opposition readily understood if one bears in mind that Europe at this time was heading towards one of the most brutal periods of carnage in all its history, the Second World War, in which Ireland remained neutral. However, while neutrality was de Valera's position with regard to the war, this stance did not cancel its economic or its moral effects.

The Abbey now, it is generally agreed, entered a decade of steady if lacklustre productions. O'Connor in *My Father's Son* argues, reasonably enough, that with Yeats—the last of the founders—gone, and with no one in place with the necessary skill and force, it was inevitable that the theatre should run out of steam. In the broader context it should also be recalled that de Valera's neutral Ireland was undergoing a phase of withdrawal, not just from the European conflict, but from Britain's influence and power, a phase in which the Free State looked inward. With partial independence gained, with a bloody civil war uneasily settled, with a new state beginning, slowly, to find its way in a world which was dangerous, complex, and strange, it was inevitable that there would be a period of internalization, a period marked by ever-increasing uniformity in matters of morals and political outlook, while, at the same time, fear and doubt deepened with the realization that life could easily become very precarious indeed. Jobs could be (and often were) as quickly lost as they were hard won; the dark quays of Corkery's play, which are haunted by prostitutes, are the Cork quays which were, throughout the 1930s, 1940s, and the 1950s, crammed with people two nights a week, as young men and young women took the boat to what Corkery calls the kingdom of Eve: Dagenham, Coventry, Cowley, Shepherd's Bush. Ireland always was a poor country, made so, the nationalists believed, by a Britain happy to drain it dry; now the native politicians were in the saddle, and had things much improved? It was a period of doubt and self-questioning, and it lasted well into the 1950s. As anxiety increased, attitudes narrowed, a process aided by the profoundly negative reaction of the Catholic church to modernism and secular society, and this did not provide an atmosphere conducive to imaginative exploration and development.

On the surface, at least. And yet the interiority of this phase provides at least some of the background and impetus for troubled and searching work in poetry and fiction, such as Kavanagh's *The Great Hunger* and his *Lough Derg* (both 1942) and Flann O'Brien's *The Third Policeman*, completed in 1940. The theatre, however, with the marked exception of such cerebral and psychologically distressing playwrights as Yeats and Beckett (himself inspired by the gloom of 1940s Ireland), demands a kind of turbulent inter-traffic between three related arenas: what is enacted on the stage, what is currently preoccupying its audience's minds, and the nature of the body politic itself. This inter-traffic is encapsulated in Hamlet's phrase that playing shows 'the very age and body of the time his form and pressure'. If the time is such that rigid forms are needed to contain almost uncontrollable pressures, then the theatre may not find images adequate to the emotional work it needs to undertake if it is to offer the release it provides when it operates as it should. Society may, at times, become so locked and confined that the theatre cannot easily do its homeopathic prophylaxis, whereby passions, by the creation of their likeness, can be brought to a 'just measure', as Milton puts it in his introduction to *Samson Agonistes*.

Nevertheless, as is evident from George Shiels's *The Rugged Path* (5 August 1940), the war in Europe haunted the imagination even of this playwright, one so apparently steeped in Irish rural conventions. The play is a profoundly disturbing one which Hugh Hunt admired, even going so far as to endorse a contemporary judgement in the *Irish Independent* that it revealed Shiels as a 'great dramatist'. The play is a violent study of political and social demoralization in Free State Ireland. A rural community 5 miles south of the border with Northern Ireland is terrified to reveal to the police who has killed an old, widowed, defenceless pensioner for £2. The old man, John Derrie, had his dog poisoned by the Dolis family, wild mountain people who terrorize the locality by the speed with which they resort to physical force when anyone stands against them. Also, locals are in dread of being known as informers in a society where to be called such was a mark of the deepest shame. There are continuous references to the Troubles of twenty years back, the War of Independence, and the Civil War—in which the fathers of the Tanseys, a respectable family, and of the mountain men, the Dolises—were comrades. There is a deep distrust of the police, represented by the Sergeant (played in 1940 by Austin Meldon), who is paying court to Michael Tansey's daughter Sara (played by Ria Mooney); this is a world given over, to a large degree, to misrule; there are no forms of social cohesion backed up by impartial law. The police themselves are spies, so that the only means of control in this society are those implemented by force, and the readiness to use violence. The wild men from the mountain rule by fear; if their demands are not met those who offend them are dealt with brutally. The play is an uncompromising study of the social and psychological mechanics of fascism. The second act, which takes place up the mountain, in the Dolises' house, is melodramatic in its crude brutality, as father and son work out their plot, with the connivance of the sinister Marcy (played by F. J. McCormick). Marcy is an old, wandering, so-called 'holy' man, who provides an alibi for the murderer, the son of the family, so he can wangle his way out of the crime he has committed. But this is one of those plays where the conventions of melodrama are consonant with the theme, here that of the danger of lawless force. This is a world where wives get beaten; there is impulsive, uncaring, physical damage: an incriminating wound on the son's hand is replicated on the spot by the father on his own as they pretend to be fixing a door which they tear off its casing as the Sergeant approaches. All that matters is that they corroborate each other's story. Eventually the Tansey men refuse to take the women's advice, that they stay out of it, and they decide to 'inform' on young Dolis, who is arrested and tried. The play ends with the Tanseys listening to the wireless for news: the first item is the war in Europe and at sea (the play has many references to the conflict), but then it is announced that the jury has returned a verdict of Not Guilty on Peter

Dolis. Mrs Tansey speaks to her daughter: 'Thank God for it! I've been praying for it late and early . . . If the case finished early this afternoon, your father and Sean should be home tonight. They've got a fine lesson in good citizenship.' The stage direction reads: '*There are a few moments of silence, then the window is shattered by a shot.*'[82] The retribution has begun.

This play proved extraordinarily popular, and had the longest run at the Abbey of any to that date, concluding on 26 October, having opened on 5 August. Patrick Kavanagh told Holloway, when they met in Fred Hanna's bookshop in Nassau Street, that he did not think it was a good play; however he did also remark that there must be some merit in it which he could not fathom.[83] Shiels wrote a sequel, *The Summit* (10 February 1941), in which the Dolises get their come-uppance.

At the end of 1940 the novelist Francis Stuart had a surprise success with *Strange Guest* (9 December) in which a nun, played by Ria Mooney, turned out from her convent, finds refuge in the house of the Chartes. There, her spiritual intensity has a profound and life-altering effect on the lives of those she comes into contact with. It is a theme, that of the effect profoundly intuitive people can have on the psychological and nervous systems of others, to which Stuart was continuously drawn in his fiction, and which informs the novels he was to write based on his experiences in wartime Germany. Stuart left Ireland in 1939 to take up a teacher's post at Berlin University.

The audience on the opening night was profoundly affected by the play's atmosphere. The play is set in an Ireland run by an extreme government, which has closed the convents of contemplative orders. The strange guest of the title, Mairead, intends to become a saint by dedicating her life to truth and simplicity. Her total honesty and sincerity act as a rebuke to the affluent but meaningless lives of the Chartes family. When Betty (Eithne Dunne), the daughter of the household, says that Mairead knows nothing of the world, the nun replies: 'I know nothing of tennis or dancing or flirting if that's what you mean. But I know what goes on in the heart and in the secret places of the mind. I know all the wickedness and vice. . . The Devil takes a lot of trouble with [nuns].'[84] Mairead (whose pre-nunnery name was, oddly, Miss Derviloba, perhaps a glancing hint at de Valera?) is aided in her task of restoring her order's fortunes by the jockey Ossie Grink (Joseph Linnane), who throws a crucial race so she can win 50 : 1 on a stake of £35, a familiar linking, in Stuart, of faith and gambling. Grink is injured in the race, and at the end is miraculously cured by Mairead, who is, now, on the road to sainthood. Her presence also reawakens the jaded marriage of Max (Austin Meldon), the head of the family, and Illyria (Eileen Crowe), his wife.

The play is an impressive exercise in a realism imbued by spirituality. It offers an unusual perspective on the religious impulse as one involving openness and the readiness to endure discomfort and incomprehension. Stuart's own position at the time, as an Irish neutral in Nazi Germany, was one which (then and now) invites at least incomprehension. But his objective had always been not entirely of this world, like his heroine. In a sense, the play offers a not entirely unsympathetic view of the otherworldliness that was part of the vision that sustained the Irish state and the Catholic church in times which were full of difficulty, hardship, and accusation.

F. R. Higgins died of a heart attack on 8 January 1941, having been at work the previous day in the theatre. He was succeeded as managing director by Ernest Blythe on 28 January, a post Blythe held until 1967, so that he saw the Abbey through its years of exile in the Queen's Theatre after it was burned down in 1951, to its re-establishment on the old site in 1966, to mark the fiftieth anniversary of the Easter Rising, in which he had been active.

Blythe, according to Tomás Mac Anna, ruled the theatre by 'force of character at once down-to-earth and commonsensical', in contrast to Yeats who ruled 'by a sort of aloof awareness'.[85] This seems to be a most accurate appraisal of the two men who, between them, dominated the policy and practice of the theatre for well over half its history in the first century of its existence. Blythe was a strange successor to Yeats: a northerner, he had a tough determined will, and he was convinced that the theatre should both be representative of the Irish people, and play its part in the continuing development of a distinctively Irish theatrical tradition. For these reasons he set about remedying a, to him, most serious omission in the Abbey's policy since its inception: the failure effectively to nurture dramatic writing in Irish and the related absence of plays in Irish from the repertoire. This concern of Blythe's is often categorized as fanatical or obsessive, but in fact he was attempting to put into place the contemporary government policy with regard to Irish, the official first language. In any case these aspirations of his also animated the original founders of the theatre, and their supporters—Yeats, Lady Gregory, Martyn, and Martyn's cousin Moore—so that in a sense he could claim, and did, that his mission was to carry through to accomplishment what they had not succeeded in doing. Blythe was working to draw into the Abbey's coffers the government money annually earmarked for An Comhar Drámaíochta, with the Comhar itself having an imperfect grasp of what was going on, until, that is, they submitted to government a proposal for expansion in autumn 1941. They were told to talk to Blythe. They did, and in a series of meetings agreed to a complicated arrangement whereby the Abbey (now known as Amharclann na Mainistreach as from 23 April 1942, another move of Blythe's to show commitment to Irish) undertook to produce, for An Comhar, five major performances in Irish each year for two years. For this the Abbey would absorb An Comhar's grant. Tomás Mac Anna wrote of this as follows: 'Ernest swallowed the poor Comhar and their grant into the jaws of the Abbey'.[86] There was a complicated agreement about committee representation and shared responsibility, but essentially Mac Anna would seem to have the situation to rights. Frank Dermody was to direct the first ten productions. There was an understanding that the Abbey production would bring the semi-professional actors from An Comhar on board; but this was allowed to lapse, as Blythe built up a Gaelic-speaking company of his own at the Abbey. And he set about this campaign of Gaelicization immediately. From 1942, unless there were special circumstances, no actor could be employed who could not speak Irish.

Blythe himself translated the medieval morality play *Everyman*, as *Cách* (22 February 1942), and from that time onwards there were two or three, and sometimes more, plays in Irish. From 1942 onwards, there were five or six productions annually in Irish. Dermody remained as director of plays in Irish until 1946. He also produced plays in English, but in 1947 he created a new post, that of Gaelic producer, to which he appointed Tomás Mac Anna, who was to serve the Abbey for many years. He was responsible for many of the pantomimes in Irish which had begun in 1945 with Mícheál Ó hAodha's *Muireann agus an Prionnsa* (26 December). These were performed both in the Abbey and at the Queen's Theatre and Blythe gave Mac Anna a free hand to develop various production styles; these were often experimental in his adaptations of European classics and in his direction of contemporary plays. Such an opportunity to experiment freely allowed Mac Anna to develop a sophisticated stagecraft which was to be put to good effect when he began directing plays in English in styles that departed from what was now the standard Abbey realistic style, derived from Murray, Ervine, and Shiels.

The decade of the 1940s, while often regarded as a period of relative inaction, nevertheless saw the emergence and maturity of a number of significant dramatists: amongst these were Louis D'Alton, Joseph Tomelty, and M. J. Molloy, as well as other writers, better known for their work in different forms, but who, during this time, with Blythe's encouragement, wrote interesting plays. Into this category fall the verse plays of Austin Clarke and work by the painter Jack B. Yeats, and by the academic B. G. MacCarthy.

Louis D'Alton was the son of Frank D'Alton, a well-known actor-manager. His first play, *The Man in the Cloak*, about the *poète maudit* James Clarence Mangan, had considerable success in 1937 with Cyril Cusack in the part of Mangan. He followed this with *Tomorrow Never Comes* (13 March 1939), which he directed and acted in himself. He was made director of plays when Hugh Hunt left in 1938, but resigned after a period of five months to be replaced by Frank Dermody. He continued to write for the Abbey and Lennox Robinson produced *The Spanish Soldier* (29 January) and Dermody his *Lovers' Meeting* (20 October 1941).

Lovers' Meeting could be used as an example of the typical Abbey play of this period. It has all the classic ingredients: matchmaking, forced marriages, the land, young versus old, illegitimacy, boozing, and incest. It is set in a place called Teremon in the midlands, and revolves around the fate of three married sisters. Hannie Martin (played by Ria Mooney) married the man she loved but he has deserted her, and she now spends her demented days at the post office waiting for a letter from him. Frances Linehan accepted the made marriage with Mossy, an alcoholic, and they spend their time together in monosyllabic and indifferent coexistence. Jane Sheridan also entered an arranged marriage, finding it convenient to do so because she was, at the time, pregnant with a child by her true love, Mick Hession. This child, Mary, is now a young woman, in love with Joe, a penniless young man. Mary's mother (played by Eileen Crowe) is bitterly opposed to this liaison, and desperately tries to persuade Mary (played by Phyllis Ryan) to marry the old but well-off farmer Batt Seery. Joe, driven to distraction by his poverty, murders an old uncle so he can inherit the land and marry the girl he loves, but their designs are thwarted when her mother tells Mary that Joe is her half-brother. Joe is arrested and sentenced to death, and Mary hangs herself on her wedding day.

This play has, in spite of its somewhat predictable plot, a brooding power deriving from its concentration on those forces, sexual, emotional, and psychological, which can usurp the stability of what were then perceived as the key institutions of Irish society: the family, the land, and a code of strict morality enjoined by a vigilant church.

In May 1942 five or six lorry-loads of papers, books, programmes, and pictures were removed from Joseph Holloway's house at 21 Northumberland Road to the National Library of Ireland. His diaries, which are an extraordinarily valuable resource for Irish theatre history, record his impressions and judgements of all the plays he went to see in Dublin from 1895 to his death in 1944. The holdings in the National Library's manuscript collection also contain correspondence, character-sketches, and vivid observations of minute and seemingly trivial events and encounters that bring the entire theatrical and cultural scene in Dublin at that time to life. There are also numerous books of cuttings and other memorabilia. The diary alone comprises 221 volumes and contains some 25 million words.

La La Noo (May 1942) is probably the best known of Jack B. Yeats's plays. It has a strange and inscrutable air in its mixture of meditations on technology, sexuality, and death. A stranger arrives at a remote public-house after viewing the local sports-day events. A group of women visitors also come by, making their way back to the bus, and get soaked in a sudden downpour. They go into the barn next door, while the stranger goes up to the forge to dry their clothes over the fire: the smith (a kind of oblique death-symbol) is not at work, but the stranger dries the clothes anyway. While this is happening the women are naked in the haybarn (the audience sees a bare arm dropping the bundle of clothing in): hence *La La Noo*, the nude. When their clothes are dry the stranger takes the smith's lorry and drives them to their bus, and is killed. The sudden irruption of the starkness of death into the dreamlike atmosphere Yeats evokes is extraordinary. The play has a slow, erotic, lethargic pace, as if there is all the time in the world to do all that may be wished; and then there is death. The mystery of being alive is solemnly, carefully, put before us. Jack Yeats once declared that he was one of those who live in the spirit, and this play sketches the mysteriousness of life, implying an essentially spiritual reality. He and his brother are not so far apart at root. The publican describes the great hosts of the ancient heroes whose presence still haunts existence:

in their battles fought among themselves—God rest their great souls, in the crevasses of the mountains back from us. They never took a sight nor a hearing of these paths. I believe I have the feeling in the palm of my hand if I put it down on a path, and it was the Great ones that are gone over passed over that path, I would feel it trembling under my hands.[87]

Against this there is the common-sense view, expressed by the same man, that 'a good road's a good road', and no more about it.

This play is a subtle piece, mixing serenity with the brute harshness of violence and death, and at the back of it all is the enigmatic sense of sexuality, eroticism, danger: seven naked women, and an absent smith. There is also, somewhere implicated in the resonance, awareness of the contemporary bestiality taking place in Germany and Poland; a hint of stripping naked under compulsion, of the way in which modern transport can facilitate death

The Whip Hand (6 July 1942) was written by Brigid G. MacCarthy, a lecturer in English at University College, Cork, where she later became professor, and the author of a number of ground-breaking studies of women's fiction in English. *The Whip Hand* was another typical Abbey play, a comedy dealing with the domineering widow Mrs Fogarty (played by Eileen Crowe), whose authoritarian ways cannot finally control her spirited son who stands up to her, and insists on marrying the girl he loves instead of the daughter of the rich farmer she has picked for him. Dan Keogh, the miserly neighbour, whose wealth Mrs Fogarty wants to secure for her own family, was played by F. J. McCormick, who told Holloway at the stage door that his tireless acting commitments had him worn out. His daughter Maureen was played by Maureen O'Sullivan. The play is of interest in that it shows the young, for once, turning upon their elders, and having the energy and determination to shape their own futures.

Walter Starkie, who was professor of Romance languages at Trinity, became director of the British Institute in Madrid in 1940, a post he held during the war years in neutral Spain to 1945. This post, as a servant of the British crown, was one which would hardly appeal to an Abbey directorate which now consisted of Blythe, Ó Faracháin, and Richard Hayes, men of strong nationalist views. Lennox Robinson, who was still in post, had by now become almost entirely ineffectual. In any case, Starkie found it increasingly difficult to attend board meetings, and the directors brought in a clause making it a dismissible offence to miss more than a certain percentage of these. Starkie was compelled to resign on 17 September 1942. Robinson spoke up for him but was talked down and withdrew his opposition to the move to get rid of Starkie. Eventually Starkie had to face the humiliation of choosing between resigning or what was, in effect, expulsion.[88] Holloway tells how he suggested to Hayes that T. C. Murray or Lord Longford (one of the founders of the Gate Theatre) be approached as possible directors, but neither suggestion met with much enthusiasm. There was in Holloway and amongst his friends such as John Burke and some Abbey actors with whom they fraternized a sense that the theatre was in the doldrums. In September 1942 Burke sent a parody of Yeats's 'September 1913' to Holloway:

Long years ago when we were young
And Ireland had an English King
We loved each week to pay our bob
And see a play by Yeats or Synge.
But now we're told by those in charge
Such authors don't deserve renewal.
The Abbey Theatre's dead and gone.
It's with Her Ladyship in Coole.[89]

Where 'Coole' is meant to be pronounced with a Dublin accent. However, Mícheál Mac Liammóir, in a lecture at the Municipal Art Gallery (5 December 1942), defended the Abbey and his own theatre, the Gate, against charges that they had become too commercial, arguing that all theatres needed long runs (such as was the case with Shiels's latter comedies) and big houses to keep going, and to ensure the financial stability necessary for experimentation to be carried out.

In 1943–4 there were a number of original plays in Irish, among them *An Bhean Chródha* (30 January) by Piaras Béaslaí, a revolutionary who had fought in the Easter Rising, later becoming a general in the Irish army. Another was *Stiana* (26 March, 1944) by Peadar Ó hAnnracháin, in which Siobhán McKenna appeared on the Abbey stage for the first time. These plays in Irish, mostly directed by Frank Dermody (1938–46), were not proving very popular, and they had poor houses, much to the disappointment of Blythe, Ó Faracháin, and Hayes. Holloway wrote in his diary about this period as follows:

It is a pity to see the childish efforts of the Gaelic three Directors of the Abbey to graft on the Gaelic theatre to the far-famed Abbey, and to behave like children in interfering with the regular work of the theatre by encroaching on their rehearsals and interfering in many ways with the Abbey Players' progress. They have also been calling the theatre by a Gaelic name on the cover of the programme and printing Gaelic poems in the ordinary Abbey programmes. All three Directors have the Gaelic bee in their bonnets and behave like children in foisting Gaelic plays on the Gaels who have no love for sitting out Gaelic plays. I hope that the season's failure to create an audience for such plays may put a little sense into the heads of the Directors.[90]

Curiously enough, the language here mirrors the satire on the Irish-language movement fiercely expressed in Flann O'Brien's mockery of the idealization of Gaels and Gaeldom in *An Béal Bocht* (1941), where 'Gaeilgeoirí' ('Ireeshans') do nothing except speak about Gaelic, lament the state of the Gael, complain that the government have deserted the cause of Gaelic, and console themselves with the thought that Gaelic is the perfect language for lamenting its own decline. Clearly, a neutral Ireland bred a renewed enthusiasm for concepts of identity based on Gaelicization, which in turn spawned its own reaction. The difficulty Blythe was contending with was that while there was a good deal of lip-service being paid to the special place of the Irish language in Irish culture, very little real commitment to it was evident in the values and attitudes of ordinary people so

that, while many would applaud the idea of the National Theatre becoming a
Gaelic one, very few actually went to see the plays.

But again, the oversimplification of the history of the theatre in the 1940s, as a
phase when inspiration was interred with 'Her Ladyship' at Coole, is not entirely
satisfactory. Louis D'Alton was a popular and considerable dramatist, as has
been indicated, but Joseph Tomelty, from Portaferry in Co. Down, was a playwright of real power, whose first play for the Abbey was *The End House* (28
August 1944), directed by Frank Dermody. Tomelty left school aged 12 and became a house-painter. His writing combines a sense of the effectiveness of natural
speech with an ability to develop mood and atmosphere that is poetic and, at his
best, technically accomplished. This play depicted, in a bleak and comfortless
manner, the claustrophobia and oppression in the Catholic ghetto of the Falls
Road in Belfast for the first time. Wallace MacAstocher (played by F. J.
McCormick), the head of the household, is a local handyman and painter with
anticlerical views and a sceptical attitude towards militant republicanism.
However, he remains susceptible to romantic notions of an idealized southern
Ireland. His son Seamus (played by Cyril Cusack) has just served a prison term for
IRA activities and is under suspicion for the recent execution of the informer
Mickey Fruin against the gable wall of their house. Monica, the daughter (played
by Siobhán McKenna), is an independent woman, heartless towards her family,
who falls for a British army deserter. He absconds with the money she keeps for
others in a savings club, and the horror of her situation is brought home to her
when Stewartie Pullar, a Protestant cornet-player from Sandy Row, who is lodging
in the attic, needs the money she holds to take up a job in a circus band. Seamus
has recourse to the local IRA fund to help her pay him and other, equally exiguous, neighbours. Meanwhile further disaster strikes: Wallace, the father, falls
from a roof while erecting a wireless aerial, and the threatened police raid starts.
Seamus is found with the money and is shot when he rushes out to his dying father. The play offers no solution to the intractable situation of oppression and
poverty it depicts. Though melodramatic in its ending, it forcefully revealed the
abject powerlessness of the northern nationalist community to a southern audience which had, twenty years after the Treaty, all but forgotten them. The *Irish
Press*, the organ of de Valera's Fianna Fáil government, praised it as showing
'what once was true here, and a daily fact of life there, because it is a call from our
own in Belfast . . . [It is] a play which asks for our understanding, presents the
problem, offers no solution. It is a picture of what happens.'[91]

The dialogue and characterization are sharp and accurate. Here is an exchange
between the Republican die-hard Mrs Griffith (played by Eileen Crowe) and Mrs
Fruin, the informer's widow (played by Bríd Ní Loingsigh):

Mrs Griffith. Time heals many a wound.
Mrs Fruin. That's true. I thought twelve years ago when they shot my sister in York Street,
    I thought when I saw her lying in the Mater Hospital, with the dum dum bullets burning
    her stomach, that the look on her face would never leave my sight. It has left me, only to

be replaced by the look of agony on the face of my husband. Why did they do it? Will his poor life bring them the freedom they want? Will it? Will it? Will it?

Mrs Griffith. There were other lives lost as well as his. I had two of my own drilled in North Howard Street.

Mrs Fruin. You've had your fill of trouble, too. Will it never cease? What did Ireland want with his life? What did Ireland do for him the three long years he tossed and tumbled on the *Argenta* in Larne Lough and I had to turn out and slave in the mill to feed our weans? What has Ireland done for me? Filled me with hate and tortured me. God curse Ireland. I've cried salt tears and so have my orphans.[92]

Monica was Siobhán McKenna's first part in English. Siobhán McKenna (Siobhán Nic Cionnaith) was a beneficiary of a scholarship scheme established by Ernest Blythe for young actors from the Gaeltacht (and other areas) in 1942 with extra money won from the government for this purpose. Specifically geared to improving the quality of acting in Irish, this was an example of Blythe's industry and commitment, but the scheme had the effect of weakening still further the link between An Comhar Drámaíochta (whose actors were made to feel even more irrelevant) and the Abbey. Another recipient of a Blythe scholarship was Seán Mac Labhraidh, later Tarzan in the US television series, where the language of the jungle that he spoke to the animals was, in fact, his own native Irish.[93]

Tomelty returned to the Abbey in 1949 with his best-known play *All Souls' Night* (16 April), although it had been presented by the Ulster Group Theatre in September 1948 when it was directed by Harold Goldblatt. Goldblatt and Tomelty were on the board of directors of the Ulster Group Theatre, which aimed to present Ulster plays, including in its repertory the work of Shiels and Ervine.

All Souls' Night was directed at the Abbey by Ria Mooney. Kathrine Quinn and her husband John (played by Máire Ní Chatháin and Michael J. Dolan) have lost one son, Stephen, and the play is concerned with how they lose their second, Michael. Kathrine is a woman who craves money, as the only security in a world she has never trusted: she was a foundling and has had a viciously cruel and hard life, so that she finds it difficult to trust anyone, even her husband. She sent Stephen to his death by insisting he row out to fetch lobsters for the local gentry even though he was terrified of the sea. When Michael, the second son (played by the young Ray MacAnally), begs her to finance the purchase of a bigger boat so they can expand their fishing business, she refuses, driving him to take part in Tom Byers's reckless expedition to loot a ship that has run aground. The coastguards come on the scene, Michael tries to swim ashore, and is drowned. Kathrine clings to her pocket book throughout the play, as to a lifeline, but she cannot contain the eruption of guilt and sorrow, embodied first in the ghost of Stephen who comes on stage, then in that of Michael, who appears almost immediately he is drowned. This supernatural element is not melodramatic, because through it the sorrow of Kathrine's and John's lives, and their helplessness, is conveyed. The ghosts are, strangely, at peace with themselves and each other, while the living are full of strife. In this regard it is different from the play to which it has some resemblance and to which it probably owes some inspiration, Yeats's *Purgatory* (1938), because in that play the nightmares do not cease after death. . In the following exchange John the husband accuses his wife of greed and heartlessness:

John. Did Stephen say he was frightened of the sea? Kathrine, why did you force him out?
Kathrine. I didn't force him out.
John. It was never to his liking to search the creels. Why did you force him out? You greedy bitch. . . It's as Michael says, you were never fit to mother children.
Kathrine. Not your children, anyway—
John. Nobody's children.
Kathrine. Not yours, I repeat.[94]

This cut is because John has always loved the girl who left him when his brother was hanged in a land agitation murder.

However, this play is not just about the meanness of a life lived in the fear of poverty, in the same way as *The End House* is not just another play dealing with the brutality of the Anglo-Irish conflict. Both plays contextualize, by the subtlety of characterization and the tension of the plot, the human situations with which people have to deal, so that the drama focuses not on politics and justice in the abstract, but in how these are lived through in the welter of experience. In *All Souls' Night* Kathrine's behaviour and Michael's anger are understandable reactions to the life-denying reality of an existence in which survival comes only from desperate effort and extreme caution. The play is a study in the fear created by dependency in the victims of the power-structure that generates, necessarily, a situation of oppression. It is a study in the obsessions spawned by colonialism: money, secrecy, superstition, pointless longing.

With Tomelty, another major dramatist to emerge in the 1940s was M. J. Molloy. From Co. Galway, Molloy trained for the priesthood at St Columba's College in Derry, but had to give up his studies due to illness. *The Old Road* (24 April 1943), Molloy's first Abbey play, was directed by Frank Dermody. It showed that Molloy had learned from the work of Synge and Fitzmaurice, in that he adapted the use of rich and colourful language to express traditional Irish rural life. In *The Old Road* Patrick Walsh, a fierce old bachelor farmer, wanders the countryside, craving female affection. Walsh (played by F. J. McCormick) is contrasted with the young lovers, Myles (played by Cyril Cusack) and Brigid (played by Bríd Ní Loingsigh), who have no money, and who realize that their situation is one with little prospect of hope. Molloy, in this play, is as concerned to analyse the emotional starvation that accompanied economic hardship in de Valera's Ireland as he is to memorialize Irish tradition and country ways.

He went on to write *The Visiting House* (18 November 1946), an evocation of a tradition in rural Ireland, where certain houses were known as places to be adjourned to at night in the sure expectation of storytelling, dancing, music, song, and dramatized amusements. Each such house had a master of ceremonies; in Molloy's play he is Broc, the Merryman, and was played by Denis O'Dea. This character is a re-creation of the Gaelic *reacaire*, or entertainer, a mixture of storyteller, stand-up comic, verbal improviser, and on-the-spot deviser of dramatic scenarios and entertainments involving known foibles and traits of neighbours and visitors. Broc's daughter Mary resists an offer of marriage from Tim Corry (played respectively by Máire Ní Dhomhnaill and Ronnie Walsh) on the grounds that she would have to give up the fun and freedom of the visiting nights. The Man of Learning (played by F. J. McCormick) is a strange and melancholy figure. He is full of a folkloric wisdom, based upon Molloy's own researches into Irish lore and folkways, and provides a homely and moralizing choric commentary on the action and the way of life it depicts. His sayings and prayers are reminiscent of the piety and spiritual immediacy of Douglas Hyde's *Religious Songs of Connacht*, collected at the turn of the century in Galway, Mayo, and Roscommon. It is a strange fact, but in this, his last but one appearance on the Abbey stage before his untimely death on 24 April 1947 (his last role was Bartley Murnaghan in Louis D'Alton's *They Got What They Wanted*, 18 February 1947), F. J. McCormick, as Mickle Conlon, the Man of Learning, has the final speech and it is a meditation on the peace to be found in death:

now you can die away for yourself, asthore. . . (*Gravely*.) For the first while right enough you'll be lonesome for the village; and lonesome for the Visiting House, too. (*Nodding*.) You will, in throth, asthore. . . But wance you have the lonesomeness and your Purgatory over, you'll be all right? (*In great humour*.) You'll be as snug as a lamb in a shed; you will, asthore. . . ashore. . .[95]

There is a sense in which Molloy wanted the Abbey to become the Visiting House of a new Ireland, one not entirely dissevered from its previous life; a wish that Yeats and Lady Gregory too shared, and one which F. J. McCormick, one of the great Abbey players, helped, more than most, to realize. He was 58 years of age when he died, and had first appeared on the Abbey stage in Edward F. Barrett's *The Grabber* (12 November 1918), directed by Fred O'Donovan.

Molloy's *The King of Friday's Men* (18 October 1948) is set in the late eighteenth century in the Connacht midlands to which Molloy's imagination constantly turned, Hyde's Connacht, where 'Mayo, Galway, and Roscommon meet', as the stage directions say. Una Brehony (Ríte Ní Fhuaráin), a young girl, has promised herself to Owen Fenigan (Mícheál Ó hAonghusa), the son of one of the tenants of the local landlord of Kilmacreena, Caesar French. French is an ageing buck, a typical eighteenth-century Anglo-Irish rake, who sends out Boorla, his bailiff, to select a 'tallywoman' for him: 'tallywomen' were mistresses of the gentry, and their culling from the ranks of the tenantry a survival of the feudal system of *droit du seigneur* that lasted in Ireland into the eighteenth century. Una, who is chosen by French, is persuaded to enlist the services of Bartley Dowd, the bully (a word in fact deriving from the Irish 'bullaí') who leads the faction fighters of Kilmacreena against their old enemies, the fighters of Tulrahan. Dowd (played by author/playwright Walter Macken) falls for Una's stratagem: she pretends to be in love with him to get him to defend her, which he does. The Bully leads

Kilmacreena to victory, and Una begins to conceive a true affection for this wild but ageing and battle-scarred heroic figure. Boorla, however, does not give up, nor does French. Una and Owen are abducted and they are promised freedom if she will admit that she duped Bartley; she does this and returns to her first love, but French reneges on his word and attempts, after all, to get her back as his tally-woman. Dowd rescues her once more, kills the landlord and takes to the hills with Rory Commons, the son of the last of the bards, where they will live out a wild and savage existence.

It is an impressive mix of Boucicault, Synge, and tales of faction fights from folklore. Dowd is a figure out of the eighteenth century glimpsed in William Carleton's 'The Party Fight and Funeral' in *Traits and Stories of the Irish Peasantry* (1843–4), but hardly realized at all in literature, with the notable exception of Donncha Ó Céileachair's short story 'Bullaí Mhártain', published in 1955, and in this play of Molloy's. Part of its interest and achievement, therefore, is its evocation of pre-Famine Ireland, a depiction which is larger than life, and full of energy and excess. But there is another side, indicated by the title. In this aspect the play explores the idea that character is created by a divine destiny: that certain individuals are charged with carrying out God's will, and that they cannot escape from their given path. Bartley explains this to Rory and Gaisceen Brehony, Una's uncle (played by Harry Brogan), at the end:

Bartley. Rory, you have the same mistake made as me. 'Tisn't for good fortune God put our like into the world, but only to do odd jobs for Him. Yourself to give good minding to His composer that was blind [Rory's father, the bard Cormac], and myself to snatch a girl from the pressgang, and to keep hunger from my sister-in-law and her orphans. We can no way complain. Himself gave His life for us of a Friday.

Gaisceen. It appears all right ye're picked amongst the King of Friday's men. But if ye are itself, He'll reward ye highly when your life is over at last.[96]

Seamus Byrne's *Design for a Headstone* (8 April 1950) was a play that came as something of a surprise. If Johnston's line, from *The Moon in the Yellow River*, that the birth of a nation is 'no immaculate conception' was a view that struck a nerve in the 1930s, then Byrne's difficult, recalcitrant, and uncompromising play of 1950 showed that the aftermath was, in many respects, savage and sordid. Byrne was himself an enigmatic character, and deeply out of kilter with the Ireland of the mid-century, with its sanitized nationalist sentiment, its piety, its lack of nerve, its institutionalized instinct for subservience. He was a solicitor and legal adviser, and worked in Co. Leitrim. In the 1940s he joined the IRA and during the Second World War was interned for his membership of an illegal organization. Like Terence MacSwiney before him, and Bobby Sands afterwards (and many others) he went on hunger strike, going without nourishment for twenty-one days.

Design for a Headstone reflects these experiences. It is set in the early 1940s and tells how Conor Egan (Mangan in the stage version, played by Mícheál Ó hAonghusa) goes on hunger strike in protest over the issue that surfaced again in 1981 in the north: whether paramilitary internees should be accorded political status—'politicals' in the lingo of the play (and of Long Kesh in the 1980s). The plot is complex and intensely imagined: the warder Pat Geraghty (Philip O'Flynn) is a tremulous collaborator with the IRA, scared into a reluctant compliance with an escape plot which involves him smuggling six revolvers into the prison; Jakey, 'an ordinary decent criminal' (as they came later to be known), is another collaborator, but both he and Geraghty are also under suspicion of being informers. Geraghty and Jakey are brutally executed, even though it is made clear to the audience, and to some of the protagonists, that they have not betrayed the IRA. A priest, Fr. Maguire, puts the Catholic church's point of view to the republicans that hunger-strikers are guilty of suicide, and of sinning against the sanctity of life; there is a Jew, Bayer (Michael J. Dolan), who only dimly apprehends what is going on; and there is Mrs Egan, Conor's wife, who is the real informer, acting as she does only to try and save her man. The play is copious, nervous, and hectic; full of action and teeming with ideas, it is a restless exploration of the tumult of anger and opinion that, at the time, lay relatively quiescent in the Irish mind, south of the partitioned north. Here, in this troubled play, the whole thing flares up again, making it, by my reckoning (and here Robert Hogan's judgement was, as is so often the case, absolutely correct), one of the most interesting plays between *The Plough and the Stars* and *The Freedom of the City*. Irish and French jostle with English in this many-voiced and intricate play. Its structure and theme are symbolized in the Celtic ring Tommy McGovern (Ronnie Walsh), the amateur smith, is fashioning with a bolt from a metal stool, the metal mounted on a tapered stick. It is a design with a dragon in its mouth. Ructions McGowan (Walter Macken) gives him instructions, another prisoner, O'Shea, interrupting and providing commentary at the same time:

Ructions. Wrap the tail round him a few times—interlace it, if you like—and finish it up with his tail in his mouth. . . And stick in a bit of green for an eye. . .
O'Shea. Is this dragon trying to choke himself?
Ructions (denunciatory). He is the symbol of passive resistance—the sufferer unto death—the Christ-like worm who never turns—the monster consuming his own tissue.
O'Shea (uncomprehending levity). Oh, Mother Ireland, get off my back!
Ructions. Symbol of the hunger striker, who turns his violence against himself—whose mortal wound is self-inflicted. . .[97]

In spite of these sceptical denunciations, Ructions is willing to take Egan's place at the end of the play when he dies. However, it is O'Leary, another prisoner, who takes on this mantle, ordering Ructions to take part in the escape in which he and the others are mown down. O'Leary fiercely attacks Fr. Maguire's doctrinal pronouncements, even denouncing Raissa Maritain, the neo-Thomist Catholic theologian who was very influential in the mid-century. Maguire's riposteis: 'Young man, take care that your ability to read—and, as you think, to understand Maritain, is not the guise of spiritual pride.'[98]

On 14 April, another night of protest at the Abbey, a group of republican supporters ran down the aisle shouting: 'Maritain was wrong.' On the other side,

Maria Duce, a branch of the Legion of Mary, staged a demonstration against what they perceived as the anticlericalism of the play. But the piece is far from being anti-ecclesiastical Fenian propaganda. It is a tormented work, in which the human dereliction wrought by conflict, misprision, hate, treachery, and sincerity, in their dragon-like contorted shapes, is fully (and bravely) registered. The play was directed by Ria Mooney.

From 1942 to late 1946 Frank Dermody directed all the Abbey plays in Irish. For a short period he was succeeded by Liam Ó Laoghaire, who staged a number of translations including one of his own of a play by Maurice Baring, *Caitríona Parr* (19 May 1947), but he and Blythe were at odds from the start, and Ó Laoghaire resigned. He was followed by Tomás Mac Anna, who directed Mícheál Mac Liammóir's *Diarmuid agus Gráinne* (3 November 1947), and J. M. Barrie's *Máire Rós* (15 March 1948), in a translation by Siobhán McKenna.

Mac Liammóir's version of this famous story from the Fionn cycle of tales is very different from the treatment of it by Yeats and Moore in 1901. Where they mixed symbolism and psychology Mac Liammóir sought to capture the atmosphere of the Fionn cycle, which is romantic and poetic, but disturbing also because these tales have to do with mythic patterns and tensions in the nature of consciousness itself. Curiously, by being faithful to the tale, Mac Liammóir's adaptation acquires modernity and an abrupt and telling relevance. Gráinne is, amongst other things, the anima or female energy that a male world devoted to the values and mores of the warrior code attempts to keep under control. She is doomed to be the possession of the ageing Fionn, and is confined until she is ready to be married. She describes her condition:

Tara, by the gods! a place where you'd be staring at a ray of sunlight, lying motionless on the wall, or listening to the minutes labouring past on heavy stone feet, or gazing at the white clouds looking for each other over the mountains, or the drops dancing on the drinking horns in the afternoon; a place where you'd see a shadow, the guardsman's shadow, perhaps, going past your door in the night, so you know how always they're watching you, as your life goes past, always, like your own shadow.[99]

This poetic treatment is actually profoundly in touch with the mythic patterns that surface everywhere in the Ossianic (or Fionn) cycle. Gráinne drugs the company at Tara and puts Diarmuid under taboo so that he cannot resist her challenge that he defy his chieftain's authority, and take her with him. They flee across Ireland, the old King in pursuit always. Eventually, an uneasy peace is made, but Gráinne cannot settle to the banal routines of normality. Diarmuid knows this: 'You're thinking of the days when you were free, when we'd sleep in the hills or the woods, or on beds of rushes amongst lonely rocks. . . with the stars shining in the skies above us.'[100] Diarmuid is gored by the boar of Ben Bulben, his own brother in animal form: Fionn could save him by giving him a magic drink, but he refuses, taking his revenge for his betrayal, and claiming back the woman he lost. But she is not his either. As the play ends she tells the old man she is with her dead lover. Mac Liammóir's spare poetic version allows the drama of the unconscious, the struggle between female principle and male ego that informs the structure of the myth, to shine through, giving the play an eerie power and troubled atmosphere.

The National Library of Ireland holds the typescript of Siobhán McKenna's translation of J. M. Barrie's *Máire Rós*. Like many in this archive, it is charred and water-stained from the fire of 1951, so that the smell of burning assails the nostrils when the reader opens the box. The play tells a strange tale of young love, death, and abduction into the otherworld. Mary Rose is a young girl loved by Simon, a navy officer. They plan to get married but Mary Rose's parents tell Simon the strange story of how, as a young girl, she disappeared for twenty days on a small island in the Hebrides. They marry and they return to the island with a 4 year-old boy, Harry. Once again the island works its magic. It is a place where birds come in great numbers. Mary Rose says: 'I love the story of the birds. I suppose the gentle creatures come, just as certain visitors are drawn here.'[101] She is abducted once more, save that now she disappears for twenty-five years. Her son Harry returns to the family home, years later, to find his mother haunting him. It is a wild play, somewhat incoherent, but McKenna's Irish translation is forceful and full of vivid imagery, an appropriate instrument for conveying Barrie's unique view of time and relativity.

Frank Dermody left the theatre in February 1947 to take up an appointment in Gabriel Pascal's film company; in that year also, Siobhán McKenna, Denis O'Dea, and Cyril Cusack left; and F. J. McCormick died. And it was in 1947 that, on 7 November, before the final act of a production of *The Plough and the Stars*, Valentine Iremonger, then a promising poet, rose to his feet in the stalls to make a speech lambasting the present directorate's artistic policy, describing it as being characterized by 'utter incompetence'. A controversy ensued, in which the newspapers engaged with their customary enthusiasm, opening the letter pages to the many perorations of dignified (and not-so-dignified) disdain and indignation. It certainly does seem to have been the case that Blythe was overworking both actors and directors, and, even more dispiriting, perhaps, many found his remote but forceful manner demoralizing.

The old days were well and truly passed. Máire Nic Shiubhlaigh struck a valedictory note in a speech to the Women Graduates' Association in Galway at the Great Southern Hotel, reported in the *Connacht Tribune* for 13 March 1948, and preserved amongst her papers in the National Library. She underlined her own view, expressed also in *The Splendid Years* (1955), that the Fays and Dudley Digges were the real *animateurs* of the Irish Theatre Movement. She concluded by recalling her friends, many now dead:

Of her great personal friends in the Irish Theatre Movement Dudley Digges came first, and his going was a great loss, but he made a great name for himself in films, dying last year. To Frank and Willie Fay the Abbey Theatre is entirely indebted for the tradition it has created. F. J. McCormick, so lately dead, is a loss beyond all telling. And Sara Allgood, with whom [she] had very close connection from the beginning, was a gifted and beautiful actress whose name is now known all over the world.[102]

Her greatest drama, she recalled, was her part in 1916, when she saw active service in Jacob's Biscuit Factory. For her part in the rebellion she was given a 1916 medal and ribbon. She was always proud of her Cumann na mBan badge. From her correspondence in the National Library it is evident that she was at work on *The Splendid Years* from around this time. She was moved to begin by a letter from Lennox Robinson, dated 9 March 1947, asking for recollections of the early years, and confessing that he was 'very ignorant' of them.[103]

In the small hours of Wednesday, 18 July 1951, the Abbey was burned to the ground with the loss of all the scenery, props, many costumes, play scripts, records, and so on, although a good deal was saved as well, including the portraits of the founders that hung in the vestibule and which can still be seen in the new foyer. Many legends and stories are told of the old building. There were supposed to be ghosts: the dog that Yeats heard barking during *Oedipus* and which also loomed over Ambrose Power in a photograph taken of him in the theatre; an irate revenant of an old programme seller clicking his fingers, heard once by J. M. Kerrigan and Dr Larchet, who conducted the orchestra; and Tomás Mac Anna has recalled how he heard a ghost walking the stage many times, late in the evening, after the performances.[104]

Walter Macken's description of the atmosphere of the old building is evocative:

There was a sort of dirty glamour about the place. I think it was the wardrobe room that gave it this. The costumes seemed to be always old, shabby and dirty—tenement clothes if you like for that was the sort of play we always seemed to be doing. We always seemed to be dirty but still the glamour of the place was always there.[105]

Tomás Mac Anna describes its effectiveness as a theatre: 'what a wonderful acoustic it had, a whisper on that old familiar stage [was] heard in every corner, and what a wonderful intimacy'.[106] During the fire Robinson was reported to have been pleased when the place went up in flames, on the grounds that now the government would, at last, honour the promise made at the outbreak of the Second World War, that a new theatre would be built to house the Abbey. But this was not to happen for many years.

5

1951–1966

'I remember everything'

More than any other of the literary or verbal arts, theatre is a business. Budgets must be planned and approved by boards of directors and sanctioned by funders; income must be projected and projected realistically; the choice of plays to go on cannot be made without the most serious consideration being given to their likely appeal; salaries must be found, protected, and enhanced where necessary to retain the best artists; and there needs to be careful and enthusiastic publicity as well as good public relations. A theatre, like a business, is an incorporation of interests needing, on the one hand, a visionary expansiveness, but on the other, steely management. Actors and artists need to be led with an almost dictatorial firmness and yet they need, also, to be cajoled and charmed. Small wonder that the theatre exhausts, frustrates, drives to drink, madness, or eccentricity. And inter-involved with everything there are the human considerations of flailing ego and utter vulnerability. It is a job hardly anyone with any sense would ever take on, without there being some driving motivation engaged at a very deep level: in their different ways the artistic directors, directors, managers, producers, managing directors of the Abbey have shown this depth of commitment—from Yeats to Blythe; Macken to Mason. Yeats had this, as did Lady Gregory; their objectives were national and, to a not inconsiderable degree, nationalistic. Lennox Robinson's animating motivation was less patriotic: more than anything Robinson was a man of the theatre, fascinated by what it could reveal of the pressures of society as they operate upon individual lives. As is evident from his involvement in the Dublin Drama League, his vision was more European and internationalist than Yeats's or Lady Gregory's, although he too had in him elements of that spirit of the early years of the century in Ireland which sought to create a cultural movement which would reflect indigenous temperament and aspiration. Hugh Hunt, who also for a time directed the Abbey's fortunes, while sympathetic to Ireland's artistic ambitions (as was evident in his ability to create a new style of poetic realism for the traditional repertoire) was really, first and foremost, a man of the theatre, with his eyes set on little else. This was why, probably, he and Frank O'Connor got on so well together: O'Connor grateful for Hunt's vision of artistic purity as he reacted from the anxious costs of republican ideology; Hunt mindful of O'Connor's native power and force of intelligence.

With Ernest Blythe, after Higgins's brief tenure as manager, another forceful individual emerged, just as patriotic as Yeats and Lady Gregory (if anything even more so) but imbued with the animus, the impatience, and the brusque intolerance of the old revolutionary idealist, bereft in a society swiftly, to his view, going to the dogs of vulgarity and opportunism. As is said in Irish: 'Oisín i ndiaidh na Féinne'—Oisín after the Fianna. Little difference that the government that retained power during most of the period of his directorship, from 1941 to 1967, was called, invoking the Fianna, Fianna Fáil: this party, while attentive to the old revolutionary values and paying homage to the Irish language, strove, like any political party must do if it is to retain office, let alone do its job, to improve the financial situation of the country, and in this case one emerging from colonial dependence. Emigration, unemployment, the health service, the hardship of subsistence farmers, inner-city deprivation: all these problems made the rebuilding of a cultural shrine, such as the Abbey, not a matter of high priority in the 1950s and 1960s. And there were many, in Ireland of that time, who thought culture was a suspect activity anyway, practised by atheists and inverts. This same harsh and utilitarian attitude was one commonly adopted towards the Irish language amongst a population many of whom were intent on survival and money-making, rather than the improvement of their sensibilities. The Abbey represented both culture and the Irish language, and it also carried an ineradicable smear, in the minds of many, of West-Britishness, snobbery, and (even worse) smart-aleckery, especially in the figure of Sean O'Casey. O'Casey was Godless and, on top of that, a nay-sayer to things dear to Irish feelings, such as the Irish struggle for independence, the Catholic church, a generalized and comfortable conformity. This was a society of large fried breakfasts for parish priests, nuns praying in their convents in the deep aroma of pure beeswax; careful saving in the new private estates going up on the edges of towns where, at night, despite assiduous exhortations to celibacy on the part of the clergy, large families were being begotten; emigrant ships hooting at quaysides as young men wept, holding their caps, looking down from the gunwales at their parents below, waving; and violence and terror in the overcrowded classrooms as children were inducted into a world that, everyone knew, was ferocious and unkind.

What use was theatre or Irish or anything that you could not eat or sell? The history of the impoverishment of that period in Irish life remains to be written. And yet Blythe won immediate support from Seán McEntee, Minister of Finance, to plan for a new building on the old site, rather than attempting to rebuild the remaining structure. This was, undoubtedly, a great pity: the back stage and the auditorium roof were destroyed, but from photographs and oral evidence, it is quite clear that the building was easily salvageable. Tomás Mac Anna has declared that one of his 'strong beliefs, after fifty years with the Abbey, is that the old building should have been restored as it was'.[1] Meanwhile, the Minister suggested, they should seek temporary accommodation while the building of a new prestigious national theatre was being carried out. Lord Moyne of the Guinness family offered the use of the Rupert Guinness Hall, where the company played for two months, while they also made use of the Peacock Theatre, which had survived the fire. In August 1951 Blythe negotiated a five-year lease with Louis Elliman of Odeon (Ireland) for the old Queen's Theatre in Pearse Street.

The Queen's was opened as the Adelphi Theatre in 1829 and rebuilt as the Queen's Royal Theatre in 1844. From about 1880 the Queen's became the venue for popular melodrama, which included standard imported fare of the kind the Irish Literary Theatre was established to combat, but also the patriotic melodramas of J. W. Whitbread as well as Boucicault and P. J. Bourke. The building, by the time the Abbey leased it, was in poor repair: there was damp on the walls; it was shabby and poorly lit; it was draughty; and it was big, too big for the Abbey's purposes. It could accommodate 50 per cent more than the capacity audience the Abbey had enjoyed on its most successful nights. This had obvious consequences for programming policy. At Abbey Street, if a play was a success, it could be revived at a later stage, but at the Queen's the business generated by a popular show was used up that much more quickly, so that revivals became much rarer and tended to be confined to those plays that could be relied upon to pull in the crowds. This pressure, to fill a theatre which was big and expensive to maintain, inevitably led to a lowering of standards, in acting, in the plays selected, and, crucially, in the direction. A tendency always present in the Abbey company, towards playing for laughs no matter what the play, was exacerbated, as the actors themselves inevitably responded to the new economic pressures. Audiences also developed increased expectations of a good laugh at reliable old troopers, who they encouraged, by applause and rumbustiousness, to overact and do little bits of business of their own devising that the audience were (not without subtlety) trained to relish. This contract, of hilarity, indulgence, and actors getting reputations for being 'great characters', was, of course, not without its attractions in a theatre which needed some such vitality to counteract the physical drawbacks of the place itself and the lack of intimacy which had been a characteristic of Abbey Street. What were needed were plays which would have long runs; and this in turn began to affect the quality of the plays submitted.

There was a bad start: the Queen's opened with O'Casey's *The Silver Tassie*, which was a complete disaster, Blythe commenting that 'we have done our duty by *The Silver Tassie* and we should never see it again'.[2]

For the first newly staged play at the Queen's the Abbey had recourse to the author of successes such as *They Got What They Wanted* and *Lovers' Meeting*, Louis D'Alton. He supplied an odd theological farce, *The Devil a Saint Would Be* (10 September 1951), which is concerned with post-war relativism and doubt. Stacey, an old Kerry woman, has a vision of a saint who tells her to give her money away to the poor, with disastrous results. She also hands over ownership of the shop and pub to her daughter Ellie and son-in-law Sean. Once he is in charge he puts a stop to her generous acts: it is the time of post-war rationing, and he makes sure he keeps his surplus tea and sugar under the counter so he can sell it at black-market prices. Ellie asks him what madness has got into him to have changed so much. He replies: 'Aye. . . for the better. an' you may change too. Or if not you'd better resign your share of the place over to me an' let me see after our prosperity. Anyway, keep Stacey out o' the shop or there'll be trouble.'[3] When Stacey is duped by the Cassidys, two roguish tinkers, into parting with her pension arrears, they get bawdy and drunk, and when she reproves them fighting breaks out. The play, in a somewhat cumbersome way, is seeking to make a comedy out of the problem of evil, and the inscrutability of human motive. The Saint lectures Stacey on moral relativism, how the Devil's best ploy is the appeal to virtue: 'His appeal is to virtue not vice. That is why the greatest scoundrels in history have all been honest men proceeding from virtuous motives and why more throats have been cut for virtue than ever were for vice.'[4] Strangely enough, in the exchange that takes place between Stacey and Dr Nolan, who is assessing her sanity, there occurs a passage which points to the moral issue that lies, largely unexplored, at the heart of this odd farce. She tells the doctor of a discussion she has overheard between two students in the bar on the nature of atomic structure and on nuclear fission. These are the post-Hiroshima years of the Cold War, and Stacey's conclusion, that the whole world is mad, was not an uncommon view. Her Saint is revealed to have been a Devil all along, when a true one comes to bring her to heaven. At the gates she upbraids Peter and angers him when she refers to his own failures on earth.

Walter Macken's *Home is the Hero* (28 July 1952) ran for seventeen weeks and became one of the company's most popular plays. Macken came from Galway, where he worked as a clerk after leaving school, joining An Taibhdhearc, the Gaelic theatre in Galway where Frank Dermody was a director, in 1933. Macken assisted Dermody in the production of Gaelic plays, in which he acted as Uaiteár Maicín. After a period in London, whither he had fled in 1936 when he eloped with a local girl, he returned to Galway in 1939 to take over as director when Dermody moved to the Abbey, encouraged by Blythe. While working as manager of the Taibhdhearc Macken wrote a number of plays in Irish, translated Boucicault's *Arrah-na-Pogue*, and developed the peculiar kind of contemporary melodrama that was to be the genre he deployed in his English plays. Macken followed Dermody to Dublin, where he became a member of the Abbey company in 1948 and, glad to relinquish the manifold duties that fell to him in the Taibhdhearc, concentrated on acting and writing. He had, however, of course already had a play performed at the Abbey. *Mungo's Mansion* (11 February 1946) is set in the Galway slums of the Claddagh at the time and evokes the vigour and colour of the life to be found on the margins of society and amongst the poor, whilst also recognizing the human tragedies that such conditions breed. Mungo King (F. J. McCormick) works in the docks and lives in Buttermilk Lane, where the houses are so crowded together that the air is unhealthy, causing his youngest boy Tomeen to contract diphtheria. Laid up with an accident, he has given 5s. to his friend Mowleogs (Harry Brogan) to put on a horse that has romped home as an outsider. Mowleogs has disappeared and the family are under pressure to find the rent. However, he turns up to tell them that he has won a sweepstake ticket on a horse at the Leopardstown races, which comes in second, bringing £2,000 to Mungo. There is a good deal of comic business as they try to rig up an electric connection to a wireless they have rented from the pawnshop by climbing out the window to the tenement next door. However, Tomeen's illness is not the only infection that the slums breed: Jack Manders (Denis O'Dea) upstairs has gone mad from the frustrations of poverty and unemployment, and kills his sad wife (Bríd Ní Loingsigh). He now makes an attempt on Mungo's life, but the latter is saved by Mowleogs. At the end of the play Mungo is finally persuaded to move out of Buttermilk Lane to the new corporation houses going up in Shantalla. The character of Manders, as a psychopath driven crazy by social conditions, is powerfully drawn and he is given his own kind of deranged poetry:

'Twas all in a kind oo a dream, Mister King, because such a pain in me head you never felt the like oo it, and then I put me hand over her mouth and pushed back her head and I knew all the time she was afraid of me and I had the do it, Mister King, I had the do it! And when she fell down, Mister King, with only a noise, a small noise, out oo her mouth, do you know that the pain in me head stopped dead. . .[5]

The play was directed by Macken's old mentor at the Taibhdhearc, Frank Dermody. Macken himself played the son, Willie, in *Home is the Hero* and the play was directed by Ria Mooney. Paddo, the father (Brain O'Higgins), returns to the family's council house in Galway, having served a prison term for the manslaughter of a neighbour. His wife Daylia (Eileen Crowe) is an alcoholic, while Willie (Mícheál Ó hAonghusa), the son, wants to marry the daughter of the man he killed. The play ends with Paddo leaving once more, his anger and solitude making him an outcast in a world that has no place for his primeval force.

At the Queen's Blythe continued a policy begun at Abbey Street, of presenting short one-act plays in Irish after the main evening performances to encourage interest in Gaelic theatre, and to develop a tolerance for it in Dublin. It met, it has to be said, with only partial success. However, the Abbey pantomimes in Irish became more popular at the Queen's, the traditional atmosphere and design of the theatre suiting their combination of song, dance, and colour. In 1952 the Abbey staged *Setanta agus an Chú* (26 December), based on the Cuchulain story; and in following years there were *Blíthín agus an Mac Rí* (26 December 1953), *Sonia agus an Bodach* (21 December 1954), and *Ulysses agus Penelope* (26 December 1955).

M. J. Molloy, author of *The King of Friday's Men*, returned to the Abbey with *The Wood of the Whispering* in 1953, directed by Ria Mooney. This play, with impressive fidelity, captures the mood and anxiety of the post-war Ireland of emigration, celibacy, and rural depopulation. In his preface Molloy wrote: 'There are countless dying villages and townlands in rural Ireland . . . The death of a village, like the death of an individual, is usually a painful business.'[6] This dereliction Molloy linked to the slow afterwave of colonialism, and argued that Ireland was a country which had failed to free herself emotionally and psychologically.

As late as 1961, in the same preface to the published version of *The Wood of the Whispering*, he wrote:

For forty years Ireland has been free and for forty years it has wandered in the desert under the leadership of men who . . . could never free their own souls and minds from the ill-effects of having been born in slavery . . . the worst disaster that can befall a nation is not conquest but colonisation.

The play mostly comprises old and deranged misfits, the wrecks of a society which has been leached of its energy and lifeblood. These are people who have given up on the challenge of reality and have retreated into sentiment, drink, and illusion. Sanbatch Daly (played by Philip O'Flynn) lives in a coffin-like box in a clearing in the wood, because his house has become a shambles for the want of care and attention. These woods were once animated by the whispering of lovers in the night, but now they are silent, save for the distant lumbering of lorries bringing drink to the pubs. Daly has his funerary habitation outside the gates of a deserted big house, potent images of ghostly longing, disappointed passion, and wasted money. Paddy King (played by Brian O'Higgins) is an 80-year-old who still fancies himself the most eligible man in the area; while his brother Jimmy (Harry Brogan) is wandering in his mind. Sadie Tubridy (Bríd Ní Loingsigh), left in the lurch by the man who had courted her for twenty years, now also lives in a deserted gardener's hut in the woods, a mute who has forsaken speech.

Daly tries to change this situation of aphasia, stasis, emotional underdevelopment, by assuming the role, incongruous in the circumstances in which he has to work, of matchmaker. There are younger people, Sheila Lanigan (Doreen Madden) and Con Kinsella (Ray MacAnally), who have returned from England because different necessities and obligations draw them back. Another, Mark Tristnan (played by the young Joe Lynch), is a potential suicide. However, amongst these young people the act of faith required for marriage seems an impossibility, even a comic one. Daly's all-but-impossible undertaking and his designs for accomplishing his objectives provide the engine of the comic plot that accelerates out of the dismal lethargy that is the mood for the first half of the play. Eventually this growing animation speeds up into farce as Daly, despairing of his task, pretends to be mad in order that he be certified and admitted to Ballinasloe asylum, where at last there will be comfort and warmth. This desperate recourse has the unexpected consequence of getting the younger characters to marry, and the play ends, not happily, but with a sense that life's unpredictabilities may evolve into surprise and joy. Mark Tristnan and Sheila agree to marry, and her melancholic young man starts a celebration: 'Girls, bring these to the drink shop, and put a fire in the snug for us, and chairs and porter and whiskey and lemonade and biscuits and red-meat and the loaves there, and we'll have a night till morning.'[7] This, a most searching work, is a sombre meditation on the relationships between social and individual liberty, the power of money, and the destructive force of repressed sexuality. Its comedy, while vivid and humane, is dark.

John D'Alton's *This Other Eden* (1 June 1953) is also a meditation on Irish dis-illusion, as the Treaty was receding into the past, and the Ireland that had come into being was more than ready for appraisal. It is a reworking of Shaw's *John Bull's Other Island* to some extent, although it moves to a more moralizing stand-point than Shaw's play allows itself; the latter is content to reflect the interplay of oppositional stereotypes, and to allow the dramatic excitement to build as the tension of uncertainty tightens. D'Alton's play is cruder, though forceful too in its own way. Roger Crispin, the Englishman, arrives in Ballymorgan intending to buy the estate of Commandant Carberry, a republican hero killed by the Black and Tans. Carberry, it turns out, was a hypocrite and had fathered a bastard, Conor Murphy, who burns down the memorial hall erected in honour of his father. Crispin, who turns out to be more patriotic than the Irish themselves, and also speaks the native tongue, offers to rebuild the hall, and he marries Maire, a local girl planning to emigrate, saving her from the liberty and licence of an England that has grown depraved. The play is an odd mixture: a critique of nationalist pieties and also of English modernization and secularism.

The 'Abbey style', of deliberate cultivation of character-acting and playing to the gallery, found its dramatist in John McCann. A journalist and politician (he served as Dublin's Lord Mayor 1966–7), he had a play, *The Dreamer*, performed at the Peacock as early as 1930. He returned with *Twenty Years A-Wooing* (29 March, 1954), which has an entirely conventional plot with stock situations: the exiguous bachelor, a prolonged engagement, the doting mother. He also worked into the plot and dialogue references to contemporary politicians, public figures, and events, increasing the sense, obviously attractive to an audience looking for an entertaining night out, of belonging to a coterie of theatregoing folk who were in the know, and who were quick to pick up the broad hints and satirical thrusts. Strangely for a national theatre with a state subsidy it was wilfully becoming more and more provincial and self-referring, in that its field of reference was tend-ing to become very Dublin-centred. There were, as has been indicated, economic reasons for this lowering of standards, and it would appear as if Ria Mooney, the main producer of plays since January 1948, had, through sheer pressure of work, been forced to allow the actors their head. In an unpublished autobiography, 'The Days before Yesterday', she described her situation: 'I had to direct from twelve to seventeen productions every ten months with a company of young people who had to be trained and disciplined as well.'[8] Robert Hogan once asked her what her job was like in these years, and she said: 'there's nothing to do with these plays. One's just like another. You rack your mind trying to think of something new, but it boils down to last week you put the door over here, so now you'll put it over there.'[9] Further, in the unpublished autobiography, she makes a revealing comment, which may serve to explain something of the demoralized mood of these years of waiting, frustration, and anger. She says that the directors held the view that the theatre was biding its time until a fully Gaelic-speaking company and management could be put into place. This may have been no more than resentment on her part, and yet it is not impossible that some such idealism animated Blythe, Ó Faracháin, and Hayes. The 1950s was a period in which it was becoming evident that the official policy of the state with regard to Irish (that it was the national tongue, and that the Republic would never be truly Irish until it was Gaelic as well) was far short of realization. This disappointing reality had the entirely predictable effect of fuelling into greater intensity the commitment of old idealists such as Blythe, compelling them to the bleak heroism of warriors fighting the waves of modernity and indifference. From being a national theatre representing the full extent of Irish creativity, the Abbey, in these years, became a kind of secret society devoted to an increasingly abstract ideal—Gaelic Ireland—while purveying, cynically almost, shoddy and often poorly-written formulaic plays in English. As if to say: that will do for now, the real thing will come later when the true ideals are realized. This attitude, in artistic matters, was not unknown in other spheres of Irish life: economic policy itself was in these years a matter of deferring and waiting. Molloy's *The Wood of the Whispering* captures this mood of anticipatory expectation, in which the life being lived is as nothing compared to what may be when the true order reveals itself. But the other and, this time, great play that rises from this mood of waiting, this *parousia* of these years, was written first in French, and not staged at the Abbey until 1969. That play was *En attendant Godot* (*Waiting for Godot*) by Samuel Beckett, and it opened in Paris in 1953, the same year as Molloy's play.

Nevertheless, Ria Mooney, Tomás Mac Anna, and the company laboured in these circumstances year in, year out, as the building of the new theatre, which, it was hoped would realize so many expectations, was continuously deferred. McCann, once he hit his stride in *Twenty Years A-Wooing* continued to supply predictable but popular entertainments in the following years: *Blood is Thicker than Water* (25 July 1955), *Early and Often* (16 July 1956), *Give Me a Bed of Roses* (25 November 1957), *I Know Where I'm Going* (26 January 1959), *It Can't Go on Forever* (31 January 1960), and so on. Denis Donoghue, looking back on the 1950s at the Abbey in 1961, attacked the whole mélange—the Abbey 'style', Harry Brogan, and John McCann; Brogan he especially excoriates as turning all his parts into the famous O'Casey boozer: 'The actor who sums up these procedures most revealingly is Harry Brogan, to whom every character is Joxer. The most cunning Abbey dramatist is John McCann.'[10]

One of his later plays in this genre, the prompt-copy of which is now preserved in the National Library of Ireland, is *A Jew Called Sammy* (27 August 1962), directed by Tomás Mac Anna. The play is set in contemporary Dublin. Peter Cartney (played by Harry Brogan) and his wife Martha (Eileen Crowe) have four children: Alphonsus at university who is involved in various projects and causes, including 'Ban the Bomb'; Johnny, who is at Maynooth studying for the priesthood; Maudie (Angela Newmann), who looks after the house; and Dolores, who has taken up with a chancer called Gerry Fitzgerald, played by the young Vincent Dowling. Sammy Rosenberg (T. P. McKenna) is the Jew who acts as a kind of fixer of all the problems, financial and emotional, that surface in the play. There is a plot, of sorts, but it is very clumsy. For example, we expect Sammy to become engaged to Maudie, whom he instructs in the mysteries of the second-hand furniture trade, but McCann seems to have thought better of developing that line. It would have been an interesting twist but there is a sense that McCann is not sufficiently involved with his characters or the play to go to the trouble of dealing with a Judaeo-Christian marriage. Instead Maudie and Patrick Glynn (Patrick Layde) find themselves courting each other in a curious poetry of used tables and chairs:

Patrick. What about the tables you have for sale?
Maudie. You said you didn't want them.
Patrick. I changed my mind. I asked Sammy to see them and he told me you had them.
Maudie. Sammy just told me. He says they're worth fifty pounds. I think that's too much.[11]

And so on. Patrick, incidentally, has by now learned to overcome his anti-Semitism. The play, like all McCann's, has a relaxed air, a sense that the audience knows what it is getting, and that the world depicted on stage is one that will cause no surprises, open up no emotional or imaginative dangers. The plot here, clumsy as it is, is of interest precisely because nothing happens. The Jew stays outside the world of the Cartneys, even though the play offers the *frisson* that something different may come about. The nothing that happens is, needless to say, far less compelling than the nothing that happens twice in *Waiting for Godot*.

Joseph Tomelty returned to the Abbey company with *Is the Priest at Home* (8 November 1954), originally produced at the Group Theatre in Belfast in May that year. It dealt with homely issues on the role of the priest in Irish society; but here Tomelty depicts his priest in a problematic way, and projects no comforting images of the Catholic church and its pastors. There is a realism about the limits of priestly influence in a society increasingly charged with tension and frustration. The play's method, in which the scenes illustrate the priest's reflections, show Tomelty making effective dramatic use of dreamscapes, as he had done in *All Souls' Night*.

The Abbey celebrated its Golden Jubilee in 1954, marking the fiftieth anniversary of the opening of the theatre on Abbey Street, although it would, perhaps, have been more appropriate to have marked that occasion in 1949, as the Abbey had its origins in the Irish Literary Theatre of 1899. The gala evening featured productions of *In the Shadow of the Glen*, *On Baile's Strand*, and *Spreading the News*.

The year 1955 saw little of value on the Abbey stage. However, the following year, the year of rock 'n' roll, Elvis Presley, and James Dean's death, saw first plays by three major talents, *The Big Birthday* by Hugh Leonard (23 January), *The Quare Fellow* by Brendan Behan (8 October), and *Gunna Cam agus Slabhra Óir* by Seán Ó Tuama. The year 1956 also saw the return of Denis Johnston to the Abbey, with a reworking of his *Blind Man's Buff* (26 December 1936) as *Strange Occurrence on Ireland's Eye* (20 August 1956).

Behan was a Dubliner born into an intensely republican family, which also had, coincidentally, deep theatrical associations. His uncle was Peadar Kearney, composer of the Irish National Anthem, but also part-time actor with the company and general handyman. Another uncle was P. J. Bourke, who wrote patriotic melodramas for the Queen's Theatre, such as *In Dark and Evil Days* (1914) and *For the Land She Loved* (1915), and who managed that theatre for a time, producing, as well as his own plays, work by Boucicault and J. W. Whitbread. Behan followed his father into the house-painting trade (a profession, it would seem, that produces reflective people), and then into the IRA. At the age of 16 in 1939 he was arrested in Liverpool and found in possession of a suitcase full of explosives to be used in the IRA bombing campaign in England. He was also later imprisoned for being a member of the IRA in Ireland, and was held at the Curragh, as were other writers such as Máirtín Ó Cadhain and Seamus Byrne, later to become another Abbey playwright. While there and in Borstal in England he began to write in English and in Irish.

Probably while detained in the Curragh he began work on a satirical and black adaptation of Hyde's seminal Gaelic play *Casadh an tSúgáin* (where the rope, in Behan's version, becomes the hangman's noose), first produced by the Irish Literary Theatre in 1901. Behan's version was called *Casadh Súgáin Eile* (*The Twisting of Another Rope*). This one-acter was rejected by the Abbey and by the Gate. Behan rewrote it in English as a three-act play and gave it the title *The Quare Fellow*, but it too was rejected by the Abbey and produced at Alan Simpson and Carolyn Swift's new theatre, the Pike, in Herbert Lane (19 November 1954). This theatre, founded in 1953, premièred Beckett's *Waiting for Godot* in 1955. Joan Littlewood took *The Quare Fellow* on for her Theatre Workshop in London, and then the Abbey accepted it, at last, after it had had rave notices at Stratford East.

Behan and the Pike Theatre were like portents of energy in a Dublin theatre scene that by the mid-1950s had, with some exceptions, subsided into lethargy and repetitiveness. However, we must be careful of accepting too readily a simplistic view of the Abbey's work at any period of its history, even at this time, in the doldrums of the 1950s. Behan was at first rejected by the Abbey, but he was put on, albeit two years after the première of *The Quare Fellow* at the Pike.

The year 1956 was also the year in which Tomás Mac Anna staged, at the Queen's, a celebrated production of Bertolt Brecht's great theatrical epic *The Life of Galileo* (21 September), which demonstrated how the modern stage could be used for all kinds of effect—argument, farce, reflection—while at the same time deliberately drawing attention to the activity of theatre as work, in which actors and audience are kept fully aware of the fact that they are watching a performance, not an imitation of life.

As in the theatre of Brecht, Behan's *The Quare Fellow* makes use of a variety of effects from popular theatre, music-hall, and melodrama: the songs, jokes, slapstick humour, and cross-talk reflect Behan's absorption of these techniques as he attended his uncle's shows at the old Queen's Theatre. It is also, like Brecht's, political theatre, but at a level much deeper than propaganda: it shows how the laws and ordinances of society condemn people to our rejection of them. Society, in sentencing people to imprisonment and death, also compels us to a collusion with these dictates. *The Quare Fellow*, to many, appeared to be without structure: there are ruminations, business, reflections, discussions, and the interpolation of song and poetry reflecting the preoccupation of the human animal with sex and food. But the 'quare fellow', off stage, is sentenced to death, and the play—exhibiting classic unity of time—is an embodiment of the process of waiting in its mixture of pity, fear, and excitement. The moral structure of the play revolves around Behan's central conviction: that we condemn others by virtue of the power-arrangements of the society we require and uphold. This is not propaganda, but political awareness made complex to the point of art by the diversity of views that theatre can present.

Tomás Mac Anna was responsible for producing *The Quare Fellow* at the Abbey, and he, too, undertook Ó Tuama's *Gunna Cam agus Slabhra Óir* (21 October). Ó Tuama was born in Blackpool in Cork to republican parents, his father's people coming from the west Cork Gaeltacht, where he spent many summers as a child on the family farm. After rigorous academic training at University College, Cork, where he was taught by Daniel Corkery, author of the Abbey plays *Fohnam the Sculptor* and *The Yellow Bittern,* he spent nine months in 1955–6 in Paris studying the theory and practice of contemporary theatre and writing *Gunna Cam agus Slabhra Óir.*

Ó Tuama's play is a brilliant historical drama, exploring questions of identity and tradition (concerns that preoccupied his teacher, Corkery) in surprising and troubling ways. The play is set in the mid-sixteenth century, at the time when Henry VIII was carrying out his policy of 'surrender and regrant' in Ireland, whereby Irish chieftains who had inherited the headship of their sept or clan according to the traditional Gaelic style were invited (or rather compelled) to surrender their native titles to the King who then reinstalled them as lords in their own lands under his protection. Mánas Ó Domhnaill, in this play, reluctantly agrees to go through this procedure, to the disgust and outrage of his son Calbhach, the fiery Franciscan, Fr. Eoghan, and certain of his subchieftains. The O'Donnells with their castle at Lifford (where the play is set), like the O'Neills of Tyrone and the MacCarthys of Cork, were one of the great Gaelic families, with overlordship over other subsidiary families—such as the Sweeneys, the O'Gallaghers, and the MacAwards, all of whom feature in this play. Indeed the action of the plot brings onto the stage, in Brechtian carnivalesque, the Gaelic world before its downfall at Kinsale: rushes on the floor of the castle, the power of the church embodied in the Franciscan, the fooling of the *crossán* (a kind of Irish *jongleur*), music and banter, and all the time the ferocity of *realpolitik* as England presses ever more insistently its advantage as a modern state, fully armed, ready to destroy any opposition to its colonial expansion. Ó Tuama's play takes the

Anglo-Irish question right back to its roots in the Tudor reconquest of Ireland, and lays bare the choices open to Ó Domhnaill then, choices crucial to any individual or any country at any time. The choice is between resistance or accommodation, where the accommodation is conceived of as being tactical in order to buy time so the resistance can be more effective in the future. That is Ó Domhnaill's dilemma, and he chooses accommodation. He is a Machiavellian figure, a Renaissance man, whose instinct is to comply with necessity and take what steps he may to secure a position he is only too aware is desperately fragile. Even his marriage to Eileanór Nic Gearailt, a Geraldine from the prestigious Norman family of Kildare, is to buttress his safety against the incursions of Lord Grey, Henry's Viceroy, as he forays through the country, enforcing submission, by conflict or treachery, to his master's will. Calbhach is disgusted at his father's tactics, and early in the play declares: 'No son ever attends his father's marriage— unless he's a bastard.'[12] As the play play develops, its complexity opens up: Eileanór's acceptance of Ó Domhnaill's offer of marriage is triggered by her own desire to protect her son by another marriage, Gearóid Óg, through an alliance with the O'Donnells of Donegal. Is this, the idealistic Calbhach asks Fr. Eoghan, what love is: dynastic manœuvring? The priest and the young Ó Domhnaill find themselves in league, and in an extraordinary scene, following the giving of absolution by Fr. Eoghan to Calbhach, the priest expounds a dark and terrible theology to the young man, declaring that the sins of the fathers do visit themselves on the sons, and that a son must do a barbarous act to clean the tainted blood he inherits. Nothing like this had been staged in drama in Irish before; and only in Yeats and in Synge do we find anything like this excitement, as theatre moves deliberately into the dark forests of the human heart:

When a man fathers a son he also initiates the basic templates of his blood. If the father's blood is blackened with wrong then so also will the son's blood be tainted in the same way. Nothing to be done. But he on whom the misfortune of inheriting bad blood falls, there also comes to him the opportunity of sweetness and grace. And he will be asked, he'll get the chance, of doing the terrible deed, the barbarous act, that act which will clean the blood, that will make it bright red again. That man may be asked to trample over his mother's body; or maybe to shackle his father in darkness. If he backs away from this test, he's damned; and the blood will turn even blacker in his veins.[13]

Ó Domhnaill constantly invokes reason as his guiding principle, and it is reason, rationality, that leads him to submit to Grey's emissaries in the last act. He ignores Fr. Eoghan's advice: 'I'm tired from telling you, Mánas, and all of you, that if you pay a levy today to avoid a fight, you'll pay another tomorrow, and twice that the day after.'[14] But the priest's resolve and his certainty that to give in once is to give in forever is not lost on Calbhach. When his father submits formally to the Latin ordinances of the terms of his acceptance of Henry as his overlord, Calbhach declares that in so doing he has relinquished the title of O'Donnell, claiming it now as his. He has a body of men, armed, outside; and he finishes by locking his father in the tower of the castle. The play ends, powerfully, with the iron door clanging, and the priest and Calbhach on their knees, praying for mercy and for help in the future; but we know that what awaits them is their doom.

The play, as will be evident from the above rather summary account, is a most impressive piece of work. It is utterly contemporary in technique and in the daring of its thought; the characters, as in Brecht, are not of great psychological interest: Ó Tuama is much more concerned to show human dilemma as it is experienced at moments of national and personal conflict. There is, also, a most effective theatrical objectivity in the piece: we look at the characters as phenomena caught in the complexities of a historical situation, but one which we recognize as being very familiar to us in our own experience.

Nothing as sophisticated had been written for the theatre in Irish, up to that point. Ó Tuama was to go on to write further plays, but this was his only piece for the Abbey. It is an indication of the failure of the Abbey's Irish policy that Ó Tuama was not given greater encouragement to write more for the national theatre company. But, aside from that, the fact that he did not achieve recognition as the major dramatist he undoubtedly was points up the problem which confronted the writer in Irish in the 1950s and 1960s: the lack of an audience.

Strange Occurrence on Ireland's Eye (20 August 1956) marked Denis Johnston's return to the Abbey stage after an absence of sixteen years from the Dublin theatre: *The Dreaming Dust*—his Swift play—had been performed at the Gate in 1940. *Strange Occurrence* was a reworking of *Blind Man's Buff* (26 December 1936), itself a piece part-based on *Die blinde Göttin* by the German expressionist Ernst Toller and on a radio play by Johnston himself about the trial of William Burke Kirwan for murder in 1852. The play ran for seven weeks, due, perhaps, to the popularity of the kind of play which this is: a trial-piece, in which the tensions of the court-room are dramatized and argument and the analysis of motive and event become matters of life and death. Kirwan is wrongly accused of murdering his wife, and convicted, but eventually has the judgement overturned when new evidence comes to light through the efforts of his mistress, the doctor Teresa Kenny. Their affair, in fact, was the apparent motive underlying his initial conviction. Johnston's analytic temper is everywhere at work in this curiously harsh and brilliant play: there is no subsiding into the softness of romantic love between Kirwan and the doctor, and she is revealed to have aborted her child. Furthermore, having freed her lover, she abandons him as a 'cheap Narcissus', too full of self-regard to be capable of viewing either himself or their relationship with any steadiness or resolve.

In 1958, Johnston produced his theatrical reply to O'Casey's *The Plough and the Stars*, giving it the title *The Scythe and the Sunset* (19 May). Johnston himself said of his play that it follows O'Casey's 'like the smell following a motor car'[15], but also acknowledges that it was a theatrical argument with *The Plough* rather than an attempt to usurp that play's vision or undermine its power. However, it is a critique: Denis Johnston was profoundly ambivalent about O'Casey's pacifist moralizing, and argued that war does change situations, and may often have positive outcomes. His is a bleaker and more realistic attitude, recognizing the inevitability of conflict, reflecting undoubtedly Johnston's experience as a BBC correspondent in the Second World War, and the shock of seeing Buchenwald after it was taken by the Allied Forces in 1945. Indeed his treatment, in the play, of revolutionaries and soldiers was based on first-hand experience: in 1916 the family home was commandeered by the IRA, 'soft-spoken young men' who did little damage, while the army men were friendly and incompetent.[16]

Johnston saw the Easter Rising itself. He was 14 at the time, and was excited and intrigued by the heroism of the insurrection and by the contrasting behaviour of many Dubliners. He later told, how, when Joseph Mary Plunkett came out of the GPO to read the Proclamation at the foot of Nelson's Pillar, the crowd dispersed quickly when someone shouted that Noblett's Toffee Shop was being looted, a detail he inserts into his play. Family memory also recalled how Johnston's mother brought tea to the republicans in the house as they were rearranging furniture upstairs.

In the play Palliser, an Anglo-Irish British army officer, wounded while leading a cavalry assault on the GPO, is captured by the rebels and taken to a republican Red Cross station across the street, located in an upstairs café. Johnston takes care to immerse his action in the actualities of event, so that human motivations, ranging from idealism to callow opportunism, are seen arising from the play of contingency and the unavoidable differences between people and between national persuasions. The dramatic interest is focused on the developing relationship and understanding between Palliser, the professional soldier, embarrassingly incapacitated by a fall from his horse in the charge, and Tetley, the revolutionary modelled on Pearse, who does not know how to assemble a captured machine-gun.

Tetley is honest in his appraisal of the circumstances of war, and develops a clear-eyed sense of the lack of expertise shown by the rebels while not discounting their valour: 'Dammit, we're only taking on the British Empire in open warfare for the first time in three generations. It takes us a little time to learn. But we'll never learn by pretending that we've done things we haven't.'[17] This he says to the more ideologically bound Williams, who maintains that the revolutionaries should not be discouraged by too frank an admission of shortcomings. Tetley also refuses to idealize the Irish people. He was watching their faces during the reading of the Proclamation, he says: 'and there was nothing but derision in their eyes—derision, and that murderous Irish laughter. It was as if we were putting on a rather poor entertainment for them, and they wanted their money back.'[18]

Palliser is egged on by Emer, an extremist republican (modelled on Maud Gonne and Constance Markievicz), and in a moment of outrage and anger he assembles the machine-gun, which she then trains on a truce across the street. Emer and Róisín, the waitress in the café, are intended contrasts on Johnston's part to O'Casey's women, who invariably speak the language of feeling and compassion: in *The Scythe* they are 'killers', Johnston's own word. Emer, in fact, in goading

Palliser, saying to him that he, unlike Tetley, does not have the courage to submit
to martyrdom, drives the Anglo-Irishman to the act, the assembling of the gun,
which will ensure that events drive forward to Tetley's execution and indeed the
beginning of the end of British rule in Ireland, and of the role his own class played
in administering it. He then also touches the gun, and it spurts into fire again.
Palliser, through Act III, moves to his own kind of martyrdom. He recognizes that
his world is passing and chooses to die in the building where the action is set,
which eventually collapses. He explains his complexity of motive to Tetley:

When we built an Empire. . . we didn't have much in the way of big battalions. But we had
life and an interest in ourselves. Now we're tired of being what we are, and we play the
other fellow's game because we're sick of winning. . . Ireland's only the start. . . piece by
piece we're going to give it all away—not because we're licked, but because we're bloody
well bored. So don't be too proud of yourselves.[19]

This insight into a self-destruction at the heart of authority, which collaborates in
its own betrayal, is one which is entirely characteristic of the force of Johnston's
theatre and the acuity of his intellect. His drama, like Shaw's, encourages the audience into watchful adjudication, but unlike Shaw's, it is far from being as ebullient or as confident in its deployment (and advocacy) of reason. Johnston
distrusts rationalism as much as he distrusts emotion, so his theatre, and this play,
is, in its own way, an advance both on Shaw and on O'Casey.

In 1958 Richard Hayes died and the government appointed Dr Séamus Wilmot,
registrar of the National University of Ireland, to the Abbey directorate in his
stead. Wilmot had been the author of a number of plays in Irish. On 14 October
Lennox Robinson died, and he was replaced on the board on 7 January 1959 by
Gabriel Fallon, a civil servant, but also a distinguished and perceptive critic.

In 1959 the year opened with John McCann's popular comedy *I Know Where
I'm Going* (26 January), followed by Tomás Mac Anna's production of Eugene
O'Neill's *Long Day's Journey into Night* (28 April), a play that had a profound
impact on the Dublin theatre of the time, revealing, as it does, an American family very like many Irish ones, riddled with guilt, obsession, fear, and haunted by
alcoholism and depression.

John Murphy's *The Country Boy* (11 May 1959) dealt with the phenomenon,
much in evidence in the Ireland of the 1950s, of the returned 'Yank'. Irish towns
and the countryside were, each year, invaded by returned emigrants, showing off
their garish suits, loud ties, and two-tone shoes. Murphy's play subjects them to a
realistic but not unsympathetic analysis—that it struck a chord in the Ireland of
the time is evident from the fact that the play ran for seventy nights at the Queen's.
The sadness and exhaustion of life in the USA for Irish emigrants who do not have
a clear idea of what they hope to achieve in their new situation is well presented.
Eddie Maher the Irish American, with his rented camera, is a drunk who cannot
keep a job, and knows what it is to be one of the 'country boys' in America who
cannot fit in: 'they just work because they have to eat. . . or drink. And that's no

living for any man. . . unless he's chasing ulcers.'[20] Tom Coffey's *Stranger Beware* (17 August 1959) dealt with a murder in a north Kerry village and explores the darker side of small-town Ireland. Coffey was born in Ennis, Co. Clare, and wrote in Irish as well as English. His best-known play, *Anyone Could Rob a Bank* (1 August 1960), was a farce.

Bryan MacMahon, from Listowel, became a teacher, and then headmaster, in his native town. He began writing plays for the local drama group before submitting to the Abbey *The Bugle in the Blood* (14 March 1949). His next play for the Abbey was *The Song of the Anvil* (12 September 1960). This play deals with subjects and themes that fascinated MacMahon as a short-story writer and realist: the interplay between pagan and Christian values, storytelling, passion, and primitive urges that issue in brutality. *The Honey Spike* (22 May 1961) draws upon MacMahon's deep knowledge of Gaelic folklore and his sympathetic appreciation of the life, culture, and language of the Irish tinkers.

Breda and Martin Claffey set out from the Giant's Causeway in Co. Antrim for the Dunkerron hospital near Kenmare, Co. Kerry, the 'honey spike' (a good and lucky maternity hospital in the tinkers' language), where she wants to have their child. On the way they encounter a variety of incidents.

In the south of Northern Ireland they encamp in the middle of an area notorious for cross-border trafficking and guerrilla action. They rescue an IRA recruit from Kerry from a B-Special patrol. They go on south until they come to Puck Fair in Killorglin, Co. Kerry, where Breda encounters Winifred McQueen, an old flame of Martin's. Winifred boasts that she could take Martin from Breda because 'there's some say you can't trust a man as long as he's able to pick up a sop. And there's more say that where women are concerned you couldn't trust a man until he's seven years dead.'[21] When Breda finally gets to the 'honey spike', her time has come, but the hospital is closed. The old porter takes pity on her and allows her into a shed where she can give birth. She has the child, but the old tinker-woman who assists cannot save her: 'I whispered in her ear and she went out the gap of life.'[22] Martin's final speech of grief is harrowing, as it mounts into a strange dignity of crazed loss:

Ye that are calm and still let me say this to ye. I'll take the child till Puck comes round again, and then, when time has done its best, we'll see what we can do. . . Cry her along the floor of heaven up to the footstool of the Livin' God. . . Cry her until the earth and sea and sky itself are full of travellers' tears.[23]

MacMahon, in the play, has deliberately chosen a theme which will allow him to create a broad tapestry of the whole of Ireland, including that harrowing reminder of border violence. His language, and the vitality of the dialogue, draw upon folklore and the eloquence and linguistic energy of the people of the roads. In him we encounter once more that fiery and brooding power, a capacity for shock and surprise, we see in that group of writers, almost a school, who come from the Listowel area of Co. Kerry.

MacMahon is better known as a novelist than as a writer of plays (indeed he turned *The Honey Spike* into a novel in 1967), nevertheless his two plays for the Abbey of the early 1960s, in their evocation of expansive imaginative arenas of experience and energy, their vivid depictions of country life, and their portrayals of visceral passion, mark him out as a serious dramatist, and one who, had not the denser and more cerebral effects of fiction proved more satisfying, could have developed into a playwright of the very highest order.

In 1962, the year after *The Honey Spike*, three new dramatists had their debut at the Abbey, three who were to become, in different ways, significant writers in the years ahead. One of these never achieved the international acclaim that was his due; the second attained national celebrity, but with only a grudging recognition of his talent; while the third turned out to be an Irish playwright of world stature. They were: Liam Lynch, with *Do Thrushes Sing in Birmingham?* (8 May); John B. Keane, with *Hut 42* (12 November); and Brian Friel, with *The Enemy Within* (6 August).

Do Thrushes Sing in Birmingham? is set in a boarding house in England. Paddy, a young man in search of a future, has just emigrated from Mayo, seeking to forget the misery and sadness of his family: a mother worn out from child-bearing and a father wrecked from work and drink. Of his father Paddy says: 'He's the grandest of men, no one can get as much out of the biteen of mountain-land we have but what he earns from the sweat of his body he hands over the counter of every pub in the village.'[24] However, in Act II any expectation that Paddy is an object of pity is dashed when he is revealed to be hard and unfeeling beneath his ready sentiment. He makes Lily, the serving girl, pregnant, and rejects her. In Act III he returns from a visit back home, where his extra money has ruined the family: 'the house was like a sty with the smell of sweat an' dirty clothes hangin' about the place.'[25] Lily has lost the child, and has been away in a convalescent home. She returns and Johnnie, Paddy's drinking partner, who loves the girl, wants to marry her, but she is in love with Paddy. The two men go on a binge for New Year's Eve, and Paddy is killed in a brawl. The ending is undramatic, but the writing conveys the force and shock of male violence. The play cuts against conventional characterizations: the emigrants are violent and pathetic, the women strong and resourceful; and both men and women are condemned to emotional patterns they find hard to break free from.

Brian Friel was born in Omagh, and grew up in Derry. After a period studying for the priesthood at Maynooth, he worked as a teacher, giving up in 1960 to devote himself full-time to writing. *The Enemy Within* was his first play to be professionally produced at the Abbey. Produced by Ria Mooney, and featuring Ray MacAnally as Columba, the play deals with the private life of the saint (also known as Colmcille) who is identified with the foundation of Derry city and the expansion of the Irish church's influence throughout Scotland and the islands of Britain and Ireland. Friel focuses on the conflict between Columba's love for Ireland and his desire to cultivate a spiritual life, free from the strong attractions of political and military involvement. He admits the fierce grip Ireland has on him, the overwhelming and terrible love of the place and a profound entanglement with its problems and enmities: 'I remember everything. The beech trees and the chestnuts and the flat, green plains and the silver of the Boyne water on a good summer's day.'[26] Eventually he renounces this attachment and chooses the life of the soul, cursing the expense of blood and sweat that is Ireland: 'You soaked my sweat! You sucked my blood! What more do you demand of me, damned Ireland? My soul? My immortal soul?'[27] Columba's rejection is, of course, not unrelated to Friel's own choices as an artist at this time, as he decided to follow his creative instinct and its lonely freedom, as against the trouble of a life immersed in society, fully engaged with its vociferations and demands. Furthermore, Columba's anger and frustration at the hold Ireland has on his emotional life reflect a dilemma that confronted many Irish intellectuals (and non-intellectuals) in the 1960s, a decade ferociously intent on modernization and internationalism. Many younger Irish men and women at that time had grown heartily sick of what Columba calls 'damned Ireland' and the jejune patriotism purveyed in the sanctimonies of priests and politicians of all parties. Indeed, at that time, many believed, with John Montague, that

> Puritan Ireland's dead and gone,
> A myth of O'Connor and O'Faolain.[28]

But it was not, needless to say. Puritan Ireland of the Protestant rather than the Catholic variety resurrected itself, with amazing and utterly unforeseen violence, in the northern conflict, as unionists reacted forcefully to what they considered to be the destruction of the purity and integrity of Northern Ireland. Whatever about Columba, and his choice of the way of the soul, Friel himself was far from finished with 'damned Ireland': his engagement with the renewed debate over identity, and the forms of government best fitted to represent it, was only beginning. The damnation (or purgatory, as Yeats saw it in 1938) of having to live through again the unresolved traumas of the Treaty and partition was to be the determining condition of cultural and artistic life in Ireland up to the end of the millennium, or at least to the ceasefires of the mid-1990s, and the Good Friday Agreement of 1998. Here, in Friel's early play, the 'damned' condition of Ireland is adduced only to dramatize Columba's rhetorical renunciation of it; but the matter was not to be so easily settled, as Friel himself well knew.

J. B. Keane was born in Listowel in 1928. He worked in a variety of jobs—as an assistant to a fowl-buyer, a chemist's help, a clerk, etc.—before settling down as a publican in his native town. One night, having returned from a performance of Joseph Tomelty's *All Souls' Night* by the Listowel Drama Group, he started writing his first major play, *Sive*, which was rejected by the Abbey. However the Listowel Drama Group won the All-Ireland Drama Finals with it in 1959, and it featured on Radio Éireann as well as on the Abbey stage as the winning play.

Hut 42 was accepted by the Abbey and produced on 12 November 1962. It deals with the contemporary social reality of emigration, and is partly based on Keane's own experience as an emigrant worker in England, also the background to his musical play *Many Young Men of Twenty* (produced in Cork and at the Olympia, Dublin, 1961).

The Man from Clare was first produced by the Southern Theatre Group at the Fr. Matthew Hall in Cork in July 1962, and then was accepted for production at the Abbey (5 August 1963). A Gaelic football team from Cuas in Co. Clare cross the Shannon to play their old rivals at Bealabann in north Co. Kerry. Padraic O'Dea, the man from Clare, is the star of the team from Cuas, but his days as a champion are numbered: in the game, which the Claremen lose, he plays badly and is outclassed by Jim Flynn, the rising hero. There is a wild night of drinking and carousing during which Flynn and O'Dea fight and O'Dea takes a terrible battering. However, O'Dea, who has never paid court to a girl, proposes to Nellie Brick, a plain-looking ex-nun, and has his offer accepted. It is a formless play, and there is little attention given to the motivation behind the actions and words of the characters: for example, O'Dea at first refuses Flynn's challenge, then changes his mind, but there is little attempt to show what lies behind this renewal of courage. The motivation remains arbitrary, inscrutable. In part this suddenness is the strength of the play, as it is of much of Keane's theatre. People act precipitately, like surges of natural energy. And their speech communicates this force with a surprising and, at times, shocking eloquence. Here is Padraic O'Dea on the women of Clare, as he explains to Nellie why he does not bother with them: 'the ones that don't show themselves off at all are ones with collops like thighs and thighs like bellies by them an' thick red legs with rings o' fat on their ankles so much that the whole lot of' em would turn a man totally against women.'[29] As in the other writers of the Listowel 'school', such as George Fitzmaurice, Bryan MacMahon, and Brendan Kennelly, there is, in Keane, a relish in wildness and fantasy, and a rich and irreverent humour. Daigan, O'Dea's mentor, says of fear

Daigan. Sure, there's nothing to be afraid of in this world. I was only afraid of three things in my life.
Padraic. What?
Daigan. Rusty blades, casky porter an' parish priests' housekeepers. . . Come on![30]

Here Keane is wittily using the old Irish convention of the triad, whereby three things are linked together in surprising juxtaposition, but in this case the tradition is given a more than usually bizarre breadth of reference.

The Man from Clare was directed by the long-suffering Ria Mooney, who resigned as producer of plays in 1963, the year in which this play was staged. Frank Dermody had been working as a film director with Gabriel Pascal's Irish Film Company since 1947; he returned in 1956 as a guest director, to stage Tomás Mac Anna's play *Winter Wedding* (26 November), and from then on staged occasional productions. When Ria Mooney resigned he was appointed senior play-director, allowing Mac Anna to concentrate on Irish plays and set design, although he too would sometimes do work in English.[31] Blythe and the board retained control of all matters relating to the selection of plays and the hiring and firing of actors. Indeed at this time and before written contracts were unknown; as Mac Anna put it: 'the word of Blythe was all you got.' Contracts only came in with the new theatre in 1967.[32] Essentially, we are dealing here with a 'top-down' style of management, with its origins in the hieratic style of Yeats and Lady Gregory, which Blythe translated into a mild version of a Stalinist bureaucracy. It was a style of management that continued into the Abbey's reincarnation in the new building in 1966, and was to persist into the 1990s. The longevity of this overweening kind of management was, to some extent, facilitated by the development, in the 1980s, of a fetish for authoritarian methods of compelling and motivating subordinates in the public and private sectors. So that, in a curious way, Blythe's dictatorial approach to the direction of the Abbey's activities anticipated so-called modern managerialism. As ever, its effects were disastrous: a company of creative people cannot be run by a board under a chairman who continually tells them what to do. A board and a chairman who do not allow as much freedom to their employees as is consistent with probity and efficiency will invariably produce a culture of wariness and cynicism, which in turn will result in fatigue and frustration. Ria Mooney resigned, but not before she had suffered a breakdown in her physical and mental well-being. An environment where there is no trust destroys the soul.

On 3 September 1963 Eamon de Valera, as President of Ireland, laid the foundation stone of the new Abbey Theatre. Present were the Taoiseach, Seán Lemass, Mrs W. B. Yeats, and Gerard Fay, son of Frank Fay. Past and present actors and directors who were also there included Fred Johnson, Ria Mooney, Eileen Crowe, and Siobhán McKenna. The stone was inscribed with the names of Yeats, Lady Gregory, Synge, and the two Fay brothers, but the names of Edward Martyn and Miss Horniman were omitted. The new building opened on 18 July 1966, exactly fifteen years after the fire. Why did it take so long? Michael Scott, who had designed the Peacock Theatre in 1927, was appointed as architect, the French theatre designer Pierre Sonrel acting as consultant. Scott's instructions were to design a theatre with a proscenium arch which would accommodate 650 people, and an experimental theatre to seat 150. Dublin Corporation refused planning permission to the proposal that the main theatre be built over the smaller one, and this meant that additional space was required. It now became essential that the Abbey purchase the Abbey Bar, Tommy Lennon's public house next door; and he, needless to say, pressed them for the best price he could get. His premises were valued at £7,000 but this did not prevent him from demanding £40,000. It took until 1957 for these negotiations to conclude, Lennon eventually wearing down the opposition and getting them to settle on a figure of £32,000. And a tobacconist, also adjoining, struck a tough bargain too. All the time the government's Department of Finance was proving most reluctant to countenance what they considered (rightly) to be opportunistic sharp practice on the part of the business people

whose properties it was essential for the Abbey to acquire, with the result that de-
lays were unavoidable while building costs spiralled. Meanwhile Scott was eager
to extend the design even further, and incorporate a site on the river front at Eden
Quay, which would give Dublin one of the best theatre complexes in the world,
but his plan would have involved yet more negotiations with cagey landlords and
tenants. Blythe vetoed this proposal, and pressed Scott to come up with a work-
able plan that could be carried through quickly. In 1959 revised plans were approved by the Corporation and estimates submitted to government, which voted
a sum of £25,000 towards the cost of the new theatre, now running in the region
of £385,000. In February 1962 tenders were invited and in June the contract was
awarded to A. J. Jennings & Co., who submitted the lowest bid. Meanwhile the
company's accumulated deficit at the Queen's Theatre was £33,000; it was to rise
to about £70,000 by 1966.

Further problems lay ahead. In 1964 the Abbey were asked to present O'Casey's
Juno and the Paycock and his *The Plough and the Stars* as part of a World Theatre
Season in London. O'Casey had, in 1958, withdrawn permission for his plays to
be performed in Ireland or by Irish players. This was a protest against John
Charles McQuaid, Archbishop of Dublin, who had refused to allow a votive mass
to be offered at the cultural festival (An Tóstal) which was to feature O'Casey's
The Drums of Father Ned. O'Casey's interdict was one of the reasons for the
Abbey's deficit, as his plays were always box-office successes. Now, however, he relented, and the Dublin plays were seen again at the Queen's preparatory to their
prestigious London showing. But the actors, whose salaries had been frozen for
years and whose contract status was, to say the least, irregular, decided to strike
just before their opening at the Aldwych, in London, with the support of the Irish
Transport and General Workers Union. Dr. C. S. Andrews was appointed media-
tor by the Irish Labour Court and Blythe, reluctantly, agreed to enter negotiations
which Andrews chaired. The strike was called off and the London performances
went ahead, but the expectations aroused by the Abbey players' return to
O'Casey in the full glare of international publicity were disappointed. O'Casey
himself laid the blame squarely at the door of Ernest Blythe: 'Let them think what
they like, but the Directors have been dead for years. They know nothing at all
about acting or the drama. No more does Ernest Blythe who may be a good manager, but who is an absolute monarch. All the Directors do is what he tells them.'[33]
O'Casey died shortly after this controversy (on 18 September 1964), which ran for
days in the Dublin papers.

C. S. Andrews's enquiry into the terms and conditions of the players greatly ex-
ceeded his initial brief. He concluded that the Abbey should be completely taken
over by the state and run by a government-appointed board. James Ryan, the
Minister of Finance, did not accept this recommendation, although he did sub-
stantially accept Andrews's proposals to improve the actors' working conditions
and career structures. Ryan also decided that, in order to make the Abbey board
less hermetically sealed and self-perpetuating, the number of shareholders be

increased: since 1924, when Robinson was made a director, the number of share-holders had varied, but the majority remained in the hands of the directors. Ryan also decided that the government should have the power to nominate two directors to the board instead of one. Blythe consented to these instructions, anticipating (correctly) that the pill diluting his personal authority would be sweetened by extra finance from the Minister. In 1964 the directors forwarded, to the Minister, forty names as possible new shareholders, nominations responding to Ryan's suggestion that they should be people of recognized artistic or creative achievements. Twenty-five were selected and included playwrights such as Máiréad Ni Ghráda, Bryan MacMahon, Brian Friel, and Seán Ó Tuama, as well as actors and directors such as Cyril Cusack, Ria Mooney, and Denis O'Dea. In July 1965 Walter Macken was appointed as the second governmental director, the other one remaining Dr Séamus Wilmot.

The background to all this manœuvring and artistic politicking was the steadily rising deficit, and the increasing costs of the building work, now under way. At one point it seemed as if the experimental theatre, the Peacock, adjoining the new Abbey was to be abandoned but the new shareholders, at their inaugural meeting in May 1965, declared that a national theatre without an experimental adjunct could not function effectively. This resolve from a body it itself had in-stalled persuaded the government to relax the constraints it was trying to impose.

The enlarged Irish National Theatre Society now attempted to curtail the authority of the managing director by the appointment of an artistic director. This Blythe bitterly opposed. At a meeting of the enlarged board on 15 May 1965 at Wynn's Hotel, the concept of an 'artistic adviser' was broached; the chairman, Roibeárd Ó Faracháin, declared that an artistic director with full powers would leave the directors without a function. The matter was left there until Brian Friel, one of the new shareholders, raised the issue again on 9 October. It was agreed that the matter be placed on the agenda for the next meeting, which took place on 4 December. Friel was absent, and the board adopted a resolution welcoming the appointment of Walter Macken as assistant manager and artistic adviser.[34] The artistic adviser would function on a consultative basis, and report to the board. Macken, the government director, declared that he would approach his duties in an entirely collaborative manner. He took up office in November 1965 but re-signed in June the following year, on the grounds that 'he was not the man for the job'. He agreed to remain as second government director until the new theatre opened the following year. To replace him Mícheál Ó hAodha, head of drama at Radio Telefís Éireann, was appointed as director, while Tomás Mac Anna took over the post of artistic adviser in December 1966. There was a good deal of dis-content amongst the shareholders at this move, which was seen as a tactical one, by Blythe, to retain his influence, he and Mac Anna having had a good working re-lationship over the years at the Queen's Theatre.

The last pantomime at the Queen's Theatre was *Emer agus an Laoch* (28 December 1965) written and directed by Tomás Mac Anna with the help of the poet and novelist Eoghan Ó Tuairisc, who had been involved as an on-the-spot writer since 1955. These pantomimes were a team-effort, with actors, the writers, the composer, Mac Anna, and often Blythe himself participating in the day-to-day development of the shows. Ó Tuairisc (also well known as a writer in English as Eugene Rutherford Watters) described the enjoyable and creative atmosphere in which the pantomimes were put together in the Gaelic magazine *Comhar* in 1977:

Tomás directing everything. Him sitting at a table at the side of the stage, his secretary beside him jotting down notes, while a scene is being rehearsed, people around practising dance-steps, or at the piano with Seán Ó Riada going through songs, another fellow in the corner trying to walk on stilts, another two in another corner learning Irish words. . . and me in another corner of the stage writing fast and to order as the need arose. A shout from Tomás: 'Ó Tuairisc six lines for the giant. . . Verse, please, and let it be funny by the way. . .' I'd write out the verse, three copies, one for the giant, another for Tomás, another upstairs to Blythe who'd examine the grammar carefully. . . the saw and the hammer increasing the cacophony. . . 'Ó Tuairisc, what song did the sirens sing?' No one knows. And then, someone (I think it was Ray MacAnally) suggests a pop-song of the day: 'Come Along-a my House'.[35]

Ó Tuairisc is here describing the compilation of *Ulysses agus Penelope* (26 December 1955), but the working methods remained just as enjoyable and stimulating in the years that followed. The pantomines were festive occasions for actors as well as for the audience, and there is little doubt that they provided a valuable opportunity for the company to work together in a relaxed and trusting way. *Emer agus an Laoch* is fairly typical of these pantomimes staged at the old Abbey, the Queen's, and the new Abbey for some years after it opened in 1966. In this one Cú Chulainn is born at the start of the play and it is said that 'his fame will last as long as grass will grow, water run, or the cost of living increase'. Or says Bricriu: 'Until *Tolka Row* will come to an end on Telefís Éireann'.[36] *Tolka Row* was a long-running and very popular series on Irish television. There is also some hefty punning on geas/taboo with jokes about Calor Gas. Or there were topical references to B-Specials, Ian Smith, Dickie Rock (an Irish showband star) as Dicí Carraig. The issue of partition and the, at that time, apparently quiescent issue of the north surface in this story of Cú Chulainn and Emer. Medbh's Connacht forces invade the province to the tune of 'Slattery's Mounted Foot' by Percy French. The wit is clumsy. Although these shows were written for children nevertheless the topical, knowing, and fairly leaden references were meant to keep the adults amused. It is quite clear, from *Emer agus an Laoch* and the other pantomines, that enjoyable as they may have been to put on, and valuable as they were as exercises in corporate morale, they leave a good deal to be desired as works of theatre, no matter how ephemeral.

On 9 July 1966 the Abbey company gave its final performance at the Queen's, which was soon to be demolished.

6

1966–1985

'History is personal'

It was a race against time for the new Abbey to open on 18 July. All kinds of difficulties surfaced. It turned out that the Abbey's patent had run out after the fire in 1951, and its renewal had been overlooked. Problems about being licensed for performance might be overcome, but permission to sell drink was another matter. For a time the grim prospect presented itself of there being no bar on the opening night; the authorities relented and a temporary licence was issued. The electricians trying to finalize the installation of the lighting system threatened to strike if the actors rehearsing the opening show dared to set foot upon the stage; the sound system came to life only half an hour before curtain up.

A fanfare of trumpets heralded the inauguration of the new theatre and President Eamon de Valera declared it open. Seaghan Barlow, the stage carpenter and erstwhile part-time actor, now 86 years of age, struck the gong that had been salvaged from the old building, and the performance began. This was *Recall the Years* by Walter Macken, the artistic adviser, and was what would now be termed a multi-media celebration and record of the theatre's past successes and controversies, including the riots about the *Playboy* and *The Plough and the Stars*, and the case taken against the Abbey players in Philadelphia for producing the 'blasphemous' *Playboy*. This compilation was intended to reveal the variety of effects which the new theatre was capable of, but as Tomás Mac Anna described it, there were many, unintentionally comic, hitches: 'the news stopped right in the middle of announcing King Edward's death and Miss Horniman's huff, away back in 1910. . . Then the sound went.' The performance included staged extracts from, among others, *The Countess Cathleen*, Yeats and Moore's *Diarmuid and Grania*, Russell's *Deirdre*, *Cathleen Ni Houlihan*, *In the Shadow of the Glen*, *Spreading the News*, and *The Playboy*.[1]

The new building, it is generally agreed, is ugly on the outside, being a fairly typical example of 1960s brutalism influenced by the need to make economies in materials and finish. Inside, however, it is a different story. The auditorium, which is fan-shaped, can hold 628, a size which, at the time, was thought to be too small for a theatre with the prestige of a national institution. Now, however, it is eminently clear that a larger auditorium would have been a liability, as theatre design has altered to adjust to changes in the theatregoing habits of city-dwellers. Fewer people go to the theatre now than did so in the 1950s and 1960s, and when they do go they expect an intimate theatre environment and sophisticated effects. The new theatre's equipment was state of the art at the time and, because it was constructed with foresight, allows for modification and adaptation. The stage has a fore-stage on lifts that can descend to form an orchestra-pit; the stage-floor itself can be raised or lowered or cantilevered in sections or together; the lighting and sound rooms are at the back of the auditorium so the engineers can see what they are doing from the vantage of the audience; the lighting was extensive and flexible; and the ceiling (which fell down when it was being fitted) can be moved, so that lights can be recessed at great height. However Tomás Mac Anna is firmly of the view that the new building is a 'monstrosity': it has poor acoustics, no intimacy, 'just four walls dead as mutton'. As for atmosphere, 'no self-respecting theatre ghost would find himself (or herself) dead in the place'.[2]

The Peacock did not open until 23 July 1967. The ceremony was conducted by Charles J. Haughey, Minister of Finance, someone very supportive of the arts in Ireland during his long political career, then in its early stages. The Peacock had 157 seats and a very flexible staging structure, whereby all sorts of spatial possibilities could be explored.

The building, which is four storeys high, also contains rehearsal rooms, administrative offices, and a board room on the third floor, and features a roof terrace. There is a private suite on the balcony, used by the President of the Republic and other distinguished guests. The side walls of planked pine in the auditorium are sound-reflecting and designed to provide maximum acoustic efficiency.

What were the policies and objectives this theatre set out to implement? At extraordinary general meetings held at Wynn's Hotel on 8 and 15 May 1965 a number of policy resolutions were adopted. These included statements on: financial matters, urging that the government clear the present overdraft; the obligation the Abbey had to serve only the 'highest artistic standards' as a national theatre; the need to mix Irish and foreign plays; the desirability that producers be given the opportunity to work abroad; the importance of a training school in the new Abbey; the necessity of touring; and the need to improve conditions of work, both material and financial, for the actors. All of these aspirations are, needless to say, unexceptional. In the commemorative programme produced for the reopening Roibeárd Ó Faracháin, Chairman of the board of directors, was given the task of writing the renewed aims of the Abbey. It does not make especially inspiring reading, although, to be fair, it is hard to rise to this kind of occasion—a Yeats or a Lady Gregory was called for, someone able to imbue rhetoric with vision. What Ó Faracháin provided was sentiment, goodwill, and reverence.

The National Theatre Society will 'begin again'; they come to the new building 'gratefully'; the Abbey will rededicate itself to its role of being a 'hospitable home' for Irish theatre; it will continue the 'tradition'; it will make fruitful use of the Peacock as a nursery for new talent, and for remustering Yeatsian verse drama; Gaelic theatre will be promoted; and the Abbey school will be re-established. These statements are worthy and valuable, and at an inaugural occasion such as that which took place on the evening of 18 July these were what was required. But there is little pressure of thought or emotion behind these sentiments. They are entirely anodyne and formal. We should not, however, be too critical of Ó Faracháin. If the debate that ran in The *Irish Times* from 18 to 20 July is in any way indicative of the level of thinking about the aims and objectives the new Abbey should set itself then it is very clear that there was an extraordinary dearth of originality in current thinking about what a national theatre should be or do. The debate involved individuals who should have known something about such matters: directors—Hilton Edwards of the Gate, Jim Fitzgerald of the Abbey and elsewhere, Tomás Mac Anna of the Abbey, Barry Cassin, a freelance, an actor, T. P. McKenna, and the *Irish Times* drama critic Seamus Kelly.

The debate makes dispiriting reading. Mac Anna wonders if the writers are there to sustain the new Abbey; he thinks the classics of the Irish theatre should be played; he is convinced that doing Brecht is a good thing; and the new theatre will 'communicate something theatrically'. Hilton Edwards's response to this latter point is heartening: 'I've been aware of this for thirty-five years, and look where I am now. In a feature in The *Irish Times*.'[3] Edwards, in fact, is very sensible. He holds that one must retain what is best in what is traditional, and that everything comes down to dedication and cash, two factors permanently in short supply. And while others stress content, youth, and European drama, he emphasizes technique. Fitzgerald longs for English and European daring (Max Frisch and Peter Brook keep surfacing throughout the debate), denies the value of tradition for young players, and, as a 'good Marxist', thinks that actors should have short-term contracts. He also wants the universities to be involved. Barry Cassin barely enters the discussion, save to call for theatre scholarships to be set up. T. P. McKenna has lots to say but it seems to boil down to two fairly self-evident truths: a theatre needs writers and an audience, so the Abbey will need these. McKenna also admires the recently funded English National Theatre; and, like Fitzgerald, he thinks European plays and involvement by the universities would be good things.

If this is a representative sampling of the thinking about theatre current in Dublin in 1966 it will be evident that the Abbey itself had a crucial role to play in developing a culture of critical and informed opinion about what theatre was, how it acted upon the individual, and the relationship between its representations and the society it represented. A paragraph from any of Yeats's writing in *Samhain* or from one of the short prefaces by Synge has more self-awareness and consequence than the entire contents of this tedious 'debate'.

When Tomás Mac Anna directed *Recall the Years*, he had assistance from Frank Dermody and Edward Golden. Dermody produced the first new play at the new Abbey, Louis MacNeice's *One for the Grave*, a strange choice. MacNeice died in 1963. He had worked as a radio producer in the BBC, but was an admired and respected poet and writer of radio plays. Born in Belfast in 1907, the son of a Church of Ireland bishop, he was educated at Marlborough public school and at Oxford. He is often grouped with W. H. Auden and Stephen Spender, and characterized as one of the 'poets of the 1930s', but he is now recognized as a major Irish writer, all the more compelling because of his mixed allegiances to Ireland and Britain. The double inheritance is well represented in *One for the Grave*, a modern morality play closely modelled on the late medieval English morality *Everyman*, which had its first performance in Ireland's new National Theatre.

One for the Grave was written in 1960–1, but never fully completed. Although based on the famous medieval predecessor, its conception was entirely modern and innovative. Everyman has died, or is in the process of dying. He is being judged in the afterlife, and his behaviour, his mental and emotional attitudes, his motivations, and his integrity are subjected to interrogation, using the format of a live television show, an 'actuality show', very much in the mould of the popular English TV series of the time, hosted by the Irishman Eamonn Andrews, *This is your Life*.

The play is typical of MacNeice, concerned as it is with questions of personal integrity and what constitutes correct action. The form of the modernized morality allows him to present these issues very directly; and the contemporary idiom he employed, where the Floor Manager acts as God's interrogating angel, increases the theatrical impact. Dermody also made full use of different stage levels to suggest, for example, the Director's raised box with its consoles, and heaven. The confusion of modern life, with its distractions, preoccupations, and forgetfulness, are suggested in the rapid verse couplets of the character called Career, who asks Everyman:

> What is it you propose to do:
> (*very fast*) To build a new town or destroy an old
> Or found a college or a zoo
> Or turn a screw or dissect a mouse
> Or launch a rocket or sell a pup
> Or breed a team for the Davis cup
> Or chart the stars on screen or sky
> Or manage a bank or write an ad
> Or cook an account or an oyster pie
> Or make a film of the Shropshire Lad
> Or gather plankton from the brine
> Or drill for oil or lift a face
> Or start one more uranium mine. . .[4]

Sean Bull, the stereotypical Irish tenor, extols the virtues of Irish (or Scotch) whiskey in a sequence devoted to exploring the manifold illusions of the world of advertisements, consumerism, and television as he sings the following to the air of 'The Rose of Tralee':

> The green moon is settin' beyond the dark pylon
> But still in ould Ireland the whiskey flows free,
> With all the colleens wearin' stockin's of nylon
> And Father O'Flynn rollin' down to the sea. . .
> (*Speaking, in brogue*) Dhrink Irish whiskey—
> (*Speaking, in Scots*) When ye canny get Scotch.[5]

While there may not have been, in the Abbey's opening years, anything remotely resembling an agreed artistic policy intended to carry vision into reality, nevertheless the opportunities for experimental staging and lighting in the new theatre led to considerable achievements in directing and imaginative effect. In this context Tomás Mac Anna's background in drama in Irish, where he was encouraged by Blythe to mount Gaelic versions of European masterpieces, stood him in good stead. This training meant that he enjoyed some limited freedom from the all-too-easily formulaic method of Abbey naturalism. Mac Anna was eager to make the best use of the Abbey's physical resources to show what a modern theatre can achieve in its physical realizations of situation and emotion denied to film and television.

In these years some of the most notable theatrical successes were adaptations of novels, in which flexible staging, lighting, and other effects were used to present the private density of effect fiction achieves in a theatrical context. The first of these adaptations was P. J. O'Connor's version of Patrick Kavanagh's *Tarry Flynn* (2 November 1966), directed by Mac Anna, with the young Donal McCann playing the lead.

An experiment in another direction was the staging of Dion Boucicault's *The Shaughraun* (31 January 1967), with Hugh Hunt returning to direct for the theatre for the first time since he had left in 1938. The part of Conn the Shaughraun was played by Cyril Cusack, also returning to the new Abbey, and the play proved a remarkable popular and critical success. Boucicault's play, first performed in 1875, was written to feature the playwright himself in the part of Conn. Its mixture of melodrama and political intrigue (it is strongly pro-Fenian) as well as the opportunity for flamboyant and colourful acting it provided meant that the Abbey company was here rediscovering one of the masters of the Irish stage from before the establishment of the Irish Literary Theatre in 1899. Furthermore, the play was given an entirely traditional production, even re-creating successfully the footlit theatre of the Victorian period and of the old Queen's in its heyday.

Siobhán McKenna also returned to the Abbey for its production of Brian Friel's *The Loves of Cass McGuire* (10 April 1967), directed by Tomás Mac Anna. The play had already opened in New York the previous year, directed by Hilton Edwards, with Ruth Gordon in the title role. McKenna played the ferocious Cass, who is characterized by Friel as follows on her first entrance: 'Ugly is too strong a word to describe her, and plain not nearly strong enough.'[6]

Friel's staging here, as in his earlier play *Philadelphia, Here I Come* (1964, Abbey production 1972), is adventurous but entirely in line with the theme of the play. Cass McGuire, an Irish-American, has returned to Ireland after fifty-two years working as a waitress near Skid Row in New York. She has a 'past'. She tells her story directly to the audience, and her contact with them is her hold on reality. At first she is put up in her brother Harry's house, but her unpredictable and violent behaviour and drunkenness become too much for Harry and his family, and they put her into the Eden nursing home. The staging is such that the main playing area serves as both the common-room in the old people's home and the living room of the McGuire family. The action brilliantly intersects Cass's narration of events with enactments of those events themselves; she tries to hold on to her version of what happened and her authority while the action unfolding on stage shows her becoming a victim to her own wilfulness and rage, as well as her increasing senility. The stagecraft is most impressive and the new Abbey was a perfect vehicle for its realization. In the following Harry has heard about Cass's violent outburst the previous night and confronts her with it; she is both with him in his house and at the same time in the nursing home telling her story. The action bristles with excitement and surprise:

Harry. I've just been told what happened this morning, Cass.
Cass. So now you know it all.
Harry. And I will not have you insult Alice about her father.
Cass. Harry's four kids, boy, they got on good: Betty, she's a doc in London, and Tom's a
   priest, and Aidan's an architect, and Dan—
Harry. But this is only the last of many, many insults. . .
Cass. (*unable to hold her own line*) So I left a note for momma and one for Connie. . .

Cass is remembering the circumstances of her leaving. This memory collides with the pain of the rejection taking place now and she, in the words of Friel's stage direction, '*cannot fight the memory any longer. She suddenly wheels wildly round to him. She almost screams her lines.* Say out what you're trying to say, Harry! Speak up and say it out straight!'

   Cass McGuire's attempt to suppress the searing pain of the conjunction of painful memories is counterpointed, in the Eden home, by the manner in which two other inmates, Trilbe and Ingram, try to blot out reality by living in the world of Wagner's *Tristan und Isolde*, a golden anaesthesia of fantasy. Again, the dramatic structure is such that Friel underlines his point about this attempt to erase memory by intercutting Cass's urgent narration's with their poetic delusions. The problem being anatomized is a human one, but it has political dimensions, all the more forceful for being implicit: Friel's entire preoccupation is with how the past is recalled; in the Ireland of the 1960s, which saw the fiftieth anniversary of the Easter Rising and the related recrudescence of the unsettled question of the partition of Ireland, the social and political amnesia necessary to cope with unresolved matters pertaining to freedom, justice, and the nature of civil and political representation was lifting. *Cass McGuire* is a play in which historical memory insists on being recalled. She cannot cope with this recollection and eventually submits to the allure of Wagnerian fantasy. One of the achievements of Friel, and he manages it very early in his work as a playwright, is to create a theatre which becomes an arena for this recall and judgement of memory. Cass's link with sanity, the way in which she keeps a hold on her story, is the relationship between her and her audience, the people sitting in the dark of the auditorium. As the ungovernable nature of her scarred past becomes ever more insistent, she loses her capacity as a storyteller and becomes a fantasist, unable to sustain a proper connection with the texture of reality. Her condition, but this is implied always, never spelt out, is an emblem for the condition of a colonized country, incapable of resisting the soft attractions of amnesia. In a sense this play, in its depth of resonance, and its invitation to reflect on the nature of the past and its influence on the present, is a mature re-creation of the kind of theatre imagined and realized by Yeats and Synge.

On 31 July *Red Roses for Me*, O'Casey's play about the 1913 lockout strike, was produced, but the success of the year was Frank MacMahon's adaptation of Brendan Behan's *Borstal Boy* (10 October 1967), directed by Tomás Mac Anna. This production made full and elaborate use of the Abbey's complex lighting rig: a bare stage allowed for total absorption in the character of Behan himself, split between his younger and older selves, while the lighting concentrated on atmosphere, shadow, and mood. Here again, as with *Cass McGuire*, the real subject was memory, and its corollary, continuity between past experience and present reality. Added to this was Behan's spendthrift personality, his energy, his talent, and his undaunted republicanism; this mixture was both an enquiry into and a record of the intensity of nationalism and its effects upon a deeply creative personality, while also celebrating Behan's ebullient humanity. The older Behan was played, with uncanny accuracy, by the great actor Niall Tóibín, and his younger self by Frank Grimes.

The new Peacock Theatre was to be, amongst other things, a nursery for theatre in Irish. In 1958 Blythe wrote:

It is proposed when the new Abbey is erected to use the Peacock . . . mainly . . . for the production of plays in Irish . . . The Directors are satisfied that it is only in a smaller theatre run in conjunction with the Abbey that really first-class dramatic work in the Irish language can be hoped for.[7]

The Peacock, when it opened, began with another adaptation (by Seán Ó Briain) of a novel, this time of Flann O'Brien's comic masterpiece *An Béal Bocht* (26 July 1967), first published in 1941. The production was by Frank Dermody. The work set an irreverent, gleeful tone. A satire on the Gaelic movement, it takes the autobiographical genre of Irish-language writing, as in Tomás Ó Criomhthain's superb *An tOileánach* (*The Islandman*), and subjects it to the most cruel humour by pushing the conventions of the form to absurd lengths. In the typical Blasket-island autobiographical narrative (another example is Muiris Ó Suilleabháin's *Fiche Blian ag Fás, Twenty Years Agrowing*) the harshness and bleakness of a life lived at subsistence level are conveyed with a kind of Sophoclean aloofness from the hardship; in O'Brien (and in the adaptation) this aloofness is turned into a kind of dumb vacancy, as if to say: these people are so reduced that they are unconscious of what has happened to them, and of how miserable their existence is. A ferocity underlies the humour, a pity disturbs the hilarity. And through it all there drives a relentless awareness that these are people on the verge of extinction; they are marginalized by loss; and they have no sense of who or what they are. There was an uproar over this production, and it was withdrawn after the opening night.

Later in the season Tomás Ó Murchadha, a young producer from Cork, made his directorial debut with Séamus Ó Néill's *Faill ar an bhFeart* (9 October 1967) at the Peacock. The play was another reappraisal of the consequences of history, in this case dealing with the United Irishmen rebellion of 1798. The Reverend Seamus Póirtéir is a Presbyterian minister at Grey Abbey, Co. Down, who writes in support of the United Irishmen in their Ulster newspaper, the *Northern Star*. His son Alastar is a member of the organization and joins in the rising. The Battle of Ballinahinch takes place, off stage; Alastar survives the conflict but his father is arrested when he refuses to co-operate with the authorities who are hunting down the young man. Póirtéir is tried, and on the evidence of lying witnesses condemned to be hanged as a traitor. Although a worthy attempt at historical drama by a respected novelist in Irish (Ó Néill came from Co. Down, and much of his work reflects his concerns with the roots of sectarian conflict), nevertheless the play does not convey anything of the pressure and urgency of events as they unfold.

This rehearsal, in fairly obvious terms, of the trauma of a crucial phase of Irish history was followed by the first production at the Abbey, in the Peacock Theatre, of the work of Samuel Beckett, a writer deeply enmeshed in the tangles and confusions of the past as they work upon memory and the present. The pieces were *Play* and *Film*. *Play* was directed by Edward Golden, a member of the company. *Film* was a showing of a short cinematic piece Beckett had made with Buster Keaton in New York in 1964. These are examples of Beckett's later work, which strives for the starkest and most uncompromising minimalism, where character is reduced to the briefest utterances, and voices insistently repeat their formulaic, and invariably futile, attempts to remember correctly what was said and done. Indeed *Film* is completely silent save for one 'shh', uttered by Keaton. There is no need to labour the pertinence and challenge of these 'shorts' to Irish society of the 1960s when there was, on the one hand, fairly rhapsodic celebrations of the legacy of the 1916 rebellion; while on the other there was a profound questioning of the relevance and complexity of remembrance itself. Confident memorializing invariably proceeds on the assumption that what we think reality is is fairly unproblematic: the past happened as people say it did. However, Beckett's rebuking presence, in modern European as much as modern Irish culture, is an insistence that reality (as he once put it) isn't that kind of girl, and that what is recalled may involve as deep a fictionalizing as the headiest romantic fantasy.

Máiréad Ní Ghráda had written plays in Irish for the Gate and the Abbey since *An Udhacht* (22 April, 1931, the Gate), which became one of the most popular

Gaelic one-act plays for amateurs for many years. Directed by Mícheál Mac Liammóir, it dealt with the classic Irish and international theme concerning wills and the competing claims of family members. Ní Ghráda, before this time, had been a teacher, then Ernest Blythe's secretary in the first Dáil and during the Civil War. In 1920 she was imprisoned in Mountjoy Jail for selling flags for the Gaelic League, at that time an illegal organization. She was a member of An Comhar Drámaíochta, the body annexed by Blythe in the 1940s, back in the 1920s. She worked, thereafter, as an editor for Brown & Nolan, publishers, as a scriptwriter and editor on Radio Éireann, and she continued to write plays. Her most successful play, *An Triail* (22 September 1964), was produced at the Irish-language theatre An Damer, which had been established in 1955 by Gael-Linn. Gael-Linn was an organization founded in 1953 to promote the Irish language by practical means, including the channelling of resources to the Gaeltacht areas, Irish-language industrialization, and an ambitious cultural programme devoted to music, handicrafts, and the theatre. Ní Ghráda, the writer and broadcaster Seán Mac Réamoinn, and Siobhán McKenna were amongst the *animateurs* of a Gaelic drama movement, seeking to do for the Irish language what the Gate had done for European drama and what the Abbey (in spite of its Gaelicized title) was failing to do, to a great extent. Ní Ghráda's *An Triail*, which in the writing had the benefit of close advice from Tomás Mac Anna (who also directed the play), dealt with a feature of Irish society which was, during the 1960s, becoming an outrage: the inhumane treatment and public shame experienced by unmarried mothers. The play created an extraordinary impact: even Harold Hobson, the reviewer for the *Sunday Times*, who was ignorant of Irish, found it very moving.

Breithiúnas (10 February 1968), directed by Tomás Mac Anna in the Peacock, was Ní Ghráda's last play. Mac Anna produced it in the round, in the centre of the Peacock's acting space, so that the audience surrounded the actors. He also used mirrors, to heighten, in the manner of Brecht, the audience's self-consciousness, their awareness that they were in a theatre watching a version of reality, coming to a judgement about characters, history, and themselves.

The play deals with the character of Marcas de Grás, a politician who enjoys the reputation of having had a heroic past in the Anglo-Irish War of Independence. He is now dying, and the play is a re-enactment of his history: once again we see the Abbey, in these years, drawn to the theme of memory, judgement, and the appraisal of the past. His wife, his mistress, his sons—all recall their experiences of de Grás; the sons, in particular, are tormented by their recollection of how they disappointed him. Gearóid recalls how his father taunted him into riding a wild horse in a circus once:

You made me get up on the bloody horse and he tearing around in circles, out of control. 'Don't be a funk', you said. . . while I shrank with fear. And you, terrified, that someone would say you had a son a coward. You, the hero, the brave soldier who fought the British on your own. I got dizzy, then, and I fell off.[8]

But it turns out that de Grás himself was a coward during the Civil War, and that his reputation rests on false reports. Here, in this play, and in the more celebrated *An Triail*, Ní Ghráda raised fundamental questions about the quality of the moral integrity the Irish state had retained from its founding acts. These were deeply probing plays, of a piece with the best achievements of the 1960s by Friel, Thomas Murphy, and Thomas Kilroy.

Tomás Ó Murchadha, a trainee producer at the Abbey from 1967, directed *The Tailor and Ansty* (3 October 1968), with the brilliant actor Eamon Kelly playing the part of Timothy Buckley, the Tailor. This play was another adaptation, this time of Eric Cross's book of the same title, which had caused an uproar when first published in 1942. It was then banned under the Censorship Act for its supposed obscenity and blasphemy, although it did no more than memorialize the vivid speech and anecdotes of a west Cork *seanchaí* from Gougane Barra. When the book appeared it provided an occasion for a bout of communal indignation at the highest level: it was debated in the Irish Senate (or upper house of parliament), and a priest turned up at Buckley's doorstep demanding that the book be burned. P. J. O'Connor's adaptation and Ó Murchadha's stage realization captured the humour and comedy of the Tailor's speech; the success the play enjoyed revealed that the Ireland of the 1960s was a vastly different place from that of the 1940s. *The Tailor and Ansty* went on tour and also transferred to the main theatre of the Abbey.

In 1970 the Abbey revived a play first put on at the Gaiety in 1964, Eugene MacCabe's remarkable *King of the Castle* (14 September), directed by Alan Simpson. MacCabe was born in 1930 in Glasgow but around this time settled on the family farm near Clones, Co. Monaghan, the border country where this play is set. It deals with a theme which in the 1960s and 1970s many found deeply shocking. Maguire (Peadar Lamb), a rich 59-year-old farmer and a complete authoritarian, has married young Tressa (Aideen O'Kelly), a standard plot in the Abbey plays of the 1950s. But there the resemblance ends. MacCabe creates a brutal realism, comparable to Patrick Kavanagh's *The Great Hunger*, which conveys the meanness and begrudgery of a rural existence where Maguire stands out for his ability to triumph where others fail, his success often the direct result of his ability to take advantage of other's misfortunes. He is R. J. Ray's 'gombeen man' turned militant capitalist. He and his young wife, however, cannot have a child, and he is taunted by the men whom he employs that for all his 'power to buy' he has no one to leave his wealth to. This inadequacy torments a man who believes that to 'fail is a disease'.

The play, like so many Abbey plays, is preoccupied with the economics of survival, of gaining and retaining land, and with the nature of luck and necessity. MacCabe's purchase on these issues derives from Martyn, Colum, Murray, and Ray, but he presents his world with the sharp and violent energy of a Synge. Here is Maguire describing the atavistic (and also economic) pull of the land to Matt Lynch (Liam O'Callaghan), shortly to leave for Canada:

Your uncle he had a place—you growin' into it—a poor pocket maybe, but *land*. Yours, not a mornin' but you could look about you—the fields—the yard—you know the lofts where swallows come—the chimleys where daws racket—the lime tree near the chicken run that hawks light on—you know every gap and ditch and what grows on them: this holly shows berries at Christmas, this one's bare. . .[9]

Maguire now decides to force through yet another deal, after a bitter exchange with his frustrated wife: he asks young Lynch to sire a child on her for him, as if he were a bull or a stallion. To the horror of Tressa and Lynch they find themselves complying, victims to their own powerlessness and to the urgings of sex. The play ends grimly in the dereliction of the aftermath of these inhuman manœuvres, Tressa saying to Maguire: 'You've locked us both in hell: we're not yesterday's people: (*Long pause*) We're alone.' MacCabe's study in sterile authoritarianism encapsulates the rigidity and hidden angers and violence of a whole period of Irish life, stretching from the end of the Second World War to the late 1960s. It was not only goods and materials that were at first rationed, and then scarce; there was a lack of comfort, of giving, of accommodation, which the structure and institutions of the state in part reflected, in part created. Amongst those structures were the authoritarian practices of the Abbey itself, only in the late 1960s emerging from a period of over-vigilant control. But as is evident now, towards the end of the millennium, managerial practices, like all forms of social behaviour, reflect underlying economic and emotional patterns.

The older Ireland, of the 1940s and 1950s, was the one in which Tom Murphy grew up. He was born in Tuam, Co. Galway, became an apprentice fitter, then gained a schoolteaching scholarship, after which he became a metalwork teacher in Co. Galway. He sent his play *A Whistle in the Dark* to the Abbey in 1961, only to have it rejected by Ernest Blythe for its brutality and violence. Blythe found it difficult to believe that the loutish behaviour of the characters bore any resemblance to the actualities of Irish life. The play was staged by Joan Littlewood's Theatre Royal at Stratford East in 1961. This play, with a commanding abruptness, immediately set the tone and colour of Murphy's particular world; another major dramatist had arrived, although his next play, *The Fooleen* (later called *A Crucial Week in the Life of a Grocer's Assistant*), was also rejected by the Abbey in 1961. He then left Ireland, and worked in London as a freelance writer for a number of years. *Famine* (18 March 1968) was directed at the Peacock by Tomás Mac Anna and it transferred to the main theatre. It was a Brechtian, epic-theatre account of the Great Famine of 1845–50, in which the main characters have to choose between loyalty to a cause and their own personal freedom.

A Crucial Week in the Life of a Grocer's Assistant (10 November 1969) dealt with the emotional as distinct from the economic causes of emigration. It was directed by Alan Simpson and had Donal McCann in the title role of John Joe Moran. Harry Brogan played his uncle Mr Brody, and Eamon Kelly played Brown, the shopkeeper and skinflint he worked for. The scene and setting are typical Abbey depictions, save that in Murphy's treatment rural realism acquires a nightmarish horror and savagery. John Joe, the 33-year-old grocer's assistant, is caught in the grip of the meanness, spite, and anger of small-town life. The reality of emigration in this play is that the young leave because to stay would mean submitting their individuality entirely in order to bow to economic conditions. You either fit in, or get out. To leave is to face the terror of loneliness and lack of security; to stay means accepting the nightmare of worry and frustration. Frank, John Joe's brother, has gone to America, driven out by the incessant misery of a life without happiness or content. John Joe describes this experience as follows:

John Joe. Wives and husbands up and down the road, pots calling kettles black; the poor eating the poor. Anybody's business but our own. Not content with the hardships of today, the poor-mouth whining about yesterday as well. Begrudging, back-biting, hypocrisy; smothering and slobbering in some cunning 19th century way. And you thought you'd keep Frank here like that?

Mother. Well, you'd better follow your brother if that's the way you feel.

John Joe. You—drove—him—away! And Pakey Garvey didn't want to go. And it wasn't the money. It isn't a case of staying or going. Forced to stay or forced to go. Never the freedom to decide and make the choice for ourselves. And then we're half-men here, or half-men away, and how can we hope ever to do anything?[10]

The play is a devastating attack on the smallness of soul that is one of the consequences of subjection and poverty. The obsessive craving for respectability drives out all spirit; the dominant emotions are hate and envy. These conditions make people almost incapable of sustaining anything remotely resembling normal human relationships; men and women turn on those closest to them with a visceral ferocity, as if to spite all fine feeling and humanity. Murphy's Ireland, full of rage, is an emotionally famished place. The eloquence of his characters is almost entirely rooted in bitterness. But this work performs what Antonin Artaud (and Milton) claimed the theatre did at its most effective: it revealed the diseases of society to itself, and administered a kind of homeopathic prophylactic to its ills. Like cures like; the theatre's cruelty may release and relieve the cruelty society carries around inside itself, unacknowledged.

Hugh Hunt directed Murphy's next play at the Abbey, *The Morning after Optimism* (15 March 1971), which turned a cold eye on love and love's illusions. Its main characters, James and Rosie, are a pimp and his whore, and in a dream-forest they encounter their idealized selves, Edmund and Anastasia. While the play makes ironic use of the conventions of *commedia dell'arte* to point up the gulf between dream and reality, a more sombre set of meditations is proceeding, in which the expense and degradation which idealism can exact from the merely human are explored. One would not wish too blithely to politicize Murphy's drama, but his play's emotional energies and their frantic frustrations are connected to the tensions at work on an island where the impulses towards secularism, modernism, and individuality were being checked by the unresolved and ever-deepening conflict in the north. The first years of the new Abbey, from 1966 to, say, 1970, are marked by an emphasis on the nature of memory and the effect of the past upon character. The period from about 1970 to 1985 may be thought of as one in which those memories awaken into new life, energized by conflict and doubt, and remain, in a very literal sense, ungovernable. Murphy is, more than any other dramatist of this period, the playwright of a turbulence that cannot be subdued to form and control. His brutality and frankness are often shocking, but the strivings and the urges that usurp the stability of his characters have a tectonic energy, a telluric power that were also in evidence in the atrocities of the Shankhill Butchers, the bombing of the La Mon House Hotel, and the nightly vociferations of the Revd Ian Paisley on the television screens. Murphy is the surgeon of these disturbances of the 1970s and 1980s; Friel their psychoanalyst or Lacanian statesman.

Murphy's *The Sanctuary Lamp* (6 October 1975) was directed for the Dublin Theatre Festival by a visiting producer, Jonathan Hales. It is an attack on the idea of sanctuary, the notion that somehow there may be a place where all things will be resolved, and be at peace. The ostensible target is Christian belief, and the play did cause some outrage at the time for its fierce anticlericalism; but the real object of Murphy's turbulent rage is the closed mind, the emotional inertia that clings to fixed ideas, and refuses the challenges of reality.

The play is set in a church in a city. Harry is a Jewish ex-strong man from a circus; Francisco is his Irish partner, a seedy and disillusioned juggler, who has had an affair with Harry's dead wife Olga; and there is also Maudie, a 16-year-old, who has been sexually and physically abused. The cast is representative of a suffering and derelict humanity, tormented by unresolved pain which drives them into angry revolution, diatribe, and sorrow. Olga, we learn, from Francisco's nightmarish sermon in Act II, overdosed, after she and Francisco had done a private show at a society party, one which included opportunities for public sexual licence. It also seems as if Teresa, Harry and Olga's daughter, is dead. Her father questions the sanctuary lamp: 'Are you dumb, are you dead?. . . And once, in the morning actually, towards the end, little girl—y'know?—got out of her cot, out of her cot, all by herself—I was very surprised—some music was playing, and danced, actually. Danced.'[11] The play ends in a mixture of hope and savagery: hope that something may permanently survive out of human experience; and the evocation of a savage and malign god. There is a wilful and deliberate attempt in this play to subvert pious and idealistic beliefs about humanity, and yet there is also a deep sense of the sadness of much human experience. Murphy's theatre is a place of angry engagements, where hatred, disappointment, fear, and sorrow are let loose, a place of suffering and not of enchantment or sanctuary. It is a transgressive act and a profoundly disturbing one.

In *The Blue Macushla* (6 March 1980) Murphy uses a night-club setting to explore a world of gangsterism and betrayal that was intended as an allegory of an Ireland frantic for money and success and careless of the human cost of political and economic unscrupulousness. Paramilitary involvement in crime, money-laundering, racketeering, sex, and violence are the activities that the night-club of the title provides a front for. The play was directed by Jim Sheridan and had Stephen Rea in the role of Danny Mountjoy. *The Blue Macushla* is a melodramatic black farce, darkened by an awareness that the Irish state, the Republic, had, by the late 1970s, failed to achieve a reality commensurate with the longing and idealism (to adopt a phrase from Brian Friel's *Translations*, also first staged in 1980 by the Field Day Theatre Company) that had marked its beginnings. The northern 'Troubles' were a violent reminder of the actuality of this failure, and the catalogue of deaths and atrocities in the 1970s were a testament to the fact that something lay deeply unresolved in the Irish body politic. There were two ways of dealing with the moral and intellectual problems with which these evidences of deeply implicated stress confronted Irish society: one was to face the trouble (and tedium) of having to rethink all over again the form or forms of government which would allow Irish people, north and south, to live together in some kind of mutuality; the other was (if one lived in the south) to ignore the whole sorry fiasco, and wish that the northern 'question' would go away. The latter was, by far, the most common attitude of these years from 1968 to 1981 and the beginning of the hunger strikes at Long Kesh.

The Gigli Concert (19 September 1983) was directed by Patrick Mason, and had Tom Hickey in the part of an English 'dynamatologist', J. P. W King, Godfrey Quigley as the Irish Man, and Kate Flynn as Mona. It is a complicated and, to some extent, disorderly play. Frequently read as a hymn to the irrepressible instinct for creativity and imagination, it is also a representation of the consequences of the psychological and societal traumas manifesting themselves in an Ireland undergoing profound change and division. The Irish Man, a successful builder, has all kinds of problems: he is an alcoholic in denial, a wife-beater, a depressive, and he entertains a fantasy that the dynamatologist, King, may train him to sing not *like* Gigli the famous Italian tenor, but *as* Gigli.

From the 1930s to the 1970s, Gigli was a name to conjure with in Ireland; his emotional energy and force were idolized almost to a sacramental extent by men for whom he represented culture, colour, and a European liberty and spaciousness. Pubs all over Ireland were full of people, around closing time, shouting their renditions of arias he had made famous, rapturously applauded by their fellow-drinkers, who translated the rough screamings into their imagined beauty. In those moments the singers *became* Gigli. Murphy takes this enthusiasm and translates it into a series of encounters between the English quasi-alchemist and the depressive Irish entrepreneur. Although the play does celebrate the allure of the imagination it also registers its poisonous and toxic dangers. The Irish Man recovers from his depression and the urge to be Gigli leaves him; he returns to the terrors of normality at the end of the play. But King, under the influence of drugs and alcohol, becomes infected with his patient's bizarre aspiration, and, at the close, becomes Gigli. It is as if Murphy is saying to us: there is a terrible and Faustian poison which entices us to believe in the limitlessness of our reach and capacity; this poison is also, in a different form, one of our greatest powers, the human imagination. But over it there is written a health warning: beware the attractions of an imagining which arises from a dereliction of life, because its effectual outcome may be to leave life more derelict than ever. It is no accident that King is a 'dynamatologist', someone who alchemicizes experience by destroying it: is his method not cognate, Murphy is implying, with those paramilitaries who claim that their actions are sponsored by vision? Murphy's play, for all its structural obliquity and intellectual obscurity, is really, at root, a rather straightforward dramatic morality about the dangers of extremism, a strangely liberal and conservative position for a dramatist whose earlier work was driven by a radical and disturbing anger.

Murphy's next Abbey play was *A Thief of a Christmas* (30 December 1985), directed by Ray Heayberd, with Mick Lally and Bob Carlile playing the parts of Costello and the Stranger. It is a companion piece to *Bailegangaire*, produced by the Druid Theatre Company of Galway in the same year, Murphy having been writer-in-residence with the company from 1983 to 1985. *Bailegangaire* had the famous Abbey actress Siobhán McKenna in the part of Mommo, her swan-song in the Irish theatre before her death from cancer the following year. Mommo is both a reprise and interrogation of the great female roles in Irish theatre from Cathleen Ni Houlihan through Synge's Deirdre to O'Casey's women of the 1920s. She is larger than life, emotional, and indomitable. The play, the title of which means The Town without Laughter, tells the story of how the place got its name; a terrible laughing contest was entered into in which the mirth is triggered by the miseries of Irish history. *A Thief of a Christmas* makes the laughing contest the central focus of its action. Its subtitle is: *The Actuality of How Bailegangaire Came by its Appellation*. In this play (and indeed in *Bailegangaire*) Murphy revisits the folkloric dramatic realizations of Synge, Fitzmaurice, M. J. Molloy, and Bryan MacMahon, and the gombeenism of Ray, Murray, and Ervine, charging them with a new mythic and symbolic power.

It is Christmas in about 1935. The scene is a combined pub and grocery store in the west of Ireland, run by a gombeen man, John (Peadar Lamb), and his wife (Bríd Ní Neachtain). There is desultory badinage, music, and singing; but there is also a general air of poverty, penny-pinching, and malice underneath the superficial good nature. Into this brittle evocation of rural Ireland come the Stranger and his wife (Joan O'Hara), who, in the bad weather, cannot make it back to their home where their grandchildren have been left to fend for themselves while they have been to the Christmas fair at Tuam. The fair has been a disaster; so much produce was brought that over-supply drove prices down. Nevertheless the denizens of the pub intend to have a good night, and musicians draw in as night falls. The Stranger and his wife are a kind of crude analogy to the Holy Family and the pub stands for the inn of the New Testament. Costello is famous for his laugh, but the Stranger, egged on by his wife in a fit of guilt when the sticks of rock she has bought for her starving grandchildren are crushed, takes him on in a laughing contest, defeats him, and eventually kills him by a paroxysm of uncontrolled mirth. It is all very strange, and the subject of the laughter is stranger still, because what they laugh at is their own pain, misery, and suffering:

Costello. Oh, sure, the decline—TB—lost to the water—tuberculosis—lost across
    the sea, in England—
Stranger's Wife.⎱ An' America!—
Stranger.   ⎰ An' America!—
Stranger's Wife. One after the other!
Costello. One after the other!— . . .
Stranger's Wife. The unbaptized an' stillborn—
Costello.The unbaptized an' stillborn—
Stranger's Wife.Buried in unconsecrated ground—Hih-hih-hih!—
Costello.In shoe-boxes planted—Mary's the neighbour I went with—Hickle-ickle-
    ickle!—Didn't we Martin John?
Martin John. At the dead hour of night—Jasus!—
Costello. Treading softly the Lisheen—
Martin John. That field haunted by infants—
Costello. Too afeared to speak or pray—
Stranger's Wife. Ye were fearful for yere ankles. . .[12]

And so the horrifying laughter goes on, making desperate and hilarious the hidden miseries of Irish life; its abandonment, at the deepest human level in many instances, of the ideals of community, accord, identity, and love which nationalism and Catholicism professed to espouse and inculcate. Murphy's rage is towering and impressive, but the attack is unbalanced and obsessive. Behind the above passage is the horrific court case of the Kerry babies trial of the mid-1980s, in which a girl confessed to murdering and burying her own child and also to the murder of a second child that was not hers, driven to these desperate acts because the father of the first child was a relative. Bailegangaire is Ireland, a place without true laughter, only the shriek of a lunatic hysteria that cannot cope with reality. Hence the tendency, explored in *The Gigli Concert*, to opt for a transcendence and hectic abstraction that itself is a form of toxic derangement, a Faustian opt-out. These ambiguities, this rage, despair, and insatiable craving for something outside the daily tedium of the actual facts of bombing, cruelty, and atrocity, are gathered into the heaving and inchoate drivings of emotion in Murphy's theatre.

    Friel returned to the Abbey stage in 1972, four years after the production of *The Loves of Cass McGuire*, with the internationally successful *Philadelphia, Here I Come* (30 October), directed by Tomás Mac Anna and with Eamon Kelly in the role of S. B. O'Donnell, reprising his performance in the first production by the Gate Theatre in 1964. The principal dramatic force of *Philadelphia* derives from the pain of not being sure that it is possible to remember correctly: this is why Edmund Burke's famous passage from the *Reflections on the Revolution in France* about it being fifteen or sixteen years 'since I last saw the Queen of France' haunts the fissured consciousness of Public and Private Gar. The disjunctions of memory are the emotional reason why Friel, technically, splits the character in two; however, although Friel's dramatic focus is here on psychological and emotional issues nevertheless the grip of memory, and the urgent requirement to recall exactly, has a more than personal intensity in an Ireland now being drawn back into reliving and re-enacting concerns and conflicts that had not been resolved even though the opposing vociferations had seemed to lie quiet for a long time.

On 30 January 1972, 'Bloody Sunday', thirteen civilians were shot dead in Derry by the Parachute Regiment, following a civil rights march in the city. In February the British embassy in Dublin was burned down; an IRA reprisal unit killed seven people in a bomb attack on Aldershot, HQ of the paratroopers; in March Stormont, the Northern Ireland Parliament, was prorogued; and on 21 July, 'Bloody Friday', nine people were killed in twenty-two bomb attacks in Belfast. It looked as if anything remotely resembling civil society was breaking down in the north. As these events unfolded, Brian Friel was writing *The Freedom of the City* (17 January 1973), his first play expressly for the new Abbey.

Technically, the play is extremely adroit: the split personality of Gar in *Philadelphia* has fractured into a multiple scenario in *The Freedom of the City* where short scenes follow each other with great rapidity to give a sense of temporal counterpoint. Three protesters in a civil rights march take refuge in the mayoral parlour of Derry's Guildhall. Their reactions to each other and to what happens to them are juxtaposed with: the judicial inquiry launched into their deaths; media commentary on the events leading to their killing by British soldiers; a sociological analysis of the relation between class tension and political and civil unrest; and the fear and anger of the soldiers themselves. In spite of the complex ambition of the stagecraft, the action moves with a breathtaking impetus and a steady clarity and focus. The depiction of the tribunal which intercuts the actions that prompted it reflects the sense of disgust and outrage that greeted the report of Lord Widgery's inquiry which exonerated the action of the paratroopers on Bloody Sunday. As the action develops, and as events are analysed and distorted by the tribunal, we see, enacted before our eyes, the ways in which history gets rewritten, for convenience, cynicism, fear, or out of sheer blind prejudice. Oddly enough, although this play's content is all political, its concerns are not really political at all, save in a very deep exploratory sense. Friel is much more concerned with how people see things, how they think they see things, and how facts prove to be the most unstable objects of recollection and memory. Not only that, the scientific evidence and forensic testimony relating to whether or not the three who took refuge in the Guildhall were killed are shown to be in error, despite the machinery of apparently scrupulous analysis and witness. And the judgement pronounced on the killings, based on error and unwarranted assumption, is no more than the enactment of prejudice, and the closing of ranks by the authorities, the police, and the security forces. Skinner (played by Eamon Morrisey), one of the protesters, describes his last thoughts as the soldiers opened fire when they came out of the Guildhall: 'two thoughts went through my mind: How seriously they took us and how unpardonably casual we were about them; and that to match their seriousness would demand a total dedication, a solemnity as formal as theirs.'[13] It may seem an exaggeration to say that this moment of deathly illumination marks a turning point in Friel's writing life: a profound seriousness is now to be fully engaged; and this exemplary commitment, not to politics but to creativity as understanding, also affected the ways in which modern and contemporary Irish theatre addressed the issues that underlay the renewal of conflict in Ireland. How may Irish society, north and south, be formally represented? What signs are commensurate with the sense of wrongs done and with the labyrinth of misprision that has been Anglo-Irish relations for longer than most people would wish to remember? Who speaks for whom and for what?

Friel returned to the Abbey with *Volunteers* (5 March 1975), which was directed by Robert Gillespie. A play set on an archaeological dig in Dublin, it has an immediate contemporary resonance in relation to the controversy over Wood Quay, where, during the digging of foundations for a new hotel, extremely complex and hugely significant deposits were unearthed. In the play the volunteers of the title are political prisoners who, because of their collaboration with the authorities, are now fallen from grace with their own people. When they go back to prison, at the end of the play, they are certain to be tried and executed by their comrades inside.

On stage, under a tarpaulin, are the exhumed remains of a sacrificial victim, a reference to the poem 'Tollund Man' in *Wintering Out* (1972) by Seamus Heaney, to whom Friel dedicated the play. Heaney's image of the victim, interred near present-day Aarhus in Denmark, functions as an evocation of the way in which society often requires savagery and sacrifice as a means of cohesion, while also reminding us that past atrocities may resurface to trouble the present. Similarly, Friel's theme, as with so much Irish drama of the 1970s and 1980s, has to do with the potentially terrible effects of memory. Keeney (played by Donal Donnelly), one of the 'volunteers', and the joker amongst them, says to his straight man Pyne (Raymond Hardie), referring to the exhumed corpse they have carefully exposed:

Keeney. That. . . is the genie of the land.
Pyne. Is he. . . dead?
Keeney. Ah, there are two schools of thought about that.[14]

Earlier, Keeney, again jokingly, speculates about the corpse, saying that he may have been 'a casualty of language', implying, in the rich semantic and symbolic weave of the play, that violence and language are profoundly related, in that all victimage is a product of language. What someone says to or about one may (and often does) kill. The volunteers themselves are under a sentence, the meaning of which will be realized physically when they go back to the prison. Language imprisons as much as it liberates; it is a curse as well as being an instrument of delight or edification, a *pensum* learned from Samuel Beckett, whose *Waiting for*

Godot was directed by Seán Cotter at the Abbey for the first time on 1 December 1969. Friel, while an intensely literary playwright (some of the speeches he gives characters are complex ruminations on issues of perception and relativity), is deeply distrustful of language, and an element of his theatrical development from the 1970s onwards is a technical sophistication that allows him to play disruptive games with how and what people mean when they speak.

These concerns, to do with power, freedom, and identity, are carried forward into *Living Quarters* (24 March 1977), which was directed by Joe Dowling. Dowling had been appointed director of the Peacock in 1974, where he had previously directed Shakespeare, Molière, and Tennessee Williams, among others.

The action of *Living Quarters* (which is based on the *Hippolytus* of Euripides) is controlled by a kind of on-stage director, the figure of Sir (played by Clive Geraghty), who is a corrective and authoritarian presence, reminding characters of what they are consigned to enact, and rebuking them if they show any twitches of initiative. He is a personification of Fate, in that in him destiny is given character; and he also underlines the point that character is, almost ineluctably, one's fate. The action is set in the living quarters of the army Commandant, Frank Butler, newly returned from heroic and selfless action in the Middle East with the UN forces. Played by Ray MacAnally in the Abbey production, he is the Theseus figure, the hero who confronted the minotaur in Crete, according to Greek myth. Here, the labyrinth he must face is in his own household in the dreary army living quarters at Ballybeg, Friel's microcosm of Ireland.

Celebrations are afoot, the Taoiseach is to arrive, there are expectations of promotion, and the long-wished-for translation to Dublin. All this is in Butler's grasp, but the action, managed by Sir, develops to reveal that his son Ben (Stephen Brennan) has been involved in an incestuous liaison with Anna (Dearbhla Molloy), the Commandant's young wife, while the father was on active service. Butler, when he finds out that his living quarters are a nest of misery, deceit, and remorse, goes off stage and shoots himself.

The tissue of meanings in the play vibrates with resonances, and one of its fields of inference is the changing nature of family life and parental authority in the Ireland of the 1970s, the Ireland of rapid economic expansions and just as swift collapses, as the Republic modernized itself at a terrific pace. The Butler family is riven, not just by emotional differences and discontents, but also by emigration; a marriage contracted to a daughter's financial disadvantage, against parental wishes; as well as the malformations of distorted and frustrated love. But at the heart of this family 'romance' is a brooding concern with loyalty, and as to whether or not our actions can conform to the idealistic notions we entertain about ourselves. Against this idealism are set the turns and twists of character, the labyrinth of damaged love, and the malevolence that may flow from accident and chance. Friel's drama achieves a fluid objectivity in which the divagations of emotion stand utterly revealed. After Frank's suicide, Ben, preoccupied with himself, as ever, mixes sorrow, love, remorse, and self-regard:

I had some intimation of a moment being missed forever—because there was the sudden necessity to blurt out, to plunge some over-simplification into him before it was too late. And what I was going to say to him was that ever since I was a child I always loved him and always hated her [his mother]—he was always my hero. And even though it wouldn't have been the truth, it wouldn't have been a lie either: no, no; no lie.[15]

It is as if Friel is saying, look into the narrow living quarters of your life; stop and think how easy it is to betray yourself and others, even for a moment's release; consider, even, that the betrayal may be, in part, sincere, that a lie may not really be a lie. As Seamus Deane puts it, in a poem in *History Lessons* (1983): 'History is personal; the age, our age.'[16] History pushes us at moments of crisis into the labyrinth where Theseus may sometimes kill the minotaur; or at others, as in Friel's play, be killed. Private agony and betrayal have their origins, in considerable part, in the public deceptions that are transacted in the name of truth and sincerity. While not being explicitly political at all this play may, in fact, be one of Friel's deepest anatomies of the political unconscious, an analysis provoked by, but by no means confined to, Ireland's civil and constitutional crisis throughout the 1970s.

In 1980 Friel founded, in Derry, the Field Day Theatre Company, with the actor Stephen Rea from Belfast. This company, whose inaugural production was Friel's *Translations* (23 September 1980) at the Guildhall in Derry, soon became a cultural movement of immense significance for Ireland, north and south. Friel and Rea were joined on the board by Seamus Heaney, Seamus Deane, Tom Paulin, and David Hammond; to their number was later added the playwright Thomas Kilroy, the only non-northerner. The Field Day aim was to provide an arena, on the stage and in print, for realizations of different kinds of alternatives in the imaging of identity. Its stimulus was the question continually raised by the reality of public disorder and violent conflict, mostly in the north, though not exclusively. What might be the form (or forms) of representation that would not inaccurately reflect how Irish people, of all traditions, feel about their lives in the present and their relationship with the past? The Field Day cultural movement combined formal experiment in language and imagery with a thoroughgoing reappraisal of how the past was interpreted in Ireland. It was a cultural movement which stood comparison with that which Yeats and Lady Gregory inaugurated in 1899 with the Irish Literary Theatre, whose home became the Abbey in 1904. But Field Day studiously avoided the Abbey, and deliberately planned its opening nights to take place in Derry. It also sought, as part of its reappraisal of the entire structure of Irish feeling and thought, to dislodge the concentrations of gravity, in the field of culture, from Dublin and Belfast, to have a 'field day' in which new openings for thinking, for play, for creativity, could be made; in which new alignments could be drawn up, and perspectives (including historical and political ones) altered. This enterprise created an arena of debate, controversy, and cultural activism which had a profound effect on Irish intellectual and artistic life; and its consequences persisted right up to the end of the millennium, although the movement had, more or less, run its course by 1991, when Seamus Deane published his *Field Day Anthology of Irish Writing* in Derry, London, and New York.

One of the last productions of Field Day was Thomas Kilroy's *Madam McAdam's Travelling Show* (1992), a writer who had his first major Abbey production with *The Death and Resurrection of Mr Roche* (8 May 1973). The play had previously been staged by the Gate in 1969, and Kilroy's interpretation of the life and significance of Hugh O'Neill, Earl of Tyrone, was presented at the Peacock (26 May, 1969).

Kilroy, from Callan, Co. Kilkenny, is one of three major theatrical talents to come to maturity in the Abbey of the 1970s, the others being Friel and Murphy. If Murphy's theatre was one which offered a release of repressed emotion and energy, and Friel's one which provided sketches of the internal psychoses caused by public tensions, then Kilroy brought a moral and ethical intelligence to bear upon the nature of responsibility. Friel and Murphy are, perhaps, stoics—for them character is eventually fate, and fate is history—but Kilroy explores the reality of guilt and the feeling, not just of being wronged (which is easy enough to convey), but of having done wrong. Damnation is not an outmoded condition in Kilroy's plays: he contemplates (and gets his audience to contemplate) what it is to do something the consequences of which may be that all will be lost.

The actor T. P. McKenna directed the 1973 production of *The Death and Resurrection of Mr Roche*, subtitled 'a comedy'. But it is a sour comedy. A group of Dublin 'lads' have come back to Kelly's flat after a Saturday night out for 'a few jars'. They are in their thirties, so they are of a generation young enough to be boisterous but old enough to be aware that life is beginning to pass them by. Myles (played by Joe Dowling), a car salesman from down the Dublin quays, tells Kelly (Mícheál Ó hAonghusa), who is a middle-ranking civil servant, that he is behind the times:

You're not with it. The country is on the move, man. On the up and up. For those that are on the move, that is. Fellows that dig. Fellows with savvy. Get me? You've got to be moving too or you'll be left behind. It's the lad with the go that's going to get the gravy, Kelly.[17]

The pathetic anxiety of this reflects the panic to be 'with it', in the horrible phrase of the times. This was the Ireland that had discovered 'liberation', that had discovered it was possible to smuggle in contraceptives from the north and that it was not impossible to make use of them on a fairly casual basis. There were rising generations of young (and not-so-young) people who had a good deal of money to spend on entertainment and pleasure. And this world is the one Kilroy creates.

However, into the midst of this freebooting and somewhat hysterical exhilaration comes Mr Roche (Eamon Kelly), a homosexual, and Kevin (Bosco Hogan), a young man who is much the worse for wear from drink. The 'lads', however, especially Kelly (who, it turns out, has his own special reasons), resent homosexuals. They push the mild-mannered Mr Roche about, eventually forcing him into a basement; he has a seizure and they think they have killed him. Now the real

panic of fear and self-interest takes over; Myles disappears, and Kelly persuades
the superannuated medical student, known as 'Doc', and Kevin to take the body
off the premises. In Act II Kelly tells Seamus, his old but now married friend, that
he has known Roche, that he wants to confess to someone what he did with him:
'God forgive me. I let him handle me—'. Seamus responds as follows: 'I'd prefer if
you hadn't said anything at all like that.'[18] Act III opens with Kelly on his knees,
praying, alone, for forgiveness. Myles returns from having had sex with a woman
down Mount Street. Now, to their amazement, Mr Roche returns with the two
sent off to get rid of the body, saying: 'I am a little ghosty-ghost. Boo—hoo!', The
play ends with the characters trying to resume their lives: Kelly tries to organize
them into a party, where they will wash, shave, go to a match, catch evening mass,
and end the day with 'a few jars'. The tedium of their lives is well caught, and
Kilroy, in the play, offers a sketch of an Ireland still in the grip of conventions and
mores that have little correspondence to the way people think and feel in reality.
Kelly is a secret homosexual; his friends live their lives according to cliché and expectation; the way to deal with trouble is to take any means of avoiding it. And for
frustration and disappointment there is always the anaesthesia of the 'few jars'.

Tea and Sex and Shakespeare (6 October 1976), directed by Max Stafford-
Clark, dealt with the figure of the writer and his relation with contemporary Irish
society, but Kilroy's major theatrical impact arrived with Talbot's Box the following year, at the Peacock, as part of the Dublin Theatre Festival (10 October 1977).
Directed by the young Englishman Patrick Mason (newly arrived from
Manchester University, where he had taught Performance), it dealt with the figure
of the Dublin mystic and ascetic Matt Talbot. Talbot, who died in 1921, was a
labourer and a reformed alcoholic, famous for his piety and his mortifications of
the flesh.

Kilroy's play is about the humanity of Talbot, about the suffering caused when
an individual is caught up into the mechanism of a force or institution intent upon
using a person's uniqueness and vulnerability for its own purposes. On the one
hand Talbot is a figure despised by his fellow-workers, because he was 'down on
his knees' in the Lockout Strike of 1913 when his 'comrades' were 'tryin' to get up
off them'; on the other, he is exploited by the church and his employers as a symbol of devotion to duty and to obedience. One of the 'crame of the crame' of
Dublin municipal society, while out riding at Enniskerry, Co. Wicklow (his stage-
mount is in fact another man), says: 'If there was more praying and less marching
around with placards we'd soon beat inflation in this country'.[19] Needless to say,
Kilroy's focus is as much upon the inflationary spirals and social upheavals of the
1970s as it is upon the condition of Irish society during the Anglo-Irish and the
Civil Wars. He uses the particular instance of Talbot to express a series of dramatic realizations about human injustice and cruelty, and shows that individual
holiness and integrity are continuously usurped by the clashing greeds of those
with the loudest voices. The very moving and semi-comic account (done in the
style of a sports commentary) of Talbot's mass-race every morning for forty years

from Gardiner Street to Clarendon Street to the quays, in order to attend three
masses in under two hours, creates a powerful image of compulsion, distress, and
terror. Talbot's pietistic frenzy becomes an image of the condition of those who
are oppressed and exhausted by the never-ending demands society makes upon
their energies and goodwill. When Talbot drops from exhaustion, worn out by
the strenuous effort to cope with the drives of his obsession and by the chains he
wears to teach him the darkness of his own body, we are told that he smells most
horribly. The smell is of mortality, and it offends those very people who need him,
and who cheer him on to his destruction.

However, this is not a bitter play; nor does it indulge in any modish anticlericalism, rampant in 1970s Ireland, and since. Talbot emerges, strangely, as a figure
commanding admiration mixed with pity and compassion; at the end he rises into
the dignity of Christ, the heroic silent man who heads from Nazareth into the city,
where already they are preparing the instruments of his torture and death. This is
Talbot's last speech, from his box, the box where his energy and beauty are kept;
it is a speech in which the love for humanity is paramount, but which is also not
without hope for a world which can contain such love:

The old man worked at his bench, shavin' the yellow timbers in the sunlight. An' the boy
used to help him. They worked together. They niver spoke. No need for words. Nothin'
was heard but the sound of timber. Then wan day. . . wan day, the boy left. He put down the
tools outta his hands. Again, nare a word. The old man came to the door with him. They
kissed wan another. Then the mother came like a shadda from the house an' she kissed the
boy too. Then the boy walked down the road in the dust 'n the hot sun. 'N way in the far
distance of the city he could hear them, the sound of the hammers 'n they batin' the timbers into the shape o' the cross.[20]

Kilroy, in his author's note to the play, wrote that the work represents his interest
in 'the way individuals of exceptional personality invite manipulation and the
projection of the needs of others', a theme extremely relevant in a century which
has seen a terrible flourishing of dictators and victims. Dictators flourish in a
moral climate where the individual is deeply convinced of his or her own emptiness and so looks to a powerful figure to fill the void. And victims often are such
because they have surrendered that vulnerability which was their uniqueness, pre-
ferring instead to be subject to others. Kilroy's moral and ethical universe is subtle: he is well aware of the abuse of power and the self-abuse of delusion, but he
never loses sight of the pity that can arise to cancel our worse endeavours of contempt and self-contempt. There is a sense in which Christ remains at the heart of
his depiction of suffering. His concern in *Talbot's Box* (and in *Double Cross*, the
play he later wrote for Field Day in 1986) extends from an Irish set of conditions
to a moral universe unbounded by national preoccupations, one in which the nature of freedom and the problems of power are weighed and measured. But there
is, in Kilroy, a specific Irish focus, which acts as a paradigm for moods, obsessions,
and delusions that trouble action and torment the soul. Kilroy's Irish people (even
his Irish 'Russians' in his version of *The Seagull* in 1981) are driven people,

individuals who are compelled into their actions by forces they can scarcely name; thus giving his theatre a psychoanalytic temper, calmer than Murphy's releases, more forgiving than Friel's cold eye, where pity, though longing to be abroad in the world, is kept under strict lock and key.

Seán Cotter, a young trainee director from Cork, had joined the Abbey production team in 1967, directing first stagings of George Fitzmaurice's *The King of the Barna Men* and *The Magic Glasses* (18 September), reviving an Abbey playwright long neglected. Cotter directed, at the Peacock, *An Deisceart Domhain* by Diarmuid Ó Súilleabháin (1 May 1969), the brave and experimental novelist from Eyeries in west Cork. The Peacock also staged the brilliant and affecting *Soldier* (11 July 1969) by Liam Lynch, directed by Tomás Ó Murchadha, who had been responsible for *The Tailor and Ansty* the previous year. *Soldier* was a sombre and exciting theatrical event, with an outstanding performance from Robert Carlile in the lead part. Lynch used monologue and flashback to convey the sufferings of conscience and the scald of remorse. His first play, *Do Thrushes Sing in Birmingham?*, had been produced at the Queen's as far back as 1962. Lynch, who died in 1989, was born in Dublin and later wrote a couple of masterful novels, of which *Tenebrae* (1985), a searching study of the play of conscience in a priest stricken by guilt and love, is perhaps the finest.

This play, like many produced in the early years of the new Abbey, is concerned with memory, and the influence of the past upon character. In many respects *Soldier* perfectly illustrates this obsession. It is set in 1954, in London, although the characters are from the north of England. The Soldier of the title, Timothy Gates, is receiving psychoanalytic treatment and his doctor is using drugs to allow him access to the buried memory and hurt that afflict him. The action of the play is constructed contrapuntally, so that as memories surface they are performed on stage. Gates recalls the disintegration of his mother's personality which occurred when he was a boy; he remembers his own fear, and his father's helpless love and inability to get through to a woman caught in the grip of a suffering she cannot cope with. His mother's mind gives way because she cannot come to terms with the death of her brother Will in the First World War. Soldier, under the memory-drug, relives the Remembrance Day parade when her mind started to go: 'Only mum, she didn't stand with us. She stood away, on her own you could say. Only that weren't her that weren't the really mum. That were a right fucking bitch. Way out beyond us: and she wanted neither of us, see. Neither dad nor me.'[21] She is taken to 'Bixley' for treatment and she is alright for a while, but she comes in again, one evening, the scene brilliantly created in a combination of monologue and flashback:

her shoulders are going up and down. Started at her I did. What in the name of Christ could I say, there were nothing to say. . . Couldn't say it will pass Mum cause I knew fucking well it wouldn't. . . Just then Dad he came in. Takes it all in at a glance he does. Takes off jacket, real slowly like there were no hurry. . . She slips out hand. He takes it real gentle like. Great bloody big hands he had. Think he couldn't do nothin right with hands that size.[22]

This depiction of the affliction of the past, how the mind can be scarred with hurt and limitless sorrow, is, strangely, all the more effective on the Irish stage for having an English context, with English voices. The problems of memory, the pain of remembrance, are not the sole property of any one culture; the Irish are, Lynch is implying in writing this play of English duty and sadness, simply amongst those this century who carry within them reservoirs of remorse and anger that lie often unplumbed. These hidden darknesses have the power to impair the capacity for love and, even, for life itself.

Heno Magee, another Dublin writer, made an impact with *Hatchet* (2 May 1972), with its combination of urban violence, realism, and unabashed dialogue. This play was directed by Roland Jaquarello at the Peacock. It reflects, to some extent, Magee's own background. Set in 1970, in a 'working-class' area of Dublin, it depicts a life of brutality, drinking, sexual frustration, and personal and social derangement. Hatchet (so called because he once, aged 14, set upon a gang who were beating up his father, with a hatchet) is married to Bridie (Terri Donnelly), who is so fed up with living with her husband's family that she has lost all interest in sex. Hatchet (John Kavanagh) works down the docks, but his mother drinks and gambles away the money he brings in. Mrs Bailey (May Cluskey), the alcoholic mother, is widowed but has a 'fancy-man', Joey (Arthur O'Sullivan), back from England on holiday. One of the Mulallys has insulted her in the pub the night before the action begins, and the play is concerned with Hatchet's vengeance on him, and the Mulally family's reprisal. The play ends with mother and son going out to face the Mulallys brandishing broken bottles as weapons. The following is from the scene in which the Mulally brothers come to take their revenge on Hatchet:

Johnnyboy. When I get him I'm going to cut his head off (*suddenly displays a large knife*). I'm going to carve your bleedin' son up. Who are you?
Bridie (Hatchet's wife). They're just friends.
Johnnyboy. Ye know my brother?
Hairoil (friend of Hatchet). Yeah sure.
Freddie. Seen him around.
Johnnyboy. Well he was jumped on last night by a few bastards. The Hatchet fella was one. Yous are mates of his, are'n't yis?
Hairoil. You could say that.
Freddie. We hang around together.
Johnnyboy. Were yis with him last night? (*neither reply*) Were yis bleedin' with him?
Mrs Bailey. So you're a Mulally, I should've known by your big nose. Don't worry, Hatchet done him on his own. It was easy. He didn't need anyone. And he won't need anyone for you either.[23]

This unsparing depiction of sheer brutality was, in 1972, quite a shock, although it was in no way bolder in its frank treatment of violence than Synge's *Playboy* of almost seventy years earlier. What was shocking was the play's refusal to provide any but the most rudimentary evidence of kindness and humanity among the tenement dwellers. Magee, in his vigorous demotic dialogue, creates a raw and forceful set of people, animated by sensation, and indifferent to anything remotely resembling finer feelings. It is a bleak, harsh triumph.

The play also showed that there was a new daring in evidence in the Abbey's programme as the theatre gradually gained in confidence in the 1970s. A further indication of their adventurousness was the fact that Yeats's *The Herne's Egg* had its first Abbey production at the Peacock (18 September 1973), along with *Purgatory*, both directed by Jim Fitzgerald.

James McKenna, a Dubliner, best known as a sculptor, wrote *The Scatterin'* in 1959; it was directed by Alan Simpson for the Dublin Theatre Festival at the Pike Theatre, which also produced plays by Beckett and Behan in those years. Simpson revived the play at the Abbey on 4 December 1973. *The Scatterin'*, as its title indicates, is a play about emigration, and, though possibly more relevant to the Ireland of the late 1950s, nevertheless its pertinence had not faded by 1973, when Ireland was beginning to experience one of those phases of financial uncertainty that were a feature of its economic life from 1922 to the mid-1980s.

Influenced as much by pantomime as by Brecht, McKenna's play mixes energetic vernacular speech with music and song to evoke a lost world of Dublin Teddy boys. They hang around, get drunk, listen to music, go into the Dublin hills, and eventually emigrate. Their hopes and vitality are destined to be confounded by the realities of poverty and unemployment. On the other hand, the Ireland they leave is an Ireland of furtive sex and joyless scrounging, of orphanages and child abuse, and they are glad, though rueful also, to be out of it:

after a short stay with the nuns, the kids were torn from their mothers an' sent in droves to the country. An' that was the last the mothers ever saw of them. . . They became the property of the State—the Free State: their keep was paid for. By God they were kept alright. Kept starved; kept naked; kept terrified. . .[24]

Simpson, the director of *The Scatterin'*, was by 1972 a freelance working for the Abbey, but he had, in 1968, taken over as artistic adviser when Tomás Mac Anna accepted a post as director of drama at Carleton College, Minnesota, in the USA on a year's leave. However, at the end of a year his contract was not renewed because of differences with the Abbey board. Blythe retired on 31 August 1967, but he maintained an office and kept a watchful eye on the ever-changing alliances of Abbey politics, and advised the reinstatement of O'Connor's old friend and colleague of over thirty years before, Hugh Hunt, the professor of drama at Manchester University. He returned, on a part-time basis, with Seán Cotter as his assistant. Hunt's term of office was for two years, beginning 1 December 1969, and he insisted on being given the title artistic director, common in British theatre. Hunt was responsible for a number of innovative productions in this period: Murphy's *The Morning after Optimism* (15 March 1971, with Cotter); *Macbeth* (28 September 1971); and Boucicault's *Arrah-na-Pogue* (4 January 1972). He also wrote *The Abbey: Ireland's National Theatre, 1904–1979* (1979), a history and a documentary record of the latter years. In 1973 Mac Anna returned to the company as artistic director.

Drama in Irish, still a poor cousin of the work in English, returned with Pádraig Ó Giollagáin's *Fleá* (25 September 1972). Directed by Eamon Kelly, the actor, it was a Rabelaisian comedy of Irish rural life. Furze Conor (played by Peadar Lamb) has a card through the post following his attendance at a mass X-ray clinic, which convinces him he is to die. During the *fleá ceoil* (music festival) which is the background to the play he gets drunk, goes to confession, tells his son Christy (Bosco Hogan) that Mary (Máire Ní Dhomhnaill), the girl he wants to marry, is actually his sister, sells off his land, and burns the proceeds so as to deprive his wife of any benefit from his demise. It turns out that the card was meant for another Furze Conor, and that Christy is not his son, so the couple can marry after all. The play is a fine, and almost unique, example of the carnivalesque tradition in modern theatre in Irish.[25] This goliardic playfulness, which is an integral part of Gaelic tradition, had all but died out, in Irish, in the twentieth century, with the notable exceptions of Máirtín Ó Cadhain and Flann O'Brien, the novelists. Ó Giollagáin's drama is a significant moment, culturally speaking; but his example, in theatre, is not taken further until Alan Titley's *Tagann Godot* (1990).

Criostóir Ó Floinn was given a drama scholarship by the Abbey board in 1972–3 to allow him to concentrate on writing full-time. In the previous decade Ó Floinn had been working tirelessly writing in Irish, developing his craft in poetry, fiction, and drama. Interestingly also, like Eoghan Ó Tuairisc, he wrote both in Irish and English, and *Cóta Bán Chríost*, the play that won the Oireachtas (an annual literary competition for works in Irish) in 1966, was staged in English as *The Order of Melchizedek* (1967). Ó Floinn's *Is é a Dúirt Polonius* (6 May 1968) was directed by Frank Bailey at the Peacock. The 1972–3 scholarship allowed Ó Floinn to devote time and energy to a subject he had had in mind a long time as a theme for a play: the life, work, and significance of the nineteenth-century poet Antoine Raifteirí (or Raftery). The result, *Mise Raifteirí An File* (22 October 1973), was an impressive historical montage, a kind of documentary drama, in which Raifteirí's personality is memorably sketched, his support for the French Revolution celebrated, and his later transformation into a symbolically charged cultural figure by Lady Gregory and Douglas Hyde analysed. It is lovingly (and accurately) done, and shows the sureness and grasp of careful scholarship. For example, the friendship between Raifteirí and James Hardiman, his contemporary who was a scholar and a public man, is skilfully integrated into the scene where the poet is tried (and found guilty) for writing verses urging sedition. The last scenes, when Raifteirí (who spent his life as a kind of impoverished Bashó, tramping the harsh roads of the west) sets out, knowingly, to meet his death, are harrowing and exciting at once, as Hyde steps forward out of the collective persona of those listening to Raifteirí's great poem of encounter with death, 'An Cholera Morbus', to comment, chorically, on the human deprivation involved in the cultural and linguistic distance of modern Ireland from this man. Lady Gregory's informant Bríd tells her, intriguingly, how blind Raifteirí would compose at night, in his bed, and that in the morning 'all he had to do was lay his finger on a certain vein that was in his head and every word of the song would come back to him, even if there was a thousand verses in it, as exactly as if out from a manuscript'.[26] Meanwhile, back in his own time, heading for his death at Craughwell, Raifteirí wishes he had English, so he could enjoy success in London, like his contemporary Thomas Moore.

The play uses Irish and English to express not only the distance but also the interplay between the two main cultures in Ireland; and it is also a profound act of veneration to one of the victims of the triumph of English in the nineteenth century. As such the play, while recognizing the cultural loss of the Irish language, also performs an act of imaginative retrieval, something Brian Friel was later to do in *Translations* (1980) with the Field Day Theatre Company. The Peacock production of Ó Floinn's play was by Colm Ó Briain and had Peadar Ó Luain (Peadar Lamb) in the part of Raifteirí.

Eoghan Ó Tuairisc had been a major literary figure in the 1960s in Irish and in English. A series of brilliant narrative fictions and poems established him as a writer of powerful intelligence and emotional range; amongst them were a long poem, *The Week-End of Dermot and Grace* (1964), based on the Fionn cycle of tales, and *Dé Luain* (1966), an epic recreation in Irish of the Easter Rising, using Joycean technique and pointillist narrative effects. He was also, annually, involved in the creation of the Abbey pantomimes in Irish, as we have seen in the previous chapter. However, after his wife Una's death in 1965 he wrote little for years and went through a prolonged period of grief and breakdown. In 1972 he married the young poet Rita Kelly and his life and imaginative powers revived. A consequence of this renewal of energies was a reinvolvement in writing for the stage in Irish: as well as pantomimes for the Abbey he had contributed a number of plays to the Irish-language Damer Theatre in the 1960s. Tomás Mac Anna, an old friend, knew that Ó Tuairisc had written a new play for the Damer; Mac Anna also knew that that theatre was having financial difficulties and offered to take the work for the Dublin Drama Festival at the Abbey in 1977. *Aisling Mheic Artáin* (4 October) was directed by Peadar Lamb. The title means 'The Vision of the Artane Boy' a reference to Artane (and the famous Artane Boys' Band), an orphanage which, for many, epitomized the control the Catholic church exercised over the minds and hearts of Ireland, and had been one of McKenna's targets in *The Scatterin'*. In Ó Tuairisc's play a monk wanders through a post-Christian Ireland and encounters many wonders. Mac Anna also commissioned Ó Tuairisc to write a Gaelic pantomime for 1977: *Oisín* (26 December) was written in collaboration with Mac Anna, and did good business.

In 1977 Stewart Parker, a Belfast-born dramatist, came to the Abbey with *Catchpeny Twist* (25 August). *Catchpenny Twist* introduced a fresh perspective on the northern Troubles, which were, as we have seen in the accounts of the drama of Friel and Murphy in the 1960s and 1970s, a continuous and creative reproach and disruptive stimulus. In Parker's treatment they form a backdrop to a 'charade' (the term used in the subtitle) or farce in which three ex-teachers try to make the grade as writers of pop-songs. Sacked because Monagh does a striptease in the empty classroom at the end of term for Roy and Martyn in a bout of tipsy horseplay, the men embark on a career writing ballads for paramilitaries. They are accused by both sides of selling out and receive a death-threat; they move to Dublin, which also proves unsafe, and then to London. Eventually, as they wait for a delayed plane in a European airport, having failed to win the Eurovision song contest, they are blown up by a letter bomb. The cheap value placed on human life is hauntingly suggested by the casual and jejune lyrics they use to describe emotion in their songs: but life, Parker implies, has a way of twisting around and taking its revenges for reckless and thoughtless action. It is a brutal, sudden, and vicious play, capturing a mood of hopeless and cynical stoicism that was a not uncommon reaction to the Troubles, north and south, in the 1970s. Its fluent stagecraft, moving deftly between registers of seriousness and levity, signalled the arrival of a major talent at the Abbey.

Graham Reid, another Belfast writer, worked first in a variety of jobs (including hospital portering) before entering Queen's University, Belfast, when he was 26. His first play, *The Death of Humpty Dumpty* (6 September 1979), was directed by Patrick Mason at the Peacock. It dealt with an 'innocent victim' of the Troubles, George Samson, a schoolteacher who, while indulging in extra-marital sex with a fellow-teacher from his school, is witness to a sectarian assassination. The paramilitaries take his car number, track him down, and shoot him on his doorstep. He is crippled and badly disabled; he cannot walk or have sex, or relieve himself. He is dependent on the sadistic Willie in the hospital, who cleans him: 'I mean sweetheart that I have to put on a rubber glove and shove my hand up your smelly arse.'[27] Reid spares the audience nothing in creating a brutal realization of the aftermath of violence. Willie scoffs at George's penis as follows: 'There it is, like a member of the Unionist Party, stripped of its power of independent action. It's still there, a reminder of past glories. Like a moose head on a wall.' His friend and fellow-patient Boyce is killed in an accident, and Willie takes pleasure in revealing this to George in the harshest possible way. The sister tells Willie that he is 'like to many others in this bloody country. You're a bloody animal, limited in everything but your capacity for cruelty.'[28] Meanwhile George is becoming bitter and full of hatred. He is angry and abusive to his wife and children on his long weekends at home. His wife Heather accidentally discovers that he has been continuously unfaithful to her, and the image he projected of the exemplary father and husband is shattered. Meanwhile, he grows tyrannical and overbearing, and is eventually suffocated by his son David. The play, cruelly direct, and powerful in a visceral way, concentrates on how violence can be transmitted in society, from good fathers to killers, from killers to victims, who in turn grow cruel themselves, and learn the code by which the whole rotten circularity of hatred works. Once the virus is let loose society, Humpty Dumpty, may not repair itself without deeper and further suffering and disgrace. D. E. S. Maxwell was right to detect a Shakespearean concern with the energy evil accumulates when it is gathered: all in the end are 'injured and injuring', he writes.[29] Reid concentrates on the moral gloom and emptiness created by violence. Reid's next play *The Closed Door*, also at the Peacock (28 April 1980), is set in the illegal paramilitary drinking dives of Belfast, and also deals with the bleak consequences and human faithlessness that follow physical violence.

A very different mood was evident in the first play of another playwright who emerged in these years, Bernard Farrell's *I Do Not Like Thee, Dr Fell* (15 March 1979). Dublin-born Farrell was a clerk with the Sealink shipping line when he submitted his play to the Abbey. It was enthusiastically received by Joe Dowling, then artistic director, and the script editor, Thomas Kilroy (who, to Farrell's amazement, insisted he call him 'Tom' when they met). It opened in the Peacock, and was directed by Paul Brennan. It deals with a disastrous encounter session, in which the participants, under their group leader the American Rita Bernstein, end up at each other's throats, or else completely demoralized and distressed. The catalyst is a young man with a stammer, Joe (played by Garrett Keogh), who continuously feeds misleading information into the exchange of personal stories that forms the basis of the encounter therapy. The humour is broad, but it also cuts deeply into facile notions of truth-telling and communication. The main concern of the play is the failure of communication because individuals either cannot or will not be themselves or tell the truth about their experiences. Eventually Joe sends everyone into a blind panic by telling them that the bag he has left outside the door contains a bomb. The builder, Peter (played by Tom Hickey), becomes hysterical with fright until, aided by Roger (quiet and sensitive up to this point), he physically attacks Joe. The play is a biting satire on the notion, common in the 1970s, that social and political problems derived from a failure to 'relate', to 'open up'. Joe, the urban psychological terrorist, symbolically explodes this comfortable illusion, Farrell returned to the Abbey with *Canaries* (1980), a play about holidays abroad on the cheap package tours then becoming widely available, followed by *All in Favour Said No!* (2 April 1981), directed by Patrick Laffan. This play, set in the Donnycarney Metal Works in Dublin, was a comedy on strikes, labour relations, and office politics. Farrell is a writer who captures the texture of life's irritations and quirks; his characters are ordinary and surprising at once; and his theatre has the attraction of what is recognizable being given a bizarre and sometimes edgy and disturbing turn.

Hugh Leonard, pseudonym of John Keyes Byrne, had written for the Abbey as far back as *The Big Birthday* (23 January 1956), and his famous adaptation of Joyce's *A Portrait of the Artist as a Young Man, Stephen D*, was revived there on 19 May 1978: it was first directed at the Gate Theatre in 1962. Leonard, a former civil servant, returned to the Abbey with *A Life* (4 October 1979), a play of suburban disappointment and rueful retrospection. Drumm (played by Cyril Cusack) appraises a life of bureaucratic service and entrapment as follows: 'I spend a third of my life in a hot-house of intrigue and skulduggery which would make the court of the Borgias look like a whist-drive, and, I do work of doubtful value for a government of doubtful morality. Cogito ergo sum. I am a cog, therefore I am.'[30] Leonard captures a world of middle-class frustrations and discontents. His are lives lived in a kind of torpor of wild expectation, resignation, and sadness. There is a Chekovian stoicism in his work, a grip on the misery of the daily grind.

Drama in Irish continued to subsist. It should be said, however, that the problem in the 1970s and the 1980s was the same problem that bedevilled Gaelic drama from the days of An Comhar Drámaíochta, and which still remains unsolved: that is, the comparative dearth of good dramatic writing in Irish. There have been exceptions (such as Mícheál Mac Liammóir's *Diarmuid agus Gráinne* and Seán Ó Tuama's *Gunna Cam agus Slabhra Óir*) but on the whole the standard of theatrical effectiveness in Gaelic drama leaves much to be desired. However, a writer of real promise and energy arrived on the scene from the Aran Islands in the 1980s, and his ability was swiftly identified by Seán MacCarthy, the script editor at the time. MacCarthy directed Antoine Ó Flatharta's *Gaeilgeoirí* (29 September 1981). This play brings onto the stage the world of the contemporary Gaeltacht. It is set in the Connemara house of Máire and Jimmy, a couple of returned exiles, who take on 'gaeilgeoiri' (the learners of Irish of the title) to supplement their income. Unlike traditional depictions of people from this world Máire and Jimmy are well-off; he is a local builder, and has put up most of the new houses in the area. Jimmy is cynical about what is expected of them by the organizers of the language scheme and is irked that they are required to speak 'pure' Irish to the students and that they should behave 'traditionally': 'Ah, says Éamonn, says Éamonn. Easy enough for him. It's not lodging houses he's after but shebeens. Full of goms letting on that yesterday's today and that they can't see tomorrow. Hand me down me bodhrán and put the television under the bed.'[31] The play is written in a patois of Irish-English, very much the kind of normal speech to be heard in the Gaeltacht of today. The students are far from dewy-eyed: 'oh Jesus Christ fuck the Gaeltacht I want to go home,' one of them says.[32] However, into all this cynicism there erupts something very old, untamed, and dangerous, all the more so for being ignored and repressed. On bonfire night Jimmy falls under the spell of some energy that surfaces from the unconscious. He goes half-demented, striping his face with black wood-ash: 'It's here still. It's still in us and if we don't allow it out it'll smother us. . . kill us. . . the ones who first lit these fires knew this. . . barbarians?. . . we are finishing with what is barbaric? We're finishing ourselves as well.'[33] Jimmy and Máire, it turns out, have lost their son Brendan, who was killed in a road accident in London. When this is revealed, one of the students takes pity on him, and Jimmy and she have sex. The play moves to a weird climax in which the students are being taught Irish dancing as a kind of hideous enforcement; Máire hears that her sister has died; and she and Jimmy resolve to recover their sexual lives together. It is a play in which the metaphor of language imperfectly understood and incorrectly transmitted stands in for the imperfection of the whole network of affective interaction between people, and between different levels of consciousness. It is a strong and effective realization of the emptiness of contemporary life in the Gaeltacht, but elsewhere also; while it also hints at the possibility of reclaiming that which was thought to be lost.

The mid-1980s saw the emergence of another major talent from a younger generation to set alongside Brian Friel, Tom Murphy, and Thomas Kilroy. This was Frank McGuinness, from Buncrana in Co. Donegal. After beginning as a poet he was inspired by a performance of Friel's *Faith Healer* to write for the stage, and *Factory Girls* (11 March 1982) opened at the Peacock, directed by Patrick Mason. This showed McGuinness to have an ear for dialogue and was based on his mother's experiences while working in the shirt factory in Buncrana. Next he wrote a commissioned piece for Field Day, which failed to reach production, eventually appearing at the Abbey (26 September 1988) as *Carthaginians*, directed by Sarah Pia Anderson. But his shattering and commanding play *Observe the Sons of Ulster Marching towards the Somme* at the Peacock (18 February 1985), directed by Patrick Mason, took everyone by surprise, and marked a profound shift in Irish theatrical thought, practice, and intent.

It is now clear, in retrospect and from hindsight, that the Abbey, the Irish National Theatre, was, from its re-establishment in 1966 in the new building, occupied with a number of key concerns. One had to do with the kind of theatre that would adequately reflect and respond to life in an Ireland undergoing far-reaching social change; this concern had formal as well as thematic ramifications and influenced the evolution of imaginative approaches to staging, design, and lighting evident in the work of Tomás Mac Anna, Patrick Mason, Joe Dowling, and others. Another preoccupation focused upon political and cultural matters, in particular the seemingly intractable nature of the renewed conflict in Northern Ireland and its southern reverberations and manifestations. At first there was a tendency to see the 'Troubles' as a northern dysfunction, best kept up there: a point of view expressed, though not necessarily endorsed, in Bryan MacMahon's *The Honey Spike* as far back as 1961. The burning down of the British embassy in Dublin on 2 February 1972 in the wake of the Bloody Sunday outrage in Derry, the bombings in Dublin and Monaghan on 17 May 1974 when thirty-three people were killed, and the Birmingham bomb which killed nineteen people on 21 November in the same year showed that the social structures of the islands of Ireland and Britain were subject to seismic upheavals the origins of which lay along a fault-line less than 100 miles north of the Abbey itself. Friel, Murphy, and Kilroy, in their different ways, reflect these realizations. The Troubles and their implications also raised afresh the issue of identity, and the relationship between culture, territories, and traditions. Public events and political statements were seen to be intimately bound up with private obsessions, fears, prejudices. What was remembered and how it was remembered became a matter of moral and civic responsibility. Statesmen, historians, academics, authority-figures could be, and often were seen to be, liars; how good, then, can words and images be, in a darkened theatre, in recognizing the play of truth and half-truth and falsity upon which public and private languages are constructed? In some sense, the story of the Abbey from 1966 to 1985 is the story of the whole of Irish theatre and Irish writing in those years, in which the literary arts acquired a terrible and resistless urgency. The 1966 commemorations of 1916 were entered into in a buoyant spirit of freshened anticipation of the future, a spirit animated by a sense that the past was over; that modernity, liberalism, and the flood of money had arrived. But it was far from being the case: the whole bloody business was starting all over again because the central issue, the fault-line itself, the border, had not been faced.

Friel's theatre of memory, in which recollection is searched and questioned, had, as we saw, a major influence on Frank McGuinness, and turned him towards the stage. But another significant influence on McGuinness was the work of Samuel Beckett, his prose as much as his drama. McGuinness learned from Beckett a technique of agonized and doubtful reminiscence, in which the torment of the memory becomes a goad to ever more urgent excavation: he also learned a method of terse and gnomic utterance, in which human exchange becomes fissured with doubt, animated by rage, or impacted with defensiveness or anxiety. It may seem a bold assertion but it seems to me that Beckett's practices had not, in any fully integrated way, entered the Irish theatre until McGuinness discovered him for his own purposes in *Observe the Sons of Ulster Marching towards the Somme*.

McGuinness deployed Beckett's techniques of horrified recollection about the surges of remorse and sorrow and curt exchange (that conceal as much as they reveal) to deal with the intimate hatreds and misprisions that are the psychological realities of the Ulster 'trouble'. As an Ulsterman, from outside the six counties of Northern Ireland, McGuinness knows, in his nerves, the pitch and fall of the internal misgivings and rages that drive the sectarian cleavages and fissures of the northern conflict. His play ventures right into one flank of the cleavage, one side of the rank ditch: that of the Protestant majority in Northern Ireland. And he uses Beckett's plangency and curtness to accomplish this extraordinarily stalwart piece of empathy. He once, in a seminar at the University of Ulster at Coleraine, said that the play began in a rumination in the Diamond at Coleraine over the names on the cenotaph of those who had fallen in the First World War. What is remarkable and decisive about this play, what distinguishes it as a conclusion of one phase of dramatic development and the inauguration of another, is the effort of its moral realization: McGuinness's dramatic art crosses over, not merely from a Catholic mind-set to Protestant ones, but into a world where the difference is fully valued. The heroism of the Protestant achievement, its fierce bravery, its courage devoid of the comfort of 'good works' is given fully human voice; but it achieves this latitude and generosity while not neglecting the fissures and discontents that disrupt what, from the outside, would seem settled convictions. The two Belfast men, Anderson (Oliver Maguire) and McIlwaine (Ian McElhinney), are at the

Twelfth Field, while on leave back home from the Somme. Anderson and McIlwaine fear that Ulster is doomed:

McIlwaine. Every nail they hammered into the *Titanic*, they cursed the Pope. That's what they say.
Anderson. And he still wasn't cursed enough
McIlwaine. Every nail we hammered into the Titanic, we'll die in the same amount in this cursed war. That's what I say.
Anderson. What are you talking about?
McIlwaine. The war's cursed. It's good for nothing. A waste of time. We won't survive. We're all going to die for nothing. . . we're on the *Titanic*. We're all going down.[34]

The play's action comprises the remembrance of one man, Pyper (played by Geoff Golden), whose recollections of his seven comrades who fell at the Somme come to life: Pyper is a cynic, an apostate, an artist of sorts, but at the end he dons the sash to march into battle at the Somme, alongside his 'brethren'. He prays to God to deliver Ulster from her enemies:

Let this day at the Somme be as glorious in the memory of Ulster as that day at the Boyne, when you scattered our enemies. Lead us back from this exile. To Derry, to the Foyle. To Belfast and the Lagan. To Armagh. To Tyrone. To the Bann and its banks. . . Lord, look down on us. Spare us. I love—. Observe the sons of Ulster marching towards the Somme. I love their lives. I love my own life. I love my home. I love my Ulster.[35]

The man from Buncrana speaks to the men of Ulster through the Ulster voices he creates on stage. There is a confluence of views and of feelings in the dramatic evocation. Here, in the play, a line is well and truly crossed; it is a transgression, but a positive one, to observe, in admiration, the lines of men marching to a different set of drums. In Coleraine, when the play toured the north in 1985, at the Riverside, when Pyper delivered this speech before the last diversified fragments of northern voices that conclude the play, there was a hush, that black hush of deepest concentration and impact. And when the final darkness came, there were those few moments of baffled delight and emotion, when an audience knows it has shared something entirely new and unsubduable.

1985–1999

'The dead are not the past,
the dead are the future'

In 1994 Patrick Mason was appointed artistic director at the Abbey, succeeding Garry Hynes, who returned to the Druid Theatre in Galway, whence she had come in 1991. After Mason's appointment there followed a period of stability in the management of the theatre which was in marked contrast with what had gone before. In an interview with me on 5 November 1998 Mason singled out, as the single most important factor in establishing this stability, the quite deliberate policy he and James Hickey, chairman of the board since 1993, adopted whereby they resolved always to speak as with one voice, whatever their disagreements in private. This meant that management and the person responsible for realizing the visionary and pragmatic goals of the Abbey, the artistic director, were in harmony. Such a united front must have involved a great deal of restraint on both sides but it meant the organization had a rock-solid foundation. It may be appropriate to give here a brief account of the vicissitudes of the artistic directors at the Abbey, to show how uncharacteristic Mason's tenure was.

On 10 December 1998 Tomás Mac Anna replied, most generously, to a series of questions on the subject of the role of the artistic director and its status in the period from 1966 onwards. When Mac Anna was made artistic adviser in 1966 Walter Macken had held two positions: that of assistant manager and artistic adviser. The intention was that Macken succeed Ernest Blythe as managing director. When Macken resigned, there were two appointments made: manager (Phil O'Kelly) and artistic adviser (Mac Anna). The term 'adviser' was used rather than 'artistic director', to avoid confusion with the directors of the board; however Mac Anna's (clearly correct) view is that the board wanted to retain control of artistic policy and feared the designation 'director' might give whoever was appointed ideas above his or her station. Once Blythe resigned in 1967 the directors assumed greater control: his 'undoubted powerful presence' exercised some restraint on their authority up to then. The thirty shareholders held 25 shares each, a total of 750; whereas the five directors held 200 each; so that the board could outvote the shareholders if they remained unified. This situation continues to this day.

Mac Anna took leave of absence at Carleton College in the USA in 1968 and was succeeded as artistic adviser by Alan Simpson, who left in 1969, to be followed by the return of Hugh Hunt. Hunt, however, insisted he be designated artistic director, a term in common use in British theatre management. When Mac Anna returned in 1970 he was made director of the Peacock, with Joe Dowling as his assistant. Lelia Doolin was made artistic director in December 1971; she resigned in 1973 and Mac Anna was appointed in her stead, a position he retained until February 1978. Joe Dowling was then made artistic director, resigning in March 1985 after a clash with the board. Once again Mac Anna assumed the position, to be replaced, in December 1985, by Christopher Fitzsimon. Fitzsimon remained in post until May 1987 when he was succeeded by Vincent Dowling. Dowling was followed by Noel Pearson in April 1989, who combined the position with the responsibilities of chairman of the board until December 1990. Then Garry Hynes of Druid took over until December 1993, when she was followed by Patrick Mason.[1]

Mason had his inaugural production at the Peacock with Thomas Kilroy's *Talbot's Box* (13 December 1977), from which time his work, often in collaboration with actors such as Tom Hickey, made free use of experimentation, and displayed considerable inventiveness in stagecraft, lighting, voicing, making full use of the resources of the physical space of the theatre itself and of the human body as an instrument of dramatic realization. In the most recent phase of the history of the Abbey Mason's presence and his example have been extremely influential. He has been an inspiration to actors, and writers have found in him a collaborator who assisted in bringing their imagined forms into that alternative reality which is the stage.

The Abbey tradition is commonly defined as being predominantly realistic and verbal; its effects are often thought to be most satisfactory when poetry is mixed with scenes of real life, as in the theatres of Sean O'Casey and M. J. Molloy. However, such a characterization of the Abbey was, and still remains, inadequate: Yeats always insisted that the plays of a national theatre should not merely reflect life's surfaces; they should question them, and probe deeper, into complex, dangerous, and unsettled arenas of the mind and consciousness—which was, of course, what Synge did, and many others after him, such as Lennox Robinson, Denis Johnston, and Teresa Deevy. Furthermore, the stagecraft of Tomás Mac Anna, schooled as it was in European practice and experiment, and tried and tested in his sustained endeavour to find arresting ways of presenting plays in Irish from the 1950s onwards, from 1966 had exhibited a readiness to create a theatre for the Abbey which used images, design, and movement in a manner which extended well beyond the boundaries of literary and verbal dramatic effects. So that when Mason assumed the artistic directorship in 1994 he did so in a theatre which was, by 1993, well accustomed to employing the full resources of all the elements of performance.

Nevertheless Mason's work, from the mid-1980s onwards, signalled a new departure, and a turning point in his own development as a director and in the theatre's own imaginative practice was his production of Tom MacIntyre's *The*

Great Hunger. This play, a very free adaptation of Patrick Kavanagh's poem of 1942, transformed that basic material, which was an attack upon the repressive puritanism of mid-century Catholic Ireland, into a carnivalesque evocation of primal human urges. Kavanagh's bleak and sterile pastoral world becomes animated with energies that refuse to stay dormant. Mason discovered a way of working with the author and the main actor, Tom Hickey, to create a collaborative event, based on Kavanagh's text, but which entered into an alliance with the creative impulse that drove the poet to confront those taboos that threaten creativity itself. To evoke powerfully negative conditions requires a force of humanity and imagination: and that is what this collaboration realized.

Making daring use of the stage space as an arena of emotion, and recognizing the force of mime, lighting, and bizarre bodily movement to convey extreme states of feeling, the play became a kind of exorcism of the dark gods of Kavanagh's repressive world, that of the small farmer Patrick Maguire, his mother, and his sister. It was a kind of exorcism of the repression and inhibitions of the Ireland that created Kavanagh, and that hurt him into poetry. MacIntyre's *The Great Hunger* opened in the Peacock on 23 May 1983, but the production did not achieve its full impact until the revised revival in the Abbey (9 July 1986).

Mason and MacIntyre collaborated on *Rise up Lovely Sweeney* (2 September 1985), a play which placed the mad Sweeney from the medieval tale *Buile Shuibhne* in a contemporary setting in which the zany hero is lost in a world of conflicting loyalties and insatiable demands. From the mid-1980s Mason's readiness to return to myths and folklore has had the effect of restoring to the theatre one of its sources of power and surprise, to some extent in abeyance in the modernist strivings of the 1960s and 1970s.

The Abbey went on a Russian tour in February 1988 and performed MacIntyre's *The Great Hunger* and John B. Keane's *The Field* (first produced at the Olympia, 1 November 1965). In St Petersburg (then Leningrad) Mason addressed the audience on the opening night of *The Great Hunger* at the Gorky Bolshoi Theatre, saying what a great honour it was to play in 'the hero city of Leningrad'. Niall Tóibín (who played the Bull McCabe in *The Field*) and Tom Hickey as Patrick Maguire faced up to each other for a photo session in Red Square on the day before they left, dressed in full stage costume.[2]

The Mason, MacIntyre, and Hickey collaboration continued for two further productions: *Dance for your Daddy* (23 February 1987) and *Snow White* (20 June 1988). The former was a profoundly disturbing piece on an issue that had begun to generate a great deal of controversy in the mid-to-late 1980s: the (often-related) problems of child sexual abuse and incest in Ireland. Throughout the period from about 1984 to the mid-1990s a series of revelations, followed by accusations and criminal proceedings, made it clear that the family, traditionally regarded as the keystone of Irish Catholic society, was, in some cases, an institution of tyranny, lust, and exploitation. In one miserable court case after another fathers, uncles, friends of the family, and priests were revealed as sex-driven destroyers of innocence and vulnerability. This collapse in the apparent integrity of the family unit was paralleled by an unprecedented breakdown of trust in the Catholic church, itself traditionally a bulwark of the family and family values. Priests were revealed as abusers of children, fornicators, liars, and embezzlers. The steady grip which the church had held on the emotional lives and moral persuasions of Irish people was loosening, and the startling thing about this, as it was happening, was how quickly society was adjusting to a different and more cynical appraisal of authority and absolute values. The temper of moral and religious outlook, more or less settled for the 150 years since the Famine, moved, and moved with an amazing swiftness. Although it would be impossible to fix dates to this process, in a matter of years Irish society underwent a profound shift from being theocentric to being, to all intents and purposes, secular. If the northern 'Troubles' inaugurated an appraisal of issues of identity in the period from 1970, say, to 1985, then from that date to 1995 the horrifying details of child abuse cases or the (sometimes) graphically amusing particulars of clerical sexual shenanigans eroded a long-established trust in religious adherence as a reliable means of social cohesion.

This pell-mell revision of attitudes, feelings, intimacies, affections, traditions, and politics was reflected, naturally enough, in the work of the National Theatre, and Tom MacIntyre's dramatic 'events', from *The Great Hunger* through to *Snow White* and beyond, seemed to catch the flux of that period with its edge of panic and hysteria.

Sheep's Milk on the Boil (17 February 1994) is both a parody of and homage to Synge. The action takes place on an island off the west coast of Ireland. Matt comes back from the mainland with a clock and a mirror (a coy reference to Christy Mahon's bit of looking-glass in *The Playboy*), and a good deal of the play is concerned with hiding and discovering the latter. There is no plot, as such: the play is an onrush of bewildering energy, violence, sex, and verbal fireworks. A male visitor arrives and a female 'Inspector of Wrack'; these make game of and make free with Matt and his wife Biddy. The Inspector, inscrutably, says she has come to the island to relieve Matt of everything his father has left him. She is a kind of embodiment of hectic disruption, a Lady of the Misrule that is Ireland, and she is after 'everything':

Every hairy acre. The birthmark before and the birthmark behind. . . that's lonesome for lack of endearments. The sour in yer sweat, the groan in yer sigh, the dint in yer eye. I'm here to collect the entire cargo your silvered father—tight as Christy's britches—wouldn't loose, and my red information is. . . one right splash of the dew just under the curly bush and you'll stream the sweets I'm after like the mushroom droves of mornin'.[3]

Synge's presence is very much in evidence (even Christy's britches are mentioned) but at a more searching level the play examines the meaning of inheritance, tradition, paternity: all concerns being tried in public and private in the most disturbing manner in the early to mid-1990s.

The play was directed by Tom Hickey, the actor who had such a triumph in *The Great Hunger* and who had been MacIntyre's acting collaborator and sounding-board. The piece is startlingly physical as well as maintaining a Synge-like density of language: however, it may be that the concern to deal with so many twists and turns in the unconscious of contemporary Ireland led MacIntyre into a maelstrom of whirling energy that departs from a central animating focus—a bewilderment all the more evident because of the somewhat self-conscious attempts to drive home allegorical points and evoke literary echoes.

The unconscious made a Jung-like entry, MacIntyre tells us, when he was working on his next play for the Abbey, *Good Evening, Mr Collins* (5 October 1995). This was a play about the Collins 'myth' in Irish historical memory; once again the theatre is divining a current of tension at work in the community, and giving it form and body. The mid-1990s was the time when the nigh-on thirty-year conflict in the north was winding down in a mixture of exhaustion, resignation, and muted hope. It was a period when Collins's participation in the discussions of 1921 that led to the Treaty and the cessation of the Anglo-Irish War came under the closest scrutiny it had ever received in modern Irish history. There was a popular film made by Neil Jordan and starring Liam Neeson (an ex-Abbey actor), which contrived to be made against competition by the Irish controversialist Eoghan Harris. Tim Pat Coogan's careful biography of Collins stayed in the bestseller lists in Ireland for months on end, all evidence of the renewed enquiry into the nature of the contract Collins signed with Britain and its consequences for Ireland in the twentieth century.

MacIntyre tells us that while he was

in the deeps of writing the play, I was aroused from sleep one night by a clap of thunder. Every stone in the house turned over, settled. Stillness again. Next morning, I enquired. My companion had heard nothing. No one in the townland had heard anything. Fine. What I'd heard, I'd heard. And it didn't surprise me. Collins was—is—the *coup de tonnerre*, the *coup de foudre*. If you're dealing with that kind of energy, expect a visitation. A nod in your direction, yours to interpret.[4]

What MacIntyre does not tell us is what interpretation he placed on the visitation, but presumably he felt it a benign one, as he went on to finish the play and have it produced, directed by Kathy McArdle.

The play concentrates on Collins's energy and force of character, contrasting him with de Valera, who is presented as methodical, cautious, and Machiavellian. Collins is lucky, a quality evoked in a recollection of childhood, when he fell through the trapdoor of a loft, the floor of which he and his sisters have strewn with flowers, into the hay beneath:

There was this trapdoor at one end of the loft and nothing would do me but to find it—even if I didn't know I was searching for it. . . the foxglove looking at me, the clover smelling, the daisies basking, the buttercups shiny. . . I'm gone, fifteen-foot drop to the stable below. A lap of hay was all that saved me. It wasn't, they said, supposed to be there. . .[5]

The piece does not seek to psychologize Collins or analyse him, or turn him into a mythic figure. Impressionistically, his telluric force is sketched by means of vignette, vigorous speech, bristling and harsh encounters. MacIntyre is drawn to the oral tradition about Collins, that he was a lady's man ('Mick and the women'), and he makes much of an alleged sexual relationship with Lady Lavery, who says: 'As for fucking me three times a day—I love the eternal accountant in you—the relish evident on both sides suggests to me, at any rate, considerable commitment in the endeavour.'[6]

John B. Keane's *The Field*, as we saw, toured Russia with *The Great Hunger* in 1988. By then Keane had, at last, been drawn into the repertoire of the Abbey, from which he had long been a conspicuous absence, apart from *The Man from Clare* in 1963. His work was considered crude, melodramatic, and shapeless; and he was under suspicion because his plays were very popular in the amateur movement, enough to make him a dubious case in the eyes of a theatrical profession ever on the watch to protect its own notions of itself.

Joe Dowling, artistic director of the Abbey 1978–84, decided, as one of his last policy resolutions before leaving to join the Gaiety, to bring Keane onto the stage of the National Theatre. Ben Barnes directed a production of *Sive* (10 June 1985), a play which had, as performed by the Listowel Drama Group in 1959, won the All-Ireland amateur championship, and was presented at the Queen's Theatre. Thereafter, Keane sent the play to Ernest Blythe, followed by four or five others, only to have each of them rejected, without, Keane suspects, being read.

Ben Barnes cut the original three acts of *Sive* to two, and made some other changes. It had an immediate and extraordinary impact, and the reasons were not hard to seek. Here, as with Eugene MacCabe and M. J. Molloy, was a dramatist capable of writing about Irish country life with complete understanding from the inside. Molloy and MacCabe have this familiarity, but Keane is closer to his material, and intelligent enough to comprehend it as it was, without romanticism, moralizing, interpretations, or contempt. The irony of this recognition of Keane's power was that the National Theatre had developed, out of the work of Synge, Colum, and Fitzmaurice, a tradition of peasant plays which were authentic enough in their way, but these plays often fell short of the intensity and power of that early work; while with Keane, the real thing was, more or less entirely, kept from the stage for over twenty-five years.

The Abbey production showed that Keane's popularity over the years in rural Ireland and in the world of amateur theatre rested upon his clear-eyed understanding of the forces at work in his own society: the pressures of economic necessity pitted against the need of the young for love and affection. In *Sive* the old woman Norma Glavin, who smokes her clay-pipe surreptitiously for fear she will be seen by her bossy and sterile daughter-in-law Mena, belongs to an older world of communal feeling and sincerity before land, money, and a profitable marriage were everything. She is on the side of Sive, the young schoolgirl, who is to be sold off like an animal to the lecherous old man Sean Dofa, for 200 sovereigns. Sive's

uncle Mike is resistless before the urge of grim necessity that drives his wife. With
the connivance of a pair of wandering tinkers, Liam Scuab, Sive's sweetheart,
plans an escape from their destiny, but the plot is foiled and Sive rushes out, bare-
foot and half-clothed, into the bog where she drowns. Thus her life is snuffed out,
a life that really had very little chance of amounting to anything, given her family's circumstances, and the fact that she lacks the protection of a mother and a father. She is illegitimate; her mother is dead, and her father gone. Sive is a helpless
victim, a casualty of the brutality of a society impervious to human needs and
feelings. But the code Mena and Mike live by was the one that dominated the
Ireland of the years from 1922 into the mid-1980s; so that another reason for
Keane's failure to get a proper airing on the Abbey stage may very well have been
because, for all his melodrama and raw energy, he was cutting uncomfortably
close to the sharp truth of the heartlessness of many Irish people, where survival
overrode all other considerations in the battle to emerge from poverty. It would be
inaccurate to dismiss as melodramatic the great scene at the end of the play when
Liam Scuab brings his dead girl in from the boghole where she has drowned; he
dries the hair on her lifeless body, and when Mena, the aunt, comes near he roars:
'You killed her! You. . . you. . . you. . . you killed her! You horrible filthy bitch!
That the hand of Jesus may strike you dead where you stand. You heartless wretch
that hunted the poor little girl to her grave.'[7] This is towering, humanitarian rage;
it is how people speak when they are hurt and wronged and cannot forgive, and it
is also emotionally and technically exact, in that it provides a release for the now
almost unbearable tension in the audience. Nor does Keane's evisceration of the
corrupt soul of this society stop here; when Mike, the uncle, distractedly reminds
them that they need a priest, Liam growls back at him, pagan and inconsolable:
'Go for the priest, then!. . . Go on!. . . Go!' Eamon Kelly, the great Kerry actor,
played the part of Pats Bocock, the wandering tinker, and brought a touch of mystery into this choric (and humane) role.

One of the reason's why *Sive* was a huge success in 1985, as Anthony Roche
pointed out, was because its portrayal of a girl victimized by a society terrified of
sexuality, and driven by money and necessity, gave expression to a complicated
tangle of feelings in the mid-1980s aroused by the 'Kerry babies' case. Keane's
play from the 1950s, his first, was still therapeutic for a society locked in stresses
of anxiety and lovelessness, in which the events leading up to the Kerry infanticide
could take place.[8] But it was as if the urgency of Keane's insight had to wait until
the oppressiveness that created the situation in which a girl would kill her own
child rather than face public humiliation had begun to break down before his
message could be heard.

Ben Barnes went on to direct Keane's *The Field* (2 February 1987) and his *Big
Maggie* (15 November 1988) at the Abbey with similar success. *The Field*, in particular, created a major cultural stir in the 1980s. It was first staged at the Olympia
(1 November 1965), with Ray MacAnally playing the leading character of the Bull
McCabe. At the Abbey the Bull was played in softer, more insidious, but no less

violent style by the Cork actor Niall Tóibín. Tóibín is also a brilliant stand-up comic and his one-man show includes many typical Kerryman jokes, a game of wit especially favoured in Cork; but here the Kerry life and tectonic power, the fear of which lies behind the Kerry joke, was given awesome portrayal in Tóibín's performance, which conveyed a steady, brooding, savage, and remorseless energy. When, for example, the Bull describes how he and his son Tadhg, after a three-month wait, killed a donkey 'with a single ear and the eyes of a saint', because he had eaten the grass of their beloved 'field', the writing goes beyond black humour or farce into something elemental and wild:

The first time I met that stallion was on Stephen's Day and he staring through one of the gates of the field we're buying now. You'd think butter wouldn't melt in his mouth. To look at his face you'd think grass was the last thing in his head. He gave me a look and he trotted off. That night he broke the gate. Three months we watched him until we cornered him. Tadhg there beat him to death. He was a solid hour flaking him with his fists and me with a blackthorn.[9]

This is the force that Maggie Burke, the owner of the field, is against as she tries to put it up for open auction, a plan foiled by the Bull, who has everyone scared to death. However, a young man, William Dee, arrives in the pub where the fixed auction is to take place, and outbids the Bull, ignoring all warnings. He is killed, by night, at the end of Act II, Scene iii, a piece of writing remarkable for its emotional and structural daring and force. The Bull and Tadhg are alone, waiting for their victim; the Bull tells his son how he has not spoken to or slept with his wife for eighteen years because he once shot a tinker's pony she had allowed to graze on his land; a jet passes over, the tiniest rumour of a reminder that the backdrop to all our technologies and mechanical wizardry is just precisely this scene, with its mixture of death and sex and spoiled love; then Tadhg tells his father how he stands fair with Paddy Finnerty's daughter ('a bit red in the legs but a good wedge of a woman') who will come with 9 acres of land; and then, at last, William Dee arrives to meet his fate. He has, as the Irish country saying goes, walked into it: he did not know that in purchasing a piece of land he was entering a force-field that would annihilate him. Money and greed are factors in the Bull's obsession, but there is more to what drives him than material conditions: the Bull is a phenomenon of nature.

The play revolves around a subject profoundly unpopular with the liberal-minded, modernist, and secular society emerging at the time in which it was written: the early to mid-1960s. The revisionist school of historians, for example, were beginning to become established in academia at that time, and one of their concerns was the degree to which nationalist attitudes were defined by equating the nation with territory. Nationalism, according to the revisionist analysis, sees Ireland as an entity comprising four provinces, not Éire and the six counties of Northern Ireland. Revisionism, then, in the 1960s, in the 1980s (when Keane's play was revived), and now, argues for a severance between nation and land and posits new sets of relations that make the so-called 'partitionist' nationalist mentality outmoded. It can be no accident (although one is not attributing design) that Keane's powerful depiction of the elemental and tectonic forces at play in the way Irish people (be they Kerry or Tyrone) feel about land surfaced at a time in which the founding traditions of the Irish state were being re-examined. And by the mid-1980s it was very evident that the passion to regain the territory of Ireland, a sub-theme of Keane's play, was still very much alive, in spite of the cerebrations of politicians and revisionist historians. These energies (atavisms, if one wishes, in the jargon) give the Bull McCabe his awesome power. With him we are in the presence of a personality where will and mind are conjoined to an urge which arises from a communal source of feeling to do with belonging, possession, and the need to expel the intruder. Exogamy, to make affiances outside one's field of force, is to be resisted in the world Keane brings into being; in *Translations* (1980) Friel wittily engages the problem through the mouth of a half-cracked old pedant who is in love with Athene. Keane's venture into the terrain of territoriality and nationhood is more disturbing than Friel's tense but balanced appraisals, its melodramatic violence and lawless humour contributing to its disruptive urgency.

In the Keane trilogy staged at the Abbey by Ben Barnes, *Sive* and *The Field* were followed by *Big Maggie*. *Big Maggie* was first played at the Opera House, Cork (20 January 1969), with the young Brenda Fricker in the role of Mary Madden, the girl whom Big Maggie's son Maurice makes pregnant. She also featured in Ben Barnes's production, but this time played magnificently in the title role.

Big Maggie, recently widowed, takes control of the shop and the farm which had been neglected by her philandering and alcoholic husband. One by one she ejects or subdues to her will all her children until, finally, she is left alone. She remains proof against romantic or humanitarian arguments, believing that these are invariably driven by disguised self-interest or greed. The play is an antidote to the notion of the good-natured Irish, dreamily susceptible to longing and notions of freedom. Maggie is a study of a person hardened by necessity and the need to survive. For example, to teach her daughter Gert hardness and resolve, she allows the traveller Teddy Heelin to make an assignation with her instead of keeping his date with Gert; only to arrange to have the girl come back and discover her in Teddy's arms. When Teddy remonstrates with her, shocked at what she is prepared to do to teach her daughter not to fall for a philanderer, she says: 'Don't give me that stuff about human beings, because that's the biggest lie of all. If a man or a woman hasn't self-respect they have nothing. You should know that, because you are nothing, you have nothing, and God pity you, you never will.'[10] And when Maurice, her son, gets Mary Madden pregnant, and sends her to his mother to plead for clemency and help, she appals the girl by guessing exactly why she has come to see her, saying that it is inevitable 'because it always happens after everything else fails. . . Whenever I see a poorly-off slip of a girl like yourself now, knocking around with a well-off young lad, I do be on the look-out, so to speak.'[11]

While this play is, on the one hand, concerned with the human suffering brought about by a suspicion of feeling and generosity of spirit in family life, in society, and in religion, on the other it recognizes the uncomfortable realities Big Maggie lives by: trust no one because life is hard; indulge yourself or your children and destruction will surely follow. By the time Barnes produced *Big Maggie* Ireland was beginning its ascent into the prosperity of the 1990s and the 'Celtic Tiger' economy, so that Maggie provided a retrospect to a world and set of attitudes apparently in decline. Yet the play haunts the mind and imagination, and it had its success in the 1980s because it wins us over to the feeling that Maggie, like the Bull McCabe, embodies some basic truth about human nature. Blandishments may come in the form of a Common Agricultural Policy from Brussels, but they too may turn out to be 'nothing' in the end.

Keane understands completely the conservatism, narrowness, and coldness of the Irish mind, and his plays depict it brilliantly. Very few dramatists have shown this aspect of the Irish so convincingly (among these would be R. J. Ray and Eugene MacCabe), which makes him a radical and daring presence; and this surely is the main reason why he was slow to reach the centre of Irish dramatic life represented by the Abbey stage.

Frank McGuinness, after the success of *Observe the Sons of Ulster*, began to write across a broad range of subjects, as if he wished to test his imaginative energies to the limit. He wrote *Innocence* for the Gate (1986), and adapted Lorca's *Yerma* for the Abbey (1987), Ibsen's *Rosmersholm* for the National Theatre in London (1987), and Ibsen's *Peer Gynt* for the Gate (1988). In the midst of these hectic demands Field Day approached him, and he undertook a commission for a play on the Bloody Sunday shootings in Derry for the 1987 season, to be staged alongside Stewart Parker's *Pentecost*, which was based on the Ulster Workers' Council strike of 1974 that ended the power-sharing Assembly that followed the Sunningdale Agreement. There are different versions as to what happened between McGuinness and the board of Field Day, but whatever the difficulties the outcome was that McGuinness withdrew his play, *Carthaginians*. He had much to occupy him, managing to combine the life of a busy academic at St Patrick's College, Maynooth, with the kind of work-schedule that would be exhausting even for a full-time writer. (In interviews he has indicated that one of the reasons he meets his crushing commitments and fearsome deadlines is the fact that he suffers from chronic insomnia.) He did not delay in having *Carthaginians* produced, and on 26 September 1988 it was staged at the Peacock, directed by Sara Pia Anderson.

The play is set in a graveyard in Derry where the characters are keeping an unexplained vigil in memory of the dead of Bloody Sunday, and in expectation of some form of change or resurrection: in the words of the Creed: 'et expecto resurrectio mortuorum' ('I await the resurrection of the dead'). This play is an exploration of the Catholic experience of suffering and its psychology of mourning, remorse, and hope, to balance the attempt at investigating a Protestant sense of destiny and despair in *Observe the Sons of Ulster*. The play's structure, as Hiroko Mikami has pointed out, follows the rituals of Holy Week from Spy Wednesday, the day on which Christ was betrayed in the Passion story, to the vigil of Easter Saturday night and Sunday morning.[12] Beckett's theme of anxious waiting (as in *Waiting for Godot*) is allied to the Christian hope of deliverance. However, *Carthaginians* delivers no reassuring anodyne; instead it offers a comfortless, fraught depiction of the hope that hopes against hope, a condition not a million miles removed from Pyper's bleak endurance in *Observe the Sons of Ulster*.

The characters of *Carthaginians* are not fully-featured human personalities: they are indications of character, traces of temperament, scraps of individuality, loosely gathered in a communal sense of grief and waiting. They, like Beckett's tramps, pass the time in banter, canters of riposte, play-acting, memory. Three girls, Maela, Greta, and Sarah (recalling the three Maries who waited before the tomb of Christ), in a trauma of grief, wait in a graveyard for a sign. They are visited by Hark, who acts as their publicity agent, and a number of other men, including Dido, a homosexual.

As a diversion they perform *The Burning Balaclava* by Fionnuala McGonigle (actually Dido) in which all the characters are called Doherty: it is a cartoonish send-up of the way in which McGuinness sees the Troubles being used by self-publicists and by those who embrace the status of victim. There is, at one point, an acid joke about sado-masochism, that it is 'where the future lies'.[13] The humour of the play-within-a-play is vicious and unsettling. Dido, playing a British soldier, encounters the young man Seph, playing Doreen O'Doherty, who is walking her pet dog Boomer:

Soldier. Where the fuck do you think you're going?

Doreen. I'm going to the fish and chip shop with Boomer here. He's my wee hound of Ulster and he looks after me. I'm buying him a fish supper.

Soldier. So you call your hound of Ulster fucking Boomer then?

Doreen. Aye, it's short for Boomerang. He might run away from his Mammy, but he always comes back to her. He's a real Irishman.

The Burning Balaclava moves to an enactment of the Bloody Sunday shootings: a priest is shot, wearing a balaclava. Hark, playing the Derry mother, says: 'I depend on the dying. Nobody knew it, not even my son, but I knit all the balaclavas. The more that dies, the more I'm given.'[14] Towards the close of the play, Seph says that all along it was as if the nationalists wanted Bloody Sunday to happen, so they 'could make sense of [their] suffering' by accusations.[15] The play concludes with a moving litany of the thirteen dead, a kind of translation of Yeats's naming of the heroes of 1916 in his famous poem.

The play registers the confusion and unease that characterized attitudes regarding the northern Troubles in the mid-1980s. Exhaustion was setting in, on all sides; there were intimations of *rapprochements* between Sinn Féin, the main political arm of the republican movement, the constitutional Social

Democratic and Labour Party, elements within unionism and loyalism, and British government representatives in Northern Ireland. There was a good deal of self-questioning as well as the usual level of self-assertion. In this context McGuinness's play, which explores, fitfully, the psychodynamics of victimization and power, reflects a growing sense of doubt about fixed positions that was in the air. However, as a dramatic construct, the play is not grounded firmly enough in the humanity of the characters, who remain ciphers, to carry the burden of a psychoanalytic approach to conflict, with the result that the play seems to skitter from one occasion to another, without the vertiginous falls and sudden psychic starts that Beckett can give to the realization of sporadic situations and abrupt transitions.

In 1992, with *Someone Who'll Watch over Me*, McGuinness widened the perspective on the central core of traumatized paralysis that is the theme of *Carthaginians*. *Someone Who'll Watch over Me* was catalysed by the incarceration and release of Brian Keenan, the Northern Irish lecturer in English, who had been held hostage by fundamentalist Shi'ite Muslims in Beirut for four and a half years. McGuinness, basing his play loosely on Keenan's story (told in *An Evil Cradling*, 1992), sets his play in the room where at first two, then three hostages are held: Adam, an American doctor, and Edward, an Irish journalist, are joined by Michael, an English lecturer in medieval literature. Like *Carthaginians*, it is a play of waiting; unlike it, it translates the misapprehensions and misprisions of Irish and English history into a parable of the possibility of kindness and courage in even the most appalling circumstances. The play opened at the Hampstead Theatre (10 July 1992), directed by Robin Le Fevre, and transferred to the Abbey Theatre on 13 April 1993.

The three hostages are shackled to the wall by chains, and divert themselves by make-believe, physical exercises, and bitter exchanges, the latter most often revolving around racial stereotypes. Each one is shackled to a mental prison-house, as well as to the wall of the room in Beirut. But the situation between the three is more fluent, unstable, and fully realized than that somewhat programmatic statement might suggest For example, Edward, responding to an extract from the Koran which Adam is reading, reflects on the danger to be feared from those who always think they are right: 'Save us from all who believe they're right. Right, in the name of God Who is not merciful and compassionate, for he is like them, always right. I've seen it at home before. Scared wee shits, panting with fear, ready to make the big sacrifice. . .'[16] However, a few moments later, this rejection of one-sidedness and obsessive hatred evaporates when Michael, the Englishman, makes a disparaging comment about Irish coarseness of speech. The Irishman in Edward explodes:

times have changed, you English mouth, and I mean mouth. One time you and your breed opened that same mouth, you ruled the roost, you ruled the world, because it was your language. Not any more. We've taken it from you. We've made it our own. And now, we've bettered you at it. . . I speak as a man who is one generation removed from the dispossessed.

Edward lapses back into the accusatory, triumphalist stereotype, which is fuelled by a sense of grievance, that he has somehow been wronged by the English, a feeling he visits upon his developing relationship with Michael. So that the play enquires into the entire nexus of British–Irish relations, the American lending a distancing element, and an irritant, thereby allowing for Anglo-Irish stand-offs, engagements, and raillery, while also facilitating concerted anti-American broadsides. This mazurka of shifting antagonism, opposition, and alliances becomes a complex pattern of human interaction that gravitates towards friendship, even love, after the American is taken away to his death. Towards the end of the play the Englishman's courage is celebrated, his Spartan capacity to sustain pain. Michael recalls his father telling him 'there is a place called Sparta. Brave soldiers come from there. When they have pain they show it by controlling it. We [the English] long for our dear life, lamenting great loss. . . but accepting fate.'[17] The Irishman and the Englishman end up combing each other's hair, as the Spartans did before battle; they do this as the Irishman prepares to depart for freedom, and the Englishman readies himself for his fate, which is death. After his meditations on Protestant and Catholic identities and traumas, McGuinness, in this play set in Beirut, expands the field of vision to encompass racial stereotypes whilst retaining a firm grip all the time on the shifting nature of human personality, giving the play weight and energy.

Keenan's release in 1990, the changes in Eastern Europe following the breaking-down of the Berlin Wall, the growing sense that accommodations might be possible in the north, are reflected in McGuinness's writings for the Abbey (and elsewhere) from 1985 onwards. The plays, in their transgression of traditional boundaries, whether political, social, or sexual, offer a moving image of the transformations taking place in Irish life at the end of the century, changes deeply related to others occurring on a European and global scale. This sense of imagined reality coming directly off the historical moment gives McGuinness's theatre immediacy and point.

Joe Dowling, the artistic director from 1978 to 1985, appointed Christopher Fitzsimon as script editor in 1984, succeeding Seán MacCarthy in a position inaugurated by Thomas Kilroy. When Mac Anna resigned in 1985 Fitzsimon became artistic director to 1987, and when Garry Hynes of Druid took over in 1991, Fitzsimon continued as script editor. That the institution of such a post was essential is evident from the statistics relating to the job the script editor had to carry out: by 1990 some 400 scripts were arriving at the Abbey annually; each play was read by two voluntary readers; and the script editor also read it, before making a recommendation (very infrequently) to accept, or to reject. At that time once a play was accepted an author would be paid £3,000 and a further £2,000 advance on royalties once the play went into rehearsal.[18] At the time of writing the initial payment is £3,500 with royalties of 1 per cent of box office receipts. Commissions are: £1,500 on signing the contract, £500 on delivery of first draft, £500 on delivery of final text.[19]

One script which the Abbey was glad to see was Brian Friel's *Dancing at Lughnasa* in 1989, marking his return to the Abbey after devoting his playwriting talents and personal energies to the Field Day company since its beginnings in 1980. With the exception of *Fathers and Sons*, an adaptation of Turgenev, which was staged at the British National Theatre (8 July 1987), Friel's plays of the 1980s had opened in Derry with Field Day, and then toured Ireland. These were: a version of Chekhov's *Three Sisters* (8 September 1981), *The Communication Cord* (21 September 1982), and *Making History* (20 September, 1988).

If *Translations*, and the Field Day enterprise which it initiated, confirmed a fresh examination of the form or forms of representation which would most appropriately reflect a divided Ireland, *Dancing at Lughnasa* (24 April 1990), directed by Patrick Mason, translated the tensions arising from past trauma into new and exciting registers of theatrical language. Friel returned to the Abbey with a play that introduced radical new perspectives on how people saw things, and why they did or did not remember the past. The play is set in August 1936; Michael, the narrator, is the same age Friel would have been in that year, and there is a sense that the play takes place in a kind of between-time, between the momentous events that led to the founding of the state, and the recurrence of violent conflict that re-emerged in the north as Friel began to enter middle age. It is not an autobiographical play, but it is personal and its themes and language are knit into Friel's own creative processes and perceptions. Michael says, in his opening speech, that even though he was only 7 at the time of the events that are to unfold, 'I know I had a sense of unease, some awareness of a widening breach between what seemed to be and what was'.[20]

The five sisters, the 'five brave Glenties women' of the dedication, live outside of Friel's Ballybeg. Their brother Jack, a missionary priest (played by Barry McGovern), has been sent back from Uganda where he had begun to 'go native'. The boy, Michael, is the illegitimate son of Chris (Catherine Byrne) and Gerry Evans (Paul Herzborg), who is, unbeknownst to them all, married in Wales.

The network of affection and creativity that the five women have provided for the boy is about to unravel. Jack's derangement brings the family into, not disgrace, but a form of exclusion from the community; Rose (Bríd Ní Neachtain), who is mentally disabled, is raped; Rose and Agnes (Bríd Brennan) are deprived of the tiny income they derive from knitting gloves by the setting up of a factory in Donegal town; and Kate (Frances Tomelty) loses her job as a teacher due to the oddity of Fr. Jack and the rumours about him. Friel shows us his women as they undergo the process of tragedy, but the strange thing about this play is that its mood is one of pathos blended with joy. There is no defiant braving of fate; rather there is endurance, steadiness, and a readiness to respond to impulse, realized in the dancing that takes place throughout the play.

Friel once said, in an interview, that the Northern Ireland problem was one which was essentially a difficulty of language, and that its solution would depend upon the kinds of language used, permitted, and ventured. He himself is a stylist,

who writes always with economy and grace; and frequently the speeches he gives
to his characters exhibit a balanced and measured rational control and a concentrated stringency of thought. He is a dramatist of ideas, who weighs his words, all
too aware that the words we use may become our fate. But here, in this play, while
the same vigour and care is evident in the writing, he reposes an unusually strong
trust in the theatrical power of what is seen and done upon the stage rather than
in what is said. It is as if he is implying that deeds and actions, especially if they
are theatricalized in a manner that suggests a ritual import, can move beyond language and its misprisions to more open patterns of expression and meaning. This
may sound very cerebral, but the theatrical impact of the play, as directed by
Patrick Mason and designed by Joe Vanek, was deeply emotional and affecting.
The women were not depicted as victims of history and deprivation, which in any
common-sense appraisal of their condition they are; they came across as emblems of humanity and gentleness, real women who had inscribed in their fates a
kind of sacrificial dignity and a remote but luminous joy. The sense of ancient patterns evolving in the sadness of their stories, suggested by the background of rituals being carried on in the 'back hills' above the town or in Jack's Uganda,
provides an air of inscrutability and mystery to human action, which carries an
uplift of dignity. Though we are embroiled in event, mired in history, that, Friel's
stagecraft intimates, is not the whole story about these women. There is more to
us (the Irish, the Ugandans, the British) than history and fact. The image
Michael's narration concludes with is that of dancing, of lives

moving rhythmically, languorously, in complete isolation; responding more to the mood of
the music than to its beat. When I remember it, I think of it as dancing. . . Dancing as if language had surrendered to movement—as if this ritual, this wordless ceremony, was now
the way to speak, to whisper private and sacred things, to be in touch with some otherness.[21]

As if it might be possible to discover, in 'the hair cracks . . . appearing everywhere', an order and a resolution, not to do with the vanity of ego and assertion,
but to do with what makes us human, the impulse to form, from which all forms
(including those of governance and settlement) emerge. It is a paradigmatic play,
a shifting and elusive exemplum of how conflict and division may be absorbed
and transcended by means of creativity, while at the same time offering no jejune
flashes of consolatory solution. It is this composure, resting on tension, that gives
the play its enigmatic air of consolation fretted with joy.
    This air of mystery Friel continued into his next Abbey play, *Wonderful
Tennessee* (30 June 1993), which was, again, directed by Patrick Mason. This time
Ballybeg is extended to include a wild sea-coast, and a disused pier, from which,
at times, an island can be seen. Oileán Draíochta, translated (loosely) by one of
the characters, is an 'Island of Otherness . . . of Mystery', and Friel is deliberately
linking his action to tales of otherworld islands, the land of youth, the country
under the wave, of Irish saga and folklore. He brings three married couples to the

pier: they are Berna (Ingrid Craigie), a psychiatrist recovering from depression, and her husband Terry (Donal McCann), a failed gambler-entrepreneur; Angela (Catherine Byrne), the put-upon teacher wife of Frank (John Kavanagh), an alcoholic would-be writer; and George (Robert Black), a musician who is suffering from some terminal illness, with his wife Trish (Marion O'Dwyer). Terry is, in spite of his business collapse, lending money every week to Angela and to Trish; he is also having an affair with Angela; and he has taken a six-month option to buy the Island of Mystery. He brings them to the pier, intending an overnight pilgrimage to the island, but Carlin the boatman fails to turn up, in spite of his repeated promises and bellicose demands from Frank. Each couple are in need of something, and that need, in some way, has led them to acquiesce in Terry's pilgrimage. The opening of the play is all expectation and the anticipation of happiness. Berna says to Angela, her sister:

Berna. . . . there are times when I feel I'm. . . about to be happy. That's not bad is it? Are you laughing at me?
Angela. Of course I'm not laughing at you.
Berna. Maybe that's how most people carry on—'about to be happy'; the real thing *almost* within grasp, just a step away. Maybe that's the norm. But then there are periods—occasions—when just being alive is. . . unbearable.[22]

There is a game the women play at the end which involves throwing a stone as close as possible to a bottle without hitting it; and the play is shot through with rituals that involve a circling around the core of meaning and reality, because to touch it, to be too open about it, means disaster. Angela, who teaches classics, recalls the Eleusinian mysteries, called such because the adepts at Eleusis never revealed what went on. Terry tells a story about Oileán Draíochta itself—that once, after the Eucharistic Congress of 1932, a group of young people, returning from Dublin where they had seen the triumphalist Catholic celebrations, went to the island. While there, overnight, some ritual was enacted, some sacrifice made, and a young man was killed. The thirteen young people were summoned to the Bishop's palace, and made to swear they would never 'divulge' what happened on that night.[23] Towards the end of the play the Dionysiac sacrifice of this victim is half-parodied, half-repeated, as the others descend on Terry and pull the shirt off his back (which is what they have been doing figuratively all along).

This play is a sombre meditation on the sadness of life, but it is also a celebration of its beauty and strangeness. Frank, the drunk, failed writer, is given a vision of pure bliss when he sees a dolphin dance, as if for him alone, above the water, for almost a full minute. This experience is thrilling, but the dolphin's 'manic, leering face' is also disturbing. The play, as in *Dancing at Lughnasa*, shows the cracks, the breakdowns, in human society and relationships; but it does not forsake an intuition that the very reason creativity and its forms exist at all is because of those very cracks and fissures. This balancing act has, of course, political implications, but they are subtle and hidden, and it would injure the delicate tissue of invention that the play is, to tear them out too blatantly.

Wonderful Tennessee was followed by *Molly Sweeney* at the Gate Theatre (9 August 1994), directed by Friel himself. *Molly Sweeney* deals with the problem of perception: it concerns a woman who has her sight restored to her having been blind for many years, but this theme is opened up to fold in (in a totally implied fashion) meditations on the problem of perception (Berkeley and Locke are touchstones throughout). It is, as the blurb to the published version indicates, a 'chamber piece': indicating that its mood is intense and dark—a kind of in-depth probe into how attitudes, including psychological and political ones, are formed and imposed. It is a gathering of energies, a contraction, and the means Friel uses are those he employed in *Faith Healer* (1979)—monologue and storytelling, with the characters given scope to ramify their individual formations of the events in their stories. After this contraction of forces, he opened out again to a broader scenario with a keen attentiveness to the interaction between characters, and to the accidentality of human impulse, in his next Abbey play, a beautifully complex piece, *Give Me your Answer, Do* (12 March 1997). Here again, Friel directed.

Here Friel's theme is the question reflected in the imploring imperative of the title: what judgement can there be of a person's life and work? This problem is posed in a number of different but interacting registers: how has Tom Connolly (Tom Hickey) coped as a writer, a husband, and a father? How has he dealt with the fact of his daughter's madness? How have his wife Daisy's parents coped with her father's obsessive kleptomania? How has the ostensibly more successful writer Garret Fitzmaurice (Des McAleer) coped with the failure that dogs him, even though he has had the accolade of a prestigious sale of his papers to a Texas university? And what lies behind the malice and destructiveness of Garret's marriage to Gráinne (Frances Tomelty)? The play unfolds the strain of all these tensions on a sunny afternoon in an old manse in Ballybeg; it opens the vertiginous falls in the human pain behind these uncertainties; and yet the play retains a kind of brittle fractious composure, which only breaks when Jack, Daisy's kleptomaniac father (David Kelly), is disgraced, and when the non-speaking Bridget, the mad girl, is spoken to by her father in a wild and pathetic fantasy. This society of writers and their financial obsessions is one burdened with secrets, jealousies, and anger; there is restless hatred, and the self-disgust that follows greedy compliance. It is a play profoundly alive to moral issues, but one in which no moralizing whatsoever takes place. People flail at judgements, they posture at certainty, but a poised nonchalance at the heart of the composition leaves them alone, refuses to judge.

Again, as in *Wonderful Tennessee*, there is a kind of stillness prevailing, a holding off from closure. Eventually David Knight (Darragh Kelly), the agent for the Texas university, agrees to buy Tom's manuscripts for a large sum, having found two previously unpublished pornographic novels written after Bridget went mad. But Tom, prevailed upon by Daisy (Catherine Byrne), does not sell, because to sell would be to capitulate to some form of final estimation. Daisy's answer is as follows: somehow, somehow bills will always be met. And what does a little physical discomfort matter? Really not a lot. But to sell for an affirmation, for an answer, to be free of that grinding uncertainty, that would be wrong for him, and so wrong for his work. Because that uncertainty is a necessity.[24]

After such forgiveness, what can be known? Art and charity combine here, in a most delicate and unusual synthesis. There is a sense of accommodation, held between conflicting demands, and what we are left with, as in all the greatest drama, is the utterly human, pure and impure.

While it may be said that Friel acquires, in these late, pre-millennium plays, a kind of nonchalant detachment which is grounded in a pervasive compassion, Murphy's later work for the Abbey aspires to a condition of dark but comic frenzy. *Too Late for Logic* (3 October 1989) was part of the Dublin Theatre Festival, and directed by Patrick Mason. Christopher, a philosopher played by Tony Doyle (who was by then being recognized as one of the most commanding as well as the most versatile of the Irish actors of the 1980s), has been given a unique career break: his boss Dr Wuzzler of Trinity has been knocked down by a bus thereby giving the ambitious Christopher his chance to expound on Schopenhauer. We learn that Christopher has left his wife Patricia to concentrate on his career; that his sister-in-law Cornelia has died; and that Michael, her husband, has gone off on a drinking-spree threatening to kill himself. All of this absurdity and chaos is presented in a kind of deadpan matter-of-fact coolness, as if there is nothing to any of this but accident and happenstance. There is a radical breakdown between human behaviour and the kind of codes society insists upon so that it may continue. People say or do anything, reacting either to the press of event or some blind impulse or intuition. The philosophy of Schopenhauer acts as a kind of framing device but this does not provide any intellectual or rational framework for the action of the play, which is not wild but sporadic and morose. Christopher, paraphrasing Schopenhauer, orates, rehearsing for his big lecture:

Man is a thing that ought not to be, he said. Worse, he said. Man is a flaw containing a bigger flaw within himself, which is will, blind will, the-thing-in-itself, the ding-a-dong. . . The mindless will towards reproduction for instance, or, in other words, blindly screwing for the species. . .[25]

Christopher's son Jack visits his father with his girlfriend Petra, a relationship that exhausts itself quickly and she is replaced by someone else, somehow casually enlisted. But as the play winds down, in a kind of entropy that is meant to be a paradigm of life and its meaninglessness, Petra seems to think Jack's mother is hers as well. It is as if there is an instinct to huddle close for comfort. In the last speech of the play, another voice-over extract from the Schopenhauer lecture, Christopher cites an illustration from the philosopher to show how life tends towards separateness and alienation: a group of porcupines crowd together for warmth on a winter's day: 'soon, however, they felt each other's spines, and that drove them apart again.'[26] The only means of survival is the avoidance of closeness, of keeping a 'moderate distance from one another'.

The grim and ferocious bleakness that is at the core of this tragic farce is a form of response to the failure of Irish society to create a culture of sharing and mutuality. It is as if Murphy is still engaged in a process of trying to express a sense of communal disappointment in the wake of Ireland's inability to find forms of civic arrangement which would accommodate differences of class, religion, and gender. His plays at the Abbey and elsewhere, from the 1960s, are a sustained attempt to strip humanity back to its bare essentials, to see what may subsist when all the protective cloaks of religion, patriotism, and family are removed. The prospect becomes darker as Murphy's writing life proceeds. By *Too Late for Logic* there is more than an implication that everything is useless, which, in its surrender, shows that the playwright has, in this play, written himself into a corner where exhaustion and sadness lurk. It is 'too late for logic', but whoever thought that logic would ever be timely?

The Wake (28 January 1998), directed by Patrick Mason, presents a devastatingly bleak interpretation of the themes of the returned exile, using it to attack the banality, meaningless, and savagery of Irish society as Murphy sees it. Vera (Jane Brennan) is a New York whore who, flushed with an advance she has got for what is going to be a particularly nasty job in Atlanta, decides to revisit her hometown after learning that her grandmother, who mostly reared her, has left her the family hotel. The thought of her own people has sustained her in the fearsome humiliations of the life she has had to endure in New York, where, literally, she has been made on occasions to eat human excrement as part of her job. The world she returns to is in ruins. Henry (Stanley Townsend) is married to her bedraggled sister Marcia (Anna Healy); he is a solicitor who does not practise, an alcoholic, if an 'urbane' one, someone whom, in Murphy's terms, the 'culture has defeated'.[27] This phrase surfaces again in the play, and Murphy has a very specific idea as to what this 'culture' is: repression, madness, memories of abuse, hypocrisy, priests driven to the edge of craziness by the expectations and accusations of their congregations, the craving for money, for the instant satisfaction of drink and sex. It is a 'culture' without structure, or 'logic', or pity. Henry at one point exclaims: 'the true essence and the core of all things is the ecstasy in the act of copulation. No, there is nothing like a bit of jack.'[28] There is a good deal of it in *The Wake*. Vera takes up with Finbar (David Herlihy), a 'knacker' who lives in a corporation house on the new estate and sells gew-gaws (including holy medals) for a living. She later seduces Henry, and all three of them move to the Imperial Hotel (which Vera has inherited), where they have sex in the windows, all lights blazing. The theatrical image comes straight out of Yeats's *Purgatory* of sixty years before, and it is hard to say which play carries the darkest vision. In Murphy the rancour and vileness are registered in more human terms, because the dereliction of value that has occurred has consequences not in any genetic flaw that is passed on but in the crazed antics of those who exploit others, or in the broken minds of those who are not brutal enough to survive. Finbar describes the hell of child sex-abuse as he has known it himself:

Fuckin' clergy! Driving round the country, screwing young ones in their Volkswagens, then going home and doing their housekeepers—Sex! Christian Brothers in the schools—Fuck! Beating the children, Henry, then buggering them: I was in care, Henry, them establishments, Henry? And young ones and oul ones getting pregnant and praying to fuckin' statues about it. Country is rotten with it. . .[29]

The play concludes with a belated wake in memory of Vera's grandmother, in the hotel, as she serves drinks from a table across which, in the past, there has been skulduggery and meanness transacted. There is a ferocious parody of the Irish 'sing-song', with party-pieces and recitations, including, amongst the latter, a terrifying rendition by Mary Jane (Olwen Fouere), the most focused and intent scavenger of the lot, of James Clarence Mangan's famous nineteenth-century hymn to past glory that arose out of despair in 1848: 'A Vision of Connaught in the Thirteenth Century'. Mangan's poem was a famine poem, and 150 years later Murphy's play describes a new kind of starvation. Vera drugs them all with the pills she uses sometimes as part of her trade, to calm down violent customers. They sink into stupor and she leaves them behind, signing over the hotel to them all before she goes. The land and property are now, given the interior horror, no more than empty obsessions, crazed fetishes. As Mrs Connelly puts it at the start of the play, in a graveyard: 'how much land does anyone need? I know how much land—*and* property—a person needs.' As these lines were being written modest houses were selling in the Dublin 4 of the Celtic Tiger economy for a quarter of a million on a daily basis.

Thomas Kilroy became a director of the Field Day Theatre Company in 1988, the only member of the board from the Irish Republic. In 1986 he had contributed to Field Day one of its most significant plays, *Double Cross* (3 February), which was directed by Jim Sheridan. This play, through its two main characters, Brendan Bracken and William Joyce ('Lord Haw-Haw'), brilliantly exposed the psychological and social catastrophe brought about by fixed ideas. Both these men, played in the play's two sections with chilling force by Stephen Rea, are Irish; both transpose an imperfect sense of identity into an inflated adulation of an ideal: in Bracken's case Britain, in Joyce's Nazi Germany. Both obsessions are seen to be akin at the only level which matters, the human and the personal. Patriotism, loyalty, service—all these codes can, given the failure to resolve the hurt which often drives them, degenerate into racism. *Double Cross* is a play about the double-cross idealism can perpetrate; as well as gathering into its net of implication the notion that to be Irish may be to carry the double burden of a double cross: that of subjection and the compensating rage that is its corollary.

Kilroy, a few years later, wrote what was to be the last original play for Field Day, *The Madam MacAdam Travelling Theatre*, which reworks a theatrical idea first developed by Lennox Robinson's *Drama at Inish*, that of the effect a put-up company has on the mores and sensibilities of a provincial town. Madam MacAdam, at the opening of the play, tells how the company came to 'a crossroads somewhere in Ulster' where the action is set. The time is the 'Emergency', as

the Second World War was known in the Irish Free State; the theme is the relationship between responsibility and the nature of identity. How can you act correctly if you do not know who you are, or why you should be expected to do what
it appears you are enjoined to do? The theme crosses over into issues of identity,
carried by a sustained imagery of acting and role-play.

The concerns of these two Field Day plays are given intense focus in Kilroy's
brilliant return to the Abbey in 1997 with *The Secret Fall of Constance Wilde* (8
October), directed by Patrick Mason. The scenario is stripped down to the mini-
mum, and the only speaking parts are Oscar Wilde (Robert O'Mahoney), his wife
(Jane Brennan), and Wilde's lover 'Bosie', Lord Alfred Douglas (Andrew Scott).
Each of them is carrying the burden of a father's selfish inhumanity: Wilde, his
father's predatory sexuality; Constance, her abuse as a child by her father; and
Douglas the legacy of his father's hypocrisy and hatred. As Constance says to
Douglas, when Wilde loses his action against the Marquis of Queensberry: 'Your
father has triumphed. They always do, don't they, fathers?'[30]

Paternity, paternal law, the old fathers, the fatherland, the patria: this always
subdues that which is vulnerable, helpless, and feminine, in the male as well as
amongst women. This latter phrase, incidentally, was the title of a study of the
brutality and suffering caused and endured by a brooding father in John
McGahern's novel *Amongst Women*, published in 1990. If a preoccupation of the
Abbey during the period 1966–85 was a remembering and interrogation of the
legacy of the fathers who founded the state, then during the period from 1985 to
the end of the millennium there has been an attempt to transcend these inheritances by giving an artistic shape to the sense of trouble they awaken.

Kilroy's play on Wilde examines the dark legacies of fathers as they visit themselves on the emotion, behaviour, and mentalities of three protaganists. Wilde
dreams of the hermaphroditus, as, he claims, Leonardo, Shakespeare, and Balzac
did:

no woman, no man, no duality, no contrary. . . our frightened time cannot bear such a vision. . . our age puts on its bright red uniforms and goes out to murder its own kind. It beats
its children simply to keep the male and female in place.[31]

This is why men seek to escape from the brutal categories of exclusion, why they
seek out others driven by this need, why they grope at each other in the disgrace-
ful place in Little College Street described by Brookfield, the actor who hates
Wilde, to Constance. The men's trousers are 'cut to allow men—to fondle each
other'. Wilde and Douglas suffer, imprisoned in the tyranny of the cages created
for them by the hatred and fear in society; Constance falls down the stairs and desperately injures her back because brute reality, which women are constantly having to face, brings her down. However, she stands by Wilde at the end. Not only
that, she faces her own capacity for deluding herself. She admits, to Oscar, that
she flattered herself 'with my own—(*contempt*) goodness—'.[32] Here Kilroy, in
showing Constance giving up this final scrap of shelter, this last vestige of the

clothing of vanity, is offering his own version of Wilde's vision: that of a society relieved of the burden of lying. Falsehood comes about because the central trauma cannot be addressed, it insists on being hidden. At the close of the play Constance's abuse by her father, caricatured as a huge Victorian puppet, with puffed-up red cheeks, a bowler hat, black moustache, is shockingly revealed on stage in a stylized, crude, Jarry-like manner. He is the bogey man who has cowed her into a life of acceptance and 'goodness'; he is the British Empire; he is an Orangeman; but he is also a cardboard cut-out, animated by our fears as much as anything else. The 'great thumping beat of sound' that announces him is an image of our frightened hearts, but it is also an explosion of release as the poison is released. Wilde's infected ear, poisoned by what he has had to hear, explodes into his brain, but it kills him, the sacrificial victim of the coming hermaphrodites.

Kilroy's play bristles with implications relating to sexuality, sexual politics, gender, cultural and political amnesia, and the inherited attitudes that determine the forms of government and society we create for ourselves. This play about Wilde is a visitation into the psyche of an Ireland at the end of the 1990s, in which many of the forms that protected and imprisoned Irish people were breaking up, not least among which was that form of radical separation of the different lives of the country evident in the line drawn across the province of Ulster, the border. *The Secret Fall of Constance Wilde* is a play about transgressions and transgressors, about the legitimacy (or not) of crossing those borders prescribed to us. Profoundly alert to psychology and personal hurt and obsession, it is also intensely political in its inferences, all the more so for holding those implications well in reserve.

Looking back, it is now apparent that from the mid-1980s onwards, a peace process was under way in Ireland, involving the British and Irish governments, the SDLP, and, crucially, Sinn Féin, who spoke with the authority of a close but occluded connection with the Provisional IRA. The single most important manœuvre in these years was the meeting between John Hume, leader of the constitutional nationalist party, the SDLP, and Gerry Adams, president of Sinn Féin, which took place in January 1988. Both denied a ceasefire was on the agenda, but now it is clear, with hindsight, that it was. Hume came in for fierce criticism for his (public) meetings with Adams, predictably from the unionists, but also from voices within the nationalist community, not excluding the party which he led. A profound seismic shift in nationalist and republican attitudes was taking place, partly as a response to a seemingly endless cycle of revenge killings and bombings, but also because membership of the European Union, and the benefits very steadily flowing in the direction of the Republic, qualified issues of national sovereignty and opened up new concepts of citizenship based on values and community rather than on territory. New ideas about the perennial issues of identity were being advanced, not just by politicians, but by academics, writers, community leaders, and by the people themselves who, as atrocities such as the bombing of

the Royal Marines in Kent in September 1989 were carried out, voiced their revulsion and disgust. Unionists were slower to accommodate themselves to the changing situation: they were less than reassured, for example, by Secretary of State
Peter Brooke's statement in November 1990 that Britain had no economic or
strategic interest in Northern Ireland, and that Westminster would find it acceptable if the unification of Ireland came about by consent. Unionism felt betrayed,
under siege from within and without, a mood which McGuinness's *Observe the
Sons of Ulster* (1985) anticipated. Nevertheless by 1991, the passionate conviction of Hume, Adams's steadfast rigour, the affability of Brooke, and the pragmatic republicanism of Albert Reynolds managed to win the unionists into 'talks
about talks'. For many this was a false dawn, such as there had been in 1973–4 in
the power-sharing executive at Stormont, but now it was different; new articulate
voices were being heard from grass-roots loyalism, voices which, hitherto, had
been silenced by blind loyalist commitment and unswerving dedication to preserving the Union at all costs. These were the kind of people (David Ervine, Gary
McMichael) who commanded a power-base amongst loyalist militants, the force
whence the likes of Paisley traditionally drew their telluric power and visceral energy. The form or forms of government which would be representative of the aspirations of Irish people were changing, because the people themselves, north and
south, were changing.

The Irish economy, boosted by huge inflows of money from Brussels, skilfully
(and correctly) negotiated by Albert Reynolds, Dick Spring, and Pádraig Flynn,
was beginning to grow dramatically. The cities were full of young people whose
parents had benefited from the first waves of affluence to mark Ireland in the
1960s and the early 1970s, that generation which derived advantage from the consequences of the economic and industrial planning of Seán Lemass and T. K.
Whitaker. The young people in Dublin, Cork, and Galway of the 1980s and 1990s
were confident and questioning, and were even more unwilling than their parents
had been to accept orthodoxies of politics or belief. Not that many of them
wished to eschew an Irish identity (as some of the revisionist generation of their
parents had); rather were they evolving more complex and more flexible (but none
the less steadfast for that) characterizations of Irishness.

Irish youth culture, in any case, was energetic, attractive, 'sexy' (in the jargon
of the period); the Irish were taking the world stage in popular culture: U2, in particular, but also the Cranberries and Hothouse Flowers were attaining global cult
status; Van Morrison was 'rediscovered' as an Irish artist with an extraordinary
ability to unite Gaelic tradition, blues emotion, and a serenity derived from
Buddhist meditation techniques; while a new clutch of traditional musicians,
such as Altan and Mícheál Ó Súilleabháin, reanimated the revival inaugurated by
Seán Ó Riada and Tomás Ó Canainn in the 1960s. As an Irish sense of identity,
amongst the young, diversified and changed, it also flourished and strengthened.
The Irish language itself, long the grim linguistic precinct (to many eyes) of joyless, pallid 'Gaeilgeoirí' sporting pioneer pins and 'fáinní', became animate and

attractive. New poets and writers (Alan Titley, Nuala Ní Dhomhnaill, Cathal Ó Searcaigh) insisted on writing Irish as a world language, one capable of registering every nuance of feeling, every chamber of interior dark, all forms of desire.

As more young people began to live financially and emotionally independent lives, the family also relaxed its conservative grip on behaviour and attitude. The young were often, now, living on their own in cities, while those who remained in the country did so more as a matter of choice than necessity. In the country, too, the dramatic increase in car ownership meant that a rural existence was not necessarily a forlorn one.

Scandals concerning bishops, parish priests, and curates; the prospect of senior churchmen having affairs, fathering children, then denying parenthood; case after case of paedophilia: all of those shook the Irish Catholic church to its foundations. These revelations of the pathetic fallibility of priests served to accelerate already changing attitudes towards authority. The women's movement increased in confidence, and women began to assume senior positions in the public and private sectors of Irish institutional and corporate life. Repressive legislation about homosexuality was relaxed.

What is remarkable, contemplating these changes of the 1980s and 1990s, is how painlessly and how quickly they came about. Ireland, the south of Ireland, and the north too, are, taking the two together, amongst those societies which, while they have a latent tendency not to alter, when they do undergo change, do so very quickly.

The new dramatists that emerged in the 1980s and 1990s, needless to say, reflected these manifold shifts in perceptions and persuasions. It is not as if entirely new tracks of insight or emotion reveal themselves in these writers, because their predecessors (Friel, MacIntyre, McGuinness, Leonard, Keane, Kilroy) had themselves been interrogators of the sclerotic norms and myopic fixations of post-war Ireland. There does appear, however, in the work of Michael Harding, Neil Donnelly, Niall Williams, and Marina Carr, a marked fluidity of presentation, and a rediscovery of the resources of language.

Michael Harding, from Co. Leitrim, is almost a paradigmatic example of this new kind of writer. Harding, before becoming a full-time novelist and playwright, had been a Catholic priest, and his departure from the clerical life lies behind his novel *Priest* (1986). Amongst his plays for the Abbey were *Strawboys* (29 July 1987), evoking a semi-mythical world, where folklore, ritual, and violence mix, followed by *Una Pooka* (12 April 1990), a kind of metaphysical murder drama, dealing with a crime committed while the Pope visited Ireland in 1979. *The Misogynist* (10 October 1990), directed at the Abbey by Judy Friel, and featuring Tom Hickey in what is virtually a monologue from start to finish, is an attack on maleness: male pride, male energy, male disgust at women. Its fluent and savage poetry, written in a kind of breathless recitative of rage, focuses on the ambiguity indicated in Irish male attitudes towards women: the overvaluation of their aspect as domestic figures which is opposed by a fear of their mysterious

life-giving powers. The tension between these contradictory impulses is what
fuels the rapid and brutal violence of the male language of the play, making it an
evisceration of the hatred and self-hate of the Irish masculine psyche:

> Why don't you go down and make a sandwich or something.
> Watch the telly.
> Go out if you're going.
> Fuck off.
> I'll be down in a minute. . .
> You give a man no bloody space at all.
> None.
> Not even the fucking attic.
> Well have it.
> Have it.
> Have the whole thing.[33]

Hubert Murray's Widow (21 April 1993) continues this concern with the hatred
between men and women, and the link between gender and politics is explored as
is the relationship between frustrated sexual desire and violence. It was directed
by Patrick Mason at the Peacock.

The play is set in border country, in Co. Fermanagh. Hubert Murray, a senior
IRA officer, is married to Rhoda, who is having an affair 'on the side' with Fr.
Boyle, recently promoted to Monsignor. She is also fancied by Gene, a young
Protestant, who takes part in a republican plan to ship guns across the border to
win her approval. However Hubert and Gene are dead; or rather they are dead
some of the time, and their ghosts revisit those scenes and emotions that torment
them or which they do not understand, to take part in them again. Harding is
making use of the dreaming-back technique Yeats learned from the Japanese
Noh; but he is also creating a hallucinatory effect by means of this theatrical
fluidity, something akin to the film-worlds of David Lynch or the quirkier work of
Roman Polanski. It has all the twists and turns of a nightmarishly insoluble who-
dunnit, with the ghosts almost as baffled as the living. It turns out that Rhoda, the
widow, has killed her husband, and put his body in the freezer; it is generally believed he has blown himself up by accident, whereas the plan was that he would
pretend to be dead while actually engaged on IRA activities. The plot is strained,
but works theatrically in a Lynch-like and zany way. Sex and political violence are
explicitly linked; the Northern Ireland problem is seen to be insoluble. Gene says:

every so often it all comes together, coheres, in one beautiful, creative act of violence. I understood that a long time ago about Ulster. The problem has no solution. Violence is just a
way of imposing order on the chaos. The problem itself. . . is the solution. . . It's almost
beautiful. It's almost like sex.[34]

The characters are driven by greed and sexual jealousy; a kind of pitiless phenomenology erases distinctions between living and dead. There is only confusion
of motive; what drives people remains inscrutable. However, they *are* driven; the

obsessions and fixations provide plenty of evidence for that. Harding's theatre is a bleak one, the vision that of a disillusioned moralist.

Neil Donnelly, from Tullamore in Co. Offaly, began writing for the Abbey in the early 1980s. *Upstarts* opened at the Peacock (7 August 1980), and this was followed by *The Silver Dollar Boys* (2 November 1981). The latter was a play about school life in 1960s Ireland, and analyses the power-relations of the classroom, and the connections between repression and criminality. *The Duty Master* (8 February 1995), directed by Ben Barnes at the Peacock, returned to a school setting. However, here the school is in England; it is a public school and Patrick O'Rourke (Dermot Crowley, the Duty Master of the title, teaches English. His marriage to Sarah, an English artist, is in trouble, and he is having an affair with the school secretary. His younger brother Michael, on his way to London with some champion greyhounds, visits unexpectedly, bringing with him a young student with whom he is having an affair. Michael and his anglicized brother reach an accommodation by the end; and Patrick prepares himself to tolerate a life in which his wife too will have affairs, while he faces, with the same equanimity, the prospect of a future return to Ireland, to his parents, and to a past he would prefer to forget. It is a strange and melancholy play, extremely well crafted in an Alan Ayckbourn fashion, but also carrying in its smooth contours rifts of trouble of a dark and evasive kind.

The public school where Patrick carries out his duties at the behest of a headmaster who never actually appears suggests an arrangement of society in which people lose touch with what they feel and who they are. Michael, the brother who stayed at home, disturbs this uneasy but settled peace with his girl friend, his greyhounds, his midlands accent, and his van that breaks down. At the opening of Act II, Michael, infuriated by Patrick's attempt to soft-soap Breda, Michael's girl, attacks his sentimentality and his lazy emotionalism: 'I never heard such tripe. The same old tricks.'[35] Patrick has learned how to use stories to construct a false self-image so that he can remain impervious to the pressures of actuality. There is a physical fight between the brothers, which breaks the tension, Michael saying: 'We all know where we stand now.'

The play meditates on the emptiness of a life lived without some connection to an inner core, without a code informed by belief and commitment. Duty is empty unless it is grounded on something more enduring than exterior shows of order. Donnelly's play looks back at those values which were so often invoked in the early years of the Free State, and which dominated life in the south of Ireland until the 1970s: home, family, religion, commitment. Patrick is out of Ireland, and glad of it; he once had studied for the priesthood, but left that behind also. What is left him? The routine of duty in an English public school. Donnelly's play, a sombre and mature set of inferences, acquires a rueful and sceptical cast, as it contemplates what it means (or does not mean) to be Irish at the end of the twentieth century.

On the whole women seem less inclined to write for the theatre than for the page. Of course women involve themselves in many aspects of theatrical work:

there have been many distinguished actresses, directors, designers, promoters, patrons, and so on. But for some reason, and Irish theatre is no exception in this, there is a remarkable dearth of women playwrights in the dramatic traditions of Europe and America. Women began to make an impact as writers, especially of fiction, from the eighteenth century; and English theatre history does furnish an example of a woman gaining recognition, even notoriety, in the seventeenth century: Aphra Behn. But her example only serves to illustrate the larger reality: that until the twentieth century women did not, for whatever reason, find the theatre a congenial medium for their talents. It may be that the world of theatre, obsessed as it is with power, money, and ego, represented, in little, the structures of control by which society itself is governed. The novel, poetry, the memoir—these forms allowed the woman writer more scope for intimacy, a mood in which the world of money, anger, and contest could be inferred rather than directly confronted. Theatre, by its nature, tests the stories people tell themselves and each other against the harshness of actuality. It is a public forum in which issues of government, identity, autonomy, and freedom are publicly engaged. It is inherently political, and it is perhaps not surprising that the arrival of women playwrights in the theatre coincides with their empowerment by the franchise in Europe and America. And yet, even in the twentieth century, their involvement in writing for the theatre is a good deal less than their involvement in any of the other literary forms. In Ireland there was the extraordinarily influential figure of Lady Gregory, but after her one has to think quite hard to recall those women who wrote for the theatre: Geraldine Cummins from Cork, Dorothy Macardle from Dundalk, Teresa Deevy from Waterford, Máiréad Ní Ghráda from Clare, B. G. MacCarthy from Cork, and a handful of others, until the 1980s and the 1990s, when the situation changes radically. Two writers, in particular, Gina Moxley from Cork and Marina Carr from Offaly (where she was brought up), have displayed remarkable powers in realizing the atmosphere of their specific locales, and in rediscovering the poetic resources of Hiberno-English speech.

After *Ullalo* (1989), and *The Deer's Surrender* (1990), Marina Carr wrote *The Mai* (5 October 1994) for the Peacock, where it was directed by Brian Brady, with music by Mícheál Ó Súilleabháin. It is an ambitious play, set in Carr's midlands, though with an extraordinary grandmother from Connemara, aged over 100, who arrives at 'the Mai's' new house with the oar that once belonged to her nine-fingered fisherman husband. The Mai has been rejoined by her straying husband Robert, and the family gather in the house she has scrimped and saved to build. The old grandmother smokes opium, and in the drug-induced haze she recalls her mother, 'the Duchess', and her mother's longing for the return of her lover, the 'sultan of Spain':

she wouldn't let me call 'er Mother, no, The Duchess, that's whah I had to call her, or Duchess for short. An' the Duchess toult me me father was tha Sultan a Spain an' thah he'd hid tha Duchess an' meself an Fraochlán because we were too beautiful for tha worlt.[36]

Carr's world is a strange mix of folk tale, memory, raddled affliction and sadness, longing, and a sense that the incredible may become all too real in a world which obeys laws not subject to our will.

Marina Carr's *Portia Coughlan* (21 March 1996) is set in her native midlands. In an afterword which she contributed to a selection of new Irish plays by Frank McGuinness she describes how, even though she left the midlands in the early 1980s, she finds herself

constantly there at night: lights off, head on the pillow and once again I'm in the Midlands. I'm wrestling, talking, laughing, reeling at the nocturnal traffic the place throws up. Now I think it's no accident it's called the Midlands. For me at least it has become a metaphor for the crossroads between the worlds.[37]

In many senses this brings us back to where we started: the crossroads between the worlds. This is what Yeats and Lady Gregory hoped that theatre would be, a space for opening up an inter-traffic between the deep memories of Irish tradition, and the actuality of the present.

Portia Coughlan is set in a modern house in the midlands, on the banks of a river, and in the High Chaparral Bar. Portia's husband Raphael is a successful industrialist; her aunt is a whore; her father Sly Scully a farmer who has toiled all his life; her mother Marianne a poisonous bitch; her grandmother Blaize Scully a paraplegic with a vicious tongue. Portia's twin Gabriel was drowned when he was 15, and since then she has been haunted by his memory and by the sound of his extraordinary singing. The play is obsessed by the memory of the dead; there is hatred, violence, passion, incest. Portia is drowned at the beginning of Act II: she is lifted out of the river covered in its spawn and algae and flowers. From that point onwards until the end of the play, the action brings Portia back on stage to reveal the terrible history of her sadness, so the effect is one in which the action embraces two worlds, that of the living, and that of the dead.

Marina Carr takes great pains to get the midlands language on stage: her spelling forces the reader (and the actors) to hear the flat open nasality of the midlands, its fluid energy. She creates a medium as flexible as Synge's, one capable of intellectual force, emotional range, and the sheer exhilaration of heart-scorching anger. In the following exchange Blaize, the appalling wheelchair-bound grandmother, is attacking her daughter-in-law Marianne (née Joyce):

Cem inta this area three giniration ago wud natin' goin for yees barrin' flamin' red hair an' fah arses. . . Ah warnt ya Sly! [her son] D'ya thincke ya'd fuckin' listen! There's a divil in thah Jiyce blood, was in Gabriel, an' ud's in Portia too. . . Ya fuckin' tramp ya![38]

Portia wants to be out of this clamour and rage, with her dead brother Gabriel, who is waiting for her by the river. Tangled into this sense that the blood of the living is tainted with the badness of the past are themes and concerns of the 1980s and 1990s: incest, the family as horror story. The Irish state had consistently extolled the family as the bedrock of value and the central sponsoring agent of citizenship, morality, and conduct. The ideal of the family was a cohesive force at the very heart of the Irish social contract, and for that reason it sometimes acted as a covering device beneath which tyrannies, abuses, and perversions could take place without the restraint the danger of exposure would otherwise exercise. A society that overvalues the family will, inevitably, have certain families that are cauldrons of hell. Portia Coughlan's is such a one.

At the end of the play Maggie May and the one-eyed Stacia are watching Portia and Maggie's husband dance. Maggie makes a fearful revelation, that Portia's mother and father are brother and sister:

Maggie M. Did ya know thah Marianne, Portia's mother, war a twin too?
Stacia. No, never knew thah.
Maggie M. There's few as does, ah'm noh aven sure Marianne knows. Marianne an' Sly is brother and sister. Sum father, different mothers, born ithin a month a wan another.
Stacia. Jay, ha chome.
Maggie M. Me mother toult me an her deathbed thah Marianne was aul' Scully's childt. Born the sem time Blaize Scully was expectin' Sly. She knows, th'oul bitch!

What we have in *Portia Coughlan* is not a critique of Irish family values: nothing as crude as that. What it presents us with, bitingly, driven by a wild and turbulent comedy, is a sense of the futility of life when love's energies have been perverted. It is a play with none of the immaturity of sensation; there is no craving to blame anyone. Carr is saying: that is what it is like to be in the midlands of existence; given such circumstances maybe it is preferable to join your twin in the Belmont river than put up with the constant incursions and pressing demands of suitors, whether husbands or not. Carr's Portia does not have the tolerance of Shakespeare's.

These younger playwrights of the Abbey, Carr, Donnelly, Harding, and others such as Niall Williams or Antoine Ó Flatharta, reveal a national theatre which it is very difficult to categorize. There is, however, a good deal of courage in evidence, revealed in a maturity of response to the complexities of Irish life at the end of the twentieth century. The stagecraft of Friel and Kilroy, in particular, which is no less than a wedding of intellectual power to the expressive potential of the medium, has shown these younger writers how to face into the changing values and shifting perspectives of an Ireland that remains haunted by its past as it opens out to Europe and the world.

An intriguing feature of Irish writing towards the end of the millennium was a notable turn to the classics for models and inspiration. Friel, in *Translations* (1980), drew upon the story of the fall of Troy, Homer, and Pallas Athene, to suggest that defeat may be a more complex thing than merely losing, and that victory may involve more than simple triumph and gratification. At the end of the century in Ireland, as the distance slowly begins to lengthen between contemporary awareness and the traumas of the past, other perspectives open up. Britain itself has a changed role in the world, as its commonwealth becomes an association of independent states in friendly accord; and Ireland, in the 1990s, enjoys one of the highest rates of growth and prosperity on the globe. Ruminations about what it means to lose lead to speculations about recovery and renewal: Troy may rise again and be reborn in Rome; and that Rome may be the Troynovant that Spenser imagined London to be in his best projections, or it may be the city of Derry, awakening from the nightmare of Bloody Sunday, and the paratroopers' rifles levelled on the crowd from the city walls. Whatever the reasons, and they are manifold (and include the strengthening influence of Louis MacNeice on writers and writing in the 1980s and 1990s), the classical stories of Greece and Rome, of Troy and Ithaca, were recovered in these decades with an urgent and compelling force. Amongst the most significant explorations of these stories were the versions made by Brendan Kennelly of *Antigone* (21 April 1986) and *The Trojan Women* (2 June 1993), and by Marina Carr of *Medea* in *By the Bog of Cats* (7 October 1998). These plays are concerned with the suffering and victimage of women, and offer a sharp and brutal corrective to the assumptions of men, their confidence, their striving 'fat vanity', their rutting intrusiveness into the secret intimacies of the female body. Kennelly's *The Trojan Women*, based on Euripides, is set outside the broken walls of Troy. The women, Hecuba, her daughter Cassandra, and her daughter-in-law Andromache, are prizes to be taken back by the Greek heroes, and used as concubines and slaves. These are the women who suffer, who endure; Kennelly's dramatic point is very clear: the Trojan women are also the women of Ireland. Indeed in a preface he recalls how, back in the north Kerry of his childhood, people would say of a woman who had a heavy burden of care and worry to carry, that she was a 'Trojan' if she did it bravely. Kennelly also says that he tried to convey the 'active resolution' he discerned at the heart of the women's suffering in the play. Hecuba and her relations stand for the women of the Kerry babies shame and disgrace, the battered and rejected wives, the broken spirits and drained energies of generations of Irish women who have had to absorb their men's disappointments as well as coping with the realities of hardship, sorrow, and loss. And yet this play of Kennelly's, for all its fearsome grief, is resolute with the will to survive, to go on.

Andromache even has to endure having her little boy Astynax forced from her embrace, and thrown from the walls of Troy, because Ulysses has decided that he will, if he lives, be a danger to Greece:

> down through the air you'll plunge—
> my God, your body, my son's body,
> your back, your head, your neck,
> your neck that I have kissed
> and kissed and touched and lingered over—
> and there's no pity!
> And is it for nothing, nothing at all
> that I have reared you?
> Is it to see your body pitched from a great height
> to break on the earth?[39]

And yet, incredibly, even though Hecuba knows she is condemned to become a body to be opened up and used by Ulysses, she will not give in, finally, to despair:

The dead are not the past, the dead are the future.
They listen and watch, their eyes
like glittering jewels
in the dark streets of eternity.[40]

In the closing moments of this play situated in smoke-filled ruins, amidst scenes of bestial violence, and expected rape, scenes like those in Rwanda or in Bosnia, not just Derry or Warrington or Teebane, Hecuba insists she is 'not a thing':

I am not a thing, I am not a fuck.[41]

Fiction and poetry in Irish have seen a period of flourishing and achievement in the 1980s and 1990s. A late twentieth-century revival in poetry was inaugurated by Seán Ó Ríordáin, from Cork, who had a profound impact on a generation of poets, initially from Munster, but his influence spread, partly through the energy and advocacy of his students and followers Michael Davitt, Liam Ó Muirthile and Nuala Ní Dhomhnaill, through the rest of Gaelic-speaking Ireland. Prose, perhaps because fiction draws upon more extensive (though not necessarily more intricate) layerings and deposits of linguistic awareness than does poetry, was slower to revive than was verse. Nevertheless, the animating presence here was the daunting but hugely charismatic figure of Máirtín Ó Cadhain. And his work has been an inspiration to, amongst others, Alan Titley, Séamas Mac Annaidh, and Mícheál Ó Conghaile. Drama in Irish has been very much the poor relation, and it is a disappointment not to see the kinds of achievement that can be discerned in the other forms coming to fruition. There are, however, certain stirrings.

One of the surprises of the 1990s at the National Theatre was *Tagann Godot*, a sequel to Beckett's *Waiting for Godot* in Irish by Alan Titley. Titley, one of the most learned, challenging, and brilliant writers in late twentieth-century Ireland, is less well known than he should be simply because he writes in Irish. From Cork, he taught in Nigeria and in Dublin before lecturing in Irish at St Patrick's College in Drumcondra. He wrote novels, short stories, fables, and literary criticism before taking on the challenge of Beckett's modernist masterpiece. It was produced first on radio and then at the Peacock (15 February 1990), where it was directed by Tomás Mac Anna.

The play is an impressive achievement. It incorporates all of Beckett's terse and mordant wit into an Irish stripped back to a functional and wary intelligence. Titley's prose style in his fiction has the comic resource and verbal brilliance of Rabelais in French, Borges in Spanish, and Geoffrey Keating in Irish. But here his dialogue is hard and taut as he circles around the central questions posed by Beckett's depiction of the lack of human value in twentieth-century consciousness. In Titley's play Godot arrives; or at least we think he does. He tries to help Estragon and Vladimir out of their paralysis of inanition. As in Beckett's play, the boy arrives as a precursor to Godot. The tramps, thinking that, as before, the boy will explain that Godot cannot come after all, mock the excuses they anticipate:

Estragon. He left his copy book at home.
Vladimir. His bike is punctured.
Estragon. He forgot.
Vladimir. He was too busy. . .
Boy. Sir, he is coming.
Vladimir. As the stallion said on a bad day.
Boy. But he is coming.
Estragon. Like next year's snow.
Vladimir. The end of the world.
Estragon. Peace in our time.
Vladimir. Full employment.
Estragon. No more taxes.
Vladimir. Lady Godiva.[42]

This superbly realizes, in Irish, Beckett's 'canters' of backtalk, the games invented by Beckett's characters to pass the time. Godot does come, eventually, but he is preceded by Progastaron, a game-show host, presiding over a situation where questions that mean life or death to the contestants are answered casually even though the consequences are terrible. The tramps think that Progastaron is Godot, and that his sidekicks Unlucky and Mommo are part of Godot's entourage. When Godot arrives, at the end of Act I, Estragon has just won the ultimate prize in Progastaron's quiz show; he has been hanged. Vladimir is in an electric chair, where he is tormented every time he gives what is deemed to be the wrong answer to obvious questions.

Godot, a Chaplinesque character, now questions the questioner. Asking why Vladimir is tied up and tortured, he is told:

Progastaron. I suppose because he's a human being. . .
Godot. And what's he done wrong to deserve this?
Progastaron. He said that he had his own ideas.
Godot. But that's not a crime, or a sin.
Progastaron. It's worse than that. It's out of fashion.[43]

It will be evident even from these brief extracts that Titley's play has a more satiric, a more humanitarian edge than Beckett's. Outrage is strong in Titley; there is a sense in which his honest anger is a late twentieth-century response to Beckett's post-war nihilism and ataraxy.

Later on, when Estragon is wakened from the dead by the magic of Godot, Vladimir asks, assuming that his sojourn in the afterlife has brought him insight, why it is we are not happy in this life; to which Estragon replies in comic bombast and meaningless piffle. When Vladimir confesses that he does not understand a word, Estragon replies:

Estragon. You said you wanted an answer. I said nothing about you being able to understand it.
Vladimir. But what I wanted was understanding. Not words.
Estragon. Is there anything else? Is it that you don't like words? Or are there specific words that don't appeal to you?[44]

Godot tells a parable, about mercy and kindness, a story interpreted by Vladimir as signifying that 'a loaf of bread is better than all the talk in the world'. This humanitarianism is savagely countered by a volte-face on the part of the tramps, who turn on Godot and kill him.

Titley's play is open without being naïve, fierce without being gratuitously brutal, contradictory without being confused, intellectual without being knowing. It has a strong grip on the resources of language; Titley's dialogue flourishes under his strict and confident control. It is, in part, a meditation on the values of a society that places an ever-higher value on objects, material and sensual satisfaction, and the rituals of distraction. There is nothing specifically 'Irish' in this play, written in an Irish surging with an imaginative energy and ceaseless inventiveness.

However, Titley's play, in its confidence and the steady onward impulse of its realized world, its grasp of modernism, and its distrust of many of the implicit values in twentieth-century literature, only serves to emphasize the significant absence in modern Irish theatre: and that is a theatre in Irish worthy of the vision the first Abbey directors had.

8

Conclusion

It is a manifold, richly veined, even glorious history. From that wet afternoon in Duras House in 1897 to the closing years of this century the Irish National Theatre has provided an arena for the visions and tensions, the nightmares and rhapsodies of the Irish people in a century which has seen them go through many changes.

When the Irish Literary Theatre opened its doors on 8 May 1899 with Yeats's *The Countess Cathleen*, the country was still, in many respects, in a pre-industrial state: predominantly rural; still, especially in the west, to a considerable extent, Gaelic-speaking; economically underdeveloped; poorly educated; deeply pious and often narrowly sectarian; and driven by a tension between craven compliance to the established political system and contempt for an administration that had inflicted grievous wrong. Dublin was a city which was, on the one hand, proud of being the second city of the Empire, while on the other it was deeply conscious of the fact that it was powerless to govern itself. Its streets and suburbs contained the Catholics who worked in Dublin Castle and the law firms; the remnants of an Anglo-Irish ascendancy reduced by a land agitation that had deprived many of them of their income; enthusiastic members of the Gaelic League who were anticipating a new and confident Ireland, re-energized by a rediscovery of a cultural identity; clerks; old Fenians; incendiaries; drunks; occultists; and the dirt-poor, teeming in the alleyways, selling their souls and bodies for bread. There was in 1899 a clear sense that a number of decisions had to be made. Were the Irish going to go it alone, and opt, finally, for Home Rule? Were they going to assert a cultural and political identity separate from that of Britain? Was that identity to be expressed in Irish (in George Moore's eyes, a language fresh from the Middle Ages) or in English (in Yeats's view, the language of the newspapers and of materialism)? Was there to be a continuum between the Ireland imagined by poets and artists, and the society being realized day in, day out, in the towns and in the countryside? Was it to be souls or gold?

The first play of what was to become the Abbey went straight to the crux of the dilemma in which such choices were to be made, and depicted on stage a conflict between tradition and the marketplace. The fervour with which Yeats engaged this concern was, typically for him, absolutist and uncompromising: Ireland's soul can only be saved by the readiness of a person, animated by the highest ideals, to sacrifice herself on behalf of those less fortunate than she. Implicated in this triumph of the imagination over materialism is the complex debate, at the heart of modernism, over the role of the artist in capitalist society. The first play of the Irish Literary Theatre carries in its network of themes a concern about who should lead Ireland out of colonialism, and how that leadership should be conducted. It is not as if Yeats provides satisfactory answers to these questions, and it would be banal unthinkingly to translate an artistic exploration of an entire set of interconnected issues into a political or economic philosophy. What Yeats succeeded in doing, in exemplary fashion, was to show how theatre could become a public laboratory for issues of governance, identity, and responsibility.

Yeats and Lady Gregory and Synge wanted their theatre to be a national theatre precisely in the sense that it should reflect the issues and tensions that trouble and animate a national community at any one time. That responsibility should be the basis of its authority. Continually, they tried to hold that course, to 'keep a swallow to its first intent', as Yeats put it in his homage to Lady Gregory in 'Coole Park, 1929'. He goes on, in the same poem, to praise the efficacy of the heroic dedication of the few against the wilful indifference of the many, repeating, in essence, the sentiments of *The Countess Cathleen*:

> And half a dozen in formation there,
> That seemed to whirl upon a compass-point,
> Found certainty in the dreaming air,
> The intellectual sweetness of those lines
> That cut through time or cross it with withershins.[1]

The last two lines could be a description, not only of what true creativity, in the Yeatsian sense, should aspire to achieve, but also of what a national theatre, responsive to and responsible for its community, should bring to the stage.

How different all of this idealistic and turbulent heroism was from the actuality of 'theatre-management' is brought home to us, not just in the ranting unhappiness of some of Miss Horniman's letters to her 'dear demon', but in countless other instances of shame, folly, or connivance. As I was completing the first draft of the history, I came across Eric Bentley's recollections of his production of a translation of *The House of Bernarda Alba* by Federico García Lorca in 1950 at the Abbey (3 April). Bentley, who went on to become a great exponent of Brecht, only got to meet Ernest Blythe because he was taken up a winding stair to his office by Ria Mooney. Lennox Robinson had by then sunk into the latter stages of alcoholism:

I got to know Lennox somewhat by accompanying him home on the bus. I also discovered how far the alcoholism went: he couldn't get home in one bus ride. He kept getting off the bus to stop at another snug: he was too gentlemanly to carry a flask in his pocket. He had to stop at the snug and buy one and, of course, another for his guest. So I had to get as drunk as he was to accompany him: it was two Irish whiskies every time we got off the bus, which was four or five times before he got home.[2]

However, such instances of human folly, or vanity, or weakness could be multiplied a hundredfold from the Abbey records. And there were always, needless to say, many other countervailing instances of generosity, kindness, fellowship, such as Yeats's defence of Robinson in the Abbey boardroom in 1937, when he excused bad behaviour and treachery (Robinson had denounced Frank O'Connor and Hugh Hunt's *The Invincibles* as unpatriotic) on the grounds of diminished responsibility, and out of loyalty to the man.

Theatre is a thankless enterprise; and yet it provides some of the most glorious experiences known to the human spirit. Miss Horniman's troublesome and virtually unwilling patronage at the beginning of the Abbey Theatre shows that the financial realities of running the business of a theatre are the foundations on which artistic and imaginative creations are built, and that they are only kept in place through diplomacy, and unremitting effort. Yeats revealed these qualities in retaining Miss Horniman's support over many strenuous years, and the same dedication is revealed by the manner in which Ernest Blythe ensured that the money was in place to rebuild the Abbey Theatre in the 1960s. Theatre people spend a good deal of their time and a not inconsiderable quantity of moral and imaginative energy in trying to ensure that there is (just) enough money in the budget to allow the show to begin rehearsal in the first place.

And then, of course, there is the uncertainty. The artistic director, the board, may believe that such and such a play will be a roaring success, only to find they have a 'turkey' on their hands. And they may even know that what they are doing is outstanding, world-shattering stuff, but the critics do not like it, and the audience refuses to turn up. A theatre is an enterprise of maximum risk and challenge; in cinema, there is always the terror of catastrophic financial collapse, but the theatre presents the actors with the reality of disfavour and rejection with an immediacy unparalleled in any other form: the theatre does not fill up, the audience does not respond.

In the theatre you are only as good as your last success. The theatregoing community is all too easily susceptible to amnesia; and so each new play, and even each new revival of an old standby, is a situation of crisis. Every time a play goes on, it is as if the whole process is happening for the first time. Shakespeare, at the end of *The Tempest*, begs the audience to applaud; he wants to cajole, to charm, but there is also a sense that he is grateful for the relief of knowing he will not, ever again, have to subject himself to the humiliation of the complete uncertainty all true ventures of the spirit must involve. But in Shakespeare's case there was to be no final respite: he did return; he could not stay away; there had to be perpetual renewal, as long as life and breath remain, of the attempt at saying that which takes good care to keep itself as hidden as possible.

And that is the history of the Abbey: perpetual renewal and reinvention, so that the challenge thrown down by Yeats be continuously taken up—that the people of Ireland find form and articulation and imagery to utter and shape their self-awareness as they evolve in relationship, whether of amity or conflict, with each other and the rest of the world.

In the last decade there has been, under Patrick Mason's leadership as artistic director, a period of radical transformation and renewal at the Abbey. In 1995

Neil Wallace wrote, in an overview of theatre in Ireland for a report commissioned by the Arts Council of Ireland, that 'the society is lucky to have one of the most talented stage directors in the English-language theatre at its head'.[3] In a community such as the theatre one, which is characterized by a more than usual quotient of begrudgery, this view would, on the whole, be widely shared. Not only has Mason been extremely effective in providing inspirational examples of how the Irish theatrical tradition can be fortified through radical departures in technique and imaginative realization; he has also been capable of responding to the need for the Abbey to reconsider its role in a society where there has been an unprecedented flourishing in the theatre arts and in performance. He has been aware of the need for the National Theatre to become a resource, not just for its own company, but also, so far as it is possible, for the different theatre communities and audiences in Ireland:

I see this National Theatre as one that will be cognizant of its past, true to its best traditions, but bold enough to respond to the creative demands of a burgeoning number of theatre artists and practitioners. . . There is one essential mode of access. . . and that is the openness of the National Theatre to the best theatre talent in the country. For the resources that have been gathered over the years by the Society, its equipment, its stages, and its subsidy are there to be put at the service of the most talented, visionary, and expert of Ireland's theatres and practitioners.[4]

Neil Wallace quotes this policy statement in his essay on the resources available to theatre in Ireland in the Arts Council review of 1995, and goes on to state, correctly, that this is not an 'unconditional offer' but a 'carefully-worded challenge' to those who believe they can enhance the creative life of the Abbey. It was also strategic, because if the National Theatre is to become a resource open to this much wider constituency than hitherto, and if it is to play, as undoubtedly it should, a training and development role, then these responsibilities carry financial implications if their artistic benefits are to be realized. Again, as Mason argues:

You have to invest not just in materials but in training people in certain disciplines, certain techniques. That is something which imposes its own kind of rigours so we have a very special role quite apart from any national responsibilities.[5]

Mason himself, in an interview conducted on 5 November 1998 at the Abbey, characterized the role of the theatre as offering a 'microcosm' of the society to which it responds, and has responded, over its history. Of Ernest Blythe's record, in the long years during which he protected the theatre in a mood of gladiatorial taciturnity and bureaucratic defensiveness, Mason is, rightly, critical; however, he does say that but for Blythe's robust determination, the Abbey might well have not survived, and been rebuilt. In fact Mason characterizes the history as representing a 'miracle of survival'.[6] The theatre remains committed to being a national 'space' for self-questioning and for the continual interrogation of the nature of identity. As he has enunciated in the policy documents Mason considers the nation to be in a new phase of discovery in relation to the focus which may represent differences of identity on the island as a whole, and obviously the Abbey must reflect these movements if it is to discharge its central function of being a national space. It is now also the case that for the first time the Abbey operates in a context of very broad theatrical activity, which it will influence (and accommodate within its walls) but which it will in turn be influenced by.

The most important decision the theatre has made in its recent history was, in Mason's view, the establishment of the post of artistic director, arising out of the compromise position in 1965 when Walter Macken became artistic adviser. At that point Blythe wanted to insist that the board drive the theatre, rather than the professionals. The first artistic director, so called, was Hugh Hunt, who insisted the term be used to describe his function. It was a difficult battle, but a crucial one in ensuring that artistic policy be the responsibility of professional theatre people rather than a board which, no matter how well intentioned, could not be other than footling, at best. There was a revival of this style of managerialism in the 1980s (it came into fashion again, at this time, dressed up in the jargon of line-management etc.) when Joe Dowling, artistic director 1978–81, fell foul of a board avid to execute its powers, under the chairmanship and animated by the zeal of Ulick O'Connor. However, this period was one which Mason sees as a crucial one in bringing forward those writers of the generation which followed Friel, Kilroy, and Murphy. Seán MacCarthy, it is generally acknowledged, played a key role in this regard, during his tenure as script editor.

Of course all of this costs money. In 1995 the funding for the Abbey was £2.5 million, equivalent to 15 per cent of the total funding for the arts, by comparison to a percentage of 39 per cent of total arts funding in 1976. Secondly, the ratio of grant to earned income was 68 : 32 in 1976, as against 54 : 46 in 1993, with the injunction from the funder that the aim should be a 50 : 50 balance between funding allocation and other income. This stipulation, for increased sponsorship, more aggressive earning activity, and improved marketing of 'product', reflected an attitude towards subsidies that gained increased acceptance in the 1990s as concerted efforts were made, throughout the public sectors in the UK and Ireland, to reduce, or indeed eliminate, 'dependency' cultures. In spite of what were cuts in real terms to its budgets, there were those who felt, in the 1990s, that the Abbey was 'getting too much of a limited cake', some even calling for the disbandment of the National Theatre altogether, as an outmoded and arthritic entity, incapable of responding to the local and the regional, where untapped energies were perceived to lie.

However, the National Theatre continues to satisfy and dissatisfy its constituencies and its stakeholders. The difficulty is in the variety of those who believe, understandably, that their interests should be served by a national theatre. Neil Wallace's list is instructive, including: the ghosts of the founders; the repertoire of the Abbey; writers; directors; designers; the shareholders; employees; the independent theatre, seeking access; politicians; the media; Actors' Equity; and the Irish language and its supporters.[7] Wallace makes the point that such a diversity of interests, all of them vocal, and all of them capable of hostility, will mean that those responsible for answering these needs will, almost unavoidably, experience a funnelling away of energy and enthusiasm. He links this expense of spirit with the fact that in the decade 1985–95 there were no fewer than seven artistic directors at the Abbey. So that Mason has brought much-needed stability to a period of unprecedented challenge.

The one area where there has been conspicuous failure to realize even a reasonable level of activity within all these diverse demands is that relating to drama in the Irish language. With the notable exception of Titley's *Tagann Godot* and Antoine Ó Flatharta's *An Solas Dearg* (9 November 1995) there has been no sustained creative activity in Irish-language theatre since 1985. It may even be said that the performance of the National Theatre, in seeking to foster an Irish-language dramatic tradition, has been lamentable since 1966. There have been exceptions, and the directorial work of Tomás Mac Anna was always significant in this aspect of the Abbey's programming, but Mac Anna's main energies were devoted to theatre in English from 1966, and the new Abbey's gain was a loss to Irish theatre in this respect. When one compares the resurgence in literature in Irish, especially poetry, with writing for the theatre, the contrast is dispiriting and, perhaps, not a little baffling.

One of the surprises of the 1990s was the rediscovery of the poetic and theatrical resources of Irish speech in English: Billy Roche from Wexford, Marina Carr from the midlands, Vincent Woods from the border counties. Synge's linguistic vitality has been shown to be something not encased in the amber of tradition, but vibrant, lively, dangerous, and still current. It may be that the next phase of the Abbey's rediscovery of its tradition will be an exciting drama in Irish; not the *parousia*, the waiting for the Gaelic redeemer, of Blythe, but the insouciant fire and confidence of a Titley or a Ní Dhomhnaill, fully operative on the stage.

Epilogue

In the Minute Book (NLI, acc. 3961, NFC 98) for the years 1904–5 someone has written, opposite the records of the committee meeting for 7 January 1905, the following in pencil: 'Goodbye Ireland. I'm going to Cork.' Which only goes to show that the art of the Irish glosses continues to flourish; and that the human spirit of creativity, in laughter or in sorrow, can always escape the labyrinths of necessity where growl the minotaurs of hatred, envy, and despair.

Notes

CHAPTER I

1 Lady Gregory, *Our Irish Theatre* (Colin Smythe, Gerrards Cross, 1972), 18.
2 W. B. Yeats, *Memoirs* (Macmillan, London, 1972), 112.
3 W. B. Yeats, *Autobiographies* (Macmillan, London, 1970), 399.
4 Yeats, *Memoirs*, 89.
5 *Uncollected Prose by W. B. Yeats*, ed. J. P. Frayne (Macmillan, London, 1970), i. 104.
6 Robert Hogan and James Kilroy, *The Irish Literary Theatre 1899–1901* (Dolmen Press, Dublin, 1975) 19–20.
7 George Moore, *Ave* (William Heinemann, London, 1947) 235.
8 Ibid. 224.
9 Yeats, *Autobiographies*, 401.
10 Quoted in Hogan and Kilroy, *The Irish Literary Theatre*, 28.
11 Moore, *Ave*, 69.
12 Ibid. 12. There is a problem about this account of Moore's, however. It reads as if the author actually saw this production of *The Countess Cathleen*, but other accounts (indeed another by Moore himself) indicate that he missed the first night, coming over for the opening performance of *The Heather Field* on 9 May.
13 Robert Hogan and Michael J. O'Neill (eds.), *Joseph Holloway's Abbey Theatre* (Southern Illinois University Press, Carbondale, 1967), 8.
14 W. B. Yeats, *Essays and Introductions* (Macmillan, London, 1969), 168–70.
15 Hogan and Kilroy, *The Irish Literary Theatre*, 51.
16 *Essays and Introductions*, 170.
17 Hogan and Kilroy, *The Irish Literary Theatre*, 35.
18 Ibid. 48.
19 Moore, *Ave*, 127.
20 Ibid. 128.
21 Ibid. 187.
22 Ibid. 193.
23 Yeats, *Autobiographies*, 427.
24 Hogan and Kilroy, *The Irish Literary Theatre*, 152 w.
25 Hogan and O'Neill (eds.) *Joseph Holloway's Abbey Theatre*, 10.
26 Ibid. 11.
27 Yeats, *Autobiographies*, 427.
28 W. B. Yeats, *Collected Poems* (Macmillan, London, 1958), 348.
29 Hogan and Kilroy, *The Irish Literary Theatre*, 82.
30 Yeats, *Autobiographies*, 447.
31 *The Collected Letters of W. B. Yeats*, ed. John Kelly et al., vols. i–iii (Clarendon Press, Oxford, 1986–), ii. 493–3.
32 R. F. Foster, *W. B. Yeats: A Life*, i: *The Apprentice Mage* (Clarendon Press, Oxford, 1997), 232.
33 Ibid.
34 Moore, *Ave*, 269–70.
35 Ibid. 263.
36 Yeats, *Collected Letters*, ii. 575.
37 Foster, *W. B. Yeats*, 237.
38 Hogan and Kilroy, *The Irish Literary Theatre*, 96.

39 Ibid. 105.
40 Foster, *W. B. Yeats*, 251–2.
41 W. B. Yeats, *Explorations* (Macmillan, London, 1962), 84.
42 Ann Saddlemyer (ed.), *Theatre Business: The Correspondence of the First Abbey Theatre Directors* (Colin Smythe, Gerrards Cross, 1982), 37.
43 Yeats, *Explorations*, 74.
44 Hogan and Kilroy, *The Irish Literary Theatre*, 118–28.
45 Cited in Foster, *W. B. Yeats*, 249.
46 Yeats, *Autobiographies*, 449.
47 Anna MacBride White and A. N. Jeffares (eds.), *The Gonne–Yeats Letters* (Hutchinson, London, 1992), 176.
48 NLI, MS 10,952.
49 Foster, *W. B. Yeats*, 260.
50 Yeats, *Collected Letters*, iii. 167.
51 NLI, MS 27,634, acc. 4036a. See also Máire Nic Shiubhlaigh, *The Splendid Years* (Duffy, Dublin, 1955).
52 Quoted in Foster, *W. B. Yeats*, 262.
53 Yeats, *Collected Poems*, 393.
54 Quoted from the journals of William Bulfin in Foster, *W. B. Yeats*, 583.
55 Yeats, *Collected Letters*, iii. 175–6.

CHAPTER 2

1 J. B. Yeats, *Letters to his Son W. B. Yeats and Others 1869–1922*, ed. Joseph Hone (Macmillan, London, 1944), 71.
2 Yeats, *Explorations*, 85.
3 Ibid. 93–6.
4 Robert Hogan and James Kilroy, *Laying the Foundations* (Dolmen Press, Dublin, 1976), where a lecture Yeats gave on 15 Mar. 1902 is quoted: 'out of the dangerous life that drama has come.'
5 Christopher Murray, *Twentieth Century Irish Drama: Mirror up to Nation* (Manchester University Press, Manchester 1997), 16.
6 Hogan and Kilroy, *Laying the Foundations*, 40–1.
7 Nic Shiubhlaigh, *The Splendid Years*, 38.
8 Yeats, *Collected Letters*, iii. 285.
9 Hogan and Kilroy, *Laying the Foundations*, 51.
10 Yeats, *Collected Letters*, iii. 258.
11 Ibid. 317.
12 *The Variorum Edition of the Plays of W. B. Yeats*, ed. Russell K. Alspach (Macmillan, London, 1966), 600.
13 Yeats, *Collected Letters*, iii. 174.
14 Hogan and Kilroy, *Laying the Foundations*, 61.
15 Ibid. 84.
16 Yeats, *Collected Letters*, iii. 429 n.
17 MacBride White and Jeffares (eds.), *The Gonne–Yeats Letters*, 174.
18 Robert Welch, *Changing States: Transformations in Modern Irish Writing* (Routledge, London, 1993), 85.
19 J. M. Synge, *Plays* (George Allen & Unwin, London, 1924), 12.
20 Yeats, *Explorations*, 107.
21 Foster, *W. B. Yeats*, 299.
22 Hogan and Kilroy, *Laying the Foundations*, 76.
23 Ibid. 79–81.
24 NLI, MS 18,312.
25 Padraic Colum, *Three Plays* (Hodges Figgis, Dublin, 1963) 103.

26 Yeats, *Collected Letters*, iii. 501.

27 Foster, *W. B. Yeats*, 318.

28 W. B. Yeats, *The Shadowy Waters* (Hodder & Stoughton, London, 1901), 26–7.

29 Hogan and O'Neill (eds.), *Joseph Holloway's Abbey Theatre*, 32–3.

30 Synge, *Plays*, 44–5.

31 Foster, *W. B. Yeats*, 318–19.

32 Yeats, *Collected Letters*, iii. 568 n., quoting from Padraic Colum, 'Early Days of the Irish Theatre', *Dublin Magazine*, 20 (Jan.–Mar. 1950).

33 Hogan and O'Neill (eds.), *Joseph Holloway's Abbey Theatre*, 39.

34 Peter Kuch, *Yeats and AE* (Colin Smythe, Gerrards Cross, 1986), 225. The Abbey Minute Book, kept by the secretary at this time, George Roberts, recording the AGM of 28 May, reveals a flurry of confused emotion, but it looks as if Russell formally resigned only after this meeting, which brought forward Lady Gregory and Stephen Gwynn as vice-presidents. However, Russell stayed on the reading committee. See NLI, MS 5651, NFC.

35 Hogan and Kilroy, *Laying the Foundations*, 107.

36 NLI, MS 22,418.

37 NLI, MS 5651, NFC.

38 Robert Hogan and James Kilroy, *The Abbey Theatre: The Years of Synge, 1905–1909* (Dolmen Press, Dublin, 1978), 20.

39 Ibid. 16–17.

40 Foster, *W. B. Yeats*, 338.

41 NLI, MS 10,952 (1) i.

42 Yeats, *Explorations*, 199–200.

43 Adrian Frazier, *Behind the Scenes: Yeats, Horniman, and the Struggle for the Abbey Theatre* (University of California Press, Berkeley and Los Angeles, 1990), 77.

44 Lady Gregory, *Collected Plays* (Colin Smythe, Gerrards Cross, 1971–9), ii. 316.

45 Ibid. 333. This speech was heavily revised in 1909 and given to Malachi, as Ann Saddlemyer points out.

46 Bernie Leacock, 'D. P. Moran: Selected Writings', unpublished research towards D.Phil., University of Ulster at Coleraine.

47 Gregory, *Collected Plays*, ii. 246.

48 Saddlemyer (ed.), *Theatre Business*, 104–6.

49 NLI, MS 21,303, acc. 3250, p. 32.

50 Colum, *Three Plays*, 42.

51 Ibid. 34.

52 Hogan and Kilroy, *The Abbey Theatre: The Years of Synge*, 57.

53 NLI, MS 10,952.

54 Ibid.

55 Hogan and Kilroy, *The Abbey Theatre: The Years of Synge*, 75.

56 Ibid. 79.

57 Yeats, *Variorum Edition*, 384.

58 NLI, MS 10,952.

59 Ibid.

60 See Hogan and Kilroy, *The Abbey Theatre: The Years of Synge*, 86–94 for details of these exchanges.

61 NLI, MS 10,952.

62 Foster, *W. B. Yeats*, 359.

63 NLI, MS 10,952.

64 Synge, *Plays*, 286.

65 Hogan and Kilroy, *The Abbey Theatre: The Years of Synge*, 142.

66 NLI, MS acc. 3961, NFC 98 (vol. 2).

67 Ibid.

68 Synge, *Plays*, 266–7.

69 NLI, MS 10,952.

70 Hogan and Kilroy, *The Abbey Theatre: The Years of Synge*, 173.
71 George Fitzmaurice, *Plays* (Dolmen Press, Dublin, 1967–70), iii. 57.
72 Saddlemyer (ed.), *Theatre Business*, 229.
73 Gregory, *Collected Plays*, iv. 97.
74 Frazier, *Behind the Scenes*, 204.
75 NLI, MS 5977. Power was the actor Ambrose Power who had played Old Mahon in *The Playboy*.
76 William George Fay and Catherine Carswell, *The Fays of the Abbey Theatre* (Rich & Cowan, London, 1935), 228–9.
77 Saddlemyer (ed.), *Theatre Business*, 261.
78 NLI, MS 10,952.
79 Ibid.
80 NLI, MS 21,319, acc. 3250, p. 16.
81 Hogan and Kilroy, *The Abbey Theatre: The Years of Synge*, 243.
82 Saddlemyer (ed.), *Theatre Business*, 282.
83 Ibid. 287.
84 Ibid. 296.
85 Ibid. 298.
86 NLI, MS 21,747, acc. 3478.
87 Foster, *W. B. Yeats*, 406.
88 G. B. Shaw, *The Shewing-up of Blanco Posnet* (Constable, London, 1927), 405.
89 *The Letters of W. B. Yeats*, ed. Allan Wade (Rupert Hart-Davis, London, 1954), 537.
90 Dan H. Laurence and Nicholas Grene (eds.), *Shaw, Lady Gregory, and the Abbey* (Colin Smythe, Gerrards Cross, 1993), 8.
91 George Moore, *Vale* (William Heinemann, London, 1947), 142.
92 Conal O'Riordan, *Adam in Dublin* (William Collins, Glasgow, 1920), 124.
93 NLI, MS 8320.
94 Hogan and Kilroy, *The Abbey Theatre: The Years of Synge*, 311.
95 Foster, *W. B. Yeats*, 406.
96 Robert Hogan, with Richard Burnham and Daniel P. Poteet, *The Abbey Theatre: The Rise of the Realists, 1910–1915* (Dolmen Press, Dublin, 1979), 24.
97 Yeats, *Variorum Edition*, 452.
98 Colum, *Three Plays*, 171.
99 NLI, MS 10,952.
100 Yeats, *Essays and Introductions*, 313–16.
101 T. C. Murray, *Selected Plays*, ed. Richard Allen Cave (Colin Smythe, Gerrards Cross, 1998), 210.
102 Foster, *W. B. Yeats*, 424.

CHAPTER 3

1 Hogan et al., *The Abbey Theatre: The Rise of the Realists, 1910–1915*, 104.
2 Foster, *W. B. Yeats*, 436.
3 Ibid. 612.
4 Ibid. 450.
5 NLI, MS 18,721.
6 Hogan et al., *The Abbey Theatre: The Rise of the Realists*, 174–5.
7 Fitzmaurice, *Plays*, i. 4.
8 Foster, *W. B. Yeats*, 483.
9 NLI, MS 29,526, stage manager's TS copy, pp. 26–7.
10 Yeats, *Collected Poems*, 120–1.
11 NLI, MS 29,470, p. 21.
12 Ibid. 33.
13 Hogan et al., *The Abbey Theatre: The Rise of the Realists*, 270.

14 INTS Minutes, NLI, MS acc. 3961, NFC 98.
15 NLI, MS 21,391, acc. 3250, p. 72. This text was badly charred in the Abbey fire.
16 Gregory, *Collected Plays*, iii. 79.
17 Hogan et al., *The Abbey Theatre: The Rise of the Realists*, 384.
18 *Selected Plays of St John Ervine*, ed. John Cronin (Colin Smythe, Gerrards Cross, 1988), 194–5.
19 Ibid. 11.
20 INTS Minutes, NLI, MS acc. 3961, NFC 98, 5 June 1916.
21 Robert Hogan and Richard Burnham, *The Art of the Amateur: 1916–1920* (Dolmen Press, Dublin, 1984), 12.
22 INTS Minutes, NLI, MS acc. 3961, NFC 98, 14 July 1916.
23 Laurence and Grene (eds.), *Shaw, Lady Gregory and the Abbey*, 119.
24 G. B. Shaw, *John Bull's Other Island* (Penguin, Harmondsworth, 1992), 159–60.
25 *Selected Plays of Lennox Robinson*, ed. Christopher Murray (Colin Smythe, Gerrards Cross, 1982), 66.
26 Ibid. 85.
27 Ibid. 96.
28 Lady Gregory *The Journals*, ed. Daniel J. Murphy (Colin Smythe, Gerrards Cross, 1978, 1987), i. 22.
29 Hogan and O'Neill (eds.), *Joseph Holloway's Abbey Theatre*, 191.
30 Ibid. 193.
31 INTS Minutes, NLI, MS acc. 3961, NFC 98.
32 Hogan and O'Neill (eds.), *Joseph Holloway's Abbey Theatre*, 197.
33 NLI, MS 29,478.
34 Quoted from Robinson's Scrapbook in Michael J. O'Neill, *Lennox Robinson* (Twayne, New York, 1964), 85.
35 Brenna Katz Clarke and Harold Ferrar, *The Dublin Drama League* (Dolmen Press, Dublin, 1979), 12.
36 Yeats, *Collected Poems*, 233.
37 Hogan and Burnham, *The Art of the Amateur*, 216.
38 Gregory, *Journals*, i. 118–19.
39 Robert Hogan and Richard Burnham, *The Years of O'Casey: 1921–1926* (Dolmen Press, Dublin, 1992), 17.
40 Ibid. 35.
41 Ibid. 26.
42 Ibid. 65.
43 Ibid. 91.
44 INTS Minutes NLI, MS acc. 3961, NFC 98, 22 Nov. 1912.
45 Gregory, *Journals*, i. 606.
46 Sean O'Casey, *Two Plays* (Macmillan, London, 1926), 193.
47 Hogan and Burnham, *The Years of O'Casey*, 147.
48 Pádraig Ó Siadhail, *Stair Dhrámaíocht na Gaeilge: 1900–1970* (Cló Iar-Chonnachta, Indreabhán, 1993), 168–9.
49 Gregory, *Collected Plays*, ii. 359.
50 Yeats, *Autobiographies*, 554.
51 Hogan, 6, p. 176.
52 Thomas Kilroy (ed.), *Sean O'Casey: Twentieth Century Views* (Prentice Hall, 1975), 167,
53 Hogan and Burnham, *The Years of O'Casey*, 195.
54 Ibid. 193.
55 Gregory, *Journals*, i. 514.
56 Gregory, *Collected Plays*, iii. 309–10.
57 Hogan and Burnham, *The Years of O'Casey*, 195.
58 Hogan and O'Neill (eds.), *Joseph Holloway's Abbey Theatre*, 236.
59 Hogan and Burnham, *The Years of O'Casey*, 200.

60 NLI, MS 21,715 (ix), acc. 3350.
61 Murray, *Selected Plays* 28.
62 Ibid. 68–9.
63 Ibid. 85.
64 Hogan and Burnham, *The Years of O'Casey*, 271.
65 George Shiels, *Three Plays* (Macmillan, London, 1945), 86.
66 NLI, Earnán de Blaghd Papers, MS 20,704, acc. 3164.
67 NLI, Earnán de Blaghd Papers, MS 20,705, acc. 3164.
68 Hogan and Burnham, *The Years of O'Casey*, 280.
69 Ibid. 281 et seq.
70 *The Letters of P. H. Pearse*, ed. Séamus Ó Buachalla (Colin Smythe, Gerrards Cross, 1980), 383.
71 Hogan and Burnham, *The Years of O'Casey*, 6, p. 316.
72 Ibid. 314.

CHAPTER 4

1 NLI, MS 24,868, acc. 3832.
2 Robinson, *Selected Plays*, 181.
3 Ibid. 192.
4 Yeats, *Variorum Edition*, 851.
5 Ó Siadhail, *Stair Dhrámaíocht na Gaeilge: 1900–1970*, 65.
6 Gregory, *Journals*, ii. 161.
7 Hugh Hunt, *The Abbey: Ireland's National Theatre* (Gill & Macmillan, Dublin, 1979), 137.
8 Gregory, *Collected Plays*, iv. 361.
9 Ibid. 241.
10 Austin Clarke, *Collected Poems* (Dolmen Press, Dublin, 1974), 183.
11 Gregory, *Collected Plays*, iv. 288.
12 Ibid. iii. 365.
13 Gregory, *Journals*, ii. 160.
14 Ibid. 168.
15 Yeats, *Variorum Edition*, 869.
16 Ibid. 886.
17 Ibid. 890.
18 Ibid. 895.
19 Yeats, *Letters*, 729.
20 Gregory, *Journals*, ii. 236.
21 Sean O'Casey, *Rose and Crown* (Macmillan, London, 1952), 38.
22 Gregory, *Journals*, ii 247.
23 Ibid. 251.
24 O'Casey, *Rose and Crown*, 34.
25 Ibid. 36–7.
26 Laurence and Grene (eds.), *Shaw, Lady Gregory and the Abbey*, 184.
27 Gregory, *Journals*, ii. 462.
28 Ibid. 329.
29 Ibid. 353.
30 Yeats, *Letters*, 766.
31 Gregory, *Journals*, ii. 456.
32 Shiels, *Three Plays*, 259.
33 D. E. S. Maxwell, *A Critical History of Modern Irish Drama 1891–1980* (Cambridge University Press, Cambridge, 1984), 233.
34 W. B. Yeats, *The Tower* (Macmillan, London, 1928), 1.
35 Shiels, *Three Plays*, 233.
36 Yeats, *Variorum Edition*, 958.
37 Ibid. 967.

38 *The Dramatic Works of Denis Johnston*, ed. Joseph Ronsley (Colin Smythe, Gerrards Cross, 1977–92), ii. 144.

39 Thomas Kilroy, 'Denis Johnston's Shavianism', in Joseph Ronsley (ed.), *Denis Johnston: A Retrospective* (Colin Smythe, Gerrards Cross, 1981), 53.

40 Johnston, *Dramatic Work*, 150.

41 Ibid. 152.

42 Robinson, *Selected Plays*, 210.

43 Ibid. 229.

44 Brinsley MacNamara, *Margaret Gillan* (George Allen & Unwin, London, 1934), 79.

45 Yeats, *Variorum Edition*, 1004.

46 Yeats, *Letters*, 730.

47 Yeats, *Essays and Introductions*, 398.

48 Yeats, *Variorum Edition*, 923–5.

49 NLI, MS acc. 3961, NFC 98, 29 Aug. 1934.

50 Hunt, *The Abbey*, 149.

51 Frank O'Connor, *My Father's Son* (Macmillan, London, 1968), 159.

52 Ibid. 157.

53 Sean O'Casey, *Three More Plays* (Macmillan, London, 1968), 32.

54 Ibid. 46.

55 Ibid. 62.

56 Hunt, *The Abbey*, 152.

57 O'Connor, *My Father's Son*, 159.

58 E. H. Mikhail (ed.), *The Abbey Theatre: Interviews and Recollections* (Macmillan, London, 1988), 151.

59 Ervine, *Selected Plays*, 9.

60 Ibid. 257–8.

61 Teresa Deevy, *Three Plays* (Macmillan, London, 1939), 131.

62 Ibid. 141.

63 Ibid. 78.

64 Quoted in Cathy Leeney, 'Themes of Ritual and Myth in Three Plays by Teresa Deevy', *Irish University Review*, 25/1 (spring/summer 1995), 109.

65 O'Connor, *My Father's Son*, 184.

66 Clarke, *Collected Poems*, 183.

67 Paul Vincent Carroll, *Shadow and Substance* (Macmillan, London, 1938), 29–30.

68 Lennox Robinson, *Killycreggs in Twilight and Other Plays* (Macmillan, London, 1939), 64–5.

69 Frank O'Connor and Hugh Hunt, *The Invincibles* (Proscenium Press, Newark, Del., 1980), 72–3.

70 O'Connor, *My Father's Son*, 207.

71 NLI, MS 21,431, acc. 3250, Act I, p. 23.

72 Frank O'Connor and Hugh Hunt, *Moses' Rock* (Catholic University Press of America, Washington, 1983), 100–1.

73 NLI, MS 20,715, acc. 3164.

74 Peter Kavanagh, *The Story of the Abbey Theatre* (Devin-Adair, New York, 1950), 175.

75 Yeats, *Variorum Edition*, 1049.

76 State Papers: Dublin Castle, 'National Theatre: Establishment', MS S9863C; quoted in Ó Siadhail, *Stair Dhrámaíocht na Gaeilge: 1900–1970*, 75.

77 NLI, *Plays in Irish*, ii (1933–49), extract from a speech by Proinsias Mac Síthigh; quoted ibid. 78.

78 Hunt, *The Abbey*, 161.

79 O'Connor, *My Father's Son*, 228.

80 NLI, MS 22,559.

81 Patrick Maume, *'Life that is Exile': Daniel Corkery and the Search for Irish Ireland* (Institute of Irish Studies, Queen's University Belfast, 1993), 36.

82 George Shiels, *The Rugged Path and The Summit* (Macmillan, London, 1942), 121.
83 Robert Hogan and Michael J. O'Neill (eds.), *Joseph Holloway's Irish Theatre*, iii (Proscenium Press, Dixon, Calif., 1970), 52.
84 NLI, MS 21,481, acc. 3250, n.p.
85 Mikhail (ed.), *The Abbey Theatre*, 169.
86 Tomás Mac Anna, 'Cuimhne Earnáin', *Anois*, 13–14 Mar. 1993, p. 13; quoted in Ó Siadhail, *Stair Dhrámaíocht na Gaeilge: 1900–1970*, 79.
87 NLI, MS 29,541.
88 NLI, MS acc. 3961, NFC 98.
89 Hogan and O'Neill (eds.), *Joseph Holloway's Irish Theatre*, iii. 81.
90 Ibid. 89.
91 Joseph Tomelty *All Souls' Night and Other Plays*, ed. Damien Smyth (Lagan Press, Belfast, 1993), 14.
92 Ibid. 186.
93 Ó Siadhail, *Stair Dhrámaíocht na Gaeilge: 1900–1970*, 85.
94 Tomelty, *All Souls' Night*, 42.
95 Robert Hogan (ed.) *Seven Irish Plays* (University of Minnesota Press, Minneapolis, 1967), 95.
96 M. J. Molloy, *Three Plays* (Proscenium Press, Newark, Del., 1975), 93–4.
97 Hogan (ed.), *Seven Irish Plays*, 106.
98 Ibid. 116.
99 NLI, MS 29,337, p. 14.
100 Ibid. 51.
101 NLI, MS 21,300, p. 38.
102 NLI, MS 27,622, acc. 4036a.
103 NLI, MS 27,631 (ii).
104 Sean McCann (ed.), *The Story of the Abbey Theatre* (New English Library, London, 1967), 62, and personal communication from Tomás Mac Anna, Dec. 1998.
105 Quoted in McCann (ed.), *The Story of the Abbey Theatre*, 63.
106 Personal communication, Dec. 1998.

CHAPTER 5

1 Personal communication from Tomás Mac Anna, Dec. 1998.
2 Hunt, *The Abbey*, 178.
3 NLI, MS 21,326, acc. 3250, p. 31.
4 Ibid. 48.
5 Walter Macken, *Mungo's Mansion* (Macmillan, London, 1957), 89.
6 Molloy, *Three Plays*, 126.
7 Ibid. 191.
8 Hunt, *The Abbey*, 174.
9 Robert Hogan, *After the Irish Renaissance* (University of Minnesota Press, Minneapolis, 1967), 14.
10 Denis Donoghue, 'Dublin Letter', *Hudson Review*, 13 (winter 1960–1), 583.
11 NLI, MS 29,318, p. 32.
12 Seán Ó Tuama, *Gunna Cam agus Slabhra Óir* (Sáirséal & Dill, Baile Átha Cliath, 1967), 10.
13 Ibid. 40.
14 Ibid. 41.
15 Joseph Ronsley, 'Denis Johnston's *The Scythe and the Sunset*', in Ronsley (ed.), *Denis Johnston: A Retrospective*, 133–4.
16 Ibid. 139.
17 *The Dramatic Works of Denis Johnston*, i. 135.
18 Ibid. 139.
19 Ibid. 163–5.

20 Hogan, *Seven Irish Plays*, 81.
21 NLI, MS 29,391, p. 75 (prompt-copy).
22 Ibid. 110.
23 Ibid. 112.
24 NLI, MS. 21, 388, acc. 3250 (prompt-copy), p. 24.
25 Ibid., Act III, p. 15.
26 Brian Friel, *The Enemy Within* (Gallery Press, Oldcastle, 1979), 18.
27 Ibid. 70.
28 'The Siege of Mulligar', in John Montague, *A Chosen Light* (Macgibbon & Kee, London, 1967), 60.
29 John B. Keane, *The Man from Clare* (Mercier Press, Cork, 1962), 26.
30 Ibid. 32.
31 Personal communication from Tomás Mac Anna, Dec. 1998.
32 Ibid.
33 Quoted Hunt, *The Abbey*, 188.
34 INTS Minutes, NLI MS acc. 3961, NFC 98.
35 Eoghan Ó Tuairisc, 'Oiliúint dhrámadóra', *Comhar*, 38/10 (1977), 5–6. Quoted in Máirín Nic Eoin, *Eoghan Ó Tuairisc: Beatha agus Saothar* (An Clóchomhar, Baile Átha Cliath, 1988), 104–5.
36 NLI, MS 29,562, Sc. i.

CHAPTER 6

1 *Irish Times*, 28 July 1969. Quoted in Hunt, *The Abbey*, 196; and NLI, MS 29,555.
2 McCann, *The Story of the Abbey Theatre*, 67; and Tomás Mac Anna, personal communication, Dec. 1998.
3 Quoted in Mikhail (ed.), *The Abbey Theatre*, 221.
4 *Selected Plays of Louis MacNeice*, ed. Alan Heuser and Peter McDonald (Oxford University Press, Oxford, 1993), 212–3.
5 Ibid. 235–6.
6 Brian Friel, *The Loves of Cass McGuire* (Gallery Press, Oldcastle, 1984), 14.
7 Earnán de Blaghd, 'The Abbey Theatre and the Irish Language', *Threshold*, 2/2 (summer 1958), 33.
8 Siobhán Ní Bhrádaigh, *Máiréad Ní Ghráda: Ceannródaí Drámaíochta* (Cló Iar-Chonnachta, Indreabhán, 1996), 70.
9 NLI, MS 29,309, p. 67. In the performed version of the play the name of the main character is changed from MacAdam to Maguire.
10 Tom Murphy, *A Whistle in the Dark and Other Plays* (Methuen, London, 1989), 172.
11 Tom Murphy, *Plays* (Methuen, London 1994), ii. 155.
12 Ibid. 234.
13 Brian Friel, *Selected Plays* (Faber & Faber, London, 1984), 150.
14 Brian Friel, *Volunteers* (Gallery Press, Oldcastle, 1989), 38.
15 Friel, *Selected Plays*, 245.
16 Seamus Deane, *History Lessons* (Gallery Press, Oldcastle, 1983), 12.
17 Thomas Kilroy, *The Death and Resurrection of Mr Roche* (Faber & Faber, London, 1969), 19.
18 Ibid. 60.
19 Thomas Kilroy, *Talbot's Box* (Gallery Press, Oldcastle, 1979), 53.
20 Ibid. 62–3.
21 NLI, MS 29,305, p. 39.
22 Ibid. 56.
23 Heno Magee, *Hatchet* (Gallery Press, Oldcastle, 1988), 62.
24 James McKenna, *The Scatterin'* (Goldsmith Press, Newbridge, 1977), 38.
25 NLI, MS 29,326.

26 Criostóir Ó Floinn, *Mise Raifteirí an File* (Sáirséal & Dill, Baile Átha Cliath, 1974), 223–4.
27 Graham Reid, *The Death of Humpty Dumpty* (Co-op Books, Dublin, 1982), 21.
28 Ibid. 35.
29 Maxwell, *A Critical History of Modern Irish Drama*, 185.
30 Hugh Leonard, *Selected Plays* (Colin Smythe, Gerrards Cross, 1992), 365.
31 NLI, MS 29,430, p. 9.
32 Ibid. 13.
33 Ibid. 29.
34 Frank McGuinness, *Observe the Sons of Ulster Marching towards the Somme* (Faber & Faber, London, 1986), 49–50.
35 Ibid. 80.

CHAPTER 7

1 Interview with Mr Patrick Mason, 5 Nov. 1998; correspondence from Ms Máiréad Delaney, Abbey Archivist, and personal communication from Dr Tomás Mac Anna and Máiréad Delaney.
2 Seamus Hosey, 'The Abbey in Russia', *Theatre Ireland*, 15 (May–Aug. 1988), 15.
3 Christopher Fitzsimon and Sanford Sternlicht (eds.), *New Plays from the Abbey Theatre: 1993–1995* (Syracuse University Press, Syracuse, NY, 1996), 83.
4 Frank McGuinness (ed.), *The Dazzling Dark: New Irish Plays* (Faber & Faber, London, 1997), 233.
5 Ibid. 193.
6 Ibid. 224.
7 John B. Keane, *Sive* (Progress House, Dublin, 1959), 109.
8 Anthony Roche, 'John B. Keane: Respectability at Last', *Theatre Ireland*, 18 (Apr.–June 1989), 30.
9 John B. Keane, *The Field* (Mercier Press, Cork, 1966), 19.
10 John B. Keane, *Big Maggie* (Mercier Press, Cork, 1969), 69.
11 Ibid. 87.
12 Hiroko Mikami, 'Frank McGuinness and the Theatre of his Time', unpublished D.Phil. thesis, University of Ulster at Coleraine.
13 Frank McGuinness, *Plays*, vol. i (Faber & Faber, London, 1992), 325.
14 Ibid. 344.
15 Ibid. 370.
16 Frank McGuinness, *Someone Who'll Watch over Me* (Faber & Faber, London, 1992), 27.
17 Ibid. 51.
18 Paul Hadfield, 'Christopher Fitzsimon', *Theatre Ireland*, 21 (Dec. 1989), 42–3.
19 Personal communication from Martin Fahy, general manager, Abbey Theatre, 18 Dec. 1998.
20 Brian Friel, *Dancing at Lughnasa* (Faber & Faber, London, 1990), 2.
21 Ibid. 71.
22 Brian Friel, *Wonderful Tennessee* (Gallery Press, Oldcastle, 1993), 43–4.
23 Ibid. 74.
24 Brian Friel, *Give Me your Answer Do!* (Gallery Press, Oldcastle, 1997), 79.
25 Thomas Murphy, *Too Late for Logic* (Methuen, London, 1990), 40.
26 Ibid. 54.
27 Thomas Murphy, *The Wake* (Methuen, London, 1998), 22.
28 Ibid. 53.
29 Ibid. 65.
30 Thomas Kilroy, *The Secret Fall of Constance Wilde* (Gallery Press, Oldcastle, 1997), 42.
31 Ibid. 20.
32 Ibid. 53.
33 David Grant (ed.), *A Crack in the Emerald* (Nick Hern Books, London, 1994), 180–1.
34 Fitzsimon and Sternlicht (eds.), *New Plays from the Abbey Theatre*, 42–3.

35 Ibid. 219.
36 Marina Carr, *The Mai* (Gallery Press, Oldcastle, 1995), 59.
37 McGuinness (ed.), *The Dazzling Dark*, 310–11.
38 Ibid. 262–3.
39 Brendan Kennelly, *The Trojan Women* (Bloodaxe, Newcastle upon Tyne, 1993), 44.
40 Ibid. 74.
41 Ibid. 74.
42 Alan Titley, *Tagann Godot* (An Clóchomhar, Baile Átha Cliath, 1991), 13–14.
43 Ibid. 36.
44 Ibid. 49.

CHAPTER 8

 1 Yeats, *Collected Poems*, 274.
 2 Christopher Griffin, 'Visions and Derisions: Interview with Eric Bentley', *Theatre Ireland*,
    9–10 (1985), 146.
 3 Neil Wallace, 'Views of Theatre in Ireland', *Report of the Arts Council: Theatre Review* (An
    Chomhairle Ealaíon, Dublin, 1995), 19.
 4 Patrick Mason, *The National Theatre: Artistic Policy* (Abbey Theatre, Dublin, 1996), 1, 7.
 5 Wallace, 'Views of Theatre in Ireland', 166.
 6 Interview with Patrick Mason, 5 Nov. 1998.
 7 Wallace, 'Views of Theatre in Ireland', 20.

Bibliography

(Confined to Works Cited in the text)

PUBLISHED SOURCES

CARR, MARINA, *The Mai* (Gallery Press, Oldcastle, 1995).

CARROLL, PAUL VINCENT, *Shadow and Substance* (Macmillan, London, 1938).

CLARKE, AUSTIN, *Collected Poems* (Dolmen Press, Dublin, 1974).

CLARKE, BRENNA KATZ, and FERRAR, HAROLD, *The Dublin Drama League* (Dolmen Press, Dublin, 1979).

COLUM, PADRAIC, *Three Plays* (Hodges Figgis, Dublin, 1963).

—— 'Early Days of the Irish Theatre', *Dublin Magazine*, 20 (Jan.–Mar. 1950).

DEANE, SEAMUS, *The Field Day Anthology* (Field Day, Derry, 1991).

—— *History Lessons* (Gallery Press, Oldcastle, 1983).

DE BLAGHD, EARNÁN, 'The Abbey Theatre and the Irish Language', *Threshold*, 2/2 (summer 1958).

DEEVY, TERESA, *Three Plays* (Macmillan, London, 1939).

DONOGHUE, DENIS, 'Dublin Letter' *Hudson Review*, 13 (winter 1960–1).

ERVINE, ST JOHN, *Selected Plays of St John Ervine*, ed. John Cronin (Colin Smythe, Gerrards Cross, 1988).

FARRELL, BERNARD, *Forty-Four Sycamore and The Last Apache Reunion* (Mercier Press, Cork, 1995).

—— *I Do Not Like Thee, Dr Fell and All in Favour Said No!* (Mercier Press, Cork, 1998).

FAY, WILLIAM GEORGE, and CARSWELL, CATHERINE, *The Fays of the Abbey Theatre: An Autobiographical Record* (Rich & Cowan, London, 1935).

FITZMAURICE, GEORGE, *Plays*, vols. i–iii (Dolmen Press, Dublin, 1967–70).

FITZSIMON, CHRISTOPHER, and STERNLICHT, SANFORD (eds.), *New Plays from the Abbey Theatre: 1993–1995* (Syracuse University Press, Syracuse, NY, 1996).

FLANNERY, JAMES W., *W. B. Yeats and the Idea of a Theatre: The Early Abbey Theatre in Theory and Practice* (Yale University Press, New Haven, 1976).

FOSTER, R. F., *W. B. Yeats: A Life, i: The Apprentice Mage* (Clarendon Press, Oxford, 1997).

FRAZIER, ADRIAN, *Behind the Scenes: Yeats, Horniman, and the Struggle for the Abbey Theatre* (University of California Press, Berkeley and Los Angeles, 1990).

FRIEL, BRIAN, *The Enemy Within* (Gallery Press, Oldcastle, 1979).

—— *The Loves of Cass McGuire* (Gallery Press, Oldcastle, 1984).

—— *Selected Plays* (Faber & Faber, London, 1984).

—— *Volunteers* (Gallery Press, Oldcastle, 1989).

—— *Dancing at Lughnasa* (Faber & Faber, London, 1990).

—— *Wonderful Tennessee* (Gallery Press, Oldcastle, 1993).

—— *Give Me your Answer, Do!* (Gallery Press, Oldcastle, 1997).

GRANT, DAVID (ed.), *A Crack in the Emerald* (Nick Hern Books, London, 1994).

GREGORY, AUGUSTA, Lady, *Our Irish Theatre* (Colin Smythe, Gerrards Cross, 1972).

—— *Collected Plays*, vols. i–iv, ed. Ann Saddlemyer (Colin Smythe, Gerrards Cross, 1971–9).

GREGORY, AUGUSTA, *The Journals*, ed. Daniel J. Murphy, vols. i and ii (Colin Smythe, Gerrards Cross, 1978 and 1987).

GRIFFIN, CHRISTOPHER, 'Visions and Derisions: Interview with Eric Bentley', *Theatre Ireland*, 9–10 (1985).

HADFIELD, PAUL, 'Christopher Fitzsimon', *Theatre Ireland*, 21 (Dec. 1989).

HOGAN, ROBERT, *After the Irish Renaissance* (University of Minnesota Press, Minneapolis, 1967).

—— (ed.), *Seven Irish Plays: 1946–1964* (University of Minnesota Press, Minneapolis, 1967).

—— and BURNHAM, RICHARD, *The Art of the Amateur: 1916–1920* (Dolmen Press, Dublin, 1984).

—— —— *The Years of O'Casey: 1921–1926* (Dolmen Press, Dublin, 1992).

—— —— and POTEET, DANIEL P., *The Abbey Theatre: The Rise of the Realists, 1910–1915* (Dolmen Press, Dublin, 1979).

—— and KILROY, JAMES, *The Irish Literary Theatre 1899–1901* (Dolmen Press, Dublin, 1975).

—— —— *Laying the Foundations: 1902–1904* (Dolmen Press, Dublin, 1976).

—— —— *The Abbey Theatre: The Years of Synge, 1905–1909* (Dolmen Press, Dublin, 1978).

—— and O'NEILL, MICHAEL J. (eds.), *Joseph Holloway's Abbey Theatre* (Southern Illinois University Press, Carbondale, 1967).

—— —— *Joseph Holloway's Irish Theatre*, vol. iii (Proscenium Press, Dixon, Calif., 1970).

HOSEY, SEAMUS, 'The Abbey in Russia', *Theatre Ireland*, 15 (May–Aug. 1988).

HUNT, HUGH, *The Abbey: Ireland's National Theatre 1904–1979* (Gill & Macmillan, Dublin, 1979).

JOHNSTON, DENIS, *The Dramatic Works of Denis Johnston*, ed. Joseph Ronsley, vols. i–iii (Colin Smythe, Gerrards Cross, 1977–92).

KAVANAGH, PETER, *The Story of the Abbey Theatre* (Devin-Adair, New York, 1950).

KEANE, JOHN B., *Sive* (Progress House, Dublin, 1959).

—— *The Man from Clare* (Mercier Press, Cork, 1962).

—— *The Field* (Mercier Press, Cork, 1966).

—— *Big Maggie* (Mercier Press, Cork, 1969).

KENNELLY, BRENDAN, *The Trojan Women* (Bloodaxe, Newcastle upon Tyne, 1993).

KILROY, THOMAS, *The Death and Resurrection of Mr Roche* (Faber & Faber, London, 1969).

—— (ed.), *Sean O'Casey: Twentieth Century Views* (Prentice Hall, Totowa NJ, 1975).

—— *Talbot's Box* (Gallery Press, Oldcastle, 1979).

—— *The Secret Fall of Constance Wilde* (Gallery Press, Oldcastle, 1997).

KUCH, PETER, *Yeats and AE: 'The Antagonism that Unites Dear Friends'* (Colin Smythe, Gerrards Cross, 1986).

LAURENCE, DAN H., and GRENE, NICHOLAS (eds.), *Shaw, Lady Gregory, and the Abbey* (Colin Smythe, Gerrards Cross, 1993).

LEENEY, CATHY, 'Themes of Ritual and Myth in Three Plays by Teresa Deevy', *Irish University Review*, 25/1 (spring/summer 1995).

LEONARD, HUGH, *Selected Plays* (Colin Smythe, Gerrards Cross, 1992).

MAC ANNA, TOMÁS, 'Cuimhne Earnáin', *Anois*, 13–14 Mar. 1993.

MacBride White, Anna, and Jeffares, A. N. (eds.), *The Gonne–Yeats Letters 1893–1938: Always your Friend* (Hutchinson, London, 1992).

McCann, Sean (ed.), *The Story of the Abbey Theatre* (New English Library, London, 1967).

McGuinness, Frank, *Observe the Sons of Ulster Marching towards the Somme* (Faber & Faber, London, 1986).

—— *Plays*, vol. i (Faber & Faber, London, 1992).

—— *Someone Who'll Watch over Me* (Faber & Faber, London, 1992).

—— (ed.), *The Dazzling Dark: New Irish Plays* (Faber & Faber, London, 1997).

Macken, Walter, *Mungo's Mansion* (Macmillan, London, 1957).

McKenna, James, *The Scatterin'* (Goldsmith Press, Newbridge, 1977).

MacNamara, Brinsley, *Margaret Gillan* (George Allen & Unwin, London, 1934).

MacNeice, Louis, *Selected Plays of Louis MacNeice*, ed. Alan Heuser and Peter McDonald (Oxford University Press, Oxford, 1993).

Magee, Heno, *Hatchet* (Gallery Press, Oldcastle, 1988).

Mason, Patrick, *The National Theatre: Artistic Policy* (Abbey Theatre, Dublin, 1996).

Maume, Patrick, *'Life that is Exile': Daniel Corkery and the Search for Irish Ireland* (Institute of Irish Studies, Queen's University Belfast, 1993).

Maxwell, D. E. S., *A Critical History of Modern Irish Drama 1891–1980* (Cambridge University Press, Cambridge, 1984).

Mikhail, E. H. (ed.), *The Abbey Theatre: Interviews and Recollections* (Macmillan, London, 1988).

Molloy, M. J., *Three Plays* (Proscenium Press, Newark, Del., 1975).

Montague, John, *A Chosen Light* (Macgibbon & Kee, London, 1967).

Moore, George, *Ave* (William Heinemann, London, 1947).

—— *Vale* (William Heinemann, London, 1947).

Murphy, Tom, *A Whistle in the Dark and Other Plays* (Methuen, London, 1989).

—— *Too Late for Logic* (Methuen, London, 1990).

—— *Plays*, vol. i–ii (Methuen, London, 1994).

—— *The Wake* (Methuen, London, 1998).

Murray, Christopher, *Twentieth Century Irish Drama: Mirror up to Nation* (Manchester University Press, Manchester, 1997).

Murray, T. C., *Selected Plays of T. C. Murray*, ed. Richard Allen Cave (Colin Smythe, Gerrards Cross, 1998).

Ní Bhrádaigh, Siobhán, *Máiréad Ní Ghráda: Ceannródaí Drámaíochta* (Cló Iar-Chonnachta, Indreabhán, 1996).

Nic Eoin, Máirín, *Eoghan Ó Tuairisc: Beatha agus Saothar* (An Clóchomhar, Baile Átha Cliath, 1988).

Nic Shiubhlaigh, Máire, *The Splendid Years: Recollections of Máire Nic Shiubhlaigh, as Told to Edward Kenny* (Duffy, Dublin, 1955).

O'Casey, Sean, *Two Plays* (Macmillan, London, 1926).

—— *Three More Plays* (Macmillan, London, 1968).

—— *Rose and Crown* (Macmillan, London, 1952).

O'Connor, Frank, *My Father's Son* (Macmillan, London, 1968).

—— and Hunt, Hugh, *The Invincibles* (Proscenium Press, Newark, Del., 1980).

——and Hunt, Hugh, *Moses' Rock* (Catholic University Press of America, Washington, 1983).

Ó Floinn, Criostóir, *Mise Raifteirí an File* (Sáirséal & Dill, Baile Átha Cliath, 1974).

O'Neill, Michael J., *Lennox Robinson* (Twayne, New York, 1964).

O'Riordan, Conal, *Adam in Dublin* (William Collins, Glasgow, 1920).

Ó Siadhail, Pádraig, *Stair Dhrámaíocht na Gaeilge: 1900–1970* (Cló Iar-Chonnachta, Indreabhán, 1993).

Ó Tuairisc, Eoghan, 'Oiliúint Dhrámadóra', *Comhar*, 38/10 (1977).

Ó Tuama, Seán, *Gunna Cam agus Slabhra Óir* (Sáirséal & Dill, Baile Átha Cliath, 1967).

Pearse, P. H., *The Letters of P. H. Pearse*, ed. Séamus Ó Buachalla (Colin Smythe, Gerrards Cross, 1980).

Reid, Graham, *The Death of Humpty Dumpty* (Co-op Books, Dublin, 1982).

Robinson, Lennox, *Killycreggs in Twilight and Other Plays* (Macmillan, London, 1939).

—— (ed.), *The Irish Theatre* (Macmillan, London, 1939).

—— *Ireland's Abbey Theatre: A History 1899–1951* (Sidgwick & Jackson, London, 1951).

—— *Selected Plays of Lennox Robinson*, ed. Christopher Murray (Colin Smythe, Gerrards Cross, 1982).

Roche, Anthony, 'John B. Keane: Respectability at Last', *Theatre Ireland*, 18 (Apr.–June 1989).

—— *Contemporary Irish Drama* (Gill & Macmillan, Dublin, 1994).

Ronsley, Joseph (ed.), *Denis Johnston: A Retrospective* (Colin Smythe, Gerrards Cross, 1981).

Saddlemyer, Ann (ed.), *Theatre Business: The Correspondence of the First Abbey Theatre Directors* (Colin Smythe, Gerrards Cross, 1982).

Shaw, G. B., *John Bull's Other Island* (Penguin, Harmondsworth, 1992).

—— *The Shewing-up of Blanco Posnet: A Sermon in Crude Melodrama* (Constable, London, 1927).

Shiels, George, *The Rugged Path and The Summit* (Macmillan, London, 1942).

—— *Three Plays* (Macmillan, London, 1945).

Synge, John M., *Plays* (George Allen & Unwin, London, 1924).

Titley, Alan, *Tagann Godot* (An Clóchomhar, Baile Átha Cliath, 1991).

Tomelty, Joseph, *All Soul's Night and Other Plays*, ed. Damien Smyth (Lagan Press, Belfast, 1993).

Wallace, Neil, 'Views of Theatre in Ireland', *Report of the Arts Council: Theatre Review* (An Chomhairle Ealaíon, Dublin, 1995).

Welch, Robert, *Changing States: Transformations in Modern Irish Writing* (Routledge, London, 1993).

Yeats, J. B., *Letters to his Son W. B. Yeats and Others 1869–1922*, ed. Joseph Hone (Macmillan, London, 1944).

Yeats, W. B., *The Shadowy Waters* (Hodder & Stoughton, London, 1901).

—— *Autobiographies* (Macmillan, London, 1970).

—— *Collected Poems* (Macmillan, London, 1958).

—— *Essays and Introductions* (Macmillan, London, 1969).

—— *Explorations* (Macmillan, London, 1962).

—— *Memoirs*, ed. and introd. Denis Donoghue (Macmillan, London, 1972).

—— *Uncollected Prose by W. B. Yeats*, ed. J. P. Frayne, i (Macmillan, London, 1970).

—— *The Variorum Edition of the Plays of W. B. Yeats*, ed. Russell K. Alspach (Macmillan, London, 1966).

—— *The Collected Letters of W. B. Yeats*, ed. John Kelly et al., vols. i–iii (Clarendon Press, Oxford, 1986–).

—— *The Letters of W. B. Yeats*, ed. Allan Wade (Rupert Hart-Davis, London, 1954).

—— *The Tower* (Macmillan, London, 1928).

UNPUBLISHED SOURCES

The manuscript holdings of the National Library of Ireland are rich in materials relevant to the Abbey Theatre. There are, of course, the Holloway papers and diaries, but also: an extensive collection of playscripts, from 1904 to *c.*1972, many of them prompt-copies; the Earnán de Blaghd papers; W. A. Henderson's Cuttings Books; Máire Nic Shiubhlaigh's papers; T. C. Murray's papers and correspondence; the Abbey board's Minute Books, which are not for consultation (NFC) save by special permission; letters between Miss Horniman, Yeats, Synge, Lady Gregory, and others; and a great deal more. The manuscript sources consulted in the preparation of this work are listed here, but much else awaits the scholar and researcher in these holdings.

Interviews with and communications from: Máiréad Delaney, A. N. Jeffares, Brendan Kennelly, Liam Lynch, Tomás Mac Anna, Seán Mac Réamoinn, Patrick Mason, Tomás Ó Murchadha.

NLI, MS acc. 3961, NFC 98 (INTS Minutes)

NLI, MS acc. 3961, NFC 98 (vol. 2)

NLI, MS 5651, NFC

NLI, MS 5977

NLI, MS 8320

NLI, MS 10,952

NLI, MS 10,952 (1)

NLI, MS 18,312

NLI, MS 18,721

NLI, MS 20,704, acc. 3164

NLI, MS 20,705, acc. 3164

NLI, MS 20,715, acc. 3164

NLI, MS 21,300

NLI, MS 21,303, acc. 3250

NLI, MS 21,319, acc. 3250

NLI, MS 21,326, acc. 3250

NLI, MS 21,388, acc. 3250

NLI, MS 21,391, acc. 3250

NLI, MS 21,431, acc. 3250

NLI, MS 21,481, acc. 3250

NLI, MS 21,715 (ix), acc. 3350

NLI, MS 21,747, acc. 3478

NLI, MS 21,951

NLI, MS 22,418

NLI, MS 22,599

NLI, MS 24,868, acc. 3832

NLI, MS 27,622, acc. 4036

NLI, MS 27,631 (ii)
NLI, MS 27,634, acc. 4036a
NLI, MS 29,305
NLI, MS 29,309
NLI, MS 29,318
NLI, MS 29,326
NLI, MS 29,337
NLI, MS 29,391
NLI, MS 29,430
NLI, MS 29,470
NLI, MS 29,478
NLI, MS 29,511
NLI, MS 29,526
NLI, MS 29,555
NLI, MS 29,562

LEACOCK, BERNIE, 'D. P. Moran: Selected Writings', unpublished research towards D.Phil.,
    University of Ulster at Coleraine.
MIKAMI, HIROKO, 'Frank McGuinness and the Theatre of his Time', unpublished D.Phil.
    thesis, University of Ulster at Coleraine.

Index

Plays are referred to under their titles followed by the author's name in brackets. 'Yeats' in these citations is W. B. Yeats; other Yeatses are specifically indicated.